What Happened to the Church?

by

William L. Barth

DORRANCE PUBLISHING CO., INC.
PITTSBURGH, PENNSYLVANIA 15222

ISBN # 0-8059-4169-X
Printed in the United States of America
First Printing

For information or to order additional books, please write:
Dorrance Publishing Co., Inc.
643 Smithaaafield Street
Pittsburgh, Pennsylvania 15222
U.S.A.

Contents

Chapter One

Dispensational View of the Bible

In 2 Timothy 2:15, the Apostle Paul tells Timothy, "study to shew thyself approved unto God, a workman that needeth not to be ashamed, rightly dividing the word of truth." Paul's direction to "study . . . rightly dividing the word of truth" is just as essential today as it was to Timothy nearly 1900 years ago.

Great events have changed the course of history and serve as milestones, not only to help us reconstruct the past eras (or ages), but also to find God's will for the human family in today's age. Paul identifies one of these eras as the "dispensation of the grace of God" and states this era was a mystery, hidden to the sons of men in other ages. The dispensation of grace to which Paul was referring is the current Church Age. Ephesians 3:1-6, "(1) For this cause I Paul, the prisoner of Jesus Christ for you Gentiles, (2) If ye have heard of the dispensation of the grace of God which is given me to you-ward: (3) How that by revelation he made known unto me the mystery; (as I wrote afore in few words, (4) Whereby, when ye read, ye may understand my knowledge in the mystery of Christ) (5) Which in other ages was not made known unto the sons of men, as it is now revealed unto his holy apostles and prophets by the Spirit; (6) That the Gentiles should be fellow heirs, and of the same body, and partakers of his promise in Christ by the gospel."

The word *dispensation* in the original Greek is *oikonomia*, *oikos* meaning "a house" and *nomos* meaning "a law." The Greek word *dispensation* means "administration or management of a household." In the English language, it is defined as a general state or ordering of things, specifically a system of revealed commands and promises regulating human affairs.

In using the word *dispensation*, Paul was comparing God's management of the world, down through the ages, to a man managing his household or family. Each home is run a little differently. If we select six homes and write down all the family rules of each house, we would find many of the rules conflict. To apply all these rules to your house and force the members of your family to keep all of them would be nearly impossible. These rules only take on real meaning when they are divided and applied to the right household. For example, one of the rules in the first house may be that the son may use the family car on Saturday night. In the second house, the son may be only four years old. In the third, the son may own his own car; therefore, he can use it anytime he wishes. In the next house, the son may be driving on a learner's permit and must be accompanied by a parent. In the fifth house, the family may not have any children, and the sixth may not own a car.

The different rules in the various dispensations are not different ways to be saved. People have always been saved by believing God and placing their faith in his Word. In the Old Testament, faith in God's promise that the Redeemer would come was requisite for salvation, while in this dispensation we are required to believe that Jesus Christ was that promised Redeemer.

Confusion is introduced when we fail to distinguish the "times" when the words were spoken from the "times" to which they refer. The confusion starts when we apply something God did or said in one dispensation to what God did or will do in a later dispensation. To apply rules or doctrine of a later dispensation to an earlier era is just as confusing. Can you imagine a preacher of three thousand years ago telling his congregation that the only way to eternal life is believing that Jesus Christ died at Calvary on a cross for their sins? This was one thousand years before Jesus died. Christians readily agree that God's program for today does not include a church ceremony involving the killing and burning of animal sacrifices. On the other hand, they will not deny it was God's rule for the Jewish Nation during the Dispensation of Law. They recognize that during the era of law God was dealing with a specific nation, using specific rules, during a specific era of time. Other truths are inter-dispensational, meaning they apply to all dispensations. The laws of God which are summarized in the Ten Commandments are one example. They are house rules for God's people of all dispensational eras.

It is much easier to understand the Scriptures if we rightly divide the Word of God and think of each dispensation as a specific period of time during which man is tested in obeying God's revealed will. The word *reveal* means to make known through divine inspiration; to make publicly known, to uncover, or unveil. Through revelation, God has made known to us truths and realities which we could not discover for ourselves.

The outline of each dispensation is basically the same:

1. God reveals his will to man.
2. God promises blessings for obeying his will.

3. God promises punishment for not obeying.
4. In each dispensational era, mankind failed to obey God's will.
5. Each dispensation ends with God's judgment.

By examining history and the future through Bible prophecy, seven dispensations can be recognized. They are as follows:

1. Garden Dispensation–Genesis chapters 1-3.
2. Flood Dispensation–Genesis chapters 4-7.
3. Babel Dispensation–Genesis chapters 8-11.
4. Patriarch Dispensation–Genesis 12 through Exodus chapter 1.
5. Law Dispensation–Exodus chapter 2 through Acts chapter 1.
6. Church Dispensation–Acts chapter 2 through Revelation chapter 19.
7. Kingdom Dispensation–Revelation chapter 20.

Prior to the statement "In the beginning God created the heaven and the earth" in Genesis 1:1, we have eternity past. After the great white throne judgment in Revelation 20:11-15, we have eternity future. Between Genesis 1:1 and the white throne judgment, we have the seven-thousand-year program of God's dealings with the human family.

A concise view of the seven dispensations would be:

1. Garden Dispensation: God said don't eat. They ate; they were driven from the Garden of Eden.
2. Flood Dispensation: God said choose to do good. They chose to do evil; they were destroyed by the flood.
3. Babel Dispensation: God said scatter. They did not scatter; they were scattered by the confusion of their language at the Tower of Babel.
4. Patriarch Dispensation: God told Abram (Abraham) to leave his native land and dwell in the promised land. Abram moved to Egypt, and his descendants became slaves.
5. Law Dispensation: God gave the Jews his law and told them to obey all the law, prosper in the promised land, and wait for the Messiah. They broke the law and went into captivity. They rejected Jesus as the Messiah and were dispersed among the Gentile Nations.
6. Church Dispensation: God's will is for the whole human family to accept Jesus as Savior and Lord, be governed by his Word, and be led by the Holy Spirit. Those who accept God's plan of salvation will be saved and become members of his Church, the body or bride of Christ. The era will end with the rapture of born-again believers and the judgment of the seven-year- tribulation period for those who reject Jesus.
7. Kingdom Dispensation: God's will is for the whole human family to receive Jesus as King of Kings when he returns to the earth, in glory,

to rule the nations with a rod of iron. The Jews will accept Jesus as King and publish God's plan of salvation to the Gentile Nations, which survived the Great Tribulation Judgment. During this era Satan is bound in Hades. After living in an environment of perfect justice and peace for 1000 years, Satan will be loosed and a portion of the human family will rebel against the Kingship of Jesus. This era will end with the rebellious being devoured by fire out of heaven.

The Garden Dispensation

The first dispensation period was the Garden Era. This period started with the creation and ended when Adam and Eve were driven from the Garden of Eden. This era is recorded in the first three chapters of the Book of Genesis (Gen.).

God's will for man was to dress and keep the garden of Eden, but not to eat of the fruit of the tree of the knowledge of good and evil. Gen. 2:15-17, "(15) And the Lord God took the man, and put him into the garden of Eden to dress it and to keep it. (16) And the Lord God commanded the man, saying, Of every tree of the garden thou mayest freely eat: (17) But of the tree of the knowledge of good and evil, thou shalt not eat of it: for in the day that thou eatest thereof thou shalt surely die."

Man failed to obey God and ate. Gen. 3:6, "And when the woman saw that the tree was good for food, and that it was pleasant to the eyes, and a tree to be desired to make one wise, she took of the fruit thereof, and did eat, and gave also unto her husband with her; and he did eat."

God's judgment included the curses (Gen. 3:14-19), death (Gen. 2:17), and expulsion from the garden of Eden, Gen. 3:22-24, "(22) And the Lord God said, Behold, the man is become as one of us, to know good and evil: and now, lest he put forth his hand, and take also of the tree of life, and eat, and live for ever: (23) Therefore the Lord God sent him forth from the garden of Eden, to till the ground from whence he was taken. (24) So he drove out the man; and he placed at the east of the garden of Eden Cherubims, and a flaming sword which turned every way, to keep the way of the tree of life."

A basic outline of the Garden Dispensation would look like this:

1. The creation–Genesis 1:1-2:3.
2. Man formed of the dust of the ground–Gen. 2:4-7.
3. The garden of Eden–Gen. 2:8-15, 2:19-20.
4. Eve created to help Adam–Gen. 2:18, 2:21-22, 3:30.
5. Marriage instituted: Man and wife become one flesh–Gen. 2:23-25.
6. Probation: The Eden Covenant–Gen. 2:16-17.
7. The temptation–Gen. 3:1-5.

8. The fall–Gen. 3:6.
9. Conviction–Gen. 3:7-13.
10. Judgment–Gen. 3:14-19.
11. The promise: The Redeemer Covenant–Gen. 3:15.
12. Coats of skins–Gen. 3:21.
13. Expulsion from the garden–Gen. 3:22-24.

The Flood Dispensation

The second dispensation period was the Flood Era. This period of time started with the expulsion from the garden of Eden and ended with the universal flood. It is recorded in Genesis chapters 4 through 7.

God's will for man was to choose to do good (now that man knew the difference between good and evil). Gen. 3:5, "For God doth know that in the day ye eat thereof, then your eyes shall be opened, and ye shall be as gods, knowing good and evil." Gen. 3:7, "And the eyes of them both were opened, and they knew that they were naked; and they sewed fig leaves together, and made themselves aprons." Gen. 3:21-22a, "(21) Unto Adam also and to his wife did the Lord God make coats of skins, and clothed them. (22a) And the Lord God said, Behold, the man is become as one of us, to know good and evil:"

Man ignored the will of God and chose to do evil. Gen. 6:5-6, "(5) And God saw that the wickedness of man was great in the earth, and that every imagination of the thoughts of his heart was only evil continually. (6) And it repented the Lord that he had made man on the earth, and it grieved him at his heart." Gen. 6:11-12, "(11) The earth also was corrupt before God, and the earth was filled with violence, (12) And God looked upon the earth, and, behold, it was corrupt; for all flesh had corrupted his way upon the earth."

God's judgment was the universal flood. Gen. 6:7, "And the Lord said, I will destroy man whom I have created from the face of the earth; both man, and beast, and the creeping thing, and the fowls of the air; for it repenteth me that I have made them." Gen. 6:17, "And, behold, I, even I, do bring a flood of waters upon the earth, to destroy all flesh, wherein is the breath of life, from under heaven; and every thing that is in the earth shall die."

The details of the flood are recorded in Genesis chapters 6 and 7. The only humans who survived the flood were Noah, his wife, his three sons, and their wives.

A basic outline of the Flood Dispensation would look like this:

1. Cain and Abel–Genesis 4:1-24.
2. The generations of Adam–Gen. 4:25-5:32.
3. Spirits leave their habitation to marry humans–Gen. 6:1-13.

4. Noah and the ark–Gen. 6:14-7:3.
5. The flood–Gen. 7:4-24.

The Babel Dispensation

The third dispensation period was the Babel Era. It started with Noah after the flood and ended with the confusion of languages at the Tower of Babel. This era is recorded in Genesis chapters 8 through 11.

God's will for man was to scatter, multiply, and replenish the earth. Gen. 9:1, "And God blessed Noah and his sons, and said unto them, Be fruitful, and multiply, and replenish the earth."

Man did not scatter. Gen. 11:1-4, "(1) And the whole earth was of one language, and of one speech. (2) And it came to pass, as they journeyed from the east, that they found a plain in the land of Shinar; and they dwelt there. (3) And they said one to another, Go to, let us make brick, and burn them thoroughly. And they had brick for stone, and slime had they for mortar. (4) And they said, Go to, let us build us a city and a tower, whose top may reach unto heaven; and let us make us a name, lest we be scattered abroad upon the face of the whole earth."

God's judgment was the confusion of languages. Gen. 11:5-9, "(5) And the Lord came down to see the city and the tower, which the children of men builded. (6) And the Lord said, Behold, the people is one, and they have all one language; and this they begin to do: and now nothing will be restrained from them, which they have imagined to do. (7) Go to, let us go down, and there confound their language, that they may not understand one another's speech. (8) So the Lord scattered them abroad from thence upon the face of all the earth: and they left off to build the city. (9) Therefore is the name of it called Babel; because the Lord did there confound the language of all the earth: and from thence did the Lord scatter them abroad upon the face of all the earth."

A basic outline of the Babel Dispensation would look like this:

1. The flood ends–Genesis 8:1-20.
2. The rainbow Covenant–Gen. 8:21-9:17.
3. Noah's prophecy–Gen. 9:20-29.
4. Noah's family repopulates the earth–Gen. 9:18-19, 10:1-31.
5. The Tower of Babel–Gen. 11:1-9.
6. The generations from Shem to Abraham–Gen. 11:10-26.
7. The generations of Terah, Abraham's father–Gen. 11:27-32.

The Patriarch Dispensation

The fourth dispensation period was the Patriarch Era. This period of time started with the call of Abraham and ended with his descendants as slaves in Egypt. During this era, we have the beginning of the Nation of Israel, commonly called the Jews. This dispensation is recorded in Genesis chapter 12 through Exodus chapter 18.

God's will was for Abram (Abraham) to leave his native country and move to the land of Canaan. Gen. 12:1-7, "(1) Now the Lord had said unto Abram, Get thee out of thy country, and from thy kindred, and from thy father's house, unto a land that I will shew thee: (2) And I will make of thee a great nation, and I will bless thee, and make thy name great; and thou shalt be a blessing: (3) And I will bless them that bless thee, and curse him that curseth thee: and in thee shall all families of the earth be blessed. (4) So Abram departed, as the Lord had spoken unto him, and Lot went with him: and Abram was seventy and five years old when he departed out of Haran. (5) And Abram took Sarai his wife, and Lot his brother's son, and all their substance that they had gathered, and the souls that they had gotten in Haran; and they went forth to go into the land of Canaan; and into the land of Canaan they came. (6) And Abram passed through the land unto the place of Sichem, unto the plain of Moreh. And the Canaanite was then in the land. (7) And the Lord appeared unto Abram, and said, Unto thy seed will I give this land: and there builded he an altar unto the Lord, who appeared unto him."

Instead of dwelling in Canaan, Abram moved to Egypt. Gen. 12:10, "And there was a famine in the land: and Abram went down into Egypt to sojourn there; for the famine was grievous in the land."

God's judgment was four hundred years of Egyptian bondage for Abraham's descendants. Abraham was forewarned of the bondage, and when it would occur, in a prophecy recorded in Gen. 15:13-16, "(13) And he said unto Abram, Know for a surety that thy seed shall be a stranger in a land that is not theirs, and shall serve them; and they shall afflict them four hundred years; (14) And also that nation, whom they shall serve, will I judge: and afterward shall they come out with great substance. (15) And thou shalt go to thy fathers in peace; thou shalt be buried in a good old age. (16) But in the fourth generation they shall come hither again: for the iniquity of the Amorites is not yet full."

Abram was Abraham's Gentile name. At this point in time the entire world was Gentile (the Nation of Israel simply did not exist). In Genesis chapter 17, God made a covenant with Abram and changed his name to Abraham. In Genesis chapter 21, Abraham had a son named Isaac. In Genesis chapter 25; Isaac had a son named Jacob. In Genesis chapter 35, Jacob had twelve sons and God changed his name from Jacob to Israel. His twelve sons were the heads of the twelve tribes of Israel.

In reality, the Patriarch Dispensation ended when the children of Israel became slaves in Egypt. They were not slaves when they first entered Egypt. As we read the account of Joseph in Egypt (Gen. 39:1-45:28), we find that he was promoted to second in command of all the land of Egypt (Gen. 41:37-45). The account continues in Gen. 46:1-50:26 with Israel (Jacob) and his family entering Egypt as welcomed guests of the Pharaoh, not as slaves (Gen. 47:1-10). At some point in time during their 430-year stay in Egypt, the attitude of the king (Pharaoh) changed (Exodus 1:1-22). With this change of attitude, we have the transition period from welcomed guests to slaves.

Webster defines *transition* as the movement from one state, stage, place, or style to another. As we look at the entire Bible from a dispensational view, we can see transition periods from one dispensation to another. One dispensational era does not end at sundown and a new one began at sunup. The Patriarch Dispensation ended with the descendants of Abraham in Egyptian bondage. The Law Dispensation could not start before the law is given. This means all the events between the Egyptian bondage, in Exodus 1:1-22, and the giving of the law at Mount Sinai, in Exodus chapter 19, can be grouped together under the heading of Patriarch to Law Transition.

A basic outline of the Patriarch Dispensation would look like this:

1. The Patriarch Abraham–Genesis 12:1-25:18.
2. The Patriarchs Isaac and Jacob–Gen. 25:19-35:29.
3. The descendants of Esau–Gen. 36:1-19.
4. The descendants of Seir the Horite–Gen. 36:20-30.
5. Early kings of the land of Edom–Gen. 36:31-43.
6. Joseph sold into slavery–Gen. 37:1-36.
7. Judah and his son's wife–Gen. 38:1-30.
8. Joseph in Egypt–Gen. 39:1-45:28.
9. Israel and his family go to Egypt–Gen. 46:1-50:26.
10. Oppression of Israel–Exodus 1:1-22.

A basic outline of the Patriarch to Law Transition period would be:

1. The birth of Moses–Exodus 2:1-10.
2. God reveals himself to Moses–Exod. 2:11-4:31.
3. Pharaoh refuses to let Israel go–Exod. 5:1-7:7.
4. The plagues and signs worked in Egypt–Exod. 7:8-11:10.
5. The Passover–Exod. 12:1-13:16.
6. Crossing the Red Sea–Exod. 13:17-14:31.
7. The song of Moses–Exod. 15:1-21.
8. Israel in the wilderness–Exod. 15:22-17:16.
9. Moses visited by his father-in-law Jethro–Exod. 18:1-27.

The Law Dispensation

The fifth dispensation was the Law Era. The Children (Nation) of Israel were taken to Mount Sinai and given the law. God told them to obey all the law, prosper in the promised land, and wait for the promised Messiah. Rejection would result in their being scattered among the Gentile Nations, until the "times of the Gentiles" were fulfilled. In addition to the warning of worldwide dispersion, the Israelites were also promised that in the "latter days" they would be regathered in the promised land and given an everlasting kingdom. This promised kingdom concerns dominion and lordship in the physical realm (the land), whereas the kingdom promised to Church members (born-again believers) is dominion and lordship in the spirit realm (the heavens).

God's will was for the nation of Israel to obey all the law, that they may prosper in the promised land and function in the world as a kingdom of priests. Exodus 19:3-6, "(3) And Moses went up unto God, and the Lord called unto him out of the mountain, saying, Thus shalt thou say to the house of Jacob, and tell the children of Israel; (4) Ye have seen what I did unto the Egyptians, and how I bare you on eagles' wings, and brought you unto myself. (5) Now therefore, if ye will obey my voice indeed, and keep my covenant, then ye shall be a peculiar treasure unto me above all people: for all the earth is mine: (6) And ye shall be unto me a kingdom of priests, and an holy nation. These are the words which thou shalt speak unto the children of Israel." Notice these laws and this covenant were given to the "house of Jacob" and the "children of Israel," not the Gentile Nations.

Instead of obedience, Israel broke the law and went into captivity among the Gentile Nations. Their failures are summarized in 2 Kings 17:6-23, which ends with the statement, "So was Israel carried away out of their own land to Assyria unto this day." As we continue to follow history and prophecy, we will find the Israelites' captivity by the Assyrians was followed by captivity by the Babylonians, Medes, Persians, Greeks, and Romans.

In a prophecy in Deuteronomy, Moses told Israel its future before it even entered the promised land. The extent of this prophecy is to the "latter days tribulation," when Israel turns to the Lord and God remembers the covenant he made with the patriarchs. Deuteronomy 4:25-31, "(25) When thou shalt beget children, and children's children, and ye shall have remained long in the land, and shall corrupt yourselves, and make a graven image, or the likeness of any thing, and shall do evil in the sight of the Lord thy God, to provoke him to anger: (26) I call heaven and earth to witness against you this day, that ye shall soon utterly perish from off the land whereunto ye go over Jordan to possess it; ye shall not prolong your days upon it, but shall utterly be destroyed. (27) And the Lord shall scatter you among the nations, and ye shall be left few in number among the heathen, whither the Lord shall lead you. (28) And there ye shall serve gods, the work of men's hands, wood and stone, which neither see, nor hear, nor eat, nor smell. (29) But if from thence thou shalt seek the Lord thy God, thou shalt find him, if thou seek him with all thy heart and with all thy soul. (30) When thou art in tribulation, and all these things are come upon thee, even in the latter days, if thou turn to the Lord thy God, and shalt be obedient unto his voice; (31) (For the Lord thy God is a merciful God;) he will not forsake thee, neither destroy thee, nor forget the covenant of thy fathers which he sware unto them."

The Bible passages that speak of Israel being scattered among the nations and being regathered are numerous. Here are a few:

1. Leviticus 26:21-42 verse 33, "And I will scatter you among the heathen."
2. Deuteronomy 28:63-65 verse 64, "And the Lord shall scatter thee among all people, from the one end of the earth even unto the other."
3. Isaiah 11:10-12 verse 11, "And it shall come to pass in that day, that the Lord shall set his hand again the second time to recover the remnant of his people."
4. Isaiah 14:1-2, "(1) For the Lord will have mercy on Jacob, and will yet choose Israel, and set them in their own land: and the strangers shall be joined with them, and they shall cleave to the house of Jacob. (2) And the people shall take them, and bring them to their place: and the house of Israel shall possess them in the land of the Lord for servants and handmaids: and they shall take them captives, whose captives they were; and they shall rule over their oppressors."
5. Jeremiah 9:12-16 verse 16, "I will scatter them also among the heathen."
6. Jeremiah 30:10-11 verse 11, "thou I make a full end of all nations whither I have scattered thee, yet will I not make a full end of thee."
7. Jeremiah 31:10, "He that scattered Israel will gather him."
8. Ezekiel 6:8-10 verse 8, "Yet will I leave a remnant, that ye may have some that shall escape the sword among the nations, when ye shall be scattered through the countries."
9. Ezekiel 12:8-17 verse 15, "And they shall know that I am the Lord, when I shall scatter them among the nations, and disperse them in the countries."
10. Ezekiel 20:21-26 verse 23, "that I would scatter them among the heathen, and disperse them through the countries."

The scattering and regathering process is also discussed in Deuteronomy 30:1-7, Ezekiel 11:13-20, 20:33-38, 20:40-44, 22:13-16, 28:24-26, 34:1-16, 36:16-28, Isaiah 54:5-10, and Joel 3:1-2.

Many have erroneously taken the position that the scattering and regathering prophecies were all fulfilled in Old Testament history. This position leads to the conclusion that God has completed his program for the Jews. God did scatter and regather a remnant of Jews in Old Testament history. Disobedience of the law resulted in their being overcome by their enemies, but this "captivity" only foreshadowed their worldwide dispersion after rejecting Jesus Christ as the promised Messiah. If these prophecies had seen total fulfillment in Old Testament history, Jesus would not have spoken of the destruction of their temple and the Gentile captivity as future events during his ministry. He foretold of the temple being destroyed in Luke 21:5-6, "(5) And as some spake of the temple, how it was adorned with goodly stones and gifts, he (Jesus) said, (6) As for these things which ye behold, the days will come, in the which there shall not be left one stone upon another, that shall not be thrown down." Jesus foretold them of the captivity in Luke 21:24, "And they shall fall by the edge of the sword, and shall be lead away captive into all nations: and Jerusalem shall be trodden down of the Gentiles, until the times of the Gentiles be fulfilled."

Jerusalem and the temple were destroyed by the Roman army in A.D. 70 nearly forty years after the death of Jesus. It was at this time the Jews were dispersed, or as Jesus put it, "lead away captive into all nations." Israel ceased to exist as a nation until May 14, 1948. This scattering and regathering took place during New Testament history. Those who have taken the position that God has rejected the Jews cannot see the new Nation of Israel as a fulfillment of Bible prophecy. The Nation of Israel will play a leading role in the latter day events and could not fulfill that future role if it did not exist.

The next big event in the history of the Nation of Israel will be the Russian invasion of Palestine, called the Gog and Magog invasion in Ezekiel chapters 38 and 39. There was no way for God to fulfill this prophecy because Israel was scattered among the Gentile Nations. The Gog and Magog army is brought against the Israel which was gathered from among the nations and dwelling in their own land. Although the prophecy concerning the regathering of the Jews to their homeland will not see its final fulfillment until the start of the Kingdom Dispensation, the Jews in Palestine today are the Nation of Israel described in the Gog and Magog invasion.

The Jews had to be regathered and in control of the City of Jerusalem before the Nation of Israel could confirm a protection treaty with Antichrist. This actual event will introduce the seven-year tribulation period. Without the Nation of Israel, the events in the tribulation period could not begin to unfold. With a remnant of Jews in their land and the rise of Russia as a mighty military power north of Jerusalem, in conjunction with the formation of a ten Gentile nation confederacy, the stage is now set for God to continue his program with the Jews. Now that the Jews have been regathered, Earth is very close to Moses' "latter days tribulation," which is the seven year tribulation era. Now that the Jews control of the city of Jerusalem, Gentile world dominance is about to end, or as Jesus said, "Jerusalem shall be trodden down of the Gentiles, until the times of the Gentiles be fulfilled." Jesus and Moses were both speaking of the same period of time and we are the generation living in that time period.

Before continuing with modern Israel, let's return to our dispensational view of the Bible and take a look at Israel's history. In Exodus, chapter 19, we saw that the children of Israel were given the law. The remainder of the Old Testament is the account of the Nation of Israel living under the law dispensation. A concise view of Judaic history during this era would look like this:

1. The law is given at Mount Sinai, followed by forty years of wandering through the wilderness, under the leadership of Moses. This period of history is recorded in Exodus 19:1 through Deuteronomy 34:12.
2. Led by Joshua, the Israelites cross through the Jordan River and enter the promised land. Conquest of the promised land is recorded in the Book of Joshua.
3. Conquest of the promised land is followed by close to 450 years (Acts 13:20) during which the Jews are ruled by judges. This period of history is recorded in the Book of Judges.

At the end of the period of Judges we have the Book of Ruth (the great-grandmother of King David). In the Book of Genesis, God promised to bruise the head of the serpent by the seed of the woman, which gave us our first glimpse of his plan of redemption. God's call to Abraham to father a nation identified the Jews as the people, or nation, through which the Redeemer would enter the world. In the Book of Ruth, God identifies the family, within the nation, through which the Redeemer would come.

Samuel, the last judge, anointed Saul as King of Israel. After Saul's reign came King David's, followed by King Solomon's, which covers about 120 years of Jewish history. During the reign of these kings the Jews prospered and became a mighty nation. After the death of King Solomon, the Jewish nation was divided into two segments: the Northern and Southern Kingdoms. A basic outline of this era would look like this:

1. Israel organizes a kingdom under Samuel–1 Samuel 1:1-8:22.
2. King Saul–1 Samuel 9:1-31:13.
3. King David–2 Samuel 1:1 through 1 Kings 2:11.
4. King Solomon–1 Kings 2:11-11:43.
5. The Books of Psalms, Proverbs, Ecclesiastes, Song of Solomon.
6. The Kingdom of Israel is divided–1 Kings 12:1-24.
7. The Books of Kings and Chronicles–1 Kings 12:25 thru 2 Chron. 36:23.

Jeroboam (1 Kings 11:29-12:33) was anointed king of the ten tribes which formed the Northern Kingdom, also called the Kingdom of Israel. Jeroboam was followed by nineteen kings covering a period of approximately 200 years. The last king of the Northern Kingdom was King Hoshea. During Hoshea's reign, Shalmaneser, King of Assyria, invaded the Northern Kingdom (2 Kings 17:1-41), and eleven tribes were taken captive. This captivity marked the beginning of the "times of the Gentiles," and the first of the five fallen kings, Revelation 17:9-14 "(9) And here is the mind which hath wisdom. The seven heads are seven mountains, on which the woman sitteth. (10) And there are seven kings: five are fallen, and one is, and the other is not yet come; and when he cometh, he must continue a short space. (11) And the beast that was, and is not, even he is the eighth, and is of the seven, and goeth into perdition. (12) And the ten horns which thou sawest are ten kings, which have received no kingdom as yet; but receive power as kings one hour with the beast. (13) These have one mind, and shall give their power and strength unto the beast. (14) These shall make war with the Lamb, and the Lamb shall overcome them; for he is Lords of lords, and King of kings: and they that are with him are called, and chosen, and faithful." Verse 10 concerns the seven Gentile governments to rule during the Jewish captivity. Verse 11 is the False Prophet reign, which will be during the last half of the seven year tribulation period. His government will be the eighth and, although it is from the seventh, it will not be controlled by the Gentiles. The "times of the Gentiles" will end when he arrives on the scene and takes control of the seventh Gentile government. Verses 12 through 14 concerns the Antichrist reign during the first half of the tribulation period.

After the death of King Solomon, Rehoboam was anointed king over the two tribes (Benjamin and Judah) of the Southern Kingdom, also called the Kingdom of Judah. Rehoboam was followed by twenty kings over a period of 300 years. The Southern Kingdom (tribe of Judah only–2 Kings 17:18) continued to exist for about 100 years after the Northern Kingdom fell to the Assyrian Empire. The last king of the Southern Kingdom was Zedekiah. During his reign, Nebuchadnezzar, King of Babylon, invaded the land of Judah and the city of Jerusalem fell (2 Kings 25:1-21). With the fall of the Kingdom of Judah, we can identify the Babylonian Empire as the second of the five fallen (past) kings of Rev. 17:10.

The next Gentile world power to conquer Jerusalem was the Median Empire under King Darius (Daniel 5:30-31). The Median Empire represents the third fallen king of Rev. 17:10. The Prophet Daniel saw this world empire as a ram with two horns (kings). In Daniel 8:3-4 we read, "(3) Then I lifted up mine eyes, and saw, and, behold, there stood before the river a ram which had [two] horns: and the [two] horns [were] high; but one [was] higher than the other, and the higher came up last. (4) I saw the ram pushing westward, and northward, and southward; so that no beasts might stand before him, neither [was there any] that could deliver out of his hand; but he did according to his will, and became great." The higher horn, which came up last was Cyrus, King of Persia.

The Persian Empire represents the fourth fallen king of Rev. 17:10. King Cyrus authorized the Jews to return to Jerusalem and rebuild the temple which King Nebuchadnezzar had destroyed. Although a remnant of Jews returned during this period of time, the nation as a whole remained in captivity. Even during the Babylonian captivity, some Jews remained in the land as vine-dressers and husbandmen (2 Kings 25:11-12).

The next Gentile world power was the Greek Empire under Alexander the Great. With the rise of the Greek Empire we can identify the fifth fallen king of Rev. 17:10. Daniel saw the Greek Empire as a he goat in Daniel 8:5-8, "(5) And as I was considering, behold, an he goat came from the west on the face of the whole earth, and touched not the ground: and the goat [had] a notable horn between his eyes. (6) And he came to the ram that had [two] horns, which I had seen standing before the river, and ran unto him in the fury of his power. (7) And I saw him come close unto the ram, and he was moved with choler against him, and smote the ram, and brake his two horns: and there was no power in the ram to stand before him, but he cast him down to the ground, and stamped upon him: and there was none that could deliver the ram out of his hand. (8) Therefore the he goat waxed very great: and when he was strong, the great horn was broken; and for it came up four notable ones toward the four winds of heaven." Alexander the Great is the great horn, and at his death his kingdom was divided among his four army commanders.

The Greek Empire was replaced by the Roman Empire, which is the sixth Gentile world power. It is represented in Rev. 17:10 with the words "and one is." When the prophecy in the Book of the Revelation was given, the Roman Empire was a reality. The remainder of Rev. 17:10 deals with the future rise of the seventh Gentile world system, characterized by the formation of a ten-nation confederacy, which God described as the final state of the Roman Empire. When John received the Revelation on the Isle of Patmos at the beginning of the Church Age, the formation of this ten-nation world power was an event far in the future. Nineteen hundred years have passed since this prophecy was given to the Church. God is about to slam the Church door shut, in January 1981 Greece entered the European Common Market as the tenth nation in the revived Roman Empire. Born-again believers are about to receive their reward and the Jews are about to inherit the kingdom promised to their forefathers. Daniel puts it this way in Dan. 2:44, "And in the days of these kings shall the God of heaven set up a kingdom, which shall never be destroyed: and the kingdom shall not be left to other people, but it shall break in pieces and consume all these kingdoms, and it shall stand for ever."

In many of the visions in the Book of Daniel dealing with world history, the Gentile world powers are seen from God's point-of-view as beast kingdoms. They can be seen in the great human image in Daniel 2:31-45, "(31) Thou, O king, sawest, and behold a great image. This great image, whose brightness [was] excellent, stood before thee; and the form thereof [was] terrible. (32) This image's head [was] of fine gold, his breast and his arms of silver, his belly and his thighs of brass, (33) His legs of iron, his feet part of iron and part of clay. (34) Thou sawest till that a stone was cut out without hands, which smote the image upon his feet [that were] of iron and clay, and brake them to pieces. (35) Then was the iron, the clay, the brass, the silver, and the gold, broken to pieces together, and became like the chaff of the summer threshingfloors; and the wind carried them away, that no place was found for them: and the stone that smote the image became a great mountain, and filled the whole earth. (36) This [is] the dream; and we will tell the interpretation thereof before the king. (37) Thou, O king, [art] a king of kings: for the God of heaven hath given thee a kingdom, power, and strength, and glory. (38) And wheresoever the children of men dwell, the beasts of the field and the fowls of the heaven hath he given into thine hand, and hath made thee ruler over them all. Thou [art] this head of gold. (39) And after thee shall arise another kingdom inferior to thee, and another third kingdom of brass, which shall bear rule over all the earth. (40) And the fourth kingdom shall be strong as iron: forasmuch as iron breaketh in pieces and subdueth all [things]: and as iron that breaketh all these, shall it break in pieces and bruise. (41) And whereas thou sawest the feet and toes, part of potters' clay, and part of iron, the kingdom shall be divided; but there shall be in it of the strength of the iron, forasmuch as thou sawest the iron mixed with miry clay. (42) And [as] the toes of the feet [were] part of iron, and part of clay, [so] the kingdom shall be partly strong, and partly broken. (43) And whereas thou sawest iron mixed with miry clay, they shall mingle themselves with the seed of men: but they shall not cleave one to another, even as iron is not mixed with clay. (44) And in the days of these kings shall the God of heaven set up a kingdom, which shall never be destroyed: and the kingdom shall not be left to other people, [but] it shall break in pieces and consume all these kingdoms, and it shall stand for ever. (45) Forasmuch as thou sawest that the stone was cut out of the mountain without hands, and that it brake in pieces the iron, the brass, the clay, the silver, and the gold; the great God hath made known to the king what shall come to pass hereafter: and the dream [is] certain, and the interpretation thereof sure." In verses 37 and 38 King Nebuchadnezzar is told he is the head of gold. His breast and two arms of silver represent the inferior Media-Persia kingdom. His belly and thighs of brass represent the Greek Empire. His two legs of iron represent the Eastern and Western divisions of the Roman Empire. His feet with ten toes, part of iron and part of clay, represent the final Gentile ten king government. In verse 44 we were told that God will set up his kingdom in the days of these kings, and we are the generation living in the days of these kings.

Daniel Chapter 7 is also a look at Gentile world powers, Daniel 7:2-8 "(2) Daniel spake and said, I saw in my vision by night, and, behold, the four winds of the heaven strove upon the great sea. (3) And four great beasts came up from the sea, diverse one from another. (4) The first [was] like a lion, and had eagle's wings: I beheld till the wings thereof were plucked, and it was lifted up from the earth, and made stand upon the feet as a man, and a man's heart was given to it. (5) And behold another beast, a second, like to a bear, and it raised up itself on one side, and [it had] three ribs in the mouth of it between the teeth of it: and they said thus unto it, Arise, devour much flesh. (6) After this I beheld, and lo another, like a leopard, which had upon the back of it four wings of a fowl; the beast had also four heads; and dominion was given to it. (7) After this I saw in the night visions, and behold a fourth beast, dreadful and terrible, and strong exceedingly; and it had great iron teeth: it devoured and brake in pieces, and stamped the residue with the feet of it: and it [was] diverse from all the beasts that [were] before it; and it had ten horns. (8) I considered the horns, and, behold, there came up among them another little horn, before whom there were three of the first horns plucked up by the roots: and, behold, in this horn [were] eyes like the eyes of man, and a mouth speaking great things." Daniel is told what the beast represents in verse 17, "These great beasts, which are four, [are] four kings, [which] shall arise out of the earth." The lion of verse 4 was the Median Empire, the bear of verse 5 was the Persia Empire, and the leopard of verse 6 was the Greek Empire. The dreadful beast with iron teeth in verse 7 was the Roman Empire and its ten horns were the ten king kingdom. The "times of the Gentiles" will end when the little horn (False Prophet) arrives and eliminates three of the ten kingdoms.

A basic outline of the remaining books in the Old Testament portion of the Bible would look like this:

1. Before the fall of the Northern Kingdom, God sent the prophets Jonah, Amos, Hosea, Isaiah, and Micah.
2. As the Northern Kingdom goes into captivity we have the prophets Zephaniah, Nahum, Jeremiah, and the Book of Lamentations.
3. As the Assyrian Empire is replaced by the Babylonian Empire we have the prophets, Habakkuk and Obadiah.
4. During the Babylonian Era we have the prophets Daniel, Ezekiel, and from the text of Joel, I would include his prophecies in this era.
5. After the Babylonian captivity, a remnant of Jews returned and rebuilt Jerusalem. This era includes the Books of Esther, Haggai, Zechariah, Ezra, Nehemiah, and Malachi.
6. The date, and penman, of the Book of Job is uncertain. Many believe it was written before or during the days of Moses.

The Law to Church Transition

The announcement of the conception of John the Baptist marked the beginning of the Law to Church Transition period, and the coming of the Holy Spirit on the Day of Pentecost marked the end of the period. The entire life, ministry, death, resurrection, and ascension of Jesus is included in this period of time. The transition period includes the four gospels: Matthew, Mark, Luke, John, and the first chapter of the Book of Acts. The coming of the Holy Spirit on the Day of Pentecost marked the beginning of the Church Dispensation; thus, the entire transition period is actually part of the Law Dispensation. During this transition period, Jesus presented to the Nation of Israel his credentials as the Son of God, their King, the promised Messiah, the Redeemer, the Christ (the Anointed One), the person of whom all the Law and Prophets spoke. The Jews as a nation rejected Jesus and his ministry, which led to his death on the cross and the completion of the Father's plan of redemption.

Jesus' substitutionary death on the cross was God's plan of redemption, and by that sacrifice Jesus became the mediator of the New Covenant or Testament. Hebrews 9:13-15, "(13) For if the blood of goats and calves, and the ashes of an heifer sprinkling the unclean, sanctifieth to the purifying of the flesh: (14) How much more shall the blood of Christ, who through the eternal Spirit offered himself without spot to God, purge your conscience from dead works to serve the living God? (15) And for this cause he is the mediator of the new testament, that by means of death, for the redemption of the transgressions that were under the first testament, they which are called might receive the promise of eternal inheritance."

By rejecting Jesus the Mediator, the Jews rejected the New Covenant promise of sonship and the indwelling Holy Spirit, which resulted in their spiritual blindness. Romans 11:25-28, "(25) For I would not, brethren, that ye should be ignorant of this mystery, lest ye should be wise in your own conceits; that blindness in part is happened to Israel, until the fulness of the Gentiles be come in. (26) And so all Israel shall be saved: as it is written, There shall come out of Sion the Deliverer, and shall turn away ungodliness from Jacob: (27) For this is my covenant unto them, when I shall take away their sins. (28) As concerning the gospel, they are enemies for your sakes: but as touching the election, they are beloved for the fathers' sakes."

When the Church Dispensation ends, God will return to his program for the Jews and rebuild the Nation. That is when the "times of the Gentiles" will end and "all Israel shall be saved." Acts 15:12-17, "(12) Then all the multitude kept silence, and gave audience to Barnabas and Paul, declaring what miracles and wonders God had wrought among the Gentiles by them. (13) And after they had held their peace, James answered, saying, Men and brethren, hearken unto me: (14) Simeon hath declared how God at the first did visit the Gentiles, to take out of them a people for his name. (15) And to this agree the words of the prophets; as it is written, (16) After this I will return, and will build again the tabernacle of David, which is fallen down; and I will build again the ruins thereof, and I will set it up: (17) That the residue of men might seek after the Lord, and all the Gentiles, upon whom my name is called, saith the Lord, who doeth all these things." This will be the fulfillment of the prophecy in Amos 9:11-15, and the New Covenant promised to the Jews in Jeremiah 31:31-34 will become a reality.

The Church Dispensation

The sixth dispensation period is the Church Era. God foretold that the Nation of Israel would reject the Messiah, which resulted in their final worldwide dispersion among the Gentile Nations. Both John the Baptist and Jesus began their public ministry with the basic statement, "Repent, the kingdom of Heaven is at hand." The life, death, burial, and resurrection of Jesus completed God's plan of redemption. Those who accept Jesus as Savior and Lord and meet the requirements of the rebirth will receive the gift of the Holy Spirit and acceptance into the Kingdom of God. The Holy Spirit was poured upon 120 Jews on the Day of Pentecost and the Church was born. Some Jews accepted Jesus, but the Nation as a whole rejected Him and in A.D. 70 Jerusalem was destroyed and the Nation of Israel was dispersed among the Gentile Nations.

God's will during this era is for both Jews and Gentiles to accept Jesus Christ as Savior and Lord, and to be led by the Holy Spirit. Believers are required to live by faith in God's Word, publish the gospel, and baptize into the Kingdom of God. By the Word of God, the name of Jesus, and the power of the Holy Spirit, they are to overcome the world, the flesh, and the devil. The rejection of Jesus promises eternal damnation in the lake of fire. The Church Dispensation continues with the Church going through seven distinct periods of history and will end with the rapture of born-again believers. The rapture is recorded in 1 Thessalonians 4:13-18. It is when Jesus returns like a thief in the night to call out his believers, who meet him in the air. This will be the event that slams the Church door shut and makes possible the revealing of Antichrist to the world. The rapture will not mark the end of the world, only the end of the Church Era.

The Church Dispensation began with the arrival of the Holy Spirit in Acts chapter 2, and ended in Revelation chapter 20. In reality, the Church Era will end somewhere in the transition period between the Church to Kingdom Dispensation, with the rapture of the born-again believers. Nobody can put a date on when the rapture will occur. All we can do is watch for the signs of the end of the age and keep in mind what Jesus said in Matthew 25:13, "Watch therefore, for ye know neither the day nor the hour wherein the Son of man cometh."

Jesus gave the Church Commission in Mark 16:15-18 but instructed the disciples to dwell in Jerusalem until the arrival of the Holy Spirit (Acts 1:1-9). The Book of Acts deals with the Gospel of Jesus being published to the world and the establishment of Churches. The outline of the Book of Acts is given in Acts 1:8, "But ye shall receive power, after that the Holy Ghost is come upon you: and ye shall be witnesses unto me both in Jerusalem (Acts 2:14-8:4), and in all Judea, and in Samaria (Acts 8:5-12:25), and unto the uttermost part of the earth (Acts 13:1-28:31)." The Epistles are letters of instruction which make up the remainder of the New Testament portion of the Bible. The last book in the Bible is the Revelation of Jesus Christ, which we will deal with in later chapters.

The Church to Kingdom Transition

The transition period from the Church Dispensation to the Kingdom Dispensation will be a period of time that is filled with activity. It includes:

1. The last period of the Church Era, in which the apostate Laodicean Church will be formed. The rapture of born-again believers from the earth will leave the Laodicean congregation to enter the seven-year tribulation period. The Laodicean churches will be destroyed by Antichrist during the first three-and-one-half years of the tribulation period.
2. The last Gentile World Empire formed with the union of ten nations in the area of the old Roman Empire. This organization can be realized in the European Common Market confederacy. It is through this organization that Antichrist (in person) must enter the world. When Antichrist is given political control of this organization the stage is set for the seven year tribulation period.
3. The restoration of the Jews as a nation will occur.
4. The seven-year tribulation will be the last event in the Church to Kingdom transition period.

The arrival of the Holy Spirit on the Day of Pentecost (Acts 2:1-4) is the first day of the Church Era. This event divided the population of the earth into one of three groups:

1. The Church, born-again believers.
2. The Jews, actual descendants of Abraham.
3. The Gentiles, the remaining population.

We need to retain this distinction as we follow each group through the Church to Kingdom transition period.

The Church Era has continued for approximately 1990 years, through seven distinct periods of history which are outlined in chapters 2 and 3 of the Book of the Revelation. Each period is distinguishable by certain characteristics, which we will discuss in a later chapter. The last period of Church history will be the Laodicean Era when Jesus is presented as outside the church, at the door, knocking for admittance. During this period of time, Christendom will be infiltrated by false prophets, apostates, and antichrists, who promote false doctrines with such cunning that a large portion of the Church membership will be deceived. The rapture will be restricted to church members only and will be the event by which Jesus separates true born-again believers from the Laodicean church members. True born-again believers are members of the Body of Christ, and their names may, or may not, appear on the membership role of a church organization. Remember, it is to the Laodicean church Jesus says, "I will spue [vomit] thee out of my mouth" (Rev. 3:15). This can be understood if we remember that every church organization on the face of the earth, will continue to exist after the rapture. Those meeting the requirements that Jesus established for being saved will be removed from the earth. After the rapture all the remaining church members will be grouped together to form the one world church, identified in Rev. 17:16 as "the hated whore." This organization will be destroyed by Antichrist during the first three and one-half years of the seven-year tribulation period.

The rapture will separate the true Church, presented in the Bible as the "Bride of Christ," from the false church, presented as the hated whore. The rapture will complete the body or group of "called out ones" and the church door will be shut. Although a great multitude will be saved during the tribulation period, they will not be saved as Church members. Individuals who confess true faith must be killed by the Antichrist organization in order to inherit eternal life during the tribulation period. They are identified in the Book of the Revelation (Rev. 7:9-17) as the tribulation dead, and should not be confused with Church members who will be resurrected from the dead to receive their glorified eternal bodies at the rapture. Those saved during the church age will be honored as the Bride of Christ at the marriage supper of the Lamb, while the tribulation dead and all the saved from past dispensations, will be present as guests or friends of the Bridegroom.

The second group of people during the Church Age are the Gentiles. "The times of the Gentiles" is that period of world history when the Jewish Nation was conquered and ruled over by Gentile world powers. It is the period of time when the Jews were scattered among the nations. The terms "latter days" or "last times" usually speaks of the tribulation period, when the "times of the Gentiles" comes to an end and the "kingdom" (world dominion) is restored to Israel. The first Gentile world power was Assyria, chronologically followed by the Babylonians, Medes, Persians, Greeks, and the Romans.

The last Gentile world power will be the ten-nation confederacy, which is the final state of the old Roman Empire. When the European Common Market formed, this ten-nation world power became a reality. In 1967, the same year the Jews took control of Jerusalem, Germany, France, Italy, Belgium, Luxembourg, and the Netherlands united to form the base of the European Common Market. England, Ireland, and Denmark were added in January 1973. In January 1981, Greece became the tenth nation. It is through this organization that the Antichrist will come. He will be followed three and one-half years later by the False Prophet, who will eliminate three of the ten nations from the confederacy. Daniel put it this way in chapter 7 verse 8, "I considered the horns (the ten horns of verse 7) and, behold, there came up among them another little horn (the False Prophet), before whom there were three of the first horns plucked up by the roots: and, behold, in this horn were eyes like the eyes of man, and a mouth speaking great things." With the rise of the False Prophet I would look for the fall of Belgium, Luxembourg, and the Netherlands, which are the three nations within the union with monarchy-type governments. When control of this organization is given to the False Prophet, it will become the eighth kingdom (Rev. 17:11), and will be controlled by Satan, not the Gentiles. This is the beast kingdom of the Book of the Revelation, which is destroyed by Jesus when he returns to the earth to establish the Kingdom Dispensation.

For the Gentiles, the Battle of Armageddon will be followed by the sheep and goat judgment of Matthew 25:31-46. This judgment of Gentile Nations will be based solely on their treatment of the Jews during the last half of the tribulation period. The Goat nations represent those nations which aided the Antichrist/False Prophet organization in their efforts to exterminate the Jews. These nations will be destroyed and will not enter the Kingdom Dispensation. The sheep nations represent the Gentile Nations which helped the Jews in their flight from the organization. These nations will enter the Kingdom Dispensation, where they will be ruled over with "a rod of iron."

In addition to the sheep and goat nation judgment, there will be the tares judgment, recorded in Matthew 13:24-30 and 13:36-43. The elimination of the goat nations may account for some, but not all, of the tares that are burned. The sheep and goat judgment will involve nations, whereas the tares judgment will involve individuals. The criteria in the sheep and goat judgment will be the nations' treatment of the Jews during the last half of the tribulation era, and the criteria in the tares judgment will be "to gather out of his kingdom all things that offend, and them which do iniquity" (Matthew 13:41b). Although a nation is judged to be a sheep nation because it did not persecute the Jews, not every individual within that nation will be permitted to live and enter the Kingdom Dispensation. Individuals in a sheep nation who have persecuted a Jew will be gathered and burned with all offensive and iniquitous things. When all these have been eliminated, Earth will enter the Kingdom Dispensation.

Now, let's consider the Jews, the actual descendants of Abraham. The Nation of Israel rejected Jesus as the promised Messiah, and in A.D. 66 the Jews revolted against Rome. The Roman Army led by Titus in A.D. 70 ended the revolt by destroying the temple and the wall around Jerusalem. In A.D. 135, the Jews tried to regain control of Jerusalem, which lead to another slaughter of several thousand Jews. After this revolt, the Jews were forbidden to enter Jerusalem under the death penalty and the final world-wide dispersion of the Jews became a reality. Christians or Moslems controlled Jerusalem for the next 1897 years, and for 1878 years the Jews ceased to exist as a nation.

During World War I, Palestine was conquered by the British. The Balfour Declaration issued in 1917 pledged British support for a Jewish national home in Palestine. In the same year, the Russian Revolution occurred, which put the Communist party in control of Russia. The year 1917 put the regathered Nation of Israel and Communist Russia on a collision course which will result in the Gog and Magog invasion of Ezekiel chapters 38 and 39. In 1923 Great Britain was given a mandate of Palestine and the Jews began returning to their homeland. Jewish immigration was met with resentment by the Arabs in Palestine, which has resulted in many Jewish-Arab clashes. Palestinian Arabs and surrounding Arab countries opposed the formation of a Jewish state and demanded independence for Palestine, with the Jews as a protected minority. In 1945 the Arab League was formed by seven Arab countries (Egypt, Syria, Lebanon, Trans-Jordan, Iraq, Saudi Arabia, and Yemen). In 1947 the United Nations divided Palestine into a Jewish state and an Arab state, separated by an international zone. In 1948 the seven league countries joined with the Palestinian Arabs in an unsuccessful attack on the new state of Israel. On May 14, 1948, the Jews announced to the world that Israel was once again a Nation. In 1967 the League countries again met defeat at the hands of Israel and in this seven-day war, the Jews gained complete control over the City of Jerusalem. The year 1967 put the City of Jerusalem and the European Common Market confederacy on a collision course which will someday result in the Battle of Armageddon. Seven to fourteen years before Armageddon, Russia will invade Palestine, which is the Gog invasion described in Ezekiel chapters 38 and 39.

A remnant of the Jews must be "brought forth out of the nations" (Ezekiel 38:8), and be dwelling in the land promised to Abraham and his descendants, before the stage is set for the Russian invasion. This will be the next major event on God's calendar for the new nation of Israel. Although many of the churches have rightly identified Gog and Magog as Russia, some have erroneously placed this invasion at the end of the Millennial Reign, based on Rev. 20:7-9, "(7) And when the thousand years are expired, Satan shall be loosed out of his prison, (8) And shall go out to deceive the nations which are in the four quarters of the earth, Gog and Magog, to gather them together to battle: the number of whom is as the sand of the sea. (9) And they went up on the breadth of the earth, and compassed the camp of the saints about, and the beloved city: and fire came down from God out of heaven, and devoured them." The Revelation 20 invasion will occur at the end of the Millennium (when the thousand years are expired), while both the Ezekiel and the Armageddon invasions will occur before the Millennial reign begins. The fire that devours the Revelation 20 army will also devour the planet, Rev. 20:11, "And I saw a great white throne, and him that sat on it, from whose face the earth and the heaven fled away; and there was found no place for them." (Also Rev. 21:1 and 2 Peter 3:7-13). The confusion exists because both armies are to be destroyed by a direct intervention from God. God's people living at the end of the Kingdom Dispensation, when Satan is loosed out of Hades, will be able to look at the historical record of the destruction of Russia and see a similar intervention by God in their future.

Some churches have erred by preaching that the Ezekiel invasion is the Armageddon invasion. The Armageddon army will be assembled and destroyed at the end of the seven-year tribulation period. The Ezekiel army is already assembled in Russia and will meet its destruction seven to fourteen years before the Battle of Armageddon. The Gog invasion has several characteristics which distinguish it from the battle of Armageddon:

1. All but one-sixth of the Gog army is destroyed (Ezekiel 39:2); however, every member of the Armageddon army is killed (Rev. 19:19-21).
2. The Armageddon army is comprised of people from all nations (Rev. 16:12-14), but the Gog army is comprised of selected nations, including: Russia, Persia (Iran), Ethiopia, Libya, and Gomer (Germany) (Ezekiel 38:1-7).
3. The Gog army did not evolve from the ten nation European Common Market confederacy, which is identified in the Revelation as the Beast kingdom.
4. The Gog invasion is followed by seven years of prosperity in the land of Israel (Ezek. 39:9-10), not 1000 years of prosperity during the reign of Jesus.
5. The intent of the Gog invasion is for God to magnify and sanctify Himself (Ezek. 38:23) to the Jews and Gentiles, not to destroy the Antichrist/False Prophet organization.

When the Russian army invades Palestine, God will destroy all but one-sixth of the army and will send fire on their homeland. This invasion will be followed by seven years of prosperity in the Nation of Israel. The destruction of the Russian Army will leave Communist China the winner of the political power struggle we are currently watching between these two nations. With the Russian army destroyed, China will invade Russia and eventually become a military threat to both Europe and the Middle East. Communist China is represented as the "kings of the east" in the Book of the Revelation. The advancing Chinese Army will threaten the prosperity of Israel, and as a result, the Nation of Israel will sign a protection treaty with the European Common Market Nations. The signing of this treaty will mark the first day of the tribulation era and then Earth will be exactly seven years away from the battle of Armageddon.

The Kingdom Dispensation

The seventh dispensation period will be the Kingdom Era. The seven-year tribulation period will end with the battle of Armageddon, when Jesus will return with his army to rescue Jerusalem (Zechariah 14:1-3). He will have come at least seven years earlier as a thief in the night for his Church, but this time he will come in glory and "every eye shall see him" (Rev. 1:7). During the millennial reign the Gentile nations will be ruled over with a rod of iron. This kingdom will be a literal kingdom with Jerusalem as its capital and Jesus as its King. His reign is described in Zechariah 14:9, "And the Lord shall be king over all the earth: in that day shall there be one Lord, and his name one."

God's will for man during this era is to accept and worship Jesus Christ as King of Kings and Lord of Lords. At this time the promises made to Abraham, Isaac, and Jacob in the Patriarch Dispensation and to their descendants in the Law Era will begin to be fulfilled. The only new information the Book of the Revelation adds to the Old Testament prophecies concerning the kingdom is the length of the era (Rev. 20:1-7) and an understanding of the sequence of events surrounding its establishment. All Gentile nations will be required to visit Jerusalem on a yearly basis, to worship the King, and to keep the feast of tabernacles (Zechariah 14:16-19). After living in a world environment of perfect justice and peace for 1000 years, a portion of the human race will rebel against the Kingship of Jesus when Satan, who was imprisoned at the beginning of the era, is released from Hades. This rebellion will be stopped by fire from God sent to devour the rebellious (Rev. 20:7-10). The Kingdom Era will be followed by the great White Throne Judgment (Rev. 20:11-15) of the lost souls from all dispensational periods and the fallen angels from the spirit realm. Following this judgment we have the creation of a new Heaven and a new Earth (Rev. 21:1).

Here are a few things that will take place during the Kingdom Era:

1. Isaiah 1:24-27–The Lord of hosts, the mighty one of Israel to restore Jerusalem.
2. Isaiah 2:1-5, Micah 4:1-7–World peace, the nations will beat their swords into plowshares and learn war no more.

3. Isaiah 2:10-18–The proud to be brought low and the Lord only exalted.
4. Isaiah 4:1-6–The Jews who escape the tribulation judgment will be exalted and called holy.
5. Isaiah 11:6-12–Israel regathered from the four corners of the earth, the earth shall be full of the knowledge of the Lord, the wolf to dwell with the lamb, the leopard to lie down with the kid.
6. Isaiah 12:1-6–Israel accepts the Holy One and he dwells in their midst.
7. Isaiah 14:1-3–Captivity reversed and Israel lives in peace.
8. Isaiah 27:1-6–The Lord slays the dragon, causes Jacob to take root. Israel will bud, blossom, and fill the face of the world with fruit.
9. Isaiah 27:12-13–The children of Israel gathered and worship the Lord at Jerusalem.
10. Isaiah 33:1-24–Jerusalem brought low, then exalted, when the Lord is judge, lawgiver, and king (verse 22).
11. Isaiah 35:1-10–Prosperity when the ransomed of the Lord returns.
12. Isaiah 51:17-23–Desolation and destruction to come up on Jerusalem then they are reversed and fall on the nations.
13. Isaiah 52:7-10–Great joy over Jerusalem's redemption when God reigns.
14. Isaiah 60:1-22–Jerusalem exalted, nations to serve or perish.
15. Isaiah 66:10-14–Joy in Jerusalem during the millennial reign.
16. Jeremiah 33:1-26–The millennial blessings.
17. Ezekiel 36:1-38–Israel restored in their land, their shame reversed and placed on the nations, their land to be like the garden of Eden.
18. Amos 9:11-15–Israel restored, prosperity, the plowman shall overtake the reaper, the treader of grapes overtakes him that soweth seed.
19. Zechaniah 3:14-20–Israel regathered and ruled by the Lord dwelling in their midst.
20. Zechariah 8:1-8–Jerusalem called the city of truth when the Lord dwells in her midst.
21. Zechariah 8:20-22–Nations and many people go to Jerusalem to pray and seek the Lord.
22. Zechariah 8:23–The Jews exalted, ten Gentile men take hold of the skirt of a Jew.

Chapter Two

The Nature of Things

The Origin of Sin

It is difficult to adequately explain in a few paragraphs what God has been trying to communicate to the human race for 6000 years. The source of all problems in the human family is a little three-letter word called *sin*. The origin of sin and God's remedy for it are what the Bible is all about. At some point in eternity past within the Elohim (the Trinity or Godhead that is the union of the Father, Son, and Holy Spirit), it was determined that the Son of God would put on flesh and die to redeem those in the human family who, of their own free will, would submit to his Lordship. Not only the plan of redemption, but the entire plan of creation was conceived in the mind of the Father, and executed by Jesus, with the Holy Spirit as the life giver.

Step one in the plan of creation was for Jesus to create a race of spirit-beings called Angels, whose function in the spiritual realm was as servant or messenger–first to the Godhead and later to the human family.

Step two was for Jesus to speak the physical universe into existence. It was the voice of Jesus which said, "Let there be . . . and there was." The purpose of the physical universe was to prepare a place for the human family to dwell; and to give us our first revelation of our heavenly Father. The Holy Spirit gives us the intent of the physical universe in Romans 1:19-20, "(19) Because that which may be known of God is manifest in them; for God hath shewed it unto them. (20) For the invisible things of him from the creation of the world are clearly seen, being understood by the things that are made, even his eternal power and Godhead; so that they are without excuse:" "They" are the people who have rejected the Biblical account of the Creation for other opinions, including the theory of evolution.

Step three was for Jesus to create the human family and give them dominion over the physical universe. The human family was created on a level above spirit-beings, with the intent that they would be a race of beings with which God could have communion.

At some point an archangel named Lucifer became lawless (see Isaiah 14:12-14 and Ezekiel 28:1-19). Lucifer was the highest created being in the spirit realm. In Ezekiel 28:12b we find, "Thou sealest up the sum, full of wisdom, and perfect in beauty." My personal belief is that Lucifer realized his own wisdom, beauty, and power, and compared himself to Adam and Eve. Why should a being as beautiful, powerful, and wise as he be servant to the humans? When Lucifer acted on this thought, he stepped out of the Will of God. One-third of the angels joined Lucifer in his rebellion against God. Some of these angels crossed from the spirit realm into the physical realm by putting on flesh and mingling with the human race. At the end of the flood dispensation, these spirits were confined to a prison under the surface of the earth, a place called Hades or the bottomless pit. The False Prophet is one of these spirit-beings who will be released from Hades at midpoint in the seven-year tribulation period (Rev. 17:8). Another 200 million will be released from the pit when the fifth angel sounds in Rev. 9:1-11.

Jesus did not make a mistake when he created Lucifer. In Ezekiel 28:15 we read, "Thou wast perfect in thy way from the day that thou wast created, till iniquity was found in thee." The word *iniquity* means lawless, without law, or outside the law. All law proceeds from the mouth of the law-giver, God. If we do what God says, we are operating under the law. If we go the way God says to go, we are going the right way or righteous way. Lucifer created lawlessness (iniquity) when he knowingly acted in a manner contrary to God's revealed will. When Lucifer took God's revealed will (the right way) and turned it around, he created the wrong way or unrighteousness.

When Lucifer approached Adam and Eve in the garden of Eden, they faced the same situation every angel had faced. Since that time, every human has faced Lucifer's temptation and today, you and I face it. Did Adam and Eve choose to live by the Word of God (the tree of life, revelation knowledge) or by the knowledge of good and evil (secular knowledge)? When they ignored God's revealed will and chose to live by knowledge, they joined Lucifer in his rebellion against God. There are only two sources of wisdom in the entire universe, and the Holy Spirit reveals them in James 3:14-17, "(14) But if ye have bitter envying and strife in your hearts, glory not, and lie not against the truth. (15) This wisdom descendeth not from above, but is earthly, sensual, devilish, (16) For where envying and strife is, there is confusion and every evil work. (17) But the wisdom that is from above is first pure, then peaceable, gentle, and easy to be intreated, full of mercy and good fruits, without partiality, and without hypocrisy."

God is one source of wisdom, and Lucifer, the god of this world system, is the other. Sensual, earthly knowledge is a mixture of truth and error. It is truth if it is in agreement with revelation knowledge but is error if it contradicts the written Word of God. God's wisdom is revelation knowledge–knowledge recorded in the Holy Bible and interpreted by the Holy Spirit. The Word of God is absolute truth, completely free from imperfections, lies, and deception, therefore, it is totally trustworthy. Lucifer's wisdom is described in verse 15, "This wisdom descendeth not from above, but is earthly, sensual, devilish." Devilish knowledge is satanic or demonic in origin and totally untrustworthy. Any person with a familiar spirit, such as a witch or warlock, is given demonic knowledge or information, which is used to control any who will respond to their information. The demonic spirit called the Prince of Grecia in Daniel 10:1-21 supplied the Greek Empire with the knowledge of the gods, demigods, and heroes of Greek mythology. Through that information, the demon controlled the people of the Greek Empire.

When Adam and Eve changed their source of wisdom, they changed their god. Lucifer became ruler of the human family and of the physical realm. In 2 Corinthians 4:4, the Holy Spirit calls Lucifer "the god of this world." In Rev. 20:2, he is called the dragon, that old serpent, the devil, and Satan. The ground, which was given to man to sustain him, became a curse. The spirit-beings who followed Lucifer in his rebellion were turned loose on the human race. They are the demons identified in the Bible as fallen angels, evil spirits, unclean spirits, foul spirits, deaf and dumb spirits, spirits of infirmity, spirits of divination, or just plain devils. The singular word *devil* refers to Satan, while the plural word *devils* refers to demons. Fear, oppression, doubt, blindness, lameness, illness, and all diseases are manifestations of demonic activity. When the truth becomes known, I believe that every problem which plagues the human family can be traced back to a sin and one of the demons. The human family, although created on an authoritative level above the angels, fell to a position below them. The Holy Spirit put it this way in 2 Peter 2:19b, "for of whom a man is overcome, of the same is he brought in bondage."

The Natural Man

Physical death befell the human family after Adam and Eve turned from God in the garden of Eden. Adam was created in a sinless state, in the image and likeness of God. In his original condition Adam would never have experienced physical death. In Genesis 2:17, God told Adam that the day he ate of the tree of knowledge of good and evil, he would die. In Genesis 5:5 we find Adam lived 930 years before he died. In God's eyes, Adam died in the garden of Eden the day he disobeyed. In reality, Adam died spiritually in the garden and died physically 930 years later, outside the garden. When Adam broke communion with God by his disobedience, he separated himself from the Holy Spirit. He was no longer a being created in the image and likeness of God. He was a sinful creature, separated from the life of God, and this is the condition he passed on to his offspring: the whole human race. In Genesis 5:3 we find Adam "begat a son in his own likeness, after his image," not in the image and likeness of God.

Like Adam, all humans, are triune; they consist of a spirit, soul, and body. The body also is triune (flesh, bones, and blood). It is equipped with five senses (sight, hearing, smell, taste, and touch), and they are receptors which send impulses to the brain, where the mind interprets and stores these impulses as knowledge in the intellect portion of the soul.

The soul is triune; it is the seat of emotion, reasoning, and intellect. The soul is a total record of all impulses generated by the sense organs, your interpretation of these impulses, and your reaction. It is the total lifetime record of everything you have ever thought, said, or done.

The spirit is triune; it consists of the conscience, the spirit of life, and the spirit of man. The conscience in its purest form is basically the voice of God. If we understand how a law works, we can understand how the conscience speaks. "Thou shalt not steal" (Exodus 20:15) is a God-given law which is generally accepted and enforced by society. If you tell a person it is wrong to steal, and he accepts the idea as a truth applying to him, he places it in his moral code of ethics. As long as he governs his actions to comply with this law, his conscience is silent. If he breaks this law and steals something, he violates his code of ethics and his conscience speaks. The person either repents or begins to wrestle with his conscience. The individual is a free moral agent and may appease his conscience by either obeying the rule or amending his code of ethics to reject it. If the law preceded from God and the individual rejects it, he is telling his Creator that he will not rule over him. The conscience is the voice of God only if the code of ethics is based on the Word of God. Everybody has a code of ethics, and, if it is violated, the conscience speaks. If you accept a lie as the truth and violate the lie, your conscience reacts the same. If Satan can separate you from the truth of the Word of God and guide you with the old cliche "Let your conscience be your guide," you are being guided the way he wants you to go. The Holy Spirit puts it this way in Proverbs 16:25, "There is a way that seemeth right unto a man, but the end thereof are the ways of death." The difference between what seems right and what is right can only be found in the Word of God.

The "spirit of life" is the second unit of the spirit of a human being. The "spirit of life" should not be confused with the Holy Spirit, which is God. This "spirit of life" is simply the God-given right to exist. It is given to an individual at conception and returns to God when the individual experiences physical death. The Holy Spirit speaks of it this way in Ecclesiastes 12:7, "Then shall the dust return to the earth as it was: and the spirit shall return unto God who gave it."

The "spirit of man" is the third unit of the spirit of a human being. It is this spirit that is you as an individual, recognizable with or without flesh. Apart from the Holy Spirit and the influences of demonic spirits, this spirit is what controls the human being. This spirit does not *control* your will–it *is* your will. This spirit dictates which thoughts you will react to, and it controls what you say and do. This spirit always strives to fulfill the desires of the flesh and the lusts of the soul.

Humans are equipped with a mind which is the mechanism between the physical body and the spirit. It is in our mind that we are 'conscious' or mentally awake and alert. In our mind is where the process of thinking takes place. It is in our mind that we perceive stimuli through physical contact or through the senses.

The real problem with sensual information is that our senses can lie to us. For example, I once touched a piece of dry ice. The nerves in my finger transmitted the sensation to my brain. The sensation was compared to previously recorded experiences and a thought was formed. As a result of my mental process, I arrived at the conclusion to remove the finger quickly, because it was being burned by the object it was touching. My sense of touch lied; my finger was being frozen, not burned. Dry ice is compressed carbon dioxide used as a refrigerant and is very cold, not hot. In our search for and accumulation of knowledge, we need to be most careful of what we accept as the truth, because that is the information we will use to govern our affairs, form our opinions, and establish our beliefs. If we accept false and erroneous knowledge as the truth, our opinions and beliefs can be nothing but false and erroneous. When God's truth is presented to someone with erroneous beliefs, it is perceived as a threat and met with resistance.

The same process takes place when I read a book. By the use of my sight, I read the author's words and information is transmitted to my brain. If the author is successful, his words will reform his original thought in my mind. The author may be communicating truth, or he may be telling me a lie. My eyes, or more specifically my sight, are not responsible for making any decisions about the validity of the author's thoughts. My eyes are only physical organs which generate impulses to my physical brain. After my physical brain receives the impulses, my mind analyzes them and makes decisions. The reasoning portion of my soul takes the information transmitted by the impulse and compares it to previously stored information on the same subject. The previously stored information is the knowledge already accumulated and retained in the intellect portion of my soul. If the decision calls for a moral or religious judgment, my soul calls on the conscience portion of my spirit to make the decision. The initial impulse of information came from a physical organ, but the resulting thought is not physical. There is no way for a scientist, or anyone else, to physically remove a thought from me, put it in a test tube, and analyze it.

The information from the impulse is stored and retained in the intellect portion of my soul. The thought generated as a result of the reasoning process is also stored and retained in the intellect portion. What I do with the thought, or what the thought causes me to do, is also stored, and all three literally become a part of me–not a part of my physical body, but a part of my soul. What I thought, said, and did yesterday are just as much a part of me as the food I ate yesterday. This is why the soul can be described as a lifetime record of everything a person has ever thought, said, or done. The word *information*, according to *Webster's Dictionary*, is defined as "the communication or reception of knowledge or intelligence." *Webster's* defines the word *knowledge* as "the fact or condition of knowing something with familiarity gained through experience or association." So the senses (sight, hearing, smell, taste, and touch) are really bits of information which are stored and retained in our soul as knowledge. Wisdom is the ability to recall previously stored knowledge and apply it to a current situation. When we reason, we are forming thoughts by comparing new information to the old information already stored. When we think, we are forming thoughts by recalling, comparing, or manipulating previously stored knowledge. This is the process by which we make all our decisions, a process which totally controls our behavior.

Since our decisions and behavior are determined by knowledge, it should be obvious that knowledge controls us. God designed the process by which we acquire and accumulate knowledge; hence, there is nothing wrong with the system. The danger is not *how* we learn, but *what* we learn. What I learned during my public school years and what I have learned from the Word of God were both learned by the same process. The 'teachers' were different, not the method of learning. The process by which we acquire knowledge does not control us. Knowledge does the controlling. Once this is realized, it is obvious that the originator of the knowledge actually does the controlling. If God says to "do this, but don't do that," and you respond in obedience to what he said, he is controlling you because he supplied the knowledge. On the other hand, if a person is ignorant of the Word of God and has accumulated only knowledge that is earthly, sensual, and devilish, it will be the only information they have to call on to make decisions and govern their affairs. In James 3:15 we are told that this wisdom is not from God, so it should be evident that the individual who has gained only earthly knowledge is controlled by Satan, not God.

In the Garden of Eden when Adam disobeyed God, he separated himself from the Holy Spirit. After the Holy Spirit left his body, what remained was something altogether different than what God had originally created. The being which was left is referred to in the Bible as the *natural man*. Adam was still a living human being, yet without the indwelling Holy Spirit, he was void of spiritual enlightenment and understanding. His remaining resources were his five natural senses, natural reasoning ability, and natural mental facility. Adam used these natural abilities to rationalize: God said I would die the day I ate of the tree of knowledge of good and evil (Gen. 2:17); Satan said I would not die if I ate (Gen. 3:1-5); I ate today and did not die (Gen. 3:6); therefore, Satan spoke the truth, and God is a liar. The natural man is nothing more than a person without the indwelling Holy Spirit, a creature using its natural abilities to arrive at a conclusion. The Holy Spirit speaks of the natural man this way in 1 Corinthians 2:11-14, "(11) For what man knoweth the things of a man, save the spirit of man which is in him? even so the things of God knoweth no man, but the Spirit of God. (12) Now we have received, not the spirit of the world, but the spirit which is of God; that we might know the things that are freely given to us of God. (13) Which things also we speak, not in the words which man's wisdom teacheth, but which the Holy Ghost teacheth; comparing spiritual things with spiritual. (14) But the natural man receiveth not the things of the Spirit of God: for they are foolishness unto him: neither can he know them, because they are spiritually discerned."

When Adam disobeyed the Word of God and separated himself from the Holy Spirit, nothing remained within him to allow him to reclaim the Holy Spirit. Verse 14 states that the ideals of the Spirit of God (Holy Spirit) seem foolish to the natural man, who cannot receive or know them. In the natural man, the spirit of man governs the individual's affairs through the five senses and the mental processes (reasoning and intellect). The Word of God is one of the many things of God, and if the natural man receives the Word and classifies it as foolishness, there is no way for the Word of God to govern the person. The only things that penetrate to the spirit portion of a person are the things the person accepts as the truth. As the natural man develops a code of ethics, he must first use his intellect to determine if the ideas presented to him are the truth. If an idea is classified as the truth and the individual agrees to conduct himself according to that truth, the idea enters the spirit and becomes a part of the conscience. If the idea is regarded as foolishness, it remains in the intellect and never penetrates to the spirit. Since the Word of God was regarded as foolishness by Adam's mental processes, he had no way to redeem himself. In this natural state Adam was spiritually dead and became what the Bible calls *carnally minded.* Here is what the Holy Spirit has to say about the carnally minded person in Romans 8:5-9, "(5) For they that are after the flesh do mind the things of the flesh; but they that are after the Spirit the things of the Spirit. (6) For to be carnally minded is death; but to be spiritually minded is life and peace. (7) Because the carnal mind is enmity against God: for it is not subject to the law of God, neither indeed can be. (8) So then they that are in the flesh cannot please God. (9) But ye are not in the flesh, but in the Spirit, if so be that the Spirit of God dwell in you. Now if any man have not the Spirit of Christ, he is none of his."

The human mind becomes hostile toward God when it cannot understand things as God says they are and cannot see things as God sees them. A person without the indwelling Holy Spirit is without spiritual discernment, because our individual human spirit (the spirit of man) cannot discern the things of God from the things of Satan. This forces the human spirit to rely on only natural mental faculty, which can interpret and understand physical things but not spiritual things. The human mind can understand the words of the Bible, but it cannot understand the spiritual truth behind those words. The human mind can understand the historical events in the Bible, but it cannot understand the spiritual manipulation behind those events. The human mind can understand the physical aspects of the law of God, but it cannot see and understand the spiritual significance behind those laws. In the mind of the natural man, everything must be caused, controlled, and explained by physical laws, or it must be rejected as foolishness.

Gods original design of a human was for the spirit (our conscience, the spirit of life, the spirit of man) to control the mind (our soul, the seat of our emotion, reasoning, and intellect), which controls the body (our flesh, bones, and blood). Where God dwelt in the original design was in our spirit (the spirit of life). After humanity's fall in the Garden of Eden, God could not co-exist with sin in the human body and had to separate Himself from the human physique. After this separation, the human spirit was altered and became merely the God-given privilege to exist in the physical realm. Satan had no dwelling place in the original human design, but the fall of Adam and Eve gave him control of the physical universe and he became the god of this world. Satan changed the human constitution by reversing the original design. The five senses, which read the physical environment, were used by Satan to make demands to the human mind which, in turn, made demands to the human spirit. With God and his Word out of the way, the demands of the flesh became stronger than the demands of God, and Satan was in control. Humans existed in this condition until Jesus died in our stead to provide the way for our heavenly Father to forgive our sins and reunite us with the Holy Spirit.

Before we leave the natural man, let's take a look at how the word *heart* is used in the Bible. The word *heart* is first used in Genesis 6:5, "And God saw that the wickedness of man was great in the earth, and that every imagination of the thoughts of his heart was only evil continually." In this statement the Holy Spirit was not referring to a physical heart. All the physical heart can do is pump blood and the only thing which proceeds out of it is blood. The heart the Holy Spirit is referring to is the very center of the human being–the human spirit, which actually controls a person's thoughts, words, and actions. Mans view of the good in man is quite different from God's view of man. In Jeremiah 17:5 we have the statement "Thus saith the Lord; Cursed be the man that trusteth in man, and maketh flesh his arm, and whose heart departeth from the Lord." He continues in verse 9 with the statement, "The heart is deceitful above all things, and desperately wicked: who can know it?"

The Bible tells of a day when the Pharisees found fault with the disciples of Jesus for not washing their hands before eating (Mark 7:1-23). They accused the disciples of defiling themselves by not keeping the traditions of the elders. Much needs to be said about this portion of Scripture, but the basic problem was that the Pharisees were worshipping God in vain. They had replaced what God told them to do with traditions and were "teaching for doctrine the commandments of men." Mark 7:14-23, "(14) And when he had called all the people unto him, he said unto them, Hearken unto me every one of you, and understand: (15) There is nothing from without a man, that entering into him can defile him: but the things which come out of him, those are they that defile the man. (16) If any man have ears to hear, let him hear. (17) And when he was entered into the house from the people, his disciples asked him concerning the parable. (18) And he saith unto them, Are ye so without understanding also? Do you not perceive, that whatsoever thing from without entereth into the man, it cannot defile him; (19) Because it entereth not into his heart, but into the belly, and goeth out into the draught, purging all meats? (20) And he said, That which cometh out of the man, that defileth the man. (21) For from within, out of the heart of men, proceed evil thoughts, adulteries, fornications, murders, (22) Thefts, covetousness, wickedness, deceit, lasciviousness, as evil eye, blasphemy, pride, foolishness: (23) All these evil things come from within, and defile the man." In Matthew 15:16-20 we read, "(16) And Jesus said, Are ye also yet without understanding? (17) Do not ye yet understand, that whatsoever entereth in at the mouth goeth into the belly, and is cast out into the draught? (18) But those things which proceed out of the mouth come forth from the heart; and they defile the man. (19) For of the heart proceed evil thoughts, murders, adulteries, fornications, thefts, false witness, blasphemies: (20) These are the things which defile a man: but to eat with unwashen hands defileth not a man."

Jesus is not speaking of Satan or demonic spirits. He is talking about the human being and the things that proceed from the heart of human beings. Humans hate to admit to being as evil as Jesus says we are, nor do we like to admit that the 'will' (Spirit of Man) of the natural man is the weakest of all the 'wills' in the universe. Even the weakest demonic spirit has a stronger will than the most powerful natural human being who ever lived.

Webster's defines the word *will* as "the power that the mind has to choose, decide, determine, and control over ones own affairs." Regardless of what the natural human being wills, he can only accomplish a goal if it does not conflict with Satan's plan for his or her life. If it conflicts with what the demonic spirits want, the more powerful will of the demon nullifies the will of the natural man. This is the position to which Adam brought the human family when he sinned in the Garden of Eden. Adam was created on an authoritative level above angelic beings, but when he sinned and separated himself from the Holy Spirit, he fell to an authoritative level below angelic spirit-beings.

If it were not for the more powerful will of God, Satan could annihilate the human race, and we could do nothing about it. There exists only one weapon that the natural man can use to defeat or overcome a demonic spirit. The weapon is a sword identified in Ephesians 6:17 as "the sword of the Spirit, which is the word of God." There is only one prayer God can hear from the natural man. It is in essence, "Jesus, have mercy on me, a sinner." No matter how much a natural man moans and groans, if he (or she) will not acknowledge his sinful condition and accept God's plan of salvation in Jesus, there is nothing God can do for him.

The Satanic Scheme

When Adam sinned and separated himself from the Holy Spirit, he could do nothing to correct the situation because his spirit was being controlled by the conclusion of his natural mental process that the laws of God were foolishness. God could have restored Adam to his original created condition, but if God had done this, Lucifer would have been able to claim that God was unjust. Adam had sinned and fallen from his created position, which was no different than what Lucifer had done. Both had sinned, and if God had overlooked Adam's sin, to be a just God, he would have to overlook all sin, including Lucifer's.

The consequence of sin was death. When the Bible speaks of death, it does not mean "to cease to exist." This is man's definition of death, just a convenient way of saying there is no hereafter, no resurrection or judgment by God. The Biblical definition of death is *separation.* When Adam died in the garden of Eden, he sinned and separated himself from the Holy Spirit (this is spiritual death). When Adam died physically, 930 years later, his soul and spirit separated from his physical body. This physical death is only temporary, and the day will come when Adam's soul and spirit will reunite with his body. He will be resurrected.

Lucifer knew if he could cause Adam and Eve to sin, the act would separate the human family from God. He knew this because he had already experienced it. When Lucifer introduced iniquity into the spirit realm, every angelic being was given the opportunity to choose between what God said and what Lucifer said. The angels who chose to remain true to God were confirmed as elect angels, and today, they are "ministering spirits, sent forth to minister for them who shall be heirs of salvation." The angels who chose to follow Lucifer were free to do so. It doesn't matter whether they were deceived by Lucifer or they followed him of their own free will; the outcome was the same. They separated themselves from God to serve Lucifer.

When Lucifer introduced iniquity into the physical realm in the garden of Eden, the opportunity was the same. Adam and Eve could choose to believe God or to believe Lucifer. Eve was deceived and Adam sinned knowingly, but the outcome was the same. They separated the human family from God.

In each dispensational era we have the same basic situation. God reveals his will, and the human family is given the opportunity to do what God says or suffer the consequences. It was not God's intent to create a robot-type race of beings. He merely explains the consequences of our actions and allows us to decide for ourselves.

The word *redemption* means "the act of redeeming." The word *redeem* means "to buy back by paying the ransom." The *redeemer* is the person who pays the ransom. The word *ransom* denotes something demanded for the release of a captured person. When Adam and Eve sinned, the human family was taken captive by Lucifer and his band of demonic spirits. The spirit of fear is one of these demons, and it manifested itself in Adam when he said, "I was afraid." (Genesis 3:10). After the human family was taken captive, there was nothing they could do to free themselves. The situation could be compared to a soldier captured by the enemy during a war, except Adam and Eve had no chance of escaping. No matter how hungry the captured soldier becomes, his captor chooses when and what to feed him. The soldier's desires are superseded by what his captor wants for him. If the captor chooses not to feed him, the captive starves to death. The captor can take the prisoner and inflict pain on him, kill him, mutilate his body, or whatever else pleases him. The captive's freedom is replaced by oppression, and he is forced to live in constant fear.

Divine justice dictated the death penalty as punishment for sin. Keep in mind, the word *death* does not mean "to cease to exist," it means "separation." The death penalty for sin is separation from God. The human family remained under control of the enemy until God Himself was willing to pay the ransom. In Ezekiel 28:12b, we saw that Lucifer was the highest created being in the spirit realm. He was also full of wisdom, which included knowledge of the Elohim, the triune Godhead. He was, after all, personally acquainted with God the Father, God the Son, and God the Holy Spirit. Lucifer was holding the human family captive and his demanded ransom was the separation of God the Son from the Father and Holy Spirit. Christians know Jesus Christ was the Redeemer, and the events in the garden of Eden revealed Lucifer as Antichrist. He had taken the human family hostage in order to maneuver the Son of God into a position where he could destroy Him.

Lucifer had seen the creation of the physical universe and realized that physical life was neither permanent nor eternal. The human race was a unique creation, separate from the impermanent life in the plant and animal kingdoms. Adam and Eve were created above plants and animals and given dominion over both. When God gave them dominion over the physical creation, He held them accountable for their actions. It is this responsibility that separates man from the animal kingdom. Human beings are accountable to God, but animals are not.

Adam and Eve were created with eternal life within them (that is, the Holy Spirit dwelt in them). Lucifer realized that things died in the plant and animal kingdoms because of the absence of the indwelling Holy Spirit. An animal had only the spirit of life (the God-given privilege to exist) and when the spirit of life was removed, the animal ceased to exist. In Lucifer's depraved condition, the human 'will' was more powerful than his, but if he could make humans disobey God, they would separate themselves from the Holy Spirit, and his 'will' would overpower theirs. Deprived of the Holy Spirit, yet alive in the physical realm, Lucifer could use the physical laws that govern all physical life against the human body to destroy it. This would give Lucifer dominion over the human race and now, he could kill, or more specifically, murder, them. The word *kill* means "to deprive of life." All Lucifer had to do now was to manipulate the Son of God into entering a human body where he could murder Him.

Instead of redeeming Adam and Eve in the garden of Eden, God drove them out. They left the garden in their fallen condition, but not without hope. God promised to send a Redeemer to save them from the hand of Lucifer. God's promise to send a redeemer is the Old Covenant (Testament). Individuals who lived during the four thousand years after the departure from Eden, were saved on the basis of what they did with that promise. Those who believed God acknowledged their need for a Redeemer and repented of their evil deeds, demonstrating their faith in God's Word. The law was given in the Old Covenant to demonstrate God's holiness and man's need for a Redeemer. The law also served to protect human beings from the effects of sin, administered by Lucifer and his demons, until the Redeemer arrived. But the promises connected to the law were only prosperity and good health in the land of the living, not eternal life in the hereafter. Nobody was saved under the Old Covenant by keeping the law, nor will anybody be saved today by keeping the law. Paul puts it this way in Galatians 2:21, "I do not frustrate the grace of God: for if righteousness come by the law, then Christ is dead in vain."

The Old Covenant was based on the atonement of sins until the Redeemer paid the ransom. God did not reveal all the details of His plan of redemption to Adam and Eve. In Gen. 3:15 we learn that the Redeemer would be the seed of a woman. In Gen. 3:21 God made Adam and Eve coats of skins and clothed them, which was a demonstration of the redemption plan:

1. The seed of the woman indicated the Redeemer would enter the world as a human baby.

2. They would be redeemed by the grace and mercy of God, not by their works. Their fig leaf coverings were replaced by coats of skins.
3. God would provide the Redeemer just as he supplied the animal for the coats.
4. The innocent animal God killed to provide the covering was an indication that without the shedding of blood there could be no forgiveness of sin.
5. The innocent would die for the guilty. They sinned and an innocent substitute was killed instead of them.
6. The Redeemer was already living. The innocent animal God killed to provide their coats of skins was in existence before they had committed the sin.

God continued to unfold his plan of redemption, and His Redeemer, throughout the remainder of the Bible. The law, animal sacrifices, the Levitical priesthood, the temple services, and many of the historical events and personages, were nothing more than foreshadowing of the promised Redeemer and his ministry. God provided enough prophecies and information concerning the Redeemer that the religious community should have spotted him immediately. Yet the religious organizations of his day did not even recognize him. One of their problems was that they failed to "study, rightly dividing the word of truth" (2 Timothy 2:15) concerning his ministry. The Redeemer was also to be a Prophet, Priest, and King. The religious leaders had the Book of Deuteronomy, and could have read what God said by the mouth of Moses concerning the coming Prophet. Deuteronomy 18:15-19, "(15) The Lord thy God will raise up unto thee a Prophet from the midst of thee, of thy brethren, like unto me; unto him ye shall hearken; (16) According to all that thou desirest of the Lord thy God in Horeb in the day of the assembly, saying, Let me not hear again the voice of the Lord my God, neither let me see this great fire any more, that I die not. (17) And the Lord said unto me, They have well spoken that which they have spoken. (18) I will raise them up a Prophet from among their brethren, like unto thee, and will put my word in his mouth; and he shall speak unto them all that I shall command him. (19) And it shall come to pass, that whosoever will not hearken unto my words which he shall speak in my name. I will require it of him."

Jesus Christ was the promised Prophet. His teachings and actions are in the books of Matthew, Mark, Luke, and John. What Jesus said about his words is recorded in John 12:44-50, "(44) Jesus cried and said, He that believeth on me, believeth not on me, but on him that sent me. (45) And he that seeth me seeth him that sent me. (46) I am come a light into the world, that whosoever believeth on me should not abide in darkness. (47) And if any man hear my words, and believe not, I judge him not: for I came not to judge the world, but to save the world. (48) He that rejecteth me, and receiveth not my words, hath one that judgeth him: the word that I have spoken, the same shall judge him in the last day. (49) For I have not spoken of myself; but the Father which sent me, he gave me a commandment, what I should say, and what I should speak. (50) And I know that his commandment is life everlasting: whatsoever I speak therefore, even as the Father said unto me, so I speak."

The religious leaders during Jesus' time were familiar with the laws concerning the Levitical Priesthood, temple services, and animal sacrifices, which were all examples of the substitutionary death of the Redeemer and his work as the High Priest. John the Baptist identified Jesus as the Redeemer, in John 1:29, with the statement "Behold the Lamb of God, which taketh away the sin of the world." Jesus spoke of his own death and resurrection in Matthew 17:22-23, Mark 9:31, and Mark 10:33-34.

The religious leaders knew that the Redeemer would deliver them from the hands of their enemy. Unfortunately, they viewed the Roman Army as their enemy instead of Lucifer. The Hebrew word *Messiah* and the Greek word *Christ* have the same basic meaning, "Anointed" or "the Anointed One." The promises God made concerning his Anointed King were much more appealing than the ones he made concerning the Prophet and High Priest. A prophet would direct attention to the Word of God, a priest would focus on sin, but neither was interested in defeating the powerful Roman Army. They had adopted the observance of the law as the plan of salvation, and when Jesus told them He was the way, they simply didn't want to hear it.

The religious leaders wanted Jesus to be killed, but not as the promised Redeemer. In John 12:46 Jesus said he came into the world as a light and that light was exposing the religious leaders as antichrists. They wanted to kill Jesus to shut his mouth. Their plot to kill him is mentioned in Matthew 26:3-4, Luke 22:2, John 5:18, 7:1, 7:19-26, and 8:34-47. In Matthew 20:28 and Mark 10:45, Jesus made it clear that he came "to give his life a ransom for many." Jesus paid that ransom by his death on the cross.

The Throne Room Scene

I would love to have been standing in God's throne room when Lucifer walked in to proclaim Jesus' death as his victory. Lucifer had just seen Jesus die on the cross and watched his spirit descend into Hades. The demonic spirits imprisoned in Hades were admiring and praising Lucifer for being successful in killing the Son of God. What crazy thoughts were going through Lucifer's mind are anyone's guess. Lucifer knew Jesus had prepared an eternal lake of fire for him and his followers, but now that he had Jesus captive, perhaps the Father would change those plans. Perhaps the Father would give up the human family for the return of his only Son. For four thousand years God had been holding in Abraham's Bosom the spirits of dead humans who were bold enough to believe His promise of redemption. Since the Redeemer was dead and in Hades, all these human spirits would have to be added to the millions already in Hades. Lucifer must have been bursting with pride knowing that the millions of human spirits who had believed in God were under the same condemnation as those who had believed in Lucifer, since the Redeemer died instead of releasing himself from the cross.

Lucifer just knew the Father's heart was broken, and he couldn't wait any longer to proclaim his victory. When he entered the throne room the Father wasn't angry, he was smiling. As Lucifer presented his accusations, the Father pointed out that Lucifer's conspiracy in the garden had been discussed in the Godhead before Lucifer was even created. Jesus had willingly agreed to live, suffer, and die in a human body in order to redeem those in the human family who would choose to believe God's Word. Lucifer quickly pointed out that the Redeemer was dead and his spirit was bound in Hades. God replied that Lucifer separated himself from God by sin; the human family separated themselves from the Holy Spirit by sin; then He pointed out that death (separation) was the result of sin, and that his Son, Jesus, had not committed a single sin.

Panic must have filled the face of Lucifer, until he remembered that nobody in a human body had ever completely obeyed all the law. After the soul of Jesus was brought in, the record is examined--every thought, word, and deed checked and rechecked–but to no avail because Jesus had lived a sinless life. In panic, Lucifer reviewed the prophecies in the Book of Books, hoping that Jesus had overlooked one and it went unfulfilled.

After Lucifer confirmed they all had been fulfilled, he turned his attention to Mary. Her record was checked. She was, in fact, a virgin. She had never had sex with a man before the birth of Jesus.

Before Lucifer had sinned, he had known Jesus personally, so he knew the Deity of Jesus was unquestionable. In heaven or in a human body, Jesus was still God. Then it dawned on Lucifer: Jesus had performed miracles. He had opened eyes Lucifer had blinded. He had cast out demons Lucifer had put in people. Jesus had healed people of sicknesses Lucifer had put on them. Jesus had restored to life people deprived of life by Lucifer. He then turned to the Father and submitted his final accusation: Jesus had overcome only because he used the power of his office. He had not emptied himself of being God. Instead of laying aside his God power, he had used it to heal, raise the dead, and free people from demonic possession and oppression.

By this time three days had passed and I suspect that the Father was growing tired of Lucifer's empty accusations. He turned to Lucifer and said something like, *Now listen you hard-headed hardhead, Jesus entered the human family and fulfilled every requirement of the Redeemer. He entered the human race as a baby, his parents potty-trained him, taught him to dress himself, taught him how to talk, and taught him My precepts and laws. You enticed him with every temptation known to the human family, but not once did he submit to your temptations, not once did he use the power of his office. By the time he was old enough to enter the*

Priesthood, it was obvious to the entire Creation that he would never yield to your temptations.

By the hand of John the Baptist Jesus was baptized in the Jordan River. In that act he identified himself with the human family and I identified him as "My beloved Son." It was at that time the Holy Spirit descended upon him. His sinless life and his future sacrifice on the cross qualified him as the mediator of the New Covenant I promised to make with my people. It was by my Word and the Holy Spirit that Jesus performed those miracles. Not once, in his entire ministry, did Jesus use a power unavailable to every human being under the terms of the New Covenant. In the days to come, people will learn what my Son accomplished for them on the cross, and those who believe are going to identify themselves with my Son in baptism. As they do, I will identify them as my children by restoring to them the Holy Spirit. By my Word, the indwelling Holy Spirit, and the name of my Son, they are going to continue doing what Jesus started. These believers are going to walk all over you, Lucifer, just as my Son has done.

Now Lucifer, the case is closed. My justice dictated the death penalty for sin. My Son, willingly, separated himself from Me and paid that penalty by his death on the cross. He offered Himself as a substitute, and I accept that sacrifice. For four thousand years, many humans have lived and died believing I would keep my promise and send the Redeemer. My Son standing in Hades is the evidence that I have kept my promise. I now declare those believers innocent of all their sins by the substitutionary death of my Son.

Now, concerning my Son. Just as my justice dictated the death penalty for sin, so does my justice dictate eternal life for obedience. Sin is the transgression of my law. For three days you have examined his life and ministry without finding a single fault. Would my justice, indeed, be just if I leave His spirit in Hades?

When they turned to look upon the spirit of Jesus in Hades, they could hear the demonic spirits and the spirits of millions of humans ridiculing him: *Resurrection! Don't be foolish, there is no such thing, nobody has ever walked out of this place.* Jesus turned and lifted his eyes toward heaven, gazing across the great fixed gulf he could see the millions of human spirits who had believed God's promise that the Redeemer would come. They would accompany him to heaven when he returns to his Father. Looking beyond them, he saw the surface of the earth, where his eleven disciples hid behind closed doors paging through the Scriptures and trying to understand what went wrong. For a second he imagined the day he would sit on his throne beside his Father to begin his ministry as High Priest. Under the New Covenant, he would send the Holy Spirit to unite with the spirits of humans who followed God's Word. The new species that would result from that union would be his Church.

Jesus looked beyond the earth, and he saw his Father's throne room. As their eyes met he heard his Father's words, "Thou art my son, this day have I begotten thee." Imagine the horror on Lucifer's face as he watched Jesus leave Hades and cross the great fixed gulf! Abel, the son of Adam and Eve, had sat on the edge of Abraham's Bosom for four thousand years and watched millions of human spirits cross the great gulf, always into but never out of Hades. As Jesus approached Paradise (Abraham's Bosom), he announced, "The victory is yours." The millions of spirits in Paradise, who died in the promise that the Redeemer would come, followed Jesus to his tomb. They watched as He entered his body and it passed through the grave clothes, leaving behind an empty mummy form. Joy filled their spirits as they watched the resurrection of Jesus. They knew that following the Church age they, too, would be reunited with their bodies, never to die again. As they walked out on the surface of the earth, they looked toward heaven in anticipation of following Jesus there in forty days.

These are the captives Paul speaks of in Ephesians 4:8-10, "(8) Wherefore he saith, When he ascended up on high, and led captivity captive, and gave gifts unto men. (9) (Now that he ascended, what is it but that he also descended first into the lower parts of the earth? (10) He that descended is the same also that ascended up far above all heavens, that he might fill all things)."

Sheol, Hades, and Hell

Forty days after his resurrection, Jesus ascended into heaven from the Mount of Olives. With him were the spirits of all the believers who were saved from the Flood, Babel, Patriarch, and Law Dispensations by the Old Covenant promise that the Redeemer would come. These spirits were held captive in the section of Sheol (world of the dead) known as Abraham's Bosom, which is also called the paradise section. God could not permit them to come to heaven until the sin penalty was paid. Before Jesus died on the cross, God had no way to forgive their sins. Because they confessed their sins, God would not permit Lucifer to initiate the effect of the sin on them, but He could not forgive and forget the sins. This process was called *atonement*, which simply means "covering." God could not forgive Adam and Eve, but he did 'cover' them. The blood of the innocent animal was used to 'cover' their sin until the Redeemer's blood could be used to remove it.

The animal sacrifices during the Levitical Priesthood demonstrated the same principle. Those of the children of Israel who believed God kept his commandments. If they broke one of his laws, they went to the Priest to confess the transgression and offer the prescribed sin offering. This would cancel Lucifer's legal right to impose his will on them, and it covered the sin until the Redeemer could remove it by offering Himself as the substitute. When God recalled the spirit of life from those who had offered atonement, they experienced physical death, and their spirits were carried by angels into the Paradise section of Sheol. They were not there to be tormented in any way. They merely rested there until Jesus died and paid the penalty for their sins. When Jesus was resurrected from the dead, all the inhabitants of the Paradise section were released and accompanied Jesus when he ascended to heaven. When Jesus returns after the tribulation period, these Old Testament saints will accompany him and be reunited with their bodies. In their resurrected bodies they will never again be subject to death, and will rule with Jesus throughout eternity.

The other section of Sheol is called Hades, (the bottomless pit). This is the temporary abode of the unsaved spirits from all seven dispensations. When individuals in an unsaved condition die their physical death, their spirit and soul are confined beneath the surface of the earth in the Hades section of Sheol. Human beings who die in a lost condition will remain in Hades until the second resurrection and the white throne judgment (Rev. 20:4-15). At this judgment they will be resurrected from the dead and stand before the God they rejected for sentencing to the lake of fire.

In Luke 16:19-31 Jesus tells of two men who died. Lazarus was saved and rested in the paradise section of Sheol, but the rich man was lost and being tormented in the Hades section. The word hell, in verse 23, is actually the Greek word Hades. The torment of the lost rich man is very real, not something he is imagining. Also, after he died and was buried, he still remained conscious and mentally alert. Luke 16:19-31, "(19) There was a certain rich man, which was clothed in purple and fine linen, and fared sumptuously every day: (20) And there was a certain beggar named Lazarus, which was laid at his gate, full of sores, (21) And desiring to be fed with the crumbs which fell from the rich man's table: moreover the dogs came and licked his sores. (22) And it came to pass, that the beggar died, and was carried by the angels into Abraham's bosom: the rich man also died, and was buried; (23) And in hell (Hades) he lift up his eyes, being in torments, and seeth Abraham afar off, and Lazarus in his bosom. (24) And he cried and said, Father Abraham, have mercy on me, and send Lazarus, that he may dip the tip of his finger in water, and cool my tongue; for I am tormented in this flame. (25) But Abraham said, Son, remember that thou in thy lifetime receivedst thy good things: and likewise Lazarus evil things: but now he is comforted, and thou are tormented. (26) And beside all this, between us and you there is a great gulf fixed: so that they which would pass from hence to you cannot; neither can they pass to us, that would come from thence. (27) Then he said, I pray thee therefore, father, that thou wouldest send him to my father's house: (28) For I have five brethren; that he may testify unto them, lest they also come into this place of torment. (29) Abraham saith unto him, They have Moses and the prophets; let them hear them. (30) And he said, Nay, father Abraham: but if one went unto them from the dead, they will repent. (31) And he said unto him, If they hear not Moses and the prophets, neither will they be persuaded, though one rose from the dead."

When Jesus was resurrected from the dead, he freed the Paradise section of Sheol. The captives who were there, accompanied him to heaven when he ascended. Since His resurrection, the spirits of the saved do not go into the earth. Today when an individual dies in a saved condition, he immediately ascends to be with Jesus in heaven (2 Corinthians 5:5-8). Under the terms of the New Covenant, the reborn cannot be separated from the Holy Spirit. They experience physical death, but their soul and spirit return to Heaven. The only thing to be put in the grave is the body. Jesus moved the Paradise section of Sheol to heaven. The only part of Sheol left beneath the surface of the earth is the Hades section. The unsaved still descend into Hades at death and will remain there until they are resurrected, judged, and transferred to the lake of fire at the white throne judgment.

The Hades section of Sheol is also where the demonic spirits are imprisoned for crossing from the spirit realm into the physical realm. These are the angels Jude speaks of in Jude 1:6, "And the angels which kept not their first estate, but left their habitation, he hath reserved in everlasting chains under darkness unto the judgment of the great day." They are the same angels Peter speaks of in 2 Peter 2:4, "For if God spared not the angels that sinned, but cast them down to hell, and delivered them into chains of darkness, to be reserved unto judgment." Again, the word *hell* is Hades, more specifically, "tartaroo" meaning the deepest part of Hades. Hell and Hades are two different places. Hades is an underground prison, and its geographical location is probably near the core of Earth. Hell is the Greek word *gehenna*, and its true definition can be found in Rev. 19:20. This verse is at the end of the seven-year tribulation period, and Antichrist (the beast) and False Prophet are both "cast alive into a lake of fire burning with brimstone." This lake of fire is *hell*, the eternal abode of the condemned spirits after the white throne judgment resurrection. Hades is their underground prison until that resurrection. The word Hades paints a mental picture of floating in an endless mass of swirling molten lava. The word hell paints a mental picture of standing in the middle of the nuclear reaction taking place on the surface of the sun. Hades is also translated as *hell* in Matthew 11:23, 16:18, Luke 10:15, 16:23, Acts 2:27, 2:31, Rev. 1:18, 6:8, 20:13, 20:14, and in 1 Corinthians 15:55 it is translated as *grave*.

In chapter five of the book of the Revelation there is a search made for one worthy to open the book sealed with seven seals. In verse 5:2 we read, "And I saw a strong angel proclaiming with a loud voice, Who is worthy to open the book, and to loose the seals thereof." Verse 5:3 continues with the statement, "And no man in heaven, nor in earth, neither under the earth, was able to open the book, neither to look thereon." The phrase "neither under the earth" is just another way of saying the word *Hades*. The search included the men in heaven, in earth, and in Hades. The men in heaven are the saved. The men in earth are those living on the face of the earth at the time of the search. The men under the earth are the inhabitants of Hades who are the lost or unsaved.

There is a clear distinction made between Hades and Hell in the final sequence of events in Revelation chapters 19 and 20. Chapter 19 is the return of Jesus to destroy the Armageddon army and establish the Kingdom Dispensation. In Rev. 19:20 Antichrist and False Prophet are thrown into hell. In Rev. 20:1-3 Satan is bound and cast into Hades during the Kingdom Era (Rev. 20:4-6). From this we can see that these three individuals are confined in two different places. Antichrist and False Prophet are confined in literal hell, while Satan is confined in the bottomless pit (Hades). At the end of the Kingdom Dispensation, Satan will be released from the Hades prison, Rev. 20:7, "And when the thousand years are expired, Satan shall be loosed out of his prison." After leading the final rebellion against God (Rev. 20:8-9), Satan joins Antichrist and False Prophet in literal hell. Rev. 20:10, "And the devil that deceived them was cast into the lake of fire and brimstone, where the beast and the false prophet are, and shall be tormented day and night for ever and ever."

Incarnation, Reincarnation, Rebirth and Resurrection

From the account Jesus gave of Lazarus and the rich man, it is easy to see that soul sleep is an antichrist doctrine. Because of the great fixed gulf, it is impossible for the spirits of dead humans to return from Hades. The search for truth ends with Jesus who spoke the ultimate truth. In Luke 16:26 Jesus said, "there is a great gulf fixed: so that they which would pass from hence to you cannot: neither can they pass to us, that would come from thence." This statement makes the doctrine of reincarnation of human spirits totally antichrist. The word *incarnate* means "to take on bodily form and substance." The word *reincarnation* means "the act of taking on bodily form and substance again." The doctrine of human reincarnation is demonic. Humans are resurrected, not reincarnated. Both incarnation and reincarnation are restricted to the angelic beings. This is true for both elect angels and fallen angels.

An example of elect angels being incarnated can be found in Genesis chapters 18 and 19. The account begins when Abraham, sitting at the door of his tent, sees three men standing before him. After Abraham kills a calf and feeds them (Gen. 18:7), they tell Abraham that he and Sarah will have a son, even though Sarah is beyond the age of childbearing (Gen. 18:9-15). In verse 18:22, two of the men leave Abraham to go to the city of Sodom. In verse 19:1 these two "angels" arrive at Sodom. The man who stayed behind to tell Abraham of their mission is identified in verse 18:17 as "the Lord." Jesus tells Abraham, in verses 18:16-22, that he has come to examine the sin cry from Sodom and Gomorrah. Abraham knew Lot lived in Sodom and verses 18:23-33 are an account of Abraham interceding for the inhabitants of the cities. In verse 18:33 the Lord goes his way, and Abraham returns to his tent.

In verses 19:1-3 the two men, identified as angels, enter the city of Sodom, where they are given food and lodging by Lot. In verses 19:4-11 the inhabitants of Sodom gather against the house of Lot in an attempt to rape the two men. The crowd of Sodomites were homosexuals, and when they tried to break through the door of Lot's house, the two angels smote them with blindness. Then the angels told Lot to get his family out of the city because they were sent to destroy it (Gen. 19:13). The following morning the angels led Lot, his wife, and two daughters (Gen. 19:15-16) outside the city. In verse 19:17 they were told to flee to the mountains without looking back. In verses 19:18-21 Lot persuades the angels to let him dwell in the city of Zoar. In verse 19:22 they are told to escape in haste, for the angel could not destroy the cities until Lot was safe. In verse 19:23 Lot enters Zoar at sunup, and in verse 19:24 the Lord rains brimstone and fire out of heaven on Sodom and Gomorrah.

There are several accounts of angels appearing to people in both the Old and New Testament. Many people have taken the position that angelic activity ended at some point in the past, but the Bible does not teach this. In Psalm 91 it is clear that God's people are given angels to protect them. Jesus confirmed this statement in Matthew 18:10 when he said we should take heed not to despise children because of their angels. In Hebrews 1:14 angels are presented as "ministering spirits, sent forth to minister for them who shall be heirs of salvation." The account of Lot and his treatment of two strangers is a solemn warning to the peoples of all the ages concerning the treatment of strangers. What kind of reception would these two strangers get if they took a midnight walk through the streets of downtown New York City, or through the homosexual district of Los Angeles? Listen to the warning the Holy Spirit gives in Hebrews 13:2, "Be not forgetful to entertain strangers: for thereby some have entertained angels unawares."

An example of fallen angels being incarnated can be found in Genesis 6:1-5, "(1) And it came to pass, when men began to multiply on the face of the earth, and daughters were born unto them, (2) That the sons of God saw the daughters of men that they were fair; and they took them wives of all which they chose. (3) And the Lord said, My spirit shall not always strive with man, for that he also is flesh: yet his days shall be a hundred and twenty years. (4) There were giants in the earth in those days; and also after that, when the sons of God came in unto the daughters of men, and they bare children to them, the same became mighty men which were of old, men of renown. (5) And God saw that the wickedness of man was great in the earth, and that every imagination of the thoughts of his heart was only evil continually."

These "sons of God" are fallen angels and this demonic invasion resulted in the universal flood. The phrase "sons of God" is restricted to direct creations of God. All angels are direct creations of God and can rightfully be called "the sons of God" whether they are elect angels or fallen angels.

As we saw earlier, elect angels are incarnated in order to perform specific tasks according to the will or direction of God. Here the "sons of God" or demonic spirits put on flesh for the purpose of sinning by sexually seducing "the daughters of men." These are the angels who "left their own habitation" (Jude 1:6) and the fallen angels of 2 Peter 2:4-5, "(4) For if God spared not the angels that sinned, but cast them down to hell, and delivered them into chains of darkness, to be reserved unto judgment; (5) And spared not the old world, but saved Noah the eighth person, a preacher of righteousness, bringing in the flood upon the world of the ungodly."

The angels which left the spirit realm to mingle with the human race are now confined in Hades. However, not all the fallen angels were guilty of the sin of putting on flesh and leaving the spirit realm, and they are still free and active in our world today. The statement "and also after that" in Genesis 6:4 is a clear indication that the incarnation of demonic spirits is not an isolated event. With this in mind, reread the entire verse, "There were giants in the earth in those days; and also after that, when the sons of God came in unto the daughters of men, and they bare children to them, the same became mighty men which were of old, men of renown."

The universal flood was an act of mercy on the part of God. The demonic invasion before the flood resulted in the total corruption of all flesh on the face of the earth, except for the family of Noah (Genesis 6:6-10). This corruption resulted in the earth being filled with violence. Genesis 6:11-13, "(11) The earth also was corrupt before God, and the earth was filled with violence. (12) And God looked upon the earth, and, behold, it was corrupt; for all flesh had corrupted his way upon the earth. (13) And God said unto Noah, The end of all flesh is come before me; for the earth is filled with violence through them; and, behold, I will destroy them with the earth." The human race reached the point when it was reproducing itself only to increase the population of hell.

The phrase "sons of God" is used five times in the Old Testament. In every case it is used in connection with angelic beings, not human beings. It is used twice in the Genesis passages we just read and three times in the Book of Job. In Job 1:6 we read, "Now there was a day when the sons of God came to present themselves before the Lord, and Satan came also among them." Satan take away the prosperity of Job, in an attempt to make him sin against God. In verse 1:22 we find Satan was unsuccessful, "In all this Job sinned not, nor charged God foolishly." In Job 2:1 Satan and the "sons of God" again present themselves before the Lord, "Again there was a day when the sons of God came to present themselves before the Lord, and Satan came also among them to present himself before the Lord." As a result of this second discussion, Satan leaves the presence of the Lord and inflicts Job with the boils, Job 2:7, "So went Satan forth from the presence of the Lord, and smote Job with sore boils from the sole of his foot unto his crown."

It is debatable as to whether these "sons of God" were elect angels with good reports, fallen angels with accusations, or merely angels presenting a report of their activities. In any case, they were able to come into the presence of the Lord. At this point in time, Jesus was in heaven sitting on his throne. Members of the human family were not permitted to enter the throne room of God under the Old Covenant because of the sin problem. It was not until Jesus completed his redemptive work on the cross, and the New Covenant became effective, that man was given access to the throne room of God. Job lived several hundred years before the New Covenant was established.

The last use of the phrase "sons of God" in the Old Testament Scriptures takes us back to the time of the creation. Following Job's discussion with his three friends concerning the reason for his misfortune, the Lord speaks to Job out of a whirlwind. The discussion begins in Job 38:1-7, "(1) Then the Lord answered Job out of the whirlwind, and said, (2) Who is this that darkeneth counsel by words without knowledge? (3) Gird up now thy loins like a man; for I will demand of thee, and answer thou me. (4) Where wast thou when I laid the foundations of the earth? declare, if thou hast understanding. (5) Who hath laid the measures thereof, if thou knowest? or who hath stretched the line upon it? (6) Whereupon are the foundations thereof fastened? or who laid the corner stone thereof; (7) When the morning stars sang together, and all the sons of God shouted for joy?" Jesus is saying that the angelic host (sons of God) shouted for joy when they watched him speak the physical universe into existence. Adam and Eve were created in the latter part of the sixth day, and at this point in time, the creation of the physical universe had been completed. The only "sons of God" in existence at the beginning of the physical creation were angels.

The phrase "sons of God" is used six times in the New Testament Scriptures. In the Old Testament it is used in connection with angelic beings which were direct creations of God. In the New Testament it is used in connection with individuals who have experienced the new birth under the terms of the New Covenant. These individuals are new, distinct, direct creations of God. The Holy Spirit put it this way in 2 Corinthians 5:17, "Therefore if any man be in Christ, he is a new creature: old things are passed away; behold, all things are become new." The new creatures appeared on the earth on the Day of Pentecost, and will disappear from the face of the earth at the rapture. Here are the New Testament passages in which the phrase "sons of God" is used:

1. John 1:11-13, "(11) He (Jesus) came unto his own, and his own received him not. (12) But as many as received him, to them gave he power to become the sons of God, even to them that believe on his name: (13) Which were born, not of blood, nor of the will of the flesh, nor of the will of man, but of God."

2. Romans 8:13-14, "(13) For if ye live after the flesh, ye shall die: but if ye through the Spirit do mortify the deeds of the body, ye shall live. (14) For as many as are led by the Spirit of God, they are the sons of God."
3. Romans 8:18-19, "(18) For I reckon that the sufferings of this present time are not worthy to be compared with the glory which shall be revealed in us. (19) For the earnest expectation of the creature waiteth for the manifestation of the sons of God."
4. Philippians 2:13-16, "(13) For it is God which worketh in you both to will and to do of his good pleasure. (14) Do all things without murmurings and disputings: (15) That ye may be blameless and harmless, the sons of God, without rebuke, in the midst of a crooked and perverse nation, among whom ye shine as lights in the world; (16) Holding forth the word of life; that I may rejoice in the day of Christ, that I have not run in vain, neither labored in vain."
5. 1 John 3:1-3, "(1) Behold, what manner of love the Father hath bestowed upon us, that we should be called the sons of God; therefore the world knoweth us not, because it knew him not. (2) Beloved, now are we the sons of God, and it doth not yet appear what we shall be: but we know that, when he shall appear, we shall be like him; for we shall see him as he is. (3) And every man that hath this hope in him purifieth himself, even as he is pure."

Adam and Eve were both direct creations. Their children were the sons and daughters of Adam and Eve, not the sons and daughters of God. The parents were created by a direct act of God, while the children were created by an act of Adam and Eve. To be the children of God, we have to be born into the family of God, or as Jesus told Nicodemus in John 3:1-8, "Ye must be born again." The rebirth of which Jesus spoke is just as real as our initial birth. Our physical birth is a result of the uniting of our father and mother when a part of each of them came together to create a new and distinct individual. The difference between our initial birth and our second birth (being born-again) is that one is physical and the other spiritual. Through our physical birth we enter into the human family and through our spiritual birth we enter into the family of God. In our physical birth we are created in the image and likeness of our earthly parents. In the spiritual birth we are created in the image and likeness of our Heavenly Father. In John 3:4 Nicodemus's natural mind tries to connect being born-again to his initial birth, "Nicodemus saith unto him, How can a man be born when he is old? can he enter the second time into his mother's womb, and be born?" In John 3:6 Jesus tells Nicodemus that they are two entirely different births, "That which is born of the flesh is flesh; and that which is born of the Spirit is spirit."

Nicodemus recognized Jesus as a teacher come from God by the miracles he did. John 3:1-2, "(1) There was a man of the Pharisees, named Nicodemus, a ruler of the Jews: (2) The same came to Jesus by night, and said unto him, Rabbi, we know that thou art a teacher come from God: for no man can do these miracles that thou doest, except God be with him." Jesus begins by telling Nicodemus that unless a man is born again, he cannot see the kingdom of God, John 3:3, "Jesus answered and said unto him, Verily, verily, I say unto thee, Except a man be born again, he cannot see the kingdom of God." *See* is the Greek word *eido*, meaning to see in the sense of perceiving and understanding something with total assurance.

Jesus describes the rebirth in John 3:5, "Jesus answered, Verily, verily, I say unto thee, Except a man be born of water and of the Spirit, he cannot enter into the kingdom of God." The word *except* in Greek is *ean me* meaning "if not," which clearly means that unless a person is born again, he cannot enter into the kingdom of God. The word *of* in the phrase "of the Spirit" is in italic because it was added by the Bible translator. The word *Spirit* identifies the Holy Spirit. In total, Jesus told Nicodemus, "Unless a person is born again, of water and the Holy Spirit, they cannot see, or enter into the kingdom of God." The rebirth is twofold; that is, the person must be born of water and the Spirit. Being born-again of water and being born-again of the Holy Spirit are equally important for entrance into the kingdom of God.

Whatever is said preceding the word *and* is equal in rank, function, and importance to what is said after the word *and*. The misunderstanding of basic grammar concerning the word *and* has opened the door to heresy in which an individual or group chooses to believe and exalt part of the "and" statement but rejects the other part. Heresy then opens the door to perversion, and eventually God's message, is replaced by the imaginations of men. When Jesus said, "Except a man be born again of water and the Spirit, he cannot see or enter into the kingdom of God," he was not only explaining his ability to work miracles to Nicodemus, he was telling him what to do to be saved. Those who deny the rebirth requirement must explain away the Mark 16:17-18 signs Jesus gave us to distinguish believers from nonbelievers. Those who think they can be saved any other way must reject the entire statement. Those who deny water baptism as essential for salvation must remove "of water" from what Jesus said. Those who deny the existence or work of the Holy Spirit must remove "the Spirit" from what Jesus said. These heresies have resulted in more miscarriages than rebirths.

Part of the confusion concerning the rebirth involves who can be saved and how to be saved. There is a big difference between who and how. You and I and everyone else can be saved, but it must be done the way Jesus described. Who can be saved is best summed up in the words "whosoever will" of Rev. 22:17, "And the Spirit and the bride (Church) say, Come. And let him that heareth say, Come. And let him that is athirst come. And whosoever will, let him take the water of life freely." John 3:16 also tells us who can be saved, but it does not define how to be saved, "For God so loved the world, that he gave his only begotten Son, that whosoever believeth in him should not perish, but have everlasting life." Both statements define who can be saved, but how they are saved is by being born again of water and the Spirit.

To understand the "of water" part we need to take a look at John the Baptist. The Old Testament Scripture ends with the following statement in Malachi 4:5-6, "(5) Behold, I will send you Elijah the prophet before the coming of the great and dreadful day of the Lord: (6) And he shall turn the heart of the fathers to the children, and the heart of the children to their fathers, lest I come and smite the earth with a curse." When the Angel Gabriel announced the conception and ministry of John the Baptist he said the following in Luke 1:15-17, "(15) For he shall be great in the sight of the Lord, and shall drink neither wine nor strong drink; and he shall be filled with the Holy Ghost, even from his mother's womb. (16) And many of the children of Israel shall he turn to the Lord their God. (17) And he shall go before him in the spirit and power of Elias, to turn the hearts of the fathers to the children, and the disobedient to the wisdom of the just; to make ready a people prepared for the Lord." What John did "to make ready a people prepared for the Lord" was to introduce water baptism, which is why he is called John the Baptist.

Did John's ministry prepare people for the Lord, or was it a failure? To answer this question let's see what Jesus said concerning John and water baptism in Luke 7:24-30, "(24) And when the messengers of John were departed, he began to speak unto the people concerning John, What went ye out into the wilderness for to see? A reed shaken with the wind? (25) But what went ye out for to see? A man clothed in soft raiment? Behold, they which are gorgeously apparelled, and live delicately, are in kings' courts. (26) But what went ye out for to see? A prophet? Yea, I say unto you, and much more than a prophet. (27) This is he, of whom it is written, Behold, I send my messenger before thy face, which shall prepare thy way before thee. (28) For I say unto you, Among those that are born of women there is not a greater prophet than John the Baptist: but he that is least in the kingdom of God is greater than he. (29) And all the people that heard him, and the publicans, justified God, being baptized with the baptism of John. (30) But the Pharisees and lawyers rejected the counsel of God against themselves, being not baptized of him." Notice in verse 29 the people who believed what Jesus said, "justified God, being baptized with the baptism of John," which was water baptism. Also notice in verse 30 the people who rejected water baptism thereby, "rejected the counsel of God against themselves, being not baptized of him."

In plain words, the people who submitted to the water baptism John introduced were "made ready" or "prepared for the Lord." Those who rejected water baptism were not. In verse 30 "him" in the phrase "being not baptized of him" is John the Baptist, not Jesus. The disciples of Jesus baptized with water but Jesus did not, John 4:1-3, "(1) When therefore the Lord knew how the Pharisees had heard that Jesus made and baptized more disciples than John, (2) (Though Jesus himself baptized not, but his disciples,) (3) He left Judea, and departed again into Galilee." It is man's responsibility to preach the word and baptize with water, while it is the responsibility of Jesus to baptize with the Holy Ghost.

Both John the Baptist and the thief on the cross lived and died during the Law Dispensation. Neither were saved as born-again Church members. They were both saved as Old Testament saints. This is why Jesus could make the statement in Luke 7:28 that the least in the kingdom of God is greater than John the Baptist. It is much better to be a son or daughter than a servant–that is the difference between the Old Covenant and the New Covenant. Because of the ministry of John the Baptist and the earthly ministry of Jesus, people were prepared but their rebirth was not completed until the Day of Pentecost when Jesus began to baptize with the Holy Spirit.

At this point we could clarify the statement Jesus made to Nicodemus by adding the word *baptism*. The statement would then read "Except a man be born again of baptism with water and baptism with the Holy Spirit, he cannot see or enter into the kingdom of God." John said the one who sent him to baptize with water also described the method by which he was to identify the one "which baptizeth with the Holy Ghost." The Apostle John records John's testimony in John 1:29-34, "(29) The next day John seeth Jesus coming unto him, and saith, Behold the Lamb of God, which taketh away the sin of the world. (30) This is he of whom I said, After me cometh a man which is preferred before me: for he was before me. (31) And I knew him not: but that he should be made manifest to Israel, therefore am I come baptizing with water. (32) And John bare record, saying, I saw the Spirit descending from heaven like a dove, and it abode upon him. (33) And I knew him not: but he that sent me to baptize with water, the same said unto me, Upon whom thou shalt see the Spirit descending, and remaining on him, the same is he which baptizeth with the Holy Ghost. (34) And I saw, and bear record that this is the Son of God."

In addition to identifying Jesus as the Christ and introducing the baptism with water, John also preached of another baptism. What he preached, and how the people responded, is recorded in Mark 1:4-5, "(4) John did baptize in the wilderness, and preach the baptism of repentance for the remission of sins. (5) And there went out unto him all the land of Judea, and they of Jerusalem, and were all baptized of him in the river of Jordan, confessing their sins." With the "baptism of repentance" we can further clarify the rebirth statement. It would then read, "Except a man be born again of baptism of repentance, baptism with water, and baptism with the Holy Spirit, he cannot see or enter into the kingdom of God." What John did "to make ready a people prepared for the Lord" was to: (1) Proclaim, repent for the kingdom of heaven is at hand (Matthew 3:1-2); (2) preach the baptism of repentance for the remission of sins; (3) identified Jesus as the Son of God, the promised Redeemer; and (4) introduced water baptism. Those who rejected any one of the four elements of John's ministry were not prepared for the Lord.

When the people ask John if he is the Christ, he made this statement in Luke 3:15-16, "(15) And as the people were in expectation, and all men mused in their hearts of John, whether he was the Christ, or not; (16) John answered, saying unto them all, I indeed baptize you with water; but one mightier than I cometh, the latchet of whose shoes I am not worthy to unloose: he shall baptize you with the Holy Ghost and with fire." (Also see Matthew 3:7-12). The pronoun *he*, in the statement "he shall baptize you with the Holy Ghost and with fire" refers to Jesus. Again, the word *and* joins together two things of equal rank. Without doing damage to the statement we could change it to read, "Jesus shall baptize you with the Holy Ghost, and Jesus shall baptize you with fire." Now it is obvious that there are two different baptisms. Add these two baptisms to John's two and you have the total of the rebirth. We could revise the rebirth statement to read, "Except a man be born again of the baptism of repentance, the baptism with water, the baptism with the Holy Spirit, and the baptism of fire, he cannot see or enter into the kingdom of God."

John the Baptist began the transition from the Law Dispensation to the Church Dispensation, Luke 16:16, "The law and the prophets were until John: since that time the kingdom of God is preached, and every man presseth into it," and Matthew 11:12-13, "(12) And from the days of John the Baptist until now the kingdom of heaven suffereth violence and the violent take it by force. (13) For all the prophets and the law prophesied until John." Although the preaching of the kingdom of God started with John the Baptist, nobody entered into the kingdom until the arrival of the Holy Spirit on the day of Pentecost. The Holy Spirit's arrival ended the transition period and began the Church Dispensation. Nobody was ever born-again prior to his arrival, and nobody will ever be born-again after the rapture of the Church. Although the arrival of the Holy Spirit ended the transition period from the Law to Church Dispensation, it did not end what John the Baptist or Jesus started, nor did it alter the requirements for being born-again. In fact, the Holy Spirit's arrival was the fulfillment of what John the Baptist started and what Jesus promised. This is why Jesus stated in John 16:7, "Nevertheless I tell you the truth; It is expedient for you that I go away: for if I go not away, the Comforter will not come unto you; but if I depart, I will send him unto you." John the Baptist introduced water baptism as a requirement of the New Covenant. It was not in the Old Testament because it was not a requirement of the Old Covenant.

John the Baptist prepared people for the Lord by preaching the baptism of repentance for the remission of sins and water baptism for those who responded in repentance. John the Baptist made it possible for people to see the kingdom of God. Jesus' part in the rebirth is the baptism of the Holy Spirit and the baptism of fire (judgment), which allows people to enter into the kingdom of God. If man would continue preparing people for the Lord by preaching the baptism of repentance for the remission of sins and water baptizing those who respond in repentance, Jesus could complete the rebirth by baptizing them with the Holy Spirit and judgment. When men stop doing their part, Jesus can't do his part, so what you have is a bunch of babies playing church, and at the rapture a bunch of miscarriages. To be saved during the Church Dispensation means to be born-again.

The English word *baptize*, comes from the Greek word *baptizo*, which has its origin in the dyeing industry. It was a trade word to the dyeing industry as the word *stain* is to the furniture industry. For example, let's say you are in the business of refinishing furniture, and one day I make a footstool using pine wood. When I finish building the stool, I bring it to your shop and ask you to stain it with walnut stain. You tell me it will cost $6.00, and it will be ready in one week. In the transaction, we understand that when you finish staining the step-stool, it will look like it was made out of walnut wood instead of pine wood. Because of the stain, the pine step-stool would be identified as a walnut step-stool. That is all the word *stain* communicates. It does not dictate the method you will use or what time of day you will do the staining. You could apply the stain to the stool with your finger, a rag, a paint brush, a stain brush, or a spray gun. You could dip the stool in a container of stain, pour stain over it, or let it soak in the stain overnight.

The same thing applies to the word *baptizo* and the dyeing industry. If you own a dye shop and I ask you to *baptize* a white jacket red, in using the word *baptize* I do not dictate the method, only the fact that I wanted the white jacket identified red. All the word *baptize* communicates is that I want you to cause the white jacket to undergo a change to red. Regardless of the method you use, the white jacket will have taken on the same color as the dye.

When you are able to separate the different methods from the word *baptize*, you will see that the basic definition of baptize is "to be identified with." This would make John the Baptist, John the Identifier. John identified Jesus as the Christ and identified what the people must do to be prepared for the Lord and the kingdom of God. He preached the baptism of repentance for the remission of sins, and those who responded to his message he baptized with water. They were "identified with" repentance and "identified with" water, which would allow Jesus to "identify them with" the Holy Spirit, and "identify them with" fire, or judgment, after He was glorified (John 7:37-39).

The procedure to be used in water baptism is given in Matthew 28:19-20, "(19) Go ye therefore, and teach all nations, baptizing them in the name of the Father, and of the Son, and of the Holy Ghost: (20) Teaching them to observe all things whatsoever I have commanded you: and, lo, I am with you always, even unto the end of the world. A-men." It doesn't matter if the water is sprinkled on you, poured on you, or you are totally immersed in water, as long as it is done "in the name of the Father, and of the Son, and of the Holy Ghost." Sprinkling, pouring, and partial or total immersion are all equally effective methods. It also doesn't matter if the individual is thirty seconds old or 120 years old, the baptism is valid. The word *baptize* does not imply any specific age. The only age limitation on water baptism was put there by the Anabaptist. The second definition of the word *baptize* communicates time "from this point in time onward." For example, in a football game I was watching one Sunday afternoon, the coach of one team made a substitution, and when the announcer introduced the new player, he said, "This is his baptism into pro-football." What the announcer meant was that this was his debut, his first public appearance as a professional football player. That game was his formal entrance into society as a pro football player, so from that time forward he could identify himself as a professional football player.

When doing a word study it is essential for you to have a complete concordance to show every occurrence of a particular word in the Bible. After you determine the definition of the word, it must accurately describe what is being said every time it occurs in the Bible. If it doesn't, the definition is incorrect. For example, the Anabaptists claim the definition of the word *baptize* is "to be totally immersed in water." From this definition they teach that the only valid baptism is total immersion in water. Now read 1 Corinthians 10:1-2, "(1) Moreover, brethren, I would not that ye should be ignorant, how that all our fathers were under the cloud, and all passed through the sea; (2) And were all baptized unto Moses in the cloud and in the sea." The word *all* refers to the children of Israel who passed through the Red Sea after their exodus from Egypt. Using the Anabaptist definition of the word baptized, verse 2 would read, "And were all totally immersed unto Moses in the cloud and in the sea." Does that statement accurately describe what happened to the children of Israel at the Red Sea? Were they all totally immersed in the sea? The actual account of Israel in the sea is recorded in Exodus Chapter 14. The record calls the Anabaptists liars, because Moses and the children of Israel, literally, walked on dry land through the sea, Exodus 14:21-23, "(21) And Moses stretched out his hand over the sea; and the Lord caused the sea to go back by a strong east wind all that night, and made the sea dry land, and the waters were divided, (22) And the children of Israel went into the midst of the sea upon the dry ground: and the waters were a wall unto them on their right hand, and on their left. (23) And the Egyptians pursued, and went in after them to the midst of the sea, even all Pharaoh's horses, his chariots, and his horsemen." The ones who were totally immersed in the sea were the enemies of God, Exodus 14:27-29, "(27) And Moses stretched forth his hand over the sea, and the sea returned to his strength when the morning appeared; and the Egyptians fled against it; and the Lord overthrew the Egyptians in the midst of the sea. (28) And the waters returned, and covered the chariots, and the horsemen, and all the host of Pharaoh that came into the sea after them; there remained not so much as one of them. (29) But the children of Israel walked upon dry land in the midst of the sea; and the waters were a wall unto them on their right hand, and on their left." Here the Biblical definition of the word *baptize* teaches just the opposite of what the Anabaptist definition teaches. There were two groups of people at the Red Sea: the children of Israel, who were identified with Moses; and the Egyptians, who were identified with Pharaoh. Those identified with Moses walked through the sea on dry land, while those identified with Pharaoh were totally immersed in the sea.

I am not saying water baptism by total immersion is wrong. On the contrary, it is just as valid as pouring and sprinkling. For the first 1500 years of the Christian Era pouring and sprinkling were the most common method of water baptism; in fact, they may have been the only methods. Satan sent the Anabaptist to Church to teach "water baptism by total immersion only" in order to exclude children from entering into the kingdom of God. Satan took Jesus' statement, "He that believeth and is baptized shall be saved" and changed it to "He that believeth shall be saved." The Anabaptist began teaching that children shouldn't be baptized until after they believe and that they can't believe until after they are old enough to be taught. The end result is the "Only Believe" package being preached today. The Holy Spirit is the only teacher that teaches spiritual truth, and without Him, they are without a teacher, John 14:26, "But the Comforter, which is the Holy Ghost, whom the Father will send in my name, he shall teach you all things, and bring all things to your remembrance, whatsoever I have said unto you." In John 16:13 we are told the Holy Spirit is the guide who leads us into the truth, "Howbeit when he, the Spirit of truth, is come, he will guide you into all truth: for he shall not speak of himself; but whatsoever he shall hear, that shall he speak: and he will shew you things to come." To cause your children to go through childhood without the teaching and guidance of the Holy Spirit is to do them an injustice from which they may not recover.

Before the Anabaptist started going to Church, water baptism was considered the Christian debut into the kingdom of God as a covenant member of the Church. The Roman Emperor Constantine delayed his water baptism until he was on his death bed, in order to reduce his chances of committing a sin between his baptism and his death. Wrong, of course, but it shows how the early Church viewed the necessity of water baptism. Before you believe an Anabaptist on whether your children are saved or not, I suggest you get a copy of the New Covenant (Testament), and find the Book, Chapter, and Verse they are quoting. Search the Old Testament and see what happens to children when God moves in judgment. God will do exactly what he promised to do in Mark 16:16. Jesus said "He that believeth and is baptized shall be saved," and that's all. There is no way for anyone to amend that statement of truth to include all children.

Look at what God told Abraham about the covenant He made with him, Genesis 17:10-14, "(10) This is my covenant, which ye shall keep, between me and you and thy seed after thee; Every man child among you shall be circumcised. (11) And ye shall circumcise the flesh of your foreskin; and it shall be a token of the covenant betwixt me and you. (12) And he that is eight days old shall be circumcised among you, every man child in your generations, he that is born in the house, or bought with money of any stranger, which is not of thy seed. (13) He that is born in thy house, and he that is bought with thy money, must needs be circumcised: and my covenant shall be in your flesh for an everlasting covenant. (14) And the uncircumcised man child whose flesh of his foreskin is not circumcised, that soul shall be cut off from his people; he hath broken my covenant." "He hath broken my covenant" implies that the nine-day-old Jew broke the covenant, but the parents' disobedience to the Word of God is what placed the nine-day-old baby outside the promises of God and caused his soul to be cut off. Then, the Anabaptist would be Anacircumcisionist trying to convince the parents that children shouldn't be circumcised until after they are taught the law, and they can't be taught until after they were old enough to understand.

Circumcision, the token or seal of the Old Covenant, guaranteed acceptance or salvation until a male child reached the age of responsibility. From the time of a child's circumcision until the child reached the age of responsibility, the parents were commanded to teach their children the laws and precepts of God. After the children reached the age of responsibility, they were required to decide for themselves whether to obey or reject God. The indwelling Holy Spirit is the seal under the New Covenant, and if a child dies before he is sealed, his soul is cut off. When the New Covenant went into effect, God grouped Jews and Gentiles together in unbelief (Romans 11:32) and said the final abode of the unbelieving is hell in Rev. 21:8. This is why we must "enter into" the kingdom of God by being born again "of water and the Spirit." Since the Holy Spirit is the seal of the New Covenant, it is important to get sealed as soon as possible.

The act of water baptism 'identifies' the human with Jesus Christ, and because baptism is done in obedience to the Word of God, Jesus promises acceptance, John 6:37, "All that the Father giveth me shall come to me; and him that cometh to me I will in no wise cast out." If the person being baptized is a child (or baby), the parents' demonstration of faith in the Word of God guarantees acceptance (salvation) until the individual reaches the age of responsibility. At that time he will be required to decide for himself whether to believe or disbelieve Jesus. In the act of water baptism the person being baptized is being identified in Christ, or literally, in the redemptive work of Christ–his death, burial, and resurrection. The guilt of original sin is removed, all previous sins are forgiven, and the person is given the privilege to become a child of God. This is what the Holy Spirit is saying in John 1:12, "But as many as received him, to them gave he power to become the sons of God, even to them that believe on his name." The word *power* is the Greek word *exousia*, meaning the right or privilege.

Whether the individual exercises that right or privilege to become a child of God is determined by the way of Jesus, not His (redemptive) work. If a person wants to sell his birthright, as Esau did, it is one of his options. If a person believes in Jesus, he will walk in obedience to the way He said to go. If an individual doesn't believe in Jesus, he will ignore what Jesus said. This is what Jesus is saying in Luke 6:46-49, "(46) And why call ye me, Lord, Lord, and do not the things which I say? (47) Whosoever cometh to me, and heareth my sayings, and doeth them, I will shew you to whom he is like: (48) He is like a man which built an house, and digged deep, and laid the foundation on a rock: and when the flood arose, the stream beat vehemently upon that house, and could not shake it: for it was founded upon a rock. (49) But he that heareth, and doeth not, is like a man that without a foundation built an house upon the earth; against which the stream did beat vehemently, and immediately it fell; and the ruin of that house was great." Until you act on the Word of God by being obedient to it, you are nothing more than a hearer only. Good advice is useless information until you act on it.

Jesus set the example. All four gospels record the fact that God the Father identified Jesus as his Son, with the Holy Spirit, when John the Baptist baptized Jesus with water in the Jordan River (Matthew 3:13-17, Mark 1:1-11, Luke 3:21-22, John 1:15-34). After his water baptism and the receiving of the Holy Spirit, Jesus went into the wilderness to be tempted of Satan. After the temptations Jesus came out of the wilderness preaching "the kingdom of God is at hand" and went on to complete his three-and-one-half year miracle working ministry.

No one can overcome Satan in the temptations without a working knowledge of the Word of God. That is the weapon Jesus used to defeat Satan, and it is the only weapon we can use to defeat him. The Holy Spirit guides and teaches us how to use this sword against the enemy. The Holy Spirit entered into Jesus's life at his water baptism. You can expect the Holy Spirit to arrive into your life at the time of your baptism and into the life of your children at the time of theirs. Until that point in time you and they cannot see the kingdom of God, much less enter into it. In the act of water baptism, Jesus was identifying himself with the human family in order to fulfill the requirement of our Kinsman Redeemer. In water baptism we are identifying ourselves with the completed redemptive work of the Redeemer and the New Covenant, which was purchased by his bloodshed.

In addition to water baptism, each individual must be identified with repentance. When they become aware of an area in their life that is contrary to the Word of God, they must confess it as sin, abandon it, and go God's way. The individual must also be identified with judgment in the daily baptism of fire. The daily baptism of fire is God's method of communicating our faithfulness or unfaithfulness to his Word. In the results of the dailty baptism, we can also see the sincerity of our commitment to Jesus. 'Test results' in the baptism of fire which show us unfaithful or insincere must be corrected with the baptism of repentance for the remission of sins. In every baptism of fire the 'test results' put us in one of the four categories described in the parable of the sower. Luke 8:11-15, "(11) Now the parable is this: The seed is the word of God. (12) Those by the way side are they that hear; then cometh the devil, and taketh away the word out of their hearts, lest they should believe and be saved. (13) They on the rock are they, which, when they hear, receive the word with joy; and these have no root, which for a while believe, and in time of temptation fall away. (14) And that which fell among thorns are they, which, when they have heard, go forth, and are choked with cares and riches and pleasures of this life, and bring no fruit to perfection. (15) But that on the good ground are they, which in an honest and good heart, having heard the word, keep it, and bring forth fruit with patience."

Without the Holy Spirit, your baptisms of fire will be one failure after another. When we get to the letter to Smyrna, we will see that the baptism of fire is the doctrine of being tried, tempted, or tested by Satan. If you have completed the first three elements of the rebirth (baptism of repentance, water baptism, and baptism of the Holy Spirit), we could reclassify the baptism of fire (judgment) as what traditional Christianity calls *progressive sanctification.* The word *sanctification* basically means "to set apart as holy." The word *progressive* implies going on, advancing, or gradual betterment. Progressive sanctification is your Christian (or spiritual) growth, or more accurately, growing in grace and knowledge of Jesus Christ (2 Peter 3:18).

When you heard the gospel and initially approached Jesus, he gave you the right to become a child of God (John 1:12). Don't confuse being given the opportunity to become a child of God with becoming an instant mature adult born-again Christian. There is a growing process before a child becomes an adult. A quick trip to the altar will not get you a lifetime fire insurance policy against going to hell. Many people mistake emotional release as receiving salvation, when more than likely, all they received was the opportunity to become a child of God. When you initially approached Jesus, he gave you the power to become a child of God by releasing you from the bondage of sin. Your body, mind, and spirit had been under the dominion of Satan, and whatever he wanted you to do, you did. When your parents or some preacher got the Word of God to you, the Holy Spirit convicted you and you judged yourself guilty by approaching Jesus, in repentance, for forgiveness. Your repentance was a commitment to turn from sin and obedience to Satan, to righteousness and obedience to God. You took God at his word, he took you at your word, and he forgave you. Now for the first time in your life you have the right to choose not to sin. You are now ready for the baptism of fire, when Satan is permitted to tempt and test your faithfulness to the commitment you made to Jesus in repentance. You judge yourself sincere on that commitment when you choose obedience to the Word of God. In these baptisms of fire, you either overcome Satan and go on to become a child of God, or Satan overcomes you and you give up your right to become a child of God. People who were called but never chosen because they were unfaithful (Rev. 17:14) never 'lost' their salvation because they never had it to lose. When Jesus raptures the Church, they will be left behind, and the only way I know how to describe them is *miscarriages.*

To be counted among the called and chosen, you must be faithful and that translates into obedience to the Word of God. One of the first questions you will have to settle is water baptism, Matthew 28:19, "Go ye therefore, and teach all nations, baptizing them in the name of the Father, and of the Son, and of the Holy Ghost." This is a commandment of Jesus and it is what he told men to do. Jesus is the only person in the universe who can baptize you with the Holy Spirit (Matthew 3:11), so you can erase any doubts as to whether this verse is speaking of water baptism or Holy Spirit baptism. If you will identify yourself with repentance and water baptism, Jesus will identify you by giving you the Holy Spirit. When Jesus baptizes you with the Holy Spirit is when he "set you apart as holy," and then you receive the opportunity to become a child of God.

Here begins your progressive sanctification. As the Word of God identifies areas of your being, which are not properly aligned to God's revealed will, you "set them apart as holy" by conforming to the Word of God. The daily baptisms of fire are now opportunities for rewards, and failures mean the loss of rewards, not the loss of your salvation. The rapture will end the Church Dispensation and complete all the promises made to Church members. If you have had sufficient opportunity to mature before the rapture but refused to do so, the reward you will lose at the rapture is your Church membership. You will enter the tribulation era as a member of the lukewarm Laodicean congregation, with no guarantee that your name will not be blotted out of the Book of Life (Rev. 3:5). How long "sufficient opportunity" is, can be found in Hebrews 5:11-14. If you have been calling yourself a Christian long enough to be a teacher of the Word of God, you have already had sufficient opportunity.

To be born-again a person must be baptized, or identified with, repentance, water, the Holy Spirit, and fire or judgment. The rebirth is not a step one, step two, step three, step four-type situation. However, for the purpose of discussion, let's assign repentance as step one, water baptism as step two, Holy Spirit baptism as step three, and the baptism of fire as step four. The Church Dispensation began on the day of Pentecost when the 120 in the upper room were baptized with the Holy Spirit (Acts 1:1-2:13). They were the first Church members and they had obviously already completed steps 1, 2, and 4. Their baptism with the Holy Spirit, which we assigned as step number 3, completed their rebirth. Simon Peter left the upper room and preached the first Church sermon, which is recorded in Acts 2:14-36. When Peter finished preaching, the people asked what they should do, Acts 2:37, "Now when they heard this, they were pricked in their heart, and said unto Peter and to the rest of the apostles, Men and brethren, what shall we do?" In essence, Peter told them they must be born again, Acts 2:38, "Then Peter said unto them, Repent, and be baptized every one of you in the name of Jesus Christ for the remission of sins, and ye shall receive the gift of the Holy Ghost." Step 1, "Repent," step 2 water baptism, "and be baptized every one of you in the name of Jesus Christ." Notice that Peter identifies both as necessary "for the remission of sins." Peter goes on to say if you do steps one and two, Jesus will do step three, "and ye shall receive the gift of the Holy Ghost." This would allow Jesus to begin the baptisms of fire (step four), which are the lifelong progressive sanctification process or what the Bible calls *edification*, which basically means building yourself up. About 3000 people responded in obedience, Acts 2:41, "They that gladly received his word were baptized: and the same day there were added unto them about three thousand souls." If you want to be saved, do the same–receive the Word, repent, be baptized–and you will receive the gift of the Holy Ghost. Then edify yourself by studying the Word of God, and when Satan comes to tempt you in the baptism of fire, be an overcomer.

The first Gentile to be saved as a Church member was an Italian named Cornelius. He was a proselyte, which is a Gentile who has been converted to Judaism. Cornelius was sincere to the God of the Jews, but what he didn't know was the Old Covenant had been superseded by the New Covenant when Jesus said "It is finished" on the cross. Cornelius had proven himself sincere in the baptism of fire (step four) and he had completed step one (repentance), which is obvious from Acts 10:2, "A devout man, and one that feared God with all his house, which gave much alms to the people, and prayed to God always." To be born-again he had to complete steps two and three (water and Holy Spirit baptism). The principality angel of the Ephesus Church Era appeared to him, told him to send for Simon Peter (Acts 10:3-8), and stated that "he (Peter) shall tell thee what thou oughtest to do." In the meantime, Peter was given the vision of the sheet containing unclean things, which alerted him that Gentiles are acceptable in the kingdom of God under the New Covenant (Acts 10:9-18). When Peter arrived at the house of Cornelius (Acts 10:19-32), he was told of the angel that appeared to Cornelius, and in verse 33, "Immediately therefore I sent to thee; and thou hast will done that thou art come. Now therefore are we all here present before God, to hear all things that are commanded thee of God."

Now that Cornelius is about to be saved, it is important that we see what Peter "commanded" Cornelius to do. In Acts 10:34-41 Peter tells Cornelius that Jesus was the promised Redeemer, how he died and rose from the dead, and that Jesus had commanded Peter to preach the gospel, Acts 10:42-48 "And he (Jesus) commanded us to preach unto the people, and to testify that it is he which was ordained of God to be the Judge of the quick and dead. (43) To him give all the prophets witness, that through his name whosoever believeth in him shall receive remission of sins." The account continues in Acts 10:44 "While Peter yet spake these words, the Holy Ghost fell on all them which heard the word. (45) And they of the circumcision which believed were astonished, as many as came with Peter, because that on the Gentiles also was poured out the gift of the Holy Ghost. (46) For they heard them speak with tongues, and magnify God. Then answered Peter, (47) Can any man forbid water, that these should not be baptized, which have received the Holy Ghost as well as we? (48) And he commanded them to be baptized in the name of the Lord. Then prayed they him to tarry certain days." When they were baptized with the Holy Spirit, step 3 was completed. Then what was missing in Cornelius' being born-again was step two, water baptism, and that's what Peter "commanded" Cornelius to do in Acts 10:47-48. Speaking in tongues (verse 10:46) is the second sign listed in Mark 16:17, "they shall speak with new tongues," which is how Peter recognized them as believers, "And these signs shall follow them that believe" (Mark 16:17a).

The absence of the Mark 16:17-18 signs may have been what alerted the Apostle Paul that the twelve men in Ephesus had not completed the rebirth. They had completed step one (repentance) and step two (water baptism), but step three (Holy Spirit baptism) had not been completed. Step three was not completed because step two was not performed in compliance with Matthew 28:19, "baptizing them in the name of the Father, and of the Son, and of the Holy Ghost." They believed and were obedient to what John the Baptist taught but were unfamiliar with what Jesus taught. When Paul explained that Jesus was the Christ, the men were baptized in compliance with Matthew 28:19 and received the Holy Spirit. The account is recorded in Acts 19:1-7, "(1) And it came to pass, that, while Apollos was at Corinth, Paul having passed through the upper coasts came to Ephesus: and finding certain disciples, (2) He said unto them, Have ye received the Holy Ghost since ye believed? And they said unto him, We have not so much as heard whether there be any Holy Ghost. (3) And he said unto them, Unto what then were ye baptized? And they said, Unto John's baptism. (4) Then said Paul, John verily baptized with the baptism of repentance, saying unto the people, that they should believe on him which should come after him, that is, on Christ Jesus. (5) When they heard this, they were baptized in the name of the Lord Jesus. (6) And when Paul had laid his hands upon them, the Holy Ghost came on them: and they spake with tongues, and prophesied. (7) And all the men were about twelve." Invalid water baptism would have canceled their Church membership, had the rapture occurred before they were sealed by the Holy Spirit.

Invalid water baptism has placed a large portion of the Christian population in this category. Some denominations have totally rejected water baptism as necessary for salvation, and even though the absence of the Holy Spirit and the Mark 16:17-18 signs are clear evidence of their folly, they refuse to change. Some Church groups reject other Church groups because their method of water baptism differs. One sprinkles water, one pours water, another immerses in water, and they are so busy fighting among themselves that an outsider wonders if any of them knows what they are talking about. It is as stupid as a drowning man listening to two men standing on the deck of the ship, arguing about whether they should throw him the life preserver tied with nylon rope or the one tied with hemp. As long as the water is applied to the individual, "in the name of the Father, and of the Son, and of the Holy Ghost," the water baptism is valid. Don't refuse a person entrance into the kingdom of God or deprive them of the Holy Spirit because of some private method of applying liquid in water baptism.

Other denominations have placed an age limit on water baptism which excludes infants and children from the kingdom of God. Jesus didn't put an age limit on water baptism, so neither should we. Some churches have replaced the water baptism service with a dedication-to-the-Lord-type ceremony, but unless water was applied to your child with the words, "I baptize you in the name of the Father, and of the Son, and of the Holy Ghost," the child is not a covenant member in right standing with God. A son born to a Jewish family under the Old Covenant was no more righteous or unrighteous than children born today under the New Covenant. God "cut off" the soul of the nine-day-old baby Jew because the parents refused to comply with the Word of God and enter the baby into the covenant God the Father made with Abraham. To be saved under the New Covenant, Church members are required to enter into the covenant God, the Father, made with his Son, Jesus Christ. Jesus said the way to enter this covenant is to be born again, of water and the Spirit. Your refusal to comply with what Jesus commanded will exclude you from the New Covenant. Refuse your children water baptism and you force Jesus to withhold the Holy Spirit until that requirement is met. Children are not automatically covenant members just because their parents are. Under the Old Covenant a child was automatically saved from conception until they were nine days old. If the child was uncircumcised on the ninth day, he entered an unsaved condition. Circumcision made the child a covenant member and put him in a saved condition until he reached the age of responsibility. At the age of accountability, the responsibility for salvation passed from the parents to the individual.

The time God gave for repentance during the Church Dispensation is running out. Being born-again is the Luke 13:24-27 "strait gate" you must enter to gain entrance into the kingdom of God during this Dispensation. Failure to enter, as dictated by the Word of God, will put you on the wrong side of the Church door at the rapture.

The entire population of the earth is being divided into three groups. The first group is made up of the population who have rejected Jesus Christ.

They are the non-Christian population of the planet, and none of them will participate in the rapture of the Church. The second group is made up of born-again believers. It includes all adults who meet the minimum requirements for salvation, "He that believeth and is baptized shall be saved," all water-baptized who have not reached the age of responsibility, and perhaps all infants less than nine days old. This group will be leaving Earth in the rapture of the Church. The third group is made up of the Christian population who meet only one of the minimum requirements for salvation. They have either been water baptized and have never settled the question of believing, or they believe but have never been water baptized. This group is the lukewarm Laodicean congregation which includes the deceived, the insincere, and everyone else who ever professed to be a Christian or associated themselves with the Church. None of this group will participate in the rapture of the Church. They will enter the seven-year tribulation period to face Antichrist in the 'deny or die' baptism of fire. Those who refuse to deny Jesus will be killed by the Antichrist organization and receive salvation as a member of the Rev. 6:9-11 fifth seal group. Those who deny Jesus to escape death will not survive to enter the Kingdom Dispensation. By midpoint in the seven-year tribulation, Antichrist will reduce this group to zero.

God presents those who reject his Word as the children of darkness and those who conform to his Word as the children of light. God didn't make some children of light and others children of darkness. We decide which group we are in by our rejection or obedience to the Word of God. The Church member can be identified by the presence or absence of the indwelling Holy Spirit. There is nothing complicated about distinguishing between the children of darkness and light, unless the person trying to see the difference is ignorant of the Word of God. It is because of this ignorance that Satan and his crew can deceive people into believing he is an angel of light (2 Corinthians 11:13-15). The same is true of the Christian and Antichrist. Ignorance of what Jesus said and taught has allowed Antichrist to split the Church congregation into several hundred different groups, all saying, "I am Christ" or "Follow me to Christ." Those who have buried their Bible under a layer of dust are followers who don't realize that they are being gathered into separate bundles to be burned. We are fast approaching the end of the Church Dispensation, which puts us very close to harvest time, so you need to examine the bundle in which you are wrapped. If you find a bundle of tares, get out and start following Jesus. Only then will you be able to see the difference between light and darkness, John 8:12, "Then spake Jesus again unto them, saying, I am the light of the world: he that followeth me shall not walk in darkness, but shall have the light of life." If you choose not to believe Jesus, just keep walking, but in either case you will never walk this road again. What the Holy Spirit is saying in Hebrews 9:27 is once, and only once, "And as it is appointed unto men once to die, but after this the judgment." What is between us and that judgment is the rapture or physical death and resurrection, not reincarnation.

The Bible teaches that each of us will stand before the judgment seat of Jesus to give an account of ourselves. Romans 14:10-12, "(10) But why dost thou judge thy brother? or why dost thou set at naught thy brother? for we shall all stand before the judgment seat of Christ. (11) For it is written, As I live, saith the Lord, every knee shall bow to me, and every tongue shall confess to God. (12) So then every one of us shall give account of himself to God." Also 2 Corinthians 5:10, "For we must all appear before the judgment seat of Christ; that every one may receive the things done in his body, according to that he hath done whether it be good or bad." In John 5:22 Jesus said the Father has committed all judgment to him, "For the Father judgeth no man, but hath committed all judgment unto the Son."

When you stand before Jesus to give an account of yourself will depend on whether you participate in the first resurrection or second resurrection. Daniel speaks of the tribulation period and the two resurrections in Daniel 12:1-2, "(1) And at that time shall Michael stand up, the great prince which standeth for the children of thy people: and there shall be a time of trouble, such as never was since there was a nation even to that same time: and at that time thy people shall be delivered, every one that shall be found written in the book. (2) And many of them that sleep in the dust of the earth shall awake, some to everlasting life, and some to shame and everlasting contempt." Daniel was told of the two resurrections: some to everlasting life, and some to shame and everlasting contempt. He was not told the amount of time between the two resurrections. Jesus spoke of the same two resurrections in John 5:28-29, "(28) Marvel not at this: for the hour is coming, in the which all that are in the graves shall hear his voice, (29) And shall come forth; they that have done good, unto the resurrection of life; and they that have done evil, unto the resurrection of damnation." We are not given the amount of time between the two resurrections until we get to Rev. 20:5, "But the rest of the dead lived not again until the thousand years were finished. This is the first resurrection." The first resurrection is Daniel's "some to everlasting life" and Jesus's "they that have done good, unto the resurrection of life." The second resurrection is Daniel's "some to shame and everlasting contempt" and Jesus' "they that have done evil, unto the resurrection of damnation." Those who participate in the first resurrection, the resurrection of life, are the saved, while those in the second resurrection, the resurrection of damnation, are the lost.

The resurrection of life is recorded in Rev. 20:4-6, "(4) And I saw thrones, and they sat upon them, and judgment was given unto them: and I saw the souls of them that were beheaded for the witness of Jesus, and for the word of God, and which had not worshipped the beast, neither his image, neither had received his mark upon their foreheads, or in their hands; and they lived and reigned with Christ a thousand years. (5) But the rest of the dead lived not again until the thousand years were finished. This is the first resurrection. (6) Blessed and holy is he that hath part in the first resurrection: on such the second death hath no power, but they shall be priests of God and of Christ, and shall reign with him a thousand years." Although these people stand before the judgment seat of Christ, they are not on trial for their lives. None will be judged guilty at this judgment, and none will be judged innocent at the white throne judgment. These people stand before the judgment seat of Christ for the purpose of receiving or losing rewards, 1 Corinthians 3:10-15, "(10) According to the grace of God which is given unto me, as a wise master builder, I have laid the foundation, and another buildeth thereon. But let every man take heed how he buildeth thereupon. (11) For other foundation can no man lay than that is laid, which is Jesus Christ. (12) Now if any man build upon this foundation gold, silver, precious stones, wood, hay, stubble; (13) Every man's work shall be made manifest: for the day shall declare it, because it shall be revealed by fire; and the fire shall try every man's work of what sort it is. (14) If any man's work abide which he hath built thereupon, he shall receive a reward. (15) If any man's work shall be burned, he shall suffer loss: but he himself shall be saved; yet so as by fire." At the time of the white throne judgment these individuals will have been resurrected and dwelling in their eternal bodies for some one thousand years.

The resurrection of damnation is recorded in Rev. 20:11-15, "(11) And I saw a great white throne, and him that sat on it, from whose face the earth and the heaven fled away; and there was found no place for them. (12) And I saw the dead, small and great, stand before God; and the books were opened: and another book was opened, which is the book of life: and the dead were judged out of those things which were written in the books, according to their works. (13) And the sea gave up the dead which were in it; and death and hell (Hades) delivered up the dead which were in them: and they were judged every man according to their works. (14) And death and hell (Hades) were cast into the lake of fire. This is the second death. (15) And whosoever was not found written in the book of life was cast into the lake of fire." This is not a courtroom scene where an individual presents his case and God presents his. The Judge sitting on that great white throne is the Lord Jesus Christ, the prosecuting attorney is the Word of God from the Holy Bible, and both you and everyone else will know you are guilty of rejecting Jesus by non-compliance to the Bible.

Participants of the first resurrection will live and reign with Jesus on the earth (Rev. 5:10) for a period of one thousand years. This period of earth history will be the Kingdom Dispensation. At the end of the Millennial (one thousand year) Reign we have the second resurrection and the great white throne judgment. The white throne judgment will be followed by the second death, which is eternal separation from God in the lake of fire. Every human being must be either a participant in the first resurrection to eternal life with God or a participant in the second resurrection, one thousand years later, to eternal separation from God in the lake of fire. The second resurrection will be a mass resurrection including the lost from all seven dispensations and the fallen angels. It is the resurrection of damnation and none will be judged innocent.

The first resurrection, which is the resurrection to life, is not a mass resurrection. It started with Jesus Christ nearly 2000 years ago, followed by his Church (1 Corinthians 15:23) at his coming as a thief in the night, prior to the seven-year tribulation period. This resurrection is the rapture of the Church recorded in 1 Thessalonians 4:13-17, "(13) But I would not have you to be ignorant, brethren, concerning them which are asleep, that ye sorrow not, even as others which have no hope. (14) For if we believe that Jesus died and rose again, even so them also which sleep in Jesus will God bring with him. (15) For this we say unto you by the word of the Lord, that we which are alive and remain unto the coming of the Lord shall not prevent them which are asleep. (16) For the Lord himself shall descend from heaven with a shout, with the voice of the archangel, and with the trump of God: and the dead in Christ shall rise first: (17) Then we which are alive and remain shall be caught up together with them in the clouds, to meet the Lord in the air: and so shall we ever be with the Lord." The Church members who are living at the moment of the rapture will undergo the change recorded in 1 Corinthians 15:51-55, "(51) Behold, I shew you a mystery; We shall not all sleep, but we shall all be changed, (52) In a moment, in the twinkling of an eye, at the last trump: for the trumpet shall sound, and the dead shall be raised incorruptible, and we shall be changed. (53) For this corruptible must put on incorruption, and this mortal must put on immortality. (54) So when this corruptible shall have put on incorruption, and this mortal shall have put on immortality, then shall be brought to pass the saying that is written, Death is swallowed up in victory. (55) O death, where is thy sting? O grave, (Hades) where is thy victory?" When Jesus returns to the earth, in glory, after the seven-year tribulation period to establish the Kingdom Dispensation we will have the resurrection of the Old Testament saints we saw in Daniel 12:1-2 and the resurrection of the tribulation dead we saw in Rev. 20:4.

One of the most deceiving incarnations of a demonic spirit will be in the person of Antichrist. This fallen angelic spirit has been active against the Church since the Day of Pentecost. During the Church Age he has been operating in the spirit realm through human beings. John speaks of his activity in 1 John 2:18-20, "(18) Little children, it is the last time: and as ye have heard that antichrist shall come, even now are there many antichrists; whereby we know that it is the last time. (19) They went out from us, but they were not of us; for if they had been of us, they would no doubt have continued with us: but they went out, that they might be made manifest that they were not all of us."

During the Church to Kingdom transition period this individual will be incarnated, and as a human, gain political control of the last Gentile world system. This ten nations confederacy, which is the final state of the old

Roman Empire, became a reality with the formation of the European Common Market. Daniel makes it clear that both Antichrist and False Prophet, will enter the world through an organization consisting of the union of ten Gentile Nations (Daniel 2:44, 7:8). From a historical view, the European Common Market is the first organization to develop, since the collapse of the old Roman Empire, that could rightly be labeled the Gentile ten king kingdom. The number of nations within the organization may vary, but when the time comes to fulfill this prophecy the nations will number ten. If God chooses to raise up another altogether different organization in the future to fulfill this prophecy, we can still look at the European Common Market and see the picture of the ten king kingdom striving to dominate world commerce.

In the second chapter of 2 Thessalonians, verses 1-6, the Holy Spirit speaks of a falling away from the truth before Antichrist (the man of sin) can be revealed. He continues in verse 7 by saying the "mystery of iniquity" (lawlessness), which was already at work when Paul penned these words, would continue until the ministry of the Holy Spirit concerning the Church was completed. He begins verse 8 with the words "And then" which speaks clearly that after He (the Holy Spirit) has completed the Church "then shall that Wicked be revealed." The completion of the Church will become a reality when it is raptured. After the rapture, Antichrist will be incarnated and reveal himself when, as the political leader of the European Common Market, he signs a protection treaty with the Jews in Israel. The day this treaty is confirmed will be the first day of the seven-year tribulation period.

The Holy Spirit continues the discussion on Antichrist in 2 Thessalonians 2:9-12 by saying, "(9) Even him, whose coming is after the working of Satan with all power and signs and lying wonders, (10) And with all deceivableness of unrighteousness in them that perish; because they received not the love of the truth, that they might be saved. (11) And for this cause God shall send them strong delusion, that they should believe a lie: (12) That they all might be damned who believed not the truth, but had pleasure in unrighteousness." The word *delusion* means "something accepted as true, that is actually false or unreal." Antichrist will be a miracle worker, not because he is a human being with supernatural power, but because he is a supernatural power in the form of a human being. The same will be true of the False Prophet. The only difference between these two individuals will be that Antichrist is an incarnated demonic spirit, but the False Prophet is a reincarnated demonic spirit. Neither one of these individuals is Satan in the flesh. They are three different and distinct fallen angels. As we saw in 1 John 2:18-20, the spirit of Antichrist has been active in the spirit realm against the Church since the Day of Pentecost. When the Church is removed from the earth, this individual will be given political control of the European Common Market in the form of a man. The fact that he has been free to operate against the church for 1990 years is a clear indication that this spirit did not put on flesh and cross from the spirit realm to the physical realm in the past.

As we saw in our discussion of fallen angels, when they left the spirit realm and committed the sin of putting on flesh, God imprisoned them in Hades, the bottomless pit. The False Prophet will be the beast that is released from Hades during the seven-year tribulation. Antichrist is the beast out of the sea (Rev. 13:1-10), and the False Prophet is the beast John saw "coming up out of the earth" in Rev. 13:11-18. The False Prophet is the beast described in Rev. 17:8, "The beast that thou sawest was, and is not; and shall ascend out of the bottomless pit, and go into perdition: and they that dwell on the earth shall wonder, whose names were not written in the book of life from the foundation of the world, when they behold the beast that was, and is not, and yet is." The False Prophet *was*, meaning that at some point in time past, he did exist in the flesh on the earth. He "is not," meaning that during the Church Age he is confined in Hades and unable to influence activity on the earth. "And yet is" implies the certainty of his existence in the flesh, and his activity during the tribulation period, after he "shall ascend out of the bottomless pit."

Antichrist and False Prophet do not participate in either resurrection. Their activity on earth will be during the time period of the first resurrection, but neither of these two individuals can qualify as "blessed and holy" (Rev. 20:4-6). If these two men were merely wicked human beings, their future would be: physical death when Jesus returns to the earth, resurrection and the white throne judgment one thousand years later; followed by the second death when they are cast into the lake of fire. They are both demonic spirits and neither will follow this routine. The final acts these two individuals perform will be to assemble the Armageddon Army, which will be destroyed by Jesus when he returns to Earth at the end of the sevend-year tribulation period (Rev. 19:1-18), to establish the Kingdom Dispensation (Rev. 20:1-6). When the Armageddon Army is destroyed, these two individuals will be cast alive into literal hell, the lake of fire. This event is recorded in Rev. 19:19-21, "(19) And I saw the beast, and the kings of the earth, and their armies, gathered together to make war against him that sat on the horse, and against his army. (20) And the beast (Antichrist) was taken, and with him the false prophet that wrought miracles before him, with which he deceived them that had received the mark of the beast, and them that worshipped his image. These both were cast alive into a lake of fire burning with brimstone. (21) And the remnant were slain with the sword of him that sat upon the horse, which sword proceeded out of his mouth: and all the fowls were filled with their flesh."

The last time we will see these two individuals will be one thousand years later (Rev. 20:7) when Satan is thrown into hell with them. Rev. 20:10, "And the devil that deceived them was cast into the lake of fire and brimstone, where the beast (Antichrist) and the false prophet are, and shall be tormented day and night for ever and ever." This event will be followed by the resurrection of damnation and the white throne judgment. We will take a closer look at the activity of these two individuals later, but first let's take at look at the seventy-weeks prophecy in the Book of Daniel.

Chapter Three

The Seventy Weeks Time Table

The seven-year tribulation period will be the last event in the Church to Kingdom transition period. In order to place the seven-year tribulation in God's plan of the ages correctly, we need to be familiar with the seventy week prophecy of Daniel chapter 9. In review, seventy years earlier Nebuchadnezzar, King of Babylon, had invaded Jerusalem, and destroyed the wall and temple. The Kingdom of Judah went into captivity. The Prophet Jeremiah had stayed in Jerusalem after the invasion and wrote a letter to the Jewish captives taken to Babylon.

Jeremiah chapters 29, 30, and 31 are a copy of this letter. If you will read the entire letter from your Bible in verse 29:10, you will find the Babylonian captivity was to end after seventy years, and the Jews would be permitted to return to Jerusalem. The letter states that Israel and Judah (the divided Northern and Southern Kingdoms) would return and possess the land that God gave to their fathers (Jeremiah 30:3). In chapter 31:1-10 the Jews are to be gathered from among the Gentile nations, redeemed (verse 31:11), given the New Covenant (verse 31-34), and to continue to exist as a nation forever (verse 35-37).

When the Babylonian Empire fell to King Darius, the Mede, Daniel knew from this letter the Babylonian captivity was over. However, Daniel misunderstood the remainder of the letter and assumed that the other promises in the letter were also a reality because the Babylonian captivity ended. He misunderstood the term "latter days" in Jeremiah 29:24 to mean the end of the Babylonian captivity, not the "latter days" of the "times of the Gentiles." The seventy week prophecy was given to correct this error in Daniel's thinking, by giving him "skill and understanding" of Israel's future.

An outline of Daniel chapter 9 would look like this:

1. Daniel understands the seventy years of Babylonian captivity has ended, Dan. 9:1-2.
2. Daniel's supplications and prayer, Dan. 9:3-19.
3. The angel Gabriel appears to Daniel to give him a vision, Dan. 9:20-23.
4. The seventy weeks prophecy, Dan. 9:24-27.

Daniel 9:1-2 reads as follows, "(1) In the first year of Darius the son of Ahasuerus, of the seed of the Medes, which was made king over the realm of the Chaldeans: (2) In the first year of his reign I Daniel understood by the books the number of the years, whereof the word of the Lord came to Jeremiah the prophet, that he would accomplish seventy years in the desolations of Jerusalem." In verse 1 "Chaldeans" is just another name for Babylonians. The Babylonian Empire was replaced by the Median Empire under Darius, the Mede. In verse 2 "the books the number of the years" may make reference to 2 Chronicles 36:21 which also gives the duration of the Babylonian captivity. "The word of the Lord came to Jeremiah the prophet" is a reference to Jeremiah's letter which was sent to the Jews at Babylon. Jeremiah 29:10 is the verse which tells of the end of the Babylonian captivity, "For thus saith the Lord, That after seventy years be accomplished at Babylon I will visit you, and perform my good word toward you, in causing you to return to this place." "This place" is Jerusalem from which the letter was sent. Daniel's prayer (Dan. 9:3-19) moved the God of Heaven to send the angel Gabriel to give him understanding (Dan. 9:20-23). When the Nation of Israel finds itself in the seven-year tribulation, the essence of this prayer will move the God of Heaven to deliver Jerusalem and the Jews from destruction at the hands of the Antichrist/False Prophet organization.

The seventy weeks prophecy is recorded in Daniel 9:24-27, "(24) Seventy weeks are determined upon thy people and upon thy holy city, to finish the transgression, and to make an end of sins, and to make reconciliation for iniquity, and to bring in everlasting righteousness, and to seal up the vision and prophecy, and to anoint the most Holy. (25) Know therefore and understand, that from the going forth of the commandment to restore and to build Jerusalem unto the Messiah the prince shall be seven weeks, and threescore and two weeks: the street shall be built again, and the wall, even in troublous times. (26) And after threescore and two weeks shall Messiah be cut off, but not for himself: and the people of the prince that shall come shall destroy the city and the sanctuary; and the end thereof shall be with a flood, and unto the end of the war desolations are determined. (27) And he shall confirm the covenant with many for one week: and in the midst of the week he shall cause the sacrifice and the oblation to cease, and for the overspreading of abominations he shall make it desolate, even until the consummation, and that determined shall be poured upon the desolate."

An outline of the seventy weeks prophecy would look like this:

1. Verse 24, The seventy weeks and seven accomplishments.
2. Verse 25, The first sixty-nine weeks. "From the going forth of the commandment to restore and to build Jerusalem . . . unto the Messiah."
3. Verse 26, The Messiah cut off, Jerusalem and the temple again destroyed.
4. Verse 2, The last week. The seven-year tribulation period.

Gabriel begins the seventy weeks prophecy by identifying the total amount of time and the seven accomplishments. Daniel 9:24 "Seventy weeks are determined upon thy people and upon thy holy city, to finish the transgression, and to make an end of sins, and to make reconciliation for iniquity, and to bring in everlasting righteousness, and to seal up the vision and prophecy, and to anoint the most Holy." The phrase "upon thy people" refers to the Jews and the phrase "upon thy holy city" refers to Jerusalem.

In the phrase "seventy weeks are determined" the "seventy weeks" are seventy weeks of years or more accurately seventy times seven years, specifically 490 years. To the Gentile a week is restricted to seven days, but to the Jews a week could have meant seven days or seven years. The word *week* used here is the same Hebrew word used by Jacob and Laban (Genesis 29:15-30) in determining how long Jacob would work for Laban before he would give his daughter to Jacob in marriage. In verse 29:18 Jacob agrees to work seven years for Rachel. After Jacob worked the seven years Laban deceived him by giving him Leah instead of Rachel. In verse 29:26 Laban explained that in his country the second born cannot be given in marriage until the first born is married. Laban continues in verse 27 with the statement "Fulfill her week, and we will give thee this also for the service which thou shalt serve with me yet seven other years." Jacob and Laban both understood the word week meant seven years, not seven days. The account continues with Jacob working for Laban seven more years for his daughter Rachel.

Four hundred and ninety years was the total amount of time determined by God to accomplish seven things concerning the Jews and Jerusalem. The seven things to be accomplished before the 490 years end are: (1) to finish the transgression, (2) to make an end of sins, (3) to make reconciliation for iniquity, (4) to bring in everlasting righteousness, (5) to seal up the vision, (6) to seal up prophecy, (7) to anoint the Most Holy. The first four items deal with the New Covenant God promised to make with the Jews. From Jeremiah's letter (Jeremiah 31:31-34) Daniel visualized that the New Covenant would become effective when the Babylonian captivity ended. Gabriel was basically saying, "Not now Daniel, after these seventy weeks or 490 years have passed."

Items 5 and 6 in the above list were: (5) to seal up the vision, and (6) to seal up prophecy. To *seal up* means to close in respect to understanding. Daniel as an individual was given understanding in this vision but to the nation and to the world as a whole, it was sealed; that is, they did not understand. In Daniel 12:4 and 12:9 we are told the entire Book of Daniel was sealed until "the time of the end." The visions and prophecies were sealed to prevent Satan and his demonic forces from understanding exactly how God would accomplish his plan of redemption. If Satan could have gained understanding into prophecy he would never have crucified Jesus. This is what the Holy Spirit is referring to in 1 Corinthians 2:7-8, "(7) But we speak the wisdom of God in a mystery, even the hidden wisdom, which God ordained before the world unto our glory: (8) Which none of the princes of this world knew: for had they known it, they would not have crucified the Lord of glory."

The vision concerns seventy weeks, or 490 years, of history of the Jews and Jerusalem. During this 490 year period, the Jews will not understand these prophecies. When the 490 years have past, not only the Book of Daniel, but all the prophecies relating to Jesus will be understood by the Jews. God promised one day to pour out his Spirit on the house of Israel, and when he does, the New Covenant and the truth of Jesus will be understood. When the Antichrist/False Prophet organization comes against Jerusalem, the Spirit will be poured upon the Jews and the whole house of Israel shall be saved. This is the day Zechariah spoke of in Zechariah 12:9-11, "(9) And it shall come to pass in that day, that I will seek to destroy all the nations that come against Jerusalem. (10) And I will pour upon the house of David, and upon the inhabitants of Jerusalem, the spirit of grace and of supplications: and they shall look upon me whom they have pierced, and they shall mourn for him, as one mourneth for his only son, and shall be in bitterness for him, as one that is in bitterness for his firstborn. (11) In that day shall there be a great mourning in Jerusalem, as the mourning of Hadadrimmon in the valley of Megiddon."

We should not confuse the statement "and they shall look upon me whom they have pierced" with the cross at Calvary. The Jews looked on Jesus at Calvary with mocking (Psalm 22), not mourning. This "looking" is the Rev. 1:7 account, when Jesus returns to the earth in glory with the saints to establish the Kingdom Dispensation. If we continue with Zechariah chapter 13 we will see that "in that day" both prophecies and prophets will cease. Zechariah 13:1-6, "(1) In that day there shall be a fountain opened to the house of David and to the inhabitants of Jerusalem for sin and for uncleanness. (2) And it shall come to pass in that day, saith the Lord of hosts, that I will cut off the names of the idols out of the land, and they shall no more be remembered: and also I will cause the prophets and the unclean spirit to pass out of the land. (3) And it shall come to pass, that when any shall yet prophesy, then his father and his mother that begat him shall say unto him, Thou shalt not live; for thou speaketh lies in the name of the Lord; and his father and his mother that begat him shall thrust him through when he prophesieth. (4) And it shall come to pass in that day, that the prophets shall be ashamed every one of his vision, when he hath prophesied; neither shall they wear a rough garment to deceive: (5) But he shall say, I am no prophet, I am an husbandman; for man taught me to keep cattle from my youth. (6) And one shall say unto him, What are these wounds in thine hands? Then he shall answer, Those with which I was wounded in the house of my friends."

The seventh item on the list of seven things to be accomplished at the end of the seventy weeks time table was "to anoint the Most Holy." After the first six items on the accomplishment list have been completed, the Nation of Israel will know that Jesus was their Messiah and they will anoint Him King. When Jesus returns to the earth to rule as King, we will move from the seven-year tribulation period to the Kingdom Dispensation.

Gabriel continues the seventy weeks prophecy (Dan. 9:25) by saying, "Know therefore and understand, that from the going forth of the commandment to restore and to build Jerusalem unto the Messiah the prince shall be seven weeks, and threescore and two weeks: the street shall be built again, and the wall, even in troublous times." The 490 year clock started when a decree was issued to restore Jerusalem, not when the Babylonian captivity ended. The amount of time to pass between the giving of that commandment to the coming of the Messiah was to be seven weeks (forty-nine years) plus threescore and two weeks (sixty-two weeks or 434 years) for a total of sixty-nine weeks or 483 years. Let's set aside the final week (seven years) for now and examine the first 483 years.

Gabriel did not mean issuing of the decree would be followed by 483 years of troublous times restoring Jerusalem. The time "from the going forth of the commandment to restore and to build Jerusalem" until Jerusalem's restoration would be a relatively short period of time (forty-nine years). A long lapse of time (434 years) would exist between the restoring and the Messiah. Added together, these years represent the total amount of time between the decree and the coming of the Messiah.

When did God begin to compute time against the 490 year timetable? The Bible records four different decrees, letters, or commandments from four different times. They are recorded in the books of Ezra and Nehemiah.

The first was issued by Cyrus, king of the Persian Empire (2 Chronicles 36:22-23, Ezra 1:1-4), in which Zerubbabel returned to Jerusalem with over 42,360 captives (Ezra 2:64-70). He restored the altar and laid the foundation of the temple before Israel's adversaries were able to stop him. These "adversaries. . . frustrated their purpose, all the days of Cyrus King of Persia, even until the reign of Darius king of Persia" (Ezra 4:1-6).

The second was issued by Darius, King of Persia (Ezra 6:1-12) resulting in the restoration of the temple (Ezra 6:13-15), which was completed "in the sixth year of the reign of Darius the King."

The third was issued by Artaxerxes (Ezra 7:11-26) in which Ezra returned with more captives (Ezra 8:1-23). Ezra arrived in Jerusalem in the "seventh year of Artaxerxes the king" (Ezra 7:7-8) to teach the law of God, beautify the temple, and restore temple worship.

The fourth, issued by Artaxerxes (Nehemiah 2:7-9), authorized Nehemiah to return to Jerusalem and rebuild the wall at government expense (Nehemiah 1:1-6:15). Nehemiah was given permission in the "twentieth year of Artaxerxes" (Nehemiah 2:1,) and the wall was rebuilt within fifty-two days (Nehemiah 6:15) after he arrived in Jerusalem. To get an idea of these "troublous times," read the first few chapters of the Book of Nehemiah. In Nehemiah 4:17 we are told that the wall was built by men with a tool in one hand and a weapon in the other.

Instead of assigning actual dates, the Jews compute time from the beginning of each new king. In order to assign dates we need to turn to Gentile historical records: time in the Roman Empire was based on the founding of the city of Rome, approximately 754 B.C. In the 6th century a man named Dionysius Exiguus tried to compute when the Christian Era began. As a result of his effort, we compute time from the birth date of Jesus Christ. Many Bible scholars today believe there was a miscalculation and the actual date of the birth of Christ was 4 B.C.

Assigning actual dates to the reign of the Persian kings is most difficult. It is nearly impossible to find a dozen different history books with identical dates for these kings. The dates I use may or may not be factual; however, most historical accounts are close to these dates. The first actual king of Persia was King Chambyses, the father of Cyrus. Cyrus conquered Babylon in 538 B.C. In 536 B.C. his father died and Cyrus became the sole monarch of the Persian Empire. The kings of the Persian Empire and the dates they reigned would look something like this:

538-529 B.C. Cyrus, the Great.
528-522 B.C. Cambyses, son of Cyrus (Also called Ahasuerus in Ezra 4:6) (Note: An individual named Smerdis ruled seven months in 522 B.C. He was not in the royal bloodline and many records either identify him as an impostor or ignore his seven month reign.)
485-465 B.C. Xerxes.
464-424 B.C. Artaxerxes Longimanus.
423-405 B.C. Darius Nothus.
404-359 B.C. Artaxerxes Mnemon.
358-338 B.C. Ochus.
337-336 B.C. Arses.
335-331 B.C. Darius Codomannus (dethroned by Alexander the Great, of the Greek Empire).

Using these dates, we are going to try to determine the birth date of the Messiah. The total time determined on the timetable was seventy weeks or 490 years. The event which started the 490 year countdown was the "going forth of the commandment to restore and to build Jerusalem"

(Daniel 9:25). Seven weeks or forty-nine years later, Jerusalem was restored in "troublous times." The restoration was followed by a period of sixty-two weeks or 434 years. "From the going forth of the commandment to restore . . . unto the Messiah the Prince" includes both the seven weeks (forty-nine years) and the sixty-two weeks (434 years), for a total time of sixty-nine weeks (483 years). As stated earlier, Cyrus conquered Babylon in the year 538 B.C. Let's subtract forty-nine years from that date. We should be able to say, "In the year 489 B.C. the Jews were busy restoring the city of Jerusalem." If we subtract the remaining 434 years, we should be able to determine the birth date of the Messiah. 489 minus 434 years gives us the birth date of the Messiah as 55 B.C. This is quite a discrepancy if the Bible scholars are correct in saying the Messiah was born in the year 4 B.C.

The first decree to restore Jerusalem was issued by Cyrus in the first year of his reign. Although Cyrus conquered Babylon in 538 B.C. his father was king until his death two years later. This would make the first year of the reign of Cyrus as 536 B.C. Using 536 B.C. as a starting date and subtracting 483 years (49 + 434) the birth date of the Messiah would be 53 B.C.

In Ezra 3:1 we find it took seven months for the exiles to reach Jerusalem. In Ezra 3:3 they restored the altar and began to offer "burnt offerings thereon unto the Lord." In Ezra 3:8-10, two years after their return, they laid the foundation of the temple. In Ezra 4:5 we find the "adversaries" of Ezra 4:1 "frustrated their purposes, all the days of Cyrus king of Persia, even until the reign of Darius king of Persia." The reign of Darius began near the year 521 B.C. Using 521 B.C. as a starting date (minus 483 year), the birth date of the Messiah would be 38 B.C. The temple work ceased until the second year of the reign of Darius, only two years later, making the birth date of the Messiah 36 B.C.

In Ezra 5:1 the prophets Haggai and Zechariah urged the people to continue work on the temple which resulted in a letter being sent to King Darius (Ezra 5:6-17). The letter urged Darius to search the records and confirm that King Cyrus had issued a decree to build the temple. In Ezra 6:1-2 the search was made, and a second decree (Ezra 6:8) was issued. As a result, the temple was completed in the sixth year of the reign of Darius (Ezra 6:15). The sixth year of the reign of Darius would be 515 B.C. Using 515 B.C. as a starting date (minus 483 years), the birth date of the Messiah would be 32 B.C.

In Ezra 7:1 the account of the restoration continues with the reign of Artaxerxes. Following King Darius (Hystaspes) was the reign of Xerxes (485-465 B.C.), then Artaxerxes (Longimanus) (464-424 B.C.). In Ezra 7:11-26 a third decree authorized Ezra to return to Jerusalem with a group of exiles (Ezra 8:1-23) for the purpose of teaching the people the law (Ezra 7:25-26). Ezra and the exiles arrived in Jerusalem in the seventh year of the reign of Artaxerxes. The seventh year of his reign would be 457 B.C. Using 457 B.C. as a starting date, (minus 483 years) the birth date of the Messiah would be A.D. 26.

The fourth decree is recorded in the Book of Nehemiah. In Nehemiah

1:1-3 a fellow Jew, named Hanani, advises Nehemiah that the wall of Jerusalem and the gates had not been restored. Nehemiah fasted and prayed (Nehemiah 1:4-11) and in Nehemiah 2:1-10, King Artaxerxes gave Nehemiah letters authorizing him to restore the wall at government expense. Nehemiah was given these letters in the twentieth year of the reign of Artaxerxes (Nehemiah 2:1), 444 B.C. Using 444 B.C. as a starting date (minus 483 years), the birth date of the Messiah would be A.D. 39.

With both the wall and the gates restored, the restoration of Jerusalem was complete. In Nehemiah 2:1 Nehemiah was given permission to rebuild the wall and gates in the twentieth year of Artaxerxes. In Nehemiah 2:11 he arrived in Jerusalem, and after three days the work began. In Nehemiah 6:15, the wall was finished in 52 days. This could mean the restoration may have continued into the next year, which was 443 B.C. If so, this would move the birth date of the Messiah to A.D. 40.

Regardless of our starting date, it is obvious we are not going to arrive at the exact birth date of Jesus. I honestly believe the human family has played games with dates and changed their method of computing time so often that nobody can accurately date an event in the Bible. The Babylonian calendar was based on 360 days per year. The Jewish calendar was based on lunar months only twenty-nine and a half days, which would make their year 354 days long. The old Roman calendar was basically the same as the Jewish until Julius Caesar introduced his Julian calendar on January 1, 45 B.C. To get his calendar to correspond with the seasons, Caesar simply announced that the year 46 B.C. would contain 15 months. The Julian calendar worked fine until the year A.D. 1582 when Pope Gregory XIII introduced the Gregorian calendar. To correct the discrepancy between the solar year and his calendar, he issued an edict saying the fifth day of October would be called the fifteenth. Men date events; God uses events to date. If there is a clock in the throne room of God, there is a good possibility the date and time on his clock are different than the clock in my house. If the human family would take their eyes off the clock to look at the events unfolding in our generation, they would know what time it is.

Our generation is making the same mistakes as the generation living when Jesus arrived. Jesus' generation had the seventy weeks prophecy as well as the dates of the Persian kings. From these two pieces of information, they could have known that according to the Word of God, the time was near for a major prophecy to be fulfilled. The greatest event in the history of the human race was about to take place, and the generation didn't even know what to look for. In Matthew 23:13-39 Jesus called the religious leaders of that generation hypocrites, and in verse 23:24 he labeled them "blind guides." This is also an accurate description of our generation and of the churches in the Laodicean era (Rev. 3:14-22). Prophecy is not a detailed history book written in advance. Many Bible prophecies, especially those concerning events still future, may be fulfilled somewhat differently than we might expect. Prophecy is God's method of telling his people what things will come to pass. Ignoring prophecy is like closing your eyes to what God is doing in the world today and what he plans to do in the future. Only two people in the generation living when Jesus arrived were actually expecting the Messiah when he arrived. One was Simeon in Luke 2:25-35 and the other was the prophetess Anna in Luke 2:36- 38.

Satan may have used the same tactics on that generation as he is using successfully on our generation. The carnal Bible students who subtracted the 483 years from the year 536 B.C. (when Cyrus issued the commandment to restore Jerusalem) would have published the birth date of the Messiah as 53 B.C. When he did not arrive that year, they would have been ridiculed and labeled false prophets. If they reevaluated his arrival from the completion of the temple, they would have re-published the new date of the Messiah's coming as the year 32 B.C. When the Messiah did not arrive in the year 32 B.C. the older generation would say, "We knew you were false prophets from your first prophecy." The younger generation would have replied, "We have heard that same song all the days of our lives and it is getting old." The unbelieving would have replied, "We considered his coming when you spoke back in 53 B.C., we reconsidered when you said 32 B.C. You have convinced us that the coming Messiah is a figment of your imagination."

When we consider the years A.D. 39-40 and remember the four year miscalculation Exiguus may have made, we are looking at the years A.D. 35-36 which are within two years of the death of Jesus, not the birth of Jesus. The Bible students who took the firm stand that "unto the Messiah" can mean nothing but "unto the birth of the Messiah" would have been very disappointed to find they completely missed him. Those who considered "unto the Messiah" with the fact that "after threescore and two weeks shall Messiah be cut off, but not for himself" would have viewed the prophecy differently, especially if they were familiar with the remainder of the Old Testament Scripture. To them, the Messiah would be the Redeemer, the one chosen of God to pay the penalty for their sins, the one to "be cut off, but not for himself." Even if they knew that God's plan of salvation was centered on the death of the Redeemer, they would have been ridiculed for talking about Israel's Messiah dying. Jesus own disciples didn't want to hear about Jesus' fate, even when they heard it from his own lips. Had these Bible students gone to the synagogue to discuss the Word of God with the religious leaders, they would have faced the same "hypocrites" and "blind guides" who rejected Jesus as the Messiah.

God identified Cyrus as the man who would issue the commandment to build Jerusalem, perhaps as much as 150 years before he arrived on the scene. At the time God identified Cyrus, Jerusalem had not yet been destroyed. The Prophet Isaiah spoke of Cyrus in Isaiah chapters 41, 44, and 45. In Isaiah 44:28 we have the statement, "That saith of Cyrus, He is my shepherd, and shall perform all my pleasure: even saying to Jerusalem, Thou shalt be built; and to the temple, Thy foundation shall be laid." The Prophet Isaiah lived and died some 150 years before the days of Cyrus. As you read these chapters in the Book of Isaiah, you will find that God is presenting Himself as the only one with the ability to foretell future events. Most Bible students date the ministry of Isaiah in the years near 740-700 B.C. The first year of the reign of Cyrus was near 536 B.C. From God's point of view the commandment to restore Jerusalem went forth from King Cyrus. When the "adversaries" "frustrated their purpose," other decrees were issued to either confirm or accomplish the original decree issued by Cyrus. The decree issued by Cyrus (Ezra 1:1-4) was twofold in that (1) he authorized the Jews to return to Jerusalem, and (2) he commanded them to "build the house of the Lord God of Israel." When Cyrus issued the decree, Zerubbabel returned with several thousand exiles, restored the altar, and laid the foundation of the temple. The "adversaries" were able to stop the temple work for nearly twenty-nine years. The second decree (issued by Darius) was nothing more than a letter of confirmation that Cyrus had authorized the Jews to rebuild the temple. The temple was restored near the year 515 B.C. The third decree, issued to Ezra by King Artaxerxes fifty-eight years later, was verification that the Jews who wanted to go were free to return to Jerusalem.

None of these decrees mentioned restoring the walls of Jerusalem. According to Gabriel (Dan. 9:25), the event that would start the 490 year timetable would be "the going forth of the commandment to restore and to build Jerusalem." This portion of the seventy week prophecy was fulfilled when King Cyrus issued his decree (536 B.C.) authorizing the exiled Jews to return to Jerusalem and rebuild the temple. The second decree confirmed that Cyrus had authorized the Jews to rebuild the temple, and the third decree verified that the Jews were free to return to Jerusalem. Although the restoration of the wall may be rightly considered rebuilding Jerusalem, it was not part of the prophecy connected with the decree issued by Cyrus. The rebuilding of the wall of Jerusalem was not mentioned by Cyrus in his original decree, nor was it mentioned in the two follow-up decrees. Gabriel first called our attention to the wall in Daniel 9:25 with the statement, "the street shall be built again, and the wall, even in troublous times." The fourth decree, issued by King Artaxerxes to Nehemiah, authorized him to rebuild the wall and gates of Jerusalem, because of Nehemiah's "sorrow of heart" (Nehemiah 2:2), not because of the decree issued by Cyrus. In Daniel 9:25 Gabriel had divided the seventy week timetable from "the going forth of the commandment" to "the Messiah" into two segments: seven weeks or forty-nine years; and sixty-two weeks or 434 years. The "going forth of the commandment to restore" issued by Cyrus marks the beginning of the first segment, the seven weeks or forty-nine years. The rebuilding of the wall in fifty-two days near the year 444 B.C.

marks the beginning of the second segment, the sixty-two weeks or 434 year countdown (unto) the Messiah.

The original decree was issued by Cyrus near the year 536 B.C. The wall of Jerusalem was restored near the year 444 B.C. This represents a period of ninety-two years which, according to the seventy week prophecy, it should have been only forty-nine years. In doing this God is demonstrating from past historical records that the 490 year timetable was not to be a *continuous* period of time. At some point during the ninety-two year period God stopped computing time against the 490 year clock, which necessitated the need for Gabriel to show that the clock would be started again with the rebuilding of the wall. In considering the entire seventy week prophecy, we will see that Gabriel actually divided the seventy weeks into three different time segments. By demonstrating that it was not a continuous period of time between the first and second segments, God was alerting his people of the delay between the second and third segments. In Daniel 9:25, we have a seven week (forty-nine year) segment and a sixty-two week (434 years) segment, which totals sixty-nine weeks or 483 years. Daniel 9:26 continues with the statement that "after" the sixty-nine week segment, the Messiah shall be cut off and the city and temple would again be destroyed. In Daniel 9:27 we have the final segment of one week or seven years in the statement, "And he shall confirm the covenant with many for one week." Between the second and third segments, the clock was stopped for 2000 years for the Church Dispensation. With the arrival of the Messiah, God stopped computing time against the timetable with one week (seven years) remaining. If it were possible for us to look into the throne room of God and see this unique clock today, it would still be stopped showing one week or seven years.

Gabriel continues the seventy weeks prophecy in Daniel 9:26, "And after threescore and two weeks shall Messiah be cut off, but not for himself: and the people of the prince that shall come shall destroy the city and the sanctuary; and the end thereof shall be with a flood, and unto the end of the war desolations are determined." The word *after* means, following in time or place. The phrase "threescore and two weeks" refers to the second segment of time Gabriel gave between the restoration of the wall of Jerusalem and the arrival of the Messiah. In the phrase "And after threescore and two weeks" Gabriel is basically saying the sixty-two weeks will end and be followed by four events: (1) the Messiah will be cut off, (2) Jerusalem and the temple will again be destroyed, (3) unto the end of the war desolations are determined upon the Jews, and (4) the final one week described in Daniel 9:27. The Messiah was cut off, but not for himself, by the substitutionary death of Jesus on Calvary for our sins. History shows "the people of the prince that shall come shall destroy the city and the sanctuary" to be the people of the Roman Empire. This part of the prophecy was fulfilled in A.D. 70 when Titus and the Roman Army destroyed the city of Jerusalem. This was followed by the final dispersion of the Jews, and for the next 1897 years the city of Jerusalem was under the control of the Moslems or Christians.

In 1967 we saw the Jews take control of the city of Jerusalem and "the people of the prince" began to form the European Common Market. By January 1981 the ten nation confederacy spoken of by Daniel the Prophet was completed, except for one point. The organization needs, and is looking for, an individual with the ability to organize and fulfill its goal to control world economics. This individual is too busy in the Church today but on the day of the rapture of the Church, he is going to be looking for a job. That part of the Church which he was unable to deceive as the demonic spirit Antichrist will be taken out of the way, and we will be able to watch this unique time clock in the throne room of God, in its final countdown to zero. Following the rapture, Antichrist is going to incarnate in the form of a human being and accept the position of spokesman for the European Common Market nations. From this position he will be able to destroy the Laodicean Church congregation, which missed the rapture. He will also be in a position to negotiate and confirm the protection treaty with the Jews at Jerusalem. This is the Isaiah 28:14-22 covenant with death that God disannuls during the countdown of the final week (seven years).

Isaiah ends his account of the covenant with death in Isaiah 28:22b with the statement, "for I have heard from the Lord God of hosts a consumption, even determined upon the whole earth." Gabriel ends the seventy weeks prophecy in Daniel 9:27 by saying, "And he [Antichrist, spokesman of the people of the prince who form the ten nation confederacy, the final form of the Roman Empire] shall confirm the covenant [protection treaty] with many [many Jews at Jerusalem] for one week [or seven years]: and in the midst of the week [three and one-half years later] he [the False Prophet] shall cause the sacrifice and the oblation to cease, and for the overspreading of abominations he shall make it desolate, even until the consummation, and that determined shall be poured upon the desolate." The final week in the seventy weeks prophecy is the seven-year tribulation period. The consumption begins when Antichrist confirms a seven-year protection covenant with the Nation of Israel (the Jews at Jerusalem). The first thing to be consumed will be false Christendom, which Jesus left behind at the rapture. During this three-and-one-half-year period all the other false religions of the world will be exempt since they do not hold Jesus Christ as the center and object of their worship. "In the midst of the week" (at midpoint in the seven-year period) the False Prophet ascends out of Hades and is reincarnated as a human being. He introduces the beast image and issues the ultimatum–worship or die–which condemns every religion on the planet. How the False Prophet ultimatum affects Judaism is that "in the midst of the week he shall cause the sacrifice and the oblation to cease" which breaks the Antichrist protection treaty confirmed three and one-half years earlier.

The ultimatum forbids the worship of God or any god except the image of the beast. People from all religions who refuse to worship the image will be killed. The consumption that consumed false Christendom will be expanded to include all religions, religious groups, and religious individuals on Earth, or as Isaiah says, "even determined upon the whole earth." Freedom of religion is replaced by freedom to sin "and for the overspreading of abominations he (the False Prophet) shall make it (earth) desolate." The phrase "even until the consummation" means even until the end of the seven-year tribulation period when God pours out the seven final vial judgments, or as Daniel 9:27 says, "and that determined shall be poured upon the desolate."

Chapter Four

Sequential Revelation

The majority of the Book of the Revelation is sequential, meaning the events are given in consecutive order or in succession. Revelation chapter 1 is an account of the arisen Jesus appearing to John on the Isle of Patmos. In Rev. 1:19, John is told to write the things he had seen (Chapter 1, the vision of Jesus), the things which are (Chapters 2 and 3, the Church Dispensation), and the things which shall be hereafter (events following the Church Dispensation). Revelation chapters 2 and 3 cover the entire Church Dispensation. It is an analytical view of church history from the eyes of Jesus. Chapter 4 is an uninterrupted continuation of the events after the Church age ends. In this chapter we will deal with the consecutive events and in the next chapter we will look at the Revelation flashbacks.

1. John Enters Heaven and Sees Seven Things.

Rev. 4:1-11 "(1) After this I looked, and, behold, a door [was] opened in
heaven: and the first voice which I heard [was] as it were of a trumpet talk-
ing with me; which said, Come up hither, and I will shew thee things which
must be hereafter. (2) And immediately I was in the spirit: and, behold, a
throne was set in heaven, and [one] sat on the throne. (3) And he that sat
was to look upon like a jasper and a sardine stone: and [there was] a rain-
bow round about the throne, in sight like unto an emerald. (4) And round
about the throne [were] four and twenty seats: and upon the seats I saw four
and twenty elders sitting, clothed in white raiment; and they had on their
heads crowns of gold. (5) And out of the throne proceeded lightnings and
thunderings and voices: and [there were] seven lamps of fire burning before
the throne, which are the seven Spirits of God. (6) And before the throne
[there was] a sea of glass like unto crystal: and in the midst of the throne,

and round about the throne, [were] four beasts full of eyes before and behind. (7) And the first beast [was] like a lion, and the second beast like a calf, and the third beast had a face as a man, and the fourth beast [was] like a flying eagle. (8) And the four beasts had each of them six wings about [him]; and [they were] full of eyes within: and they rest not day and night, saying, Holy, holy, holy, Lord God Almighty, which was, and is, and is to come. (9) And when those beasts give glory and honour and thanks to him that sat on the throne, who liveth for ever and ever, (10) The four and twenty elders fall down before him that sat on the throne, and worship him that liveth for ever and ever, and cast their crowns before the throne, saying, (11) Thou art worthy, O Lord, to receive glory and honour and power: for thou hast created all things, and for thy pleasure they are and were created."

John was instructed to enter a door opened to heaven. The purpose was to see "things which must be hereafter" or things to follow the rapture of the Church. After entering heaven John observes seven things: (1) a throne set in heaven, Rev. 4:2b; (2) the one on the throne, Rev. 4:2c-3, (3) twenty-four elders, Rev. 4:4, (4) seven lamps of fire, Rev. 4:5, (5) a sea of glass, Rev. 4:6a, (6) four living creatures, Rev. 4:6b-11; and (7) a book sealed with seven seals (chapter 5).

The first thing John saw was a throne set in heaven. In spirit he actually walked into the throne room of God. The second thing he saw was God the Father sitting on the throne. The third thing he saw was twenty-four elders seated around the throne. Who the twenty-four elders are is debatable. Many believe they are the twelve children of Jacob who became the heads of the tribes of Israel and the twelve Apostles of Jesus. Listen to a discussion between Jesus and Peter in Matthew 19:27-28, "(27) Then answered Peter and said unto him, Behold, we have forsaken all, and followed thee; what shall we have therefore? (28) And Jesus said unto them, Verily I say unto you, That ye which have followed me, in the regeneration when the Son of man shall sit in the throne of his glory, ye also shall sit upon twelve thrones, judging the twelve tribes of Israel." Does "ye which have followed me" mean the twelve Apostles or us?

The twenty-four elders may be the "watchers" seen in Daniel chapter 4. King Nebuchadnezzar had a vision of a great tree and asked Daniel for the interpretation. Notice the part the watchers play, Daniel 4:10-17, "(10) Thus [were] the visions of mine head in my bed; I saw, and behold a tree in the midst of the earth, and the height thereof [was] great. (11) The tree grew, and was strong, and the height thereof reached unto heaven, and the sight thereof to the end of all the earth: (12) The leaves thereof [were] fair, and the fruit thereof much, and in it [was] meat for all: the beasts of the field had shadow under it, and the fowls of the heaven dwelt in the boughs thereof, and all flesh was fed of it. (13) I saw in the visions of my head upon my bed, and, behold, a watcher and an holy one came down from heaven; (14) He cried aloud, and said thus, Hew down the tree, and cut off his branches, shake off his leaves, and scatter his fruit: let the beasts get away from under it, and the fowls from his branches: (15) Nevertheless leave the stump of his roots in the earth, even with a band of iron and brass, in the tender grass of the field; and let it be wet with the dew of heaven, and [let] his portion [be] with the beasts in the grass of the earth: (16) Let his heart be changed from man's, and let a beast's heart be given unto him; and let seven times pass over him. (17) This matter [is] by the decree of the watchers, and the demand by the word of the holy ones: to the intent that the living may know that the most High ruleth in the kingdom of men, and giveth it to whomsoever he will, and setteth up over it the basest of men." King Nebuchadnezzar's spirit is going to be changed from a human to animal for seven years, "Let his heart be changed from man's, and let a beast's heart be given unto him; and let seven times pass over him." and "This matter [is] by the decree of the watchers, and the demand by the word of the holy ones." Let's go a little further and we can see the difference between the human race and animals.

The king was told that the vision concerns the Babylonian Empire and that he is the tree, Dan 4:22 "It [is] thou, O king, that art grown and become strong: for thy greatness is grown, and reacheth unto heaven, and thy dominion to the end of the earth." In verse 4:26-27 Daniel continues, "(26) And whereas they commanded to leave the stump of the tree roots; thy kingdom shall be sure unto thee, after that thou shalt have known that the heavens do rule. (27) Wherefore, O king, let my counsel be acceptable unto thee, and break off thy sins by righteousness, and thine iniquities by shewing mercy to the poor; if it may be a lengthening of thy tranquillity." Good advice but it fell on deaf ears because one year later the prophecy was fulfilled. Dan. 4:29-33, "(29) At the end of twelve months he walked in the palace of the kingdom of Babylon. (30) The king spake, and said, Is not this great Babylon, that I have built for the house of the kingdom by the might of my power, and for the honour of my majesty? (31) While the word [was] in the king's mouth, there fell a voice from heaven, [saying], O king Nebuchadnezzar, to thee it is spoken; The kingdom is departed from thee. (32) And they shall drive thee from men, and thy dwelling [shall be] with the beasts of the field: they shall make thee to eat grass as oxen, and seven times shall pass over thee, until thou know that the most High ruleth in the kingdom of men, and giveth it to whomsoever he will. (33) The same hour was the thing fulfilled upon Nebuchadnezzar: and he was driven from men, and did eat grass as oxen, and his body was wet with the dew of heaven, till his hairs were grown like eagles' [feathers], and his nails like birds' [claws]."

Seven years later, Dan. 4:34-37 "(34) And at the end of the days I Nebuchadnezzar lifted up mine eyes unto heaven, and mine understanding returned unto me, and I blessed the most High, and I praised and honoured him that liveth for ever, whose dominion [is] an everlasting dominion, and his kingdom [is] from generation to generation: (35) And all the inhabitants of the earth [are] reputed as nothing: and he doeth according to his will in the army of heaven, and [among] the inhabitants of the earth: and none can stay his hand, or say unto him, What doest thou? (36) At the same time my reason returned unto me; and for the glory of my kingdom, mine honour and brightness returned unto me; and my counselors and my lords sought unto me; and I was established in my kingdom, and excellent majesty was added unto me. (37) Now I Nebuchadnezzar praise and extol and honour the King of heaven, all whose works [are] truth, and his ways judgment: and those that walk in pride he is able to abase." When the king's spirit was changed from an animal to a human his understanding and reasoning returned.

There are some things about the twenty-four elders we can know for sure. They have "crowns of gold" which speaks of their political authority. They are "clothed in white raiment" which says they are righteous. The day will come when the Church will dress the same way, Rev. 19:7-8 "(7) Let us be glad and rejoice, and give honour to him (Jesus): for the marriage of the Lamb is come, and his wife (the Church, the Bride of Christ) hath made herself ready. (8) And to her was granted that she should be arrayed in fine linen, clean and white: for the fine linen is the righteousness of saints." In Rev. 5:8 we can see they are involved in our prayers, "And when he had taken the book, the four beasts and four [and] twenty elders fell down before the Lamb, having every one of them harps, and golden vials full of odours, which are the prayers of saints." With those harps they sing the song of redemption so without doubt they are human spirits, not angelic beings, Rev. 5:9-10 "(9) And they sung a new song, saying, Thou art worthy to take the book, and to open the seals thereof: for thou wast slain, and hast redeemed us to God by thy blood out of every kindred, and tongue, and people, and nation; (10) And hast made us unto our God kings and priests: and we shall reign on the earth."

The fourth thing John observed were seven lamps of fire identified as the seven Spirits of God. All seven Spirits of God were the Holy Spirit, the third person in the Trinity. The number seven implies totality or completeness, in the sense of wholeness. The seven letters to seven churches in Revelation Chapters 2 and 3 represent the whole of Christendom. Later we will look at each of the seven facets to see the complete picture of the Church and Christianity. The seven Spirits of God represent the complete Holy Spirit. There are not seven different Holy Spirits, just one Holy Spirit with seven different facets. We can see these different facets by looking at what happened to Jesus, when John baptized him in the Jordan River. In Matthew 3:13-17 as Jesus "went up strightway out of the water. . . . The Spirit of God descending like a dove, and lighting upon him . . . ." In Luke 3:22 we are told "the Holy Ghost descended in a bodily shape like a dove upon him." In John 1:29-34 we are told this was the historical event that would identify the Son of God to John the Baptist, "Upon whom thou shalt see the Spirit descending, and remaining on him, the same is he which baptizeth with the

Holy Ghost. And I saw, and bare record that this is the Son of God." The "Spirit of God," the "Spirit," and the "Holy Ghost" that descended in the bodily form of a dove and rested upon Jesus, the Son of God, at his water baptism, was the Holy Spirit, the third person in the Trinity.

This event was the fulfillment of a prophecy given in Isaiah 11:1-3, "(1) And there shall come forth a rod out of the stem of Jesse, and a Branch shall grow out of his roots: (2) And the spirit of the Lord shall rest upon him, the spirit of wisdom and understanding, the spirit of counsel and might, the spirit of knowledge and of the fear of the Lord; (3) And shall make him of quick understanding in the fear of the Lord: and he shall not judge after the sight of his eyes, neither reprove after the hearing of his ears." In verse 2 you can see the seven facet Holy Spirit that rested on Jesus at his water baptism: (1) the spirit of the Lord, (2) the spirit of wisdom, (3) the spirit of understanding, (4) the spirit of counsel, (5) the spirit of might, (6) the spirit of knowledge, and (7) the spirit of the fear of the Lord.

The fifth thing John saw was a sea of glass. At this point in time we are at the beginning of the seven-year tribulation era and the sea of glass is empty. The next time John sees the sea of glass we are at the end of the tribulation era and he sees the tribulation dead standing on the sea of glass. Rev. 15:2-3, "(2) And I saw as it were a sea of glass mingled with fire: and them that had gotten the victory over the beast, and over his image, and over his mark, [and] over the number of his name, stand on the sea of glass, having the harps of God. (3) And they sing the song of Moses the servant of God, and the song of the Lamb, saying, Great and marvelous [are] thy works, Lord God Almighty; just and true [are] thy ways, thou King of saints."

The sixth thing John saw was four beasts that were full of eyes and had six wings each. The first beast was like a lion, the second a calf, the third had a face like a man, and the fourth was like a flying eagle. These living creatures were angelic beings similar to the Cherubim angels Ezekiel saw. These had six wings while the ones Ezekiel saw had only four. Ezekiel described what he saw, 1:3-10 "(3) The word of the LORD came expressly unto Ezekiel the priest, the son of Buzi, in the land of the Chaldeans by the river Chebar; and the hand of the LORD was there upon him. (4) And I looked, and, behold, a whirlwind came out of the north, a great cloud, and a fire infolding itself, and a brightness [was] about it, and out of the midst thereof as the colour of amber, out of the midst of the fire. (5) Also out of the midst thereof [came] the likeness of four living creatures. And this [was] their appearance; they had the likeness of a man. (6) And every one had four faces, and every one had four wings. (7) And their feet [were] straight feet; and the sole of their feet [was] like the sole of a calf's foot: and they sparkled like the colour of burnished brass. (8) And [they had] the hands of a man under their wings on their four sides; and they four had their faces and their wings. (9) Their wings [were] joined one to another; they turned not when they went; they went every one straight forward. (10) As for the likeness of their faces, they four had the face of a man, and the face of a lion, on the right side: and they four had the face of an ox on the left side; they four also had the face of an eagle." Ezekiel saw them again in chapter 10:14-15, "(14) And every one had four faces: the first face [was] the face of a cherub, and the second face [was] the face of a man, and the third the face of a lion, and the fourth the face of an eagle. (15) And the cherubims were lifted up. This [is] the living creature that I saw by the river of Chebar."

When the four beasts worship God, the twenty-four elders join them, Rev. 4:8b-11, "(8b) and they rest not day and night, saying, Holy, holy, holy, Lord God Almighty, which was, and is, and is to come. (9) And when those beasts give glory and honour and thanks to him that sat on the throne, who liveth for ever and ever, (10) The four and twenty elders fall down before him that sat on the throne, and worship him that liveth for ever and ever, and cast their crowns before the throne, saying, (11) Thou art worthy, O Lord, to receive glory and honour and power: for thou hast created all things, and for thy pleasure they are and were created." Describing God with the phrase "which was, and is, and is to come" is just another way of saying He is eternal. "Was" is past tense and no matter how far back you go, he was there. "Is" is present and he is alive today. "To come" is future and he will always be here.

2. The Search for one worthy to loose Seven Seals of a Book.

Rev. 5:1-14, "(1) And I saw in the right hand of him that sat on the throne a book written within and on the backside, sealed with seven seals. (2) And I saw a strong angel proclaiming with a loud voice, Who is worthy to open the book, and to loose the seals thereof? (3) And no man in heaven, nor in earth, neither under the earth, was able to open the book, neither to look thereon. (4) And I wept much, because no man was found worthy to open and to read the book, neither to look thereon. (5) And one of the elders saith unto me, Weep not: behold, the Lion of the tribe of Juda, the Root of David, hath prevailed to open the book, and to loose the seven seals thereof. (6) And I beheld, and, lo, in the midst of the throne and of the four beasts, and in the midst of the elders, stood a Lamb as it had been slain, having seven horns and seven eyes, which are the seven Spirits of God sent forth into all the earth. (7) And he came and took the book out of the right hand of him that sat upon the throne. (8) And when he had taken the book, the four beasts and four [and] twenty elders fell down before the Lamb, having every one of them harps, and golden vials full of odours, which are the prayers of saints. (9) And they sung a new song, saying, Thou art worthy to take the book, and to open the seals thereof: for thou wast slain, and hast redeemed us to God by thy blood out of every kindred, and tongue, and people, and nation; (10) And hast made us unto our God kings and priests: and we shall reign on the earth. (11) And I beheld, and I heard the voice of many angels round about the throne and the beasts and the elders: and the number of them was ten thousand times ten thousand, and thousands of thousands; (12) Saying with a loud voice, Worthy is the Lamb that was slain to receive power, and riches, and wisdom, and strength, and honour, and glory, and blessing. (13) And every creature which is in heaven, and on the earth, and under the earth, and such as are in the sea, and all that are in them, heard I saying, Blessing, and honour, and glory, and power, [be] unto him that sitteth upon the throne, and unto the Lamb for ever and ever. (14) And the four beasts said, Amen. And the four [and] twenty elders fell down and worshipped him that liveth for ever and ever."

The book sealed with seven seals was the seventh thing John saw when he entered heaven after the Church rapture. The book contains the record of the judgments recorded in the remainder of the book of the Revelation. What is needed now is someone to execute the judgments. The proclamation of the strong angel is a question, "Who is worthy to open the book, and to loose the seals thereof?" During the search, "no man in heaven, nor in earth, neither under the earth, was able to open the book, neither to look thereon." The phrase "neither under the earth" is just another way of saying the word "Hades" or "the Bottomless Pit." The search included the men in heaven, in earth, and in Hades. The men in heaven at this point are the saved from all previous dispensations and the Church. The seven-year tribulation era has just begun so the "tribulation dead" who will be saved are still alive on planet Earth. The men in earth are those living on the face of the earth at the time of the search. The men under the earth are the inhabitants of Hades who are the lost or unsaved from all previous dispensations.

John's weeping ends when Jesus Christ is found worthy to open and read the book. Jesus is the Old Testament "Lion of the tribe of Juda, the Root of David," and composer of the new song the Church is singing, Rev. 5:9-10 "(9) And they sung a new song, saying, Thou art worthy to take the book, and to open the seals thereof: for thou wast slain, and hast redeemed us to God by thy blood out of every kindred, and tongue, and people, and nation; (10) And hast made us unto our God kings and priests: and we shall reign on the earth." His worthiness was confirmed by his resurrection, Rev. 5:12, "Saying with a loud voice, Worthy is the Lamb that was slain to receive power, and riches, and wisdom, and strength, and honour, and glory, and blessing." In Rev. 5:7 there is a distinction made between God the Father on his throne and God the Son, who left his throne to redeem us, "And he came and took the book out of the right hand of him that sat upon the throne." Notice Rev. 5:13 Jesus now receives equal worship with the Father, "And every creature which is in heaven, and on the earth, and under the earth, and such as are in the sea, and all that are in them, heard I saying, Blessing, and honour, and glory, and power, [be] unto him that sitteth upon the throne, and unto the Lamb for ever and ever."

During the Law Dispensation in the Levitical Priesthood the priest was commanded to burn incense on the Altar of Incense in the temple. In Rev. 5:8 we are told what these odours represent, "And when he had taken the book, the four beasts and four [and] twenty elders fell down before the Lamb, having every one of them harps, and golden vials full of odours, which are the prayers of saints." The Church Dispensation is the fulfillment of Malachi 1:11, "For from the rising of the sun even unto the going down of the same my name [shall be] great among the Gentiles; and in every place incense [shall be] offered unto my name, and a pure offering: for my name [shall be] great among the heathen, saith the LORD of hosts." The Greek word translated as *odours* is translated as *incense* elsewhere in the Bible. The burning of incense represents the act of praying where we submit our prayers to God. The smoke contains odours, aroma, or fragrance which is the essence of our prayers as they come up before God. Prayers submitted by saints on legal grounds and in the proper format are sweet smelling to God. They are a sweet savour to God just as the burnt offering of animal sacrifices was during the Levitical Priesthood, Exodus 29:18, "And thou shalt burn the whole ram upon the altar: it [is] a burnt offering unto the LORD: it [is] a sweet savour, an offering made by fire unto the LORD." When Israel departed from God, He moved in judgment and told them not to waste their time, Leviticus 26:31, "And I will make your cities waste, and bring your sanctuaries unto desolation, and I will not smell the savour of your sweet odours." Unless you're a saint the only prayer you can submit that will come up before God is the sinner's prayer. It would appear that premature prayers are stored in golden vials and opened when the time is right. For example, no amount of praying today will move God to judge Satan and end hardships on the human race. These prayers will be stored in the golden vial and presented to God when the time to judge Satan has arrived. Burning incense to anyone or anything else is an abomination to God.

3. First Seal Opened: Rider on a White Horse.

Rev. 6:1-2, "(1) And I saw when the Lamb opened one of the seals, and I heard, as it were the noise of thunder, one of the four beasts saying, Come and see. (2) And I saw, and behold a white horse: and he that sat on him had a bow; and a crown was given unto him: and he went forth conquering, and to conquer." The rider on the white horse is Antichrist. He is given a bow and a crown for the purpose of conquering. The bow is a weapon of war signifying he has been given the ability and military force necessary to overcome all human resistance. The crown signifies political authority. At this time Antichrist has incarnated in a human body and is active with the European Common Market confederacy.

4. Second Seal Opened: The Red Horse.

Rev. 6:3-4, "(3) And when he had opened the second seal, I heard the second beast say, Come and see. (4) And there went out another horse [that was] red: and [power] was given to him that sat thereon to take peace from the earth, and that they should kill one another: and there was given unto him a great sword." The rider on the red horse was given a great sword and power for the purpose of taking "peace from the earth, and that they should kill one another." The wars and rumors of wars period started with the Laodicean Church Era and will reach full intensity when this rider goes forth. He will fulfill the prophecy given in Matthew 24:6-8, "(6) And ye shall hear of wars and rumours of wars: see that ye be not troubled: for all [these things] must come to pass, but the end is not yet. (7) For nation shall rise against nation, and kingdom against kingdom: and there shall be famines, and pestilences, and earthquakes, in divers places. (8) All these [are] the beginning of sorrows."

5. Third Seal Opened: The Black Horse.

Rev. 6:5-6, "(5) And when he had opened the third seal, I heard the third beast say, Come and see. And I beheld, and lo a black horse; and he that sat on him had a pair of balances in his hand. (6) And I heard a voice in the midst of the four beasts say, A measure of wheat for a penny, and three measures of barley for a penny; and [see] thou hurt not the oil and the wine." The rider on the black horse had a pair of balances in his hand which speaks of judgment, in the sense of MENE TEKEL, "MENE; God hath numbered thy kingdom, and finished it," and "TEKEL; Thou art weighed in the balances, and art found wanting." This rider will not weigh the Church in the balances. Jesus will put the Church in the balances by rapturing the Philadelphia congregation. The Laodicean congregation left behind will be weighed in the balance during the first half of the tribulation and will be destroyed. The Antichrist/False Prophet organization will be weighted and finished during the last half.

In Daniel chapter 5 Belshazzar had profaned articles taken by his father from the temple in Jerusalem, resulting in the hand-writing on the wall. Daniel interprets the writing for Belshazzar in Daniel 5:25-28, "(25) And this [is] the writing that was written, MENE, MENE, TEKEL, UPHARSIN. (26) This [is] the interpretation of the thing: MENE; God hath numbered thy kingdom, and finished it. (27) TEKEL; Thou art weighed in the balances, and art found wanting. (28) PERES; Thy kingdom is divided, and given to the Medes and Persians." That night Darius the Median killed Belshazzar and ended the Babylonian Empire. Profaning the temple articles was the proverbial 'straw that broke the camel's back.' After reading the entire chapter, it is obvious Belshazzar was weighed and found lacking in his lifestyle. When the cause of Belshazzar's death was made known to him, he had already been judged, "God hath numbered thy kingdom, and finished it." The handwriting was merely the announcement of a decision which had already been made. Many argue Belshazzar had the rest of the day to repent and be saved, but I don't think so. Belshazzar chose the wrong lifestyle and it would not let him repent. God had judged and announced his decision, and I doubt if Belshazzar could have said anything to change God's mind. Before God judged, yes, but after the judgment, no it's too late. If you live a lifestyle that does not include obedience to the Word of God you are not going to change anything on your deathbed. By your lifestyle, on a daily basis, you have communicated to God your choice of heaven or hell. A lifestyle that ignores or rejects God, his Word, and his ways cannot be changed on your deathbed because your lifestyle, and God's judgment are history, and God did not make a way for us to rewrite history. God made a way for us to get him to forget things we have done, but a lifelong lifestyle of rejecting Jesus is not one of those things. Don't be one of the people who gets "weighed in the balances and art found wanting."

The instructions given to the rider are recorded in Rev. 6:6, "And I heard a voice in the midst of the four beasts say, A measure of wheat for a penny, and three measures of barley for a penny; and [see] thou hurt not the oil and the wine." The rider is told to ignore the wealthy and weigh the rest of the people. Oil and wine are luxuries enjoyed by the wealthy of planet Earth, which may mean God has weighed and finished them. Remember what Jesus said about the rich in Matthew 19:23-24, "(23) Then said Jesus unto his disciples, Verily I say unto you, That a rich man shall hardly enter into the kingdom of heaven. (24) And again I say unto you, It is easier for a camel to go through the eye of a needle, than for a rich man to enter into the kingdom of God."

Measuring food or eating food by weight speaks of the hard times that come when people rejects God and He moves in judgment. Listen to what God told Israel in Lev. 26:26-29, "(26) [And] when I have broken the staff of your bread, ten women shall bake your bread in one oven, and they shall deliver [you] your bread again by weight: and ye shall eat, and not be satisfied. (27) And if ye will not for all this hearken unto me, but walk contrary unto me; (28) Then I will walk contrary unto you also in fury; and I, even I, will chastise you seven times for your sins. (29) And ye shall eat the flesh of your sons, and the flesh of your daughters shall ye eat." Israel rejected God and He executed the judgment, 2 Kings 6:24-29 "(24) And it came to pass after this, that Benhadad king of Syria gathered all his host, and went up, and besieged Samaria. (25) And there was a great famine in Samaria: and, behold, they besieged it, until an ass's head was [sold] for fourscore [pieces] of silver, and the fourth part of a cab of dove's dung for five [pieces] of silver. (26) And as the king of Israel was passing by upon the wall, there cried a woman unto him, saying, Help, my lord, O king. (27) And he said,

If the LORD do not help thee, whence shall I help thee? out of the barn-floor, or out of the winepress? (28) And the king said unto her, What aileth thee? And she answered, This woman said unto me, Give thy son, that we may eat him today, and we will eat my son to morrow. (29) So we boiled my son, and did eat him: and I said unto her on the next day, Give thy son, that we may eat him: and she hath hid her son." Without doubt these were hard times but Jesus says they are not comparable to the hard times yet to come, Matthew 24:21-22 "(21) For then shall be great tribulation, such as was not since the beginning of the world to this time, no, nor ever shall be. (22) And except those days should be shortened, there should no flesh be saved: but for the elect's sake those days shall be shortened."

Many Christians today have been deceived into believing that the Church will go through the seven-year tribulation period. To these individuals survival becomes an important factor. There *will* be a very severe food shortage during the tribulation period. This lack of food will result in hordes of hungry people raiding the homes of those who have stored food for survival purposes. Those who have stored food are going to have to fight, and perhaps kill, to defend it. How can any individual expect to stand innocent before Jesus, when he has to explain that he killed starving people because he didn't want to share his food with them? Survival is not the path to eternal life during the tribulation period. If you are not planning to leave this world with the Church, you should be planning to be slaughtered by Antichrist.

6. Fourth Seal Opened: The Pale Horse.

Rev. 6:7-8, "(7) And when he had opened the fourth seal, I heard the voice of the fourth beast say, Come and see. (8) And I looked, and behold a pale horse: and his name that sat on him was Death, and Hell followed with him. And power was given unto them over the fourth part of the earth, to kill with sword, and with hunger, and with death, and with the beasts of the earth." The rider on the pale horse was named Death, followed by a second named Hades. The Greek word translated *Hell* is Hades, the underground prison, not *gehenna* the "lake of fire burning with brimstone." It is debatable whether power was given over a fourth of the Earth's population or a fourth of the earth geographicallyl. Either way, a lot of people will be killed, and death followed by Hades indicates they died in a lost condition.

7. Fifth Seal Opened: Souls Under the Altar Seen.

Rev. 6:9-11, "(9) And when he had opened the fifth seal, I saw under the altar the souls of them that were slain for the word of God, and for the testimony which they held: (10) And they cried with a loud voice, saying, How long, O Lord, holy and true, dost thou not judge and avenge our blood on them that dwell on the earth? (11) And white robes were given unto every one of them; and it was said unto them, that they should rest yet for a little season, until their fellowservants also and their brethren, that should be killed as they [were], should be fulfilled."

These souls are the people who will be killed by Antichrist during the first half of the tribulation era. Antichrist put them in the deny or die baptism of fire and they will be killed because they will not deny "the Word of God" or "the testimony which they held." Their testimony will be that they were deceived during the Laodicean church era and were rejected as Church members when Jesus raptured the Church. After they reevaluate their beliefs and acknowledge their error, Jesus will arrange for Antichrist to locate them in order to test their sincerity. Those who test acceptable will be killed and will become the souls under the altar. Those tested unacceptable will be eternally lost. There will be no other way to salvation during this period. The Church Covenant will end with the Church rapture and the New Covenant will be with the Jews at the end of the tribulation era. Today it is easy for us to say we would die rather than deny Jesus and the Word of God. This is the same thing Simon Peter said in Mark 14:26-31, "If I should die with thee, I will not deny thee in any wise." Yet, when Simon Peter was put in a situation that represented a threat to his life, he did deny Jesus (Mark 14:66-72). I realize many people today are promoting the idea that there will be a great church revival during the seven-year tribulation period. By now you should be able to see that Antichrist is behind that teaching. The Church is completed and removed from the earth *before* the incarnation of Antichrist. There can be no great church revival on this planet if there is no church. When the Church is removed from the earth the great Church Commission of Mark 16:15-18 is finished. In the rapture Jesus separated born-again believers from the unbelieving. When Antichrist reduces the Laodicean membership to zero there will be no more Christians on Earth, only Jews and Gentiles.

Their cry to Jesus is recorded in Rev. 6:10, "And they cried with a loud voice, saying, How long, O Lord, holy and true, dost thou not judge and avenge our blood on them that dwell on the earth?" In Rev. 6:11a they are given white robes which says they have been judged righteous, 19:8b "for the fine linen is the righteousness of saints." In Rev. 6:11b they are told to rest for a little season, "and it was said unto them, that they should rest yet for a little season, until their fellowservants also and their brethren, that should be killed as they [were], should be fulfilled." The "fellow-servants" are the people who profess belief in Christ Jesus but whose Church membership will be canceled by the rapture. The brethren, or more accurately, "their brethren," are the people left on earth who will go into the last three and one-half years of the tribulation period to face the False Prophet and be killed for their refusal to worship the beast image or take the unforgivable mark. They are the people who profess belief in God, the Father. The Antichrist mission will be to destroy false Christianity, while the False

Prophet will move against every form of religion on the face of the earth. Judaism will be his prime target. During the first three and one-half years they will have been protected by the treaty with the Antichrist organization, but the False Prophet will not respect that treaty.

8. Sixth Seal Opened: Wrath of the Lamb.

Rev. 6:12-7:17, "(6:12) And I beheld when he had opened the sixth seal, and, lo, there was a great earthquake; and the sun became black as sackcloth of hair, and the moon became as blood; (13) And the stars of heaven fell unto the earth, even as a fig tree casteth her untimely figs, when she is shaken of a mighty wind. (14) And the heaven departed as a scroll when it is rolled together; and every mountain and island were moved out of their places. (15) And the kings of the earth, and the great men, and the rich men, and the chief captains, and the mighty men, and every bondman, and every free man, hid themselves in the dens and in the rocks of the mountains; (16) And said to the mountains and rocks, Fall on us, and hide us from the face of him that sitteth on the throne, and from the wrath of the Lamb: (17) For the great day of his wrath is come; and who shall be able to stand? (7:1) And after these things I saw four angels standing on the four corners of the earth, holding the four winds of the earth, that the wind should not blow on the earth, nor on the sea, nor on any tree. (2) And I saw another angel ascending from the east, having the seal of the living God: and he cried with a loud voice to the four angels, to whom it was given to hurt the earth and the sea, (3) Saying, Hurt not the earth, neither the sea, nor the trees, till we have sealed the servants of our God in their foreheads. (4) And I heard the number of them which were sealed: [and there were] sealed an hundred [and] forty [and] four thousand of all the tribes of the children of Israel. (5) Of the tribe of Juda [were] sealed twelve thousand. Of the tribe of Reuben [were] sealed twelve thousand. Of the tribe of Gad [were] sealed twelve thousand. (6) Of the tribe of Aser [were] sealed twelve thousand. Of the tribe of Nephthalim [were] sealed twelve thousand. Of the tribe of Manasses [were] sealed twelve thousand. (7) Of the tribe of Simeon [were] sealed twelve thousand. Of the tribe of Levi [were] sealed twelve thousand. Of the tribe of Issachar [were] sealed twelve thousand. (8) Of the tribe of Zabulon [were] sealed twelve thousand. Of the tribe of Joseph [were] sealed twelve thousand. Of the tribe of Benjamin [were] sealed twelve thousand. (9) After this I beheld, and, lo, a great multitude, which no man could number, of all nations, and kindreds, and people, and tongues, stood before the throne, and before the Lamb, clothed with white robes, and palms in their hands; (10) And cried with a loud voice, saying, Salvation to our God which sitteth upon the throne, and unto the Lamb. (11) And all the angels stood round about the throne, and [about] the elders and the four beasts, and fell before the throne on their faces, and worshipped God, (12) Saying, Amen: Blessing, and glory, and wisdom, and thanksgiving, and honour, and power, and might, [be] unto our God for ever and ever. Amen. (13) And one of the elders answered, saying unto me, What are these which are arrayed in white robes? and whence came they? (14) And I said unto him, Sir, thou knowest. And he said to me, These are they which came out of great tribulation, and have washed their robes, and made them white in the blood of the Lamb. (15) Therefore are they before the throne of God, and serve him day and night in his temple: and he that sitteth on the throne shall dwell among them. (16) They shall hunger no more, neither thirst any more; neither shall the sun light on them, nor any heat. (17) For the Lamb which is in the midst of the throne shall feed them, and shall lead them unto living fountains of waters: and God shall wipe away all tears from their eyes."

Jesus will open the sixth seal at midpoint in the seven-year tribulation era. The rapture of the Church and the Antichrist's destruction of Laodicean congregation will already be history. The False Prophet, reincarnated from Hades, will kill the two faithful witnesses, delete three nations from the ten king kingdom, and begin his persecution of the Jews. Being familiar with the events to occur when the sixth seal is opened will open your understanding of much of the Old Testament. A large portion of the Old Testament concerns this period of time. The Scriptures that talk of the day of the Lord, Jacob's trouble, the great day of his wrath, the day of his fierce anger, the last days, or the latter times, are speaking of this time period. The sixth seal contains seven events: (1) a great earthquake; (2) sun becomes black; (3) stars of heaven fall; (4) heaven is opened; (5) four angels stop the wind from blowing; (6) 144 thousand Jews sealed; and (7) the view of the tribulation dead.

The first thing to happen when Jesus opens the sixth seal will be a great earthquake, Rev. 6:12a "And I beheld when he had opened the sixth seal, and, lo, there was a great earthquake." This will be a worldwide earthquake and its intensity is given in Rev. 6:14b "and every mountain and island were moved out of their places." An earthquake in Biblical prophecy is an earth shaking event. It will be a literal earthquake, but it will also be God's way of saying, "Wake up, planet Earth, and look at what is happening."

The sixth seal second event concerns the sun and moon, Rev. 6:12b "and the sun became black as sackcloth of hair, and the moon became as blood."

The sixth seal third event will be the stars of heaven falling, Rev. 6:13 "And the stars of heaven fell unto the earth, even as a fig tree casteth her untimely figs, when she is shaken of a mighty wind." This will be the beginning of the judgment of Satan, as he and his demonic hierarchy are thrown out of heaven. Stars in Bible prophecy implies angels, and when they are presented as falling, they are coming down out of heaven to Earth. The details of this war in heaven are given in the flashback Chapter 12:1-17.

The sixth seal fourth event concerns heaven being opened, Rev. 6:14a "And the heaven departed as a scroll when it is rolled together." Earth dwellers will see Jesus on his throne, Rev. 6:15-17 "(15) And the kings of the earth, and the great men, and the rich men, and the chief captains, and the mighty men, and every bondman, and every free man, hid themselves in the dens and in the rocks of the mountains; (16) And said to the mountains and rocks, Fall on us, and hide us from the face of him that sitteth on the throne, and from the wrath of the Lamb: (17) For the great day of his wrath is come; and who shall be able to stand?" These are the proud who will fulfill the prophecy given in Isaiah 2:10-22, verse 10 "Enter into the rock, and hide thee in the dust, for fear of the Lord, and for the glory of his majesty," verse 19 "And they shall go into the holes of the rocks, and into the caves of the earth, for fear of the Lord, and for the glory of his majesty, when he ariseth to shake terribly the earth." These people are responding in regret, not repentance. Their regret is comparable to the thief who gets caught and begins to cry, not because he is sorry for being a thief, but because he is sorry for having been caught.

Isaiah foresaw the sun and moon darkening and the worldwide earthquake and tells us why it happened in Isaiah 13:9-16, "(9) Behold, the day of the LORD cometh, cruel both with wrath and fierce anger, to lay the land desolate: and he shall destroy the sinners thereof out of it. (10) For the stars of heaven and the constellations thereof shall not give their light: the sun shall be darkened in his going forth, and the moon shall not cause her light to shine. (11) And I will punish the world for [their] evil, and the wicked for their iniquity; and I will cause the arrogancy of the proud to cease, and will lay low the haughtiness of the terrible. (12) I will make a man more precious than fine gold; even a man than the golden wedge of Ophir. (13) Therefore I will shake the heavens, and the earth shall remove out of her place, in the wrath of the LORD of hosts, and in the day of his fierce anger. (14) And it shall be as the chased roe, and as a sheep that no man taketh up: they shall every man turn to his own people, and flee every one into his own land. (15) Every one that is found shall be thrust through; and every one that is joined [unto them] shall fall by the sword. (16) Their children also shall be dashed to pieces before their eyes; their houses shall be spoiled, and their wives ravished." The phrase "shake the heavens" means the war in heaven where Satan gets thrown out. The phrase "the earth shall remove out of her place" is the worldwide earthquake. The phrases "the wrath of the LORD of hosts . . . in the day of his fierce anger" describes the same time period we saw in Revelation 6 when they hid in "the dens and in the rocks of the mountains . . . from the wrath of the Lamb . . . for the great day of his wrath is come."

Jesus talks of the same time period in Mark 13:24-27, "(24) But in those days, after that tribulation, the sun shall be darkened, and the moon shall not give her light, (25) And the stars of heaven shall fall, and the powers that are in heaven shall be shaken. (26) And then shall they see the Son of man coming in the clouds with great power and glory. (27) And then shall he send his angels, and shall gather together his elect from the four winds, from the uttermost part of the earth to the uttermost part of heaven." The phrase "in those days, after that tribulation" brings us to the the middle of the tribulation era. "After that tribulation" is after the Antichrist reign during the first half. Verse 25 is the war in heaven when Satan gets thrown out. Verse 26 is the end of the tribulation era and the return of Jesus in glory. Verse 27 is the regathering of the Jews for the Kingdom Dispensation.

Jesus also spoke on this subject in Matthew 24:29-31, "(29) Immediately after the tribulation of those days shall the sun be darkened, and the moon shall not give her light, and the stars shall fall from heaven, and the powers of the heavens shall be shaken: (30) And then shall appear the sign of the Son of man in heaven: and then shall all the tribes of the earth mourn, and they shall see the Son of man coming in the clouds of heaven with power and great glory. (31) And he shall send his angels with a great sound of a trumpet, and they shall gather together his elect from the four winds, from one end of heaven to the other." What Jesus added in this account is heaven opening and Earth-dwellers seeing Him on his throne.

The Prophet Isaiah foresaw Earth "reel to and fro like a drunkard" in Isaiah 24:16-23, "(16) From the uttermost part of the earth have we heard songs, even glory to the righteous. But I said, My leanness, my leanness, woe unto me! the treacherous dealers have dealt treacherously; yea, the treacherous dealers have dealt very treacherously. (17) Fear, and the pit, and the snare, are upon thee, O inhabitant of the earth. (18) And it shall come to pass, that he who fleeth from the noise of the fear shall fall into the pit; and he that cometh up out of the midst of the pit shall be taken in the snare: for the windows from on high are open, and the foundations of the earth do shake. (19) The earth is utterly broken down, the earth is clean dissolved, the earth is moved exceedingly. (20) The earth shall reel to and fro like a drunkard, and shall be removed like a cottage; and the transgression thereof shall be heavy upon it; and it shall fall, and not rise again. (21) And it shall come to pass in that day, that the Lord shall punish the host of the high ones that are on high, and the kings of the earth upon the earth. (22) And they shall be gathered together, as prisoners are gathered in the pit, and shall be shut up in the prison, and after many days shall they be visited. (23) Then the moon shall be confounded, and the sun ashamed, when the Lord of hosts shall reign in mount Zion, and in Jerusalem, and before his ancients gloriously."

The opening statement in Isaiah 24:16, "From the uttermost part of the earth have we heard songs, even glory to the righteous" concerns the publicity which will be generated by the rapture of the Church. The rapture will be followed by the signing of the protection treaty between Antichrist and the Jews at Jerusalem. This treaty will exempt the Jews from the Antichrist slaughter when he destroys the Laodicean congregation. At the end of his three and one-half year reign the False Prophet will arrive on the scene and break the protection treaty, which is what Isaiah says in the remainder of verse 24:16, "But I said, My leanness, my leanness, woe unto me! the treacherous dealers have dealt treacherously; yea, the treacherous dealers have dealt very treacherously." Isaiah then foretells of the snare and the flight of the Jews. In verse 24:18b, "for the windows from on high are open" is when heaven is opened and Earth-dwellers get to see Jesus on his throne. What Isaiah describes in verse 24:18c-20 as "the foundations of the earth do shake" is the worldwide earthquake. Isaiah 24:21 concerns the judgment of Satan and his demonic hierarchy "And it shall come to pass in that day, that the Lord shall punish the host of the high ones that are on high, and the kings of the earth upon the earth." Isaiah 24:22a concerns the gathering of the Armageddon army, "And they shall be gathered together." Isaiah 24:22b is its destruction and the confinement of the participants to Hades (the prison) when Jesus returns, "as prisoners are gathered in the pit, and shall be shut up in the prison, after many days shall they be visited." From the Book of the Revelation we know that Satan will also be confined (Rev. 20:1-3) and we can amend Isaiah's statement "and after many days shall they be visited" to "after *1000 years* shall they be visited" (Rev. 20:5 and 20:7). Isaiah 24:23 concerns the Kingdom Dispensation when King Jesus will reign, "Then the moon shall be confounded, and the sun ashamed, when the Lord of hosts shall reign in mount Zion, and in Jerusalem, and before his ancients gloriously."

During the millennial reign "the moon shall be confounded, and the sun ashamed," which is quite different than what the sun and moon did when Jesus opened the sixth seal, Rev. 6:12b "and the sun became black as sackcloth of hair, and the moon became as blood." I realize there is much more to the glory of heaven than brightness, and that the brightness of heaven (Acts 26:13) exceeds the brightness of our sun, which explains why the sun is ashamed. I also realize if two lights are placed together, the brightness of one can be increased until the second light cannot be seen, but regardless of how bright the one light becomes, the second would never become black. The only way for the sun to become black or dark is to stop generating light. Joel saw the sun dark in Joel 2:10, darkened in Joel 3:15, and turned into darkness in Joel 2:30-31, "(30) And I will shew wonders in the heavens and in the earth, blood, and fire, and pillars of smoke. (31) The sun shall be turned into darkness, and the moon into blood, before the great and the terrible day of the LORD come." Atomic warfare, dust storms, and volcanic activity could all put enough particles in our atmosphere to darken the sun, but the particles cannot turn the sun into darkness or cause it to become black. Jesus told us in Luke 21:25 "there shall be signs in the sun, and in the moon, and in the stars," and I would not be surprised to see him turn off the sunlight to create a darkness so intense "they gnawed their tongues for pain"

(Rev. 16:11), or turn up the intensity to scorch them (Rev. 16:8-10).

The sixth seal fifth event concerns the four winds of the earth, Rev. 7:1 "And after these things I saw four angels standing on the four corners of the earth, holding the four winds of the earth, that the wind should not blow on the earth, nor on the sea, nor on any tree." Their purpose is to hurt the earth and the sea, Rev. 7:2-3 "(2) And I saw another angel ascending from the east, having the seal of the living God: and he cried with a loud voice to the four angels, to whom it was given to hurt the earth and the sea, (3) Saying, Hurt not the earth, neither the sea, nor the trees, till we have sealed the servants of our God in their foreheads."

The sixth seal sixth event will be the sealing of 144 thousand Jews, Rev. 7:2-8 "(2) And I saw another angel ascending from the east, having the seal of the living God: and he cried with a loud voice to the four angels, to whom it was given to hurt the earth and the sea, (3) Saying, Hurt not the earth, neither the sea, nor the trees, till we have sealed the servants of our God in their foreheads. (4) And I heard the number of them which were sealed: [and there were] sealed an hundred [and] forty [and] four thousand of all the tribes of the children of Israel. (5) Of the tribe of Juda [were] sealed twelve thousand. Of the tribe of Reuben [were] sealed twelve thousand. Of the tribe of Gad [were] sealed twelve thousand. (6) Of the tribe of Aser [were] sealed twelve thousand. Of the tribe of Nephthalim [were] sealed twelve thousand. Of the tribe of Manasses [were] sealed twelve thousand. (7) Of the tribe of Simeon [were] sealed twelve thousand. Of the tribe of Levi [were] sealed twelve thousand. Of the tribe of Issachar [were] sealed twelve thousand. (8) Of the tribe of Zabulon [were] sealed twelve thousand. Of the tribe of Joseph [were] sealed twelve thousand. Of the tribe of Benjamin [were] sealed twelve thousand." The sealing of the 144 thousand Jews is given here to show the point in the seven-year tribulation when their ministry will begin. Also God has always had his representatives on Earth. The False Prophet will kill the two faithful witnesses at this point. They will be replaced by the 144 thousand sealed Jews. The details of their ministry are-given in the flashback Chapter 14:1-20.

The sixth seal seventh event will involve the great multitude of the tribulation dead. This group will include the fifth seal group slaughtered by Antichrist and the group to be slaughtered by the False Prophet during the last half of the tribulation era. The great multitude is seen in Rev. 7:9 "After this I beheld, and, lo, a great multitude, which no man could number, of all nations, and kindreds, and people, and tongues, stood before the throne, and before the Lamb, clothed with white robes, and palms in their hands;" Next we have the worship of the tribulation dead and the angels, Rev. 7:10-12 "(10) And cried with a loud voice, saying, Salvation to our God which sitteth upon the throne, and unto the Lamb. (11) And all the angels stood round about the throne, and [about] the elders and the four beasts, and fell before the throne on their faces, and worshipped God, (12) Saying, Amen:

Blessing, and glory, and wisdom, and thanksgiving, and honour, and power, and might, [be] unto our God for ever and ever. Amen." The great multitude is identified, Rev. 7:13-14 "(13) And one of the elders answered, saying unto me, What are these which are arrayed in white robes? and whence came they? (14) And I said unto him, Sir, thou knowest. And he said to me, These are they which came out of great tribulation, and have washed their robes, and made them white in the blood of the Lamb." We are then given a look at the service of the tribulation dead, Rev. 7:15 "Therefore are they before the throne of God, and serve him day and night in his temple: and he that sitteth on the throne shall dwell among them." Next we see the care of the tribulation dead, Rev. 7:16-17 "(16) They shall hunger no more, neither thirst any more; neither shall the sun light on them, nor any heat. (17) For the Lamb which is in the midst of the throne shall feed them, and shall lead them unto living fountains of waters: and God shall wipe away all tears from their eyes."

The opening of the sixth seal will mark the move into the last three and one-half years of the tribulation period. With the removal of the Church prior to the tribulation era and the annihilation of Christianity by Antichrist we can understand why the sixth seal is presented as the wrath of the Lamb (Rev. 6:16- 17). Much is said about the wrath of God in the Bible. For example, in 1 Thessalonians 5:9-10 we are told the Church is not appointed to wrath, "(9) For God hath not appointed us to wrath, but to obtain salvation by our Lord Jesus Christ, (10) Who died for us, that, whether we wake or sleep, we should live together with him." In fact, born-again believers are already delivered from the wrath to come, 1 Thessalonians 1:9-10, "(9) For they themselves shew of us what manner of entering in we had unto you, and how ye turned to God from idols to serve the living and true God; (10) And to wait for his Son from heaven, whom he raised from the dead, even Jesus, which delivered us from the wrath to come." The wrath of God comes upon the children of disobedience, Ephesians 5:5-7, "(5) For this ye know, that no whore-monger, nor unclean person, nor covetous man, who is an idolater, hath any inheritance in the kingdom of Christ and of God. (6) Let no man deceive you with vain words: for because of these things cometh the wrath of God upon the children of disobedience. (7) Be not ye therefore partakers with them." Colossians 3:5-6, "(5) Mortify therefore your members which are upon the earth; Fornication, uncleanness, inordinate affection, evil concupiscence, and covetousness, which is idolatry: (6) For which things' sake the wrath of God cometh on the children of disobedience."

9. Seventh Seal Opened: Silence in Heaven.

Rev. 8:1-6, "(1) And when he had opened the seventh seal, there was silence in heaven about the space of half an hour. (2) And I saw the seven angels which stood before God; and to them were given seven trumpets. (3) And another angel came and stood at the altar, having a golden censer; and there was given unto him much incense, that he should offer [it] with the prayers of all saints upon the golden altar which was before the throne. (4) And the smoke of the incense, [which came] with the prayers of the saints, ascended up before God out of the angel's hand. (5) And the angel took the censer, and filled it with fire of the altar, and cast [it] into the earth: and there were voices, and thunderings, and lightnings, and an earthquake. (6) And the seven angels which had the seven trumpets prepared themselves to sound."

When Jesus opens the seventh seal the inhabitants of heaven will get a look at the next sequence of judgments. The half hour of silence may be peace in heaven resulting from Satan and his crew being thrown out during the last seal, but I tend to believe it results from the inhabitants' amazement at seeing the intensity or severity of the trumpet judgments. The first four trumpets are often referred to as the thirds trumpets, and the last three are the woe trumpets.

When the first trumpet sounds against vegetation, one-third of the trees and all green grass will be burnt. When the second trumpet sounds against the sea, a third of the sea will become blood, a third of all sea creatures will die, and a third of all ships will be destroyed. When the third trumpet sounds, a third of fresh water many die because the waters will be made bitter. When the fourth trumpet sounds against light, one-third of the sun, moon, and stars will be darkened, and day and night will be shortened by one-third.

After the seven angels are given seven trumpets, another angel will be given much incense to offer with the prayers of all saints. The phrase "all saints" tells us that every human being in heaven and every saint on Earth will then be in agreement with God's judgment. I believe the "much incense" given to offer with the incense of the saints will be from the elect angelic hosts. The saints and elect angels have put themselves in agreement with God and are urging him to judge Satan. The angel then will take the golden censer, fill it with fire from the altar, and cast it into the earth. After this "the seven angels which had the seven trumpets prepared themselves to sound." The fire from the altar cast into the earth signifies that the planet's sin and iniquity are about to be taken away. Isaiah encountered the same type situation when he saw Jesus in Isaiah 6:5-7, "(5) Then said I, Woe [is] me! for I am undone; because I [am] a man of unclean lips, and I dwell in the midst of a people of unclean lips: for mine eyes have seen the King, the LORD of hosts. (6) Then flew one of the seraphims unto me, having a live coal in his hand, [which] he had taken with the tongs from off the altar: (7) And he laid [it] upon my mouth, and said, Lo, this hath touched thy lips; and thine iniquity is taken away, and thy sin purged." Fire from the altar and burning incense covered Aaron's sins while he functioned as High Priest to Israel, Leviticus 16:11-13 "(11) And Aaron shall bring the bullock of the sin offering, which [is] for himself, and shall make an atonement for himself, and for his house, and shall kill the bullock of the sin offering which [is] for himself: (12) And he shall take a censer full of burning coals of fire from off the altar before the LORD, and his hands full of sweet incense beaten small, and bring [it] within the vail: (13) And he shall put the incense upon the fire before the LORD, that the cloud of the incense may cover the mercy seat that [is] upon the testimony, that he die not."

10. First Trumpet Sounds Against Vegetation.

Rev. 8:7, "The first angel sounded, and there followed hail and fire mingled with blood, and they were cast upon the earth: and the third part of trees was burnt up, and all green grass was burnt up."

When the first trumpet sounds, hail and fire mingled with blood will be cast upon the earth. The result will be a third of the trees and all green grass burned. I would not be surprised if the blood is the actual blood of Jesus after his sacrifice on the cross. In his duty as high priest he may be sprinkling his blood upon the altar in heaven as a sin offering for Earth. This is what priests were instructed to do with the blood during the Levitical Priesthood, Leviticus 1:5 "And he shall kill the bullock before the LORD: and the priests, Aaron's sons, shall bring the blood, and sprinkle the blood round about upon the altar that [is by] the door of the tabernacle of the congregation." This could also be the beginning of the New Covenant which Jesus intends to establish with the Jews and Earth during the Kingdom Dispensation. The law covenant with the Jews was also sealed with blood, Exodus 24:3-8 "(3) And Moses came and told the people all the words of the LORD, and all the judgments: and all the people answered with one voice, and said, All the words which the LORD hath said will we do. (4) And Moses wrote all the words of the LORD, and rose up early in the morning, and builded an altar under the hill, and twelve pillars, according to the twelve tribes of Israel. (5) And he sent young men of the children of Israel, which offered burnt offerings, and sacrificed peace offerings of oxen unto the LORD. (6) And Moses took half of the blood, and put [it] in basons; and half of the blood he sprinkled on the altar. (7) And he took the book of the covenant, and read in the audience of the people: and they said, All that the LORD hath said will we do, and be obedient. (8) And Moses took the blood, and sprinkled [it] on the people, and said, Behold the blood of the covenant, which the LORD hath made with you concerning all these words."

11. Second Trumpet Sounds Against the Sea.

Rev. 8:8-9, "(8) And the second angel sounded, and as it were a great mountain burning with fire was cast into the sea: and the third part of the sea became blood; (9) And the third part of the creatures which were in the sea, and had life, died; and the third part of the ships were destroyed."

When the second trumpet sounds against the sea, a third of the sea will become blood, a third of the sea creatures will die, and a third of the ships will be destroyed. From other prophecies we know a mountain means a government, fire means judgment, and seas represent people (the human race). The phrase "a great mountain burning with fire was cast into the sea" would be a great government burning with judgment was cast into the human race. In Genesis 9:4 we are told the life of the flesh is in the blood, "But flesh with the life thereof, [which is] the blood thereof, shall ye not eat." "The third part of the sea became blood" means that a third of humanity at this point in the seven-year tribulation era will be given the privilege of continued life from God. Only a third of the Jews will survive, Zechariah 13:8-9 "(8) And it shall come to pass, [that] in all the land, saith the LORD, two parts therein shall be cut off [and] die; but the third shall be left therein. (9) And I will bring the third part through the fire, and will refine them as silver is refined, and will try them as gold is tried: they shall call on my name, and I will hear them: I will say, It [is] my people: and they shall say, The LORD [is] my God." The passage continues with the statement "the third part of the creatures which were in the sea, and had life, died." The sea represents human beings while "the creatures which were in the sea" are the demons (in the humans). These demons will be deprived of continued life within the humans because the human body is now the property of God. They must abandon ship and look for a new vessel to call home. From the demon's point of view, "the third part of the ships were destroyed."

12. Third Trumpet Sounds Against Fresh Water.

Rev. 8:10-11, "(10) And the third angel sounded, and there fell a great star from heaven, burning as it were a lamp, and it fell upon the third part of the rivers, and upon the fountains of waters; (11) And the name of the star is called Wormwood: and the third part of the waters became wormwood; and many men died of the waters, because they were made bitter."

When the third trumpet sounds against fresh water, many will die because the waters are made bitter. Stars represent angels in prophecy and since Satan and his crew have already been confined to Earth, the angel of this prophecy must be an elect angel on a mission from God. His name is Wormwood and his mission will be to blot out the names of one-third of the human race from the land of the living. These are the individuals who walk through life in the imaginations of their own hearts with no fear of God before their eyes and without considering the judgment of God and the eternal bitterness at the end of the road. God says much about Wormwood in the Scriptures, Deuteronomy 29:18-20 "(18) Lest there should be among you man, or woman, or family, or tribe, whose heart turneth away this day from the LORD our God, to go [and] serve the gods of these nations; lest there should be among you a root that beareth gall and wormwood; (19) And it come to pass, when he heareth the words of this curse, that he bless himself in his heart, saying, I shall have peace, though I walk in the imagination of mine heart, to add drunkenness to thirst: (20) The LORD will not spare him, but then the anger of the LORD and his jealousy shall smoke against that man, and all the curses that are written in this book shall lie upon him, and the LORD shall blot out his name from under heaven." Jeremiah 9:13-16, "(13) And the LORD saith, Because they have forsaken my law which I set before them, and have not obeyed my voice, neither walked therein; (14) But have walked after the imagination of their own heart, and after Baalim, which their fathers taught them: (15) Therefore thus saith the LORD of hosts, the God of Israel; Behold, I will feed them, [even] this people, with wormwood, and give them water of gall to drink. (16) I will scatter them also among the heathen, whom neither they nor their fathers have known: and I will send a sword after them, till I have consumed them."

The preachers in the Laodicean Churches will be no different than the prophets of Israel, Jeremiah 23:14-15, "(14) I have seen also in the prophets of Jerusalem an horrible thing: they commit adultery, and walk in lies: they strengthen also the hands of evildoers, that none doth return from his wickedness: they are all of them unto me as Sodom, and the inhabitants thereof as Gomorrah. (15) Therefore thus saith the LORD of hosts concerning the prophets; Behold, I will feed them with wormwood, and make them drink the water of gall: for from the prophets of Jerusalem is profaneness gone forth into all the land." It also applies to the judges in our land that has stopped punishing criminals and turned sweet judgment into bitterness, Amos 5:6-7, "(6) Seek the LORD, and ye shall live; lest he break out like fire in the house of Joseph, and devour [it], and [there be] none to quench [it] in Bethel. (7) Ye who turn judgment to wormwood, and leave off righteousness in the earth."

13. Fourth Trumpet Sounds Against Light.

Rev. 8:12-13, "(12) And the fourth angel sounded, and the third part of the sun was smitten, and the third part of the moon, and the third part of the stars; so as the third part of them was darkened, and the day shone not for a third part of it, and the night likewise. (13) And I beheld, and heard an angel flying through the midst of heaven, saying with a loud voice, Woe, woe, woe, to the inhabiters of the earth by reason of the other voices of the trumpet of the three angels, which are yet to sound!"

When the fourth trumpet sounds against light, a third of the sun, moon, and stars will be darkened, and day and night will be shortened by a third. We saw the sun and moon darken when Jesus opened the sixth seal. Then we were at mid-point in the seven-year tribulation era and now we are in the final six months. Here the sun and moon will be darkened by shortening the day and night by a third. In other words, Jesus will change the hours in a day from twenty-four to sixteen. He will do this for the elect's sake as he promised in Matthew 24:21-22, "(21) For then shall be great tribulation, such as was not since the beginning of the world to this time, no, nor ever shall be. (22) And except those days should be shortened, there should no flesh be saved: but for the elect's sake those days shall be shortened." We will examine the shortened day in more detail when we discuss the abomination of desolation in the chapter on Daniel, but for now we need to realize Jesus' return will be six months (225 sixteen-hour days) after the shortening of the day. The tribulation era will have been severe up to this point but the worst will be yet to come. This is why the angel will announce the next three trumpets as three woes, "And I beheld, and heard an angel flying through the midst of heaven, saying with a loud voice, Woe, woe, woe, to the inhabiters of the earth by reason of the other voices of the trumpet of the three angels, which are yet to sound!"

14. Fifth Trumpet Releases Demons from the Bottomless Pit.

Rev. 9:1-12, "(1) And the fifth angel sounded, and I saw a star fall from heaven unto the earth: and to him was given the key of the bottomless pit. (2) And he opened the bottomless pit; and there arose a smoke out of the pit, as the smoke of a great furnace; and the sun and the air were darkened by reason of the smoke of the pit. (3) And there came out of the smoke locusts upon the earth: and unto them was given power, as the scorpions of the earth have power. (4) And it was commanded them that they should not hurt the grass of the earth, neither any green thing, neither any tree; but only those men which have not the seal of God in their foreheads. (5) And to them it was given that they should not kill them, but that they should be tormented five months: and their torment [was] as the torment of a scorpion, when he striketh a man. (6) And in those days shall men seek death, and shall not find it; and shall desire to die, and death shall flee from them. (7) And the shapes of the locusts [were] like unto horses prepared unto battle; and on their heads [were] as it were crowns like gold, and their faces [were] as the faces of men. (8) And they had hair as the hair of women, and their teeth were as [the teeth] of lions. (9) And they had breastplates, as it were breastplates of iron; and the sound of their wings [was] as the sound of chariots of many horses running to battle. (10) And they had tails like unto scorpions, and there were stings in their tails: and their power [was] to hurt men five months. (11) And they had a king over them, [which is] the angel of the bottomless pit, whose name in the Hebrew tongue [is] Abaddon, but in the Greek tongue hath [his] name Apollyon. (12) One woe is past; [and], behold, there come two woes more hereafter."

When the fifth trumpet sounds (the first woe), demons will be released from their prison in Hades. For the next five months they will be permitted to hurt and torment unsealed men. During this period of time people desire and seek death, without success. The star or elect angel will fall "from heaven unto the earth" with the key to the bottomless pit (Hades). Hades is the underground prison for lost human spirits and fallen angels who crossed from the spirit realm to the physical realm. They put on human flesh for the purpose of seducing the daughters of men, which corrupted the earth and resulted in the judgment of the universal flood (Gen. 6:1-7). The angel with the key will release them on the human race a second time. When the pit is opened smoke, "as the smoke of a great furnace" will darken the sun and the air. Out of the smoke will come locusts, Rev. 9:3a, "And their came out of the smoke locusts upon the earth" with shapes like horses, Rev. 9:7a "And the shapes of the locusts [were] like unto horses prepared unto battle." The demons were described as Rev. 9:7b-10a, "(7b) and on their heads [were] as it were crowns like gold, and their faces [were] as the faces of men. (8) And they had hair as the hair of women, and their teeth were as [the teeth] of lions. (9) And they had breastplates, as it were breastplates of iron; and the sound of their wings [was] as the sound of chariots of many horses running to battle. (10) And they had tails like unto scorpions." The crowns of gold gives them political authority and the breastplates of iron speaks of their strength. The king and his names are given in Rev. 9:11, "And they had a king over them, [which is] the angel of the bottomless pit, whose name in the Hebrew tongue [is] Abaddon, but in the Greek tongue hath [his] name Apollyon."

The demons will be given power as scorpion have, Rev. 9:3b "and unto them was given power, as the scorpions of the earth have power." Rev. 9:10b "and there were stings in their tails: and their power [was] to hurt men five months." Rev. 9:5, "And to them it was given that they should not kill them, but that they should be tormented five months: and their torment [was] as the torment of a scorpion, when he striketh a man." Death may be a welcome escape from intense pain but not during this five month period, Rev. 9:6 "And in those days shall men seek death, and shall not find it; and shall desire to die, and death shall flee from them." The demons will be commanded to hurt only unsealed people, Rev. 9:4 "And it was commanded them that they should not hurt the grass of the earth, neither any green thing, neither any tree; but only those men which have not the seal of God in their foreheads." When Jesus opened the sixth seal at midpoint in the tribulation era, 144 thousand Jews were sealed. Without doubt, these individuals will not be tormented. For three years they will have been warning the human race of the consequences of worshiping the beast image or taking his mark. Those who believed them will have fled and hid from the beast organization. If the fugitives are located they will be tested in the deny or die baptism of fire. If they deny God, they will take the beast mark, become unredeemable, and they will receive this fifth trumpet torment. If they do not deny, they will be killed, not sealed, and they will be saved as a member of the sixth seal tribulation dead. Those not found by the beast organization who would die rather than deny God will qualify to be sealed and survive the tribulation era to enter the Kingdom Dispensation as living human beings. They may have been sealed when the second trumpet sounded, or perhaps when this trumpet sounded. In either case we are told in Rev. 9:12 "One woe is past; [and], behold, there come two woes more hereafter."

15. Sixth Trumpet Sounds the Final Call.

Rev. 9:13-21, "(13) And the sixth angel sounded, and I heard a voice from the four horns of the golden altar which is before God, (14) Saying to the sixth angel which had the trumpet, Loose the four angels which are bound in the great river Euphrates. (15) And the four angels were loosed, which were prepared for an hour, and a day, and a month, and a year, for to slay the third part of men. (16) And the number of the army of the horsemen [were] two hundred thousand thousand: and I heard the number of them. (17) And thus I saw the horses in the vision, and them that sat on them, having breastplates of fire, and of jacinth, and brimstone: and the heads of the horses [were] as the heads of lions; and out of their mouths issued fire and smoke and brimstone. (18) By these three was the third part of men killed, by the fire, and by the smoke, and by the brimstone, which issued out of their mouths. (19) For their power is in their mouth, and in their tails: for their tails [were] like unto serpents, and had heads, and with them they do hurt. (20) And the rest of the men which were not killed by these plagues yet repented not of the works of their hands, that they should not worship devils, and idols of gold, and silver, and brass, and stone, and of wood: which neither can see, nor hear, nor walk: (21) Neither repented they of their murders, nor of their sorceries, nor of their fornication, nor of their thefts."

When the sixth trumpet sounds (the second woe), the four horns of the golden altar before God will speak, and the four angels bound in the river Euphrates will be released for the purpose of killing a third of the human race. These four angels will command an army of two hundred million horsemen. This army of two hundred million will be demonic beings, not human beings, or our war machines. Their description is, Rev. 9:17 "And thus I saw the horses in the vision, and them that sat on them, having breastplates of fire, and of jacinth, and brimstone: and the heads of the horses [were] as the heads of lions; and out of their mouths issued fire and smoke and brimstone." Rev. 9:19 "For their power is in their mouth, and in their tails: for their tails [were] like unto serpents, and had heads, and with them they do hurt." Notice what is being described is "them that sat on them," demons that sat on horses. Compare the description of these demons to the ones released from Hades when the fifth trumpet sounded. They are no longer wearing "crowns of gold" which is understandable because political authority is in the four angels commanding them. Their "breastplates of iron" have been replaced with breastplates of judgment (fire). We need to realize this army of two hundred million is not the Armageddon Army. The judgments, in the Revelation, began with the opening of seven seals, followed by the seven trumpet judgments, which will be followed by the final seven vial judgments. The Armageddon Army is not assembled until the sixth vial judgment of Rev. 16:12-16. These two hundred million demons will be present at the Battle of Armageddon, but under the fifth trumpet their mission was to torment unsealed humans for five months, and under the sixth trumpet judgment their mission is to kill a third of the earths population, Rev. 9:18, "By these three was the third part of men killed, by the fire, and by the smoke, and by the brimstone, which issued out of their mouths."

After this slaughter God gives us the reaction of the people still alive on Earth, Rev. 9:20-21, "(20) And the rest of the men which were not killed by these plagues yet repented not of the works of their hands, that they should not worship devils, and idols of gold, and silver, and brass, and stone, or wood: which neither can see, nor hear, nor walk: (21) Neither repented they of their murders, nor of their sorceries, nor of their fornication, nor of their thefts." The men who survive the plague will still refuse to repent of: (1) the works of their hands; (2) their murders; (3) their sorceries; (4) their fornications; and (5) their thefts. By "the works of their hands" they were worshiping devils and idols. The idols being worshiped which "neither can see, nor hear, nor walk" will be made of gold, silver, brass, stone, and wood. In Rev. 9:20-21 God is literally saying all the people on earth who will repent have already repented. The last person to die for their refusal to worship the beast image will have been killed. This will complete the great multitude of tribulation dead we saw when Jesus opened the sixth seal. At this point in time, there will be only two events left in the seven-year tribulation period: the blowing of the seventh trumpet, which will announces Jesus as the King of Earth, and the pouring out of the vial plagues, which will destroy the Antichrist/False Prophet organization. Then Jesus will return and destroy the Armageddon Army.

16. Mighty Angel With a Little Book.

Rev. 10:1-11, "(1) And I saw another mighty angel come down from heaven, clothed with a cloud: and a rainbow [was] upon his head, and his face [was] as it were the sun, and his feet as pillars of fire: (2) And he had in his hand a little book open: and he set his right foot upon the sea, and [his] left [foot] on the earth, (3) And cried with a loud voice, as [when] a lion roareth: and when he had cried, seven thunders uttered their voices. (4) And when the seven thunders had uttered their voices, I was about to write: and I heard a voice from heaven saying unto me, Seal up those things which the seven thunders uttered, and write them not. (5) And the angel which I saw stand upon the sea and upon the earth lifted up his hand to heaven, (6) And sware by him that liveth for ever and ever, who created heaven, and the things that therein are, and the earth, and the things that therein are, and the sea, and the things which are therein, that there should be time no longer: (7) But in the days of the voice of the seventh angel, when he shall begin to sound, the mystery of God should be finished, as he hath declared to his servants the prophets. (8) And the voice which I heard from heaven spake unto me again, and said, Go [and] take the little book which is open in the hand of the angel which standeth upon the sea and upon the earth. (9) And I went unto the angel, and said unto him, Give me the little book. And he said unto me, Take [it], and eat it up; and it shall make thy belly bitter, but it shall be in thy mouth sweet as honey. (10) And I took the little book out of the angel's hand, and ate it up; and it was in my mouth sweet as honey: and as soon as I had eaten it, my belly was bitter. (11) And he said unto me, Thou must prophesy again before many peoples, and nations, and tongues, and kings."

John saw a mighty angel come down from heaven with a little book in hand. The angel swore by God, "that there should be time no longer." In other words, the opportunity to repent will be no longer. There will be no advantage to delaying the final vial judgments any longer. The population of the earth will be so aligned that all who would worship the beast image will already be beyond repentance. The remaining population would choose to die, rather than worship the image. We are at the point where, if God doesn't destroy the beast organization, "there should no flesh be saved." After the announcement by the mighty angel with the little book, seven thunders will speak and John is told to seal up the things they said, and not to write them, Rev. 10:3b-4, "(3b) and when he had cried, seven thunders uttered their voices. (4) And when the seven thunders had uttered their voices, I was about to write: and I heard a voice from heaven saying unto me, Seal up those things which the seven thunders uttered, and write them not." If their words are sealed and unwritten no one this side of heaven know what was said. John is told to take the little book from the angel and eat it, Rev. 10:10, "And I took the little book out of the angel's hand, and ate it up; and it was in my mouth sweet as honey: and as soon as I had eaten it, my belly was bitter."

The sequential events stop here and the flashback account of the ministry of the two faithful witnesses is inserted, Rev. 11:1-13. The sequential events continue at verse 14 with the statement, "The second woe is past."

17. Seventh Trumpet Announces Jesus as King.

Rev. 11:14-19, "(14) The second woe is past; [and], behold, the third woe cometh quickly. (15) And the seventh angel sounded; and there were great voices in heaven, saying, The kingdoms of this world are become [the kingdoms] of our Lord, and of his Christ; and he shall reign for ever and ever.

(16) And the four and twenty elders, which sat before God on their seats, fell upon their faces, and worshipped God, (17) Saying, We give thee thanks, O Lord God Almighty, which art, and wast, and art to come; because thou hast taken to thee thy great power, and hast reigned. (18) And the nations were angry, and thy wrath is come, and the time of the dead, that they should be judged, and that thou shouldest give reward unto thy servants the prophets, and to the saints, and them that fear thy name, small and great; and shouldest destroy them which destroy the earth. (19) And the temple of God was opened in heaven, and there was seen in his temple the ark of his testament: and there were lightnings, and voices, and thunderings, and an earthquake, and great hail."

One of the announcements made by the mighty angel seen in the sixth trumpet concerns when the seventh angel will begin to sound, Rev. 10:7 "But in the days of the voice of the seventh angel, when he shall begin to sound, the mystery of God should be finished, as he hath declared to his servants the prophets." The phrase "the mystery of God should be finished" simply means God will no longer be a mystery. The mystery will be "finished, as he hath declared to his servants the prophets." The reason God is a mystery to most of the people on Earth is that they have never read the Bible to see what God "hath declared to his servants the prophets" and many who have read it refuse to believe what God said.

When the seventh angel sounds, Jesus will be declared King, Rev. 11:15, "And the seventh angel sounded; and there were great voices in heaven, saying, The kingdoms of this world are become [the kingdoms] of our Lord, and of his Christ; and he shall reign for ever and ever." The first one thousand years of this reign is the Kingdom Dispensation where Jesus reigns as king over Earth. It ends with the white throne judgment. This is the end spoken of in 1 Corinthians 15:24-28, "(24) Then [cometh] the end, when he shall have delivered up the kingdom to God, even the Father; when he shall have put down all rule and all authority and power. (25) For he must reign, till he hath put all enemies under his feet. (26) The last enemy [that] shall be destroyed [is] death. (27) For he hath put all things under his feet. But when he saith all things are put under [him, it is] manifest that he is excepted, which did put all things under him. (28) And when all things shall be subdued unto him, then shall the Son also himself be subject unto him that put all things under him, that God may be all in all." This end is followed by the creation of a new heaven and new earth and that is the beginning, 1 Corinthians 2:9, "But as it is written, Eye hath not seen, nor ear heard, neither have entered into the heart of man, the things which God hath prepared for them that love him."

The twenty-four elders praise the event, Rev. 11:17b, "because thou (God) hast taken to thee thy great power, and hast reigned." The nation's reaction will be just the opposite, Rev. 11:18a "And the nations were angry." We are told the reason for their anger in Rev. 19:15a, "And out of his mouth goeth a sharp sword, that with it he should smite the nations: and he shall rule them with a rod of iron." Today every nation and every individual has the free choice of obedience or disobedience to the Word of God. During the Kingdom Dispensation the nations will conduct their affairs according to the Book or get smacked with that "rod of iron." The wrath in the phrase, Rev. 11:18b, "thy wrath is come," will be directed at his enemies, Rev. 11:18d, "and shouldest destroy them which destroy the earth." The vial judgments will destroy the Antichrist/False Prophet organization; Jesus will destroy the Armageddon Army; the goat nations who persecuted the Jews will be destroyed in the sheep and goat judgment; and the tares judgment will rid Earth of all that offends and those who do iniquity.

The phrase "and the time of the dead," Rev. 11:18c, refers to the first resurrection, which is the resurrection of life. The remainder of the verse concerns the judgment seat of Christ, "that they should be judged, and that thou shouldest give reward unto thy servants the prophets, and to the saints, and them that fear thy name, small and great." It is the resurrection to eternal life and the saved are being judged for rewards, or loss of rewards, 1 Corinthians 3:10-15.

The last thing to be seen in the seventh trumpet judgment will be the opening of the temple of God in heaven, Rev. 11:19, "And the temple of God was opened in heaven, and there was seen in his temple the ark of his testament: and there were lightnings, and voices, and thunderings, and an earthquake, and great hail." The next sequential events mentioned in the Revelation are the vial judgments. We see seven angels walk out of this open temple in Rev. 15:1-8. Inserted here are four flashback topics: Rev. 12:1-17, Israel and the Great Red Dragon; Rev. 13:1-10, The Antichrist Reign; Rev. 13:11-18, The False Prophet Reign; and Rev. 14:1-20, Ministry of the 144 thousand sealed Jews.

18. Seven Angels Given Seven Vials Filled with the Wrath of God.

Rev. 15:1-8, "(1) And I saw another sign in heaven, great and marvellous, seven angels having the seven last plagues; for in them is filled up the wrath of God. (2) And I saw as it were a sea of glass mingled with fire: and them that had gotten the victory over the beast, and over his image, and over his mark, [and] over the number of his name, stand on the sea of glass, having the harps of God. (3) And they sing the song of Moses the servant of God, and the song of the Lamb, saying, Great and marvellous [are] thy works, Lord God Almighty; just and true [are] thy ways, thou King of saints. (4) Who shall not fear thee, O Lord, and glorify thy name? for [thou] only [art] holy: for all nations shall come and worship before thee; for thy judgments are made manifest. (5) And after that I looked, and, behold, the temple of the tabernacle of the testimony in heaven was opened: (6) And the seven angels came out of the temple, having the seven plagues, clothed in pure and white linen, and having their breasts girded with golden girdles. (7) And one of the four beasts gave unto the seven angels seven golden vials full of the wrath of God, who liveth for ever and ever. (8) And the temple was filled with smoke from the glory of God, and from his power; and no man was able to enter into the temple, till the seven plagues of the seven angels were fulfilled."

The fifth thing John saw in Rev. 4:6 was a sea of glass. At that point in time we will be at the beginning of the seven-year tribulation era, when the sea of glass is empty. When John sees the sea of glass a second time, we will be at the end of the tribulation era, because John sees the entire group of tribulation dead standing on the sea of glass. Notice they have the "harps of God" and sing two songs. The "song of Moses" will be sung by the sixth seal group killed for their belief in the God of the Old Testament. The "song of the Lamb" is sung by the fifth seal group killed for their belief in the Jesus Christ of the New Testament. The song of the tribulation dead is recorded in Rev. 15:3-4.

One of the things we saw in Rev. 11:19 when the seventh trumpet sounded was, "the temple of God was opened in heaven." John sees seven angels come out of the open temple. They are given "seven golden vials" which are "the seven last plagues; for in them is filled up the wrath of God." The sixth and seventh seal and the seven trumpet judgments were presented as the "wrath of the Lamb," but the seven vial judgments are presented as "the wrath of God."

19. The First Vial: A Noisome and Grievous Sore.

Rev. 16:1-2, "(1) And I heard a great voice out of the temple saying to the seven angels, Go your ways, and pour out the vials of the wrath of God upon the earth. (2) And the first went, and poured out his vial upon the earth; and there fell a noisome and grievous sore upon the men which had the mark of the beast, and [upon] them which worshipped his image." The first vial judgment is a noisome and grievous sore which will be limited to the people in the beast kingdom who had worshipped the image and taken the mark. The ulcerated sores are grievous or hurtful and the agony groans, although noisy, will fall on deaf ears and will not persuade God to stop the judgment.

20. The Second Vial: The Sea Becomes Blood: All Sea Life Dies.

Rev. 16:3, "(3) And the second angel poured out his vial upon the sea; and it became as the blood of a dead [man]: and every living soul died in the sea." The second vial will be poured upon the sea (human race) which becomes as the blood of a dead man. As we saw in Gen 9:4 the life of the flesh is in the blood. When the second trumpet angel sounded we saw "the third part of the sea became blood" which was a third of human beings becoming flesh with life as they are given the privilege of continued life from God. Here we see just the opposite. The individuals touched by this judgment have been weighed in the balances and found lacking. Although they are still physically living, God's decision has been announced, and they will be dead flesh. The phrase "and every living soul died in the sea" does not mean every living soul in the human race will die. The vial judgments will destroy the beast organization and "every living soul . . . which had the mark of the beast, and them which worshipped his image."

21. The Third Vial: Rivers and Fountains of Waters Become Blood.

Rev. 16:4-7, "(4) And the third angel poured out his vial upon the rivers and fountains of waters; and they became blood. (5) And I heard the angel of the waters say, Thou art righteous, O Lord, which art, and wast, and shalt be, because thou hast judged thus. (6) For they have shed the blood of saints and prophets, and thou hast given them blood to drink; for they are worthy. (7) And I heard another out of the altar say, Even so, Lord God Almighty, true and righteous [are] thy judgments." We saw third trumpet angel sound against fresh water and many die because the waters are made bitter. The third vial judgment turns fresh water to blood. The rivers, fountains of waters, and blood are all literal which is obvious from the declaration of the angel of the waters, "For they have shed the blood of saints and prophets, and thou hast given them blood to drink; for they are worthy."

22. The Fourth Vial: Men Scorched with Great Heat.

Rev. 16:8-9, "(8) And the fourth angel poured out his vial upon the sun; and power was given unto him to scorch men with fire. (9) And men were scorched with great heat, and blasphemed the name of God, which hath power over these plagues: and they repented not to give him glory." The fourth vial will be poured upon the sun and men will be scorched with great heat. The peoples' response to the scorching will be that they "blasphemed the name of God, which hath power over these plagues: and they repented not to give him glory."

23. The Fifth Vial: Darkness in the Beast Kingdom.

Rev. 16:10-11, "(10) And the fifth angel poured out his vial upon the seat of the beast; and his kingdom was full of darkness; and they gnawed their tongues for pain, (11) And blasphemed the God of heaven because of their pains and their sores, and repented not of their deeds." The fifth vial will cause darkness in the beast kingdom, a darkness that is so intense that the members will gnaw their tongues for pain. After both the fourth and fifth vial judgments, instead of repentance men will blaspheme the God of heaven. These people will suffer because of their sins and rejection of God. The suffering, which should have caused them to repent, will result in blasphemy, not repentance. Physical suffering will always result in either repentance or blasphemy. The author of sin and suffering is Satan, not God. Blasphemy is attributing something from God to Satan, or taking something that is of Satan, and attributing it to God. If you are one of those 'poor suffering Christians,' walking under the cloak that you are suffering for the glory of God, you are walking in blasphemy. God will get glory only when you repent. If God wanted you and I to suffer and die for our sins, he would not have sent Jesus to suffer and die in our stead. Suffering is the end result of sin and unbelief and communicates the need for God and repentance. When we say the suffering is from God and not Satan, we are guilty of blasphemy.

Don't misunderstand me. I'm not saying you are going to hell because you are suffering from sickness or a disease. I am saying they are from Satan, and God is communicating either that you have reached the "end of the road" or that some area of your being is not properly aligned to his revealed will. You could be in a situation known as the *baptism of fire*, when God allows Satan to come against you and his Word, to determine if you believe God enough to stand on his Word. If you keep and stand on the Word of God, Satan and whatever he brought with him must flee from you. In the process you are either an overcomer, or one that is overcome. I will discuss this process in more detail later, but at this point, we need to realize these two vial judgments will cause much physical suffering and pain. Man will respond to the suffering with blasphemy instead of repentance. There will be nothing else God can do, and the next event on the horizon will be Armageddon.

24. The Sixth Vial: The World Gathered to Armageddon.

Rev. 16:12-16, "(12) And the sixth angel poured out his vial upon the great river Euphrates; and the water thereof was dried up, that the way of the kings of the east might be prepared. (13) And I saw three unclean spirits like frogs [come] out of the mouth of the dragon, and out of the mouth of the beast, and out of the mouth of the false prophet. (14) For they are the spirits of devils, working miracles, [which] go forth unto the kings of the earth and of the whole world, to gather them to the battle of that great day of God Almighty. (15) Behold, I come as a thief. Blessed [is] he that watcheth, and keepeth his garments, lest he walk naked, and they see his shame. (16) And he gathered them together into a place called in the Hebrew tongue Armageddon."

The sixth vial will dry up the Euphrates River to prepare the way of the kings of the east. The kings of the east will be Communist China. When Russia invaded Palestine in the Gog Magog invasion God will have destroyed all but one-sixth of their army and homeland. I suspect, before the invasion, Russia will have eliminated the United States to prevent military intervention and will have crippled Europe for the same reason. After God destroyed all but one-sixth of Russia there will be nothing to stop Communist China from invading Russia. The Antichrist recovery plan for Europe will be successful and he will become the only person in the world who can stop the invading Red China army. The combined military forces of the European Common Market nations will stop the kings of the east from overrunning Europe. The Antichrist protection treaty signed with the Jews at Jerusalem will stop the kings of the east from overrunning the middle east. The red army will stop on the north side of the Euphrates River and the invasion will be halted. When the great river Euphrates is dried up, the red army invasion force will begin to move south toward Jerusalem.

The goal of the three miracle-working demonic spirits will be to gather the military forces of the Gentile nations for Armageddon. Notice in verse 14 they go forth unto the kings of the earth and of the whole world. This is a definite change of tactics. Previously, members of the beast organization will have been pursuing people on an individual basis, in an attempt to force them to worship the image and take the unforgivable mark. Earth is a big place and the people who believed God will be hiding. The beast organization will not be able to locate and approach every person on an individual basis in three and years. This is why the miracle-working demonic spirits from Satan, Antichrist, and the False Prophet will approach the political leaders of the nations. If all the nations and people on earth had already been approached by the beast organization, they would already have taken the unforgivable mark or would be dead for their refusal. If this were the case, there would be no need to deceive people into joining the Armageddon Army by "working miracles."

The three frog-like unclean spirits are identified as "the spirits of devils" or demons. One comes out of the mouth of Satan (the dragon), one out of the mouth of the beast (Antichrist), and the other out of the mouth of the false prophet. They will "go forth unto the kings of the earth" or principality demons of the nations to deceive them into joining the Armageddon invasion force. It will be necessary to deceive them because the pushy principality demon of Egypt will have caused a division in Satan's organization and other nation principalities may have chosen to join his rebellion against Satan. The phrase "and of the whole earth" includes every individual human on the whole earth, not just the human political rulers of the nations. They have the ability to work miracles in order to deceive and "to gather them to the battle of that great day of God Almighty," which is Armageddon.

In the final days of the Church Era, Jesus gave the people on Earth a stern warning to watch and not to be deceived into becoming a member of the Laodicean church congregation. Those who ignored the warning will be counted as one of the members of the congregation who missed the rapture, when Jesus came as a thief in the night, and suddenly removed his Church from the planet. In the final days of the seven-year tribulation era, the three miracle-working demonic spirits will be sent to the nations to deceive them into joining the Armageddon Army. In verse 16:15, Jesus gives us the final warning, "Behold, I come as a thief. Blessed is he that watcheth, and keepeth his garments, lest he walk naked, and they see his shame." Here, Jesus is basically telling the population on Earth to watch and not to be deceived into becoming a member of this invasion force. Those who reject the warning will be counted as one of the troops in the Armageddon Army. The return of Jesus will be just as sudden and unexpected to the troops in the Armageddon Army as the rapture was to the Laodicean church members. Jesus will take them by surprise, and they will find out too late that they are fighting for the wrong side. It is apparent from the next verse that the troops in the Armageddon Army will pay about as much attention to the words of Jesus as the Laodicean church membership did, Rev. 16:16, "And he gathered them together into a place called in the Hebrew tongue Armageddon."

25. The Seventh Vial Poured into the Air: It is Done.

Rev. 16:17-21, "(17) And the seventh angel poured out his vial into the air; and there came a great voice out of the temple of heaven, from the throne, saying, It is done. (18) And there were voices, and thunders, and lightnings; and there was a great earthquake, such as was not since men were upon the earth, so mighty an earthquake, [and] so great. (19) And the great city was divided into three parts, and the cities of the nations fell: and great Babylon came in remembrance before God, to give unto her the cup of the wine of the fierceness of his wrath. (20) And every island fled away, and the mountains were not found. (21) And there fell upon men a great hail out of heaven, [every stone] about the weight of a talent: and men blasphemed God because of the plague of the hail; for the plague thereof was exceeding great."

The seventh vial will be poured into the air, and a voice from the throne will announce "It is done." Among other things, Earth will experience the severest earthquake since the Garden of Eden, "and there was a great earthquake, such as was not since men were upon the earth, so mighty an earthquake, [and] so great." The result of the greatest earthquake is given in Rev. 16:20, "And every island fled away, and the mountains were not found." Mountains will no longer be found because the shaking will lower them until they are even with the surrounding terrain. Every island will disappear because all the continents will come together to form a single land mass. When the nations floated away on the continental crust was during the days of Peleg, the son of Eber, the son of Salah, the son of Arphaxad, the son of Shem, who was the son of Noah. Noah and Shem survived the universal flood which ended the Flood Dispensation. The generations of Noah are given in Genesis chapter 10 and verse 25 reads, "And unto Eber were born two sons: the name of one [was] Peleg; for in his days was the earth divided; and his brother's name [was] Joktan."

The great city that was divided into three parts is great Babylon. The details of the judgment of Babylon are given in Revelation chapters 17 and 18. Chapter 17 covers the Judgment of Babylon during the Antichrist Reign. Chapter 18 covers the Judgment of Babylon during the False Prophet Reign. Both are flashback chapters and they were inserted here because this is the end of the road for Babylon. Chapter 19 opens with a wave of praise because "It is done."

The people's response to the great hail out of heaven was blasphemy, Rev. 16:21b, "and men blasphemed God because of the plague of the hail; for the plague thereof was exceeding great." The weight of every stone was about the weight of a talent which most Bible reference books put at about one hundred pounds.

26. First Wave of Praise: The Great Whore Judged.

Rev. 19:1-3, "(1) And after these things I heard a great voice of much people in heaven, saying, Alleluia; Salvation, and glory, and honour, and power, unto the Lord our God: (2) For true and righteous [are] his judgments: for he hath judged the great whore, which did corrupt the earth with her fornication, and hath avenged the blood of his servants at her hand. (3) And again they said, Alleluia. And her smoke rose up for ever and ever." The rejoicing in heaven is praise for true and righteous judgments of God against the great whore. Satan is "the great whore, which did corrupt the earth with her fornication." Following the seven vial judgments are the flashback chapters 17 and 18, which detail the judgment of this whore. The last verse in chapter 18 reads, "And in her was found the blood of prophets, and of saints, and of all that were slain upon the earth." Part of the praise here is, "and hath avenged the blood of his servants at her hand." After the chapters concerning the vial judgments, the scene shifts to heaven and the sequential events mentioned continue there.

27. Second Wave of Praise: The Lord God Omnipotent Reigns.

Rev. 19:4-6, "(4) And the four and twenty elders and the four beasts fell down and worshipped God that sat on the throne, saying, Amen; Alleluia. (5) And a voice came out of the throne, saying, Praise our God, all ye his servants, and ye that fear him, both small and great. (6) And I heard as it were the voice of a great multitude, and as the voice of many waters, and as the voice of mighty thunderings, saying, Alleluia: for the Lord God omnipotent reigneth." The first wave of praise was for the true and righteous judgments of God. The second wave of praise was because the Lord God omnipotent reigns.

28. Marriage Supper of the Lamb.

Rev. 19:7-10, "(7) Let us be glad and rejoice, and give honour to him: for the marriage of the Lamb is come, and his wife hath made herself ready. (8) And to her was granted that she should be arrayed in fine linen, clean and white: for the fine linen is the righteousness of saints. (9) And he saith unto me, Write, Blessed [are] they which are called unto the marriage supper of the Lamb. And he saith unto me, These are the true sayings of God. (10) And I fell at his feet to worship him. And he said unto me, See [thou do it] not: I am thy fellowservant, and of thy brethren that have the testimony of Jesus: worship God: for the testimony of Jesus is the spirit of prophecy."

This marriage of the Lamb will be the formal ceremony of the union of Jesus and the Church. The rapture removed the Bride from the earth prior to the tribulation era but the formal marriage ceremony was delayed until after all the invited guests had arrived. The invited guests will include all the Old Testament saints and all the tribulation saints. Don't confuse them with the Bride. Without doubt, the highest honor in the entire universe is for the God of heaven to call us his sons and daughters. The second highest honor is for God to call someone blessed. In Rev. 19:9 we read, "Blessed are they which are called unto the marriage supper of the Lamb." In Rev. 20:6 we read the blessed will be resurrected to eternal life and will reign with Jesus in the millennial kingdom, "Blessed and holy is he that hath part in the first resurrection: on such the second death hath no power, but they shall be priests of God and of Christ, and shall reign with him a thousand years." The group called blessed in verse 19:9, is the same group called blessed in verse 20:6. The first part of this blessed group to enter heaven were the Old Testament saints who accompanied Jesus at his ascension. The Bride will be the sons and daughters of God, by the rebirth, from the Day of Pentecost to the day of the Church rapture. The second part of the blessed group are the saints who missed the rapture and were slaughtered by Antichrist. They were the souls under the altar when Jesus opened the fifth seal in Rev. 6:9-11. They were told to rest until their brethren, those who were to be killed as they were, joins them. Their brethren who were to be slaughtered by the False Prophet, complete the group called blessed. When they get to heaven, we will be ready to proceed with the formal marriage ceremony of Jesus and his Bride, and move on to the marriage supper. The Bride will be the Church, while the guests are the friends of the Bridegroom. For example, John the Baptist lived and died during the Law Dispensation. In John

3:28-29 he identifies himself not as the bride, but as a friend of the bridegroom, "(28) Ye yourselves bear me witness, that I said, I am not the Christ, but that I am sent before him. (29) He that hath the bride is the bridegroom: but the friend of the bridegroom, which standeth and heareth him, rejoiceth greatly because of the bridegroom's voice: this my joy therefore is fulfilled." It is the friends of the bridegroom that says, "Let us be glad and rejoice, and give honour to him: for the marriage of the Lamb is come."

Jesus gave us the parable of marriage invitations in Matthew 22:1-14, "(1) And Jesus answered and spake unto them again by parables, and said, (2) The kingdom of heaven is like unto a certain king, which made a marriage for his son, (3) And sent forth his servants to call them that were bidden to the wedding: and they would not come. (4) Again, he sent forth other servants, saying, Tell them which are bidden, Behold, I have prepared my dinner: my oxen and [my] fatlings [are] killed, and all things [are] ready: come unto the marriage. (5) But they made light of [it], and went their ways, one to his farm, another to his merchandise: (6) And the remnant took his servants, and entreated [them] spitefully, and slew [them]. (7) But when the king heard [thereof], he was wroth: and he sent forth his armies, and destroyed those murderers, and burned up their city. (8) Then saith he to his servants, The wedding is ready, but they which were bidden were not worthy. (9) Go ye therefore into the highways, and as many as ye shall find, bid to the marriage. (10) So those servants went out into the highways, and gathered together all as many as they found, both bad and good: and the wedding was furnished with guests. (11) And when the king came in to see the guests, he saw there a man which had not on a wedding garment: (12) And he saith unto him, Friend, how camest thou in hither not having a wedding garment? And he was speechless. (13) Then said the king to the servants, Bind him hand and foot, and take him away, and cast [him] into outer darkness; there shall be weeping and gnashing of teeth. (14) For many are called, but few [are] chosen." The first seven verses concern the invitations sent to the old testament saints. Verses 8-10 concern the invitations sent to the Laodicean congregation rejected as sons and daughters at the Church rapture. The ones who honored the invitation are the fifth seal group who were given white robes and told to wait for the brethren, the sixth seal group. When the sixth seal is open Satan is cast out of heaven and I believe he is the individual described in verses 11-13. Verse 14 not only concerns the wedding invitations but every other invitation given by God.

We are then told, "and his wife hath made herself ready." The Church making herself ready, (you making yourself ready) is a truth you don't hear in the Laodicean Church sermons. Their "only believe salvation package" is simple and is for the simple. It will never get you to heaven because it takes out all the "you have to do this." You must be born-again, you must be sincere in repentance, you must be faithful, and you must overcome in the daily baptisms of fire. You have to do these things or you do not have the right to stand with the ones who did. If you are waiting for Jesus to make you ready, you need to be told there is nothing else he can do. He provided the way but you have to walk it and if you don't go the way He said, you can't get there. "His wife hath made herself ready. And to her was granted that she should be arrayed in fine linen, clean and white: for the fine linen is the righteousness of saints." She was granted to be arrayed in fine linen because it represents the righteousness of the saints. The one who "granted that she should be arrayed" made a decision and declared that she was in right standing.

After the formal marriage ceremony is the marriage supper of the Lamb, Rev. 19:9, "And he saith unto me, Write, Blessed are they which are called unto the marriage supper of the Lamb. And he saith unto me, These are the true sayings of God." The marriage supper is comparable to the Gentile wedding reception. It is an affair that follows the formal marriage ceremony, in which the friends and guests of the bride and groom come together to receive and honor the newly married couple. The duration of the marriage supper is debatable. I personally believe it will last the entire length of the one thousand year millennial reign of Jesus on Earth. I suspect John was totally overwhelmed at seeing the Church in all its glory to fall at the feet of the individual to worship him. I say individual because I am not totally convinced the person talking to John is an angel. In the statement "I am thy fellow servant" the person is merely saying he is a partner in agreement with John in the matter of Jesus. In the statement "and of thy brethren" it would appear that the person is saying he is personally related to John, which would make him a Church member, not an angel. The person could be an angel saying "of thy brethren" in the sense that he has the "testimony of Jesus" just as they have. The angelic host had to choose between what Satan said and what Jesus said, just as we humans have to do. They are in heaven after Satan and his crew have been thrown out, so we know they decided in favor of Jesus.

The word *testimony* means open declaration or evidence. The testimony of Jesus is an open declaration of Jesus or the evidence of Jesus. When someone gives a testimony of Jesus they are making an open declaration and in that statement is the evidence. Examine the evidence, compare it to the Scriptures, and anyone can know your opinion of Jesus. Here we are told "the testimony of Jesus is the spirit of prophecy." The Old Testament portion of the Bible is filled with prophecies concerning Jesus and you can learn much about Jesus by studying them. An open declaration that contradicts the prophecies means that you are not convinced Jesus is telling the truth. For example, Isaiah 7:14, "Therefore the Lord himself shall give you a sign; Behold, a virgin shall conceive, and bear a son, and shall call his name Immanuel." The fulfillment of this prophecy was the conception and birth of Jesus given in the New Testament. From this information, you either believe Jesus was born of a virgin or you believe Jesus was a bastard. When you make an open declaration on his virgin birth you either confirm or deny the truth of the prophecy. No opinion is a denial of Jesus because he said there is no middle ground, Matthew 12:30, "He that is not with me is against me; and he that gathereth not with me scattereth abroad." You either make known your opinion of Jesus or you deny him and the day is coming when he will do the same for you, Matthew 10:32-33, "(32) Whosoever therefore shall confess me before men, him will I confess also before my Father which is in heaven. (33) But whosoever shall deny me before men, him will I also deny before my Father which is in heaven." Luke 12:8-9, "(8) Also I say unto you, Whosoever shall confess me before men, him shall the Son of man also confess before the angels of God: (9) But he that denieth me before men shall be denied before the angels of God."

29. Return of Jesus in glory to end the Great Tribulation.

Rev. 19:11-16, "(11) And I saw heaven opened, and behold a white horse; and he that sat upon him [was] called Faithful and True, and in righteousness he doth judge and make war. (12) His eyes [were] as a flame of fire, and on his head [were] many crowns; and he had a name written, that no man knew, but he himself. (13) And he [was] clothed with a vesture dipped in blood: and his name is called The Word of God. (14) And the armies [which were] in heaven followed him upon white horses, clothed in fine linen, white and clean. (15) And out of his mouth goeth a sharp sword, that with it he should smite the nations: and he shall rule them with a rod of iron: and he treadeth the winepress of the fierceness and wrath of Almighty God. (16) And he hath on [his] vesture and on his thigh a name written, KING OF KINGS, AND LORD OF LORDS."

When heaven opens this time John sees Jesus on a white horse followed by his army. We are told the rider, who was called Faithful and True, has eyes as a flame of fire and many crowns on his head. He is wearing a vesture dipped in blood and on the vesture and his thigh a name is written, KING OF KINGS, AND LORD OF LORDS. In Rev. 19:12c we are told, "and he had a name written, that no man knew, but he himself" and in Rev. 19:13b "and his name is called The Word of God."

In Rev. 19:11d we are told "and in righteousness he doth judge and make war" and in Rev. 19:15, "And out of his mouth goeth a sharp sword, that with it he should smite the nations: and he shall rule them with a rod of iron." Both statements speak of Jesus as King during the Kingdom Dispensation.

The statement "he treadeth the winepress of the fierceness and wrath of Almighty God" speaks of the judgment of his enemies in the destruction of the Armageddon army.

The army that will follow Jesus from Heaven is described in Rev. 19:14, "And the armies [which were] in heaven followed him upon white horses, clothed in fine linen, white and clean."

This time Jesus will come in "power and great glory," Luke 21:27, "And then shall they see the Son of man coming in a cloud with power and great glory." Don't confuse the return of Jesus in "power and great glory" with his coming as a thief in the night. When Jesus returns with power and great glory, he removes from Earth are "all things that offend, and them which do iniquity" (Matt 13:41b). They are removed by being killed and confined to Hades to await the great white throne judgment of Rev. 20:11-15. His coming as a thief in the night is the 1 Thessalonians 4:13-18 Church rapture, when he removes the believers and leaves the unbelieving behind. This coming is also recorded in Matthew 24:36-41, "(36) But of that day and hour knoweth no man, no, not the angels of heaven, but my Father only. (37) But as the days of Noe were, so shall also the coming of the Son of man be. (38) For as in the days that were before the flood they were eating and drinking, marrying and giving in marriage, until the day that Noe entered into the ark, (39) And knew not until the flood came, and took them all away; so shall also the coming of the Son of man be. (40) Then shall two be in the field; the one shall be taken, and the other left. (41) Two women shall be grinding at the mill; the one shall be taken, and the other left." Obviously this serene scene does not describe what will happen on Earth when Jesus destroys the Armageddon army in the tribulation era.

30. Supper of the Great God, Flesh of the Armageddon Army.

Rev. 19:17-21, "(17) And I saw an angel standing in the sun; and he cried with a loud voice, saying to all the fowls that fly in the midst of heaven, Come and gather yourselves together unto the supper of the great God; (18) That ye may eat the flesh of kings, and the flesh of captains, and the flesh of mighty men, and the flesh of horses, and of them that sit on them, and the flesh of all [men, both] free and bond, both small and great. (19) And I saw the beast, and the kings of the earth, and their armies, gathered together to make war against him that sat on the horse, and against his army. (20) And the beast was taken, and with him the false prophet that wrought miracles before him, with which he deceived them that had received the mark of the beast, and them that worshipped his image. These both were cast alive into a lake of fire burning with brimstone. (21) And the remnant were slain with the sword of him that sat upon the horse, which [sword] proceeded out of his mouth: and all the fowls were filled with their flesh."

An angel will call the fowls to the supper of the great God to eat the flesh of the Armageddon army. After disposing of Antichrist and the False Prophet, "the remnant were slain with the sword of him that sat upon the horse, which [sword] proceeded out of his mouth: and all the fowls were filled with their flesh."

The Armageddon army will be made up of both humans and demonic angels. When John foresaw the army he described it as, Rev. 19:19, "And I saw the beast (Antichrist), and the kings of the earth (demonic hierarchy), and their armies, gathered together to make war against him (Jesus) that sat on the horse, and against his army." Antichrist and the False Prophet will be the first two individuals to be thrown into literal hell, Rev. 19:20, "And the beast (Antichrist) was taken, and with him the false prophet that wrought miracles before him, with which he deceived them that had received the mark of the beast, and them that worshipped his image. These both were cast alive into a lake of fire burning with brimstone."

31. Satan Bound and Cast Into the Bottomless Pit for One Thousand Years.

Rev. 20:1-3, "(1) And I saw an angel come down from heaven, having the key of the bottomless pit and a great chain in his hand. (2) And he laid hold on the dragon, that old serpent, which is the Devil, and Satan, and bound him a thousand years, (3) And cast him into the bottomless pit, and shut him up, and set a seal upon him, that he should deceive the nations no more, till the thousand years should be fulfilled: and after that he must be loosed a little season."

Satan will be bound and cast into Hades or the bottomless pit for the next one thousand years, to stop him from deceiving the nations during the millennial reign.

32. First Resurrection and the Kingdom Dispensation.

Rev. 20:4-6, "(4) And I saw thrones, and they sat upon them, and judgment was given unto them: and [I saw] the souls of them that were beheaded for the witness of Jesus, and for the word of God, and which had not worshipped the beast, neither his image, neither had received [his] mark upon their foreheads, or in their hands; and they lived and reigned with Christ a thousand years. (5) But the rest of the dead lived not again until the thousand years were finished. This [is] the first resurrection. (6) Blessed and holy [is] he that hath part in the first resurrection: on such the second death hath no power, but they shall be priests of God and of Christ, and shall reign with him a thousand years."

The people sitting on the thrones will be the tribulation dead. "Judgment was given to them" or the responsibility to judge was given to them and they will reign with Jesus for one thousand years during the Kingdom Dispensation. The phrase "and they lived" means they were resurrected to eternal life. They are part of the first resurrection, also called the resurrection of life. It was preceded by the resurrection of Jesus and the resurrection of Church members at the rapture. This assembly will contain both the fifth and sixth seal groups. The fifth seal group (Rev. 6:9-11) killed by Antichrist are the ones beheaded for the witness of Jesus and for the Word of God. Those which had not worshipped the beast, neither his image, neither had received his mark upon their foreheads, or in their hands, are the individuals who are killed by the False Prophet during the last half of the tribulation era, which make up the sixth seal group in Rev. 7:9-17. A third group to be resurrected is the Old Testament saints. We are told of their resurrection in Daniel 12:1-2, "(1) And at that time shall Michael stand up, the great prince which standeth for the children of thy people: and there shall be a time of trouble, such as never was since there was a nation even to that same time: and at that time thy people shall be delivered, every one that shall be found written in the book. (2) And many of them that sleep in the dust of the earth shall awake, some to everlasting life, and some to shame and everlasting contempt."

Here we have a record of the completion of first resurrection and the millennial reign of Jesus, which is the Kingdom Dispensation. Notice that the participants of the first resurrection are called blessed and holy, and they are given everlasting life since the second death has no power over them. These individuals will stand before the judgment seat of Christ (1 Cor. 3:10-15) for the purpose of receiving or losing rewards. They are not on trial for their life. None will be judged guilty at this judgment, just as none will be judged innocent at the white throne judgment. Also notice in verse 5, "But the rest of the dead lived not again until the thousand years were finished." The rest of the dead will participate in the second resurrection, at the end of the millennium, which is the resurrection of damnation. The first death is the separation of the spirit and soul from the body, which we call physical death, and it is only temporary. The second death is eternal separation from God in the lake of fire (Hell). Again, do not confuse the Church with the tribulation dead. The Church members were resurrected from the dead and/or given eternal glorified bodies before the first individual in the tribulation group was ever killed.

33. Satan Released from Hades to Assemble the Final Army.

Rev. 20:7-10, "(7) And when the thousand years are expired, Satan shall be loosed out of his prison, (8) And shall go out to deceive the nations which are in the four quarters of the earth, Gog and Magog, to gather them together to battle: the number of whom [is] as the sand of the sea. (9) And they went up on the breadth of the earth, and compassed the camp of the saints about, and the beloved city: and fire came down from God out of heaven, and devoured them. (10) And the devil that deceived them was cast into the lake of fire and brimstone, where the beast and the false prophet [are], and shall be tormented day and night for ever and ever."

At the end of the Kingdom Dispensation, Satan will be released from Hades, to assemble the final army. This final army will be comprised of all human beings who rejected Jesus as King during the Kingdom era. They will assemble at Jerusalem, just as the Armageddon Army had done one thousand years earlier, and they will be destroyed by a direct act of God, just as the Russian Gog and Magog army was destroyed prior to the seven-year tribulation period. This Gog and Magog army is not the army described in Ezekiel chapters 38 and 39. Humans living on earth at the end of the millennial reign will be able to consult their history books about an event that took place in the Church to Kingdom transition period, an event which will be comparable to what is about to occur in their day. They will be able to read how God miraculously destroyed all but one-sixth of the mighty Russian army, when it tried to invade the land of Israel. The destruction of this final army at the end of the Kingdom Dispensation will be both swift and final. After this army is destroyed, Satan will join Antichrist and the False Prophet in the lake of fire.

34. The Great White Throne Judgment.

Rev. 20:11-15, "(11) And I saw a great white throne, and him that sat on it, from whose face the earth and the heaven fled away; and there was found no place for them. (12) And I saw the dead, small and great, stand before God; and the books were opened: and another book was opened, which is [the book] of life: and the dead were judged out of those things which were written in the books, according to their works. (13) And the sea gave up the dead which were in it; and death and hell delivered up the dead which were in them: and they were judged every man according to their works. (14) And death and hell were cast into the lake of fire. This is the second death. (15) And whosoever was not found written in the book of life was cast into the lake of fire."

When Jesus begins the great white throne judgment the destruction of the earth and the heaven we know today will occur. This is the literal "end of the world." This is the destruction Peter speaks of in 2 Peter 3:10, "But the day of the Lord will come as a thief in the night; in the which the heavens shall pass away with a great noise, and the elements shall melt with fervent heat, the earth also and the works therein shall be burned up." This will be followed by the resurrection of damnation. No one will be found innocent at this judgment and we see the inhabitants of Hades joining Antichrist, False Prophet, and Satan in the lake of fire. Notice it is at this point that death, the last enemy, is destroyed in the lake of fire. This is the end that Paul speaks of in 1 Corinthians 15:20-26, "(20) But now is Christ risen from the dead, and become the first fruits of them that slept. (21) For since by man came death, by man came also the resurrection of the dead. (22) For as in Adam all die, even so in Christ shall all be made alive. (23) But every man in his own order: Christ the first fruits; afterward they that are Christ's at his coming. (24) Then cometh the end, when he shall have delivered up the kingdom to God, even the Father; when he shall have put down all rule and all authority and power. (25) For he must reign, till he hath put all enemies under his feet. (26) The last enemy that shall be destroyed is death."

Revelation chapter 21:1 opens with the creation of a new heaven and a new earth, "And I saw a new heaven and a new earth: for the first heaven and the first earth were passed away; and there was no more sea." The human beings who survive the Kingdom Dispensation, will be the humans that God will use to repopulate the new creation. This was God's plan from the beginning and he has never changed direction. The wisdom of God can be seen in how he handled Satan's rebellion. The only beings, both spirit and human, in the Kingdom of God at this point, will be those who chose to be there of their own free will. They were all given the opportunity to decide for themselves whether they would believe God and do as he instructed, or reject what God said to follow Satan. He told us in advance that he would have mercy on those obedient to his voice and that he would execute judgment on the disobedient. God will do exactly what he has said he would do. It is only a matter of time.

The remainder of the Revelation gives us a look at the new creation and new Jerusalem, home of the Bride, and my new address throughout eternity. In Rev. 21:6b-7 Jesus says it can be yours also, "(6b) I will give unto him that is athirst of the fountain of the water of life freely. (7) He that overcometh shall inherit all things; and I will be his God, and he shall be my son." Rev. 21:4 lists some things you will be unable to find in this city, "And God shall wipe away all tears from their eyes; and there shall be no more death, neither sorrow, nor crying, neither shall there be any more pain: for the former things are passed away." If you find these arrangements unacceptable, you are free to follow the crowd in verse 21:8 to their eternal address, "But the fearful, and unbelieving, and the abominable, and murderers, and whoremongers, and sorcerers, and idolaters, and all liars, shall have their part in the lake which burneth with fire and brimstone: which is the second death." In the final analysis there are only two groups of people. One group has judged God faithful and trustworthy, by what he has told us in his Word. The other group refused to heed the Word of God, and thereby judged him a liar. One group will spend eternity in the new creation with God. The other group will spend eternity in hell separated from God. There will be nothing between. Judgment Day is coming, but it is merely the day you enter your final abode. Judgment Day is payday, the day God gives you what you have been working for. If you are one of those sitting around waiting day to see if you won or lost on Judgment Day, I can tell you in advance, *you have lost.* Today is the day of salvation. Today, you must communicate to God, by your thoughts, words, and deeds, your preference concerning your final dwelling place. If you have entered into the New Covenant by being born-again as Jesus instructed, you are saved. Instead of Judgment Day representing a threat, it represents a day of joy, because that is the day God makes the final separation of the righteous from the unrighteous. God is patient, but he is also truthful. He promised judgment, and he must judge. Don't misunderstand the reason for his delay; read 2 Peter 3:1-18.

Chapter Five

Revelation Flashbacks

As I stated earlier, the majority of the Book of the Revelation is sequential, meaning the events are given in consecutive order or in succession. The book also contains *flashbacks,* interruptions in the continuity of events to provide additional information on a subject. In this chapter we will look at the flashbacks, which are:

1. Rev. 13:1-10, The Antichrist Reign, first half of seven-year tribulation era.
2. Rev. 11:1-13, Ministry of the two faithful witnesses, first half of the seven-year tribulation era.
3. Rev. 17:1-18, Judgment of Babylon during the Antichrist Reign.
4. Rev. 13:11-18, The False Prophet Reign, last half of the seven-year tribulation era.
5. Rev. 14:1-20, Ministry of the 144 thousand sealed Jews, last half of the seven-year tribulation era.
6. Rev. 18:1-24, Judgment of Babylon during the False Prophet Reign.
7. Rev. 12:1-17, Israel and the Great Red Dragon, Law to Church Transition era to end of tribulation period.

The Antichrist Reign

The rise and reign of Antichrist is recorded in Revelation 13:1-10, "(1) And I stood upon the sand of the sea, and saw a beast rise up out of the sea, having seven heads and ten horns, and upon his horns ten crowns, and upon his heads the name of blasphemy. (2) And the beast which I saw was like unto a leopard, and his feet were as [the feet] of a bear, and his mouth as the mouth of a lion: and the dragon gave him his power, and his seat, and great authority. (3) And I saw one of his heads as it were wounded to death; and his deadly wound was healed: and all the world wondered after the beast. (4) And they worshipped the dragon which gave power unto the beast: and they worshipped the beast, saying, Who [is] like unto the beast? who is able to make war with him? (5) And there was given unto him a mouth speaking great things and blasphemies; and power was given unto him to continue forty [and] two months. (6) And he opened his mouth in blasphemy against God, to blaspheme his name, and his tabernacle, and them that dwell in heaven. (7) And it was given unto him to make war with the saints, and to overcome them: and power was given him over all kindreds, and tongues, and nations. (8) And all that dwell upon the earth shall worship him, whose names are not written in the book of life of the Lamb slain from the foundation of the world. (9) If any man have an ear, let him hear. (10) He that leadeth into captivity shall go into captivity: he that killeth with the sword must be killed with the sword. Here is the patience and the faith of the saints."

The Bible makes a distinction between Antichrist and False Prophet, and unless we retain this distinction, we will confuse their missions. Antichrist will be the beast that rises out of the sea, and his mission will be to stop people from confessing belief in Jesus Christ. The False Prophet will be the beast that comes up out of the earth, and his mission will be to stop people from confessing belief in God, the Father, and all other religions. Antichrist will begin the seven-year tribulation period when he confirms a protection covenant with regathered Israel. The False Prophet will appear three and one-half years later to break that covenant. The False Prophet, not Antichrist, will perform the abomination of desolation and force the earth dwellers to worship an image and receive the unforgivable mark of the beast.

The distinction between Antichrist and the False Prophet we read in the seventy weeks prophecy can also be seen in 2 Thessalonians 2:3-4, "(3) Let no man deceive you by any means: for that day shall not come, except there come a falling away first, and that man of sin be revealed," (that day will be the rapture of the Church, the falling away is the apostate Laodicean Church Era, that man of sin will be Antichrist. The remainder of the passage concerns the False Prophet.) "the son of perdition; (4) Who opposeth and exalteth himself above all that is called God, or that is worshipped; so that he as God sitteth in the temple of God, shewing himself that he is God." Verse 4 is the abomination of desolation.

During the Church Era, Antichrist is still a demonic spirit, operating in and against the Church through human beings. He and his seducing spirits (1 Timothy 4:1-5) bring about the falling away or apostasy within the Church. This is accomplished by infiltrating the churches with false prophets, apostles, and teachers who promote error and introduce damnable heresies (2 Peter 2:1, 1 John 4:1-6, 2 Corinthians 11:13-15). We will examine the apostate church in a later chapter, but for now we need to realize it is the goal of Antichrist to destroy the Church, not build one. I realize many of us have been taught that Antichrist is very busy today building a one-world church, which God is supposed to destroy in the seven-year tribulation period. The truth is, Jesus will form the one-world church by the rapture, and Antichrist will spend the next three and one-half years destroying what Jesus left behind.

A. Antichrist, Beast That Rises Out of the Sea.

Rev. 13:1-2a, "(1) And I stood upon the sand of the sea, and saw a beast rise up out of the sea, having seven heads and ten horns, and upon his horns ten crowns, and upon his heads the name of blasphemy. (2a) And the beast which I saw was like unto a leopard, and his feet were as [the feet] of a bear, and his mouth as the mouth of a lion."

In Rev. 17:15 we are told that waters in prophecy represent the human race, "And he saith unto me, The waters which thou sawest, where the whore sitteth, are peoples, and multitudes, and nations, and tongues." Antichrist is a spirit who puts on flesh (incarnates), which is why John foresaw him as coming up from among humans. Whether John actually foresaw Antichrist or just the organization he commands is debatable. I believe John foresaw only the organization because we are living in the time period of the seventh head, and I can see the ten horn organization, but it has not reached world dominance, so I cannot see the crowns or Antichrist. John foresaw the crowns, so he is describing the beast and its activity after it has reached world dominance. The beast John described represents world history from the beginning of the Jewish captivity to the end of their captivity. The seven-headed ten-horn beast represents the human race in the form of Gentile world governments or empires (Assyrian, Babylonian, Median, Persian, Greek, Roman) and the ten King Kingdom which Antichrist and the False Prophet will command. John lived during the sixth head (Roman Empire) time period when the Book of Daniel was still sealed. This is why when he looked back into history he saw what looked like a leopard with feet like a bear and a mouth like a lion. From the prophecies of Daniel Chapter 7 and world history, we know the lion was the Median Empire (third head), the bear was the Persia Empire (fourth head), and the leopard was the Greek Empire (fifth head). Daniel saw and described these same beasts but because he was looking forward in history he saw them in the reverse order. John was looking back into history and saw first the leopard, then the bear, and then the lion. Daniel was looking forward in history and saw first the lion, then the bear, and then the leopard.

Antichrist is God's rod of anger on the church population who rejected Jesus, just as the False Prophet is God's rod of anger on a world who rejected Jesus. When the church congregation reaches the point when it will no longer hear the words of Jesus and obey the Word of God, He has no choice but to send these two instruments of destruction into the world. The only other choice God has is to allow the human race to continue repopulating the earth in order to increase the population of hell. Antichrist and False Prophet will serve the same purpose during the seven-year tribulation era as the Assyrian Army did against the Northern Kingdom of Israel during the Law Dispensation when Israel refused to obey God. Here is how God describes the Assyrians in Isaiah 10:5-7, "(5) O Assyrian, the rod of mine anger, and the staff in their hand is mine indignation. (6) I will send him against an hypocritical nation, and against the people of my wrath will I give him a charge, to take the spoil, and to take the prey, and to tread them down like the mire of the streets. (7) Howbeit he meaneth not so, neither doth his heart think so; but it is in his heart to destroy and cut off nations not a few."

B. The Beast Exalted by the Dragon.

Rev. 13:2b, "and the dragon gave him his power, and his seat, and great authority." The dragon who gives Antichrist his power is Satan, (Rev. 20:2). The extent of the power is worldwide, Rev. 13:7b "and power was given him over all kindreds, and tongues, and nations." The seat Antichrist will be given is political control of the European Common Market confederacy. Through this organization, he will completely destroy what is left of false Christianity on the face of the earth, which is why he is given "great authority."

C. A Deadly Head Wound Healed.

Rev. 13:3-4, "(3) And I saw one of his heads as it were wounded to death; and his deadly wound was healed: and all the world wondered after the beast. (4) And they worshipped the dragon which gave power unto the beast: and they worshipped the beast, saying, Who [is] like unto the beast? who is able to make war with him?"

The phrase "one of his heads" eliminates Antichrist as the recipient of the head wound. Antichrist is a man, or more accurately, a demonic spirit incarnated in a human body. He only has one head. The thing being described with more than one head is the beast with seven heads and ten horns. Some are promoting the erroneous idea that the wounded head is the Old Roman Empire. John saw a beast with seven heads, ten horns and ten crowns. The heads represent Gentile world governments, the horns represent political rulers, and the crowns show where political authority is vested. The seventh head is the final Gentile world government, which is the ten king kingdom. The head wound will occur during their existence, and since the first six heads are already Gentile history, it only leaves the seventh head to receive the deadly wound. It is in this time period that John, "saw one of his heads as it were wounded to death and his deadly wound was healed," which will result in all the world wondering after the beast.

Another popular teaching is that Antichrist will receive a physical head wound, and perform a healing miracle on himself. To the carnal mind a healing miracle is rather spectacular. To the born-again believer healing miracles are, or at least should be, a common everyday occurrence. The reason a healing miracle is regarded so highly among the unbelievers is because of the publicity generated by the deceived Christian population. In the Mark 16:15-18 Church Commission one of the signs Jesus said would follow "them that believe" the gospel is that "they shall lay hands on the sick, and they shall recover." The deceived Christian population can't handle physical ailments as Jesus told them to, because they either haven't heard the gospel or they don't believe it. Rather than repent and honor Jesus by believing the gospel and doing things His way, they explain their inability by discrediting Jesus and the Word of God. The most common excuse given for their inability to work miracles is that God gave the twelve Apostles the power to work miracles in order to get the Church started, and when the Apostles died, the age of miracles ended.

This is the blasphemy Jesus warns of in Mark 3:22-30, "(22) And the scribes which came down from Jerusalem said, He hath Beelzebub, and by the prince of the devils casteth he out devils. (23) And he called them unto him, and said unto them in parables, How can Satan cast out Satan? (24) And if a kingdom be divided against itself, that kingdom cannot stand. (25) And if a house be divided against itself, that house cannot stand. (26) And if Satan rise up against himself, and be divided, he cannot stand, but hath an end. (27) No man can enter into a strong man's house, and spoil his goods, except he will first bind the strong man; and then he will spoil his house. (28) Verily I say unto you, All sins shall be forgiven unto the sons of men, and blasphemies wherewith soever they shall blaspheme: (29) But he that shall blaspheme against the Holy Ghost hath never forgiveness, but is in danger of eternal damnation: (30) Because they said, He hath an unclean spirit." They attributed Jesus' ability to work miracles to demons, and he told them that was blasphemy against the Holy Spirit. It was blasphemy then and will continue to be blasphemy until the Holy Spirit completes his mission with the Church.

Without doubt, both Antichrist and the False Prophet will be able to work miracles, but neither can work a miracle today. During the Church Dispensation, Satan will not cast out himself because a demon cannot cast out a demon, and Antichrist cannot cast out another antichrist spirit. To do so would create a division in Satan's kingdom, and like Jesus said in Mark 3:26, "And if Satan rise up against himself, and be divided, he cannot stand, but hath an end." During the Church Dispensation only born-again believers will be able to work miracles, and their power lies in the indwelling Holy Spirit, the Word of God, and the name of Jesus. The rapture of born-again believers will end the Church Age, and then the demonic spirit Antichrist is incarnated, and it is time for the "strong delusion." The word *delusion* means "something accepted as true that is actually false or unreal." The term "strong delusion" is used by the Holy Spirit in connection with the coming of Antichrist in 2 Thessalonians 2:9-12, "(9) Even him, whose coming is after the working of Satan with all power and signs and lying wonders, (10) And with all deceivableness of unrighteousness in them that perish; because they received not the love of the truth, that they might be saved. (11) And for this cause God shall send them strong delusion, that they should believe a lie: (12) That they all might be damned who believed not the truth, but had pleasure in unrighteousness."

The "strong delusion" is a big lie that will be believed by "them that perish; because they received not the love of the truth, that they might be saved." In verse 2:9 we are told Antichrist will have all "power," all "signs," and all "lying wonders" in order to do the work of Satan, which is to deceive human beings. Also, notice the words: Signs and lying wonders are in plural form, meaning more than one. Antichrist will use his power, many signs, and many lying wonders to promote a single strong delusion or one big lie. The Antichrist himself could be the delusion. Antichrist is an incarnate demon spirit in human form. When he puts on flesh he is not going to try to convince the world that he is god. He is going to use all his power, signs, and lying wonders to convince the human population that he is a human being, a mere man. *That's* the big lie. The miracles he will perform are going to be real, not magician's tricks, and they will deceive, but the big deceit will be how and why he is able to perform miracles. If you think our education has made us too intelligent to accept a big lie as the truth, consider what the school system has done with the theory of evolution. From the damage that theory has done, I would not be surprised to find that *it* is the strong delusion. It calls the God who created all things a liar, and that is a big lie.

The "strong delusion" could center on the interpretation of life and death. Antichrist is a demon spirit and very much alive today. He knows life is not determined by human flesh. Our modern definition of life is as perverted and erroneous as our modern definition of death. The human definition of death is, "to cease to exist, extinction, a permanent cessation of all vital functions: the end of life." The human definition of life is "the quality that distinguishes a vital and functional being from a dead body." Both of these definitions are based on the premise that life and death are determined by the continuance of the physical human body. A demonic spirit is a conscious, intelligent being which can see, talk, think, persuade, and will. Demonic spirits are alive and it doesn't matter if they are in a physical body or out of a physical body, in an image or out of an image, in heaven, on the earth, or under the earth. Antichrist is a created eternal spirit, and even though he has departed from God to follow Satan, he is not dead, only separated from God. A human being does not have the ability, or means, to kill a demonic spirit, even if the spirit crosses into the physical realm and puts on flesh.

Antichrist will be in a physical body during the seven-year tribulation and he will heal a deadly head wound, but not to his physical head. He will heal the seventh head on the beast representing the last Gentile world government. We know from Rev. 13:14b that the wound is caused from a sword, "saying to them that dwell on the earth, that they should make an image to the beast, which had the wound by a sword, and did live." The sword is a weapon of war so it might be the Gog and Magog (Russian) invasion of the Middle East, or something not visible yet. Regardless, the European Common Market nations will suffer a blow so severe that the whole organization nearly collapses. Their recovery from this severe blow will be what astonishes the entire world. This will be how the organization and Antichrist gains world dominance, "and his deadly wound was healed; and all the world wondered after the beast" (Rev. 13:3b).

In Rev. 13:4 we are told how they worship him, "And they worshipped the dragon which gave power unto the beast: and they worshipped the beast, saying, Who is like unto the beast? who is able to make war with him?" Notice he will not be receiving worship through an image, or a mark, or a religious ceremony. Both he and Satan will receive worship through the natural reasoning process of the human mind, and their voiced opinions, "Who is like unto the beast? who is able to make war with him?"

D. Antichrist Speaks Great Things and Blasphemies.

Rev. 13:5a&6, "(5a) And there was given unto him a mouth speaking great things and blasphemies. . . . (6) And he opened his mouth in blasphemy against God, to blaspheme his name, and his tabernacle, and them that dwell in heaven." Antichrist blasphemes three things of God: his name, his tabernacle, and them that dwell in heaven. His name is Jesus Christ. His tabernacle was the Church. Them that dwell in heaven are the Christians removed from Earth in the rapture.

E. Antichrist Given Power to Continue Forty Two Months.

Rev. 13:5b, "and power was given unto him to continue forty [and] two months." Forty-two months equal three-and-one-half years, the first half of the seven-year tribulation period. During this time period Antichrist will stamp out false Christianity from Earth. The false church will be that group of individuals left on the earth after the rapture. It does not represent any single denomination or church congregation. It does represent all that remains of Christendom after Jesus removes the true born-again believers from the earth. The Laodicean church congregation of Rev. 3:14-22 will represent Christendom in its final form, with Jesus outside the congregation (verse 20). It will be a complacent organization which Jesus describes as repulsive in Revelation 3:15-16, "(15) I know thy works, that thou are neither cold nor hot: I would thou wert cold or hot. (16) So then because thou are lukewarm, and neither cold nor hot, I will spue (vomit) thee out of my mouth." There are very few things in this world more repulsive than an organization or individual pretending to be something they are not, or professing to have something they don't have. Leaving this reprobate organization today is much easier than leaving it by laying down your life during the Antichrist reign.

F. Antichrist to War With and Overcome the Saints.

Rev. 13:7a, "And it was given unto him to make war with the saints, and to overcome them." To make war with the saints and to overcome them means to kill them. These saints are not members of the true Church or the Bride of Christ, and they never will be. The Revelation makes a clear distinction between the Bride, who was raptured during the Laodicean Church Era, and the people killed during the seven-year tribulation period. The people killed in the Antichrist slaughter during the first three and one-half years of the tribulation will become the souls seen under the altar when Jesus opens the fifth seal, in Rev. 6:9-11. They will be joined by the sixth seal multitude of Rev. 7:9-17 who are killed by the False Prophet during the last half of the tribulation era. The fifth and sixth seal groups are presented as a single group in the Rev. 20:4, "And I saw thrones, and they sat upon them, and judgment was given unto them: and I saw the souls of them that were beheaded for the witness of Jesus, and for the word of God, and which had not worshipped the beast, neither his image, neither had received his mark upon their foreheads, or in their hands; and they lived and reigned with Christ a thousand years." The fifth seal group killed by Antichrist are the ones beheaded for the witness of Jesus and for the Word of God. Those who did not worship the beast, neither his image, neither had received his mark upon their foreheads, or in their hands, are the individuals who will be killed by the False Prophet during the last half of the tribulation era. The entire group will be resurrected to life and reign with Jesus during the millennial kingdom, "they lived and reigned with Christ a thousand years." The word *beheaded* may indicate that the guillotine will be used to kill these people. Regardless of the method, to be beheaded means physical death.

Don't let the word *saint* confuse you. A saint is a spirit-being or human being who chooses to believe God and do what he says. A saint during the Church Dispensation is a born-again believer. A saint during the Antichrist reign is any person who confesses Jesus as Lord and is killed for that confession. A saint during the False Prophet reign is any person who is killed for their refusal to worship the beast image and take the unforgivable mark.

That portion of the Laodicean congregation which preaches that only God can work miracles will exalt Antichrist to position of god, by reason of the "signs and lying wonders" he works. Rather than face the truth–that they missed the glory train to heaven–the mid- and post-tribulationist will jump on the Antichrist bandwagon. Those who continue preaching salvation under the Church promises will receive Antichrist's blessing and encouragement. When the people who denied Church signs before the rapture see the "signs and lying wonders" of Antichrist, they will reverse their denial and place the signs on top of their salvation package. The entire Antichrist group will use the signs to distinguish between "them that believe" and "them that don't believe," with one minor modification: "them that don't believe" will be killed by the Antichrist organization and "them that believe" will be killed by Jesus when he returns to establish the Kingdom Dispensation.

The European Common Market recovery plan formulated by Antichrist will gain him instant recognition as a dynamic politician. Since he has already converted the Laodicean congregation to his way of thinking, it will be no trouble for him to gain their support. These two factors will take Antichrist from being a nobody to being world ruler, in a relatively short period of time. The publicity he receives will result in instant popularity, and it will make you very unpopular just to disagree with something he says. He will dominate radio and television, and he will be the topic of discussion every time someone opens his mouth. His political ambition is to conquer the world, and what Napoleon and Hitler couldn't do in years with an army, he will do in weeks with his tongue. Antichrist will exalt the government as god and will teach that every knee in society must bow to its authority for the good of all. When he fulfills his political goal and signs the protection treaty with the Jews, there will be no further need for the Laodicean congregation, so he will turn on the organization and order its destruction. What the Jews received under Hitler's regime, the Laodicean congregation will receive under the Antichrist regime, with one exception: those who deny Jesus and the Word of God will escape death under Antichrist's command.

G. All Worship the Beast Except Those in the Book of Life.

Rev. 13:8, "And all that dwell upon the earth shall worship him, whose names are not written in the book of life of the Lamb slain from the foundation of the world." All "whose names are not written in the book of life of the Lamb slain from the foundation of the world" who are living on earth during the Antichrist reign will worship him. The only way to get your name recorded in the Book of Life is to accept God's plan of salvation that was finalized before the earth was even created. God's plan of salvation during the Antichrist reign will be for the Laodicean Church membership rejected at the Church rapture to be killed by Antichrist's organization for their witness of Jesus and the Word of God.

H. The Patience and Faith of the Saints.

Rev. 13:9-10, "(9) If any man have an ear, let him hear. (10) He that leadeth into captivity shall go into captivity: he that killeth with the sword must be killed with the sword. Here is the patience and the faith of the saints." "He that leadeth into captivity shall go into captivity" is a message for the pastors of the Laodicean Churches and the congregation which follows with their eyes closed. In 2 Peter chapter 2, the Holy Spirit warns of false prophets and teachers, and the damnable heresies they bring into the church. Their purpose is to entangle the congregation in enough error to cause them to be overcome, instead of overcomers. Here is how he explains it in 2 Peter 2:17-22, "(17) These are wells without water, clouds that are carried with a tempest; to whom the mist of darkness is reserved for ever. (18) For when they speak great swelling words of vanity, they allure through the lusts of the flesh, through much wantonness, those that were clean escaped from them who live in error. (19) While they promise them liberty, they themselves are the servants of corruption: for of whom a man is overcome, of the same is he brought in bondage. (20) For if after they have escaped the pollutions of the world through the knowledge of the Lord and Saviour Jesus Christ, they are again entangled therein, and overcome, the latter end is worse with them than the beginning. (21) For it had been better for them not to have known the way of righteousness, than, after they have known it, to turn from the holy commandment delivered unto them. (22) But it is happened unto them according to the true proverb, The dog is turned to his own vomit again; and the sow that was washed to her wallowing in the mire."

Since the confirmation of the Jews' protection treaty is the first day of the seven-year tribulation period, it is obvious that Antichrist is actively and personally involved in the political affairs of the European Common Market nations *prior to* the beginning of the tribulation era. In other words, the European Common Market nations will have already received their deadly wound, Antichrist's recovery program will have already been successful, and he will already be sole political spokesman of the organization, before the tribulation period begins. Since Antichrist cannot be incarnated until after the Holy Spirit has completed and removed the Church, the rapture must occur in sufficient time to allow for the ascendancy of Antichrist to top position in the European Common Market. The obvious event to precede the seven-year tribulation period which could instigate the rise of Antichrist could be the Russian invasion of the Middle East in the Gog and Magog account.

The first strike nuclear capability of Russia could eliminate the United States as a military crutch for the Nation of Israel, which would leave Israel to the mercy of its God, and leave the armies of the European Common Market nations as the only real military threat to the invasion. The same first strike ability could be used to cripple Europe, eliminate the threat of military intervention, and provide the deadly wound needed for the Antichrist recovery program. If the rapture was to occur at the instant of the nuclear attack, the spotlight would be taken off the rapture, and Jesus would truly come as a thief in the night. He would come not only suddenly, but nearly unnoticed, since the civil authorities and the news media would be too busy with the nuclear attack reports to listen to stories of a few missing bodies. The seven years of plenty (or three and one-half, if it overlaps the tribulation era) following the attack, would give Antichrist the time he needs to accomplish his recovery program and be exalted to sole spokesman of the organization before the time of the tribulation period. Bible students know that it will be God who destroys five-sixths of the invading Russian army. Although the nations will be able to see that it was supernatural intervention, the "signs and lying wonders" of Antichrist will also be supernatural, so he may be able to steal the credit for destroying the Russian army. This publicity would make him savior of the Jews, catapult him to instant worldwide popularity, and account for why the Jews might accept him as their Messiah.

Since the Jews have already rejected Jesus, Antichrist could use their blindness and exalt them as God's chosen people. This will not only discredit Christianity, it will allow him to mix Judaism with the strong delusion. By doing this he will make it appear that anyone rejecting what he says is rejecting both Old and New Testament Scripture. He may preach that the nuclear exchange ended the tribulation era and that the Kingdom Era has begun. His recovery program with the European Common Market nations will be most convincing, as will the years of plenty in the land of Israel. By preaching that the Kingdom Era has begun, Antichrist could use the parable of the wheat and tares as justification for eliminating rebels and offenders from his kingdom when he turns on the Laodicean congregation.

In Ezekiel 38:18 we are told the Gog invasion brings fury to the face of God, "And it shall come to pass at the same time when Gog shall come against the land of Israel, saith the Lord God, that my fury shall come up in my face." This change of policy could very well mean that the rapture of the Church had already occurred before this point in time. Jesus came two thousand years ago as our Redeemer, he could say, "I came not to judge the world, but to save the world" (John 12:47). In John 5:22 we are told, "For the Father judgeth no man, but hath committed all judgment unto the Son." When Jesus completed the work of redemption he returned to heaven, where he has functioned in the office of High Priest for the Church, Hebrews 8:1, "Now of the things which we have spoken this is the sum: We have such an high priest, who is set on the right hand of the throne of the Majesty in the heavens." Jesus will continue to function in the office of High Priest until the Church Dispensation ends. During the transition from the Church to Kingdom Dispensation, Jesus will function in the office of Judge, and stain his garment with the blood of his enemies. During the Kingdom Dispensation, Jesus will function in the office of King of the Jews and of the whole earth. We are told that Jesus is the Judge of the living and dead in Acts 10:42, "And he commanded us to preach unto the people, and to testify that it is he which was ordained of God to be the Judge of quick (living) and dead." In 1 Peter 4:1-5 we are told that this is the time the enemies of the Church will give their account, "(1) Forasmuch then as Christ hath suffered for us in the flesh, arm yourselves likewise with the same mind: for he that hath suffered in the flesh hath ceased from sin; (2) That he no longer should live the rest of his time in the flesh to the lusts of men, but to the will of God. (3) For the time past of our life may suffice us to have wrought the will of the Gentiles, when we walked in lasciviousness, lusts, excess of wine, revellings, banquetings, and abominable idolatries: (4) Wherein they think it strange that ye run not with them to the same excess of riot, speaking evil of you: (5) Who shall give account to him that is ready to judge the quick and the dead." We are told "when" in 2 Timothy 4:1, "I charge thee therefore before God, and the Lord Jesus Christ, who shall judge the quick and the dead at his appearing and his kingdom." The fact that Jesus is wearing his Judge garment instead of his High Priest garment at the time of this invasion, is another good indication that the rapture of the Church will occur before the Gog invasion.

We can also see the distinction between the Church Dispensation, Jesus as Judge, and Jesus as King in Luke 4:16-21, "(16) And he came to Nazareth, where he had been brought up: and, as his custom was, he went into the synagogue on the sabbath day, and stood up for to read. (17) And there was delivered unto him the book of the prophet Esaias. And when he had opened the book, he found the place where it was written, (18) The Spirit of the Lord is upon me, because he hath anointed me to preach the gospel to the poor; he hath sent me to heal the brokenhearted, to preach deliverance to the captives, and recovering of sight to the blind, to set at liberty them that are bruised, (19) To preach the acceptable year of the Lord. (20) And he closed the book, and he gave it again to the minister, and sat down. And the eyes of all them that were in the synagogue were fastened on him. (21) And he began to say unto them, This day is this scripture fulfilled in your ears." Verses 18 and 19 are the Church Dispensation, and that is what the members should have been doing for the past two thousand years. As we read the entire passage out of the Book of Isaiah, notice that Jesus stopped reading in the middle of the passage where the Church Age ends. "The day of vengeance of our God" is the transition from the Church to Kingdom Dispensation, when Jesus is Judge. The remainder of the passage is the Kingdom Dispensation. Isaiah 61:1-3, "(1) The spirit of the Lord God is upon me; because the Lord hath anointed me to preach good tidings unto the meek; he hath sent me to bind up the brokenhearted, to proclaim liberty to the captives, and the opening of the prison to them that are bound; (2)

To proclaim the acceptable year of the Lord, and the day of vengeance of our God: to comfort all that mourn; (3) To appoint unto them that mourn in Zion, to give unto them beauty for ashes, the oil of joy for mourning, the garment of praise for the spirit of heaviness; that they might be called trees of righteousness, the planting of the Lord, that he might be glorified."

The mourners of Isaiah 61:1-3, are identified in Zechariah 12:9-14, "(9) And it shall come to pass in that day, that I will seek to destroy all the nations that come against Jerusalem. (10) And I will pour upon the house of David, and upon the inhabitants of Jerusalem, the spirit of grace and of supplications: and they shall look upon me whom they have pierced, and they shall mourn for him, as one mourneth for his only son, and shall be in bitterness for him, as one that is in bitterness for his firstborn. (11) In that day shall there be a great mourning in Jerusalem, as the mourning of Hadadrimmon in the valley of Megiddon. (12) And the land shall mourn, every family apart; the family of the house of David apart, and their wives apart; the family of the house of Nathan apart, and their wives apart; (13) The family of the house of Levi apart, and their wives apart; the family of Shimei apart, and their wives apart; (14) All the families that remain, every family apart, and their wives apart." "That day" is the day of the battle of Armageddon, when Jesus returns in great glory to end the seven-year tribulation period and to begin the Kingdom Dispensation. From this we can see, "the day of vengeance of our God" begins with the destruction of five-sixths of the Gog and Magog army and ends with the destruction of the Armageddon army. Since we already know the great tribulation covers a seven-year period of history, if we add the seven years of prosperity in Israel (Ezekiel 38:8-10) following the destruction of the Gog and Magog army, we can see that the "day of vengeance of our God" may cover a fourteen year period of human history. This seven years of plenty followed by seven years of famine is in agreement with the revelation of Jesus in the life of Joseph.

In review, Joseph was one of the twelve sons of Israel (or Jacob). In Genesis 37:5-8, Joseph had a dream in which his sheaf stood upright and the eleven sheaves of his brothers did obeisance to it. In Genesis 37:9-11, he had a dream in which the sun, moon and eleven stars made obeisance to him. His brothers understood the dream of the sheaves as Joseph reigning over them. The family understood the second dream as them bowing before Joseph. Because of the dreams, Joseph's brothers envied him and plotted to kill him to make sure the dream didn't come true (Genesis 37:20). Reuben persuaded them to throw Joseph, alive, into a pit so his blood would not be on their hands. Reuben intended to rescue Joseph from the pit and deliver him to his father (Genesis 37:21-22). While Joseph's brothers were eating bread they noticed a company of Ishmeelite merchants en route to Egypt. They took Joseph out of the pit and sold him to the merchants. In Egypt, Joseph was sold to Potiphar as a slave. When Joseph refused the advances of Potiphar's wife, she accused him of rape, and he ended up in prison (Gen.

39:1-23). In prison he interpreted the dreams of the butler and baker, (Gen. 40:1-23). Two years later, when Pharaoh had dreams the butler remembered Joseph in prison and told Pharaoh how Joseph had correctly interpreted his dream (Gen. 41:1-13).

Pharaoh dreamed of seven fat cows being eaten by seven lean cows (Genesis 41:1-4). In his second dream he saw a stock of corn with seven full ears. After a blast of east wind he saw a second stock spring up, with seven empty ears. He then saw the seven empty ears devour the seven full ears, (Genesis 41:5-8). Joseph interpreted his dreams as seven years of plenty, followed by seven years of famine. Joseph then recommended that Pharaoh select a man to oversee storing twenty percent of the food and grain during the seven years of plenty, which could be used for survival during the seven years of famine (Genesis 41:25-36). Pharaoh selected Joseph and exalted him to the highest position in the land, second only to himself (Genesis 41:37-46). The seven years of plenty is recorded in Genesis 41:46-52. The seven years of famine is in Genesis 41:53-57, "(53) And the seven-years of plenteousness, that was in the land of Egypt, were ended. (54) And the seven years of dearth began to come, according as Joseph had said: and the dearth was in all lands; but in all the land of Egypt there was bread. (55) And when all the land of Egypt was famished, the people cried to Pharaoh for bread: and Pharaoh said unto all the Egyptians, Go unto Joseph; what he saith to you, do. (56) And the famine was over all the face of the earth: and Joseph opened all the storehouses, and sold unto the Egyptians; and the famine waxed sore in the land of Egypt. (57) And all countries came into Egypt to Joseph for to buy corn; because that the famine was so sore in all lands."

The famine account continues in Genesis 47:13-26. Joseph sold the stored grain for money. When the money failed he traded the grain for the Egyptians' livestock. When their livestock was gone, he traded the Egyptian's grain for their land. In the process the Egyptians lost everything they owned, and Pharaoh owned everything. Joseph then redistributed the people, Genesis 47:21, "And as for the people, he removed them to cities from one end of the borders of Egypt even to the other end thereof." He then gave them seed and made it a law that 20 percent of their increase would be given to Pharaoh. During the process the priests were excluded, Genesis 47:22, "Only the land of the priests bought he not; for the priests had a portion assigned them of Pharaoh, and did eat their portion which Pharaoh gave them: wherefore they sold not their lands." Genesis 47:26, "And Joseph made it a law over the land of Egypt unto this day, that Pharaoh should have the fifth part; except the land of the priests only, which became not Pharaoh's."

Genesis 41:57-47:13 is the record of Joseph being reunited with his family. During the seven years of famine Jacob, Joseph's father heard that grain was available in Egypt. He sent Joseph's brothers to Egypt to purchase grain. They brought the grain from Joseph, and although they didn't recognize Joseph as their brother, he recognized them. Eventually, Joseph revealed himself to them, and had the family move to the land of Goshen, in Egypt, where he sustained them through the famine.

Jesus is the one selected by the Sovereign Father to rule during the Kingdom Dispensation as Joseph ruled Egypt during the famine. When Jesus came to his 'brothers' (the Jews) they rejected that revelation, plotted his death, and threw him in the pit to die. Three days later, he came out of the pit, very much alive, and disappeared from their sight, as the veil of spiritual blindness covered the Nation. Unbeknown to his 'brothers,' Jesus has been exalted to the highest position in the creation, second only to the Father, and a people called Gentiles will bow to him. When the seven years of plenty after the Gog and Magog invasion ends, Jesus' 'brothers' will be in the famine of the great tribulation, and they will call on their God for deliverance. Their God will say, "Go unto Jesus; what he saith to you, do." It is during that famine that Jesus will reveal himself to his 'brothers', and they will become the mourners of Zechariah 12:9-14.

The pronoun "I", representing the speaker in the account of the Gog and Magog invasion, is Jesus Christ. He is the one with the holy name, the Lord, and the Holy One in Israel. There is no mention of mourning in the Gog and Magog account, because in Israel it will be a time of rejoicing. Their God has just stopped the mighty Russian army from invading their land. The Gog and Magog account is Jesus beginning to "build again the tabernacle of David" (Acts 15:16). Some in the Nation will be repeating Matthew 21:5, "Tell ye the daughter of Sion, Behold, thy King cometh unto thee, meek, and sitting upon an ass, and a colt the foal of an ass." The majority of the Nation will be repeating Matthew 21:9, "And the multitudes that went before, and that followed, cried, saying, Hosanna to the son of David: Blessed is he that cometh in the name of the Lord; Hosanna in the highest." The last time the Jews sang that song, it took Satan and his crew exactly one week to change their tune. Seven days later, Jesus heard the very same crowd crying, "Crucify him, crucify him." When the number of Jews accepting Jesus as King Jesus reaches 144 thousand (twelve thousand from each tribe), they will be sealed. This puts Earth at midpoint in the seven-year tribulation period, and three and one-half years from the Armageddon invasion, the return of Jesus in glory, and the Kingdom Dispensation. When Jesus returns in glory after the tribulation period, the Jews will look on him whom they have pierced, and they will mourn. The Gentiles will see the final fulfillment of the prophecies concerning regathering the Jews. At this point Earth will enter the Kingdom Dispensation, and King Jesus will rule the Gentile nations with a rod of iron, from the City of Jerusalem. That rod of iron is the Word of God being published by the Jews and enforced by King Jesus.

Three and one-half years prior to the sealing of the 144 thousand Jews, the scornful men at Jerusalem (Isaiah 28:14-22) will confirm the protection treaty with Antichrist, the spokesman for the ten nation European Common

Market. Although this event will introduce the seven-year tribulation period, Jews will be unaffected during the first half of the tribulation period because they will be protected from the Antichrist massacre by the protection treaty confirmed at the beginning of his reign. Many wonder why the Jews will not recognize Antichrist as the enemy. The basic answer to this question is that they did not recognize Jesus. In rejecting Jesus, they alienated themselves from the New Covenant promise of the indwelling Holy Spirit. Without the Holy Spirit, an individual does not have the capability to understand spiritual truth, let alone prophecy. Jesus put it this way in John 16:12-13, "(12) I have yet many things to say unto you, but ye cannot bear them now. (13) Howbeit when he, the Spirit of truth, is come, he will guide you into all truth: for he shall not speak of himself; but whatsoever he shall hear, that shall he speak: and he will shew you things to come."

The covenant protects them from physical death by the Antichrist organization, but they must watch the slaughter of the Laodicean congregation. What they see is distasteful, but what they don't see is God provoking them to jealousy, Deuteronomy 32:21, "They have moved me to jealousy with that which is not God; they have provoked me to anger with their vanities: and I will move them to jealousy with those which are not a people; I will provoke them to anger with a foolish nation." One thousand nine hundred and ninety-six years of history show that the Church is not going to provoke the Jews to jealousy. I see worldwide judgment on the horizon, not worldwide Church revival. The Prophet Joel spoke of a former and latter rain in Joel 2:23-24, "(23) Be glad then, ye children of Zion, and rejoice in the Lord your God: for he hath given you the former rain moderately, and he will cause to come down for you the rain, the former rain, and the latter rain in the first month. (24) And the floors shall be full of wheat, and the vats shall overflow with wine and oil." The former rain came on the Day of Pentecost when God poured out his Spirit on 120 Jews in the upper room, which began the Church Dispensation. We just saw the beginning of the latter rain in the Gog and Magog account in Ezekiel 39:29, "Neither will I hide my face any more from them: for I have poured out my spirit upon the house of Israel, saith the Lord God." The downpour on the house of Israel will be in the first month (or beginning) of the Kingdom Dispensation. That is when "the floors shall be full of wheat, and the vats shall overflow with wine and oil." This latter rain will be the fulfillment of Jeremiah 31:31-34 and 33:37-41.

Another reason why I don't see a worldwide revival preceding the rapture is because a dispensational period ends in judgment, not revival. The moderate latter rain came in the Gog and Magog invasion. According to Jeremiah, the downpour of the latter rain came with the return of Jesus and the destruction of the Armageddon army, which begins the Kingdom Dispensation. What God pours out at the end of the one thousand years is fire, not the Holy Spirit, Rev. 20:7-9, "(7) And when the thousand years are expired, Satan shall be loosed out of his prison, (8) And shall go out to deceive the nation which are in the four quarters of the earth, Gog and Magog, to gather them together to battle: the number of whom is as the sand of the sea. (9) And they went up on the breadth of the earth, and compassed the camp of the saints about, and the beloved city: and fire came down from God out of heaven, and devoured them." In Ezekiel 39:7b Jesus said, "and the heathen shall know that I am the Lord, the Holy One in Israel." God never calls his sons or daughters heathens. In Ezekiel 38:23, God says, "Thus will I magnify myself, and sanctify myself; and I will be known in the eyes of many nations, and they shall know that I am the Lord." In Ezekiel 39:21, he says, "And I will set my glory among the heathen, and all the heathen shall see my judgment that I have executed, and my hand that I have laid upon them." The heathen nations need to be alerted to the fact that Jesus is God, the Holy One in Israel, because when He returns after the tribulation they must stand before him in the Matthew 25:31-46, sheep and goat nation judgment. This judgment will be based solely on how the nations treated the Jews during the tribulation period. At midpoint in the tribulation the False Prophet will break the Antichrist protection covenant, demand that the mark of the beast be taken, introduce the beast image, and issue the ultimatum to worship or die. This is the abomination of desolation that will cause the flight of the Jews, when they go into hiding. To hide or help a Jew at this point in time will mean risking your own life. The nations will be judged on how they handled that situation in the sheep and goat judgment by King Jesus (Matthew 25:31-46). Individuals from every nation who persecuted the Jews will be gathered and burned as tares, along with "all things that offend and them which do iniquity" (Matthew 13:24-30 and 13:34-43). These judgments will decide who enters the Kingdom Dispensation and who doesn't. Because of the Gog and Magog invasion, no one will be able to stand before King Jesus and say, "I didn't know."

How long God will be able to continue working with a generation of Christians, and a generation of Jews, before the two different programs clash, is an unknown factor. The Philadelphia congregation already know that Jesus will be the Holy One in Israel. In fact, they have already completed the Revelation chapter 5 search, and their search for the worthy One has ended with Jesus. I am not trying to date the rapture, I know and believe, Matthew 24:36, "But of that day and hour knoweth no man, no, not the angels of heaven, but my Father only." and Matthew 24:44, "Therefore be ye also ready: for in such an hour as ye think not the Son of man cometh." I also know the fig tree is the Nation of Israel, and being a farm boy, I know what season it is when the trees, "putteth forth leaves." If Jesus doesn't rapture the Church before the Gog and Magog invasion is stopped, I will be able to say "the day of vengeance of our God" has already begun. Knowing that this is a fourteen year period, seven years of plenty, plus seven years of famine for Israel–it would be obvious that the Jews are fourteen years away from the Kingdom Dispensation. The Church must be raptured within the next seven years.

What isn't obvious is that this fourteen year period can be shortened by three and one-half years and still be accurate from a prophetic viewpoint. When the Jews confirm the protection covenant with Antichrist, will the next three and one-half years be both a period of physical prosperity and spiritual famine, because of their spiritual blindness? In other words, when the Russian army is stopped, the Jews could have three and one-half years of prosperity, and then confirm the Antichrist protection covenant. That covenant would give them three and one-half more years of prosperity, while Antichrist eliminates the Laodicean congregation. At the end of that period the Jews would have had their seven years of prosperity. When the False Prophet breaks the Antichrist covenant, the Jews see that "the treacherous dealer dealeth treacherously" (Isaiah 21:1-10). Realizing their error, they would have been living in the famine of spiritual blindness for three and one-half years, with three and one-half years to go until the Kingdom Dispensation, for a total of seven years of famine. If this were the case, when the Gog and Magog invasion is stopped, I would say the Jews are ten-and-one-half years from the Kingdom Dispensation, and the Church must be raptured within the next three and one-half years.

Regardless of how that prophecy is fulfilled, the Philadelphia congregation must be raptured before, or when, the Jews confirm the Antichrist protection covenant. The last person saved in the Philadelphia congregation will be the last Church member. The first person from the rejected Laodicean congregation to be killed by the Antichrist organization, for their refusal to deny Jesus and the word of God, will be the first person in the Revelation 6:9-11 fifth seal group. During the Church Dispensation all the people on earth have been categorized into three groups: Jews, Gentiles, and the Church. This division can be seen in 1 Corinthians 10:32, "Give none offense, neither to the Jews, nor to the Gentiles, nor to the church of God." The Church group will consist of born-again believers; the Jews are actual descendants of Abraham; and the Gentiles are everyone else. When the Church leaves the planet in the rapture, the remaining population will be divided into two groups: the Jews and the Gentiles. The rejected Laodicean church congregation will be included in the Gentile group. The Laodicean Church will be the segment of the Gentiles to provoke the Jews to jealousy, not the Church. If the Church has any part in provoking the Jews to jealousy, it will be in the instant it is raptured.

Reconsider Deuteronomy 32:21, "They have moved me to jealousy with that which is not God; they have provoked me to anger with their vanities: and I will move them to jealousy with those which are not a people; I will provoke them to anger with a foolish nation." Since when is God's opinion of born-again believers "those which are not a people"? From God's point of view, that describes them who say they are, but are not. Listen to how

God described the Jewish Nation, just before he made that statement, Deuteronomy 32:18-20, "(18) Of the Rock that begat thee thou are unmindful, and hast forgotten God that formed thee. (19) And when the Lord saw it, he abhorred them, because of the provoking of his sons, and his daughters. (20) And he said, I will hide my face from them, I will see what their end shall be: for they are a very foward generation, children in whom is no faith." God was describing the nation at the point in time when their disobedience to his Word makes them no different than the heathen Gentile. That is also the description of the Laodicean church congregation at the time of the rapture. It is these "children in whom is no faith" who provokes God to the judgment of the Church in the rapture, when he separates the faithful from the faithless.

When the fake Christians face Antichrist, they gladly deny Jesus because they never believed in him in the first place. When the deceived Christians face Antichrist, many refuse to deny, which results in their death and salvation as members of the Rev. 6:9-11 fifth seal group. This slaughter will touch the Jewish population and move them to jealousy. The event will take place in the seven-year tribulation period after the Church leaves Earth. "Those which are not a people" are the Laodicean congregation which was rejected by God at the rapture of the Church. The statement "I will provoke them to anger with a foolish nation" will be fulfilled during the last half of the tribulation period. The Jews are provoked to anger when the Antichrist protection covenant is broken by the False Prophet, and he starts slaughtering them. The foolish nation will be the remains of the European Common Market nations, after the False Prophet eliminates three of the ten nations. In the Rev. 17:9-18 account of world history it is the eightth kingdom listed in verse 17:11. The destruction of false Christianity by Antichrist will open the door, or more precisely, the bottomless pit (Rev. 17:8, 13:11-18), for the reincarnation of the False Prophet and his three and one-half year (Daniel 12:7) reign of terror on Earth.

Ministry of the Two Faithful Witnesses

The ministry of the two faithful witnesses is recorded in Revelation 11:1-13, "(1) And there was given me a reed like unto a rod: and the angel stood, saying, Rise, and measure the temple of God, and the altar, and them that worship therein. (2) But the court which is without the temple leave out, and measure it not; for it is given unto the Gentiles: and the holy city shall they tread under foot forty [and] two months. (3) And I will give [power] unto my two witnesses, and they shall prophesy a thousand two hundred [and] threescore days, clothed in sackcloth. (4) These are the two olive trees, and the two candlesticks standing before the God of the earth. (5) And if any man will hurt them, fire proceedeth out of their mouth, and devoureth their enemies: and if any man will hurt them, he must in this manner be killed. (6) These have power to shut heaven, that it rain not in the days of their prophecy: and have power over waters to turn them to blood, and to smite the earth with all plagues, as often as they will. (7) And when they shall have finished their testimony, the beast that ascendeth out of the bottomless pit shall make war against them, and shall overcome them, and kill them. (8) And their dead bodies [shall lie] in the street of the great city, which spiritually is called Sodom and Egypt, where also our Lord was crucified. (9) And they of the people and kindreds and tongues and nations shall see their dead bodies three days and an half, and shall not suffer their dead bodies to be put in graves. (10) And they that dwell upon the earth shall rejoice over them, and make merry, and shall send gifts one to another; because these two prophets tormented them that dwelt on the earth. (11) And after three days and an half the Spirit of life from God entered into them, and they stood upon their feet; and great fear fell upon them which saw them. (12) And they heard a great voice from heaven saying unto them, Come up hither. And they ascended up to heaven in a cloud; and their enemies beheld them. (13) And the same hour was there a great earthquake, and the tenth part of the city fell, and in the earthquake were slain of men seven thousand: and the remnant were affrighted, and gave glory to the God of heaven."

A. John Told to take Measurements.

Rev. 11:1-2, "(1) And there was given me a reed like unto a rod: and the angel stood, saying, Rise, and measure the temple of God, and the altar, and them that worship therein. (2) But the court which is without the temple leave out, and measure it not; for it is given unto the Gentiles: and the holy city shall they tread under foot forty [and] two months." John was instructed to measure three things: the temple of God, the altar, and them that worship therein. The outer court was not measured because it was given to the Gentiles for forty-two months, or the first half of the seven-year tribulation era.

B. The Two Witnesses to Prophesy 1260 Days (three and a half years).

Rev. 11:3-6, "(3) And I will give [power] unto my two witnesses, and they shall prophesy a thousand two hundred [and] threescore days, clothed in sackcloth. (4) These are the two olive trees, and the two candlesticks standing before the God of the earth. (5) And if any man will hurt them, fire proceedeth out of their mouth, and devoureth their enemies: and if any man will hurt them, he must in this manner be killed. (6) These have power to shut heaven, that it rain not in the days of their prophecy: and have power over waters to turn them to blood, and to smite the earth with all plagues, as often as they will."

Power will be given to the two witnesses to prophecy for 1260 days or three and one-half years, which is the first half of the tribulation period. They will foretell that what Antichrist is doing to the deceived Christians is going to happen to all the deceived, "We-believe-in-God" crowd.

In verse 4 we are told, "These (the two witnesses) are the two olive trees, and the two candlesticks standing before the God of the earth." Zechariah saw these witnesses in Zechariah Chapter 4. Verse 2 and 3 reads, "(2) And said unto me, What seest thou? And I said, I have looked, and behold a candlestick all [of] gold, with a bowl upon the top of it, and his seven lamps thereon, and seven pipes to the seven lamps, which [are] upon the top thereof: (3) And two olive trees by it, one upon the right [side] of the bowl, and the other upon the left [side] thereof." From Rev. 4:5b we know the seven lamps represent the Holy Spirit, "and [there were] seven lamps of fire burning before the throne, which are the seven Spirits of God." The discussion between Zechariah and the angel continues in verse 4:11-14, "(11) Then answered I, and said unto him, What [are] these two olive trees upon the right [side] of the candlestick and upon the left [side] thereof? (12) And I answered again, and said unto him, What [be these] two olive branches which through the two golden pipes empty the golden [oil] out of themselves? (13) And he answered me and said, Knowest thou not what these [be]? And I said, No, my lord. (14) Then said he, These [are] the two anointed ones, that stand by the Lord of the whole earth."

It is obvious from verses 5 and 6 that these two witnesses will be a major problem for Antichrist and his organization, "(5) And if any man will hurt them, fire proceedeth out of their mouth, and devoureth their enemies: and if any man will hurt them, he must in this manner be killed. (6) These have power to shut heaven, that it rain not in the days of their prophecy: and have power over waters to turn them to blood, and to smite the earth with all plagues, as often as they will."

C. The Two Witnesses Killed by the False Prophet.

Rev. 11:7, "And when they shall have finished their testimony, the beast that ascendeth out of the bottomless pit shall make war against them, and shall overcome them, and kill them." When they have finished their testimony is a midpoint in the tribulation era. This means Laodicean congregation has been reduced to zero and the fifth seal group of tribulation dead is completed. The "beast that ascendeth out of the bottomless pit" will be the reincarnated False Prophet. Everything the Antichrist organization does to destroy the two witnesses will backfire, but the False Prophet will war with them, overcome them, and kill them.

D. Treatment of their Dead Bodies.

Rev. 11:8-10, "(8) And their dead bodies [shall lie] in the street of the great city, which spiritually is called Sodom and Egypt, where also our Lord was crucified. (9) And they of the people and kindreds and tongues and nations shall see their dead bodies three days and an half, and shall not suffer their dead bodies to be put in graves. (10) And they that dwell upon the earth shall rejoice over them, and make merry, and shall send gifts one to another; because these two prophets tormented them that dwelt on the earth."

The False Prophet will kill them and let the world look on their dead bodies in the streets of Jerusalem for three and one-half days. The world will celebrate their death with a celebration comparable to Christmas season in the United States.

E. The Two Witnesses Resurrected to Life After Three and a Half Days.

Rev. 11:11-12, "(11) And after three days and an half the Spirit of life from God entered into them, and they stood upon their feet; and great fear fell upon them which saw them. (12) And they heard a great voice from heaven saying unto them, Come up hither. And they ascended up to heaven in a cloud; and their enemies beheld them." At the end of the three and one-half day period the two witnesses will be resurrected to life and ascend into heaven as their enemies watch. The death of these two witnesses and their resurrection three and one-half days later will definitely be a sign to the Nation of Israel that they are three and one-half years away from the kingdom God promised their forefathers. The two witnesses' resurrection is God's stamp of approval on the truth of their ministry.

F. Seven Thousand Die in an Earthquake.

Rev. 11:13, "And the same hour was there a great earthquake, and the tenth part of the city fell, and in the earthquake were slain of men seven thousand: and the remnant were affrighted, and gave glory to the God of heaven."

This great earthquake is the same worldwide earthquake we saw when Jesus opened the sixth seal in Rev. 6:12-17. In Jerusalem one-tenth of the city will fall and seven thousand will die. The survivors will be affrighted and will give glory to the God of heaven. This brings us to the last three and one-half year period of the tribulation era, under the reign of the False Prophet. The flashback account of the two witnesses ends in Rev. 11:13, and verse 14 continues with the statement, "The second woe is past; and, behold, the third woe cometh quickly." In the sequential events of Revelation the second woe is the sixth trumpet and the third woe is the seventh trumpet.

Who these two witnesses will be is debatable. We know they will be fearless in speaking out against the corruption in both political and religious circles, as were the Prophet Elijah and John the Baptist. Because of the similarity between their miracles (Rev. 11:6) and the miracles in Egypt (Exodus chapters 7-11), many believe one of the witnesses will be Moses. Enoch (Genesis 5:21-24) and Elijah (2 Kings 2:1-18) are the only two human beings in the entire recorded history of man, who never experienced physical death. Because both of these men were translated, I believe they will return to the earth as the two witnesses and experience physical death at the hand of the False Prophet. I also believe they are "the two anointed ones" Zechariah saw. This prophesy is still too far in the future to focus clearly on their names. It doesn't have to be any of the men I have mentioned. God could fulfill this prophesy with you and your next door neighbor, if both of you have the knowledge and faith in the Word of God needed to accomplish the task.

Judgment of Babylon During the Antichrist Reign

The judgment of Babylon will occur throughout the entire seven-year tribulation era. The part judged during the Antichrist reign is recorded in Revelation 17:1-18, "(1) And there came one of the seven angels which had the seven vials, and talked with me, saying unto me, Come hither; I will shew unto thee the judgment of the great whore that sitteth upon many waters: (2) With whom the kings of the earth have committed fornication, and the inhabitants of the earth have been made drunk with the wine of her fornication. (3) So he carried me away in the spirit into the wilderness: and I saw a woman sit upon a scarlet coloured beast, full of names of blasphemy, having seven heads and ten horns. (4) And the woman was arrayed in purple and scarlet colour, and decked with gold and precious stones and pearls, having a golden cup in her hand full of abominations and filthiness of her fornication: (5) And upon her forehead [was] a name written, MYSTERY, BABYLON THE GREAT, THE MOTHER OF HARLOTS AND ABOMINATIONS OF THE EARTH. (6) And I saw the woman drunken with the blood of the saints, and with the blood of the martyrs of Jesus: and when I saw her, I wondered with great admiration. (7) And the angel said unto me, Wherefore didst thou marvel? I will tell thee the mystery of the woman, and of the beast that carrieth her, which hath the seven heads and ten horns. (8) The beast that thou sawest was, and is not; and shall ascend out of the bottomless pit, and go into perdition: and they that dwell on the earth shall wonder, whose names were not written in the book of life from the foundation of the world, when they behold the beast that was, and is not, and yet is. (9) And here [is] the mind which hath wisdom. The seven heads are seven mountains, on which the woman sitteth. (10) And there are seven kings: five are fallen, and one is, [and] the other is not yet come; and when he cometh, he must continue a short space. (11) And the beast that was, and is not, even he is the eighth, and is of the seven, and goeth into perdition. (12) And the ten horns which thou sawest are ten kings, which have received no kingdom as yet; but receive power as kings one hour with the beast. (13) These have one mind, and shall give their power and strength unto the beast. (14) These shall make war with the Lamb, and the Lamb shall overcome them: for he is Lord of lords, and King of kings: and they that are with him [are] called, and chosen, and faithful. (15) And he saith unto me, The waters which thou sawest, where the whore sitteth, are peoples, and multitudes, and nations, and tongues. (16) And the ten horns which thou sawest upon the beast, these shall hate the whore, and shall make her desolate and naked, and shall eat her flesh, and burn her with fire. (17) For God hath put in their hearts to fulfil his will, and to agree, and give their kingdom unto the beast, until the words of God shall be fulfilled. (18) And the woman which thou sawest is that great city, which reigneth over the kings of the earth."

Revelation chapter 17 is a flashback which gives us the judgment of the great whore, in which the mystery of the woman and the beast are revealed. Chapter 18 deals with the judgment of the Babylon organization. The information is given after the last vial judgment was executed and the last verses in chapter 18 brings us back to the point in time when the last vial judgment was executed. The next sequential event in the Revelation is recorded in Rev. 19:1-3 and is a record of the inhabitants of heaven rejoicing over the destruction of the great whore.

A. John to See the Judgment of the Great Whore.

Rev. 17:1-2, "(1) And there came one of the seven angels which had the seven vials, and talked with me, saying unto me, Come hither; I will shew unto thee the judgment of the great whore that sitteth upon many waters: (2) With whom the kings of the earth have committed fornication, and the inhabitants of the earth have been made drunk with the wine of her fornication."

John is to be shown "the judgment of the great whore that sitteth upon many waters." The woman labeled the great whore is Satan which is obvious from Rev. 17:5, "And upon her forehead [was] a name written, MYSTERY, BABYLON THE GREAT, THE MOTHER OF HARLOTS AND ABOMINATIONS OF THE EARTH." In Rev. 17:15 the waters are identified, "And he saith unto me, The waters which thou sawest, where the whore sitteth, are peoples, and multitudes, and nations, and tongues." The phrase, "peoples, and multitudes, and nations, and tongues" includes all the different social orders on Earth, the whole human race, not just the deceived Christian population. Also notice that the whore is sitting, which means society is supporting her.

In 17:2 the angel continues the description of the great whore by saying, "With whom the kings of the earth have committed fornication, and the inhabitants of the earth have been made drunk with the wine of her fornication." The inhabitants of the earth are human beings, while the kings of the earth are the fallen angels who joined Satan's rebellion. The kings of the earth committed fornication with the great whore when they ignored what God said and began doing what Satan said. These demonic spirits are placed in positions of authority, for the purpose of accomplishing the will of

Satan on the earth. Satan's authority over them can be seen in Rev. 17:18, "And the woman which thou sawest is that great city, which reigneth over the kings of the earth."

Babylon is an outlaw organization operating within the kingdom of God with Satan as its god. The kings in the kingdom are the fallen principality angels which rule as upper management over a specific geographical territory. The fallen powers or dominion angels are the work force. In Rev. 18:17 they are presented as shipmasters, the company in ships, and sailors. In Ezekiel 27:26 they are called rowers and in verse 29a "and all that handle the oar, the mariners, and all the pilots of the sea." All these sea men are demonic angels which enter human bodies, claim them as their ship or vessel, and guide or direct their movement though the sea or fellow human beings (seas are waters). Satan seduced these seaman away from God and he is now using them to seduce humans away from God. It is because of this seduction that Satan is called a great whore.

In Ephesians 6:12, we are told that the spiritual hierarchy consists of principalities and powers, "For we wrestle not against flesh and blood, but against principalities, against powers, against the rulers of the darkness of this world, against spiritual wickedness in high places." The power demonic spirits are Satan's work force, while the principalities are the spirits ruling over a certain territory. In Ezekiel 9:1-11, we are told of the activity in the spirit realm which brought about the destruction of Jerusalem in the physical realm. When the Greek Empire replaced the Persian Empire, a demonic spirit called the prince of Persia had to be fought and defeated, before a second demonic spirit called the prince of Grecia could be enthroned. This change of command in the spirit realm is recorded in Daniel 10:1-21. Verse 10:20 reads "Then said he, Knowest thou wherefore I come unto thee? and now will I return to fight with the prince of Persia: and when I am gone forth, lo, the prince of Grecia shall come." Our history books tell us the Persian Empire was conquered by Alexander the Great, but they don't tell that the motivating force behind Alexander was a demonic spirit called the prince of Grecia. If you want to know more about this demonic spirit, all you have to do is study the Greek society and culture. God had scattered the Israelites among the Persian population, so they had the knowledge of the God of heaven. They rejected God to follow the demon, as did the Greeks, Romans, and every other society on Earth. The Nation of Israel stumbled over Christ, so it is easy to see that the demonic spirit responsible for tripping them was Antichrist.

It is because of this spiritual hierarchy that the Holy Spirit urges us to pray for our government rulers and people in authority over us. 1 Timothy 2:1-2, "(1) I exhort therefore, that, first of all, supplications, prayers, intercessions, and giving of thanks, be made for all men; (2) For kings, and for all that are in authority; that we may lead a quiet and peaceable life in all godliness and honesty." When a people and their government respond to the Word of God and follow his precepts, they place themselves in a position where God can bless, prosper, and protect them. When they reject the Word of God, they place themselves under the control of the demonic hierarchy. It doesn't matter if the subject is Earth, a nation, a church, or an individual, the same principle applies. The spiritual authority ruling over us is determined by our obedience or disobedience to God. When we turn from the precepts of God, to follow any other precepts, in God's eyes we are guilty of adultery.

A "woman" in Bible prophecy represents a religious people or person. If the woman is presented as a chaste virgin (2 Corinthians 11:1-4), or bride (Rev. 18:23, 21:2, 21:9, 22:17), the religious people are truly God's people. If the woman is presented as a whore, the religious people (or person) she represents are not God's people. They are God's people who have left him for something else, or they were never God's people, but in either case, they are presenting themselves as something they are not. The true Church is presented as the Bride, with Jesus as the bridegroom. When the Holy Spirit completes the Church, Jesus will call out his Bride at the rapture. Everybody left on the face of the earth at that point in time will be members of the false church, represented as the hated whore in Rev. 17:16.

A whore is a woman who takes what God has given her, rejects his commandments, and substitutes Satan's motives of lust and greed for pleasure and gain. After the decision to be a whore, she continues with no fear of God before her eyes. The residing demon (seaman) can use the vessel (her body) he now commands to corrupt and destroy whoever they can attract. Proverbs chapter 7 describes the activity of a whore and says, "(21) With her much fair speech she caused him to yield; with the flattering of her lips she forced him. (22) He goeth after her straightway, as an ox goeth to the slaughter, or as a fool to the correction of the stocks." The last three verses of the chapter contain some good advice. Proverbs 7:25-27, "(25) Let not thine heart decline to her ways; go not astray in her paths. (26) For she hath cast down many wounded; yea, many strong men have been slain by her. (27) Her house is the way to hell, going down to the chambers of death." It is important to God that we look at the whore and understand what she is, how she got there, what motivates her, and what God plans to do with her when he moves against this planet in judgment. Once you understand how a whore operates you can take the same principles and apply them to Satan, the demons, this world system, your church, and yourself to understand what Babylon is all about. You don't have to be a woman to be a whore from God's point of view. All you have to do is present yourself as something you are not, claim to have something you don't have, or use the tactics they use. The church organization Jesus leaves on earth at the rapture, he labels a whore, because they presented themselves as born-again Christians, when they were not. They claimed to have the indwelling Holy Spirit when, in fact, they did not. Keep in mind that every church denomination and religious organization existing on the face of the earth before the rapture will continue to exist after the rapture. The only difference is that they are all fakes, and Jesus groups them all together into a single organization, which he calls a whore.

We are a sex-oriented society, so when we think of seduction, we usually think of physical sex. When we speak of fornication, we normally think of illegal sex involving two unmarried people. When we speak of adultery, we normally refer to illegal sex involving two people each married to someone else or sex involving a married person with an unmarried person. For the purpose of our discussion we will use the words adultery and fornication interchangeably. From God's point of view one is just as illegal as the other, and both are illegal because they are contrary to the law of God. Because society permits or tolerates them doesn't make them right. When two humans commit physical adultery or fornication from God's point of view they become one, 1 Corinthians 6:15-17, "(15) Know ye not that your bodies are the members of Christ? shall I then take the members of Christ, and make them the members of an harlot? God forbid. (16) What? know ye not that he which is joined to an harlot is one body? for two, saith he, shall be one flesh. (17) But he that is joined unto the Lord is one spirit." It is the only sin we can commit that defiles our physical bodies, 1 Corinthians 6:18-20, "(18) Flee fornication. Every sin that a man doeth is without the body; but he that committeth fornication sinneth against his own body. (19) What? Know ye not that your body is the temple of the Holy Ghost which is in you, which ye have of God, and ye are not your own? (20) For ye are bought with a price: therefore glorify God in your body, and in your spirit, which are God's." In Leviticus chapter 18, after discussing unlawful marriages and illegal sexual practices, God sums them up in verse 18:26 as abominations, "Ye shall therefore keep my statutes and my judgments, and shall not commit any of these abominations; neither any of your own nation, nor any stranger that sojourneth among you." *Abomination* means extreme disgust and hatred. God established and ordained the institution of marriage and that is the only legal means to satisfy the sexual lust of the body. To indulge in unlawful sex, one must ignore or reject God's guidelines concerning marriage and sex. This departure from the revealed will of God is whoredom because the individual has been seduced into submitting to another's will.

In 1 Corinthians 6:16 we are told when two humans commit physical adultery or fornication from God's point of view they become one. The same is true in the spirit realm. If you can be seduced (lead away) from God, you and the seducing demon become one. In the process the human becomes a servant to the demon, Romans 6:16, "Know ye not, that to whom ye yield yourselves servants to obey, his servants ye are to whom ye obey; whether of sin unto death, or of obedience unto righteousness?" The end result is demon possession, where the demonic spirit actually takes up residency within the human and claims the human's body as his vessel or house. The will of the demonic spirit is stronger than the human will, so the human will becomes a slave to the demon. An insincere person faking

Christianity and people deceived into thinking they are Christians both run the risk of entering into a second condition, one worse than their original condition. Jesus explains it this way in Matthew 12:43-45, "(43) When the unclean spirit is gone out of a man, he walketh through dry places, seeking rest, and findeth none. (44) Then he saith, I will return into my house from whence I came out; and when he is come, he findeth it empty, swept, and garnished. (45) Then goeth he, and taketh with himself seven other spirits more wicked than himself, and they enter in and dwell there: and the last state of that man is worse than the first. Even so shall it be also unto this wicked generation."

These fallen angelic spirits form the demonic spiritual hierarchy, which Satan has used throughout human history, to promulgate his propaganda. In publishing his deceit, lies, and perversions, the propaganda is designed to discredit the God of heaven by discrediting his Word and his ways. In the garden of Eden Satan seduced the human race from the Lord their God. As a result of that seduction, the human race died spiritually as they separated themselves from the Life of God, and departed from his Word, to drink the wine resulting from Satan's fornication in the spirit realm. The wine of Satan's fornication has been distributed by the demonic hierarchy (kings of the earth) down through the ages in order to keep the human race drunk. In this drunken condition we are spiritually dead, mentally confused, and stumbling around in darkness worshipping all kinds of gods, sometimes even trying to worship the God of heaven in every conceivable way, *except* doing what he says the way he says to do it.

The inhabitants of Babylon are divided into three distinct groups: Satan (the woman or the great whore), the demonic hierarchy (the fallen angels or the kings of the earth), and the drunk inhabitants of the earth (spiritually dead humans who support Satan by doing things his way instead of God's way). These individuals make up Babylon, the outlaw organization, that has been operating within and against the kingdom of God. This is the organization being judged in Revelation chapter 18. They are all whores because they departed from their lawful God, to whore around with the servant exalting himself as a god. At this point in time they are all nearly dead drunk. The sober inhabitants of the Earth left the planet in the rapture of the Church. At the time of the rapture the remaining inhabitants of the earth were all drunk on Satan's wine (his false doctrines and perverted knowledge) instead of what God offered them in his Word and his Son Jesus Christ. The rapture sobered up a multitude of drunk deceived Christians who repented, turned to Jesus, and were slaughtered by the Antichrist organization. It is during this three and one-half year period that Satan and his demonic hierarchy consumes a large amount of blood in a relatively short period of time. We are told in Rev. 17:6, the blood of God's people is the ingredient that causes drunkenness in Satan and his demonic hierarchy, and this blood is supplied by the repentant deceived Christians who sobered up, after the rapture of the true Church. With the destruction of the hated whore (the false Christianity portion of Babylon), we come to the middle of the seven-year tribulation era, and the rise of the False Prophet. He introduces the image of the beast and performs the abomination of desolation by issuing his ultimatum to worship the image or die. This is the event that sobers up the drunken deceived Jewish Nation, but it is too late for them to do anything but run (the flight of the Jews), hide, and wait for Jesus to return, destroy this outlaw organization, and establish the Kingdom Dispensation.

B. John Sees a Woman Sitting on a Scarlet Coloured Beast.

Rev. 17:3-7, "(3) So he carried me away in the spirit into the wilderness: and I saw a woman sit upon a scarlet coloured beast, full of names of blasphemy, having seven heads and ten horns. (4) And the woman was arrayed in purple and scarlet colour, and decked with gold and precious stones and pearls, having a golden cup in her hand full of abominations and filthiness of her fornication: (5) And upon her forehead [was] a name written, MYSTERY, BABYLON THE GREAT, THE MOTHER OF HARLOTS AND ABOMINATIONS OF THE EARTH. (6) And I saw the woman drunken with the blood of the saints, and with the blood of the martyrs of Jesus: and when I saw her, I wondered with great admiration. (7) And the angel said unto me, Wherefore didst thou marvel? I will tell thee the mystery of the woman, and of the beast that carrieth her, which hath the seven heads and ten horns."

The great whore of verse 1 is now seen as a drunken woman sitting upon a scarlet colored beast. She did not change her position, she is just being presented in more detail. In verse 1 we saw her sitting upon many waters, which were identified in verse 17:15 as the human race (peoples, multitudes, nations, and tongues). The scarlet colored beast with seven heads and ten horns, on which the woman is sitting in verse 17:3, is also the human race, but now Jesus is moving forward in history to when the Jews went into captivity. The history of the scarlet colored beast is the history of the human race from the beginning of the Jewish captivity until the end of their captivity. During this period of world history, we have the rise and fall of the seven Gentile world governments (the seven heads on the beast).

Names are given to people for the purpose of identifying them. *Harlot* is another name for *whore*. The great whore is the mother of the harlots because they had their origin in Satan. The first of her offspring were the fallen angels which make up the spiritual hierarchy. The first inhabitants of the earth to be made drunk with the wine of her fornication (Rev. 17:2) were our ancestors Adam and Eve. The first human being to sober from this drunkenness was Abel, who was killed by his brother Cain. Cain never sobered up, for in 1 John 3:12, the Holy Spirit makes the statement that Cain was of that wicked one. The great whore is the mother of the abominations of the earth, which also had their origin in Satan. The abominations of the earth are the things we humans do that God tells us not to do. They are the things God calls sins.

The whore was drunk with the blood of the saints and martyrs of Jesus. Since the blood of God's people makes Satan drunk, it would have the same effect on the spirits in his demonic hierarchy. In Rev. 17:2 we saw "the inhabitants of the earth have been made drunk with the wine of her fornication." The inhabitants of the earth who have been made drunk includes not only the societies of our day, but all past societies. Most of us have seen a drunk person and are familiar with how the alcohol affects the human body. If a person consumes enough alcohol, it will ultimately take control of the individual. It takes control of the tongue, so the person's way of talking becomes altered. It takes control of the eyes, and the blurring continues to worsen, until the person can't even focus his eyes on the person sitting across the room. It takes control of the feet, so the person can't walk the way he wants, and his hands, so he can't do the things he would like to do. It takes control of the brain and the mental processes become confused and literally useless. If enough alcohol is consumed, the individual passes out, falls from the bar stool and takes on the appearance of a dead person. We even describe them as 'dead drunk'. In this condition the drunkard is unquestionably useless, totally defenseless, with no will whatsoever.

The ingredient that causes spiritual drunkenness is sin. The ingredient that causes psychological drunkenness is secular knowledge. The ingredient in grape wine that produces physical drunkenness is alcohol. I can drink fresh grape juice all evening and remain sober. If I would take that same grape juice and cause it to ferment it would turn into wine, and I would not be able to drink it all evening without getting drunk. The same thing is true concerning knowledge. It was God's design for the human family to govern their affairs by the truth of His revealed will, which is revelation knowledge. When Satan or a human takes the truth of God's revelation knowledge, and causes it to undergo change, it becomes unreliable erroneous knowledge or a plain lie. Once you see the effect of alcohol on our physical bodies, you can visualize the condition of the human mental process when it consumes knowledge which contradicts the truth of the Word of God. Lies and error mixed with revelation knowledge is garbage and creates the same drunken condition in our mental process as alcohol creates in the human body. The garbage creates a condition of uncertainty, a wavering of opinions and beliefs, a state of confusion, literally, Babylon. The drunken condition intensifies as more of this mixture is consumed, until, like the drunk who passed out, humans pass a point where they become totally insensitive to Bible truth.

Describing Babylon as a person or nation governing its affairs by secular knowledge instead of the Word of God is close, but it still misrepresents Babylon. Satan has successfully separated entire nations from God by using the Word of God deceitfully. The basic meaning of the word *deceive* is to lead astray. The principle of deception is to convince someone to accept something as true or valid, when it is false or invalid. In the Garden of Eden, Satan used the revelation knowledge of God recorded in Genesis 2:16-17, "(16) And the Lord God commanded the man, saying, Of every tree in the garden thou mayest freely eat: (17) But of the tree of the knowledge of good and evil, thou shalt not eat of it: for in the day that thou eatest thereof thou shalt surely die." He then mixed it with his knowledge, which was a lie, Genesis 3:4, "And the serpent said unto the woman, Ye shall not surely die." This mixture created doubt in Eve's mind as to the truthfulness of God. When she compared the two knowledges, she found them conflicting. What Satan fed Eve was actually a mixture of good and evil. Eve knew she could eat of every tree in the garden except one and live. The knowledge Lucifer mixed with this truth is that she could eat of every tree, including the tree of knowledge of good and evil, without dying. What her mental process told her, was different than what God had said, and she made the wrong choice. You are not in the Garden of Eden, but the only thing that has changed is the scenery. The decision you are being asked to make is the same. Will you choose to live by revelation knowledge from the tree of life or by secular knowledge, the knowledge of good and evil?

You see Babylon when you see Christian businessmen using the same deceit tactics to acquire gain as the non-christians use. You see Babylon when you elect Christian government officials and they vote to legalize murder by supporting abortion. We send politicians to Washington believing they will honor and defend the Constitution, and they jump on the bandwagon to take away our birthright to keep and bear arms. In Luke 11:21 Jesus says, "When a strong man armed keepeth his palace, his goods are in peace" but they don't believe him. They read the Bible where it says "if any would not work, neither should he eat" (2 Thess. 3:10), and they see people abusing the welfare system until they get elected and then they go totally blind to everything except votes. It is impossible to be a Christian one day a week and a sinner the other six. That is confusion and that describes Babylon.

This mixture of good and evil is confusion, which is the basic meaning of the word *Babylon.* The confusion may be easier to understand if we use the words *truth* and *error* to describe the mixture. For something to be the truth the information on the subject must be presented without distortion or misrepresentation. Revelation knowledge is the revealed will of God recorded in the Holy Bible. In his written Word, God teaches truths and realities which humans could not discover for themselves. Satan takes revelation knowledge and mixes it with enough error to deceive humans into thinking they are worshipping God, when in fact, they are not. He takes the Word of God and adds something to it or takes something away, a little overemphasis on one point, a little neglect on another, enough truth to pacify, but enough error to render the truth ineffective.

The truth and error mixture is not limited to the Word of God. We were all born in Babylon, and the human soul is contaminated with falsehood before we are old enough to recognize the difference between a lie and the truth. How old were you when you stopped believing in Santa Claus, fairy-tales, and the theory of evolution? Our entire education is a mixture of fact and fiction. This is true concerning our generation and every generation before us. It is true for our society and every other society that ever existed on Earth. The confusion began in the Garden of Eden when the human family took the directions of God and mixed them with directions from Satan. The process continued through seven different human kingdoms or world governments, where a part of the culture and intellect of the last society was retained and mixed with the next. These are the seven heads John saw on the scarlet colored beast, directing the movement of its body, which is the human race. The final result of mixing culture and intellect is pure humanism, when the human race reaches a point when they will no longer respond to, or be influenced by, the truth of the Word of God. At this point God will move in judgment against Earth and destroy Babylon.

The revelation knowledge in the Word of God is taught by the Holy Spirit and is spiritually discerned. Without the Holy Spirit, which is received in the rebirth process, a person does not have the ability to understand the Word of God. They continue to learn but truth and understanding evades them. They are the people the Holy Spirit speaks of in 2 Timothy chapter 3 as having corrupt minds, "Ever learning, and never able to come to the knowledge of the truth." He describes them in verses 1-9, "(1) This know also, that in the last days perilous times shall come. (2) For men shall be lovers of their own selves, covetous, boasters, proud, blasphemers, disobedient to parents, unthankful, unholy, (3) Without natural affection, trucebreakers, false accusers, incontinent, fierce, despisers of those that are good, (4) Traitors, heady, highminded, lovers of pleasures more than lovers of God; (5) Having a form of godliness, but denying the power thereof: from such turn away. (6) For of this sort are they which creep into houses, and lead captive silly women laden with sins, led away with divers lusts, (7) Ever learning, and never able to come to the knowledge of the truth. (8) Now as Jannes and Jambres withstood Moses, so do these also resist the truth: men of corrupt minds, reprobate concerning the faith. (9) But they shall proceed no further: for their folly shall be manifest unto all men, as theirs also was." Their folly shall be manifest unto all, by Jesus, when he calls the believers out of the world and leaves them behind to face Antichrist.

Notice in verse 3:5 this group is described as, "Having a form of godliness, but denying the power thereof: from such turn away." There is a big difference between having a form of godliness, and having true godliness. The power and the difference in a church congregation, or an individual, is the Holy Spirit. Jesus made this point clear to his Apostles in Acts 1:4-8, when he commanded them that they should not depart from Jerusalem, but wait for the promise of the Father. He continues in verse 8 by saying, "But ye shall receive power, after that the Holy Ghost is come upon you."

Without the Holy Spirit, a person is not only powerless, his form of godliness is counterfeit. That is what separates the members of the kingdom of Babylon from the members of the kingdom of God. We have all been born in the kingdom of Babylon. To get out of Satan's kingdom, we must "enter into" the kingdom of God, through the John 3:5 rebirth, "Jesus answered, Verily, verily, I say unto thee, Except a man be born of water and of the spirit, he cannot enter into the kingdom of God." Notice Jesus did not say, "only believe and you may enter." You can eat that garbage if you choose, but it won't save you anymore than it will save the believing demons described in James 2:19, "Thou believest that there is one God; thou doest well: the devils also believe, and tremble." If salvation was only a matter of believing, these demons would have nothing to tremble about. Buy the "Only Believe" package and the day will come when you, too, will tremble.

The "last days perilous times" of 2 Timothy 3:1 are here, and you don't have to be a Bible student to know that. Just watch the television news broadcast and read the daily newspaper. We have allowed our government to throw God out of the public school system, so the teachers can corrupt the minds of our children with carnal knowledge. The knowledge explosion of today is not only one of the characteristics of Babylon, it is clearly one of the signs of the time of the end. This increase of knowledge was foretold in Daniel 12:4c, "But thou, O Daniel, shut up the words, and seal the book, even to the time of the end: many shall run to and fro, and knowledge shall be increased." The angel continues in verses 9 and 10 with the statement, "(9) And he said, Go thy way, Daniel: for the words are closed up and sealed till the time of the end. (10) Many shall be purified, and made white, and tried; but the wicked shall do wickedly: and none of the wicked shall understand; but the wise shall understand." The Laodicean apostate church era (Rev. 3:14-22) is also here, and the false teachers are busy throwing Jesus out of the church. This is why he is presented in Rev. 3:20 as standing at the door knocking for admittance.

As we saw in Rev. 17:6, Satan and the demonic hierarchy were made drunk by the blood of the saints and martyrs of Jesus. Anybody who has ever gotten drunk knows you don't just walk into a bar and become drunk. You have one drink, then another, then another, and gradually over a period of time you become drunk. If you want to become really drunk quickly, all you need to do is to consume a large quantity of alcohol in a relatively short period of time. The same thing is true of the drunkenness of Satan and the demonic hierarchy. The woman was drunken with the blood of the saints. They had their first drink of a saint's blood when Cain killed Abel. They have continued their drinking for nearly six thousand years, and will continue in a partially drunken condition, until the rapture of the Church. Then they become really drunk in the next three and one-half years, because they consume a large quantity of blood in a relatively short period of time. This blood is the martyrs of Jesus and is supplied by the deceived Laodicean congregation who missed the rapture. A *martyr of Jesus* is someone who is killed for his testimony of Jesus. John's reaction at seeing Satan, the drunken woman, at the middle of the tribulation period is recorded in Rev. 17:6b, "I wondered with great admiration."

Rev. 17:7 reads, "And the angel said unto me, Wherefore didst thou marvel? I will tell thee the mystery of the woman, and of the beast that carrieth her, which hath the seven heads and ten horns." John is to be told the mystery of two things: the woman, and the beast with seven heads and ten horns that carrieth her. This drunken woman is the great whore we saw in Rev. 17:1, but the angel does not begin to tell the mystery of her until we get to the end of the chapter at verse Rev. 17:18. Chapter 17 mentions two whores representing two different things, the hated whore is the deceived Laodicean congregation rejected at the Church rapture, and the great whore is Satan.

C. The Beast Identified as the False Prophet.

Rev. 17:8, "The beast that thou sawest was, and is not; and shall ascend out of the bottomless pit, and go into perdition: and they that dwell on the earth shall wonder, whose names were not written in the book of life from the foundation of the world, when they behold the beast that was, and is not, and yet is."

John is to see the judgment of the great whore (Rev. 17:1), so the angel begins at the point in time when her judgment begins, which is at the middle of the seven-year tribulation period. This is when the False Prophet is reincarnated from Hades. The beast is the False Prophet. He "was," which is a verb in the past tense, meaning that at some point in time past, he did exist in the flesh on the earth. He "is not," meaning that during the Church Age he is confined in Hades, unable to influence activity on the earth. "And yet is" speaks of the certainty of his existence in the flesh and his activity during the tribulation period, after he "shall ascend out of the bottomless pit." The phase "was, and is not; and shall ascend out of the bottomless pit" is the reincarnation of the False Prophet and the phrase is there so you don't confuse him with Antichrist, who is incarnated, not reincarnated. Before the actual reincarnation the False Prophet is "the beast that was, and is not, and yet is." Where the False Prophet is going is "into perdition" which means into total utter ruin.

The earth-dwellers who wonder are the people living during the False Prophet reign, "whose names were not written in the book of life from the foundation of the world." The only way to get your name recorded in the book of life is to denounce Satan and sin, repent, and accept God's plan of salvation that was finalized before the foundation of the earth. God's plan of salvation during the False Prophet reign is to be killed by the organization for obedience to the messages of the three proclaiming angels being expounded by the 144 thousand sealed Jews. Their ministry is the everlasting gospel, the reality of God's judgment on rebellious Earth, and they warn of the consequences of worshipping the beast or his image, and taking his unforgivable mark. During the False Prophet reign the statement reads, Rev. 18:8b, "and they that dwell on the earth shall wonder, whose names were not written in the book of life from the foundation of the world." During the Antichrist reign the statement is, Rev. 13:8 "And all that dwell upon the earth shall worship him, whose names are not written in the book of life of the Lamb slain from the foundation of the world." The phrase "of the Lamb" is missing from the statement applying to the False Prophet reign because his mission is not against the Lamb (Jesus Christ).

D. The Mystery of the Beast Revealed.

Rev. 17:9-14, "(9) And here [is] the mind which hath wisdom. The seven heads are seven mountains, on which the woman sitteth. (10) And there are seven kings: five are fallen, and one is, [and] the other is not yet come; and when he cometh, he must continue a short space. (11) And the beast that was, and is not, even he is the eighth, and is of the seven, and goeth into perdition. (12) And the ten horns which thou sawest are ten kings, which have received no kingdom as yet; but receive power as kings one hour with the beast. (13) These have one mind, and shall give their power and strength unto the beast. (14) These shall make war with the Lamb, and the Lamb shall overcome them: for he is Lord of lords, and King of kings: and they that are with him [are] called, and chosen, and faithful."

The angel told John that he would show him the mystery of the woman and the seven headed beast with ten horns. This is where he begins to reveal the mystery of the beast. He starts by saying the seven heads are seven mountains, on which the woman (Satan) sitteth. In Daniel 2:34-35 we can see how the Holy Spirit uses a mountain in Bible prophecy to describe a world empire or government, "(34) Thou sawest till that a stone was cut out without hands, which smote the image upon his feet [that were] of iron and clay, and brake them to pieces. (35) Then was the iron, the clay, the brass, the silver, and the gold, broken to pieces together, and became like the chaff of the summer threshingfloors; and the wind carried them away, that no place was found for them: and the stone that smote the image became a great mountain, and filled the whole earth." At the time of Satan's judgment, which begins at midpoint in the seven-year tribulation era, there will have been seven major Gentile world governments, and they will have all supported or upheld Satan. Verse 10 begins with the statement "And there are seven kings". These seven kings or kingdoms are the Assyrian Empire, Babylonian Empire, Median Empire, Persian Empire, Greek Empire, Roman Empire, and the European Common Market. The angel continues by saying "five are fallen" which means five have emerged and fallen, or more specifically, five are history. These are the Assyrian, Babylonian, Median, Persian, and Greek Empires. This would bring us up to the time of the Roman Empire and the angel's statement, "and one is." In other words, when the Book of the Revelation was given to John, the sixth world government was still a reality.

The angel continues in Rev. 17:10 with the statement, "and the other is not yet come," meaning at the time the Revelation was given, the seventh king was a future Gentile world government. From the view of world history in the great image of Daniel 2:31-45, the final Gentile world power would be a confederacy of ten kings. In explaining the world governments the angel began with the head of the image, identified it as the Babylonian Empire, and moved down its body ending with its ten toes. The ten toes represent ten kings which are the final Gentile world government. God has promised the Jews a kingdom throughout the Old Testament Scriptures and this is where he keeps his Word, Daniel 2:44, "And in the days of these kings shall the God of heaven set up a kingdom, which shall never be destroyed: and the kingdom shall not be left to other people, but it shall break in pieces and consume all these kingdoms, and it shall stand for ever." This ten king kingdom is the European Common Market, and we are living in the days of these kings. So get ready, Jesus is coming soon. In John's day he could say, "And there are seven kings: five are fallen, and one is, [and] the other is not yet come; and when he cometh, he must continue a short space," Rev. 17:10. Today we would say, "And there are seven kings: six are fallen, and one is," (the ten king kingdom). The phrase "[and] the other is not yet come" is no longer valid because the one yet to come in John's day has arrived in our generation.

The last Gentile world government has arrived and the last part of verse 17:10 reads, "and when he cometh, he must continue a short space" (or short time). How much time a "short space" represents is debatable. A short time can mean a different amount of time to different people. I do believe God is communicating by implication that the ten king kingdom will continue to exist for a short period of time, but I believe he is also saying something else. With the coming of the ten king kingdom, Antichrist is coming, and I believe the pronoun *he* represents both the last Gentile world government and Antichrist, "and when he (Antichrist) cometh, he must continue a short space (his three and one-half year reign during the first half of the seven-year tribulation era)." The life span of the ten king kingdom is a single generation. Jesus told His disciples of these days in Luke chapter 21 and told them to watch for Israel the fig tree to bud, "(28) And when these things begin to come to pass, then look up, and lift up your heads; for your redemption draweth nigh. (29) And he spake to them a parable; Behold the fig tree, and all the trees; (30) When they now shoot forth, ye see and know of your own selves that summer is now nigh at hand. (31) So likewise ye, when ye see these things come to pass, know ye that the kingdom of God is nigh at hand. (32) Verily I say unto you, This generation shall not pass away, till all be fulfilled. (33) Heaven and earth shall pass away: but my words shall not pass away." The formation of the European Common Market began in 1967 and was completed in January 1981, when Greece entered the confederacy to complete the ten nations. The year 1967 is also significant because it was the year the Jewish Nation reclaimed the city of Jerusalem, in the seven day war. The year 1967 put this organization and the city of Jerusalem on a collision course that will meet in the battle of Armageddon. If the last generation didn't start in the year 1918, my next choice would be 1967. Rev. 17:10 is the "times of the Gentiles" from start to finish. Rev. 17:11 is the False Prophet reign from start to finish during the last half of the tribulation era. In verse 17:12 Jesus goes back to the ten king kingdom to provide more information on the Antichrist reign.

The European Common Market will remain in the hands of the Gentiles, from God's point of view, even after they turn political control over to Antichrist. He will use this organization to destroy false Christianity after the rapture, and in the middle of the tribulation period the False Prophet will take control. The rise of the False Prophet will end the seventh ten nation Gentile world government and will begin the eighth world power, which is really the seventh under the leadership of the False Prophet. This is what the angel is saying in Rev. 17:11, "And the beast (the False Prophet of verse 17:8) that was, and is not, even he is the eighth, (government) and is of the seven, (government) and goeth into perdition (total utter ruin)." When control of this organization is given to the False Prophet, it is controlled by Satan, not the Gentiles. This is the beast kingdom of the Book of the Revelation, which is destroyed by Jesus when he returns to the earth in glory with his saints to establish the Kingdom Dispensation.

One of the first things the False Prophet does is to remove three of the ten nations from the confederacy, so the organization changes from a ten king kingdom to a seven king kingdom. Therefore, all the prophecies concerning the ten king kingdom and ten horns must be fulfilled before the arrival of the False Prophet at the middle of the tribulation period. The False Prophet is the little horn of Daniel 7:7-8, "(7) After this I saw in the night visions, and behold a fourth beast, dreadful and terrible, and strong exceeding; and it had great iron teeth: it devoured and brake in pieces, and stamped the residue with the feet of it: and it was diverse from all the beasts that were before it; and it had ten horns. (8) I considered the horns, and, behold, there came up among them another little horn, before whom there were three of the first horns plucked up by the roots: and, behold, in this horn were eyes like the eyes of man, and a mouth speaking great things." The fourth beast in Daniel's vision is the Roman Empire, which is also the sixth head on the beast in Revelation Chapter 17. In Daniel 7:23-24 he is given the interpretation of the fourth beast, "(23) Thus he said, The fourth beast shall be the fourth kingdom upon earth, which shall be diverse from all kingdoms, and shall devour the whole earth, and shall tread it down, and break it in pieces. (24) And the ten horns out of this kingdom are ten kings that shall arise: and another shall rise after them; and he shall be diverse from the first, and he shall subdue three kings."

When it is realized that the ten king kingdom will cease to exist when the False Prophet rises to power, it should be easy to understand Rev. 17:12-17. In these verses the angel is telling the mystery of the ten horns John saw on the scarlet colored beast, so he is describing an organization and its activity from the year 1967 to the middle of the seven-year tribulation. Revelation 17:12-17, "(12) And the ten horns which thou sawest are ten kings, which have received no kingdom as yet; but receive power as kings one hour with the beast. (13) These have one mind, and shall give their power and strength unto the beast. (14) These shall make war with the Lamb, and the Lamb shall overcome them: for he is Lord of lords, and King of kings: and they that are with him are called, and chosen, and faithful. (15) And he saith unto me, The waters which thou sawest, where the whore sitteth, are peoples, and multitudes, and nations, and tongues. (16) And the ten horns which thou sawest upon the beast, these shall hate the whore, and shall make her desolate and naked, and shall eat her flesh, and burn her with fire. (17) For God hath put in their hearts to fulfill his will, and to agree, and give their kingdom unto the beast, until the words of God shall be fulfilled."

In the first part of verse 17:12 the angel is saying the ten horns are ten kings which form a kingdom, "And the ten horns which thou sawest are ten kings, which have received no kingdom as yet." This kingdom is the seventh head on the scarlet colored beast, representing the last Gentile government. In the year 1967, this ten king kingdom became visible in the European Common Market. The last part of verse 17:12 reads, "But receive power as kings one hour with the beast." The beast here is the incarnate Antichrist, not the scarlet colored beast. The angel is telling the mystery of the ten horns, and now he begins to show the connection between the 10 king kingdom and Antichrist. The angel continues in Rev. 17:13 by saying, "These have one mind, and shall give their power and strength unto the beast." "These" are the political rulers (horns) of the European Common Market. "They have one mind" simply means they are all in agreement to "give their power and strength unto the beast" (Antichrist). The reason is given in verse 14, "These shall make war with the Lamb, and the Lamb shall overcome them: for he is Lord of lords, and King of kings: and they that are with him [are] called, and chosen, and faithful." When Antichrist, or for that matter anyone else, declares war on a saint they are, in reality, declaring war on God. This is why the angel revealing the mystery of the beast says Antichrist and his organization are warring with Jesus. The last part of the verse, "they that are with him are called, and chosen, and faithful" takes us to the end of the tribulation era, and the return of Jesus (Rev. 19:11- 21) to Earth with his army.

E. The Waters Represent the Human Race.

Rev. 17:15, "And he saith unto me, The waters which thou sawest, where the whore sitteth, are peoples, and multitudes, and nations, and tongues." The angel tells John the waters which the great whore sits on, in verse 17:1, represent the human race. The angel gave John this information to allow him to understand what he saw. God gave it to us as a key to allow us to understand that waters represent people in Bible prophecy. The next time you are reading your Bible and waters are used in a prophecy, remember that seas and waters represent people. If the sea is presented as calm, the people are content and living in peace. If the sea is foaming or waves roaring, the people are perplexed and living in turmoil.

F. The Ten Horns Hate and Destroy the Whore.

Rev. 17:16-17, "(16) And the ten horns which thou sawest upon the beast, these shall hate the whore, and shall make her desolate and naked, and shall eat her flesh, and burn her with fire. (17) For God hath put in their hearts to fulfil his will, and to agree, and give their kingdom unto the beast, until the words of God shall be fulfilled."

The ten horns are the ten political rulers of the last Gentile world government, which is the seventh head on the beast. From this information we can determine the time period the angel is describing. Since there are ten horns, the time period is just prior to or during the first half of the seven-year tribulation when Antichrist reigns. We know this because one of the first things the False Prophet does when he arrives at midpoint in the tribulation era is to eliminate three of the ten nations in this confederacy. The word *beast* appears in both verse 16 and 17 but it represents two different things. The beast in verse 16 has ten horns, which we saw earlier on the seven headed scarlet colored beast representing Gentile world governments during the Jewish captivity. The beast in verse 17 is Antichrist, "For God hath put in their [the ten horns or political rulers] hearts to fulfil his will, and to agree, and give their kingdom [the ten Gentile nations] unto the beast [Antichrist], until the words of God shall be fulfilled." The will of God is for Antichrist, in command of the ten king kingdom confederacy, to destroy the Laodicean congregation Jesus left behind at the Church rapture. "And the ten horns" (political rulers of the ten king kingdom) "which thou sawest upon the beast" (the scarlet colored 7 headed beast), "these shall hate the whore" (false Christianity, the Laodicean congregation), "and shall make her desolate and naked, and shall eat her flesh, and burn her with fire." Don't confuse the hated whore with the great whore of verse 17:1. The great whore is Satan, whose judgment begins at midpoint in the tribulation, when he and his crew get thrown out of heaven and the False Prophet ascends out of the bottomless pit.

The false church organization Jesus left on Earth after the rapture is presented as a hated whore, in contrast to the virgin Bride He took home to Heaven with him at the rapture. The false church organization, even though it is false, is hated by Antichrist because of his extreme hatred of Jesus

Christ. He hates everything Jesus stands for and everything that stands for Jesus. When this slaughter begins, hordes of unbelievers will storm every church building on Earth. After they get their hands on the membership roll, before the church building finishes burning, another mob will be pounding on your home door. If you were a born-again believer you won't be there; you'll be in heaven. If you're home, they are going to give you the choice of denying Jesus and living, or confessing Jesus and be killed. When they are finished with you, they will move on to the next person whom they suspect of being a believer of Jesus. It will be a crime, punishable by death, to own a Bible, breath the name of Jesus, or mention the word Church.

It is not a question of *if* they locate you, only *when*. If you believe in Jesus and sober up on the wrong side of the rapture, God is going to arrange a way for Antichrist to find and kill you. It is his way of offering you an invitation to the marriage supper of the Lamb. If you have been pretending to be a Christian, or playing around with Christianity, it is His way of saying "get serious." It is time to find out what the "only believe" crowd really believes. If you were deceived, He is giving you a last opportunity to re-evaluate your opinion. The only way to inherit eternal life, during this three and one-half year period, is to be murdered by the Antichrist organization. If you are not planning to leave Earth in the rapture, you should be planning to be murdered by Antichrist. It is his job to "hate the whore, and shall make her desolate and naked, and shall eat her flesh, and burn her with fire." The rapture of the Church will end the Church Dispensation, and nobody, throughout eternity, will ever again be saved as a member of the Church. When Antichrist finishes this slaughter at midpoint in the tribulation, the last chapter has been written in Christianity and Earth will be ready for God to continue his program with the Jews.

G. The Woman Described as a Great City.

Rev. 17:18, "And the woman which thou sawest is that great city, which reigneth over the kings of the earth." With this verse we move into the second half of the seven-year tribulation era. This woman is Satan, the great whore of verse 17:1 which John saw sitting upon many waters. Now John is told she "is that great city, which reigneth over the kings of the earth." The "kings of the earth" Satan is reigning over here are the fallen angels in the demonic hierarchy. They are the same "kings" we saw in Rev. 17:2, "With whom the kings of the earth have committed fornication, and the inhabitants of the earth have been made drunk with the wine of her fornication." Satan dwells in the spirit realm which is where the judgment of Babylon "that great city" takes place. God compares the judgment of Satan to a great city so that we can look at his judgments against cities in the physical realm to understand what is happening in the spirit realm. The judgment of Nebuchadnezzar's Babylon is covered in Jeremiah chapters 50 and 51. The judgment of the city of Tyre in Ezekiel chapters 26, 27, and 28 parallels the judgment of Revelation Babylon. The lamentation upon the king of Tyre in Ezekiel 28:11-19 is actually directed at Satan himself. We will see more details on Satan's judgment in Revelation chapter 18.

The False Prophet Reign

The rise and reign of the False Prophet is recorded in Revelation 13:11-18, "(11) And I beheld another beast coming up out of the earth; and he had two horns like a lamb, and he spake as a dragon. (12) And he exerciseth all the power of the first beast before him, and causeth the earth and them which dwell therein to worship the first beast, whose deadly wound was healed. (13) And he doeth great wonders, so that he maketh fire come down from heaven on the earth in the sight of men, (14) And deceiveth them that dwell on the earth by [the means of] those miracles which he had power to do in the sight of the beast; saying to them that dwell on the earth, that they should make an image to the beast, which had the wound by a sword, and did live. (15) And he had power to give life unto the image of the beast, that the image of the beast should both speak, and cause that as many as would not worship the image of the beast should be killed. (16) And he causeth all, both small and great, rich and poor, free and bond, to receive a mark in their right hand, or in their foreheads: (17) And that no man might buy or sell, save he that had the mark, or the name of the beast, or the number of his name. (18) Here is wisdom. Let him that hath understanding count the number of the beast: for it is the number of a man; and his number [is] Six hundred threescore [and] six."

A. The False Prophet, Beast Out of the Earth.

Rev. 13:11, "And I beheld another beast coming up out of the earth; and he had two horns like a lamb, and he spake as a dragon."

This is the arrival of the False Prophet at midpoint in the seven-year tribulation era. He is seen "coming up out of the earth" in contrast to Antichrist who rises up out of the sea. He is the beast we saw in Rev. 17:8 that "was, and is not; and shall ascend out of the bottomless pit" and the beast that "was, and is not; and yet is" which says he is reincarnated. The beast is seen as having two horns, implying that the government has two political rulers. This is the same arrangement we saw with the Median/Persian government, the ram with two horns, Dan. 8:3-4. The False Prophet joins Antichrist and has joint political authority in the European Community Market confederacy, the ten king kingdom. It is the False Prophet who eliminates three nations from the confederacy, which changes the organization from a ten king to a seven king kingdom. In the interpretation of the vision of 4 beasts out of the sea, following the fourth beast (the Roman Empire), Daniel is told, "And the ten horns out of this kingdom are ten kings that shall arise; and another shall rise after them, and he shall be diverse from the first, and he shall subdue three kings." (Daniel 7:24). At this point in time all the prophecies concerning the ten king kingdom and the seven headed beast with ten horns will have been fulfilled.

Another thing that happens at midpoint in the tribulation is Satan and his crew are thrown out of heaven, Rev. 12:7-9. In the phrase "he spake as a dragon," the dragon is Satan. During this period of time Satan's mouth is silenced in heaven and the False Prophet becomes the mouthpiece of Satan. Listen to how Daniel describes the False Prophet in Dan. 7:25, "And he shall speak great words against the Most High, and shall wear out the saints of the Most High, and think to change the times and the laws; and they shall be given into his hand until a time and times and the dividing of time."

B. Earth Dwellers Deceived.

Rev. 13:12-14, "(12) And he exerciseth all the power of the first beast before him, and causeth the earth and them which dwell therein to worship the first beast, whose deadly wound was healed. (13) And he doeth great wonders, so that he maketh fire come down from heaven on the earth in the sight of men, (14) And deceiveth them that dwell on the earth by [the means of] those miracles which he had power to do in the sight of the beast; saying to them that dwell on the earth, that they should make an image to the beast, which had the wound by a sword, and did live."

The "first beast before him" was Antichrist and since "he exerciseth all the power of the first beast" he is equal in power to Antichrist. Rather than compete with Antichrist for top political position, The False Prophet uses the power to cause "the earth and them which dwell therein to worship the first beast, whose deadly wound was healed." The first beast was Antichrist but the beast "whose deadly wound was healed" is the organization, the seventh head on the seven headed beast. The ten king kingdom is history but the excitement of slaughtering thousands of deceived Christians who missed the rapture will be fresh in their minds. The Christians are all gone but the False Prophet has a plan that will outlaw all religions and result in millions of deceived humans being slaughtered. He puts the plan in operation by "saying to them that dwell on the earth, that they should make an image to the beast, which had the wound by a sword, and did live." Again we are told the image is to the organization, "which had the wound by a sword, and did live." The sword is a weapon of war, which tells us how the European Common Market nations will receive their deadly wound.

The False Prophet will be a miracle worker, Rev. 13:13-14a, "(13) And he doeth great wonders, so that he maketh fire come down from heaven on the earth in the sight of men, (14) And deceiveth them that dwell on the earth by [the means of] those miracles which he had power to do in the sight of the beast." This is not a magician's trick, nor is there anything supernatural about lightning. Lightning is simply a natural phenomenon. God is a spirit being, and he created the physical universe by speaking it into existence. In this truth, we can see the power of words from the mouth of a spirit. God not only created the physical universe, he also devised all the natural laws which govern its behavior. It should be easy to see that the spiritual laws God used to create the physical universe are superior to the natural laws which govern its behavior. The use of a spiritual law to control or supersede a natural law is called a *miracle.* In the garden of Eden, when God created Adam, he gave him dominion over the physical universe. Adam was able to use spiritual laws to reign as king over the physical creation until he departed from the revealed will of God. When he sinned and separated himself from God, he died spiritually. A spiritually dead human has no more control over spiritual laws than a physically dead human body has over natural laws.

Both Antichrist and the False Prophet will be miracle workers. With the expulsion from the garden of Eden came the promise of the Redeemer, and with the Redeemer, the promise of a New Covenant. Under the New Covenant, through the rebirth, humans can be separated from their sins and reunited with God. The New Covenant members make up the organization called the Church. The organization, as well as each of its members, has been given both the ability and responsibility to work miracles. This is obvious from the Mark 16:15-18 Church Commission. There remains a faithful remnant, but Christendom as a whole has become a hearer of the Word only, and not a doer of the Word. What do you do Church, when Satan touches one of your members with a sickness or disease? Are you a doer of James 5:14-15 or a hearer only, "(14) Is any sick among you? let him call for the elders of the church; and let them pray over him, anointing him with oil in the name of the Lord: (15) And the prayer of faith shall save the sick, and the Lord shall raise him up; and if he have committed sins, they shall be forgiven him." And what about you, born-again believer? In Mark 16:18 Jesus said one of the signs that would follow you is "they shall lay hands on the sick, and they shall recover." Are you a believer of the Word or a hearer only? Adam's disobedience in the garden of Eden allowed Satan to take what God intended for his good, and use it against him until he was destroyed. When the doers of the Word are raptured, Antichrist is going to take the miracles God intended for the Church's good, and destroy what is left of Christendom with them. When he is finished the False Prophet will take the same miracles, and try to destroy what is left of the human family.

Spiritual laws are activated by what we say, literally by the words that come out of our mouths. In Matthew 21:17-21 (Mark 11:11-23) Jesus spoke to a fig tree and killed it. When His disciples marveled at how quickly the fig tree died, Jesus made the following statement in Matthew 21:21, "Jesus answered and said unto them, Verily I say unto you, If ye have faith, and doubt not, ye shall not only do this which is done to the fig tree, but also if ye shall say unto this mountain, Be thou removed, and be thou cast into the sea; it shall be done." Let's not explain our inability to move mountains and kill fig trees with our words by accusing Jesus of being deceitful in saying something he didn't really mean. He said we could if "ye have faith, and doubt not" so if we can't, it is because of our lack of faith or the presence of doubt. In Romans 10:17 we are told faith comes from the Word of God, "So then faith cometh by hearing, and hearing by the word of God." The absence of the Word of God is the absence of faith, and the Word of God mixed with doubt is unbelief. Jesus came out of the spirit realm and told us how spiritual laws operate. Both Antichrist and the False Prophet will come out of that same environment, already knowing how those laws operate. The deceit lies in the *means*, the answer to, "How can they do that?"

It is important to remember that during the last three and one-half years of the tribulation period, and especially near its end, there will be many great signs and wonders which the Antichrist/False Prophet organization may use to their advantage to lure people from their hiding places. In Matthew 24:24 we are told false christs and prophets will be showing great signs and wonders. In Luke 21:11, Jesus says, "fearful sights and great signs shall there be from heaven." Both sights and signs are plural meaning more than one. Daniel's advice to wait, and Jesus' advice to hide and stay hidden are indeed good advice. The best advice Jesus gave is not to be deceived. In Luke chapter 21 the disciples of Jesus ask him a question, (verse 7) "what sign will there be when these things shall come to pass?" Jesus begins by saying, "Take heed that ye be not deceived:" and ends the answer with Luke 21:34-36, "(34) And take heed to yourselves, lest at any time your hearts be overcharged with surfeiting, and drunkenness, and cares of this life, and so that day come upon you unawares. (35) For as a snare shall it come on all them that dwell on the face of the whole earth. (36) Watch ye therefore, and pray always, that ye may be accounted worthy to escape all these things that shall come to pass, and to stand before the Son of man."

C. The Ultimatum: Worship the Beast Image Or Die.

Rev. 13:15-18, "(15) And he had power to give life unto the image of the beast, that the image of the beast should both speak, and cause that as many as would not worship the image of the beast should be killed. (16) And he causeth all, both small and great, rich and poor, free and bond, to receive a mark in their right hand, or in their foreheads: (17) And that no man might buy or sell, save he that had the mark, or the name of the beast, or the number of his name. (18) Here is wisdom. Let him that hath understanding count the number of the beast: for it is the number of a man; and his number [is] Six hundred threescore [and] six."

The most common teaching today is that the image will be a sophisticated computer of some type, used to control the population of the earth.

That's not what is being taught here. We humans are continuously trying to reduce the operation of God and angels to the natural laws that control us. Consider the fact that Satan controls most of the population on Earth today, just as he always has, and he never needed a computer, then or now, in order to control. Why would he need a sophisticated computer to control the population during the tribulation era? The Greek word translated as *image* is the same word the translators used to describe the Israelites worshipping the idol Baal in Romans 11:4, "But what saith the answer of God unto him? I have reserved to myself seven thousand men, who have not bowed the knee to the image of Baal." The Greek word translated as *life* is used over a hundred times in the New Testament, where it is translated as *spirit.* This is the only place where it is translated as *life.* It is translated with a capital *S* (Spirit) when referring to the Holy Spirit or the Spirit of God, and with a small *s* (spirit) when referring to a human spirit or a demonic spirit. What the False Prophet introduces is going to be a living, talking idol, which will be indwelt by a demonic spirit.

Man can build talking computers, but regardless of how sophisticated the computer becomes, it is still nothing more than a machine. The intelligence of a computer is limited to the information stored in the memory unit by man, and the programs we write to retrieve or manipulate that information. The intelligence of these living idols will surpass anything we humans could build, but it will all be based on deception. Again, we are not discussing the type of deception used by magicians to perform tricks. The life in these idols will be just as genuine as the lightning used by the False Prophet to impress people. If you were to be hit by one of his bolts of lightning, you would be killed because the lightning is genuine. If you were to talk to one of these idols, you would be talking to a genuine living being.

Neither Satan, nor the False Prophet, has the ability or power to create life. The way the False Prophet gives life to the idol, will be by taking a living spirit created by God and putting it in the image. The spirit will be one of the fallen angelic spirits, but it is and will be very much alive. This is why the life or spirit in the image will be genuine. It is also its ability to "both speak, and cause that as many as would not worship the image of the beast" to be killed. There will be no way to fool the image by pretending to worship it. When a crowd gathers to worship the image, the demon spirit residing in the image will be able to screen the minds of the humans in the crowd and identify fakers by name. The ability of a demonic spirit to access the soul of a human is the reason a person with a familiar spirit can tell you things about yourself that you have forgotten, or that nobody could have known. This deception will be most convincing. For example, if a person would ask the image a question concerning Alexander the Great, the demons who inhabited his body would enter the image, and be able to tell him things about Alexander that were never recorded in history books. This is the experience a person who claims to have returned to a previous life, or lived at some point in history, as someone else has. The demonic spirit, who inhabited the body of the person they claim to have been, is now residing in their body.

The intent of giving life to the image was "that the image of the beast should both speak, and cause that as many as would not worship the image of the beast should be killed." The goal of the ultimatum is to stop the worship of the God of heaven and redirect that worship to the image of the beast. The people killed for their refusal to worship the image are the great multitude we saw in the opening of the sixth seal, in Rev. 7:9, which will be made up of all nations, kindreds, people, and tongues. Although the ultimatum will be worldwide, the prime goal of the False Prophet will be to exterminate the Jews so Jesus cannot establish the Kingdom Dispensation. Today Jesus may not be precious in the eyes of the Jews, but his Father is, and so is his Father's Word. The image and ultimatum will be in direct opposition to the first three commandments of the law under the Old Covenant. They are recorded in Exodus 20:1-6, "(1) And God spake all these words, saying, (2) I am the Lord thy God, which have brought thee out of the land of Egypt, out of the house of bondage. (3) Thou shalt have no other gods before me. (4) Thou shalt not make unto thee any graven image, or any likeness of any thing that is in heaven above, or that is in the earth beneath, or that is in the water under the earth: (5) Thou shalt not bow down thyself to them, nor serve them: for I the Lord thy God am a jealous God, visiting the iniquity of the fathers upon the children unto the third and fourth generation of them that hate me; (6) And shewing mercy unto thousands of them that love me, and keep my commandments." The False Prophet ultimatum to worship the beast image or die outlaws Judaism, but it also outlaws Muslims, Hinduism, Buddhism, Humanism, Communism, Satan worship, all the occults, and anything else you want to add. The ultimatum forbids every form of worship except the worship of the beast image. No group or individual will be excluded from the ultimatum. It will include the atheist, agnostics, and everybody else who claims to worship nothing or something. The image itself will demand worship and it will identify anyone who will not worship, causing them to be put to death. It is the False Prophet who commits the abomination of desolation, by his announcement that the God of heaven will no longer be worshipped. The only way to be saved during the last half of the tribulation period will be to be killed for refusal to worship the image, or to be one of the sealed 144 thousand Jews. These Jews are direct descendants of Abraham and represent the first fruits (Rev. 14:4) of the group to be saved at the end of the Kingdom Dispensation.

The mark of the beast will be required to buy or sell. The mark will be displayed on the right hand or in the forehead. Those who worship the image will be identified by, either the mark of the beast, the name of the beast, or the number of his name. The message of the third proclaiming angel, which will be published by the sealed 144 thousand Jews, is that anyone who worships the beast or takes the mark will be unredeemable. Without the mark you will not be able to buy or sell. Take the mark and God promises you a permanent position in hell. What do you do? Do you really think you could watch your children starve to death? Could you starve to death? What would you do if the government changed your social security number to a mark? Would you walk away from your business, job, and paycheck, or take the mark? After spending your life accumulating money, what will your reaction be when you walk into your bank and find the only way to get to your wealth is to take the mark? What are you going to do when you can't own anything without taking the mark? What will you do if you are ill: take the mark and get medical attention, or suffer? How much pain can you take before you sell your soul? What are you going to do when they give you the choice to worship the beast image, or die? Would you die, or would you choose survival, and take the mark? If you don't care enough about Jesus today, to do what he says, what makes you think you'll love him enough tomorrow, to die for him? What will your decision be? Joel called it right, when he called it the valley of decision in Joel 3:14, "Multitudes, multitudes in the valley of decision: for the day of the Lord is near in the valley of decision."

I'm not saying your social security number, your credit cards, your bank account number, or any other number used today to identify you, or what belongs to you, is the mark of the beast. They are merely examples God has given us to look at, in order to understand what is on the horizon for earth. Take your social security number, for example. If you are a part of the work force in the United States, you are required to pay income taxes. Try getting a job and paying your income tax without a social security number. We are the computer generation. It was our generation who traded our name identification for numbers. We traded our money for a number on a little plastic credit card. We are the generation grooming society for Antichrist. If you think we are too civilized to be a part of such a slaughter, take a good look at Adolf Hitler, Nazi Germany, and their slaughter of the Jews. It is a very accurate picture of Antichrist and the False Prophet, their organization, and their respective missions. When Antichrist arrives, society will welcome him with open arms. Three and one-half years after his arrival the False Prophet will walk into human history and issue the ultimatum to worship the beast image and take the unforgivable mark, or die. Refusal to take the mark will be a capital offense punishable by death. It is at this point in history that the mark of the beast will be placed visibly on ones forehead or right hand, and that act is unforgivable (Rev. 14:9).

The unforgivable mark will be any one of the three things listed in Rev. 13:17, "And that no man might buy or sell, save he that had (1) the mark, or (2) the name of the beast, or (3) the number of his name." The number of his name is given in Rev. 13:18 as 666, "Here is wisdom. Let him that hath understanding count the number of the beast: for it is the number of a man;

and his number is Six hundred three-score and six." The name of the beast may be False Prophet, or perhaps Antichrist, or it may prove to be the name they choose to call the Organization. The mark may be an insignia or emblem of some type, which represents the organization. The only good advice I can give you is, never, under any condition, for any reason, let anyone print a mark, name, or number upon you. I know this is good advice because it came from the mouth of God, and is recorded in Leviticus 19:28, "Ye shall not make any cuttings in your flesh for the dead, nor print any marks upon you: I am the Lord." Don't misunderstand me. It is only during the reign of the False Prophet that a person can print something on their body, that makes them unredeemable. Until that time the only unforgivable sin is blasphemy against the Holy Spirit.

Until the actual printing of the mark, name, or number on your body is made mandatory by the False Prophet, it is what's behind the mark that makes you a member of the Antichrist organization. The printing will be a visible sign of a person's allegiance to the Antichrist organization. What's behind the mark on the forehead is the brain or mind, our thought processing center. We work and do things with our hands, so the mark on the right hand or forehead would indicate that the person had pledged allegiance to the Antichrist's way of thinking and his way of doing things. The mandatory printing of the mark on the body will be visible evidence of allegiance to Antichrist, but even without the mark, the evidence will still be visible. The Antichrist organization is a reality in our world today, but the only people who can see it clearly are true born-again believers. The plain truth is, unless you are born again as Jesus instructed, you are already a member of the Antichrist organization. We have the same situation with the signs Jesus said would follow believers, in the Mark 16:15-18 Church Commission. The signs identify believers, but by their absence, they also identify the unbelieving. Believers belong to Jesus and the unbelieving belong to Antichrist. To join an Antichrist group, a person must ignore, reject, or explain away what Jesus said concerning the five Church Commission signs, and replace it with the excuses of the unbelieving. That is your valley of decision. You can choose to believe what Jesus said, or you can choose to believe something else. The only problem is, if you decide against Jesus, you are putting yourself in agreement with Antichrist.

Words are nothing more than a vehicle to transfer or communicate thoughts. It doesn't matter if they are written or spoken, the result is the same. When people talk to us, their thoughts are being transferred to us. By their words we can actually look into their mind and know what they believe. When we read the Bible the thoughts of God are being transferred to us. The more a person talks, the more we can know about him. The same thing is true with the Bible: The more you read, the more you can know about God. When an individual claims to be a Christian, they are presenting themselves as one who believes and follows the opinions and teachings of Jesus Christ. In talking to you, they are communicating thoughts which agree or disagree with the opinions and teaching of Jesus. If they disagree with what Jesus said, they are not followers and are attempting to deceive you by presenting themselves as something they are not. In Luke 11:23, Jesus said, "He that is not with me is against me." Thoughts are invisible, but the evidence is very clear. When someone tries to tell you something different than what Jesus said, the question is simple. Either Jesus is a liar, or the person you are listening to is a liar. If your opinion of Jesus is that he is a liar, you are in total agreement with Antichrist. Since you already agree with Antichrist, it will represent no threat to you to have his mark printed on your body. In fact, you will welcome the mark, because it will allow you to keep the things you value, and permit you to continue pursuing the things your soul and body lust after.

During the Church Dispensation, Jesus will not force his opinions and teachings on you. You are in the valley of decision and completely free to decide for yourself what you will believe. Your belief will determine your attitudes, opinions, and values. When you translate any of them into words or conduct, anyone can compare them to the Bible and identify you as, in Christ, or in Antichrist. If you leave your Bible at home, you can attend or join any Church, without any problems. You only get in trouble when you compare what they teach to what God teaches in his Word and challenge the discrepancies. For example: If the Mark 16:15-18 signs are not practiced, take them to the passage, and show them where Jesus said the signs would follow them that believe. If they deny the signs, it is apparent that they are not believers. After listening to their excuses, you must decide whether you are going to believe Jesus or them. If you decide in their favor you will be welcomed in the congregation. If you voice a decision to believe Jesus, they will not welcome you. If you try to deceive yourself by thinking you can join and convert them to Jesus, you have made a grave mistake. If they refuse to hear what Jesus said, there is nothing you can say to cause them to believe. They have made their decision, and if you stay, you are supporting not only their decision, but also their cause. If they are unable to convert you to their way of believing, they will remove you from the congregation. The method may be subtle persecution, open hostility, or excommunication, but the reason will be clear: They don't want you there, and neither does Jesus.

If the signs are not practiced, you don't have to sit there and wonder what the congregation believes. Jesus said the signs would follow them that believe, and if the signs are not there, it is because they don't believe. If you choose to join yourself with non-believers, Jesus will honor your decision at the rapture. During the Church Dispensation, Jesus will not separate you from anything, against your will. The rapture ends both the Church, and your opportunity to walk away from the Antichrist organization. To get out of the Antichrist organization after the rapture will cost you your life. Your rejection of Jesus has resulted in his rejection of you, and the subtle persecution of the Antichrist will turn into open hostility. Had you heeded the words of Jesus, you could have avoided being deceived, and would have left Earth in the rapture. It will be too late after you have been caught in the snare and left in the valley of decision. Now they are going to remove you from the organization by killing you, unless you are willing to again, reject Jesus and the Word of God. You will not be given the opportunity to walk away this time. You will either deny Jesus or die. Your only means of salvation will be repentance, your refusal to deny Jesus, and your death at the hands of the Antichrist organization. The unbelieving will be so deceived at this point in time that they will actually think they are doing the will of God by killing you. Here is how Jesus described the situation in John 16:1-3, "(1) These things have I spoken unto you, that ye should not be offended. (2) They shall put you out of the synagogues: yea, the time cometh, that whosoever killeth you will think that he doeth God service. (3) And these things will they do unto you, because they have not known the Father, nor me." When Antichrist is finished using the deceived church, he will turn on it, and destroy it (Rev. 17:16). So the entire deceived church membership will be faced with the same decision in the valley of decision. It is debatable, but I believe the deceived Christians who denied Jesus in order to avoid physical death during the Antichrist reign, will be beyond redemption by the time the False Prophet arrives. I believe they will be first in line to take the mark.

Make no mistake about the Church and the Kingdom of God on Earth. The Church is part of the Kingdom of God, but not the part, promised to the Nation of Israel. God is working with a generation of Israelites in answer to the prayer, "Thy kingdom come. Thy will be done in earth, as it is in heaven" (Matthew 6:10). Jesus is also working with a generation of Church members in fulfillment of the promise in John 14:2-3, "I go to prepare a place for you, I will come again, and receive you unto myself; that where I am, there ye may be also." It is the generation of the ten virgins of Matthew 25:1-13. The unfolding of these events is the midnight cry "Behold, the bridegroom cometh; go ye out to meet him." The members of this generation indwelt by the Holy Spirit are "they that were ready went in with him to the marriage." The remainder of this generation will recognize the rapture, but they will find the door was shut. Their cry, "Lord, Lord, open to us" will be answered by the bridegroom, "Verily I say unto you, I know you not." The people of this generation on the wrong side of the closed door got there because they refused to open their church door when Jesus was standing outside knocking. It is this generation who makes up the Laodicean church membership of Rev. 3:14-22. To this generation Jesus is saying "Behold, I stand at the door, and knock: if any man hear my voice, and open the door, I will come in to him, and will sup with him, and he with me" (Rev. 3:20). It is our generation that saw the events begin to unfold, and I suspect it will be our generation that will see Jesus wrap it up. Whether you let Jesus in or not will determine if you will be caught in the deceivers snare (Luke 21:35), or whether you will be accounted worthy to escape all these thing that shall come to pass (Luke 21:36). Those who escape will leave Earth in the rapture of the Church before the seven-year tribulation begins. The rapture will complete the true Church, and in the twinkling of an eye, we're gone (1 Corinthians 15:51-55).

Ministry of the 144 Thousand Sealed Jews

The ministry of the 144 thousand sealed Jews is recorded in Revelation 14:1-20, "(1) And I looked, and, lo, a Lamb stood on the mount Sion, and with him an hundred forty [and] four thousand, having his Father's name written in their foreheads. (2) And I heard a voice from heaven, as the voice of many waters, and as the voice of a great thunder: and I heard the voice of harpers harping with their harps: (3) And they sung as it were a new song before the throne, and before the four beasts, and the elders: and no man could learn that song but the hundred [and] forty [and] four thousand, which were redeemed from the earth. (4) These are they which were not defiled with women; for they are virgins. These are they which follow the Lamb whithersoever he goeth. These were redeemed from among men, [being] the firstfruits unto God and to the Lamb. (5) And in their mouth was found no guile: for they are without fault before the throne of God. (6) And I saw another angel fly in the midst of heaven, having the everlasting gospel to preach unto them that dwell on the earth, and to every nation, and kindred, and tongue, and people, (7) Saying with a loud voice, Fear God, and give glory to him; for the hour of his judgment is come: and worship him that made heaven, and earth, and the sea, and the fountains of waters. (8) And there followed another angel, saying, Babylon is fallen, is fallen, that great city, because she made all nations drink of the wine of the wrath of her fornication. (9) And the third angel followed them, saying with a loud voice, If any man worship the beast and his image, and receive [his] mark in his forehead, or in his hand, (10) The same shall drink of the wine of the wrath of God, which is poured out without mixture into the cup of his indignation; and he shall be tormented with fire and brimstone in the presence of the holy angels, and in the presence of the Lamb: (11) And the smoke of their torment ascendeth up for ever and ever: and they have no rest day nor night, who worship the beast and his image, and whosoever receiveth the mark of his name. (12) Here is the patience of the saints: here [are] they that keep the commandments of God, and the faith of Jesus. (13) And I heard a voice from heaven saying unto me, Write, Blessed [are] the dead which die in the Lord from henceforth: Yea, saith the Spirit, that they may rest from their labours; and their works do follow them. (14) And I looked, and behold a white cloud, and upon the cloud [one] sat like unto the Son of man, having on his head a golden crown, and in his hand a sharp sickle. (15) And another angel came out of the temple, crying with a loud voice to him that sat on the cloud, Thrust in thy sickle, and reap: for the time is come for thee to reap; for the harvest of the earth is ripe. (16) And he that sat on the cloud thrust in his sickle on the earth; and the earth was reaped. (17) And another angel came out of the temple which is in heaven, he also having a sharp sickle. (18) And another angel came out from the altar, which had power over fire; and cried with a loud cry to him that had the sharp sickle, saying, Thrust in thy sharp sickle, and gather the clusters of the vine of the earth; for her grapes are fully ripe. (19) And the angel thrust in his sickle into the earth, and gathered the vine of the earth, and cast [it] into the great winepress of the wrath of God. (20) And the winepress was trodden without the city, and blood came out of the winepress, even unto the horse bridles, by the space of a thousand [and] six hundred furlongs."

A. The Lamb and 144 Thousand Sealed Jews on Mount Sion.

Rev. 14:1, "And I looked, and, lo, a Lamb stood on the mount Sion, and with him an hundred forty [and] four thousand, having his Father's name written in their foreheads."

The 144 thousand are Jews, actual descendants of Abraham after the flesh, not Gentiles. They were sealed when Jesus opened the sixth seal in Rev. 6:12-7:17 which will be midpoint in the seven-year tribulation era. Their sealing will be identical to the sealing of certain Jews just prior to the destruction of Jerusalem by Nebuchadnezzar, King of Babylon. The Jews who were sealed, were selected to survive the destruction of Jerusalem. God pouring out his fury on the God-rejecting Jerusalem is also a picture of God pouring out his fury on the Christ-rejecting world during the tribulation era.

Ezekiel gives us the description of what took place in the spiritual realm to bring about the destruction of Jerusalem in the physical realm. The account is given in Ezekiel 9:1-11, "(1) He cried also in mine ears with a loud voice, saying, Cause them that have charge over the city to draw near, even every man with his destroying weapon in his hand. (2) And, behold, six men came from the way of the higher gate, which lieth toward the north, and every man a slaughter weapon in his hand; and one man among them was clothed with linen, with a writer's inkhorn by his side: and they went in, and stood beside the brazen altar. (3) And the glory of the God of Israel was gone up from the cherub, whereupon he was, to the threshold of the house. And he called to the man clothed with linen, which had the writer's inkhorn by his side; (4) And the Lord said unto him, Go through the midst of the city, through the midst of Jerusalem, and set a mark upon the foreheads of the men that sigh and that cry for all the abominations that be done in the midst thereof. (5) And to the others he said in mine hearing, Go ye after him through the city, and smite: let not your eye spare, neither have ye pity: (6) Slay utterly old and young, both maids, and little children, and women: but come not near any man upon whom is the mark; and begin at my sanctuary. Then they began at the ancient men which were before the house. (7) And he said unto them, Defile the house, and fill the courts with the slain: go ye forth. And they went forth, and slew the city. (8) And it came to pass, while they were slaying them, and I was left, that I fell upon my face, and cried, and said, Ah Lord God! wilt thou destroy all the residue of Israel in thy pouring out of thy fury upon Jerusalem? (9) Then said he unto me, The iniquity of the house of Israel and Judah is exceeding great, and the land is full of blood, and the city full of perverseness: for they say, The Lord hath forsaken the earth, and the Lord seeth not. (10) And as for me also, mine eye shall not spare, neither will I have pity, but I will recompense their way upon their head. (11) And, behold, the man clothed with linen, which had the inkhorn by his side, reported the matter, saying, I have done as thou hast commanded me."

Sion is the Greek word for the Hebrew name *Zion*. In prophecy, Mount Zion speaks of the mountain of the Lord. This mountain is the kingdom in which the Lord Jesus is King. He is the chief stone in this mountain. This kingdom was promised to the descendants of Abraham throughout the Old Testament. When the Jews rejected this stone, Jesus became the cornerstone of a new building called the Church. The seat of government during the Church Dispensation is in heaven, where the building is being constructed of living stones. These living stones are members of the human family who will accept the redemptive work of Jesus, and enter into the New Covenant via the rebirth. With the rapture of the Church this building is completed, and suddenly the stone falls on the Christ-rejecting church members and grinds them to powder. This wlil be the end of the times of the Gentiles and God will begin to fulfill his promise to make a New Covenant with the Jews. The Jews will be redeemed, receive the New Covenant promise of the Holy Spirit, and the Kingdom promises will become a reality on Earth. The seat of government will be the City of Jerusalem, and all nations will be subject to the Lordship of King Jesus. The prophecies concerning Mount Zion, the mountain of the Lord, and the Kingdom promises all speak of the Kingdom Dispensation. The actual Kingdom Dispensation will only cover the first 1000 years, because at the end of the millennial reign, we have the judgment of the lost, and the creation of a new heaven and new Earth. The saved of Kingdom Era will populate the new creation as living human beings throughout eternity. Here is how the Holy Spirit explains it in Isaiah 59:20-21, "(20) And the Redeemer shall come to Zion, and unto them that turn from transgression in Jacob, saith the Lord. (21) As for me, this is my covenant with them, saith the Lord; My spirit that is upon thee, and my words which I have put in thy mouth, shall not depart out of thy mouth, nor out of the mouth of thy seed, nor out of the mouth of thy seed's seed, saith the Lord, from henceforth and forever."

In another passage in Isaiah, we can see how Jerusalem, the Jews, Zion, the Gentile Nations, the mountain of the Lord, and the kingdom promises all come together, Isaiah 2:1-5, "(1) The word that Isaiah the son of Amoz saw concerning Judah and Jerusalem. (2) And it shall come to pass in the last days, that the mountain of the Lord's house shall be established in the top of the mountains, and shall be exalted above the hills; and all nations shall flow unto it. (3) And many people shall go and say, Come ye, and let us go up to the mountain of the Lord, to the house of the God of Jacob; and he will teach us of his ways, and we will walk in his paths: for out of Zion shall go forth the law, and the word of the Lord from Jerusalem. (4) And he shall judge among the nations, and shall rebuke many people: and they shall beat their swords into plowshares, and their spears into pruning hooks: nation shall not lift up sword against nation, neither shall they learn war any more. (5) O house of Jacob, come ye, and let us walk in the light of the Lord."

From King Nebuchadnezzar's dream of the great image, we know at what point in human history the stone will do its crushing, Dan. 2:31-35, "(31) Thou, O king, sawest, and behold a great image. This great image, whose brightness was excellent, stood before thee; and the form thereof was terrible. (32) This image's head was of fine gold, his breast and his arms of silver, his belly and his thighs of brass, (33) His legs of iron, his feet part of iron and part of clay. (34) Thou sawest till that a stone was cut out without hands, which smote the image upon his feet that were of iron and clay, and brake them to pieces. (35) Then was the iron, the clay, the brass, the silver, and the gold, broken to pieces together, and became like the chaff of the summer threshing floors; and the wind carried them away, that no place was found for them: and the stone that smote the image became a great mountain, and filled the whole earth." Gentile world dominion is about to collapse and pass out of existence. The stone that smote the image will became a great mountain (government) and fill the whole Earth as the planet enters the Kingdom Dispensation.

B. The 144 Thousand Sing a New Song.

Rev. 14:2-5, "(2) And I heard a voice from heaven, as the voice of many waters, and as the voice of a great thunder: and I heard the voice of harpers harping with their harps: (3) And they sung as it were a new song before the throne, and before the four beasts, and the elders: and no man could learn that song but the hundred [and] forty [and] four thousand, which were redeemed from the earth. (4) These are they which were not defiled with women; for they are virgins. These are they which follow the Lamb whithersoever he goeth. These were redeemed from among men, [being] the firstfruits unto God and to the Lamb. (5) And in their mouth was found no guile: for they are without fault before the throne of God."

These 144 thousand Jews will be to the Kingdom Dispensation, what the upper room 120 were to the Church Dispensation, on the Day of Pentecost. They are the first subjects of the Kingdom Era, the first fruits (Rev. 14:4) of many to be saved during the Kingdom Dispensation under the New Covenant God promised the Jews. The New Covenant song these Jews sing is not the same New Testament song the Church is singing. The promises are altogether different. I have been redeemed under the Church New Covenant promises. At the rapture this mortal will put on immortality and enter Heaven to reign with Jesus in the spirit realm throughout eternity as a king and priest to my heavenly Father. These 144 thousand Jews will be redeemed under the Jews' New Covenant promises. At their sealing, these mortals put on immortality, but they will continue to exist throughout eternity in the physical realm as immortal human beings in their human bodies. After they are sealed they will be comparable to Adam and Eve in the Garden of Eden before the fall. Sin kills and these Jews, "are without fault before the throne of God" (Rev. 14:5). What I will be like at the rapture is only comparable to what Jesus was when he walked out of the closed tomb, in his glorified human body. Church members will enter the Kingdom of God via the rebirth, while the people on earth during the kingdom era will, literally, be living in the Kingdom of God. The 144 thousand sealed Jews will not be counted among the tribulation dead. The False Prophet, time, or nothing else in the universe can kill them. Nor can anything separate them from God, "These are they which follow the Lamb whithersoever he goeth" (Rev. 14:4b).

The immortality of the 144 thousand sealed Jews, may be more understandable, if we examine what it means to be saved during the Kingdom Dispensation, from the resurrection point of view. In Daniel 12:2 we saw two resurrections: some to everlasting life; and some to shame and everlasting contempt. In John 5:28-29, Jesus spoke of the same two resurrections: they that have done good, unto the resurrection of life; and they that have done evil, unto the resurrection of damnation. In Revelation chapter 20, we saw where the first resurrection was the resurrection to life, and the second resurrection was the resurrection to damnation. The resurrection to life occurs at the beginning of the Kingdom Era, and the resurrection to damnation occurs at the end of the Kingdom Dispensation. If you are an individual living during the Kingdom Dispensation, and you die physically, the only resurrection you would have to look forward to would be the resurrection to damnation at the end of the era. The resurrection to life would have been past, and it will be an historical event that will never be repeated. The only people who will suffer or die during the Kingdom Dispensation are those who refuse to obey the Word of God. Law breakers will receive swift and just punishment for their disobedience. If the offense is worthy of death, the only resurrection the individual will have to look forward to, will be the resurrection of damnation. I personally believe accidental death will be a thing of the past, but even if it isn't, it will be no problem for Jesus or one of his representatives to restore the individual to life. Don't confuse being restored to life with being resurrected. When an individual is resurrected, it is eternal, while being restored to life, is only temporary, as in the raising of Lazarus from the dead in John 11:1-46. When you read this account, take close notice of the statement Jesus made to Martha in verses 25-26, "(25) Jesus said unto her, I am the resurrection, and the life: he that believeth in me, though he were dead, yet shall he live: (26) And whosoever liveth and believeth in me shall never die. Believest thou this?" Verse 25 applies to Old Testament saints, Church members who died in Christ, and the tribulation dead. Verse 26 applies to the last generation of Christians, the 144 thousand sealed Jews, and those who will survive the Kingdom Dispensation.

Another characteristic of the sealed Jews is given in Rev. 14:4a, "These are they which were not defiled with women; for they are virgins." Jesus is not saying these Jews are unmarried men; in fact, he is not even saying they are men. When dealing with a woman in Bible prophecy, the subject is God's people, or people claiming to be God's people. If they are truly God's people, the woman is presented as a virgin. If the woman is presented as a whore, the people claiming to be God's people are presenting themselves as something they are not. The 144 thousand Jews are virgins, which merely says they are truly God's people. God established and sanctioned marriage, so a man is not defiled with women simply because he is married to one. These Jews were not defiled with women because they refused to join themselves with the Laodicean church congregations, who were presenting themselves as God's people, when they were nothing but fakes, literally, whores. Had the Jews bought what the whore was trying to sell, they would have been destroyed by Antichrist, as she was in Rev. 17:15-16. The Greek word translated as *women* is the same word translated as *woman* in Revelation chapter 17 verses 3, 4, 6, 7, 9, and 18 which describes the judgment of the great whore. The Greek word translated as *virgins* is used elsewhere in the Bible to describe unmarried women, Acts 21:9, 1 Corinthians 7:25, 34, 36, 37 and in verse 28 we have the statement "if a virgin marry, she hath not sinned." The same Greek word is used to describe the true Church in 2 Corinthians 11:2, "For I am jealous over you with godly jealousy: for I have espoused you to one husband, that I may present you as a chaste virgin to Christ."

The Greek word translated as *man*, in the phrase "no man could learn that song" (Rev. 14:9) denotes mankind in the sense that no person, man, woman, or child could learn that song. Jesus used the same Greek word in John 6:44 when he said, "No man can come to me, except the Father which hath sent me draw him," and in John 14:6, "Jesus saith unto him, I am the way, the truth, and the life: no man cometh unto the Father, but by me." The same thing applies to the word *men* in Rev. 14:4, "These were redeemed from among men." The Greek word translated as *men* denotes men in the sense of human beings. Jesus used the same Greek word to tell Peter and Andrew, "Follow me, I will make you fishers of men" (Matthew 4:19), and also in Matt. 6:14-15, "(14) For if ye forgive men their trespasses, your heavenly Father will also forgive you: (15) But if ye forgive not men their trespasses, neither will your Father forgive your trespasses."

C. Message of the First Proclaiming Angel.

Rev. 14:6-7, "(6) And I saw another angel fly in the midst of heaven, having the everlasting gospel to preach unto them that dwell on the earth, and to every nation, and kindred, and tongue, and people, (7) Saying with a loud voice, Fear God, and give glory to him; for the hour of his judgment is come: and worship him that made heaven, and earth, and the sea, and the fountains of waters."

The ministry of the 144 thousand sealed Jews during the False Prophet reign will be three-fold. What they say to the human family will be the messages given by the three proclaiming angels. They will preach the ever lasting gospel, the reality of God's judgment on rebellious Earth, and they will warn of the consequences of worshipping the beast, his image, and taking his unforgivable mark. The everlasting gospel is the unchanging Word of God, literally, the Holy Bible revelation of the God of heaven. It includes the Old Testament account of what he has done and will do, plus the New Testament record of Jesus, who he is, what he did, and what he is going to do. From the statement, "worship him that made heaven, and earth, and the sea, and the fountains of waters," it is plain to see that even at this late date, the evolutionists are still calling God a liar. Also notice their ministry is worldwide, "to every nation, and kindred, and tongue, and people." A great multitude will believe, repent, and turn to the God of the Bible. Many of them will be slaughtered by the Antichrist/False Prophet organization and resurrected to everlasting life at the end of the tribulation era. This is the great multitude of tribulation dead, we saw after Jesus opened the sixth seal.

It is these sealed Jews who will fulfill the prophecy Jesus gave in Matthew 24:14, "And this gospel of the kingdom shall be preached in all the world for a witness unto all nations; and then shall the end come." Notice Jesus begins verse 24:15 with the statement, "When ye therefore shall see the abomination of desolation, spoken of by Daniel the prophet," and continues with the warning for the Jews to flee and hide until they see him coming in the clouds of heaven with power and great glory (Matt. 24:30). The kingdom they are a witness to is the literal Kingdom of God on Earth, with King Jesus ruling from Jerusalem. His subjects, the Nation of Jews, will teach the principles of the kingdom to the Gentile Nations, while Church enjoys her marriage feast.

The Laodicean church membership has thrown a lot of confusion on this subject, but the basic mission is the Mark 16:15-18 Church Commission. Their gospel is the good news of Jesus, as recorded in Luke 24:45-49, "(45) Then opened he their understanding, that they might understand the Scriptures, (46) And said unto them, Thus it is written, and thus it behooved Christ to suffer, and to rise from the dead the third day: (47) And that repentance and remission of sins should be preached in his name among all nations, beginning at Jerusalem. (48) And ye are witnesses of these things. (49) And, behold, I send the promise of my Father upon you: but tarry ye in the city of Jerusalem, until ye be endued with power from on high." There is a world of difference between entering the Kingdom of God, via the rebirth and the Church, and entering the Kingdom of God, via the seven-year tribulation period.

D. Message of the Second Proclaiming Angel.

Rev. 14:8, "And there followed another angel, saying, Babylon is fallen, is fallen, that great city, because she made all nations drink of the wine of the wrath of her fornication."

We are given the details of this judgment in the Revelation chapter 18 flashback. Babylon is the story of Lucifer and his followers in rebellion against God. The human race entered the rebellion in the Garden of Eden, when the human family took the commandments of God and mixed them with directions from Lucifer. The process continued through seven different human kingdoms, or world governments. The culture and intellect of each era, came forward and mixed with the following era. The end result is pure humanism, when the human race reaches the point where they will no longer respond to, or be influenced by, the Word of God. At this point God moves in judgment against Earth, destroys Babylon, and sends his King to rule the planet.

What is said here, in one verse, is expounded in two verses in Revelation chapter 18. The first part of verse 14:8a, "Babylon is fallen, is fallen, that great city" is expounded in verse 18:2, "And he cried mightily with a strong voice, saying, Babylon the great is fallen, is fallen, and is become the habitation of devils, and the hold of every foul spirit, and a cage of every unclean and hateful bird." This is the woe of Rev. 12:12, "Woe to the inhabiters of the earth and of the sea! for the devil is come down unto you, having great wrath, because he knoweth that he hath but a short time." The fall of Babylon, that great city, began when Michael and his angels threw Satan and his angels out of heaven in Rev. 12:7-12. The second part of verse 14:8b, "because she made all nations drink of the wine of the wrath of her fornication" is expounded in verse 18:3, "For all nations have drunk of the wine of the wrath of her fornication, and the kings of the earth have committed fornication with her, and the merchants of the earth are waxed rich through the abundance of her delicacies." The pronoun *her* in verse 18:3 refers to

Satan. The kings of the earth are Satan's angels (the demonic hierarchy), and the merchants of the earth are the human inhabitants who have chosen what Satan offered over what God offered.

E. Message of the Third Proclaiming Angel.

Rev. 14:9-11, "(9) And the third angel followed them, saying with a loud voice, If any man worship the beast and his image, and receive [his] mark in his forehead, or in his hand, (10) The same shall drink of the wine of the wrath of God, which is poured out without mixture into the cup of his indignation; and he shall be tormented with fire and brimstone in the presence of the holy angels, and in the presence of the Lamb: (11) And the smoke of their torment ascendeth up for ever and ever: and they have no rest day nor night, who worship the beast and his image, and whosoever receiveth the mark of his name."

The message of the third proclaiming angel is a warning not to "worship the beast and his image, and receive [his] mark in his forehead, or in his hand." Those who refuse to heed the warning will experience the "wrath of God" in judgment and spend eternity in the torment of literal hell. That act makes them unredeemable.

F. The Fate of the Tribulation Dead who Die in the Lord.

Rev. 14:12-13, "(12) Here is the patience of the saints: here [are] they that keep the commandments of God, and the faith of Jesus. (13) And I heard a voice from heaven saying unto me, Write, Blessed [are] the dead which die in the Lord from henceforth: Yea, saith the Spirit, that they may rest from their labours; and their works do follow them."

The saints during the last half of the tribulation era are "they that keep the commandments of God, and the faith of Jesus." The definition of the word *patience* is "cheerful (or hopeful) endurance" and they are either Jews participating in the flight of the Jews or Gentiles trying to survive without access to the property or wealth they had and without the ability to buy or sell anything. Both are trying to avoid contact with anyone involved with the beast organization and both are being hunted and killed for their refusal to worship the beast image. Many will not survive and God's message to them is "Blessed [are] the dead which die in the Lord from henceforth." The dead who die from henceforth will be counted among the sixth seal group of tribulation dead. At this point in time the entire world population is in the valley of decision, which brings us to harvest time.

G. The Harvest Reaped by the Son of Man on a Cloud.

Rev. 14:14-16, "(14) And I looked, and behold a white cloud, and upon the cloud [one] sat like unto the Son of man, having on his head a golden crown, and in his hand a sharp sickle. (15) And another angel came out of the temple, crying with a loud voice to him that sat on the cloud, Thrust in thy sickle, and reap: for the time is come for thee to reap; for the harvest of the earth is ripe. (16) And he that sat on the cloud thrust in his sickle on the earth; and the earth was reaped."

This reaping is followed by the reaping at Armageddon in Rev. 14:17-20, which will take place at the end of the tribulation era. The reaping by the Son of man on the cloud will start at midpoint in the tribulation era and stop when the Armageddon reaping begins. The Son of man with the golden crown and sharp sickle is Jesus Christ. He is sitting on the white cloud above the earth because his actual return to earth is still three and one-half years in the future. This "harvest of the earth" will be worldwide and will include every nation regardless of their religious heritage. They are not being judged on their religious heritage, only on whether they will or will not worship the beast image and take the mark. The only voice saying, "Don't worship or take the mark" will be from the 144 thousand sealed Jews. Their opinion of the Jews and the God of the Jews will determine their decision. This harvest will result in the sixth seal great multitude of tribulation dead, (Rev. 7:9-17), "of all nations, and kindreds, and people, and tongues." Don't confuse this harvest with the fifth seal group killed during the first half of the tribulation era. This harvest will be worldwide with no limitations, while the Antichrist slaughter will be limited to the Laodicean congregation rejected at the Church rapture.

H. The Reaping at Armageddon.

Rev. 14:17-20, "(17) And another angel came out of the temple which is in heaven, he also having a sharp sickle. (18) And another angel came out from the altar, which had power over fire; and cried with a loud cry to him that had the sharp sickle, saying, Thrust in thy sharp sickle, and gather the clusters of the vine of the earth; for her grapes are fully ripe. (19) And the angel thrust in his sickle into the earth, and gathered the vine of the earth, and cast [it] into the great winepress of the wrath of God. (20) And the winepress was trodden without the city, and blood came out of the winepress, even unto the horse bridles, by the space of a thousand [and] six hundred furlongs."

Judgment of Babylon During the False Prophet Reign

The judgment of Babylon will occur throughout the entire seven-year tribulation era. The part judged during the False Prophet reign is recorded in Revelation 18:1-24, "(1) And after these things I saw another angel come down from heaven, having great power; and the earth was lightened with his glory. (2) And he cried mightily with a strong voice, saying, Babylon the great is fallen, is fallen, and is become the habitation of devils, and the hold of every foul spirit, and a cage of every unclean and hateful bird. (3) For all nations have drunk of the wine of the wrath of her fornication, and the kings of the earth have committed fornication with her, and the merchants of the earth are waxed rich through the abundance of her delicacies. (4) And I heard another voice from heaven, saying, Come out of her, my people, that ye be not partakers of her sins, and that ye receive not of her plagues. (5) For her sins have reached unto heaven, and God hath remembered her iniquities. (6) Reward her even as she rewarded you, and double unto her double according to her works: in the cup which she hath filled fill to her double. (7) How much she hath glorified herself, and lived deliciously, so much torment and sorrow give her: for she saith in her heart, I sit a queen, and am no widow, and shall see no sorrow. (8) Therefore shall her plagues come in one day, death, and mourning, and famine; and she shall be utterly burned with fire: for strong [is] the Lord God who judgeth her. (9) And the kings of the earth, who have committed fornication and lived deliciously with her, shall bewail her, and lament for her, when they shall see the smoke of her burning, (10) Standing afar off for the fear of her torment, saying, Alas, alas that great city Babylon, that mighty city! for in one hour is thy judgment come. (11) And the merchants of the earth shall weep and mourn over her; for no man buyeth their merchandise any more: (12) The merchandise of gold, and silver, and precious stones, and of pearls, and fine linen, and purple, and silk, and scarlet, and all thyine wood, and all manner vessels of ivory, and all manner vessels of most precious wood, and of brass, and iron, and marble, (13) And cinnamon, and odours, and ointments, and frankincense, and wine, and oil, and fine flour, and wheat, and beasts, and sheep, and horses, and chariots, and slaves, and souls of men. (14) And the fruits that thy soul lusted after are departed from thee, and all things which were dainty and goodly are departed from thee, and thou shalt find them no more at all. (15) The merchants of these things, which were made rich by her, shall stand afar off for the fear of her torment, weeping and wailing, (16) And saying, Alas, alas, that great city, that was clothed in fine linen, and purple, and scarlet, and decked with gold, and precious stones, and pearls! (17) For in one hour so great riches is come to nought. And every shipmaster, and all the company in ships, and sailors, and as many as trade by sea, stood afar off, (18) And cried when they saw the smoke of her burning, saying, What [city is] like unto this great city! (19) And they cast dust on their heads, and cried, weeping and wailing, saying, Alas, alas, that great city, wherein were made rich all that had ships in the sea by reason of her costliness! for in one hour is she made desolate. (20) Rejoice over her, [thou] heaven, and [ye] holy apostles and prophets; for God hath avenged you on her. (21) And a mighty angel took up a stone like a great millstone, and cast [it] into the sea, saying, Thus with violence shall that great city Babylon be thrown down, and shall be found no more at all. (22) And the voice of harpers, and musicians, and of pipers, and trumpeters, shall be heard no more at all in thee; and no craftsman, of whatsoever craft [he be], shall be found any more in thee; and the sound of a millstone shall be heard no more at all in thee; (23) And the light of a candle shall shine no more at all in thee; and the voice of the bridegroom and of the bride shall be heard no more at all in thee: for thy merchants were the great men of the earth; for by thy sorceries were all nations deceived. (24) And in her was found the blood of prophets, and of saints, and of all that were slain upon the earth."

A. The Fall of Babylon the Great Announced.

Rev. 18:1-3, "(1) And after these things I saw another angel come down from heaven, having great power; and the earth was lightened with his glory. (2) And he cried mightily with a strong voice, saying, Babylon the great is fallen, is fallen, and is become the habitation of devils, and the hold of every foul spirit, and a cage of every unclean and hateful bird. (3) For all nations have drunk of the wine of the wrath of her fornication, and the kings of the earth have committed fornication with her, and the merchants of the earth are waxed rich through the abundance of her delicacies."

We are at midpoint in the seven-year tribulation era, and the phrase "after these things" refers to the things we saw in Revelation chapter 17, which was the judgment of the Laodicean segment of Babylon during the first half of the tribulation era. Chapter 17 ends with the statement, 17:18, "And the woman (Satan) which thou sawest is that great city, which reigneth over the kings of the earth." The judgment we are going to see here is organizational Babylon consisting of Satan, his spiritual hierarchy (18:1-3, 18:9-10, 18:17-19), and the human element of his organization (merchants and their merchandise, 18:11-16). One of the things seen in the opening of the sixth seal at midpoint in the tribulation was the sealing of 144 thousand Jews. Their three-fold ministry to the world was given by the three proclaiming angels, the second being, "And there followed another angel, saying, Babylon is fallen, is fallen, that great city, because she made all nations drink of the wine of the wrath of her fornication" Rev. 14:8.

The statement "Babylon is fallen" or "Babylon the great is fallen", in essence, is the message that God has begun his judgment of Satan by throwing him and his crew out of Heaven. They are the stars of heaven falling to the earth in the opening of the sixth seal, Rev. 6:13, "And the stars of heaven fell unto the earth, even as a fig tree casteth her untimely figs, when she is shaken of a mighty wind." We learn in Rev. 12:4a that his crew consists of one-third of the created angels, "And his tail drew the third part of the stars of heaven, and did cast them to the earth." More details are provided in Rev. 12:7-9, "(7) And there was war in heaven: Michael and his angels fought against the dragon; and the dragon fought and his angels, (8) And prevailed not; neither was their place found any more in heaven. (9) And the great dragon was cast out, that old serpent, called the Devil, and Satan, which deceiveth the whole world: he was cast out into the earth, and his angels were cast out with him." The information added in Rev. 18:2 is that after being cast out of heaven, they are confined to Earth, "And he cried mightily with a strong voice, saying, Babylon the great is fallen, is fallen, and is become the habitation of devils, and the hold of every foul spirit, and a cage of every unclean and hateful bird." The Greek word translated as *bird* means bird in the sense of "lifting itself up" as it begins to fly. A spirit (human or angelic) lifting itself up denotes pride or the proud boasting themselves against God. At this time the proud humans have been caught in the deceivers snare and the proud demons are in a cage with no way out.

Isaiah saw this time period in Isaiah 13:9-16 and begins by saying "Behold, the day of the LORD cometh." He gives the reason for his coming in verse 11, "And I will punish the world for [their] evil, and the wicked for their iniquity; and I will cause the arrogancy of the proud to cease, and will lay low the haughtiness of the terrible." The reason given in Rev. 18:3 is "For all nations have drunk of the wine of the wrath of her fornication, and the kings of the earth have committed fornication with her, and the merchants of the earth are waxed rich through the abundance of her delicacies."

B. The Call for Separation or Suffer Her Judgment.

Rev. 18:4-8, "(4) And I heard another voice from heaven, saying, Come out of her, my people, that ye be not partakers of her sins, and that ye receive not of her plagues. (5) For her sins have reached unto heaven, and God hath remembered her iniquities. (6) Reward her even as she rewarded you, and double unto her double according to her works: in the cup which she hath filled fill to her double. (7) How much she hath glorified herself, and lived deliciously, so much torment and sorrow give her: for she saith in her heart, I sit a queen, and am no widow, and shall see no sorrow. (8) Therefore shall her plagues come in one day, death, and mourning, and famine; and she shall be utterly burned with fire: for strong [is] the Lord God who judgeth her."

Those who respond to the call from God will be those who listened and obeyed the 144 thousand sealed Jews who were saying, "Don't worship the beast or take the mark." They were called out of Babylon and placed in the sixth seal group of tribulation dead. During this three and one-half year period Jesus opened the seventh seal and the seven trumpet judgments were executed. These judgments were basically concerned with the human element of the population on Earth. Although Satan and his demons were cast out of heaven and restricted to Earth, the only restriction they have on Earth is that they cannot touch the 144 thousand sealed Jews. When the fifth trumpet angel sounds, the demons or fallen angels now imprisoned in Hades are released on the human population. The unsealed are tormented five months and are not allowed to escape the torment through physical death. When the sixth trumpet angel sounds we have the invasion of the 200 million horsemen, which are demonic beings, and a third of the earth's population will be killed. Listen to how Joel describes their invasion in Joel 2:1-10, "(1) Blow ye the trumpet in Zion, and sound an alarm in my holy mountain: let all the inhabitants of the land tremble: for the day of the Lord cometh, for it is nigh at hand; (2) A day of darkness and of gloominess, a day of clouds and of thick darkness, as the morning spread upon the mountains: a great people and a strong; there hath not been ever the like, neither shall be any more after it, even to the years of many generations. (3) A fire devoureth before them; and behind them a flame burneth: the land is as the garden of Eden before them, and behind them a desolate wilderness; yea, and nothing shall escape them. (4) The appearance of them is as the appearance of horses; and as horsemen, so shall they run. (5) Like the noise of chariots on the tops of mountains shall they leap, like the noise of a flame of fire that devoureth the stubble, as a strong people set in battle array. (6) Before their face the people shall be much pained: all faces shall gather blackness. (7) They shall run like mighty men; they shall climb the wall like men of war; and they shall march every one on his ways, and they shall not break their ranks: (8) Neither shall one thrust another; they shall walk every one in his path: and when they fall upon the sword, they shall not be wounded. (9) They shall run to and fro in the city; they shall run upon the wall, they shall climb up upon the houses; they shall enter in at the windows like a thief. (10) The earth shall quake before them; the heavens shall tremble: the sun and the moon shall be dark, and the stars shall withdraw their shining."

The statement, "A fire devoureth before them; and behind them a flame burneth," in Joel 2:3, is the spread of wickedness across Earth. The Holy Spirit describes it this way in Isaiah 9:18-20, "(18) For wickedness burneth as the fire: it shall devour the briers and thorns, and shall kindle in the thickets of the forest, and they shall mount up like the lifting up of smoke. (19) Through the wrath of the Lord of hosts is the land darkened, and the people shall be as the fuel of the fire: no man shall spare his brother. (20) And he shall snatch on the right hand, and be hungry; and he shall eat on the left hand, and they shall not be satisfied: they shall eat every man the flesh of his own arm." Also, notice the statement made in Joel 2:8, "when they fall upon the sword, they shall not be wounded." A human being does not have the ability, or means, to kill a demonic spirit even if they cross into the physical realm and put on flesh. These demons are fallen angels, and they know life is not determined by human flesh. Can you imagine the horror on a soldier's face when he empties his automatic weapon into the body of an incarnate or reincarnated demonic spirit, and the demon just keeps coming at him?

Also take notice of the phrase, "the day of the Lord" in Joel 2:1. Many of the promises God made to the Jews by the mouth of their prophets did not see fulfillment during the period of Old Testament history, specifically, those concerning the tribulation era and the Kingdom era. Many of the prophecies concerning this period of time are identified by the opening statements, "the day of the Lord, in that day, or at that time." The day of the Lord is a key phrase, since the day of the Lord covers both the tribulation and kingdom eras. The day of the Lord will cover at least 1007 years of human history, and it is all still future. A Gentile day starts at midnight and ends at midnight the following night. A Jewish day starts at sundown and ends at sundown the following day. The Jewish day begins with a period of darkness followed by a period of sunlight. The day of the Lord will begin with the period of darkness called the seven-year tribulation era, followed by a 1000 year period of light called the Kingdom Dispensation. If the day of the Lord is being presented as a time of judgment, a time of trouble, a dark or cloudy day, the prophecy is dealing with the tribulation period. If the day of the Lord is being presented as a time of peace, joy, happiness, prosperity, or a time of blessing, the prophecy is dealing with the Kingdom era.

The "day" in the Revelation account is the last day of the tribulation era. Listen to the boast of Babylon and her last day, Rev. 18:7-8, "(7) How much she hath glorified herself, and lived deliciously, so much torment and sorrow give her: for she saith in her heart, I sit a queen, and am no widow, and shall see no sorrow. (8) Therefore shall her plagues come in one day, death, and mourning, and famine; and she shall be utterly burned with fire: for strong [is] the Lord God who judgeth her." "Utterly burned with fire" means she was utterly consumed with judgment. This is where she went into perdition, "total utter ruin." Listen to her boast and God's accusations in Isaiah 47:7-15, "(7) And thou saidst, I shall be a lady for ever: [so] that thou didst not lay these [things] to thy heart, neither didst remember the latter end of it. (8) Therefore hear now this, [thou that art] given to pleasures, that dwellest carelessly, that sayest in thine heart, I [am], and none else beside me; I shall not sit [as] a widow, neither shall I know the loss of children: (9) But these two [things] shall come to thee in a moment in one day, the loss of children, and widowhood: they shall come upon thee in their perfection for the multitude of thy sorceries, [and] for the great abundance of thine enchantments. (10) For thou hast trusted in thy wickedness: thou hast said, None seeth me. Thy wisdom and thy knowledge, it hath perverted thee; and thou hast said in thine heart, I [am], and none else beside me. (11) Therefore shall evil come upon thee; thou shalt not know from whence it riseth: and mischief shall fall upon thee; thou shalt not be able to put it off: and desolation shall come upon thee suddenly, [which] thou shalt not know. (12) Stand now with thine enchantments, and with the multitude of thy sorceries, wherein thou hast laboured from thy youth; if so be thou shalt be able to profit, if so be thou mayest prevail. (13) Thou art wearied in the multitude of thy counsels. Let now the astrologers, the stargazers, the monthly prognosticators, stand up, and save thee from [these things] that shall come upon thee. (14) Behold, they shall be as stubble; the fire shall burn them; they shall not deliver themselves from the power of the flame: [there shall] not [be] a coal to warm at, [nor] fire to sit before it. (15) Thus shall they be unto thee with whom thou hast laboured, [even] thy merchants, from thy youth: they shall wonder every one to his quarter; none shall save thee."

The judgment of Babylon we just saw was the last day of the tribulation era when the seventh vial judgment was executed, Rev. 16:17-21, "(17) And the seventh angel poured out his vial into the air; and there came a great voice out of the temple of heaven, from the throne, saying, It is done. (18) And there were voices, and thunders, and lightnings; and there was a great earthquake, such as was not since men were upon the earth, so mighty an earthquake, [and] so great. (19) And the great city was divided into three parts, and the cities of the nations fell: and great Babylon came in remembrance before God, to give unto her the cup of the wine of the fierceness of his wrath. (20) And every island fled away, and the mountains were not found. (21) And there fell upon men a great hail out of heaven, [every stone] about the weight of a talent: and men blasphemed God because of the plague of the hail; for the plague thereof was exceeding great." In Rev. 17:18 we were told the woman John saw was that great city, "And the woman (Satan) which thou sawest is that great city, which reigneth over the kings of the earth." After her judgment is completed, the organization (the great city) is divided into three parts. The first part is Satan its god, the second part is the demonic hierarchy which abandoned him (standing afar off for the fear of her torment), and the third part of the city is the human beings. The remainder of the chapter is their lament for her and the result of the judgment.

Babylon is a great city because it includes the entire planet. It is planet Earth that has become "the habitation of devils" (demons) as a result of Satan and his angels being thrown out of heaven. God speaks to the entire human population of Earth in Rev. 18:4-8, "(4) And I heard another voice from heaven, saying, Come out of her, my people, that ye be not partakers of her sins, and that ye receive not of her plagues. (5) For her sins have reached unto heaven, and God hath remembered her iniquities. (6) Reward her even as she rewarded you, and double unto her double according to her works: in the cup which she hath filled fill to her double. (7) How much she hath glorified herself, and lived deliciously, so much torment and sorrow give her: for she saith in her heart, I sit a queen, and am no widow, and shall see no sorrow. (8) Therefore shall her plagues come in one day, death, and mourning, and famine; and she shall be utterly burned with fire: for strong is the Lord God who judgeth her." God's people will be the individuals who respond to the message of the 144 thousand sealed Jews, by repenting and accepting the everlasting gospel. The individuals who repent and turn to God will do the same thing Jesus told the Jews to do: flee and hide. If any of the repentant can be located by the False Prophet/Antichrist organization, their sincerity will be put to the test. They will be given the opportunity to worship the beast image and take the unforgivable mark, or die. Nobody on Earth will be permitted to worship anything except the image, and nobody will be able to buy or sell anything except those who have taken the mark.

C. Reaction of the Principality Demons, Kings of the Earth.

Rev. 18:9-10, "(9) And the kings of the earth, who have committed fornication and lived deliciously with her, shall bewail her, and lament for her, when they shall see the smoke of her burning, (10) Standing afar off for the fear of her torment, saying, Alas, alas that great city Babylon, that mighty city! for in one hour is thy judgment come." The demonic hierarchy is composed of principalities and powers. The principalities demons are management ruling over a particular geographical territory. The powers demons are the work force. This lament is from the kings of the earth or principalities demons. When these individuals see God judging Satan, they will abandon him. They don't repent and turn to God; they merely move away from Satan because of fear, and watch his judgment from a distance. Demons are beyond repentance and unredeemable.

D. Reaction of Humans to the Judgment of Babylon.

Rev. 18:11-17a, "(11) And the merchants of the earth shall weep and mourn over her; for no man buyeth their merchandise any more: (12) The merchandise of gold, and silver, and precious stones, and of pearls, and fine linen, and purple, and silk, and scarlet, and all thyine wood, and all manner vessels of ivory, and all manner vessels of most precious wood, and of brass, and iron, and marble, (13) And cinnamon, and odours, and ointments, and frankincense, and wine, and oil, and fine flour, and wheat, and beasts, and sheep, and horses, and chariots, and slaves, and souls of men. (14) And the fruits that thy soul lusted after are departed from thee, and all things which were dainty and goodly are departed from thee, and thou shalt find them no more at all. (15) The merchants of these things, which were made rich by her, shall stand afar off for the fear of her torment, weeping and wailing, (16) And saying, Alas, alas, that great city, that was clothed in fine linen, and purple, and scarlet, and decked with gold, and precious stones, and pearls! (17a) For in one hour so great riches is come to nought." The merchants of the earth are human beings who watch the judgment of Satan and the collapse of his organization. They react in much the same way as the demons. Keep in mind, God is not describing those in the human race, who hungered and thirsted after righteousness. If you see this, it should help in reevaluating your values and priorities.

E. Reaction of the Power Demons to the Judgment of Babylon.

Rev. 18:17b-19, "(17b) And every shipmaster, and all the company in ships, and sailors, and as many as trade by sea, stood afar off, (18) And cried when they saw the smoke of her burning, saying, What [city is] like unto this great city! (19) And they cast dust on their heads, and cried, weeping and wailing, saying, Alas, alas, that great city, wherein were made rich all that had ships in the sea by reason of her costliness! for in one hour is she made desolate."

This lament is from the powers demons which are the work force in the demonic hierarchy. The principalities demons manage and govern over a particular geographical territory. The powers demons manage and govern human beings. They "trade by sea" (water which represents peoples). *Shipmasters*, *sailors*, and *rowers* are demons that have taken up residency in a human body and claimed it as their ship or home. They are "all the company in ships." They maneuver the body through the sea of other people as the person works, shops and goes about his daily routine. The phrase "as many as trade by sea" are wandering demons that move from one human body to another. These demons are disembodied spirits, so the only way they can get enjoyment or satisfaction is through the sense organs of a human body. Depending on their appetite one night they may occupy the body of a young girl so they can play the whore, the next night a homosexual, the next night an alcoholic, the next night a thief, and the next night they team up with a resident demon to rape and murder a child. When the human gets caught, he answers the question "Why did you do it?" with "I don't know" and being ignorant of the Word of God, he is telling you the absolute truth. The demons move in and out of human bodies or take them captive anytime they want to, 2 Timothy 2:25-26, "(25) In meekness instructing those that oppose themselves; if God peradventure will give them repentance to the acknowledging of the truth; (26) And [that] they may recover themselves out of the snare of the devil, who are taken captive by him at his will." There is only one way to keep demons from overcoming you and taking control of your body, 1 John 4:4, "Ye are of God, little children, and have overcome them: because greater is he that is in you, than he that is in the world." The greater in you is the Holy Spirit given to the born-again believer in the rebirth. Otherwise you have no say in the matter, and there is no third choice.

Throughout the Old Testament Scriptures God has used events and figures in human history as a means of communicating with his people. One such example is in Ezekiel chapters 26 through 28 where God uses the judgment of the city of Tyrus to demonstrate what we just read in Revelation chapter 18. Tyre was a seaport city on the Mediterranean Sea which was going to be destroyed by the Babylonian Army (Ezekiel 26:7). In describing the judgment of the city of Tyrus God is giving us a look at the judgment of Babylon the Great. God divides the city of Tyrus into three distinct groups: its king which God uses to describe Satan; the demonic hierarchy, its prince the principality demon enthroned by Satan to rule over the city and its princes, the dominion demons; and, the inhabitants of the city which are the human beings. Listen to the lamentation upon the king of Tyrus and God's description of Satan, Ezekiel 28:11-19, "(11) Moreover the word of the Lord came unto me, saying, (12) Son of man, take up a lamentation upon the king of Tyrus, and say unto him, Thus saith the Lord God; Thou sealest up the sum, full of wisdom, and perfect in beauty. (13) Thou hast been in Eden the garden of God; every precious stone was thy covering, the sardius, topaz, and the diamond, the beryl, the onyz, and the jasper, the sapphire, the emerald, and the carbuncle, and gold: the workmanship of thy tabrets and of thy pipes was prepared in thee in the day that thou wast created. (14) Thou art the anointed cherub that covereth; and I have set thee so: thou wast upon the holy mountain of God; thou hast walked up and down in the midst of the stones of fire. (15) Thou wast perfect in thy ways from the day that thou wast created, till iniquity was found in thee. (16) By the multitude of thy merchandise they have filled the midst of thee with violence, and thou hast sinned: therefore I will cast thee as profane out of the mountain of God: and I will destroy thee, O covering cherub, from the midst of the stones of fire. (17) Thine heart was lifted up because of thy beauty, thou hast corrupted thy wisdom by reason of thy brightness: I will cast thee to the ground, I will lay thee before kings, that they may behold thee. (18) Thou hast defiled thy sanctuaries by the multitude of thine iniquities, by the iniquity of thy traffick; therefore will I bring forth a fire from the midst of thee, it shall devour thee, and I will bring thee to ashes upon the earth in the sight of all them that behold thee. (19) All they that know thee among the people shall be astonished at thee: thou shalt be a terror, and never shalt thou be any more."

In Ezekiel 28:1-10 we have God's description of the principality demon, the prince of Tyrus, "(1) The word of the Lord came again unto me, saying, (2) Son of man, say unto the prince of Tyrus, Thus saith the Lord God; Because thine heart is lifted up, and thou hast said, I am a God, I sit in the seat of God, in the midst of the seas; yet thou art a man, and not God, though thou set thine heart as the heart of God: (3) Behold, thou art wiser than Daniel; there is no secret that they can hide from thee: (4) With thy wisdom and with thine understanding thou hast gotten thee riches, and hast gotten gold and silver into thy treasures: (5) By thy great wisdom and by thy traffick hast thou increased thy riches, and thine heart is lifted up because of thy riches: (6) Therefore thus saith the Lord God; Because thou hast set thine heart as the heart of God: (7) Behold, therefore I will bring strangers upon thee, the terrible of the nations: and they shall draw their swords against the beauty of thy wisdom, and they shall defile thy brightness, (8) They shall bring thee down to the pit, and thou shalt die the deaths of them that are slain in the midst of the seas. (9) Wilt thou yet say before him that slayeth thee, I am God? but thou shalt be a man, and no God, in the hand of him that slayeth thee. (10) Thou shalt die the deaths of the uncircumcised by the hand of strangers: for I have spoken it, saith the Lord God."

In Rev. 18:11-17a we just read about the "merchants of the earth" and identified them as those in the human race who did not "hunger and thirst after righteousness." In the Revelation account we saw the things the inhabitants of Babylon hungered and thirsted after, which are summed up in Revelation 18:14 as "the fruits that thy soul lusted after." There is nothing wrong or sinful about the merchandise, but when the lust for these things begins to drive you, it's time to consider who is in control. Disembodied demons cannot have or own anything so the only way for them to satisfy their craving for things in the physical realm is to drive a human. If the lust is compulsive and against your will, it should be obvious you are not rowing your own boat. The inhabitants or merchants of Tyrus trafficked in these same commodities and in reading Ezekiel 27:1-36 it looks like business as usual until we reach verse 26 and the statement "Thy rowers have brought thee into great waters." While the merchants were busy merchandising, the rowers were busy rowing. The merchants of the earth are the human beings, and the rowers are demonic spirits. These demons have successfully separated the inhabitants of Tyrus from God and rowed or carried them away by the cares of this world, the deceitfulness of riches, and the lust of other things (Mark 4:19). We would be accurate to describe the merchants of Tyrus as demon-possessed human beings. In looking at the inhabitants of Babylon, we saw that this type seduction results in the human and demon becoming one. In this condition, from God's point of view, they are so much alike that when He is talking about them, it is sometimes difficult to distinguish between the human and the demon.

We could also make the statement "they are all in the same boat" which is accurate today but at the end of the judgment of Babylon the Great this statement would be inaccurate. When the principality demons (the kings of the earth, Rev. 18:9-10) see the judgment of Satan they are going to abandon him, "standing afar off for the fear of her torment." When the powers demons see Satan's judgment, they abandon ship by leaving the human bodies in which they have been residing. The abandonment is recorded in Rev. 17b, "And every shipmaster, and all the company in ships, and sailors, and as many as trade by sea, stood afar off." Their lament starts in verse 18 "And cried when they saw the smoke of her burning, saying, What city is like unto this great city! (19) And they cast dust on their heads, and cried, weeping and wailing, saying, Alas, alas, that great city, wherein were made rich all that had ships in the sea by reason of her costliness! for in one hour is she made desolate."

Compare their abandonment and lament to Ezekiel 27:26-36, "(26) Thy rowers have brought thee into great waters: the east wind hast broken thee in the midst of the seas. (27) Thy riches, and thy fairs, thy merchandise, thy mariners, and thy pilots, thy calkers, and the occupiers of thy merchandise, and all thy men of war, that are in thee, and in all thy company which is in the midst of thee, shall fall into the midst of the seas in the day of thy ruin.

(28) The suburbs shall shake at the sound of the cry of thy pilots. (29) And all that handle the oar, the mariners, and all the pilots of the sea, shall come down from their ships, they shall stand upon the land; (30) And shall cause their voice to be heard against thee, and shall cry bitterly, and shall cast up dust upon their heads, they shall wallow themselves in the ashes: (31) And they shall make themselves utterly bald for thee, and gird them with sackcloth, and they shall weep for thee with bitterness of heart and bitter wailing. (32) And in their wailing they shall take up a lamentation for thee, and lament over thee, saying, What city is like Tyrus, like the destroyed in the midst of the sea? (33) When thy wares went forth out of the seas, thou filledst many people; thou didst enrich the kings of the earth with the multitude of thy riches and of thy merchandise. (34) In the time when thou shalt be broken by the seas in the depths of the waters thy merchandise and all thy company in the midst of thee shall fall. (35) And the inhabitants of the isles shall be astonished at thee, and their kings shall be sore afraid, they shall be troubled in their countenance. (36) The merchants among the people shall hiss at thee; thou shalt be a terror, and never shalt be any more."

Notice what the rowers did in Ezekiel 27:29 "And all that handle the oar, the mariners, and all the pilots of the sea, shall come down from their ships, they shall stand upon the land." This is a description of the demonic spirits separating themselves from the human bodies in which they have been residing and controlling. They are the "princes of the sea" leaving their thrones in Ezekiel 26:13-21, "(13) And I will cause the noise of thy songs to cease; and the sound of thy harps shall be no more heard. (14) And I will make thee like the top of a rock: thou shalt be a place to spread nets upon; thou shalt be built no more: for I the Lord have spoken it, saith the Lord God. (15) Thus saith the Lord God to Tyrus; Shall not the isles shake at the sound of thy fall, when the wounded cry, when the slaughter is made in the midst of thee? (16) Then all the princes of the sea shall come down from their thrones, and lay away their robes, and put off their broidered garments: they shall clothe themselves with trembling; they shall sit upon the ground, and shall tremble at every moment, and be astonished at thee. (17) And they shall take up a lamentation for thee, and say to thee, How art thou destroyed, that wast inhabited of seafaring men, the renowned city, which wast strong in the sea, she and her inhabitants, which cause their terror to be on all that haunt it! (18) Now shall the isles tremble in the day of thy fall; yea, the isles that are in the sea shall be troubled at thy departure. (19) For thus saith the Lord God; When I shall make thee a desolate city, like the cities that are not inhabited; when I shall bring up the deep upon thee, and great waters shall cover thee; (20) When I shall bring thee down with them that descend into the pit, with the people of old time, and shall set thee in the low parts of the earth, in places desolate of old, with them that go down to the pit, that thou be not inhabited; and I shall set glory in the land of the living: (21) I will make thee a terror, and thou shalt be no more: though thou be sought for, yet shalt thou never be found again, saith the Lord God." The demons clothe themselves with trembling and will never again sing the songs you are hearing today. If you have chosen to dance to the songs they are singing, the day will come when you, too, will clothe yourself with trembling.

F. The Result of the Judgment of Babylon.

Rev. 18:20-24, "(20) Rejoice over her, [thou] heaven, and [ye] holy apostles and prophets; for God hath avenged you on her. (21) And a mighty angel took up a stone like a great millstone, and cast [it] into the sea, saying, Thus with violence shall that great city Babylon be thrown down, and shall be found no more at all. (22) And the voice of harpers, and musicians, and of pipers, and trumpeters, shall be heard no more at all in thee; and no craftsman, of whatsoever craft [he be], shall be found any more in thee; and the sound of a millstone shall be heard no more at all in thee; (23) And the light of a candle shall shine no more at all in thee; and the voice of the bridegroom and of the bride shall be heard no more at all in thee: for thy merchants were the great men of the earth; for by thy sorceries were all nations deceived. (24) And in her was found the blood of prophets, and of saints, and of all that were slain upon the earth."

In Romans 12:19 we are told, "Dearly beloved, avenge not yourselves, but [rather] give place unto wrath: for it is written, Vengeance [is] mine; I will repay, saith the Lord." It is written in Deuteronomy 32:41-43, "(41) If I whet my glittering sword, and mine hand take hold on judgment; I will render vengeance to mine enemies, and will reward them that hate me. (42) I will make mine arrows drunk with blood, and my sword shall devour flesh; [and that] with the blood of the slain and of the captives, from the beginning of revenges upon the enemy. (43) Rejoice, O ye nations, [with] his people: for he will avenge the blood of his servants, and will render vengeance to his adversaries, and will be merciful unto his land, [and] to his people." This is the day Jesus gets blood stains on his garment, Isaiah 63:2-4, "(2) Wherefore [art thou] red in thine apparel, and thy garments like him that treadeth in the winefat? (3) I have trodden the winepress alone; and of the people [there was] none with me: for I will tread them in mine anger, and trample them in my fury; and their blood shall be sprinkled upon my garments, and I will stain all my raiment. (4) For the day of vengeance [is] in mine heart, and the year of my redeemed is come." The rejoicing in heaven is because God has avenged.

The mighty angel who cast the stone into the sea said, "Thus with violence shall that great city Babylon be thrown down, and shall be found no more at all." Jeremiah wrote a letter concerning the judgment of the Babylon Empire and had Seraiah, a prince on King Zedekiah's staff, take the letter to the City of Babylon and read it. Jeremiah told him how to dispose of the book in 51:63-64a, "(63) And it shall be, when thou hast made an end of reading this book, [that] thou shalt bind a stone to it, and cast it into the midst of Euphrates: (64a) And thou shalt say, Thus shall Babylon sink, and shall not rise from the evil that I will bring upon her." Jeremiah Chapter 51 is a copy of the letter and it parallels the judgment in the Revelation account. The reason for God's avenging is given in Rev. 18:23c-24, "(23c) for thy merchants were the great men of the earth; for by thy sorceries were all nations deceived. (24) And in her was found the blood of prophets, and of saints, and of all that were slain upon the earth." The things missing in Babylon after the judgment are, Rev. 18:22-23a, "(22) And the voice of harpers, and musicians, and of pipers, and trumpeters, shall be heard no more at all in thee; and no craftsman, of whatsoever craft [he be], shall be found any more in thee; and the sound of a millstone shall be heard no more at all in thee; (23a) And the light of a candle shall shine no more at all in thee; and the voice of the bridegroom and of the bride shall be heard no more at all in thee."

Israel and the Great Red Dargon

The account of Israel and the Great Red Dragon is recorded Revelation 12:1-17, "(1) And there appeared a great wonder in heaven; a woman clothed with the sun, and the moon under her feet, and upon her head a crown of twelve stars: (2) And she being with child cried, travailing in birth, and pained to be delivered. (3) And there appeared another wonder in heaven; and behold a great red dragon, having seven heads and ten horns, and seven crowns upon his heads. (4) And his tail drew the third part of the stars of heaven, and did cast them to the earth: and the dragon stood before the woman which was ready to be delivered, for to devour her child as soon as it was born. (5) And she brought forth a man child, who was to rule all nations with a rod of iron: and her child was caught up unto God, and [to] his throne. (6) And the woman fled into the wilderness, where she hath a place prepared of God, that they should feed her there a thousand two hundred [and] threescore days. (7) And there was war in heaven: Michael and his angels fought against the dragon; and the dragon fought and his angels, (8) And prevailed not; neither was their place found any more in heaven. (9) And the great dragon was cast out, that old serpent, called the Devil, and Satan, which deceiveth the whole world: he was cast out into the earth, and his angels were cast out with him. (10) And I heard a loud voice saying in heaven, Now is come salvation, and strength, and the kingdom of our God, and the power of his Christ: for the accuser of our brethren is cast down, which accused them before our God day and night. (11) And they overcame him by the blood of the Lamb, and by the word of their testimony; and they loved not their lives unto the death. (12) Therefore rejoice, [ye] heavens, and ye that dwell in them. Woe to the inhabiters of the earth and of the sea! for the devil is come down unto you, having great wrath, because he knoweth that he hath but a short time. (13) And when the dragon saw that he was cast unto the earth, he persecuted the woman which brought forth the man [child]. (14) And to the woman were given two wings of a great eagle, that she might fly into the wilderness, into her place, where she is nourished for a time, and times, and half a time, from the face of the serpent. (15) And the serpent cast out of his mouth water as a flood after the woman, that he might cause her to be carried away of the flood. (16) And the earth helped the woman, and the earth opened her mouth, and swallowed up the flood which the dragon cast out of his mouth. (17) And the dragon was wroth with the woman, and went to make war with the remnant of her seed, which keep the commandments of God, and have the testimony of Jesus Christ."

A. The Sun-Clothed Woman and the Great Red Dragon.

Rev. 12:1-6, "(1) And there appeared a great wonder in heaven; a woman clothed with the sun, and the moon under her feet, and upon her head a crown of twelve stars: (2) And she being with child cried, travailing in birth, and pained to be delivered. (3) And there appeared another wonder in heaven; and behold a great red dragon, having seven heads and ten horns, and seven crowns upon his heads. (4) And his tail drew the third part of the stars of heaven, and did cast them to the earth: and the dragon stood before the woman which was ready to be delivered, for to devour her child as soon as it was born. (5) And she brought forth a man child, who was to rule all nations with a rod of iron: and her child was caught up unto God, and [to] his throne. (6) And the woman fled into the wilderness, where she hath a place prepared of God, that they should feed her there a thousand two hundred [and] threescore days."

The woman is the Nation of Israel, her child is Jesus Christ, and the great red dragon is Satan. Joseph saw the Nation of Israel presented this way in the book of Genesis, when the nation was only he, his eleven brothers and their parents. Genesis 37:9-11, "(9) And he (Joseph) dreamed yet another dream, and told it his brethren, and said, Behold, I have dreamed a dream more; and, behold, the sun and the moon and the eleven stars made obeisance to me. (10) And he told it to his father, and to his brethren: and his father rebuked him, and said unto him, What is this dream that thou hast dreamed? Shall I and thy mother and thy brethren indeed come to bow down ourselves to thee to the earth? (11) And his brethren envied him; but his father observed the saying."

The Nation of Israel, this woman, is going to do two different things, separated by two thousand years of human history. The first thing she does is already history, and if we look at the event in its proper sequence, we would read Revelation 12 verses 1, 2, and 5, "(1) And there appeared a great wonder in heaven; a woman clothed with the sun, and the moon under her feet, and upon her head a crown of twelve stars: (2) And she being with child cried, travailing in birth, and pained to be delivered. (5) And she brought forth a man child, who was to rule all nations with a rod of iron: and her child was caught up unto God, and to his throne." The second thing this woman (Nation) does will happen two thousand years later, when she sees the False Prophet and the abomination of desolation. The second event is the flight of the Jews, Revelation 12 verses 1, 2, and 6, "(1) And there appeared a great wonder in heaven; a woman clothed with the sun, and the moon under her feet, and upon her head a crown of twelve stars: (2) And she being with child cried, travailing in birth, and pained to be delivered. (6) And the woman fled into the wilderness, where she hath a place prepared of God, and they should feed her there a thousand two hundred and three-score days." These 1260 days will be the last half of the seven-year tribulation era. In Matthew 24:15-22 Jesus told us the event that would trigger the flight of the Jews will be the abomination of desolation spoken of by Daniel the prophet. Keep in mind that Daniel lived during the days of the Babylonian Empire when the calendar was based on 360 days a year, not 365. 3.5 years times 360 days equals 1260 days.

Needless to say, both events speak of the coming of the Lord Jesus. The first event was the first coming of Jesus as a baby (man-child) in the flesh to suffer and die, in order to pay the ransom for our sins and redeem us. The Jewish Nation stumbled over Jesus and didn't recognize him as the promised Messiah, but they will recognize him at his second coming as King of Kings and Lord of Lords, to end their Gentile captivity and establish the Kingdom Dispensation. Isaiah chapter 66 deals with the transition to the Kingdom era and in verse 7, the Nation of Israel is presented as a woman who got her labor pains after she gave birth, "Before she travailed, she brought forth; before her pain came, she was delivered of a man child." Her pain and travail here refer to the suffering and prayers of the Nation of Israel during the last half of the tribulation era. Their anguish, during this period of time, is being compared to the anguish of a woman giving birth. The difference is that 2000 years ago the woman was delivered of a man-child, and during the last half of the tribulation era, the woman will be crying to the man-child to deliver her. Another comparison is in Jeremiah 30:6-7, "(6) Ask ye now, and see whether a man doth travail with child? wherefore do I see every man with his hands on his loins, as a woman in travail, and all faces are turned into paleness? (7) Alas! for that day is great, so that none is like it: it is even the time of Jacob's trouble; but he shall be saved out of it." Jeremiah chapter 4 also deals with this period of time, and the chapter ends with, "(31) For I have heard a voice as of a woman in travail, and the anguish as of her that bringeth forth her first child, the voice of the daughter of Zion, that bewaileth herself, that spreadeth her hands, saying, Woe is me now! for my soul is wearied because of murderers." Isaiah chapter 24 also deals with this period of time.

The great red dragon of Rev. 12:3-4 is identified in verse 12:9 as Satan. Rev. 12:3-4, "(3) And there appeared another wonder in heaven; and behold a great red dragon, having seven heads and ten horns, and seven crowns upon his heads. (4) And his tail drew the third part of the stars of heaven, and did cast them to the earth: and the dragon stood before the woman which was ready to be delivered, for to devour her child as soon as it was born." Again, this same dragon is going to do two different things, separated by some two thousand years of human history. Two thousand years ago "the dragon stood before the woman (Israel) which was ready to be delivered, for to devour her child as soon as it was born." At that time he killed all the children in or near the city of Bethlehem two years old and under (Matthew 2:16-18), but during the last half of the tribulation era he will try to exterminate the entire Nation of Jews. In reading Jeremiah chapter 4, and Isaiah chapter 24, it would appear that Satan's goal is to exterminate the entire human race. In speaking of this same period of time, Jesus said if these days were not shortened, the human race would be annihilated. Matthew 24:21-22, "(21) For then shall be great tribulation, such as was not since the beginning of the world to this time, no, nor ever shall be. (22) And except those days should be shortened, there should no flesh be saved: but for the elect's sake those days shall be shortened."

Notice how Satan the "great red dragon" is described. He is seen as "having seven heads and ten horns" which describes the beast we saw during the Antichrist reign in Rev. 13:1-10. It is the same beast organization, just two different time periods. We know this prophecy concerns the period of human history when Jesus was born by where the crowns are located on the great red dragon, "seven crowns upon his heads." Political authority was with the Roman Empire, the sixth Gentile world power to rule during the Jewish captivity. The ten horns represent the future political system described in Rev. 17:12, "And the ten horns which thou sawest are ten kings, who have received no kingdom as yet, but receive power as kings one hour with the beast." When Antichrist walks into human history the political authority will shift from the heads to the horns. Notice where the crowns are located when Antichrist arrives in Rev. 13:1, "And I stood upon the sand of the sea, and saw a beast rise up out of the sea, having seven heads and ten horns, and upon his horns ten crowns, and upon his heads the name of blasphemy."

The statement "his tail drew the third part of the stars of heaven, and did cast them to the earth" speaks of the rebellion in heaven. The stars of heaven he drew with his tail are the angels who aligned themselves with Satan in his rebellion against God. One-third of the angels of heaven are fallen angels, which form Satan's demonic hierarchy. In Isaiah 9:15 we are told "the prophet that teacheth lies, he is the tail," so the angels who were drawn away, believed Satan's lies.

B. War in Heaven.

Rev. 12:7-12, "(7) And there was war in heaven: Michael and his angels fought against the dragon; and the dragon fought and his angels, (8) And prevailed not; neither was their place found any more in heaven. (9) And the great dragon was cast out, that old serpent, called the Devil, and Satan, which deceiveth the whole world: he was cast out into the earth, and his angels were cast out with him. (10) And I heard a loud voice saying in heaven, Now is come salvation, and strength, and the kingdom of our God, and the power of his Christ: for the accuser of our brethren is cast down, which accused them before our God day and night. (11) And they overcame him by the blood of the Lamb, and by the word of their testimony; and they loved not their lives unto the death. (12) Therefore rejoice, [ye] heavens, and ye that dwell in them. Woe to the inhabiters of the earth and of the sea! for the devil is come down unto you, having great wrath, because he knoweth that he hath but a short time."

Notice it is Michael and his angels that throw Satan and his demonic hierarchy (his angels) out of heaven, not the Church. The statement, "And the stars of heaven fell unto the earth" when Jesus opened the sixth seal in Rev. 6:12-13, brought us to the midpoint in the seven-year tribulation era. The phrase in verse 12:8, "Neither was their place found any more in heaven" means that from this point in time, on throughout eternity, Satan and his angels (the fallen angels in the demonic hierarchy) are no longer permitted to enter heaven. Up to this point in time Satan and crew were permitted to enter heaven and present themselves (Job 1:6, 2:1) before the throne of God, to submit accusations (Rev. 12:10) against God's people, which is presented in Colossians 2:14 as "handwriting of ordinances that was against us, which was contrary to us." When Satan and crew are thrown out of heaven, the inhabitants of heaven rejoice, and a woe is pronounced to the inhabiters of Earth because, "the devil is come down unto you, having great wrath, because he knoweth that he hath but a short time." The changes that took effect when Satan is cast out of heaven are given in the first part of verse 10, "And I heard a loud voice saying in heaven, Now is come salvation, and strength, the kingdom of our God, and the power of his Christ." What made the changes possible is explained in the last part of the verse, "for the accuser of our brethren is cast down, which accused them before our God day and night."

C. The Dragon Turns His Wrath on the Remnant of Her Seed.

Rev. 12:13-17, "(13) And when the dragon saw that he was cast unto the earth, he persecuted the woman which brought forth the man [child]. (14) And to the woman were given two wings of a great eagle, that she might fly into the wilderness, into her place, where she is nourished for a time, and times, and half a time, from the face of the serpent. (15) And the serpent cast out of his mouth water as a flood after the woman, that he might cause her to be carried away of the flood. (16) And the earth helped the woman, and the earth opened her mouth, and swallowed up the flood which the dragon cast out of his mouth. (17) And the dragon was wroth with the woman, and went to make war with the remnant of her seed, which keep the commandments of God, and have the testimony of Jesus Christ."

This describes the activities of the Antichrist/False Prophet organization against the Nation of Israel during the last half of the tribulation era. At this point in time the False Prophet is reincarnated, three of the ten nations in the European Common Market are eliminated, the image of the beast is introduced, and the abomination of desolation occurs as he issues the ultimatum to worship the image and take the unforgivable mark or die. The ultimatum breaks the Antichrist protection covenant, which causes the flight of the Jews. The False Prophet (the serpent) propaganda will result in the worldwide persecution of the Jews. This will be the way Jesus lets individual Gentiles and Gentile nations determine if they want to be counted with the sheep nations or the goat nations (Matthew 25:31-46).

Jesus spoke of the flight of the Jews during the great tribulation era and the abomination of desolation in Mark 13:14-27 and Matthew 24:15-27, "(15) When ye therefore shall see the abomination of desolation, spoken of by Daniel the prophet, stand in the holy place, (whoso readeth, let him understand:) (16) Then let them which be in Judaea flee into the mountains: (17) Let him which is on the housetop not come down to take any thing out of his house: (18) Neither let him which is in the field return back to take his clothes. (19) And woe unto them that are with child, and to them that give suck in those days! (20) But pray ye that your flight be not in the winter, neither on the sabbath day: (21) For then shall be great tribulation, such as was not since the beginning of the world to this time, no, nor ever shall be. (22) And except those days should be shortened, there should no flesh be saved: but for the elect's sake those days shall be shortened. (23) Then if any man shall say unto you, Lo, here [is] Christ, or there; believe [it] not. (24) For there shall arise false Christs, and false prophets, and shall shew great signs and wonders; insomuch that, if [it were] possible, they shall deceive the very elect. (25) Behold, I have told you before. (26) Wherefore if they shall say unto you, Behold, he is in the desert; go not forth: behold, [he is] in the secret chambers; believe [it] not. (27) For as the lightning cometh out of the east, and shineth even unto the west; so shall also the coming of the Son of man be."

When Antichrist turns on the Church he will cause a "flight of the deceived Christians" just like the flight of the Jews from the False Prophet when he issues his ultimatum. The Jews living on Earth, when the False Prophet rises to power will have three and one-half years to watch the slaughter of Christians by the Antichrist organization and to benefit from the ministry of the two witnesses of Rev. 11:1-13. These two events may alert many as to the signs of the time and cause them to take notice of what is happening. Those who take notice will flee from the False Prophet and hide as Jesus told them to do. Many, if not all, of them will "be accounted worthy to escape all these things that shall come to pass, and to stand before the Son of man" (Luke 21:36), as living human beings to enter the Kingdom Dispensation. The fact the deceived Christians woke up on the wrong side of the rapture is proof that they did not heed the signs of the time. They are equal to the group Jesus spoke of in Luke 21:34-36, "(34) And take heed to yourselves, lest at any time your hearts be overcharged with surfeiting, and drunkenness, and cares of this life, and so that day come upon you unawares. (35) For as a snare it shall come on all them that dwell on the face of the whole earth. (36) Watch ye therefore, and pray always, that ye may be accounted worthy to escape all these things that shall come to pass, and to stand before the Son of man." Had they been obedient to the words of Jesus, they could have entered the kingdom of God via the Church. Then they would have been "accounted worthy to escape all these things that shall come to pass, and to stand before the Son of man" as a member of the Bride of Christ. Like the five foolish virgins of Matthew 25:1-13, they are going to be found void of the Holy Spirit and not ready to go with him to the marriage, or more specifically, to leave Earth in the rapture of the Church. By the time they come to the realization that Jesus had told them the truth, the Church door will be shut, and the Antichrist mob will find and kill them for their testimony of Jesus and the Word of God. This way they will become members of the fifth seal tribulation dead of Rev. 6:9-11.

The Jews who refuse to heed the warning of Jesus to hide and those captured by the False Prophet/Antichrist organization will be faced with the same decision the deceived Christians faced with Antichrist. They must either deny the Word of God and the testimony of Jesus by bowing to the beast image or be killed. The advice Jesus gave the Jews to follow during this period of time is recorded in Luke 21:12-19, "(12) But before all these, they shall lay their hands on you, and persecute you, delivering you up to the synagogues, and into prisons, being brought before kings and rulers for my name's sake. (13) And it shall turn to you for a testimony. (14) Settle it therefore in your hearts, not to meditate before what ye shall answer: (15) For I will give you a mouth and wisdom, which all your adversaries shall not be able to gainsay nor resist. (16) And ye shall be betrayed both by parents, and brethren, and kinsfolk, and friends; and some of you shall they cause to be put to death. (17) And ye shall be hated of all men for my name's sake. (18) But there shall not an hair of your head perish. (19) In your patience possess ye your souls." The same time period is covered in Matthew 24:9-14, "(9) Then shall they deliver you up to be afflicted, and shall kill you: and ye shall be hated of all nations for my name's sake. (10) And then shall many be offended, and shall betray one another, and shall hate one another. (11) And many false prophets shall rise, and deceive many. (12) And because iniquity shall abound, the love of many shall wax cold. (13) But he that shall endure unto the end, the same shall be saved. (14) And this gospel of the kingdom shall be preached in all the world for a witness unto all nations; and then shall the end come." Both the Luke and Matthew accounts continue with the warning to flee to the mountains and hide.

The 144 thousand sealed Jews will be as much of a problem to the False Prophet as the two witnesses were to Antichrist. During the entire three and one-half year period, the False Prophet has been trying to persuade earth dwellers to join his organization and take the mark. At the same time, the 144 thousand Jews were saying, "Take the mark, and you'll spend eternity in hell." The Antichrist/False Prophet propaganda will be designed to lure the Jews from hiding, but the 144 thousand urge them to stay hidden. The words that come out of the mouth of Satan will cause many people to pursue the woman, for the purpose of destroying her. The earth will help the woman in her efforts to avoid the organization and wherever she goes someone will give her nourishment and a cup of cold water. This woman not only includes the sealed 144 thousand, but all the Jews fleeing from the False Prophet. Satan eventually will realize that regardless of how many people he sends after the 144 thousand, they cannot be captured or killed. In anger, he will change his tactics and turn his attention to destroying the unsealed Jews, by making war with the remnant of her seed.

Chapter Six

Daniel

The Book of Daniel and the Book of the Revelation are both called apocalyptic books, because they are mainly concerned with prophetic revelation. The Book of Daniel is to the Jews as the Book of the Revelation is to the Church. By the Prophet Daniel, God reveals the entire period of the "times of the Gentiles" or from their view, the Jewish captivity. The "times of the Gentiles" began when Shalmaneser the King of Assyria, invaded the Northern Kingdom of Israel (2 Kings 17:1-41), and eleven tribes were taken captive. One hundred years after the Northern Kingdom fell to the Assyrian Empire, Nebuchadnezzar, the King of Babylon, invaded the Southern Kingdom, and the tribe of Judah (2 Kings 17:18) went into captivity. Daniel was one of the captive children of Israel chosen to work in the King's palace (Daniel 1:1-21) during the Babylonian captivity. The "times of the Gentiles" will end at midpoint in the seven-year tribulation era when the False Prophet arrives.

In giving us the ministry of Antichrist in Rev. 13:1-10, the first thing John sees and describes is the scarlet colored beast, Rev. 13:1-2, "(1) And I stood upon the sand of the sea, and saw a beast rise up out of the sea, having seven heads and ten horns, and upon his horns ten crowns, and upon his heads the name of blasphemy. (2) And the beast which I saw was like unto a leopard, and his feet were as the feet of a bear, and his mouth as the mouth of a lion: and the dragon gave him his power, and his seat, and great authority." This beast represents world history from the beginning of the Jewish captivity to the end of their captivity. How you see the beast depends on where you are standing in history. I am standing in the seventh head, and since the time period from the formation of the ten king kingdom to the Kingdom Dispensation covers only a single generation, I can see relatively clearly in both directions. I can look at recent history and see the Nation of Israel and the Jews returning to their homeland to await the Gog and Magog (Russian) invasion. I can see the apostate church era, the Church rapture, and the destruction of the remains. I can look forward in history and see the European Common Market as the ten King Kingdom that will be turned over to Antichrist, his three and one-half year reign and activity, the reign and activity of the False Prophet, the events that will transpire during the seven-year tribulation era, and the return of Jesus to destroy this beast and establish the Kingdom Dispensation. I can look back into history and see all seven heads on the scarlet colored beast. I would start describing the beast by saying the seventh head is the ten king kingdom manifest in the European Common Market confederacy. The head next to it is the sixth head or the Old Roman Empire. The next head is the Greek Empire, the next is the Persian, the next is the Median, the next is the Babylonian and the first head is the Assyrian Empire into which eleven of the twelve tribes of the children of Israel went into captivity.

The Apostle John was standing at a different point in history, so when he looked back into history he saw and described the beast using first a leopard, then a bear, and then a lion (Rev. 13:2). If John were to turn and look into the immediate future, from where he stood, he would have seen the seventh head as the ten king kingdom. He would then be able to look at current history, and see he was standing in the history period of the Roman Empire or the sixth head on the beast. Then looking back into history, he would have seen the fifth head (the leopard) as the Greek Empire, the fourth head (the bear) as the Persian Empire and the third head (the lion) as the Median Empire. Had he looked further back into history, he would have seen the second head as the Babylonian, and the first head as the Assyrian Empire. Needless to say, John would have had no idea as to what the leopard, bear, and lion represented unless he was familiar with the Book of Daniel. Daniel saw and described these same beasts, but from where he was standing, he was looking forward in history so he saw them in the reverse order. John was looking back into history and saw first the leopard, then the bear, and then the lion. Daniel was looking forward in history and saw first the lion, then the bear, and then the leopard.

The Prophet Daniel was standing in the period of history of the Babylonian Empire. Had he looked back into history he would have seen the Assyrian Empire, and the eleven tribes of the children of Israel in captivity. He could have looked at current history and seen when the Assyrian Empire had fallen to the Babylonian Empire, and the last tribe (Judah) of the children of Israel carried away captive (2 Kings 17:6-23). It was at this point in time God gave the prophecies in the Book of Daniel. Daniel lived to see the fall of the Babylonian Empire, to Darius the Median (Daniel 5:1-31), and then the rise of the Persian Empire under King Cyrus (Daniel 10:1). These prophecies enabled Daniel to look forward into history. His first look was when he was given the interpretation of King Nebuchadnezzar's dream of the great image (Daniel 2:1-49). We have already discussed this image, but in review, the head of gold represented the Babylonian Empire, which is the second head on the scarlet colored beast. The first head was the Assyrian Empire, which was history at Daniel's point in time. The silver breast and two arms represent the Media-Persian Empire, which are the third and fourth head on the scarlet colored beast. His brass belly and thighs represented the Greek Empire which is the fifth head. The iron legs represented the Roman Empire the sixth head, and his ten toes represent the ten king kingdom which is the seventh head. In Daniel 2:41-43 he even saw the demon invasion, as beings from the spirit realm (the iron), again leave their habitation to "mingle themselves with the seed of men" (the clay). He sees the judgment of Babylon, as Jesus, the stone cut out without hands, smites the image in the time period of the ten toes (Daniel 2:34-35), and on into the Kingdom Dispensation as "the stone that smote the image becomes a great mountain, and filled the whole earth."

Daniel's second look into history is given in Daniel 7:1-28, and this is when he sees the lion, bear, and leopard in the reverse order John saw looking back in history in Rev. 13:1-2. In this prophecy Daniel sees four great beasts come up out of the sea (Daniel 7:1-3). In Daniel 7:15-16 he asked for the interpretation, which is given in Daniel 7:17-18, "(17) The great beasts, which are four, are four kings, which shall arise out of the earth. (18) But the saints of the most High shall take the kingdom, and possess the kingdom for ever, even for ever and ever." In Daniel 7:1 we are told the prophecy was given "in the first year of Belshazzar king of Babylon," so the entire prophecy covers the time period between the Babylonian Empire to the Kingdom Dispensation where "the saints of the most High shall take the kingdom," and on into eternity, following the great white throne judgment where the saints "possess the kingdom for ever, even for ever and ever." Since Daniel was told in verse 7:17 the four beasts are four kings (or kingdoms) "which shall arise." All four will be future to the Babylonian Empire where Daniel was standing. The first of the four beast was a lion representing the Median Empire, Daniel 7:4, "The first was like a lion, and had eagle's wings: I beheld till the wings thereof were plucked, and it was lifted up from the earth, and made stand upon the feet as a man, and a man's heart was given to it." The second beast was a bear representing the Persian Empire, Daniel 7:5, "And behold another beast, a second, like to a bear, and it raised up itself on one side, and it had three ribs in the mouth of it between the teeth of it: and they said thus unto it Arise, devour much flesh." The third beast was a leopard representing the Greek empire, Daniel 7:6, "After this I beheld, and lo another, like a leopard, which had upon the back of it four wings of a fowl; the beast had also four heads; and dominion was given to it." The fourth was a dreadful and terrible beast with great iron teeth and ten horns representing the Roman Empire, Daniel 7:7, "After this I saw in the night visions, and, behold a fourth beast, dreadful and terrible, and strong exceedingly; and it had great iron teeth: it devoured and brake in pieces, and stamped the residue with the feet of it: and it was diverse from all the beasts that were before it; and it had ten horns."

Notice Daniel saw the Roman Empire as a monstrous beast kingdom having ten horns, but he was not able to see the ten horns as a distinct ten king kingdom or world government, separated by some 2000 years of human history. When Daniel focused his attention on the ten horns, what he saw was the rise of the False Prophet at the middle of the seven years tribulation era, and the ten king kingdom being changed to a seven king kingdom, Daniel 7:8, "I considered the horns, and, behold, there came up among them another little horn, before whom there were three of the first horns plucked up by the roots; and, behold, in this horn were eyes like the eyes of man, and a mouth speaking great things." What Daniel was unable to see was the Church Dispensation and the Antichrist reign during the first half of the seven-year tribulation era. This is because the Antichrist mission is against the Church, not the Jews. Their time of trouble comes at the middle of the tribulation era when the False Prophet enters the world and breaks the protection covenant. Jesus was the first person to ever speak the word "church" (Matthew 16:18). Daniel could not see the Church Dispensation because God did not reveal the Church to the people who lived in past dispensations (Ephesians 3:1-6).

The next thing Daniel was able to see after the reign of the False Prophet was his judgment which takes place at the end of the seven-year tribulation era. Daniel 7:9-11, "(9) I beheld till the thrones were cast down, and the Ancient of days did sit, whose garment was white as snow, and the hair of his head like the pure wool: his throne was like the fiery flame, and his wheels as burning fire. (10) A fiery stream issued and came forth from before him: thousand thousands ministered unto him, and ten thousand times ten thousand stood before him: the judgment was set, and the books were opened. (11) I beheld then because of the voice of the great words which the horn spake: I beheld even till the beast was slain, and his body destroyed, and given to the burning flame." This scene is repeated with additional details in Rev. 19:11-21. Again, notice that Daniel could see the False Prophet being cast into hell, "the burning flame," but he could not see that he was accompanied by the Antichrist. Daniel saw "his body destroyed," which we can see now as the killing of the people in the Armageddon Army and all the people who had taken the unforgivable mark of the beast. This judgment and their death is recorded in Rev. 19:20-21, "(20) And the beast was taken, and with him the false prophet that wrought miracles before him, with which he deceived them that had received the mark of the beast, and them that worshipped his image. These both were cast alive into a lake of fire burning with brimstone. (21) And the remnant were slain with the sword of him that sat upon the horse, which sword proceeded out of his mouth: and all the fowls were filled with their flesh."

The next event Daniel saw was the sheep and goat judgment, Daniel 7:12, "As concerning the rest of the beasts, they had their dominion taken away: yet their lives were prolonged for a season and time." The sheep and goat judgment is given in more detail in Matthew 25:31-46. During this judgment, all nations on Earth are gathered before Jesus (verse 25:31) at the end of the seven-year tribulation era, and judged on their treatment of the Jews during the reign of the False Prophet. The sheep nations helped the Jews in their time of trouble and are permitted to enter the Kingdom Dispensation. The goat nations are those who refused to help the Jews and they are killed and confined to Hades to await the white throne judgment at the end of the millennial reign. The next thing Daniel sees is the Kingdom Dispensation, Daniel 7:13-14, "(13) I saw in the night visions, and, behold, one like the Son of man came with the clouds of heaven, and came to the Ancient of days, and they brought him near before him. (14) And there was given him dominion, and glory, and a kingdom, that all people, nations, and languages, should serve him: his dominion is an everlasting dominion, which shall not pass away, and his kingdom that which shall not be destroyed." In the last part of verse 14, Daniel is able to see the survivors of the millennial reign, going on into eternity to populate the new creation of Revelation chapter 21.

In Daniel 7:15-16 he asks for the interpretation of the prophecy and is told in verses 17-18, "(17) These great beasts, which are four, are four kings, which shall arise out of the earth. (18) But the saints of the most High shall take the kingdom, and possess the kingdom for ever, even for ever and ever." Daniel then asks for the truth concerning the fourth beast and the events which followed. Daniel 7:19-22, "(19) Then I would know the truth of the fourth beast, which was diverse from all the others, exceeding dreadful, whose teeth were of iron, and his nails of brass; and stamped the residue with his feet; (20) And of the ten horns that were in his head, and of the other which came up, and before whom three fell; even of that horn that had eyes, and a mouth that spake very great things, whose look was more stout than his fellows. (21) I beheld, and the same horn made war with the saints, and prevailed against them; (22) Until the Ancient of days came, and judgment was given to the saints of the most High; and the time came that the saints possessed the kingdom." The explanation begins in Daniel 7:23, "Thus he said, The fourth beast shall be the fourth kingdom upon earth, which shall be diverse from all kingdoms, and shall devour the whole Earth, and shall tread it down, and break it in pieces." Looking back into history, we can see this fourth beast kingdom as the Old Roman Empire, which has continued to devour, tread down, and break in pieces the whole Earth for two thousand years. The final expression of the old Roman Empire will be in the formation of the ten king kingdom described in Daniel 7:24a, "And the ten horns out of this kingdom are ten kings that shall arise." Since it is in the days of these kings that Jesus sets up His kingdom, the prophecies to be fulfilled in their days will be: the Gog and Magog invasion; the rapture of the true Church; the turn-over of the European Common Market to Antichrist; Antichrist's signing of the protection treaty with the Jews; and the slaughter of deceived Christians during the three and one-half year Antichrist reign. After these things the False Prophet will enter the world and turn the ten king kingdom into a seven king kingdom, which is the remainder of the Daniel 7:24 verse, "and another shall rise after them; and he shall be diverse from the first, and he shall subdue three kings."

The explanation continues with a description of the activity of the False Prophet and the length of his reign, Daniel 7:25, "And he shall speak great words against the most High, and think to change times and laws: and they shall be given into his hand until a time and times and the dividing of time." From other prophecies we can see that "a time and times and a dividing of time" is a year, and a plural year or two years, and a dividing of a year, which equals three and one-half years, specifically, the last half of the seven-year tribulation era. By the prophecies in Rev. 13:11-18 we know it is the False Prophet who will introduce the beast image and issue the ultimatum to worship the image or die. This is the means by which he "shall wear out the saints of the most High." In reading Daniel 7:20-22 it is apparent that he saw the saints losing this war, "(20) And of the ten horns that were in his head, and of the other which came up, and before whom three fell; even of that horn that had eyes, and a mouth that spake very great things, whose look was more stout than his fellows. (21) I beheld, and the same horn made war with the saints, and prevailed against them; (22) Until the Ancient of days came, and judgment was given to the saints of the most High; and the time came that the saints possessed the kingdom." He was not able to see these killings as God's means of salvation during the False Prophet reign. The people in the beast kingdom doing the killing will not be able to see it either. We would not have been able to see it either, if Jesus had not told us they will be resurrected to life at the end of the tribulation era, Rev. 20:4, "And I saw thrones, and they sat upon them, and judgment was given unto them: and I saw the souls of them that were beheaded for the witness of Jesus, and for the word of God, and which had not worshipped the beast, neither his image, neither had received his mark upon their foreheads, or in their hands; and they lived and reigned with Christ a thousand years." The deceived members of the beast organization during the reign of both Antichrist and the False Prophet will actually think they are doing the will of God by killing the saints. Jesus told of this time in John 16:1-3, "(1) These things have I spoken unto you, that ye should not be offended. (2) They shall put you out of the synagogues: yea, the time cometh, that whosoever killeth you will think that he doeth God service. (3) And these things will they do unto you, because they have not known the Father, nor me." The first part of John 16:2, "They shall put you out of the synagogues" refers to the persecution to be suffered by believers during the Church Dispensation, while the remainder of the verse refers to the killings of the seven-year tribulation era. The Greek word translated as synagogues is *aposunagogos* meaning excommunicated, to be put out of or turned away from an assemblage of persons. We already saw during the Laodicean church era that Jesus is outside the church knocking at the door. Don't worry about being "put out" because all they did was put you where Jesus is.

At the end of the three and one-half year reign of the False Prophet, his dominion to consume and destroy is stopped by judgment, Daniel 7:26, "But the judgment shall sit, and they shall take away his dominion, to consume and to destroy it unto the end." Following this judgment we move into the Kingdom Dispensation, Daniel 7:27, "And the kingdom and dominion, and the greatness of the kingdom under the whole heaven, shall be given to the people of the saints of the most High, whose kingdom is an everlasting kingdom, and all dominions shall serve and obey him."

Two years later "in the third year of the reign of king Belshazzar," Daniel sees the vision of the ram and he goat. The vision is recorded in Daniel 8:1-14, "(1) In the third year of the reign of king Belshazzar a vision appeared unto me, even unto me Daniel, after that which appeared unto me at the first. (2) And I saw in a vision; and it came to pass, when I saw, that I was at Shushan in the palace, which is in the province of Elam; and I saw in a vision, and I was by the river of Ulai. (3) Then I lifted up mine eyes, and saw, and, behold, there stood before the river a ram which had two horns: and the two horns were high; but one was higher than the other, and the higher came up last. (4) I saw the ram pushing westward, and northward, and southward; so that no beasts might stand before him, neither was there any that could deliver out of his hand; but he did according to his will, and became great. (5) And as I was considering, behold, an he goat came from the west on the face of the whole earth, and touched not the ground: and the goat had a notable horn between his eyes. (6) And he came to the ram that had two horns, which I had seen standing before the river, and ran unto him in the fury of his power. (7) And I saw him come close unto the ram, and he was moved with choler against him, and smote the ram, and brake his two horns: and there was no power in the ram to stand before him, but he cast him down to the ground, and stamped upon him: and there was none that could deliver the ram out of his hand. (8) Therefore the he goat waxed very great: and when he was strong, the great horn was broken; and for it came up four notable ones toward the four winds of heaven. (9) And out of one of them came forth a little horn, which waxed exceeding great, toward the south, and toward the east, and toward the pleasant land. (10) And it waxed great, even to the host of heaven; and it cast down some of the host and of the stars to the ground, and stamped upon them. (11) Yea, he magnified himself even to the prince of the host, and by him the daily sacrifice was taken away, and the place of his sanctuary was cast down.

(12) And an host was given him against the daily sacrifice by reason of transgression, and it cast down the truth to the ground; and it practised, and prospered. (13) Then I heard one saint speaking, and another saint said unto that certain saint which spake, How long shall be the vision concerning the daily sacrifice, and the transgression of desolation, to give both the sanctuary and the host to be trodden under foot? (14) And he said unto me, Unto two thousand and three hundred days; then shall the sanctuary be cleansed."

In Daniel 8:15-19, Daniel questions the meaning of the vision and is told it concerns "the time of the end." In Daniel 8:20 the ram with two horns is identified as the kings of Media and Persia. In Daniel 8:21 the he goat is identified as the king of Grecia (Greece) with the great horn being its first king, which history shows was Alexander the Great. In viewing the scarlet colored beast we would be looking at its third, fourth, and fifth heads. The vision deals with the period of human history between the Babylonian Empire (the second head) and the Roman Empire (the sixth head). Since Gabriel alerted Daniel that the vision concerns "the time of the end," it is obvious God will use events and figures from this period of human history to communicate knowledge and truths which will apply to the seven-year tribulation period. The phrase "the last end of the indignation" in Daniel 8:19 may be limiting these truths to the last half of the tribulation, for this is the period when God will deal with the Jews and the Nation of Israel.

The historical interpretation of the vision is relatively simple. Daniel 8:20 tells us, "The ram which thou sawest having two horns are the kings of Media and Persia" which explains Daniel 8:3-4, "(3) Then I lifted up mine eyes, and saw, and, behold, there stood before the river a ram which had two horns: and the two horns were high; but one was higher than the other, and the higher came up last. (4) I saw the ram pushing westward, and northward, and southward; so that no beasts might stand before him, neither was there any that could deliver out of his hand; but he did according to his will, and became great." The fall of the Babylonian Empire is recorded in Daniel chapter 5 with Belshazzar and the hand writing on the wall. The chapter ends with the statement, Daniel 5:30-31, "(30) In that night was Belshazzar the king of the Chaldeans slain. (31) And Darius the Median took the kingdom, being about threescore and two years old." King Darius the Median is the first horn on the ram. The ram had two horns, "and the two horns were high; but one was higher than the other, and the higher came up last." refers to the rise of Cyrus king of Persia. We see Cyrus ruling in Daniel chapter 10. These two different kings or horns are presented on a single ram to show the uniqueness of the kingdom. The Medes and Persians had a single goal and they united to conquer the world. The Median Empire was absorbed and united with the Persian Empire, but not through force. The relationship between the Medes and Persians can be seen in Daniel chapter 6. This chapter deals with the trickery that causes Daniel to be thrown into the lion's den. When king Darius becomes aware of the trickery and tries to deliver

Daniel, he is told in Daniel 6:15, "Then these men assembled unto the king, and said unto the king, Know, O king, that the law of the Medes and Persians is, That no decree nor statue which the king establisheth may be changed." The unique relationship between the Medes and Persians is the same type of arrangement that will exist between Antichrist and the False Prophet. Antichrist will arrive on the scene first, and three and one-half years later, will be joined by the more powerful (the higher one) False Prophet. During the last half of the tribulation era, they will be united in a single cause and reign together.

Daniel 8:21, "And the rough goat is the king of Grecia: and the great horn that is between his eyes is the first king." explains Daniel 8:5-7, "(5) And as I was considering, behold, an he goat came from the west on the face of the whole earth, and touched not the ground: and the goat had a notable horn between his eyes. (6) And he came to the ram that had two horns, which I had seen standing before the river, and ran unto him in the fury of his power. (7) And I saw him come close unto the ram, and he was moved with choler against him, and smote the ram, and brake his two horns: and there was no power in the ram to stand before him, but he cast him down to the ground, and stamped upon him: and there was none that could deliver the ram out of his hand." The great horn was Alexander the Great, the Greek king who defeated the kings of Media and Persia, and established the Greek Empire. Between the years 334 B.C. and 327 B.C. Alexander conquered the world, and in the prime of his life at the age of 33 (356-323 B.C.) he became sick and died. Alexander's four chief army commanders had gone into different parts of the empire as governors, and at his death they assumed the title of kings. Lysimachus took the northern portion of the empire (Thrace or Asia Minor), Seleucus the eastern part (Syria and Babylon), Ptolemy the southern part (Egypt), and Cassander the western regions consisting of Greece and the neighboring countries. This is what is being said in Daniel 8:8, "Therefore the he goat waxed very great: and when he was strong, the great horn was broken; and for it came up four notable ones toward the four winds of heaven," explained in Daniel 8:22, "Now that being broken, whereas four stood up for it, four kingdoms shall stand up out of the nation, but not in his power."

Daniel 8:23 continues with the statement, "And in the latter time of their kingdom, when the transgressors are come to the full, a king of fierce countenance, and understanding dark sentences, shall stand up." The phrase "in the latter time of their kingdom" means in the latter time of the Greek Empire. The "king of fierce countenance" is the little horn of Daniel 8:9, "And out of one of them came forth a little horn, which waxed exceeding great, toward the south, and toward the east, and toward the pleasant land." History shows this individual to be Antiochus Epiphanes, the king of Syria. His goal was to unite the people in his kingdom by Hellenizing them. The word *Hellenize* means to make Greek in character, by adopting the Greek language, customs, ideals, ethics, and religion. His effort caused a division among the Jews. Those who rejected the God of the Scriptures and the Holy Covenant were converted to Greek thought and became Hellenized Jews. Those who chose to remain true to God and the Holy Covenant became a problem to Epiphanes. Since he could not convert them, he chose to exterminate both them and their religion. The Jews who resisted Epiphanes were forced to flee into the hills, where they waged the Maccabean Wars in an effort to regain the city of Jerusalem. Knowing in advance this vision concerns the time of the end, it is obvious to see that God is using Antiochus Epiphanes, his persecution of the Jews, and the events surrounding that persecution, to paint a picture of the False Prophet and his persecution of the Jews during the last half of the tribulation era.

From the book of the Revelation we have already seen the rise of the False Prophet, Satan and his angels being thrown out of heaven, and the massive demonic activity during the last portion of the tribulation era. We had this same type of situation in the days of Antiochus Epiphanes. The fact that demons crossed from the spirit realm into the physical realm to assist Epiphanes is recorded in Daniel 8:10, "And it waxed great, even to the host of heaven; and it cast down some of the host and of the stars to the ground, and stamped upon them." In Daniel 8:11 we are told Epiphanes would stop the daily sacrifices and cast down the sanctuary, "Yea, he magnified himself even to the prince of the host, and by him the daily sacrifice was taken away, and the place of his sanctuary was cast down." Daniel 8:12 concerns the host that was given him, "And an host was given him against the daily sacrifice by reason of transgression, and it" (the demonic host) "cast down the truth to the ground; and it" (the demonic host) practised, and prospered." In verses 8:13-14, Daniel questions how long Epiphanes will be permitted to continue, and is told 2300 days or just over six years. These 2300 days is the length of the persecution of the Jews during the reign of Epiphanes, not the length of the persecution during the reign of the False Prophet. Daniel had already been told that the length of the False Prophet reign would be three and one-half years, back in Daniel 7:24-25, "(24) And the ten horns out of this kingdom are ten kings that shall arise: and another shall rise after them; and he shall be diverse from the first, and he shall subdue three kings. (25) And he shall speak great words against the most High, and shall wear out the saints of the most High, and think to change times and laws: and they shall be given into his hand until a time and times and the dividing of time." Don't lose sight of the fact Daniel died long before the latter end of the Greek Empire, when Epiphanes walked onto the pages of human history. The knowledge God is communicating to Daniel is intended for the generation of Jews who will be living in the days of Epiphanes. It is also intended for the generation of Jews who will be living when the False Prophet walks onto the pages of human history. They will be able to look at the prophecies in the Book of Daniel, examine the historical record of Antiochus

Epiphanes, and put together a clear picture of what is happening on Earth.

In explaining this vision to Daniel, Gabriel makes it clear the mighty power of Epiphanes is not his own human power. Daniel 8:23-25, "(23) And in the latter time of their kingdom, when the transgressors are come to the full, a king of fierce countenance, and understanding dark sentences, shall stand up. (24) And his power shall be mighty, but not by his own power: and he shall destroy wonderfully, and shall prosper, and practise, and shall destroy the mighty and the holy people. (25) And through his policy also he shall cause craft to prosper in his hand; and he shall magnify himself in his heart, and by peace shall destroy many: he shall also stand up against the Prince of princes; but he shall be broken without hand." What is said here concerning Epiphanes will also be true of the False Prophet except the phrase "And in the latter time of their kingdom." The pronoun "their" represents Alexander's four successors. If we were to use the word "their" to represent the ten king kingdom, the entire passage would be true concerning the False Prophet. The "Prince of princes" that both Epiphanes and the False Prophet stand up against is the Lord Jesus Christ. Epiphanes stopped the daily sacrifices which was the "transgression of desolation" of Daniel 8:13. These animal sacrifices demonstrated God's plan of redemption in the substitutionary death of Jesus. The first animal sacrifice was performed by God Himself in the garden of Eden. From the garden, to the sacrifice of the Lamb of God, the people on earth worshipped God by demonstrating their belief in His promise of redemption by duplicating that ceremony. In stopping the daily sacrifices, Epiphanes, in essence, was forbidding the worship of the God of Heaven. The False Prophet will do the same thing when he issues the ultimatum to worship only the beast image.

Daniel Chapter 9 contains the prophecy of the seventy weeks, which we have already examined. Daniel chapters 10, 11, and 12 are, in reality, a more detailed look at the ram and he goat prophecy. As we examine these chapters keep in mind God is using events and personages in Israel's immediate future to communicate an understanding as to what the Jews will face during the three and one-half year reign of the False Prophet in the last half of the tribulation era. The intent of these chapters is given in Daniel 10:14, "Now I am come to make thee understand what shall befall thy people in the latter days: for yet the vision is for many days." Due to the length of these chapters we will use outline form, but you should read the passages not quoted here. The three chapters would be labeled, "Daniel's last vision: Israel's future." They are subdivided into: (A) Israel's future to the rise of Antiochus Epiphanes, Daniel 10:1-11:20; (B) The vial Syrian: A picture of the great tribulation False Prophet, Daniel 11:21-35; (C) The King at the time of the end: The great tribulation False Prophet, Daniel 11:36-12:3; and (D) The Book of Daniel sealed until the time of the end, Daniel 12:4-13. Israel's future to the rise of Antiochus Epiphanes is sub-divided as follows:

1. The time and place of the vision, Daniel 10:1, 10:4.
2. Daniel fasts for three weeks, Daniel 10:2-3.
3. Daniel describes a man he saw in white linen, Daniel 10:5-6.
4. Daniel's reaction to the man clothed in white linen, Daniel 10:7-11.
5. The angel sent on the day Daniel asks God for understanding, Daniel 10:12, "Then said he unto me, Fear not, Daniel: for from the first day that thou didst set thine heart to understand, and to chasten thyself before thy God, thy words were heard, and I am come for thy words."
6. The angel delayed twenty-one days by the demonic prince of the kingdom of Persia. Daniel 10:13, "But the prince of the kingdom of Persia withstood me one and twenty days: but, lo, Michael, one of the chief princes, came to help me; and I remained there with the kings of Persia."
7. Daniel to understand what will befall the Jews in the latter days. Daniel 10:14, "Now I am come to make thee understand what shall befall thy people in the latter days: for yet the vision is for many days."
8. The angel strengthens Daniel when his strength fails, Daniel 10:15-19.
9. Spiritual change of command: Prince of Greece replaces the Prince of Persia. Daniel 10:20-21, "(20) Then said he, Knowest thou wherefore I came unto thee? and now will I return to fight with the prince of Persia: and when I am gone forth, lo, the prince of Grecia shall come. (21) But I will shew thee that which is noted in the scripture of truth: and there is none that holdeth with me in these things, but Michael your prince."
10. The same angel stands by Darius the Mede during his first year, Daniel 11:1.
11. Darius the Mede followed by four Persian kings. Daniel 11:2a "And now will I shew thee the truth. Behold, there shall stand up yet three kings in Persia." The first of the three kings was Cyrus, the Great, who reigned from 538-529 B.C. He was followed by his son Cambyses (528-522 B.C.) who is also called Ahasuerus in Ezra 4:6. In the year 522 a man named Smerdis reigned for seven months, but he was an impostor and was not in the royal bloodline. The third king of Persia was Darius Hystaspes who reigned from 521-486 B.C. The fourth king was Xerxes.
12. The wealth of the fourth Persian king contributes to the Greek invasion. Daniel 11:2b "and the fourth shall be far richer than they all: and by his strength through his riches he shall stir up all against the realm of Grecia." The fourth Persian king was Xerxes who reigned from 485-465 B.C. It is during his reign that the angel talking with Daniel begins to suppress the principality demon over the Persian Empire. This suppression allows the principality demon of Greece to strengthen his kingdom for the change of command we saw in 9 above (Daniel 10:20-21). Xerxes was followed by Artaxerxes Longimanus 464-424 B.C., Darius Nothus 423-405 B.C., Artaxerxes Mnemon 404-359 B.C., Ochus 358-333 B.C., Arses 337-336 B.C. and then Darius Codomannus (335-331 B.C.) who was dethroned by

Alexander the Great. The dethroning of this last Persian king also marks the dethroning of the principality demon, the prince of Persia, and the end of the angel's fight he spoke of in Daniel 10:20-21.

13. The mighty king, Alexander the Great. Daniel 11:3 "And a mighty king shall stand up, that shall rule with great dominion, and do according to his will."

14. The Greek kingdom to be divided into four parts. Daniel 11:4 "And when he shall stand up, his kingdom shall be broken, and shall be divided toward the four winds of heaven; and not to his posterity, nor according to his dominion which he ruled: for his kingdom shall be plucked up, even for others beside those." We have already seen where Alexander conquered the world between the years 334-327 B.C., and at the age of 33 he became sick and died. The Greek Empire was divided into four parts under the rule of Alexander's four chief army commanders (or Governors). Lysimachus took the northern portion of the empire (Thrace or Asia Minor), Seleucus the eastern part (Syria and Babylon), Ptolemy the southern part (Egypt), and Cassander the western regions consisting of Greece and the neighboring countries. This division in the Greek Empire set the stage for a power struggle between the four commanders or kings. Lysimachus conquered Cassander and added Greece and Macedon to his kingdom. Lysimachus was then conquered by Seleucus, and three of the four sections of the Greek Empire came under the control of the king of Syria. Since this territory lies north of the land of Palestine, we can now identify the king of Syria as the king of the north. Ptolemy had taken the southern portion of the Greek Empire which was Egypt. He strengthened his kingdom by adding Cyprus, Phoenicia, Cyrenaica, and the land of Palestine. The Book of Daniel continues with the power struggle between these two kingdoms, to the rise of Antiochus Epiphanes.

15. The power struggle between Egypt (king of the south) and Syria (king of the north). Daniel 11:5 "And the king of the south shall be strong, and one of his princes; and he shall be strong above him, and have dominion; and his dominion shall be a great dominion." Ptolemy I (Soter, 323-285 B.C.) was the general in Alexander's army who took Egypt, the southern portion of the Greek Empire. He was followed by his son Ptolemy II (Philadelphus) who was given the great dominion of Daniel 11:5. He reigned in Egypt from 285-247 B.C. and it was during his reign the Punic Wars started. The Punic Wars were a series of three contests between Rome and Carthage for dominance of the Mediterranean Sea. Egypt, under Ptolemy II, helped Rome in the First Punic War, which took place between 264-261 B.C. The greatness of Egypt, at this point in time, can be seen in the library founded at Alexandria. These kings introduced Greek culture, ideals, and philosophy into the land of Palestine, which gave birth to the Hellenistic Jews who adopted the Greek thought, patterns of life, and their many gods.

In the meantime, the king of the north, Seleucus I (Nicator), was busy bringing most of the remaining Greek Empire under his control as the king of Syria. He was followed by his son Antiochus I (Soter) who reigned as King of Syria from 280-261 B.C. He was followed by his son Antiochus II (Theos) who turned his attention toward Egypt, which was the last remaining portion of the original Greek Empire not under the control of the king of Syria.

Daniel 11:6, "And in the end of years they shall join themselves together; for the king's daughter of the south shall come to the king of the north to make an agreement: but she shall not retain the power of the arm; neither shall he stand, nor his arm: but she shall be given up, and they that brought her, and he that begat her, and he that strengthened her in these times." The power struggle between the king of the north, Antiochus II, and the king of the south, Ptolemy II, ended with an agreement of marriage. The warring ended when Ptolemy II married his daughter Berenice to Antiochus II. Ptolemy III (Euergetes), the son of Ptolemy II and the brother of Berenice, became the king of the south (Egypt) in 247-222 B.C. The condition of peace lasted until the death of Antiochus II, when his son Seleucus 2nd seized the throne. He killed his stepmother, Berenice, and his infant half-brother, before Berenice's brother, Ptolemy III, could arrive with an army.

Although Ptolemy III did not arrive in time to save his sister, his invasion of Syria was very profitable. Daniel 11:7-9, "(7) But out of a branch of her roots shall one stand up in his estate, which shall come with an army, and shall enter into the fortress of the king of the north, and shall deal against them, and shall prevail: (8) And shall also carry captives into Egypt their gods, with their princes, and with their precious vessels of silver and of gold; and he shall continue more years than the king of the north. (9) So the king of the south shall come into his kingdom, and shall return into his own land."

Seleucus II was replaced as the king of the north by Seleucus III who reigned from 226-223 B.C. He was followed by Antiochus III (the Great), son of Seleucus II, who reigned from 223-187 B.C. His goal was to restore the crumbling Seleucid Empire. Ptolemy III was replaced as the king of the south by his son Ptolemy IV (222-205 B.C.), who was outraged by Antiochus's efforts to rebuild the Seleucid Empire. Ptolemy IV assembled an army and defeated Antiochus III at Raphia in the year 217 B.C. Daniel 11:10-12, "(10) But his sons shall be stirred up, and shall assemble a multitude of great forces: and one shall certainly come, and overflow, and pass through: then shall he return, and be stirred up, even to his fortress. (11) And the king of the south shall be moved with choler, and shall come forth and fight with him, even with the king of the north: and he shall set forth a great multitude; but the multitude shall be given into his hand. (12) And when he hath taken away the multitude, his heart shall be lifted up; and he shall cast down many ten thousands: but he shall not be strengthened by it."

Ptolemy IV was replaced as king of the south by his son, Ptolemy V (205-182 B.C.), who was six years old when his father died. Ptolemy V became interested in the ancient Pharaohs of Egypt and their priesthood rituals. When he became of age he was crowned at Memphis using the ceremonies of the ancient Pharaohs. It was his decree on the Rosetta Stone (discovered in the year 1799) that led to an understanding of the ancient Egyptian Hieroglyphics. He had recorded the same decree in ancient Egyptian Hieroglyphics, in Demotic (the popular language of Egypt at that time), and at the bottom of the stone the same message was recorded in Greek. During the days of Ptolemy V, the Egyptian Empire began to weaken through internal civil wars. This allowed Antiochus the Great (III) to launch an invasion, in the year 198 B.C., against Egypt in which the land of Palestine was reclaimed by Syria. It was Antiochus the Great who forced Ptolemy V to marry his own daughter Cleopatra. This invasion is recorded in Daniel 11:13-19, "(13) For the king of the north shall return, and shall set forth a multitude greater than the former, and shall certainly come after certain years with a great army and with much riches. (14) And in those times there shall many stand up against the king of the south: also the robbers of thy people shall exalt themselves to establish the vision; but they shall fall. (15) So the king of the north shall come, and cast up a mount, and take the most fenced cities: and the arms of the south shall not withstand, neither shall there be any strength to withstand. (16) But he that cometh against him shall do according to his own will, and none shall stand before him: and he shall stand in the glorious land, which by his hand shall be consumed. (17) He shall also set his face to enter with the strength of his whole kingdom, and upright ones with him; thus shall he do: and he shall give him the daughter of women, corrupting her: but she shall not stand on his side, neither be for him. (18) After this shall he turn his face unto the isles, and shall take many: but a prince for his own behalf shall cause the reproach offered by him to cease; without his own reproach he shall cause it to turn upon him. (19) Then he shall turn his face toward the fort of his own land: but he shall stumble and fall, and not be found."

Antiochus the Great was replaced as the king of the north by his son, Seleucus IV, who reigned from 187-175 B.C. His reign is recorded in Daniel 11:20, "Then shall stand up in his estate a raiser of taxes in the glory of the kingdom: but within few days he shall be destroyed, neither in anger, nor in battle." Daniel 11:21 opens with the statement "And in his estate shall stand up a vile person" which introduces the next king of the north who was Antiochus (IV) Epiphanes, the brother of Seleucus IV and the son of Antiochus the Great (III). This is the same Antiochus Epiphanes presented in Daniel 8:23-25 as the "king of fierce countenance."

The next part of our outline (The vile Syrian: A picture of the great tribulation False Prophet.) deals with Daniel 11:21-35, and the reign of Antiochus Epiphanes, the king of the north, who rules the Greek Syrian Empire from 175-164 B.C.

1. A vile person stands up to whom they shall not give the honor of the kingdom. Daniel 11:21a, "And in his estate shall stand up a vile person, to whom they shall not give the honour of the kingdom."
2. Peaceable, he obtains the kingdom by flatteries. Daniel 11:21b, "but he shall come in peaceable, and obtain the kingdom by flatteries."
3. He works deceitfully. Daniel 11:22-23, "(22) And with the arms of a flood shall they be overflown from before him, and shall be broken; yea, also the prince of the covenant. (23) And after the league made with him he shall work deceitfully: for he shall come up, and shall become strong with a small people."
4. He scatters the spoils among his followers. Daniel 11:24, "He shall enter peaceable even upon the fattest places of the province; and he shall do that which his fathers have not done, nor his fathers' fathers; he shall scatter among them the prey, and spoil, and riches: yea, and he shall forecast his devices against the strong holds, even for a time."
5. He defeats the king of the South. Daniel 11:25-26, "(25) And he shall stir up his power and his courage against the king of the south with a great army; and the king of the south shall be stirred up to battle with a very great and mighty army; but he shall not stand: for they shall forecast devices against him. (26) Yea, they that feed of the portion of his meat shall destroy him, and his army shall overflow: and many shall fall down slain." The king of the south is still Egypt. Ptolemy V was replaced as king of the south by his son Ptolemy VI who reigned from 182-146 B.C. This invasion took place in 170 B.C.
6. Lies spoken at the peace table. Daniel 11:27, "And both these kings' hearts shall be to do mischief, and they shall speak lies at one table; but it shall not prosper: for yet the end shall be at the time appointed."
7. He returns to his own land with great riches. Daniel 11:28, "Then shall he return into his land with great riches; and his heart shall be against the holy covenant; and he shall do exploits, and return to his own land." The "holy covenant" Epiphanes was against is the Old Testament (Covenant) promise of God to send his Redeemer, which the Jews were demonstrating in their ceremonial animal sacrifices and temple services. It was at this point Epiphanes realized, that because of their religion, some of the Jews were not conforming to his efforts to Hellenize them.
8. He returns southward but not as the former or the latter. Daniel 11:29, "At the time appointed he shall return, and come toward the south; but it shall not be as the former, or as the latter." First we need to realize, we are dealing with three separate and distinct invasions: the former, this one,

and the latter one. The former invasion was successful as we saw in verses 11:25-26, and Epiphanes returns to his own land with great riches (11:28). This invasion ends when the "ships of Chittim" come against him and sends him home grieving. Daniel 11:30 begins with the statement, "For the ships of Chittim shall come against him: therefore he shall be grieved, and return." As we have already seen, when the Greek Empire was divided four ways, Egypt ended up with a large portion of the southern and eastern coastline of the Mediterranean Sea and with many of the islands, including Cyprus. By this point in time, the second Punic War between Rome and Carthage had ended, which gave the Roman Empire dominance in the Mediterranean Sea. This invasion by Epiphanes represented a threat to the commerce between Egypt and the Roman Empire. History records this incident as Epiphanes arriving at Egypt, where he is met by a Roman ambassador. In essence, he was told to go home and leave Egypt alone, unless he wanted to fight the entire Roman Empire. Needless to say, Epiphanes heads for home, grieved. This is the last incident in the power struggle within the Greek Empire between Syria, king of the north, and Egypt, king of the south. The latter invasion will be the latter days invasion, which this entire prophecy is pointing to. This latter invasion will be launched by the False Prophet during the last half of the tribulation era.

9. Indignation against the Holy Covenant. Daniel 11:30b, "and have indignation against the holy covenant: so shall he do; he shall even return." Epiphanes had to pass through the land of Palestine to get from Egypt to Antioch, the capital city of the Syrian Empire. As we have already seen, his last campaign into Egypt had been successful, and on the return trip home his heart was against the holy covenant (Daniel 11:28). On this trip home he is grieved by the embarrassment he suffered in Egypt by the Roman ambassador. His state of mind is further aggravated when he arrives at Jerusalem and finds the Jews still worshipping God. The number of Jews he killed varies from history book to history book, but most agree that at this time, Epiphanes stripped the temple of its gold, silver, precious vessels and furniture, and ordered the Jews to abandon the religion of their forefathers and conform to Greek thought.

10. Forsakers of the Holy Covenant accept his way of thinking. Daniel 11:30c, "and have intelligence with them that forsake the holy covenant." The forsakers of the holy covenant were the Jews, who turned from the truth of the word of God, to Greek philosophy. The intelligence the Greeks valued and exalted so highly was secular knowledge acquired by use of the human natural mental process, not revelation knowledge. The emphasis these Greeks put on education is being repeated in our generation. It destroyed the Greek Empire, corrupted the Hellenized Jews (Daniel 11:32), and it is corrupting and destroying our generation. The danger is not in getting an education, it is what the education does to you. The Hebrew word translated as have intelligence is *biyn* which speaks of something that separates mentally from understanding. The intelligence of Epiphanes would have been rejected by the Jews as foolishness if they had not forsaken the God of the holy covenant.

11. Epiphanes performs the abomination of desolation. Daniel 11:31, "And arms shall stand on his part, and they shall pollute the sanctuary of strength, and shall take away the daily sacrifice, and they shall place the abomination that maketh desolate." We will look at what Epiphanes did in more detail later.

12. Those who do wickedly against the covenant are corrupted by his flatteries. Daniel 11:32a, "And such as do wickedly against the covenant shall he corrupt by flatteries." These are the Hellenized Jews who turned from the truth of the Word of God to conform to Greek thought. They supported the views of the government, and in turn, they received the support of the government. The federal religion was the many gods, demigods, and heroes of Greek mythology. Our federal religion is humanism. The government crammed our heads with this religion through the public school system, and it is still cramming it into our children. The corrupting effect of humanism is far worse than that of Greek mythology. You will probably find this hard to believe, unless you have made a sincere commitment to return to God and the truth of the Holy Scriptures. I am not speaking here of the "Only Believe" salvation package. I am speaking of that portion of the rebirth called the baptism of fire where the new convert is required to take the Word of God and wash the flatteries, including humanism, from his mind. I am talking about Romans 12:1-2, "(1) I beseech you therefore, brethren, by the mercies of God, that ye present your bodies a living sacrifice, holy, acceptable unto God, which is your reasonable service. (2) And be not conformed to this world: but be ye transformed by the renewing of your mind, that ye may prove what is that good, and acceptable, and perfect, will of God," and 2 Corinthians 10:3-6, "(3) For though we walk in the flesh, we do not war after the flesh: (4) (For the weapons of our warfare are not carnal, but mighty through God to the pulling down of strong holds;) (5) Casting down imaginations, and every high thing that exalteth itself against the knowledge of God, and bringing into captivity every thought to the obedience of Christ; (6) And having in a readiness to revenge all disobedience, when your obedience is fulfilled."

13. Those who know God shall be strong and resist. Daniel 11:32b, "but the people that do know their God shall be strong, and do exploits."

14. They that understand shall instruct many and die for their resistance. Daniel 11:33, "And they that understand among the people shall instruct many: yet they shall fall by the sword, and by flame, by captivity, and by spoil, many days."

15. Through their death they are tried, purged, and made white. Daniel 11:34-35a, "(34) Now when they shall fall, they shall be holpen with a little help: but many shall cleave to them with flatteries. (35a) And some of them of understanding shall fall, to try them, and to purge, and to make them white."

16. These prophecies point to the time of the end. Daniel 11:35b, "even to the time of the end: because it is yet for a time appointed."

Epiphanes's goal was to Hellenize (make Greek) all the people in his kingdom. The Jews who were familiar with God's views, resisted what Epiphanes was trying to accomplish. Their resistance resulted in Epiphanes issuing an ultimatum commanding all the people in the kingdom to conform to the government religion or die. Epiphanes used federal troops to enforce the ultimatum and it became a federal crime to worship the God of the Bible. The federal troops were sent to the city of Jerusalem to stop the temple services and to force the Jews into conforming. The Jews who resisted Epiphanes were forced into the hills where they waged the Maccabean Wars. The Jews who would not conform were hunted down and put in the deny or die baptism of fire, "to try them, and to purge, and to make them white." This scene will be repeated during the last half of the seven-year tribulation period. Those who refuse to conform to the ultimatum of the False Prophet will be hunted down and put in the same situation. Those who were made "white" died because they would not deny the Word of God and their testimony.

Trying to reconstruct the dates and events during the latter end of the Greek Empire is nearly impossible. You can get a variety of dates depending on which history book or historical record you examine. I included dates to give you an idea of when these events took place, not to invoke an argument. If you disagree with the dates I use, ignore them or mentally insert the word *approximately* after you read a date. We humans date events, while God uses events to date. The sequence in which these events occurred is also difficult to reconstruct. The rise and decline of the Greek Empire, as well as the rise of the Roman Empire, occurred in the time period between where the Old Testament Scriptures end and the New Testament Scriptures begin. The last book in the Hebrew Bible is the Book of Malachi, which many date near 455 B.C. The New Testament actually began when the angel Gabriel announced the conception of John the Baptist. Between Gabriel's announcement and the Book of Malachi we have a period of approximately 455 years in which the Hebrew prophets were silent. They were silent because God was silent.

It was probably during this period of silence, the Hellenized Jews tampered with the sacred Holy Scriptures. When God finished speaking to the Prophet Malachi, the Hebrew Old Testament Scripture was completed. The original Hebrew Bible contained twenty-four books, which correspond to the thirty-nine Old Testament Books in the King James Version (KJV) of the English Bible. They are as follows:

Book No. 1, Genesis, same in both bibles.
Book No. 2, Exodus, same in both bibles.
Book No. 3, Leviticus, same in both bibles.

Book No. 4, Numbers, same in both bibles.
Book No. 5, Deuteronomy, same in both bibles.
Book No. 6, Joshua, same in both bibles.
Book No. 7, Judges, same in both bibles.
Book No. 8, Samuel, in the KJV Samuel is divided into two books, 1st and 2nd Samuel.
Book No. 9, Kings, in the KJV Kings is divided into two books, 1st and 2nd Kings.
Book No. 10, Isaiah, same in both bibles.
Book No. 11, Jeremiah, same in both bibles.
Book No. 12, Ezekiel, same in both bibles.
Book No. 13, The Twelve, in the KJV the Twelve are the twelve minor prophets which were separated into twelve separate books. They are: (1) Hosea, (2) Joel, (3) Amos, (4) Obadiah, (5) Jonah, (6) Micah, (7) Nahum, (8) Habakkuk, (9) Zephaniah, (10) Haggai, (11) Zechariah, and (12) Malachi.
Book No. 14, Psalms, same in both bibles.
Book No. 15, Proverbs, same in both bibles.
Book No. 16, Job, same in both bibles.
Book No. 17, Song of Songs, entitled Song of Solomon in the KJV.
Book No. 18, Ruth, same in both bibles.
Book No. 19, Lamentations, same in both bibles.
Book No. 20, Ecclesiastes, same in both bibles.
Book No. 21, Esther, same in both bibles.
Book No. 22, Daniel, same in both bibles.
Book No. 23, Ezra-Nehemiah, in the KJV this book is divided into two separate books.
Book No. 24, Chronicles, in the KJV they are divided into two books, 1st and 2nd Chronicles.

During the days of Ptolemy II (285-247 B.C.), the Hebrew Bible was translated into the Greek language. This translation became known as the Septuagint. Following the invasion of Alexander the Great (334-327 B.C.), the Greek language became the international language of the Mediterranean area, until it was replaced in the second century A.D. by Latin. Whether the seventy (or seventy-two) translators were responsible for adding books to the original Hebrew Bible is debatable. Some of the books that were added are dated around 100 B.C. and one is dated A.D. 100, so it is obvious the Septuagint underwent several changes during the next 250 years. In either case, in its final form, the Septuagint contained fourteen books which were not part of the original Hebrew Bible.

In the Septuagint the Book of Daniel was changed to include the Song of the Three Hebrew Children, The History of Susanna, and Bel and the Dragon. The other books that were added are:

the Book of Baruch, date and author unknown.
1st Esdras, date and author unknown.
2nd Esdras, date (approx) A.D. 100, author unknown.
Book of Judith, date (approx) 100 B.C., author unknown.
Book of Tobit, date (approx) 300 B.C., author unknown.
Book of Sirach (Ecclesiasticus), date 180 B.C., believed to be written by a Jewish philosopher.
Book of Wisdom, date (approx) 100 B.C., written in Greek by an Alexandrian Jew who impersonates himself as Solomon.
Rest of Esther, date and author unknown.
Prayer of Manasses, date and author unknown.
1st Maccabees, written about 100 B.C. by a Palestinian Jew.
2nd Maccabees, date (approx) 100 B.C., author unknown.

Latin translations of the Bible began to appear in the second century A.D. as the international language changed from Greek to Latin. We need to remember there were no printing presses in those days, so the copies of the Bible were handwritten and many were incomplete and inaccurate. In the year A.D. 382, Damasus, the Bishop of Rome, commissioned Jerome to produce a stable Latin version of the Bible. His work resulted in the Vulgate Bible, which became the common version for the next one thousand years. In doing his work Jerome used the text of the original Hebrew Bible, the Greek Septuagint, and other Latin versions. Because Jerome used the original Hebrew Bible, he was able to detect the discrepancies between the original Hebrew Bible and the Greek Septuagint. He identified the fourteen added books and labeled them *Apocrypha*, meaning separate, hidden, or concealed writings. He expressed doubt as to their validity in being the inspired Word of God, but lost his argument to the theologian Augustine and the Greek-speaking population who had been using the Septuagint for nearly seven hundred years. The Vulgate became the common Bible in the Roman Catholic Church, and the Apocrypha writings went unchallenged until the days of the Reformation. When the Roman Church called the Council of Trent in 1546 to combat the Reformation, it gave formal recognition to the Apocrypha writings.

The "Reformers" goal was to cleanup the Roman Catholic Church by removing false doctrines, many of which entered the Church through the Apocrypha writings. Among them were the doctrine of purgatory, prayers for the dead, the worship of saints, the justification of suicide, the end justifies the means, and alms giving as atonement for sin. Rather than be reformed the Roman Catholic Church labeled the reformers as "protestors," their Churches Protestant, and tried to put down the rebellion by force. When the Reformation blood stopped flowing, the English speaking population of the world had a Bible in which the Old Testament portion corresponded to the original Hebrew Bible.

It isn't difficult to understand that a return to the Hebrew God would require a return to the original Hebrew Bible. For the return to be accurate, we must go all the way back to the year 455 B.C. and the Book of Malachi, where God completed his Old Testament revelation. The Apocrypha Books were never a part of the Hebrew Bible, then or now, and they were never considered inspired by the Jews. God entrusted his Word to the Jews, not only to record it, but to preserve it for future generations. I personally believe the Jews who translated the Hebrew Bible into the Greek language during the days of Ptolemy II were faithful and translated only the books in the original Hebrew Bible. I say this because several of the Apocrypha Books were not even written until nearly 150 years after they had completed their work on the Septuagint. This is enough evidence to see the original Septuagint had to be amended by somebody, at a later point in history, to include the Apocrypha writings. The next obvious question is, Who did it? It was during this 150 year period Antiochus Epiphanes (175-164 B.C.) had "intelligence with them (Jews) that forsake the holy covenant" (Daniel 11:30). It was these Hellenized Jews who were corrupted by what Epiphanes considered intelligence, Daniel 11:32a "And such as do wickedly against the covenant shall he corrupt by flatteries." Notice the Hellenized Jews not only forsook the holy covenant, they did wickedly against it. I believe when the truth is known, we will find the wickedness the Hellenized Jews did against the holy covenant was to change the Sacred Holy Scriptures to include the Apocrypha writings.

The intelligence the Greeks valued and exalted was knowledge acquired through the natural mental process. The knowledge and wisdom they lusted after was earthly, sensual, and devilish (James 3:15). From a look at Greek history, it is obvious, they put no value whatsoever on the revelation knowledge contained in the Hebrew Bible. They did not believe the Hebrew God, nor did they serve, worship, or fear Him. Their education was based on secular knowledge, apart from the revelation knowledge of the Word of God, and it set the Greek Empire on a course leading to its own destruction. Under the disguise of higher learning and more education, the Hellenized Jews were able to modify the Septuagint to include the Apocrypha writings.

Oddly enough it was the rebirth of "learning" nearly 1800 years later that led to the Apocrypha writings being separated from the Sacred Holy Scriptures. This rebirth or revival of learning was called the Renaissance. It began in Italy in the 14th century, and during the 15th and 16th centuries it spread across Europe. It was during this re-emphasis on learning the people began comparing what the papacy (the office of the pope, head of the Roman Catholic Church) taught, to what the Word of God taught. Their evaluation was the Reformation. The Renaissance was a mental movement, a return to intellectual knowledge and the exaltation of humanism and materialism. The Reformation was a spiritual movement, a return to revelation knowledge and the exaltation of God's written Word as the sole rule of belief and life.

It is not my intent to bad-mouth the papacy or the Roman Catholic Church. Its own history speaks more clearly than I ever could. Anyone who examines the history of the papacy and cannot see an Italian political organization that interposed itself between God and God's people, is being dishonest to themselves and the historical record. The papacy empowered itself by separating God's written Word from the people and presenting Christianity as obedience to the organization. It maintained its power by murdering anyone who would not bow the knee to Papal authority. It exalted the head of the organization above the throne of God, and what he said above what Jesus said. Compare what the papacy accomplished by the Inquisition to what Jesus told it to do in the Mark 16:15-18 Church Commission. The Reformation did not result in a reformed Roman Catholic Church, because it refused to be changed. The papacy power to kill people for translating and reading the Bible was eventually taken away, but it still exercises control over the lives and destiny of several million people. The Reformers who survived the Inquisition left the Roman Catholic Church, and began preaching and urging the people to read and study the Bible. The most outstanding accomplishment of the Reformers was that they took the Bible from the papacy and put it back into the hands of the Church members. Since that time the Church membership has been without a legitimate excuse for being deceived.

During the Reformation the Apocrypha writings came under attack and were rejected as part of the inspired Word of God. The rejection was so complete, that much of the Protestant Church membership still consider them taboo. As a result many have never heard of the man Antiochus Epiphanes, and are totally unfamiliar with what he did, to cause Jesus to call the Jews attention to it in Matthew 24:15-18, "(15) When ye therefore shall see the abomination of desolation, spoken of by Daniel the prophet, stand in the holy place, (whoso readeth, let him understand:) (16) Then let them which be in Judea flee into the mountains: (17) Let him which is on the housetop not come down to take anything out of his house: (18) Neither let him which is in the field return back to take his clothes."

Daniel spoke of two different abominations of desolations, one in Daniel chapter 8 which was to last 2300 days (8:14), and the second in Daniel chap ter 12 which was to last 1290 days (12:11). The first was to be performed by the "little horn" or king of Daniel 8:9, who would come out of the Greek Empire after "the great horn was broken" and it was divided among the "four notable ones" of Daniel 8:8. The prophecies in Daniel chapter 10:1-11:35 provide more information on what would take place during this period of history. When Jesus made the statement we just read in Matthew 24:15-18, the 2300-day abomination of desolation was history, the Greek Empire had fallen to the Roman Empire, Antiochus Epiphanes was dead, and all the prophecies in Daniel chapter 8 and Daniel 10:1-11:35 were fulfilled. The phrase "shall see" is in the future tense, in the statement "When ye therefore shall see the abomination of desolation." This makes what Jesus said a prophecy (something that will come to pass or happen in the future). Jesus was actually speaking of the 1290-day abomination of desolation which is the three and one-half year reign of the False Prophet, during the last half of the seven-year tribulation period. In the prophecies in the Book of Daniel, God has told us in advance, what would happen in both the 2300-day and the 1290-day abomination of desolation. Since an abomination of desolation is the same regardless of who performs it, by looking at what Epiphanes did, we can gain an understanding as to what the False Prophet will do. What we need is a history book account of what Epiphanes actually did, to compare it to what God said he would do.

There is a historical record of what Epiphanes did, but unfortunately, it was part of the Apocrypha Books and was literally discarded by a large portion of the Protestant church population. I am speaking specifically of the Book of 1st Maccabees. This book is historical in content, not doctrinal. The book contains the history of the Jews from the year 175 to 134 B.C. It is believed to have been written by a Palestinian Jew near the year 100 B.C. Being written by a Jew doesn't make it the inspired Word of God, nor does is make it any more reliable than any other historical record. If you are not mature enough in your Christian growth to read the first chapter in the Book of 1st Maccabees for its historical value, skip over it, but before you do let me ask you to consider two things. The first is that neither Jesus nor his Apostles ever made a direct statement from any of the Apocrypha writings. This not only shows us their doctrinal value, but also introduces the possibility that the Greek Septuagint may not have been changed to include the Apocrypha writings until a much later date in history.

The second thing to consider is that if direct revelation stopped with the Book of Malachi in the year 455 B.C., and did not start again until the announcement of the conception of John the Baptist, the Book of 1st Maccabees is, in fact, uninspired. This fact also makes all other historical accounts between the year 455 B.C. and John the Baptist uninspired. This means a college textbook on the Greek Empire is no more trustworthy than the Book of 1st Maccabees, and vice versa. You read a school history book for its historical value, and if you approach the first chapter of 1st Maccabees the same way, you will be able to see what the abomination of desolation was, without having to worry about getting tangled up in false doctrine.

The first nine verses of 1st Maccabees concern Alexander the Great, "(1) After Alexander the Macedonian, Philip's son, who came from the land of Kittim, had defeated Darius, king of the Persians and Medes, he became king in his place, having first ruled in Greece. (2) He fought many campaigns, captured fortreses, and put kings to death. (3) He advanced to the ends of the earth, gathering plunder from many nations; the earth fell silent before him, and his heart became proud and arrogant. (4) He collected a very strong army and conquered provinces, nations, and rulers, and they became his tributaries. (5) But after all this he took to his bed, realizing that he was going to die. (6) He herefore summoned his officers, the nobles, who had been brought up with him from his youth, to divide his kingdom among them while he was still alive. (7) Alexander had reigned twelve years when he died. (8) So his officers took over his kingdom, each in his own territory, (9) and after his death they all put on royal crowns, and so did their sons after them for many years, causing much distress over the earth."

Verse 10 introduces Antiochus Epiphanes, "(10) There sprang from these a sinful offshoot, Antiochus Epiphanes, son of King Antiochus, once a hostage at Rome. He became king in the year one hundred and thirty-seven of the kingdom of the Greeks."

Verses 11-15 introduce the apostate Jews, "(11) In those days there appeared in Israel men who were breakers of the law, and they seduced many people, saying: "Let us go and make an alliance with the Gentiles all around us; since we separated from them, many evils have come upon us." (12) The proposal was agreeable; (13) some from among the people promptly went to the king, and he authorized them to introduce the way of living of the Gentiles. (14) Thereupon they built a gymnasium in Jerusalem according to Gentile custom. (15) They covered over the mark of their circumcision and abandoned the holy covenant; they allied themselves with the Gentiles and sold themselves to wrongdoing."

Verses 16-19 deal with the successful invasion of Egypt, "(16) When his kingdom seemed secure, Antiochus proposed to become king of Egypt, so as to rule over both kingdoms. (17) He invaded Egypt with a strong force, with chariots and elephants, and with a large fleet, (18) to make war on Ptolemy, king of Egypt. Ptolemy was frightened at his presence and fled, leaving many casualties. (19) The fortified cities in the land of Egypt was captured, and Antiochus plundered the land of Egypt."

Verses 20-28 deal with Epiphanes robbing the temple, "(20) After Antiochus had defeated Egypt in the year one hundred and forty-three, he returned and went up to Israel and to Jerusalem with a strong force. (21) He insolently invaded the sanctuary and took away the golden altar, the lampstand for the light with all its fixtures, (22) the offering table, the cups and the bowls, the golden censers, the curtain, the crowns, and the golden ornament on the facade of the temple. He stripped off everything, (23) and took away the gold and silver and the precious vessels; he also took all the hidden treasures he could find. (24) Taking all this, he went back to his own country, after he had spoken with great arrogance and shed much blood. (25) And there was great mourning for Israel, in every place where they dwelt, (26) and the rulers and the elders groaned. Virgins and young men languished, and the beauty of the women was disfigured. (27) Every bridegroom took up lamentation, she who sat in the bridal chamber mourned,

(28) And the land was shaken on account of its inhabitants, and all the house of Jacob was covered with shame."

Verses 29-40 deal with the federal troops sent to Jerusalem, "(29) Two years later, the king sent the Mysian commander to the cities of Judah, and he came to Jerusalem with a strong force. (30) He spoke to them deceitfully in peaceful terms, and won their trust. Then he attacked the city suddenly, in a great onslaught, and destroyed many of the people in Israel. (31) He plundered the city and set fire to it, demolished its houses and its surrounding walls, (32) took captive the women and children, and seized the cattle. (33) Then they built up the City of David with a high, massive wall and strong towers, and it became their citadel. (34) There they installed a sinful race, perverse men, who fortified themselves inside it, (35) storing up weapons and provisions, and depositing there the plunder they had collected from Jerusalem. And they became a great threat. (36) The citadel became an ambush against the sanctuary, and a wicked adversary to Israel at all times. (37) And they shed innocent blood around the sanctuary; they defiled the sanctuary. (38) Because of them the inhabitants of Jerusalem fled away, and she became the abode of strangers. She became a stranger to her own offspring, and her children forsook her. (39) Her sanctuary was as desolate as a wilderness; her feasts were turned into mourning, Her sabbaths to shame, her honor to contempt. (40) Her dishonor was as great as her glory had been, and her exaltation was turned into mourning."

Verses 41-63 deal with enforcing the ultimatum, "(41) Then the king wrote to his whole kingdom that all should be one people, (42) each abandoning his particular customs. All the Gentiles conformed to the command of the king, (43) and many Israelites were in favor of his religion; they sacrificed to idols and profaned the sabbath. (44) The king sent messengers with letters to Jerusalem and to the cities of Judah, ordering them to follow customs foreign to their land: (45) to prohibit holocausts, sacrifices, and libations in the sanctuary, to profane the sabbaths and feast days, (46) to desecrate the sanctuary and the sacred misisters, to build pagan altars and temples and shrines, (47) to sacrifice swine and unclean animals, (48) to leave their sons uncircumcised, and to let themselves be defiled with every king of impurity and abomination, (49) so that they might forget the law and change all their observances. (50) Whoever refused to act according to the command of the king should be put to death. (51) Such were the orders he published throughout his kingdom. He appointed inspectors over all the people, and he ordered the cities of Judah to offer sacrifices, each city in turn. (52) Many of the people, those who abandoned the law, joined them and committed evil in the land. (53) Israel was driven into hiding, wherever places of refuge could be found. (54) On the fifteenth day of the month Chisleu, in the year one hundred and forty-five, the king erected the horrible abomination upon the altar of holocausts, and in the surrounding cities of Judah they built pagan altars. (55) They also burnt incense at the doors of houses and in the streets. (56) Any scrolls of the law which they found they tore up and burnt. (57) Whoever was found with a scroll of the covenant, and whoever observed the law, was condemned to death by royal decree. (58) So they used their power against Israel, against those who were caught, each month, in the cities. (59) On the twenty-fifth day of each month they sacrificed on the altar errected over the altar of holocausts. (60) Women who had had their children circumcised were put to death, in keeping with the decree, (61) with the babies hung from their necks; their families also and those who had circumcised them were killed. (62) But many in Israel was determined and resolved in their hearts not to eat anything unclean; (63) they preferred to die rather than to be defiled with unclean food or to profane the holy covenant; and they did die. Terrible affliction was upon Israel."

From the prophecies in the Book of Daniel and the historical record of Epiphanes, we can put together a fairly clear picture of an "abomination of desolation." It begins with apostasy, a departure of God's people from his revealed Will. This is followed by the rise of a powerful political figure with a strong federal force. This organization interposes itself between God's revealed Will and God's people. The organization then demands allegiance, and uses its power to kill those who resist. This is the basic routine Epiphanes followed. The Papacy was another picture of the abomination of desolation. The Church will be in the apostasy stage as it waits for Antichrist to take political control of the ten king kingdom. Following the rapture of born-again believers, Antichrist will complete the procedure by destroying false Christianity. At the middle of the tribulation period the False Prophet will take control of the Antichrist organization, and will put the Jews and everyone else who professes belief in the God of the Scriptures or any other god through the same persecution.

In our outline look at the prophecies in the Book of Daniel we have seen: Israel's future to the rise of Antiochus Epiphanes, Daniel 10:1-11:20; and The vile Syrian: a picture of the great tribulation False Prophet, Daniel 11:21-35. The last part of the verse in Daniel 11:35 reads, "even to the time of the end: because it is yet for a time appointed." This statement marks the ends of the prophecies concerning Epiphanes, the Greek Empire, and the 2300 day abomination of desolation. With verse 11:36 the angel moves to the last half of the seven-year tribulation period, the reign of the False Prophet, and the 1290 day abomination of desolation. This was the prime reason for the vision as we saw in Daniel 10:14, "Now I am come to make thee understand what shall befall thy people in the latter days: for yet the vision is for many days." This part of our outline is labeled, "The king of the time of the end: the great tribulation False Prophet."

1. The king shall do according to his will. Daniel 11:36a, "And the king shall do according to his will." Needless to say, Epiphanes was not a king who did according to his will. He had many things his own way, but the two things he wanted most were both beyond his power to accomplish. In Daniel 11:29-30 his will to reunite the Greek Empire was broken when he was sent home grieving. His goal to Hellenize all the people in his kingdom was frustrated and brought to nothing by a remnant of God-fearing Jews. The king being spoken of here that "shall do according to his will" is the False Prophet of Rev. 13:11-18. He will arrive on the scene at the middle of the seven-year tribulation period. His kingdom will be the European Common Market confederacy after he eliminates three nations, which turns the organization into a seven king kingdom. In Rev. 13:12a we are told, "And he exerciseth all the power of the first beast before him." The beast before him was Antichrist who reigned during the first half of the tribulation period. The False Prophet's power will be worldwide, Rev. 13:7, "And it was given unto him to make war with the saints, and to overcome them: and power was given him over all kindreds, and tongues, and nations." This power will allow him to "do according to his will."

2. He shall exalt himself and magnify himself above every god. Daniel 11:36b, "and he shall exalt himself, and magnify himself above every god." It is easy to see that the False Prophet will be full of self pride, for this is what causes individuals to exalt themselves.

3. He shall speak marvelous things against the God of gods. Daniel 11:36c, "and shall speak marvelous things against the God of gods." In Rev. 13:11b we are told that "he spake as a dragon" or literally, as Satan. Antichrist will be a blasphemer as we saw in Rev. 13:5-6, "(5) And there was given unto him a mouth speaking great things and blasphemies; and power was given unto him to continue forty and two months. (6) And he opened his mouth in blasphemy against God, to blaspheme his name, and his tabernacle, and them that dwell in heaven." I suspect that the False Prophet will come up with some new angles on blasphemy that the human race hasn't even thought of yet. Daniel heard some of the "great words" he spoke, and they held his attention. Here is how he described it in Daniel 7:11, "I beheld then because of the voice of the great words which the horn spake: I beheld even till the beast was slain, and his body destroyed, and given to the burning flame."

4. He shall prosper until God's will is accomplished. Daniel 11:36d, "and shall prosper till the indignation be accomplished: for that that is determined shall be done." The False Prophet will be able to "do according to his will" until the very end of the tribulation period. Consider this statement with Daniel 9:27, "And he (Antichrist) shall confirm the covenant with many for one week: and in the midst of the week he (the False Prophet) shall cause the sacrifice and the oblation to cease, and for the overspreading of abominations he shall make it desolate, even until the consummation, and that determined shall be poured upon the desolate." What has been determined to be "poured upon the desolate" is "the wrath of God upon the earth" in the seven vial judgments of Revelation chapter 16.

5. He shall not regard the God of his fathers. Daniel 11:37a, "Neither shall he regard the God of his fathers." The word translated as God is Elohim, meaning the Trinity or Godhead. It is the same Hebrew word translated God in the phrase, "In the beginning God created" in Genesis 1:1. The False Prophet has no regard for the living and true God. The statement "the God of his fathers" needs to be considered in light of the fact the False Prophet enters the world from Hades ("up out of the earth," Rev. 13:11, "the bottomless pit," Rev. 17:8). As we have already seen, Hades is a prison under the surface of the earth where lost human spirits and fallen angels are confined. The fallen angels are demonic spirits who sinned by incarnating and crossing from the spiritual realm to the physical realm (Genesis 6:1-5, 2 Peter 2:4-5). They literally put on flesh and impersonate a human being. The fact that the False Prophet ascends out of Hades means that he is reincarnated or incarnated again. Which ethnic race he incarnated into originally, is debatable, but there is no doubt that his reincarnation will be as a Jew. As a Jew, he will naturally be expected to worship and exalt the God of his fathers. The word translated as God identifies the God of heaven, the God of the Holy Scriptures, and the God of the Jews. Since it is this God that the False Prophet does not regard, nor does he regard the God of his fathers, we can expect him to reincarnate as a renegade Jew.

6. Nor will he regard the desire of women: whore religious organizations. Daniel 11:37b, "nor the desire of women." In the first part of this verse we saw how the False Prophet did not regard the true God or His religion. Now we are being told he has no regard for any of the false gods or false religions. As we have already seen, a woman in Bible prophecy represents a religion, its god, or a religious organization. The word women is the plural form of woman, and speaks of more than one. In reality, it speaks of all. In the False Prophet ultimatum to worship the image of the beast or die, no person, group, or religion is excluded. Some have used this statement to teach that the False Prophet will be a homosexual. He may be, but that is not what God is teaching in this verse. The subject of this verse is the False Prophet and which god he regards. Read the entire verse and keep this statement in context, Daniel 11:37, "Neither shall he regard the God of his fathers, nor the desire of women, nor regard any god: for he shall magnify himself above all."

7. He will magnify himself above all gods. Daniel 11:37c, "nor regard any god: for he shall magnify himself above all." He will magnify himself above all gods by convincing people that what he says is above what God or gods say. He will increase the size of himself to a degree larger or greater than all gods. Most of us have viewed an object under a magnifying glass, and can understand the difference between actual size and apparent size. The people who are unfamiliar with the Word of God have never viewed the False Prophet, or what God says about him. The only picture they have of him will be what he says about himself.

8. He honors the God of forces. Daniel 11:38a, "But in his estate shall he honour the God of forces." The phrase "in his estate" means that in the place where the God of Heaven should stand, the False Prophet will cause the God of forces to stand. Instead of honoring the God of heaven as Deity, he will honor forces as deity. As political ruler of seven nations in the European Common Market he will have control over a mighty military force, but the forces he honors will not stop with military might. In Rev 13:13-14a we are told, "(13) And he doeth great wonders, so that he maketh fire come down from heaven on the earth in the sight of men, (14a) And deceiveth them that dwell on the earth by the means of those miracles which he had power to do in the sight of the beast:" This is not a magician's trick, and there is nothing supernatural about lightning. Lightning is one of the natural laws of nature, but it does give us a glimpse of the powers the False Prophet honors as deity.

The basic meaning of the Hebrew word translated as *forces* is "a fortified place," but the meaning goes beyond a physical location. It is also the word translated as *fortress* in Jeremiah 16:19a, "O Lord, my strength, and my fortress, and my refuge in the day of affliction," and *stronghold* in Nahum 1:7a, "The Lord is good, a stronghold in the day of trouble," or the *strong rock* of Psalms 31:2, "Bow down thine ear to me; deliver me speedily. Be thou my strong rock, for an house of defense to save me." Today these passages speak of Jesus Christ, our God, and the security promised for obedience to his Word. It allows born-again believers to stand in a fortified place because Jesus commands an innumerable elect angelic force to protect them. The False Prophet will be promoting himself as god, making the same promises to his followers, with the same success because of the demonic angelic force at his disposal. It is not the fortified place the False Prophet is promoting as god, it is the means, the forces that make it fortified. The translators would have been correct to say "But in his estate shall he honour the God of fortress" or the "God of strength." The Holy Spirit used the "God of forces" to communicate that it is the forces behind the fortress, the forces behind the strength, that the False Prophet will promote as god. I know the God of strength and Jesus is my fortress, but I would have been confused to find the False Prophet honoring Him.

9. He introduces a new god. Daniel 11:38b-39a, "(38b) and a god whom his fathers knew not shall he honour with gold, and silver, and with precious stones, and pleasant things. (39a) Thus shall he do in the most strong holds with a strange god, whom he shall acknowledge and increase with glory." The new god the False Prophet introduces will be the living image of Rev. 13:14b-15, "(14b) saying to them that dwell on the earth, that they should make an image to the beast, which had the wound by a sword, and did live. (15) And he had power to give life unto the image of the beast, that the image of the beast should both speak, and cause that as many as would not worship the image of the beast should be killed."

10. With these two gods he rules over many. Daniel 11:39b, "and he shall cause them to rule over many." The two gods are the god of forces and the image of the beast. In Daniel 11:36 we were told the False Prophet would "exalt himself, and magnify himself above every god." His manipulation of the natural laws of nature, and of the living image, are designed to convince people that he is god. He will be so convincing, in fact, that Jesus said if it were possible even the very elect would be deceived in Matthew 24:24-25, "(24) For there shall arise false Christs, and false prophets, and shall shew great signs and wonders; insomuch that, if it were possible, they shall deceive the very elect. (25) Behold, I have told you before."

The convincing power of the two gods will be seen in what they do. One speaks and the other works miracles, and together they will convince people that the False Prophet is god. "Together they convince" will be effective because Satan copied the idea from God. We could describe the ministry of Jesus as one of speaking and working miracles. Jesus preached The Word (speaking) and worked miracles: casting out demons, raising the dead, healing the sick, walking on water, calming the storm, turning water into wine, etc. The miracles confirmed The Word, and "together they convinced" people Jesus was who he claimed to be. Jesus was doing what his Father told him to do, and the miracles were the Father's stamp of approval as to the truth of what his Son said. This is why Jesus could say "though ye believe not me, believe the works" in John 10:37-38, "(37) If I do not the works of my Father, believe me not. (38) But if I do, though ye believe not me, believe the works: that ye may know, and believe, that the Father is in me, and I in him."

The intent of the miracles is given in the last part of the verse, "believe the works: that ye may know, and believe, that the Father is in me, and I in him." Jesus repeated what his Father said, the Father confirmed the truth of what Jesus said by the miracles, and together they convinced, or as Jesus said, "that ye may know, and believe that the Father is in me, and I in him." Jesus and the Father were one because the Father dwelt in him, just as the Holy Spirit dwells in born-again believers. Jesus spoke the truth and the Father dwelling in him did the miracles. This is exactly the way Jesus intended the Church to operate. Born-again Church members speak the truth, and the Holy Spirit dwelling in them does the miracles, and together they convince, because you and I can look, listen, know, and believe they are of Jesus. The miracles confirm they are doing what Jesus told them to do, just as the miracles confirmed Jesus was doing what the Father told him to do. Jesus puts this altogether in John chapter 14, when he answered Philip's request for Jesus to show him the Father. John 14:8-12, "(8) Philip saith unto him, Lord, shew us the Father, and it sufficeth us. (9) Jesus saith unto him, Have I been so long time with you, and yet hast thou not known me, Philip? he that hath seen me hath seen the Father; and how sayest thou then, Shew us the Father? (10) Believest thou not that I am in the Father, and the Father in me? the words that I speak unto you I speak not of myself: but the Father that dwelleth in me, he doeth the works. (11) Believe me that I am in the Father, and the Father in me: or else believe me for the very works' sake. (12) Verily, verily, I say unto you, He that believeth on me, the works that I do shall he do also; and greater works than these shall he do; because I go unto my Father."

The "together they convince" concept is clear in the Mark 16:15-18 Church Commission. In verse 15 Jesus told his followers to "preach the gospel" and in verse 17 "these signs shall follow them that believe." We can describe the ministry of Jesus as one of speaking and working miracles, because he spoke the truth and the Father confirmed what he spoke by the miracles. We can describe the ministry of the Church as one of speaking and working miracles, because it is speaking the truth and the Holy Spirit is confirming what is being spoken as the truth by the miracles. There are no miracles in the congregation of the unbelieving, because as long as the Church is on the earth, the working of miracles is restricted to "them that believe." The absence of miracles is the way Jesus identifies the people on both sides of the pulpit as unbelievers.

"Together they convince" is just another way of saying "Together they conquer." The definition of *convince* is "to persuade by argument or evidence; overcome the doubts of; cause to feel certain." The word *convince* is a Latin word with the prefix *con* meaning with or together, and *vincere* meaning to conquer. That person behind the pulpit is conquering you. They are speaking words which form thoughts, and if you accept those thoughts as the truth, it will conquer you. If the person is of God, they are repeating what Jesus said and attempting to convince you that Jesus spoke the truth. Accept that as the truth, and you are being conquered by Jesus Christ. If the person is not of God, they are taking what Jesus said and attempting to convince you that Jesus didn't say what he means or didn't mean what he said. Accept that as the truth, and you are being conquered by Antichrist. The miracles are manifestations of the Holy Spirit, which dwells in the believers and operates in the congregation of believers. The Holy Spirit and the miracles are Jesus' way of convincing you that one congregation is made up of "them that believe," and the other congregation is made up of them that do not believe. When the congregation of believers leaves Earth in the rapture, the congregation of unbelieving will see many miracles performed by the unholy spirit of Antichrist. They will be the recipients of the 2 Thessalonians chapter 2 strong delusion.

11. He divides the land for gain. Daniel 11:39c, "and shall divide the land for gain." Dividing the spoils is a way of rewarding followers for faithful service. Allegiance motivated by greed is effective in a materialistic society, because of the emphasis put on material gain. It is also effective in the political realm, because it satisfies the politicians craving for status. When a new area of land is conquered, the False Prophet strengthens his kingdom by putting his people in charge, and controlling them with the threat of losing their material gain or status. You can see the success of this tactic in the Communist party. When a new country is conquered the political and religious leaders are classified as enemies of the state and imprisoned or killed. Their vacated positions are filled with faithful party members who clean up their domain by executing those who represent a threat to communism.

12. At the time of the end the king of the south pushes at him. Daniel 11:40a, "And at the time of the end shall the king of the south push at him." This is one of the most significant events in the history of Earth. In Matthew 12:22-37 Jesus healed a man who was blind and dumb by casting out the demon. The Pharisees accused Jesus of casting out the demon with the aid of Beelzebub, the prince of the demons. In Matthew 12:25 Jesus makes this statement, "And Jesus knew their thoughts, and said unto them, Every kingdom divided against itself is brought to desolation; and every city or house divided against itself shall not stand." In verse 26 He follows this statement with a question, "And if Satan cast out Satan, he is divided against himself; how shall then his kingdom stand?" The answer to the question is obvious: His kingdom can't stand, because "every kingdom divided against itself is brought to desolation." This is the division in the kingdom of Satan that sets his kingdom on a course leading to its own destruction.

This division is actually a disagreement within the demonic hierarchy that starts a rebellion, which Satan is unable to control. In review, the demonic hierarchy consists of Satan as the sovereign authority. Immediately under Satan are the principality demons which are the "kings of the earth" we saw in Revelation chapters 17 and 18. Each Gentile nation has a principality demon enthroned by Satan, who directs the affairs of the nation according to the will of Satan. They are also referred to as the prince of the nation, prince of Tyrus in Ezekiel 28:1-10, prince of the kingdom of Persia in Daniel 10:13, and the prince of Grecia in Daniel 10:20 over the realm of Greece. Immediately under the principality demons are the dominion demons or the work force.

The principality demon that "gets pushy" with the principality demon False Prophet will be the prince of Egypt, the king of the south. When he pushes will be "at the time of the end." If we would place this event in the Book of the Revelation, it would fall at the very end of the seven-year tribulation era, after the blowing of the seventh trumpet, and just before the pouring out of the seven vial judgments. Needless to say, Satan must move against this principality demon and dethrone him, in order to restore tranquillity in his kingdom. This is the first time in history that Satan is fighting against himself, and like Jesus said, "every kingdom divided against itself is brought to desolation."

13. An invasion force sent to Egypt. Daniel 11:40b-41a, "(40b) and the king of the north shall come against him like a whirlwind, with chariots, and with horsemen, and with many ships; and he shall enter into the countries, and shall overflow and pass over. (41a) He shall enter also into the glorious land, and many countries shall be overthrown." The king of the north is the Antichrist/False Prophet organization made up of the remaining seven European Common Market nations. They are en route to Egypt to dethrone the pushy principality demon. Their invasion of Egypt will be successful, but this invasion force will never return home. The navy will cross the Mediterranean Sea while the land forces move south along the coast through Turkey, Syria, Lebanon, and the land of Israel, the glorious land.

14. He will not conquer Edom, Moab, or the Ammonites. Daniel 11:41b, "but these shall escape out of his hand, even Edom, Moab, and the chief of the children of Ammon." The invasion force will move south through the land of Israel, between the Jordan River/Dead Sea and the Mediterranean Sea. The land of Edom, Moab, and Ammon lie on the east side of the Jordan River, and make up present day Jordan and perhaps the northeastern edge of Saudi Arabia. These countries "escape out of his hand" because the invasion force will move past them on the west side of the Jordan River. The target of the invasion force is Egypt, and Satan must get his military force to Egypt as quickly as possible, to defeat the pushy principality demon by putting Egypt under the control of the False Prophet. From the events surrounding Antiochus Epiphanes, I seriously doubt if the city of Jerusalem will come under attack during the southern movement of the invading army. But that army will return, so get out of the city of Jerusalem and the land of Israel, and get on the other side of the Jordan River and the Dead Sea. The principality demon of Jordan will be neutral in the argument between the False Prophet and the prince of Egypt, and as the division in Satan's kingdom widens, he will side against the False Prophet.

15. Countries controlled include Egypt, Libya, and Ethiopia. Daniel 11:42-43, "(42) He shall stretch forth his hand also upon the countries: and the land of Egypt shall not escape. (43) But he shall have power over the treasures of gold and of silver, and over all the precious things of Egypt: and the Libyans and the Ethiopians shall be at his steps." By the time the Antichrist/False Prophet invasion force reaches Egypt the principality demons of Libya, Sudan, and Ethiopia will have sided with the prince of Egypt. Egypt will be defeated, Sudan will fall, and the battle front in north Africa will extend from Ethiopia to Libya. The False Prophet invasion of north Africa will be stopped by bad news.

16. Tidings from the east and north trouble him. Daniel 11:44a, "But tidings out of the east and out of the north shall trouble him." The tidings out of the north that will trouble the False Prophet concern what is happening back home. God is pouring out the Revelation vial judgments. In review, the first vial judgment (Rev. 16:2), will be a noisome and grievous sore, limited to the people in his kingdom who worshipped the image and took the unforgivable mark. The second vial (16:3) will be poured upon the sea, which becomes as the blood of a dead man, and all sea life dies. The third vial (16:4-7) will turn fresh water to blood, for the purpose of giving the people in his kingdom who killed the saints and prophets blood to drink. The fourth vial (16:8-9) will be poured upon the sun, and men will be scorched with great heat. The fifth vial (16:10-11) will cause darkness in his kingdom, that is so intense, the members will gnaw their tongues for pain.

The tidings out of the east that trouble the False Prophet will be the mighty Red Chinese army coming at him, and there is no Euphrates River to slow them down. God will have poured out the sixth vial judgment, Rev. 16:12, "And the sixth angel poured out his vial upon the great river Euphrates; and the water thereof was dried up, that the way of the kings of the east might be prepared." Satan's kingdom is really in a mess now. It is time to call in reinforcements, and make a last stand, which is what we see if we continue reading in Rev. 16:13-14, "(13) And I saw three unclean spirits like frogs come out of the mouth of the dragon, and out of the mouth of the beast, and out of the mouth of the false prophet. (14) For they are the spirits of devils, working miracles, which go forth unto the kings of the earth and of the whole world, to gather them to the battle of the great day of God Almighty."

17. With great fury he goes forth to destroy.
Daniel 11:44b, "therefore he shall go forth with great fury to destroy, and utterly to make away many." The False Prophet will abandon his north Africa campaign and begin to retreat, destroying everything in his path, and killing every human he finds. He will march through Egypt and northward through the land of Israel.

18. His camp will be between the seas in the glorious holy mountain.
Daniel 11:45a, "And he shall plant the tabernacles of his palace between the seas in the glorious holy mountain." When the False Prophet reaches the valley of Megiddo, north of Jerusalem, he will stop and set up camp to prepare for the last battle of the war. Between the seas means between the Dead Sea and the Mediterranean Sea. At this time the city of Jerusalem will come under attack, Zechariah 14:2, "For I will gather all nations against Jerusalem to battle; and the city shall be taken, and the houses rifled, and the women ravished; and half of the city shall go forth into captivity, and the residue of the people shall not be cut off from the city." Here comes Jesus! Zechariah 14:3, "Then shall the Lord go forth, and fight against those nations, as when he fought in the day of battle." This will end the seven-year tribulation period. This will be the return of Jesus recorded in Rev. 19:11-16, to destroy the Armageddon army (Rev. 19:17-21) and establish the Kingdom Dispensation (Rev. 20:1-6).

19. None shall help him when he comes to his end. Daniel 11:45b, "yet he shall come to his end, and none shall help him." This will be the end of the Antichrist and the False Prophet reign, and from here they will go directly to hell, Rev. 19:20, "And the beast was taken, and with him the false prophet that wrought miracles before him, with which he deceived them that had received the mark of the beast, and them that worshipped his image. These both were cast alive into a lake of fire burning with brimstone." In Rev. 20:1-3 Satan will be bound, and cast into Hades, until the end of the Millennial Reign of Jesus.

20. At that time Michael shall stand up for the Jews. Daniel 12:1a, "And at that time shall Michael stand up, the great prince which standeth for the children of thy people." Michael is an elect principality angel. The fact that he is a great prince means he is a very powerful being with much authority. In Jude 1:9 he is called "the archangel" which may identify him as a ruler over angels, instead of a territory. The phrase "thy people" refers to Daniel's people which are the Jews. The children of Daniel's people are their descendants and needs to be considered with the statement "at that time." Michael will stand up for the Jewish descendants, "at that time" during the great tribulation period, when the False Prophet is persecuting them.

21. It will be a time of great trouble: The great tribulation. Daniel 12:1b, "and there shall be a time of trouble, such as never was since there was a nation even to that same time." The fact Jesus spoke of this same "time of trouble" is clear evidence it did not see fulfillment prior to A.D. 30-33. This "time of trouble" will be the great tribulation Jesus spoke of in Matthew 24:21, "For then shall be great tribulation, such as was not since the beginning of the world to this time, no, nor ever shall be."

22. The Jews in the book shall be delivered at this time. Daniel 12:1c, "and at that time thy people shall be delivered, every one that shall be found written in the book." The Jews will be delivered during the seven-year tribulation period. During the first half they will be protected by the Antichrist protection covenant (Daniel 9:27, Isaiah 28:14-15). During the second half God will disannul the protection covenant (Isaiah 28:18-22) and the persecution of the Jews will begin. In reality, they will be delivered in the last day of the tribulation era (Zechariah 14:2-3), when Jesus returns and destroys the Armageddon Army.

23. Many to participate in the first resurrection to everlasting life. Daniel 12:2a, "And many of them that sleep in the dust of the earth shall awake, some to everlasting life." "Them that sleep in the dust of the earth" are humans who have experienced physical death prior to this point in time. "Shall awake" is the resurrection from the dead. "Many of them," instead of "all of them," can be understood if you remember there are two different resurrections. We have more visibility on the subject than Daniel had. He could say "some" to participate in the first and "some" to participate in the second. We can say "some" to participate in the first and "everyone else" will participate in the second a thousand years later. The time period between the two resurrections is revealed in Rev. 20:4-5, but Daniel was not told and he had no other way of knowing.

This is the first resurrection which Jesus called the resurrection of life in John 5:29. Jesus was the first to be resurrected. He was the first fruit of them that slept, 1 Corinthians 15:20, "But now is Christ risen from the dead, and become the first fruits of them that slept." The resurrection will continue with the Church, 1 Corinthians 15:23, "But every man in his own order: Christ the first fruits; afterward they that are Christ's at his coming," which is the 1 Thessalonians 4:13-18 rapture. At the end of the seven-year tribulation period the first resurrection will be completed with the Old Testament saints and the tribulation dead.

24. Some to participate in the second resurrection of shame and everlasting contempt. Daniel 12:2b, "and some to shame and everlasting contempt." Jesus called this resurrection "the resurrection of damnation" in John 5:29. It will take place at the end of the Kingdom Dispensation, one thousand years after the resurrection of life. The people who participate in this resurrection will be the lost from all seven dispensations. They will stand before the great white throne of Rev. 20:11-15. At this point in time, all lost human spirits and all demonic spirits will be cast into the lake of fire.

25. The wise to shine like the brightness of the firmament. Daniel 12:3a, "And they that be wise shall shine as the brightness of the firmament." The wise are they with wisdom. In James 3:14-17 we saw that there are two sources of wisdom. One is from the God of heaven and is found in his written Word. It is a straight and narrow path which will led you to the first resurrection. The wise are following this path. The other source of wisdom is from Satan, the god of this world. It is a broad path which will led you to the second resurrection. The fool follows this path. Proverbs 9:10 identifies the beginning of wisdom, "The fear of the Lord is the beginning of wisdom: and the knowledge of the holy is understanding."

26. Those who turn many to righteousness to shine as the stars forever. Daniel 12:3b, "and they that turn many to righteousness as the stars for ever and ever." "Those who turn many to righteousness" are they who know "the knowledge of the holy is understanding," and that "the fear of the Lord is the beginning of wisdom." "Those" are they who are exalting, preaching, and teaching the Word of God, urging the hearers to turn, or return, to the God of the holy Scriptures. The "many" who turn are those who repent, literally turn from their evil ways to Gods way. Those who turn to righteousness, turn to the right way, and by doing what God said, the way he said to do it, they enter into a right standing with God. This right standing with God is entering into a covenant relationship with him, not merely keeping his law. Nobody was ever saved by keeping the law, nor will there ever be. The law demonstrates our need for a Redeemer, which points us to Jesus. In Galatians 3:24 it is called our schoolmaster, "Wherefore the law was our schoolmaster to bring us unto Christ, that we might be justified by faith."

Abraham was the founding father of the nations of the Israelites. In Acts 7:8 we are told God gave Abraham the covenant of circumcision, "And he gave him the covenant of circumcision: and so Abraham begat Isaac, and circumcised him the eighth day; and Isaac begat Jacob; and Jacob begat the twelve patriarchs." Part of this covenant was that the Redeemer would enter the world through Abraham's descendants. The details of entering into this covenant is recorded in Genesis 17:1-14, "(1) And when Abram was ninety years old and nine, the Lord appeared to Abram, and said unto him, I am the Almighty God; walk before me, and be thou perfect. (2) And I will make my covenant between me and thee, and will multiply thee exceedingly. (3) And Abram fell on his face: and God talked with him, saying, (4) As for me, behold, my covenant is with thee, and thou shalt be a father of many nations. (5) Neither shall thy name any more be called Abram, but thy name shall be Abraham; for a father of many nations have I made thee. (6) And I will make thee exceeding fruitful, and I will make nations of thee, and kings shall come out of thee. (7) And I will establish my covenant between me and thee and thy seed after thee in their generations for an everlasting covenant, to be a God unto thee, and to thy seed after thee. (8) And I will give unto thee, the land wherein thou are a stranger, all the land of Canaan, for an everlasting possession; and I will be their God. (9) And God said unto Abraham, Thou shalt keep my covenant therefore, thou, and thy seed after thee in their generations. (10) This is my covenant, which ye shall keep, between me and you and thy seed after thee; Every man child among you shall be circumcised. (11) And ye shall circumcise the flesh of your foreskin; and it shall be a token of the covenant betwixt me and you. (12) And he that is eight days old shall be circumcised among you, every man child in your generations, he that is born in the house, or bought with money of any stranger, which is not of thy seed. (13) He that is born in thy house, and he that is bought with thy money, must needs be circumcised: and my covenant shall be in your flesh for an everlasting covenant. (14) And the uncircumcised man child whose flesh of his foreskin is not circumcised, that soul shall be cut off from his people; he hath broken my covenant."

Notice in verse 7 it is an "everlasting covenant," in verse 11 that circumcision was "a token of the covenant," and in verse 12 that it was to be done when the child was eight days old. Now reread verse 17:14, "And the uncircumcised man child whose flesh of his foreskin is not circumcised, that soul shall be cut off from his people; he hath broken my covenant." A nine-day-old uncircumcised Jew man child enters into a lost condition ("that soul shall be cut of from his people") because "he hath broken my covenant." In this we can not only see the parent's responsibility for their children, but the emphasis God put on becoming a "covenant child." God made the covenant and established the guidelines for entering into the covenant. The parents of a nine-day-old uncircumcised son have placed that child outside the covenant of promise. The child has no claim on anything God said or promised. The child is, literally, in the world without a covenant, having no hope, and without God.

During the period of Jewish history before Christ, all Gentiles were in this position. Ephesians 2:11-12, "(11) Wherefore remember, that ye being in time past Gentiles in the flesh, who are called Uncircumcision that which is called the Circumcision in the flesh made by hands; (12) That at that time ye were without Christ, being aliens from the commonwealth of Israel, and strangers from the covenants of promise, having no hope, and without God in the world."

When Jesus came and the Jews rejected him as the promised Redeemer, they alienated themselves from the New Covenant promise of the rebirth and the indwelling Holy Spirit. They are now walking in the vanity of their minds just as the Gentiles had done, Ephesians 4:17-18, "(17) This I say therefore, and testify in the Lord, that ye henceforth walk not as other Gentiles walk, in the vanity of their mind, (18) Having the understanding darkened, being alienated from the life of God through the ignorance that is in them, because of the blindness of their heart." Israel's blindness is only temporary, Romans 11:25-27, "(25) For I would not, brethren, that ye should be ignorant of this mystery, lest ye should be wise in your own conceits; that blindness in part is happened to Israel, until the fulness of the Gentiles be come in. (26) And so all Israel shall be saved: as it is written, There shall come out of Sion the Deliverer, and shall turn away ungodliness from Jacob: (27) For this is my covenant unto them, when I shall take away their sins."

This New Covenant, under which "all Israel shall be saved" is recorded in Jeremiah 31:31-34, "(31) Behold, the days come, saith the Lord, that I will make a new covenant with the house of Israel, and with the house of Judah: (32) Not according to the covenant that I made with their fathers in the day that I took them by the hand to bring them out of the land of Egypt; which my covenant they brake, although I was an husband unto them, saith the Lord: (33) But this shall be the covenant that I will make with the house of Israel; After those days, saith the Lord, I will put my law in their inward parts, and write it in their hearts; and will be their God, and they shall be my people. (34) And they shall teach no more every man his neighbor, and every man his brother, saying, Know the Lord: for they shall all know me, from the least of them unto the greatest of them, saith the Lord: for I will forgive their iniquity, and I will remember their sin no more."

This is not the covenant Church members enter into through the rebirth. It is a new covenant God will make with the house of Israel "after those days" (verse 33) of the great tribulation. It is when the Armageddon Army invades the city of Jerusalem that the Jews turn to Jesus, Zechariah 12:9-11, "(9) And it shall come to pass in that day, that I will seek to destroy all the nations that come against Jerusalem. (10) And I will pour upon the house of David, and upon the inhabitants of Jerusalem, the spirit of grace and of supplications: and they shall look upon me whom they have pierced, and they shall mourn for him, as one mourneth for his only son, and shall be in bitterness for him, as one that is in bitterness for his firstborn. (11) In that day shall there be a great mourning in Jerusalem, as the mourning of Hadadrimmon in the valley of Megiddon."

In comparing the Church covenant to the Kingdom covenant several differences can be seen. To the Church in Mark 16:15 Jesus said "Go ye into all the world, and preach the gospel to every creature," while the Kingdom covenant in Jeremiah 31:34 says, "they shall teach no more every man his neighbor, and every man his brother, saying, Know the Lord: for they shall all know me, from the least of them unto the greatest of them." In the Kingdom covenant (Jeremiah 31:33) God says, "I will be their God, and they shall be my people" while the Church covenant says, "He that overcometh shall inherit all things; and I will be his God, and he shall be my son" (Rev. 21:7). There is a big difference between being God's people, and being personally related to God. The Church covenant concerns whosoever will come, while the Kingdom covenant concerns the nation of Jews. During the Kingdom Dispensation Jesus and crew will rule the Gentile nations with "a rod of iron" (Rev. 2:26-29). It should be obvious that Jesus doesn't need a rod of iron to rule his people. What Jesus is going to do with that rod of iron is to force the Gentile nations to be obedient to the Word of God, whether they want to be or not. During the Church covenant, Jesus is not forcing anyone to be obedient to the Word of God.

During the Kingdom Dispensation Satan will be bound and confined to Hades "that he should deceive the nations no more" (Rev. 20:3). During the Church Dispensation Satan is free, and very active in deceiving both nations and individuals. When the Kingdom covenant becomes effective, Jesus will be ruling over Earth from a throne in the city of Jerusalem, and there will be worldwide peace and prosperity. During the Church Dispensation Jesus is sitting on a throne in heaven, and the only people promised peace and prosperity are born-again believers, which is the same thing as saying a 'covenant child.' As a Church member I can be physically located anywhere in the universe and worship Jesus. Since I am a Gentile, if I were living in my physical body on Earth during the Kingdom Dispensation, I would be required to go to the city of Jerusalem on a yearly basis to worship Jesus and keep the feast of tabernacles, or else get smacked with that rod of iron. Here is how Zechariah described it in 14:16-19, "(16) And it shall come to pass, that every one that is left of all the nations which came against Jerusalem shall even go up from year to year to worship the King, the Lord of hosts, and to keep the feast of tabernacles. (17) And it shall be, that whoso will not come up of all the families of the earth unto Jerusalem to worship the King, the Lord of hosts, even upon them shall be no rain. (18) And if the family of Egypt go not up, and come not, that have no rain; there shall be the plague, wherewith the Lord will smite the heathen that come not up to keep the feast of tabernacles. (19) This shall be the punishment of Egypt, and the punishment of all nations that come not up to keep the feast of tabernacles."

While we are in the Book of Zechariah, let's move up to verse 12 and look at "the plague" and how Jesus destroys the Armageddon army. Zechariah 14:12-15, "(12) And this shall be the plague wherewith the Lord will smite all the people that have fought against Jerusalem; Their flesh shall consume away while they stand upon their feet, and their eyes shall consume away in their holes, and their tongue shall consume away in their mouth. (13) And it shall come to pass in that day, that a great tumult from the Lord shall be among them; and they shall lay hold every one on the hand of his neighbor, and his hand shall rise up against the hand of his neighbor. (14) And Judah also shall fight at Jerusalem; and the wealth of all the heathen round about shall be gathered together, gold, and silver, an apparel, in great abundance. (15) And so shall be the plague of the horse, of the mule, of the camel, and of the ass, and of all the beasts that shall be in these tents, as this plague."

The main difference between the Kingdom covenant and the Church covenant is the Kingdom covenant is everlasting, meaning it will never end. The Church covenant is everlasting to the members who have entered into the covenant but the invitation to enter will end the instant the Church is raptured. We are the midnight hour generation and the cry that Jesus is coming is getting louder and louder. If you have entered into the Church covenant through the rebirth as Jesus instructed, you are in right standing with God and will be counted among the five wise virgins. Otherwise you are going to be counted among the five foolish virgins and find the Church covenant history, and the Church door closed. It is the midnight hour generation Jesus is describing in Matthew 25:1-13, "(1) Then shall the kingdom of heaven be likened unto ten virgins, which took their lamps, and went forth to meet the bridegroom. (2) And five of them were wise, and five were foolish. (3) They that were foolish took their lamps, and took no oil with them: (4) But the wise took oil in their vessels with their lamps. (5) While the bridegroom tarried, they all slumbered and slept. (6) And at midnight there was a cry made, Behold, the bridegroom cometh; go ye out to meet him. (7) Then all those virgins arose, and trimmed their lamps. (8) And the foolish said unto the wise, Give us of your oil; for out lamps are gone out. (9) But the wise answered, saying, Not so; lest there be not enough for us and you: but go ye rather to them that sell, and buy for yourselves. (10) And while they went to buy, the bridegroom came; and they that were ready went in with him to the marriage: and the door was shut. (11) Afterward came also the other virgins, saying, Lord, Lord, open to us. (12) But he answered and said, Verily I say unto you, I know you not. (13) Watch therefore, for ye know neither the day nor the hour wherein the Son of man cometh."

The last section of the Book of Daniel we have entitled, "The Book of Daniel sealed until the time of the end."

1. Daniel told to seal the book until the time of the end. Daniel 12:4a, "But thou, O Daniel, shut up the words, and seal the book, even to the time of the end." The sealing of the Book of Daniel means it would not be understood until "the time of the end." The phrase "the time of the end" means the same thing as "the last times" and "latter days" which speaks of the Church to Kingdom transition era. God is saying the Book of Daniel would not be understood until the time of its fulfillment. When Daniel asks for more understanding, he is told a second time the book is sealed (Dan. 12:9).
2. In the time of the end many shall run to and fro. Daniel 12:4b, "many shall run to and fro." The Bible repeatedly speaks of the restlessness of the latter day population. Many believe this passage is speaking of the movement of man. For nearly six thousand years the speed at which man was able to move was limited to the speed of a galloping horse. It was our generation that saw the movement of man increase from 30-40 miles per hour to several thousand miles per hour. We are the ones who saw a trip, which only a hundred years ago would have taken several months, reduced to a matter of hours. Amos tells us why they run to and fro in Amos 8:11-12, "Behold, the days come, saith the Lord God, that I will send a famine in the land, not a famine of bread, nor a thirst for water, but of hearing the words of the Lord: (12) And they shall wander from sea to sea, and from the north even to the east, they shall run to and fro to seek the word of the Lord, and shall not find it."
3. In the time of the end knowledge shall be increased. Daniel 12:4c, "and knowledge shall be increased." It is also our generation that experienced the knowledge explosion. The people who lived one hundred years ago could not even imagine what it would be like to live in our world today.
4. The question: How long to the end of these wonders? Daniel 12:5-6, "(5) Then I Daniel looked, and behold, there stood other two, the one on this side of the bank of the river, and the other on that side of the bank of the river. (6) And one said to the man clothed in linen, which was upon the waters of the river, How long shall it be to the end of these wonders?"
5. The answer: three and one-half years. Daniel 12:7, "And I heard the man clothed in linen, which was upon the waters of the river, when he held up his right hand and his left hand unto heaven, and sware by him that liveth for ever that it shall be for a time, times, and an half; and when he shall have accomplished to scatter the power of the holy people, all these things shall be finished." Again "a time, times, and an half" is three and one-half years. During the last half of the seven-year tribulation era in the reign of the False Prophet, "all these things shall be finished." The "holy people" (Romans 11:1-36) to be scattered will be the Jews.

The Jews will know that Jesus is Lord, their Messiah, the Christ, and their

God at least seven years prior to the arrival of the False Prophet. This is obvious from the Gog and Magog invasion in Ezekiel chapters 38 and 39 where Russia and its satellite countries invade the land of Palestine. In Ezekiel 39:2-5, God destroys all but one-sixth of the invading army. In Ezekiel 39:6, God sends fire on the homeland of the invading army. In Ezekiel 39:7, God says, "So will I make my holy name known in the midst of my people Israel; and I will not let them pollute my holy name any more: and the heathen shall know that I am the Lord, the Holy One in Israel." Ezekiel 39:8-10 continues with a description of prosperity in the land of Israel for a period of seven years. This invasion is so close it could start before I finish writing this paragraph. We are in the period of wars and rumors of wars Jesus spoke of in Matthew 24:6, "And ye shall hear of wars and rumors of wars: see that ye be not troubled: for all these things must come to pass, but the end is not yet." In the cold war arms build-up the nations responded to the call in Joel 3:9-10, "(9) Proclaim ye this among the Gentiles; Prepare war, wake up the mighty men, let all the men of war draw near; let them come up: (10) Beat your plowshares into swords, and your pruning hooks into spears: let the weak say, I am strong." The cold war has ended and the world powers are saying, "Peace and Safety," which brings us to 1 Thessalonians 5:3, "For when they shall say, Peace and safety; then sudden destruction cometh upon them, as travail upon a woman with child; and they shall not escape."

6. Daniel asks for more understanding. Daniel 12:8, "And I heard, but I understood not: then said I, O my Lord, what shall be the end of these things?" What Daniel was unable to understand was "the end of these things," the final sequence of events in the Church to Kingdom transition. Daniel did not have a problem understanding the Church Dispensation, because he could not see the Church from where he stood in human history. The prophecies God gave Daniel are primarily concerned with two things. The first is the Gentile world powers that would rise and fall during the time of the Jewish captivity and dispersion or "the times of the Gentiles." The second is the reign and activity of the False Prophet which will be limited to the last three and one-half years of the seven-year tribulation period. There is very little direct information on Antichrist in the Book of Daniel and I suspect that Daniel confused him with the False Prophet. Daniel could see the final form of the Roman Empire as a ten king kingdom, and he could see the ten king kingdom undergo the change to a seven king kingdom, but he saw only one political figure. The only direct revelation on Antichrist in the Book of Daniel is in Daniel 9:27. He is the individual that confirms the protection treaty with the Jews which introduces the seven-year tribulation period. This is the only thing Antichrist does that has a direct influence on the Jews, which is understandable when we remember his mission is against Jesus Christ and his Church, not the Nation of Israel. We can still gain a vast amount of understanding in the Book of Daniel on Antichrist when we recognize the similarity between the mission of the False Prophet and the mission of Antichrist. The attitude of the False Prophet and his treatment of the Jews is almost identical to the attitude of Antichrist and his treatment of the apostate church.

7. Daniel told the words are sealed till the time of the end. Daniel 12:9, "And he said, Go thy way, Daniel: for the words are closed up and sealed till the time of the end." Again God is telling Daniel the prophecies are sealed or closed to understanding until the time of their fulfillment. When we consider that the prophecies in the Book of Daniel were given to the Jews nearly 2600 years ago, another truth becomes evident. The Jews were God's representative people on Earth at the time the prophecies in the Book of Daniel were given. The people to whom God is referring, who would not understand the prophecies in the Book of Daniel until the time of the end, are the Jews. To understand why the Jews cannot comprehend the Book of Daniel we need to remember the statement made in Rev 19:10, "the testimony of Jesus is the spirit of prophecy." The Jews living during the Law Dispensation could not understand the Book of Daniel because the final days of the "times of the Gentiles" were too far in the future. When the Law Dispensation gave way to the Church Dispensation the Jewish Nation as a whole rejected the "testimony of Jesus." Their rejection of Jesus Christ as the promised Redeemer and their Messiah resulted in the temporary blindness the Holy Spirit told us about in Romans 11:25-27, "(25) For I would not, brethren, that ye should be ignorant of this mystery, lest ye should be wise in your own conceits; that blindness in part is happened to Israel, until the fulness of the Gentiles be come in. (26) And so all Israel shall be saved: as it is written, There shall come out of Sion the Deliverer, and shall turn away ungodliness from Jacob: (27) For this is my covenant unto them, when I shall take away their sins." Notice the blindness will continue only "until the fulness of the Gentiles be come in." The next great eye-opening event in Israel's history will be the destruction of the invading Russian army given in Ezekiel chapters 38 and 39. Either ten and one-half, or seven years later, the blindness on the Nation of Israel will be removed when the False Prophet introduces the beast image and issues his ultimatum for them to worship the image or die.

To understand why the Jews living during the Law Dispensation could not understand the Book of Daniel, and why members of past Church eras could not fully understand the prophecies in the Book of the Revelation, we need to remember Bible prophecy centers on events, not dates. Many times the amount of time between when a prophecy is given and its fulfillment determines the clarity of the event. The characteristics of prophecy and time are comparable to a physical object and distance. If you were standing at an airport at night awaiting the arrival of a certain flight from the west, the first thing you may be able to see is a dim, white light on the horizon. As the plane approached, you would realize the light is a bright light, not a dim light. Next you would be able to see the single white light as two lights, one on each wing. Soon you would be able to see other lights on the plane besides the landing lights. If you were standing at the end of the runway as the plane was about to pass overhead, you would be able to distinguish many features of the aircraft that were literally impossible for you to see with the naked eye when you first spotted the plane as a dim, white light. As the distance between the airport and the aircraft decreases, the more clearly you can see the plane.

The same thing is true with prophecy. For example, today we know from Rev. 11:1-13 that two individuals will be killed by the False Prophet (verse 7) which God calls his "two witnesses" in verse 3. We know their ministry will take place during the first half of the tribulation period during the Antichrist reign and that they will be killed at the middle of the tribulation era. World history will continue to move closer and closer to the day of their death. If not before, at the time of their death the people alive on Earth will be able to see the prophecy so clearly that they will be able to look at the man who killed them and be able to identify the False Prophet by name. We also know the two witnesses will be killed in the streets of Jerusalem (Rev. 11:8-9), "and they of the people and kindreds and tongues and nations shall see their dead bodies three days and a half, and shall not suffer their dead bodies to be put in graves." Jesus is literally saying the world will "see" their dead bodies. Can you imagine the problems preachers had describing how they would see their dead bodies, worldwide, prior to the development of television and communications satellites?

8. Many shall be purified, made white, and tried. Daniel 12:10a, "Many shall be purified, and made white, and tried."

9. The wicked shall do wickedly. Daniel 12:10b, "but the wicked shall do wickedly."

10. The wise shall understand, the wicked shall not. Daniel 12:10c, "and none of the wicked shall understand; but the wise shall understand."

Here God makes a comparison to show the similarity between the persecution of the Jews by the False Prophet and the persecution they suffered under Antiochus Epiphanes. At the time of the end "the many" which shall be purified, made white, and tried are those who are killed by the False Prophet organization for their refusal to deny the word of God, worship the beast image, or refuse to take the unforgivable mark. The wicked will accept the thinking of the False Prophet and welcome the mark of the beast in order to continue pursuing their sinful lusts and the accumulation of wealth through buying and selling. The wise are those who know God through his Word, and the wicked are those who are ignorant of the Word of God. Compare the wise and the wicked at the time of the end to the wise and wicked during the days of Epiphanes. During the reign of the False Prophet, Daniel 12:10, "Many shall be purified, and made white, and tried; but the wicked shall do wickedly: and none of the wicked shall understand; but the wise shall understand." During the reign of Antiochus Epiphanes, Daniel 11:32-35, "(32) And such as do wickedly against the covenant shall he corrupt by flatteries: but the people that do know their God shall be strong, and do exploits. (33) And they that understand among the people shall instruct many: yet they shall fall by the sword, and by flame, by captivity, and by spoil, many days. (34) Now when they shall fall, they shall be holpen with a little help: but many shall cleave to them with flatteries. (35) And some of them of understanding shall fall, to try them, and to purge, and to make them white, even to the time of the end: because it is yet for a time appointed."

11. The abomination of desolation to last 1290 days. Daniel 12:11, "And from the time that the daily sacrifice shall be taken away, and the abomination that maketh desolate set up, there shall be a thousand two hundred and ninety days." In Daniel 8:3-14 we saw the period of human history leading to the rise of Antiochus Epiphanes. In Daniel 8:14 we were told the abomination of desolation during the reign of Epiphanes would last 2300 days or just over six years. Here we are told the abomination of desolation at the time of the end, during the reign of the False Prophet, will last 1290 days.

12. Blessed are those who survive to the 1335th day. Daniel 12:12, "Blessed is he that waiteth, and cometh to the thousand three hundred and five and thirty days." "Those who survive" will be the Jews on Earth who escape death during the last half of the tribulation period, by avoiding capture by the Antichrist/False Prophet organization. Had they been captured and killed by the organization for their refusal to take the mark or worship the beast image, they would have been blessed (Rev. 14:13), in that they would have been counted among the Rev. 7:9-17 great multitude of tribulation dead. They would have been resurrected to eternal life (Rev. 20:4-6) when Jesus returned to earth at the end of the tribulation, to live and reign with Jesus during the Kingdom Dispensation. "Blessed are those who survive" the tribulation period, because they will enter the Kingdom Dispensation as living human beings who inherit an everlasting kingdom (Daniel 7:14, 7:23-28), and reign in the physical realm with Jesus throughout eternity. What it will be like to be a Jew during the Kingdom Dispensation can be seen in Zechariah 8:23 and Isaiah 4:1-3. Zechariah 8:23 reads, "Thus saith the Lord of hosts; In those days it shall come to pass, that ten men shall take hold out of all languages of the nations, even shall take hold of the skirt of him that is a Jew, saying, We will go with you: for we have heard that God is with you." Isaiah 4:1-3 reads, "(1) And in that day seven women shall take hold of one man, saying, We will eat our own bread, and wear our own apparel: only let us be called by thy name, to take away our reproach. (2) In that day shall the branch of the Lord be beautiful and glorious, and the fruit of the earth shall be excellent and comely for them that are escaped of Israel. (3) And it shall come to pass, that he that is left in Zion, and he that remaineth in Jerusalem, shall be called holy, even every one that is written among the living in Jerusalem."

13. Daniel will die and stand in his lot at the end of the days. Daniel 12:13, "But go thou thy way till the end be: for thou shalt rest, and stand in thy lot at the end of the days." At the end of these days, when the Kingdom Dispensation begins, Daniel will be "among the living in Jerusalem."

In Daniel 12:11 we were told the abomination of desolation during the reign of the False Prophet would last 1290 days, which appears to be thirty days beyond the actual three and one-half year reign of the False Prophet. We have the same situation in Daniel 12:12 in the statement, "Blessed is he that waiteth, and cometh to the thousand three hundred and five and thirty days." Here the 1335th day appears to be seventy-five days beyond the reign of the False Prophet. The first thing to remember is the prophecies in the Book of Daniel were given during the days of the Babylonian, Mede, and Persian Empires, when a year was 360 days instead of 365 days. Using their calendar year, the False Prophet reign would be 360 days multiplied by 3.5 years or 1260 days. If we subtract 1260 days from the False Prophet abomination of desolation, which is to last 1290 days, we have a remainder of 30 days. If we subtract the 1260 days from the 1335 we have a remainder of 75 days. Let's examine why.

The 360 day year is also used in the prophecies in the Book of the Revelation. In describing the reign of Antichrist in Rev. 13:1-10 we are told in verse 13:5 he would continue forty-two months (12 times 3.5). In Rev. 11:1-13 describing the ministry of the two witnesses who prophesy during his reign we are told in verse 11:3 their ministry would last 1260 days. The False Prophet will enter the picture at midpoint in the tribulation period and will issue the ultimatum to worship beast image or die, which causes the flight of the Jews. In Rev. 12:6 we saw they will flee into the wilderness to a place prepared of God where they will be fed for 1260 days.

One of the things we saw when Jesus opened the sixth seal concerns the wind and is recorded in Rev. 7:1, "And after these things I saw four angels standing on the four corners of the earth, holding the four winds of the earth, that the wind should not blow on the earth, nor on the sea, nor on any tree." The predominant winds on our planet are created by the rotation of the Earth on its axis. Should these angels stop the wind from blowing by stopping the rotation of the earth, the length of a day would be altered. A day is one complete revolution of the Earth on its axis. Whether this is the method the angels will use to stop the wind from blowing or not is debatable.

The fact that Jesus will increase the speed of the rotation of the earth is not debatable. This will be done when the fourth trumpet angel sounds in Rev. 8:12, "And the fourth angel sounded, and the third part of the sun was smitten, and the third part of the moon, and the third part of the stars; so as the third part of them was darkened, and the day shone not for a third part of it, and the night likewise." With the day and night reduced by a third, the Earth will make a complete revolution in sixteen hours instead of twenty-four hours. This means from the fourth trumpet until the return of Jesus the number of hours in a day will be sixteen. We know the False Prophet will reign for three and one-half years based on the Babylonian calendar of 360 days per year or a total of 1260 days. We also know the blessed are those who survive the tribulation when it ends with the return of Jesus on the 1335th day. With this information we can now compute at what point in the three and one-half year period the fourth trumpet angel will sound. From the opening of the sixth seal to the blowing of the fourth trumpet there will be 1110 twenty-four hour days. From the fourth trumpet until the return of Jesus there will be 225 sixteen hour days for a total of 1335 days (1110 + 225 = 1335).

One thousand one hundred and ten twenty-four hour days is just over three years; 1110 days divided by thirty days per year would equal thirty-seven months or 3.083 years. Immediately it becomes evident the most severe part of the seven-year tribulation period will be the final six months or roughly the last 225 sixteen hour days. This is why an angel announces the next three trumpet judgments as three woes in Rev. 8:13. When the fifth trumpet angel sounds, the demons will be released from Hades to torment humans for five months or 150 sixteen hour days. During this time period humans will desire and seek death without success. When the fifth trumpet judgment ends, Earth will be just 75 sixteen hour days away from the return of Jesus.

According to Daniel 12:11, the False Prophet abomination of desolation will last 1290 days. This means it will continue 1110 twenty-four hour days, plus 180 of the sixteen hour days (1110 plus 180 equals 1290 days). We also saw that the fourth trumpet reduced the number of hours in a day, followed by the fifth trumpet announcing tormenting demons and the five months or 150 sixteen-hour days when humans will be unable to die. If we subtract these 150 hours from the 180 sixteen-hour days, we can see a thirty-day period between when the fifth trumpet judgment ends and when the abomination of desolation ends. During this thirty-day period, the army of 200 million horsemen will kill a third of the Earth's population. When this slaughter is finished, the seventh trumpet angel will announce Jesus as King, and the abomination of desolation will end. At this point, the Jews will turn wholeheartedly to Jesus, and pray for his return and deliverance. Moses told them that when they find themselves in the latter day tribulation, if they would turn to the Jesus that he would hear them in Deuteronomy 4:29-31, "(29) But if from thence thou shalt seek the Lord thy God, thou shalt find him, if thou seek him with all thy heart and with all thy soul. (30) When thou art in tribulation, and all these things are come upon thee, even in the latter days, if thou turn to the Lord thy God, and shalt be obedient unto his voice; (31) (For the Lord thy God is a merciful God;) he will not forsake thee, neither destroy thee, nor forget the covenant of thy fathers which he sware unto them." This is the prayer Jesus has been waiting to hear, and when it comes, the Deuteronomy 4:29-31 prophecy will be fulfilled.

I would not be surprised to find this will be the first prayer to which God will respond since the last person saved as a Church member prayed, "I repent Jesus, have mercy on me, a sinner." When the Holy Spirit completes the Church, the rapture will have ended the Church Dispensation and the Church covenant promises. The Gentile population will have returned to the position they held before the Church Dispensation began, which is described in Ephesians 2:12, "That at that time ye were without Christ, being aliens from the commonwealth of Israel, and strangers from the covenants of promise, having no hope, and without God in the world." God promised to make a new covenant with the Jews (Jeremiah 31:31-34) and this prayer will allow God to make that covenant a reality. He will hear their prayer and answer by pouring out the seven vial judgments, which will end the tribulation era, and send King Jesus back to Earth to establish the Kingdom Dispensation. From the rapture of the Church until the Deuteronomy 4:29-31 response by the Jews, the people on Earth will be without a covenant, which means they had no basis for approaching God, and he had no basis for answering any prayers. When the members of the true Church left in the rapture, God moved against Earth in judgment. If you refused to be obedient to the Word of God and rejected Jesus, you will be the object of God's wrath and judgment. God promises that He will not hear your misery cry or your prayers. Your crying and prayers will ricochet off a heaven of brass, Deuteronomy 28:23, "And thy heaven that is over thy head shall be brass, and the earth that is under thee shall be iron."

Here are a few promises God made to the objects of his judgments: Proverbs 1:24-29, "(24) Because I have called, and ye refused; I have stretched out my hand, and no man regarded; (25) But ye have set at nought all my counsel, and would none of my reproof: (26) I also will laugh at your calamity; I will mock when your fear cometh; (27) When your fear cometh as desolation, and your destruction cometh as a whirlwind; when distress and anguish cometh upon you. (28) Then shall they call upon me, but I will not answer; they shall seek me early, but they shall not find me: (29) For that they hated knowledge, and did not choose the fear of the Lord."

Isaiah 1:15, "(15) And when ye spread forth your hands, I will hide mine eyes from you: yea, when ye make many prayers, I will not hear: your hands are full of blood."

Ezekiel 8:17-18, "(17) Then he said unto me, Hast thou seen this, O son of man? Is it a light thing to the house of Judah that they commit the abominations which they commit here? for they have filled the land with violence, and have returned to provoke me to anger: and, lo, they put the branch to their nose. (18) Therefore will I also deal in fury: mine eye shall not spare, neither will I have pity: and though they cry in mine ears with a loud voice, yet will I not hear them."

Micah 3:4, "Then shall they cry unto the Lord, but he will not hear them: he will even hide his face from them at that time, as they have behaved themselves ill in their doings."

Zechariah 7:8-13, "(8) And the word of the Lord came unto Zechariah, saying, (9) Thus speaketh the Lord of hosts, saying, Execute true judgment, and shew mercy and compassion every man to his brother: (10) And oppress not the widow, nor the fatherless, the stranger, nor the poor; and let none of you imagine evil against his brother in your heart. (11) But they refused to hearken, and pulled away the shoulder, and stopped their ears, that they should not hear. (12) Yea, they made their hearts as an adamant stone, lest they should hear the law, and the words which the Lord of hosts hath sent in his spirit by the former prophets: therefore came a great wrath from the Lord of hosts. (13) Therefore it is come to pass, that as he cried, and they would not hear; so they cried, and I would not hear, saith the Lord of hosts."

When the Jews turn to Jesus in the Deuteronomy 4:29-31 response, the seventh trumpet angel announces Jesus as King of Earth. The fact God heard their prayer is clear evidence that the Deuteronomy 28:23 heaven of brass is history. Since prayers are getting through it also means the False Prophet abomination of desolation is no longer effective. Knowing the abomination of desolation ends on the 180th sixteen hour day, we can subtract this figure from the total of 225 sixteen-hour days and see a 45 sixteen hour day period between the end of the abomination of desolation and the actual return of King Jesus to Earth. During this forty-five-day-period the seven vial judgments are executed against the Antichrist/False Prophet organization. If you are in hiding during this period of time, heed the warning of Jesus and stay hidden. Matthew 24:21-27, "(21) For then shall be great tribulation, such as was not since the beginning of the world to this time, no, nor ever shall be. (22) And except those days should be shortened, there should no flesh be saved: but for the elect's sake those days shall be shortened. (23) Then if any man shall say unto you, Lo, here is Christ, or there; believe it not. (24) For there shall arise false Christs, and false prophets, and shall shew great signs and wonders; insomuch that, if it were possible, they shall deceive the very elect. (25) Behold, I have told you before. (26) Wherefore if they shall say unto you, Behold, he is in the desert; go not forth: behold, he is in the secret chambers; believe it not. (27) For as the lightning cometh out of the east, and shineth even unto the west; so shall also the coming of the Son of man be." Those who heed the words of Jesus and stay in hiding will survive the False Prophet reign, to enter the Kingdom Dispensation as living human beings. If they can be deceived into leaving their hiding place, they will be forced to worship the beast image or be killed.

Chapter Seven

The Seven Letters to the Seven Churches

Revelation chapters 2 and 3 deal with the Church Dispensation. They are an analytical view of the Church Dispensation from the eyes of God. The Church era has continued for nearly two thousand years, with the Church going through seven distinct periods of history. In each church era the Church represents Christendom as a whole. Each church era is distinguishable by certain characteristics which Jesus gives in the form of a letter. The outline or format of each of the seven letters is basically the same in that each contains: (1) TO: information, (2) FROM: information, (3) COMMENDATION: or commendable characteristics, (4) REBUKE: for unacceptable characteristics, (5) EXHORT: or corrective steps, and (6) PROMISES: to the overcomers. We will follow this same format as we look at each church era individually. An outline of the entire Church Dispensation with the approximate dates of each era would look like this:

A. The Seven Letters to the Seven Churches–Rev. 2:1-3:22.
1. The letter to Ephesus: First century church–Rev. 2:1-7.
2. The letter to Smyrna: Persecuted church (100-300)–Rev. 2:8-11.
3. The letter to Pergamos: Marriage of church and state (300-500)–Rev. 2:12-17.
4. The letter to Thyatira: The papacy (500-1500)–Rev. 2:18-29.
5. The letter to Sardis: The reformation church (1500-1700)–Rev. 3:1-6.
6. The letter to Philadelphia: Revival and evangelism (1700-1900)–Rev. 3:7-13.
7. The letter to Laodicea: The apostate church (1900-?)–Rev. 3:14-22.

The Letter to Ephesus

1. The Letter to Ephesus: First Century Church.
Revelation 2:1-7, "(1) Unto the angel of the church of Ephesus write; These things saith he that holdeth the seven stars in his right hand, who walketh in the midst of the seven golden candlesticks; (2) I know thy works, and thy labor, and thy patience, how thou canst not bear them which are evil: and thou hast tried them which say they are apostles, and are not, and hast found them liars: (3) And hast borne, and hast patience, and for my name's sake hast labored, and hast not fainted. (4) Nevertheless I have somewhat against thee, because thou hast left thy first love. (5) Remember therefore from whence thou are fallen, and repent, and do the first works; or else I will come unto thee quickly, and will remove thy candlestick out of his place, except thou repent. (6) But this thou hast, that thou hatest the deeds of the Nicolaitanes, which I also hate. (7) He that hath an ear, let him hear what the Spirit saith unto the churches; To him that overcometh will I give to eat of the tree of life, which is in the midst of the paradise of God."

a. TO: The church at Ephesus.
Rev. 2:1a, "Unto the angel of the church of Ephesus write."

Each of the seven letters are addressed, "unto the angel of the church." As we have already seen, an angel is a being from the spirit realm. In the beginning they were created on an authoritative level below human beings and functioned as servants to both the eternal Godhead and the human family. Adam and Eve's disobedience in the garden of Eden resulted in a separation from God, which placed the human family on an authoritative level below angelic beings. Since that time the elect angels (those who remained true to God by refusing to join Satan's rebellion) have operated as messengers, watchers (Daniel 4:13, 4:17), guardians (Matthew 18:10), and ministering spirits to the heirs of salvation (Hebrews 1:13-14). The pastor of the church at Ephesus was not an angel, nor will he ever be. He was a human being with the responsibility to pastor a congregation of people in Ephesus. What had happened in his Church was typical of what was generally happening to every church established in the first century. This is why Jesus could use his Church as an example, to communicate the condition and changes in Christendom which took place during the first church era. The second letter was to the Church at Smyrna, which was undergoing persecution typical of what the Churches suffered from the years A.D. 100 to 300.

The Greek word translated as *angel* could have been translated as *messenger* or *angel*, but not *pastor* or *minister*. Jesus used the same Greek word to describe John the Baptist in Matthew 11:10, "For this is he, of whom it is written, Behold, I send my messenger before thy face, which shall prepare thy way before thee." The message of John the Baptist was from God, and John presented it correctly, which qualifies him as a "messenger of God."

The message given "unto the angel of the church of Ephesus" was from God, and the angelic being presented it correctly, which qualifies him as a "messenger of God." The next link in the chain of communications is the human minister or pastor, which may be of God or of Satan. The Greek word translated as angel here is translated as messenger in 2 Corinthians 12:7-8, where Paul describes his "thorn in the flesh" as a demon spirit of Satan, "(7) And lest I should be exalted above measure through the abundance of the revelations, there was given to me a thorn in the flesh, the messenger of Satan to buffet me, lest I should be exalted above measure. (8) For this thing I besought the Lord thrice, that it might depart from me."

For the person behind the pulpit to qualify as a "messenger of God," he must present the message exactly as it came from God. If the message is perverted, when it is presented to you, it should be obvious someone has tampered with it. You need to delay acting on the message until you examine the messenger, to determine if he is of God or of Satan. If the message is not clear, you have every right to question the messenger until the message is clear. Since you already have a written copy of the message being delivered, it should be impossible for him to deceive you. How stupid it would be for the congregation at Ephesus to be given a written copy of a message from God, and sit there and let the person behind the pulpit present or discuss the message with the attitude that the originator didn't say what he meant, or mean what he said. If the person behind the pulpit is a messenger of God, he is repeating what God has said in his written Word, and urging you to do as God has instructed.

The originator of the letter to the church at Ephesus is the originator of the entire Bible. The delivery channel or chain of communications of the Book of the Revelation is given in Rev. 1:1, "The Revelation of Jesus Christ, which God gave unto him, to shew unto his servants things which must shortly come to pass; and he sent and signified it by his angel unto his servant John." It is: (1) from God (the Father); (2) to Jesus Christ (the Son of God); (3) to his angel (his messenger, a supernatural being from the spirit realm); (4) to his servant John (the Apostle John); (5) to his servants (to those who willingly submit to the lordship of Jesus). Both the pastor of the church and the congregation would be included as his servants.

b. FROM: Jesus who holds the seven stars and walks in the midst of the church.

Rev. 2:1b, "These things saith he that holdeth the seven stars in his right hand, who walketh in the midst of the seven golden candlesticks."

The mystery of the seven stars and the seven golden candlesticks is revealed in Rev. 1:20b, "The seven stars are the angels of the seven churches: and the seven candlesticks which thou sawest are the seven churches." There are seven stars or angels because there are seven different church eras. Since Jesus holds these angels in his right hand, it is apparent that they are elect principality or ruling angels. The first of the seven angels will operate during the first church era, the second angel during the second church era, etc. We know the responsibility of each of the seven angels from the seven letters to the seven churches, because they are actually a copy of the orders given to the ruling principality angel of each era, "unto the angel of the church of Ephesus write." Think of this letter being sent marked "immediate action required" to the first principality angel and all the first century churches, with a copy marked "information" to all the churches established after the end of the first century.

The principality angel of the church of Ephesus or first century churches, would be opposed to the principality demon enthroned by Satan during that same period of time. From the instructions Jesus gave his angel, we can see the instructions Satan gave his angel. In the commendation portion of the letter we can see the satanic activity that was unsuccessful, and in the rebuke portion the satanic activity that was successful. When the first century came to a close, the principality angel of Jesus dethroned the principality demon and both gave way to the principality angels of the next era. This is the same type arrangement we saw in the Book of Daniel with the Gentile world powers. During the Persian Empire, Satan enthroned his demonic spirit called the prince of Persia, which delayed the messenger angel God sent to Daniel (Daniel 10:1-21). When the Persian Empire had run its course, the elect angel fought and dethroned the prince of Persia which ended the Persian Empire, and gave rise to the Greek Empire and Satan's principality demon called the prince of Grecia.

The seven principality angels did not preach or proclaim the message to human beings. Jesus gave the responsibility to preach the gospel to human members of the Church in Mark 16:15, "Go ye into all the world, and preach the gospel to every creature." When a human would go, the principality angel was responsible for clearing the way, by warring with the principality demon who was responsible to Satan for blocking or hindering the spread of the gospel. You can see this angel at work in the conversion of Cornelius, the first Gentile Church member, in Acts chapter 10.

Jesus is also presented as the one "who walketh in the midst of the seven golden candlesticks," which are the seven churches. Jesus is the head of the Church (Ephesians 4:15, 5:23, Colossians 1:18), and every individual member, as well as the congregation as a whole, is responsible to Him. Jesus knows what is going on in the churches. The statement "I know thy works" appears in each of the seven letters. The size of the congregation has no bearing on whether Jesus is in the midst or not. In Matthew 18:20 Jesus said, "For where two or three are gathered together in my name, there am I in the midst of them."

c. COMMENDATION: Six commendable points.

Rev. 2:2-3, "(2) I know thy works, and thy labor, and thy patience, and how thou canst not bear them which are evil: and thou hast tried them which say they are apostles, and are not, and hast found them liars: (3) And hast borne, and hast patience, and for my name's sake hast labored, and hast not fainted."

Rev. 2:6, "But this thou hast, that thou hatest the deeds of the Nicolaitanes, which I also hate."

The church at Ephesus was commended on six points: (1) their works (their toil or deeds); (2) their labor (expended energy); (3) their patience (endurance); (4) their refusal to bear evil ones; (5) for identifying false apostles as liars; and (6) their hatred of the deeds of the Nicolaitanes.

Their refusal to "bear them which are evil" means they refused to lift up or carry them which are evil, in the sense they put them down or removed them. Sin was identified as sin, and the unrepentant sinner was excommunicated, or put out of the congregation. By doing this the Church was able to keep itself clean. Jesus has placed the responsibility of judging and removing wicked members from the congregation on the church. To tolerate them is harmful to both the individual and the congregation. They are to be admonished as described in 2 Thessalonians 3:14-15, "(14) And if any man obey not our word by this epistle, note that man, and have no company with him, that he may be ashamed. (15) Yet count him not as an enemy, but admonish him as a brother." If the individual is willing, but unable to overcome the sin area, the problem may be demonic, in which case the elders educate the individual, then bind and cast out the demon. If an individual refuses to acknowledge and abandon a sin after the first or second admonition, they must be rejected and separated from the congregation. This is what the Holy Spirit is speaking of in Titus 3:10-11, "(10) A man that is an heretic after the first and second admonition reject; (11) Knowing that he that is such is subverted, and sinneth, being condemned of himself." This transfers the responsibility from the congregation onto the sinner and places the person in a position where God will do the judging. As long as the individual is in the congregation, they are responsible for the judging.

Examine the instructions given to the church at Corinth in 1 Corinthians 5:1-13, "(1) It is reported commonly that there is fornication among you, and such fornication as is not so much as named among the Gentiles, that one should have his father's wife. (2) And ye are puffed up, and have not rather mourned, that he that hath done this deed might be taken away from among you. (3) For I verily, as absent in body, but present in spirit, have judged already, as though I were present, concerning him that hath so done this deed, (4) In the name of our Lord Jesus Christ, when ye are gathered together, and my spirit, with the power of our Lord Jesus Christ, (5) To deliver such an one unto Satan for the destruction of the flesh, that the spirit may be saved in the day of the Lord Jesus. (6) Your glorying is not good. Know ye not that a little leaven leaveneth the whole lump? (7) Purge out therefore the old leaven, that ye may be a new lump, as ye are unleavened. For even

Christ our passover is sacrificed for us: (8) Therefore let us keep the feast, not with old leaven, neither with the leaven of malice and wickedness; but with the unleavened bread of sincerity and truth. (9) I wrote unto you in an epistle not to company with fornicators: (10) Yet not altogether with the fornicators of this world, or with the covetous, or extortioners, or with idolaters; for then must ye needs go out of the world. (11) But now I have written unto you not to keep company, if any man that is called a brother be a fornicator, or covetous, or an idolater, or a railer, or a drunkard, or an extortioner; with such an one no not to eat. (12) For what have I to do to judge them also that are without? do not ye judge them that are within? (13) But them that are without God judgeth. Therefore put away from among yourselves that wicked person."

The fifth point for which the church at Ephesus was commended was for identifying false apostles as liars. Any untrue statement or action which creates a false or misleading impression is a lie. This makes the lie a deception and the liar a deceiver. It doesn't matter if the individual originates the lie, or promulgates lies originated by someone else, the damage is the same and both are liars. In John chapter 8 the scribes and Pharisees rejected the teaching of Jesus as being untrue. In the discussion Jesus tells them their father is the devil and that the devil is the father of the lie, John 8:44, "Ye are of your father the devil, and the lusts of your father ye will do. He was a murderer from the beginning, and abode not in the truth, because there is no truth in him. When he speaketh a lie, he speaketh of his own: for he is a liar, and the father of it." The false apostles were exposed as liars, because the church "tried them," which means they tested or examined them to determine if they were of God or of Satan. In this way the church was able to keep doctrinally clean.

The sixth point for which the church at Ephesus was commended was their hatred of the deeds of the Nicolaitanes. The Greek word translated as *Nicolaitanes*, is Nikolaites, from Nikolaos, which is a compound word made up of *nike*, meaning victory by conquest, and *laos,* meaning a people. A Nicolaitane would be a person victorious over a people by conquest, which implies that they exercise control over the people. Jesus and the church at Ephesus hated the Nicolaitanes' *deeds*, which is the same Greek word translated as *works* in Jesus' statement, "I know thy works." Their works or deeds were the means the Nicolaitanes used to gain victory over and control the people in their congregation. Their methods and tactics are so numerous that the only sure way to avoid them is to know the way Jesus said it is to be done and do it that way.

Jesus intended the church to preach the gospel. This would allow the Holy Spirit to take the Word of God and convict sinners. If they would come to repentance, the Holy Spirit would bring them to the local church, where they would be baptized into the body of Christ and become a member of the local congregation. In the new convert (newborn baby) would be the desire for the sincere milk of the Word (1 Peter 2:2), which would be satisfied as the local congregation expounded unto them the way of God more perfectly (Acts 18:26). As the individual's knowledge of the Word of God increased their faith would increase (Romans 10:17) and the growing process would continue to maturity. As a mature Christian the individual could be used of God to assist the local congregation as described in Ephesians 4:11-16, "(11) And he gave some, apostles; and some, prophets; and some, evangelists; and some, pastors and teachers; (12) For the perfecting of the saints, for the work of the ministry, for the edifying of the body of Christ: (13) Till we all come in the unity of the faith, and of the knowledge of the Son of God, unto a perfect man, unto the measure of the stature of the fulness of Christ: (14) That we henceforth be no more children, tossed to and fro, and carried about with every wind of doctrine, by the sleight of men, and cunning craftiness, whereby they lie in wait to deceive; (15) But speaking the truth in love, may grow up into him in all things, which is the head, even Christ: (16) From whom the whole body fitly joined together and compacted by that which every joint supplieth, according to the effectual working in the measure of every part, maketh increase of the body unto the edifying of itself in love."

d. REBUKE: Because thou hast left thy first love.
Rev. 2:4, "Nevertheless I have somewhat against thee, because thou hast left thy first love."

Although the church at Ephesus had many commendable characteristics their love for Jesus, the Word, and the truth was beginning to cool off. Those who have experienced first love know the effects, the contentment of being near the loved one, and the empty feeling when separated. The loved one is able to dominate the mind so completely, that thoughts of them are entertaining. There is bliss in anticipation of one day living together forever, and there is joy in knowing they also love you. The church at Ephesus did not lose their first love, they left it. If we continue our human analogy, we would see the person marry their first love, and settle down to married life. He then gets a job or pursues a career in order to provide the loved one with the things she wants or needs. Everything seems to be just fine until the day he comes home from work exhausted, kicks off his shoes, stretches out on the couch in front of the television, and the one he loves comes to him with tears in her eyes and asks "Honey, do you still love me?" What the church at Ephesus once did out of total devotion and pure love, they were now doing out of a sense of duty or indifference. If they had looked at what thoughts dominated their minds and how those thoughts affected their mood, they would have known their situation. When you are indifferent, or lukewarm, little or no thought is given to the person. When you love someone you want to be with them and thoughts of them produce peace and contentment. When you hate someone you want to be away from them and thoughts of them produce anger and hostility.

e. EXHORT: Remember, repent, and do the first works.
Rev. 2:5, "Remember therefore from whence thou are fallen, and repent, and do the first works; or else I will come unto thee quickly, and will remove thy candlestick out of his place, except thou repent."

The church at Ephesus is urged to remember, repent, and do the first works. To remember is to bring something from the past into the mind and think on it. One of the things Jesus said the Holy Spirit would do in John 14:26 was to "bring all things to your remembrance, whatsoever I have said unto you." What Jesus said the church was to do is the Mark 16:15-18 Church Commission. In essence, Jesus is telling them to compare what he told them to do with what they were doing, so they could see "from whence thou are fallen." To repent means to turn around and go the other way. With the exhort "do the first works" Jesus was telling them to get back to their original mission. Failure to turn around and go back to the first works would result in them continuing to fall, until they were removed.

Jesus is not saying the individual members in the church would lose their salvation, by him removing the Holy Spirit from them. What he said he would do is "I will come unto thee quickly, and will remove thy candlestick out of his place." We saw in Rev. 1:20 the candlestick represents the church, in the sense, that the church is a lamp stand or light bearer. The light being radiated from the church is the pure, undiluted Word of God. The power behind that light is the Holy Spirit. When a church stops publishing the Word of God the light goes out, because they cut or turn off the power of the Holy Spirit. With the power off the church can no longer fulfill the Mark 16:15-18 commission, and the signs or manifestations of the Holy Spirit (verses 17-18) cease. This is why it is so easy to tell the difference between a true church and a false church.

Jesus warned the church at Ephesus that unless they repented he would remove "thy candlestick" or their light bearing congregation "out of his place." Unless the church at Ephesus starts doing what he told them to do, he was going to remove, eliminate, or get rid of them. Jesus did this by the persecution in the next church era, but by adding, "except thou repent," it is obvious he gave them space or time to repent. What happened during this period of time is obvious. When the pastor stopped preaching the Word of God, the power of the Holy Spirit was cut off, and the manifestation in Mark 16:17-18 could not longer be seen. If the minister had been a born-again believer, he would have been indwelt by the Holy Spirit and would have started preaching with an emphasis on repentance. If the congregation refused to repent, Jesus would remove the "flame of fire" and send him to a congregation that would respond. He would eventually be replaced with a cold cinder or perhaps even one of Satan's boys.

The Spirit filled apostles, prophets, evangelists, pastors, and teachers that Jesus put in the congregation for the perfecting of the saints, for the work of the ministry, and for the edifying of the body of Christ (Ephesians

4:11-12) would begin to leave for other churches. They would eventually be replaced with false apostles, prophets, evangelists, pastors, and teachers. The laymen in the congregation who were devoted to Jesus would recognize the deadness and start looking for a congregation in the will of God. The remainder of the congregation becomes pew-warmers with no chance of spiritual growth or maturity. They still call the building a church, but the cross on its steeple means the same thing as a cross in a cemetery. This is the condition in which Jesus found the temple of Jerusalem, which caused him to say, "There shall not be left here one stone upon another, that shall not be thrown down" (Matthew 24:1-2). His evaluation of the religious leaders is found in Matthew 23:27-28, "(27) Woe unto you, scribes and Pharisees, hypocrites! for ye are like unto whited sepulchres, which indeed appear beautiful outward, but are within full of dead men's bones, and of all uncleanness. (28) Even so ye also outwardly appear righteous unto men, but within ye are full of hypocrisy and iniquity."

f. PROMISE: Overcomers given the right to the tree of life.
Rev. 2:7, "He that hath an ear, let him hear what the Spirit saith unto the churches; To him that overcometh will I give to eat of the tree of life, which is in the midst of the paradise of God."

The statement "He that hath an ear, let him hear what the Spirit saith unto the churches" is repeated in all seven letters. In John 8:44, Jesus told a group of Jews, "Ye are of your father the devil, and the lusts of your father ye will do." If we look at the verses just before and after this statement we will see that Jesus could identify them as "of Satan" because of their inability to hear and understand his Words. John 8:41-47, "(41) Ye do the deeds of your father. Then said they to him, We be not born of fornication; we have one Father, even God. (42) Jesus said unto them, If God were your Father, ye would love me: for I proceeded forth and came from God; neither came I of myself, but he sent me. (43) Why do ye not understand my speech? even because ye cannot hear my word. (44) Ye are of your father the devil, and the lusts of your father ye will do. He was a murderer from the beginning, and abode not in the truth, because there is no truth in him. When he speaketh a lie, he speaketh of his own: for he is a liar, and the father of it. (45) And because I tell you the truth, ye believe me not. (46) Which of you convinceth me of sin? And if I say the truth, why do ye not believe me? (47) He that is of God heareth God's words: ye therefore hear them not, because ye are not of God."

The method Jesus used to distinguish between those of God and those of Satan was based on their ability to hear God. We also saw that the church at Ephesus was commended because "thou hast tried them which say they are apostles, and are not, and hast found them liars." That responsibility has never been taken from the church and the same method still works. From 1 John 4:1-6 it is apparent that it will work on both human spirits and demonic spirits, "(1) Beloved, believe not every spirit, but try the spirits whether they are of God: because many false prophets are gone out into the world. (2) Hereby know ye the Spirit of God: Every spirit that confesseth that Jesus Christ is come in the flesh is of God: (3) And every spirit that confesseth not that Jesus Christ is come in the flesh is not of God: and this is that spirit of antichrist, whereof ye have heard that it should come; and even now already is it in the world. (4) Ye are of God, little children, and have overcome them: because greater is he that is in you, than he that is in the world. (5) They are of the world: therefore speak they of the world, and the world heareth them. (6) We are of God: he that knoweth God heareth us; he that is not of God heareth not us. Hereby know we the spirit of truth, and the spirit of error."

"Him that overcometh" is obviously one that is *not* overcome or overpowered. The overcomer subdues and gains superiority, while the one overcome is conquered and brought into subjection. The principal is given in 2 Peter 2:19, "for of whom a man is overcome, of the same is he brought in bondage." In Romans 12:21 we are told, "Be not overcome of evil, but overcome evil with good." During the Church Dispensation the overcomers are born-again believers, 1 John 5:4-5, "(4) For whatsoever is born of God overcometh the world: and this is the victory that overcometh the world, even our faith. (5) Who is he that overcometh the world, but he that believeth that Jesus is the Son of God?" As we saw in 1 Peter 2:2 the newborn has a hunger for the Word of God, "As newborn babes, desire the sincere milk of the word, that ye may grow thereby." If they are fed the sincere Word they will overcome infancy and grow into little children. If anything is substituted for the sincere Word, or the sincere Word is rejected, the growth process stops, which results in a bunch of babies playing church. This situation existed in the church at Corinth which resulted in the rebuke recorded in 1 Corinthians 3:1-3, "(1) And I, brethren, could not speak unto you as unto spiritual, but as unto carnal, even as unto babes in Christ. (2) I have fed you with milk, and not with meat: for hitherto ye were not able to bear it, neither yet now are ye able. (3) For ye are yet carnal: for whereas there is among you envying, and strife, and divisions, are ye not carnal, and walk as men?"

Paul called them "brethren" so he was addressing Church members. The chapter continues with the warning they would lose rewards that could have been theirs. They were not in danger of losing their salvation, but they would never enjoy the abundant life Jesus purchased for them at Calvary. Instead of the congregation overcoming Satan and throwing him and his representatives out, the thief would continue to steal, kill, and destroy, John 10:9-11, "(9) I am the door: by me if any man enter in, he shall be saved, and shall go in and out, and find pasture. (10) The thief cometh not, but for to steal, and to kill, and to destroy: I am come that they might have life, and that they might have it more abundantly. (11) I am the good shepherd: the good shepherd giveth his life for the sheep." Babies who refuse to grow into little children, become dull of hearing and can be best described as pew-warmers. Hebrews 5:11-6:2, "(11) Of whom we have many things to say, and hard to be uttered, seeing ye are dull of hearing. (12) For when for the time ye ought to be teachers, ye have need that one teach you again which be the first principles of the oracles of God; and are become such as have need of milk, and not of strong meat. (13) For every one that useth milk is unskillful in the word of righteousness: for he is a babe. (14) But strong meat belongeth to them that are of full age, even those who by reason of use have their senses exercised to discern both good and evil. (6:1) Therefore leaving the principles of the doctrine of Christ, let us go on unto perfection; not laying again the foundation of repentance from dead works, and of faith toward God, (2) Of the doctrine of baptisms, and of laying on of hands, and of resurrection of the dead, and of eternal judgment."

The newborn babes who receive the sincere Word grow in grace and in the knowledge of Jesus Christ into little children. It is as little children that many are overcome by the spirit of error, antichrist, deceivers, and false apostles, prophets, and teachers. Tradition claims many, but many more are overcome by false doctrines. What little children need to be taught is 1 John 4:4, "Ye are of God, little children, and have overcome them: because greater is he that is in you, than he that is in the world." They need to be taught what sin is and who sinners are, 1 John 3:7-10, "(7) Little children, let no man deceive you: he that doeth righteousness is righteous, even as he is righteous. (8) He that committeth sin is of the devil; for the devil sinneth from the beginning. For this purpose the Son of God was manifested, that he might destroy the works of the devil. (9) Whosoever is born of God doth not commit sin; for his seed remaineth in him: and he cannot sin, because he is born of God. (10) In this the children of God are manifest, and the children of the devil: whosoever doeth not righteousness is not of God, neither he that loveth not his brother." Jesus warns of the consequences of causing little ones to be overcome in Matthew 18:1-14. As the little children grow they become young men, and are recognizable as such when they begin to take the Word of God and overcome Satan instead of allowing him to overcome them. As they mature they become fathers which can be used of God to work in the ministry and bring newborns into existence by the gospel. The distinction between little children, young men, and fathers can be seen in 1 John 2:12-18, "(12) I write unto you, little children, because your sins are forgiven you for his name's sake. (13) I write unto you, fathers, because ye have known him that is from the beginning. I write unto you, young men, because ye have overcome the wicked one. I write unto you, little children, because ye have known the Father. (14) I have written unto you, fathers, because ye have known him that is from the beginning. I have written unto you, young men, because ye are strong, and the word of God abideth in you, and ye have overcome the wicked one. (15) Love not the world, neither the things that are in the world. If any man love the world, the love of the Father is not in him. (16) For all that is in the world, the lust of the flesh, and the lust of the eyes, and the pride of life, is not of the Father, but is of the world. (17) And the world passeth away, and the lust thereof: but he that doeth the will of God abideth for ever. (18) Little children, it is the last time: and as ye have heard that antichrist shall come, even now are there many antichrists; whereby we know that it is the last time."

The Letter to Smyrna

2. The Letter to Smyrna: Persecuted Chruch (100-300).
Revelation 2:8-11, "(8) And unto the angel of the church in Smyrna write;
These things saith the first and the last, which was dead, and is alive; (9) I
know thy works, and tribulation, and poverty, (but thou art rich) and I know
the blasphemy of them which say they are Jews, and are not, but are the syn-
agogue of Satan. (10) Fear none of those things which thou shalt suffer:
behold, the devil shall cast some of you into prison, that ye may be tried;
and ye shall have tribulation ten days: be thou faithful unto death, and I will
give thee a crown of life. (11) He that hath an ear, let him hear what the
Spirit saith unto the churches; He that overcometh shall not be hurt of the
second death."

a. TO: the church in Smyrna.
Rev. 2:8a, "And unto the angel of the church in Smyrna write."

The Ephesus church era covers the time period between the Day of Pentecost, when the Church came into existence, to approximately A.D. 100. This era was followed by the era of great church persecution which lasted from approximately A.D. 100 to 300. Again we are dealing with Christendom as a whole. Jesus is using the local church at Smyrna as a typical example of the persecution Christendom would undergo after the Ephesus era ended. The first century churches had left their first love and lost sight of their original mission, "Go ye into all the world, and preach the gospel to every creature." In the rebuke section Jesus warned them to remember, repent, and do the first works or they would be removed out of their place. The persecution of the Smyrna era caused the insincere to be removed from the churches, and caused the sincere to be removed and scattered throughout the Roman Empire. The persecution continued until the year A.D. 313 when Constantine issued the edict of Milan.

From the letter to the angel of the Smyrna era we can see the instructions Satan issued to the principality demon he enthroned. The demon was laboring under the idea of using the power of the Roman Empire and its perverted citizens to crush the Church by persecuting or killing the members. Most of us have seen movies or read history accounts of how the Christians were tortured and killed in the Roman arenas for sport, so I won't labor the point. Needless to say, during this period of time it was most unpopular to be called a Christian. When the insincere were threatened with the loss of their possessions or death they denied Jesus and Christianity in order to survive. The sincere Christians were tortured, imprisoned, or killed for their refusal to deny Jesus. The Christians who were forced to flee for their lives actually became missionaries of the gospel and instead of destroying Christendom the persecution resulted in the spread of Christianity throughout the Roman Empire.

b. FROM: Jesus, which was dead and is alive.
Rev. 2:8b, "These things saith the first and the last, which was dead and is alive."

Jesus introduces himself as the resurrected one, which is most significant, since the churches in this era would be facing death. There is no mention of Jesus coming in this letter, because the sincere Christians would be coming to him through their death. To the church at Ephesus he said, "I will come unto thee quickly" (verse 2:5), to Smyrna "be thou faithful unto death, and I will give thee a crown of life" (verse 2:10), to Pergamos, "I will come unto thee quickly " (verse 2:16), to Thyatira, "hold fast till I come" (verse 2:25), to Sardis, "I will come on thee as a thief" (verse 3:3), and to Philadelphia, "Behold, I come quickly" (verse 3:11). His coming is not mentioned in the letter to the Laodicean church because the rapture of the Church will occur, and the sincere members who were deceived and left behind will come to him through their death at the hands of Antichrist.

c. COMMENDATION: Good works in spite of tribulation and poverty.
Rev. 2:9a, "I know thy works, and tribulation, and poverty, (but thou art rich)."

Again, Jesus knows what is going on and he is aware of their works, tribulation, and poverty. The opposite of poverty is riches, which, in the eyes of the pagan world is determined by material possessions, of which gold is considered the most precious. In 1 Peter 1:7 we are told from God's point of view "the trial of your faith" is much more precious than gold. This is why Jesus could look on their poverty and say "but thou art rich." The trying of your faith, tribulation, and poverty are all a result of Satanic or demonic activity, which is obvious from the exhort portion of the letter in Rev. 2:10, "Fear none of those things which thou shalt suffer: behold, the devil shall cast some of you into prison, that ye may be tried; and ye shall have tribulation ten days: be thou faithful unto death, and I will give thee a crown of life."

The Greek word *tribulation* means to crowd, in the sense of applying pressure. Webster defines it as "distress or suffering resulting from oppression or persecution." Webster defines the word *persecute* as "to harass in a manner designed to injure, grieve, or afflict; specifically: to cause to suffer because of belief." From the parable of the sower it is obvious that every satanic attack is directed at the Word of God. Matthew 13:18-23, "(18) Hear ye therefore the parable of the sower. (19) When any one heareth the word of the kingdom, and understandeth it not, then cometh the wicked one, and catcheth away that which was sown in his heart. This is he which received seed by the way side. (20) But he that received the seed into stony places, the same is he that heareth the word, and anon with joy receiveth it; (21) Yet hath he not root in himself, but dureth for a while: for when tribulation or persecution ariseth because of the word, by and by he is offended. (22) He also that received seed among the thorns is he that heareth the word; and the care of this world, and the deceitfulness of riches, choke the word, and he becometh unfruitful. (23) But he that received seed into the good ground is he that heareth the word, and understandeth it; which also beareth fruit, and bringeth forth, some an hundredfold, some sixty, some thirty."

In John 16:33 Jesus told his followers, "In the world ye shall have tribulation," and in 2 Timothy 3:12 the Holy Spirit repeats that truth, "Yea, and all that will live godly in Christ Jesus shall suffer persecution." In other words, if you are going to live a godly life in Jesus according to the Word of God, you can expect to be crowded and pressured by Satan and crew. When you realize the testing of your faith is more precious than gold, your attitude toward tribulations will change. The object of tribulations is given in Romans 5:3-5, "(3) And not only so, but we glory in tribulations also: knowing that tribulation worketh patience; (4) And patience, experience; and experience, hope: (5) And hope maketh not ashamed; because the love of God is shed abroad in our hearts by the Holy Ghost which is given unto us." In 2 Peter 2:9 we are told, "The Lord knoweth how to deliver the godly out of temptations, and to reserve the unjust unto the day of judgment to be punished." Tribulations are designed by Satan to overcome you, or as Jesus said in John 10:10 to steal, kill, and destroy. The tribulations are either going to make you an overcomer or one that is overcome. If the tribulations turn you from a godly life in Christ or from the Word of God, you can expect Satan to steal, kill, and destroy. It doesn't matter if the object of the tribulation is an individual, a congregation, or Christendom as a whole. This is basically what happened to Christendom by the end of the first century. They had left their first love, lost sight of their mission, and Satan moved in to steal, kill, and destroy.

d. REBUKE: None, but he knows of the blaspheming Jews of the synagogue of Satan.
Rev. 2:9b, "and I know the blasphemy of them which say they are Jews, and are not, but are the synagogue of Satan."

There is no rebuke to Christendom as a whole in the letter to Smyrna. In the words "I know" Jesus is saying he is aware of the blaspheming Jews. Some teach that the Jews were trying to put the Church under Old

Testament law, but they were guilty of blasphemy. Blasphemy is taking something that is of God and attributing it to Satan, or taking something that is of Satan and attributing it to God. How the Jews blasphemed is debatable. Since they were claiming to be Jews it is doubtful that the blasphemy involved the Father. Denying the deity of Jesus would be blasphemy, and since the Jews as a whole had already rejected Jesus as the Christ, this would only be a continuance of that rejection. The blasphemy could have been directed against the Church, its members, or the New Testament portion of the Scripture. If the blasphemy concerned the deity, existence, or work of the Holy Spirit, they had committed the unpardonable sin. The five signs Jesus said would follow believers in the Mark 16:15-18 Church Commission are manifestations of the Holy Spirit, and to attribute them to Satan, or deny them, is blasphemy against the Holy Spirit. I personally believe this is where the Jews had blasphemed. These signs were a problem to unbelievers on the Day of Pentecost when the Church walked out of the upper room, and looking back through two thousand years of Church history, they have always been a problem to the unbelieving. The key lies in the fact that Jesus said the signs would follow "them that believe," not them that don't believe, and especially not them of the synagogue of Satan. The signs separate "them which say they are" from them which are.

e. EXHORT: Faithfulness to death for a crown of life.
Rev. 2:10, "Fear none of those things which thou shalt suffer: behold, the devil shall cast some of you into prison, that ye may be tried; and ye shall have tribulation ten days: be thou faithful unto death, and I will give thee a crown of life."

The churches which were established in the first century are actually going to be destroyed during this period of persecution. The Christendom congregation was made up of some of "the synagogue of Satan," some sincere, and some insincere. Jesus begins the exhort with the statement, "Fear none of those things which thou shalt suffer" and ends it with "be thou faithful unto death, and I will give thee a crown of life." In the promise section he says, "He that overcometh shall not be hurt of the second death." When the persecution started, those of the synagogue of Satan were not able to hide under the cloak of Christianity. The sincere would remain faithful, and the insincere would, be unfaithful to escape imprisonment and death, lose the crown of life, be overcome and hurt of the second death.

As we have already seen the trying of your faith, tribulation, and poverty are all a result of Satanic or demonic activity, which is obvious from the statement "the devil shall cast some of you into prison, that ye may be tried." The Greek word translated as *tried* is the same word translated as *tempted* in James 1:13 and 1:14, and in both passages it means to be tested. In other words, to be tried, tempted, or tested is all the same thing, and it is done by Satan, not God. This is clear from James 1:12-15, "(12) Blessed is the man that endureth temptation: for when he is tried, he shall receive the crown of life, which the Lord hath promised to them that love him. (13) Let no man say when he is tempted, I am tempted of God: for God cannot be tempted with evil, neither tempteth he any man: (14) But every man is tempted, when he is drawn away of his own lust, and enticed. (15) Then when lust hath conceived, it bringeth forth sin: and sin, when it is finished, bringeth forth death."

The doctrine of being tried, tempted, or tested by Satan is the baptism of fire. In essence, fire in the Bible speaks of judgment, and the judge is Jesus. It should not be confused with the great white throne judgment day, when the lost are judged and thrown into hell. The baptism of fire is the process by which we communicate to Jesus our preference of heaven or hell, and our faithfulness or faithlessness. Jesus told the Smyrna congregation "Behold, the devil shall cast some of you into prison, that ye may be tried" (or tested), "be thou faithful unto death, and I will give thee a crown of life" and "He that overcometh shall not be hurt of the second death" (the white throne judgment of Rev. 20:11-15).

The devil, not God, cast some of them into prison. The reason they were cast into prison is "that ye may be tried" or tested to identify the sincere and insincere, and it was "unto death," to separate the faithful from the unfaithful. To all Satan imprisoned for the test Jesus said, "be thou faithful unto death, and I will give thee a crown of life." Since it was "unto death," it is a last chance or final call, when the individual is placed in an either-or situation. The prisoner is either going to be faithful unto death and get a crown of life, or be unfaithful to escape death and lose a crown of life. To see the baptism of fire "unto death," watch the prisoners being marched onto a platform in the arena above a group of hungry lions and listen to the Roman soldier say, "This is your last chance, deny Jesus and this Christianity or I'm going to feed you to the lions." The Christians who were fed to the lions were "faithful unto death" and given a crown of life. Those who denied Christianity to escape being fed to the lions were not "faithful unto death" and lost a crown of life. They were all identified with judgment in the baptism of fire, and the faithful tested acceptable while the unfaithful tested unacceptable. They were all given the opportunity to overcome, but only the faithful can be classified as overcomers. In the promise section of the letter Jesus said, "He that overcometh shall not be hurt of the second death." The faithful were the overcomers which "shall not be hurt of the second death." The unfaithful were overcome and shall be hurt of the second death.

A prison is an institution of the government for the confinement and punishment of persons convicted of crimes against the state or society. The government during this 200 year period was the Roman Empire and the statement "ye shall have tribulation ten days" can be seen in the fact that ten out of the seventeen emperors who ruled the empire during this period persecuted Christians. It is a sad situation when Satan gets enough control over a government to confiscate personal belongings, or imprison a person because they are a Christian. It is even sadder when the citizens of that government are permitted to kill Christians, merely for the sport of watching them die.

The first century churches left their first love, cut off their power, and lost sight of their mission, which resulted in the baptism of fire "unto death" for the churches in the Smyrna era. It continued until the year 313 when the Roman Emperor Constantine by the "edit of Milan" made it illegal to throw Christians to the lions. This two-hundred-year-period is relatively a short period of time, compared to the two thousand years of church history. This means the baptism of fire "unto death" is an exception, rather than the rule. There have been isolated cases throughout church history when members have been killed for the testimony of Jesus, but again, it has been the exception not the rule. It will become the rule after the rapture of the faithful Church, when the Laodicean church membership is put to the test of the baptism of fire "unto death". The first century churches left their first love and their refusal to repent is what caused the churches in the Smyrna era to face the baptism of fire "unto death." In the Laodicean church era the churches refuse to let Jesus in, or they actually threw him out, which is obvious from Revelation 3:20, "Behold, I stand at the door, and knock." This is the whore Christendom that Antichrist destroys in the baptism of fire "unto death" as he eats her flesh, and burns her with fire (Rev. 17:16).

A lack of understanding on the baptism of fire (the process of being tried, tempted, or tested by Satan) is responsible for most of today's Christian population being counted among the overcome instead of the overcomers. It has been perverted in the Laodicean congregation to the point where all you have to do to be a Christian is to say you have been born again. It's like a pauper saying he is a millionaire without the wealth to back up the statement. The heart of the problem is self-deceit, when people become so dishonest that they refuse to even consider the facts and acknowledge the truth. Satan is a deceiver and he doesn't mind you saying you are a Christian as long as you don't live like one. He doesn't even mind you taking your Bible to Church as long as you believe what he says instead of what Jesus said. The most popular gospel being published today by the Laodicean preachers is the "only believe package," but what they are not telling the congregation is that Jesus said, "these signs shall follow them that believe; In my name shall they cast out devils; they shall speak with new tongues; they shall take up serpents; and if they drink any deadly thing, it shall not hurt them; they shall lay hands on the sick, and they shall recover" (Mark 16:17-18). If the Laodicean church preacher was a believer these signs would follow him. The sad part of the situation is the signs don't follow him but the congregation does. They would rather believe a lie and be deceived, than to believe Jesus and do what he told them to do. They would rather live with the devil, than cast him out. They would rather be overcome by sickness and die, than to be an overcomer and recover.

Those who cannot see the seven letters to the seven churches as seven distinct consecutive periods of church history also have trouble seeing themselves standing in the Laodicean era. Look around and realize the people in your neighborhood are not being imprisoned or thrown to the lions today because of being called a Christian. We realize that Jesus isn't calling on church members to lay down their lives for a crown of life today and that the baptism of fire "unto death" for a crown of life is the exception rather than the rule. The obvious question is, What is the rule? Because of the persecution suffered by the Christians living in the Smyrna era, the traditional teaching on the crown of life is that it is a martyr's reward, which means you must be killed for your faith in Jesus to receive it. If this were the truth the only people in heaven to own a crown of life would be those who were put into the 'either-or' situation of deny Jesus or be killed. This would eliminate most of the Christian population who lived between the years 313 and 1996. The truth is the crown of life is both a martyr's crown and a victor's crown. It is a victor's crown to those tested acceptable in life, and a martyr's crown to those tested unacceptable in life but tested acceptable in the 'deny or die' situation.

It could also be called a victorious martyr's crown to those tested acceptable in life and in death. By this I mean the person was tested acceptable in life, and when put in a life or death situation, it would be totally impossible for them to be tested unacceptable. In other words, the person's salvation was predetermined by their lives and not in question in any way, shape, or form, at the point when they faced death. This can be seen in the life and death of the first Christian martyr. His name was Stephen and the incident is recorded in Acts 6:1-7:60. In Acts 6:5 we are told Stephen was "a man full of faith and of the Holy Ghost." In Acts 6:8 we are told "And Stephen, full of faith and power, did great wonders and miracles among the people." Stephen was a born-again believer and eternal salvation was his before he faced the mob with the stones. When Stephen was stoned to death, his faith was not being tried, tempted, or tested by Satan.

An example of a martyr's crown given to those tested unacceptable in life but tested acceptable in the 'deny or die' situation can be seen in the Smyrna congregation. The first century churches had left their first love and had failed to repent. The churches in the Smyrna era were nothing more than a continuation of the churches established in the Ephesus era. The Ephesus churches were tested unacceptable because they had left their first love, and could no longer be used as a witness for Jesus. They had judged themselves unfaithful. In the persecution that followed during the Smyrna era, what Jesus is basically saying is get serious or get out. Their moment of truth comes when they faced the 'deny or die' situation. Their eternal salvation hangs in the balances. They are no longer going to be allowed to play church, pretend to be Christians, or do damage to Christendom. In the 'deny or die' situation they are all being tried, tempted, and tested by Satan.

Needless to say, the 'deny or die' situation brings some to repentance and exposes the rest as hypocrites. The only ones who will be given a crown of life are those who repent and remain faithful until death, which is obvious from Jesus's statement, "be thou faithful unto death, and I will give thee a crown of life." The apostate churches of the Laodicean era will face this same situation following the rapture.

In the baptism of fire "unto death" the crown of life is either won or lost in the 'deny or die' decision. The phrase "crown of life" is found in the Bible only twice. It appears in the Revelation 2:10 passage we just read which is the exception, or the baptism of fire "unto death." The only other place it appears in the Bible is in James 1:12 which is the rule, or normal baptism of fire. Let's reconsider James 1:12-13, "(12) Blessed is the man that endureth temptation: for when he is tried, he shall receive the crown of life, which the Lord hath promised to them that love him. (13) Let no man say when he is tempted, I am tempted of God: for God cannot be tempted with evil, neither tempteth he any man." As we have already seen the Greek word translated as *tried* in the Revelation 2:10 statement, "behold, the devil shall cast some of you into prison, that ye may be tried," is the same Greek word translated as *tempted* in James 1:13. We can restate James 1:13 using the word *tested* without doing any damage to the text. The statement would read, "Let no man say when he is tested, I am tested of God: (or God is testing me) for God cannot be tempted (untemptable) with evil, neither test he any man: (with evil)." In either case the text is clear in the fact that God isn't trying, testing, or tempting anyone. He is watching to see what we do in the test, but the tester is Satan, not God.

The Greek word translated as *tried* in James 1:12 is a different Greek word with the same basic meaning except that it means to be tested and found acceptable. We can restate James 1:12 by saying, "Blessed is the man that endureth testing: for when he is tested acceptable, he shall receive the crown of life, which the Lord hath promised to them that love him." Now consider how many times Satan has come to tempt and test you. Consider how many times Satan met defeat because you resisted him and endured the temptation by remaining faithful to the Word of God, without it costing you your life. Anytime you have been tried, tempted, or tested by Satan you were baptized with fire, or literally, "being identified with judgment." In the judgment you are being identified as faithful, tested acceptable, or unfaithful, tested unacceptable. The object of the test is your faith in the Word of God, the tester is Satan, and the judge is Jesus. The reason for the test is to allow both you and God to see your faithfulness or unfaithfulness. The judgment is the outcome of the test, in which Jesus judges one a victor and one defeated. Again, we are not talking about the final judgment day or the day you die. We are talking about the day you met the enemy in a temptation or test and won (or lost) a battle, not the war.

The baptism of fire is the lifelong process by which a Christian grows to maturity. The conflict started when someone convinced you that, according to the Word of God, you were a sinner en route to hell and since then there has been almost continuous war. God reveals a truth to us in His Word, and allows Satan to come against us to try to separate us from that truth. I don't know of any war where the winning army lost all the battles. Both armies know at the end of each battle who won, just as we know after each temptation who won and who lost. In our war there is only one weapon and it is a sword called the Word of God. Either you are going to take that sword and defeat Satan or he is going to take the sword and defeat you. This is why being identified with judgment in the baptism of fire either makes you an overcomer or one who is overcome. This is the "trial of your faith" and the test results reveal your trust in God or your mistrust. We saw in 1 Peter 1:7 where the "trial of your faith" is much more precious than gold, but if the fire consumes you, and you yield to the temptation, the gold is counterfeit. It isn't precious to God or you. It means you have been identified with judgment and tested unacceptable.

We need to get rid of the old cliche "win a few, lose a few." That attitude is going to cause a lot of Christians to be left behind at the rapture to face the baptism of fire "unto death" at the hand of Antichrist. We are facing a different situation than our forefathers. The rapture will divide our generation into a group tested acceptable and ready to go, and a group tested unacceptable which is not ready to go. We are in the Laodicean church era and have been in it for nearly a hundred years. That's about how long Jesus tolerated the churches in the Ephesus era, who left their first love, before he allowed the tribulation to come upon the churches in the Smyrna era. Our generation is running out of time. Those who refuse to get serious and miss the rapture are going to be forced to get serious in the deny or die baptism of fire unto death during the Antichrist reign.

f. PROMISE: The overcomers shall not be hurt of the second death.
Rev. 2:11, "He that hath an ear, let him hear what the Spirit saith unto the churches; He that overcometh shall not be hurt of the second death."

As we have already seen, the second death is eternal separation from God in the lake of fire. Those hurt of the second death are those who participate in the second resurrection, which is the resurrection to damnation (Rev. 20:1-15). The overcomers participate in the first resurrection to eternal life and cannot be touched by the second death which is clear from Revelation 20:6, "Blessed and holy is he that hath part in the first resurrection: on such the second death hath no power, but they shall be priests of God and of Christ, and shall reign with him a thousand years."

The Letter to Pergamos

3. The Letter to Pergamos: Marriage of Church and State (300-500).
Revelation 2:12-17, "(12) And to the angel of the church in Pergamos write;

These things saith he which hath the sharp sword with two edges; (13) I know thy works, and where thou dwellest, even where Satan's seat is: and thou holdest fast my name, and hast not denied my faith, even in those days wherein Antipas was my faithful martyr, who was slain among you, where Satan dwelleth. (14) But I have a few things against thee, because thou hast there them that hold the doctrine of Balaam, who taught Balac to cast a stumbling block before the children of Israel, to eat things sacrificed unto idols, and to commit fornication. (15) So hast thou also them that hold the doctrine of the Nicolaitanes, which thing I hate. (16) Repent; or else I will come unto thee quickly, and will fight against them with the sword of my mouth. (17) He that hath an ear, let him hear what the Spirit saith unto the churches; To him that overcometh will I give to eat of the hidden manna, and will give him a white stone, and in the stone a new name written, which no man knoweth saving he that receiveth it."

a. TO: The church in Pergamos.
Rev. 2:12a, "And to the angel of the church in Pergamos write."

During the Ephesus era or first hundred years of Christendom we saw the churches leave their first love and refuse to repent. This departure led to the persecution Christendom suffered during the Smyrna era. The persecution lasted about two hundred years (A.D. 100-313) but instead of destroying Christianity, it actually caused it to spread. The members who were forced to flee for their lives became missionaries. When Satan realized the persecution was not destroying Christendom, he changed his approach. From the letter to the angel of the Pergamos era we can see the instructions Satan issued to the principality demon he enthroned. The demon was to marry the Church and State which would end the persecution, and then destroy the Church from within through false doctrine.

Tradition claims the Roman Emperor Constantine saw a flaming cross in the sky with the words *By this sign conquer* at sunset on the day before the battle of Milvian Bridge near Rome on October 27, 312. Constantine believed the message was from God, and that he should conquer under the sign of Christianity. He won the battle of Milvian Bridge and supposedly became a Christian. In the year 313 he issued the edit of Milan which ended the persecution of the Smyrna era by granting everyone the right to choose their own religion.

The word *pergamos* contains the Greek word *gamos* which denotes bigamy, the act of entering into ceremonial marriage with one person while still legally married to another. The Church is the Bride of Christ but during the Pergamos era Christendom entered into an illegal relationship with the Roman government. The edict of Milan put the Church and government in agreement, but the marriage was not complete until the Emperor Theodosius, who ruled from 378 to 398. He made Christianity the government religion of the Roman Empire and made Church membership compulsory. He persecuted all other religions, outlawed idol worship, destroyed heathen temples, and forced the heathens into the Christian Church. Theodosius didn't understand you can lead a horse to water, but you can't make it drink. The government can't make a person a Christian merely by making them attend Church. The Church is to be filled with "whosoever will come" which makes membership strictly voluntary. Jesus never forced Christianity on anyone and he never intended the government to force it on anybody.

In Matthew 22:21 Jesus said, "Render therefore unto Caesar the things which are Caesar's: and unto God the things that are God's," which is clearly a separation of government and Church. The government has a responsibility to the inhabitants of the land which concerns their physical well-being and the law, which rewards the good and punishes the evil doers. The responsibility of the Church concerns the spiritual well-being of the inhabitants of the land. If the Church meets its responsibility, the government officials are born-again believers with the intelligence to know the difference between what belongs to Caesar and what belongs to God. If the government meets its responsibility the inhabitants of the land enjoy a fear-free environment and prosperity, which will allow the Church to meet its responsibility of "Go ye into all the world, and preach the gospel to every creature" (Mark 16:15); "Teaching them to observe all things whatsoever I have commanded you" (Matthew 28:20). If either fails to meet its responsibility the inhabitants of the land are placed in a state of turmoil.

The Pergamos church era covers a period of about two hundred years, roughly A.D. 300 to 500. The era actually began in A.D. 313 with the edict of Milan and a bigamy marriage between the Church and State. During the Pergamos era the government supported Christianity and controlled the Church. Instead of the Church addressing itself to its commission, it became involved in a political power struggle with the government. After the fall of the Roman Empire in A.D. 476 Christendom entered the Thyatira church era. During this era Christendom, in the form of the papacy, became a strong political organization that exalted itself above all governments. During the Pergamos church era the government claimed supremacy and during the Thyatira church era the papacy claimed supremacy.

b. FROM: Jesus, which has the sharp sword with two edges.
Rev. 2:12b, "These things saith he which hath the sharp sword with two edges."

With that sharp two-edged sword, Jesus nullified the bigamy marriage and separated the Church and State. In the Rev. 19:11-21 return of Jesus, we are told in verse 13 that "his name is called The Word of God" and in verse 15, "And out of his mouth goeth a sharp sword, that with it he should smite the nations." In verse 19:21 he destroys the Armageddon Army with this same sword, "And the remnant were slain with the sword of him that sat upon the horse, which sword proceeded out of his mouth: and all the fowls were filled with their flesh." The sword out of the mouth of Jesus is his Word. It is a two-edged sword because his word is capable of both convicting and converting, condemning or setting free, killing and giving life. Jesus presents himself as "he which hath the sharp sword with two edges" to remind the Pergamos congregation of his authority over both the Church and the government.

c. COMMENDATION: Good works and faithfulness although dwelling where Satan's seat is.
Rev. 2:13, "I know thy works, and where thou dwellest, even where Satan's seat is: and thou holdest fast my name, and hast not denied my faith, even in those days wherein Antipas was my faithful martyr, who was slain among you, where Satan dwellest."

The traditional teaching on "where Satan's seat is" has been that Pergamos was Satan's headquarters or base of operation. This teaching may have gained acceptance because of the reputation Pergamos had for wickedness. The truth is Pergamos was no more of a headquarters for Satan than any other city or place on Earth, then or now. Although Satan walks to and fro in the earth, his base of operation is in front of the throne of God. It has always been there and will remain there until Michael and his angels throw Satan and his angels out of Heaven. Satan stands before God and accuses humans continuously, which is clear from Rev. 12:10, "And I heard a loud voice saying in heaven, Now is come salvation, and strength, and the kingdom of our God, and the power of his Christ: for the accuser of our brethren is cast down, which accused them before our God day and night." Satan and crew will get thrown out of heaven at the midpoint in the seven–year tribulation period, at which time his headquarters or base of operations will become Earth. Even then, if we were to choose a spot on the planet for Satan's headquarters, it would be the seven remaining nations of the European Common Market Nations under the leadership of the False Prophet, not Pergamos or the city of Babylon.

There is a better argument for Thessalonica being the base of Satan's operation in the phrase "where Satan's seat is." The Greek word translated as *seat* is the same Greek word translated as *Thessalonica* in Acts 17:1, 17:11, 17:13, Philippians 4:16, and 2 Thessalonians 4:10. The word *Thessalonica* is from the Greek word *therme* which means heat. Our English word *thermal* and the prefix *thermo-* come from the same Greek word. What Jesus is actually saying is, "I know thy works, and where thou dwellest, even where Satan's heat is." It doesn't take much Bible knowledge to see that the government of the Roman Empire was conducting its affairs according to the will of Satan, not the revealed will of God. With Satan in control of the government, he was in a position to apply enough pressure on the Church to force his will and ideas into Christendom. Pressure in the physical realm creates heat and that same truth applies to the spirit realm. Satan's pressure is designed to turn us from the revealed will of God. In the parable of the sower (Luke 8:13) we saw that some hear and receive the word with joy, "which for a while believe, and in time of temptation fall away." The temptation was Satan's pressure or the heat of the baptism of fire. Lust is also an example of Satan's pressure or heat. The lust for political power that burns in a politician, is really no different than the lust that burns in the rich for more riches, or the lust that burns in the body of adulterers or fornicators for sex. If Satan can apply enough pressure to create enough heat to cause us to ignore God's revealed will, we are operating in the realm of where Satan dwelleth.

To understand the government take-over of the Churches in the Pergamos era, consider the government take-over of the education system in the United States. Many of the schools and colleges were established by Churches for the purpose of preparing pastors and missionaries for the work of God. In the process of time the government began supporting the education system, and eventually exercised complete control over it. Today the public education system in the United States is totally anti-Christ, anti-God, and anti-Bible. It is literally against the law of the land to pray, teach, or read the Bible in a public classroom. The government allows the teachers to call themselves Christians, but they must limit Christianity to Sunday, and teach antichrist principals during the week. They can spend one day a week teaching Jesus is the Creator and he completed the creation in six days, as long as they spend five days a week discrediting the Word of God by teaching that mother nature was the creator. These teachers are a product of the Laodicean church congregation, where the separation of Church and State means that Christianity must not interfere with government, business, schools, social laws, or the judicial system. It's not a matter of compromise, because there is no compromise between Christianity and Satanism.

During the Smyrna era Satan tried to destroy Christendom from outside the Church. During the Pergamos era, he used the government to force his congregation into the Christian congregation, to destroy Christendom from within through false doctrine. One of the first false teachers to reveal himself, after Constantine granted everyone the right to choose his own religion, was a priest in Alexandria named Arius (256-336). He began teaching that Jesus is neither eternal nor equal with the Father. He taught that Jesus was a created creature. The movement became known as Arianism, and caused Constantine to call the First Council of Nicaea, where Arianism was condemned. Although the movement was condemned, the freedom of religion granted by the government allowed Arianism to continue until Theodosius became Emperor. When he made Christianity the government religion of the Roman Empire he outlawed and persecuted all other religions. By making Church membership compulsory he actually forced the Church to accept the entire population of the Roman Empire as fellow Christians.

Because this situation was forced on Christendom by the government, the Church could no longer keep itself doctrinally clean by expelling or excommunicating unrepentant sinners and false apostles, prophets, evangelists, pastors, or teachers. This is why the rebuke in the Pergamos letter is directed at those who hold false doctrine, and in the exhort Jesus says He will fight against them, "Repent; or else I will come unto thee quickly, and will fight against them with the sword of my mouth."

Those in the Church who resisted what the government was forcing on Christendom were persecuted, and at least one person named Antipas, was killed by fellow Church members, "and thou holdest fast my name, and hast not denied my faith, even in those days wherein Antipas was my faithful martyr, who was slain among you, where Satan dwellest." Notice that Antipas was slain among "you" which is a pronoun representing the "Church," "where Satan dwellest." During the Smyrna era when Satan was persecuting the Church from outside the congregation, he cast some into prison to test "their" faith. During the Pergamos era Satan is in the Church congregation and the persecution centers on the name or person of Jesus and "His" faith, "thou holdest fast my name, and hast not denied my faith."

In Philippians 2:9-11 we are told there is no name in earth, heaven, or Hades with more authority than the name of Jesus, "(9) Wherefore God also hath highly exalted him, and given him a name which is above every name: (10) That at the name of Jesus every knee should bow, of things in heaven, and things in earth, and things under the earth; (11) And that every tongue should confess that Jesus Christ is Lord, to the glory of God the Father." Jesus gave every born-again believer the authority to use his name in the earth to get things done. It is the authority in the name of Jesus that allows believers to expel demons, "In my name shall they cast out devils" (Mark 16:17). It is the authority in the name of Jesus that gets results when we pray, John 14:12-14, "(12) Verily, verily, I say unto you, He that believeth on me, the works that I do shall he do also; and greater works than these shall he do; because I go unto my Father. (13) And whatsoever ye shall ask in my name, that will I do, that the Father may be glorified in the Son. (14) If ye shall ask any thing in my name, I will do it." The only thing excluded in the "any thing" is God and his Word for they are both eternal. When this is realized we stop trying to change God, and start doing things the way he told us to do it in his Word.

The power in the authority of the name of Jesus is released by the words coming from the mouth of a person indwelt by the Holy Spirit. The Mark 16:17-18 signs are manifestations of the indwelling Holy Spirit, but they also manifest the person as a Christian. Deceivers do not have the authority to use the name of Jesus, and they are not indwelt by the Holy Spirit, so the absence of the signs is clear evidence that they do not love Jesus, believe what he said, or keep his commandments. Jesus made this clear in John 14:15-26, "(15) If ye love me, keep my commandments. (16) And I will pray the Father, and he shall give you another Comforter, that he may abide with you forever; (17) Even the Spirit of truth; whom the world cannot receive, because it seeth him not, neither knoweth him: but ye know him; for he dwelleth with you, and shall be in you. (18) I will not leave you comfortless: I will come to you. (19) Yet a little while, and the world seeth me no more; but ye see me: because I live, ye shall live also. (20) At that day ye shall know that I am in my Father, and ye in me, and I in you. (21) He that hath my commandments, and keepeth them, he it is that loveth me: and he that loveth me shall be loved of my Father, and I will love him, and will manifest myself to him. (22) Judas saith unto him, not Iscariot, Lord, how is it that thou wilt manifest thyself unto us, and not unto the world? (23) Jesus answered and said unto him, If a man love me, he will keep my words: and my Father will love him, and we will come unto him, and make our abode with him. (24) He that loveth me not keepeth not my sayings: and the word which ye hear is not mine, but the Father's which sent me. (25) These things have I spoken unto you, being yet present with you. (26) But the Comforter, which is the Holy Ghost, whom the Father will send in my name, he shall teach you all things, and bring all things to your remembrance, whatsoever I have said unto you."

I realize it is unpopular in our day to teach there are commandments placed on Christians, but that doesn't change the facts. "But the Comforter, which is the Holy Ghost, whom the Father will send in my name" is that part of the rebirth process that Jesus promises to "ye" or you of John 14:15-16, "(15) If ye love me, keep my commandments. (16) And I will pray the Father, and he shall give you another Comforter, that he may abide with you for ever." In fact, one of the commandments is that we believe on the name of Jesus. 1 John 3:18-24, "(18) My little children, let us not love in word, neither in tongue; but in deed and in truth. (19) And hereby we know that we are of the truth, and shall assure our hearts before him. (20) For if our heart condemn us, God is greater than our heart, and knoweth all things. (21) Beloved, if our heart condemn us not, then have we confidence toward God. (22) And whatsoever we ask, we receive of him, because we keep his commandments, and do those things that are pleasing in his sight. (23) And this is his commandment, That we should believe on the name of his Son Jesus Christ, and love one another, as he gave us commandment. (24) And he that keepeth his commandments dwelleth in him, and he in him. And hereby we know that he abideth in us, by the Spirit which he hath given us."

When we realize the authority in the name of Jesus, and that the power behind that name during the Church Dispensation is the Holy Spirit indwelling believers, we can see the problem Satan had after he forced the entire population of the Roman Empire into the Church congregation. His representatives were not believers, so the signs Jesus said would follow believers in Mark 16:17-18 would not follow them. Since he could not fake the signs, his only other choice was to introduce a perverted gospel that would result in a new Christianity without the signs. Since a Christian is a person who believes and follows the teachings of Jesus Christ, Satan had to discredit Jesus and his teachings. One of the easiest ways to undermine authority, destroy a person's name, or ruin his reputation, is to convince people that person is a liar. By using the government to force the Church into accepting the entire population of the Roman Empire as fellow Christians, it is obvious only a very small percentage of the Christendom congregation were born-again believers followed by the Mark 16:17-18 signs. This made it easy to convince the majority of the church population who were already non-believers that the absence of the signs was normal, no longer needed, or some other garbage like they ended when the apostles died. This made it possible to be a Christian believer without the signs following, which eliminated the need for the indwelling Holy Spirit. It was then possible to be saved and go to heaven without being born again.

The next step was to get the Scriptures out of the hands of the laymen members in order to keep them from the truth. Satan accomplished this by the papacy in the Thyatira church era (500-1500) which followed the Pergamos era. This new type Christianity plunged the world into the dark ages, and Christendom stayed in this condition until a man named Martin Luther read "The just shall live by faith" in Romans 1:17 and chose to believe God. On October 31, 1517 he posted his 95 thesis on the church door in Wittenberg, which was the beginning of the Sardis church era (1500-1700) or the reformation era. At this time the sharp sword with two edges separated the Church from the State, and the bigamy marriage of the Pergamos era ended. During the Pergamos era the government claimed to be the head of the Church. During the Thyatira era the papacy claimed to be the head. They were both wrong. Jesus is the head of the Church.

Satan undermined the authority of Jesus and his name in the Church, because he didn't want believers to use the authority in the name of Jesus to cast him or his representatives out of the congregation, or expel them from individual members. He discredited Jesus as a person by taking what Jesus said and distorting it. A false doctrine is created by taking revelation knowledge and perverting it. In the process Jesus becomes a liar and his Word becomes untrustworthy. The false doctrines were designed to give the Christendom congregation something to believe that would appease their conscience and allow them to think they were doing the will of God without doing what Jesus said. If a person is suspected of being untruthful, what they say is either ignored altogether, or we doubt them. It is literally impossible to place complete trust in what they say, or to believe them to the point of changing our opinion on any subject to totally agree with theirs.

Jesus is God and what he did and said is revelation knowledge, but if you take that truth and mix it with error or pervert it, the result is doubt, which actually neutralizes faith. Consider what Jesus said about doubt in Matthew

21:21-22, "(21) Jesus answered and said unto them, Verily I say unto you, If ye have faith, and doubt not, ye shall not only do this which is done to the fig tree, but also if ye shall say unto this mountain, Be thou removed, and be thou cast into the sea; it shall be done. (22) And all things, whatsoever ye shall ask in prayer, believing, ye shall receive." The amount of faith needed to move a mountain is given in Matthew 17:14-21, "(14) And when they were come to the multitude, there came to him a certain man, kneeling down to him, and saying, (15) Lord, have mercy on my son: for he is lunatic, and sore vexed: for ofttimes he falleth into the fire, and oft into the water. (16) And I brought him to thy disciples, and they could not cure him. (17) Then Jesus answered and said, O faithless and perverse generation, how long shall I be with you? how long shall I suffer you? bring him hither to me. (18) And Jesus rebuked the devil; and he departed out of him: and the child was cured from that very hour. (19) Then came the disciples to Jesus apart, and said, Why could not we cast him out? (20) And Jesus said unto them, Because of your unbelief: for verily I say unto you, If ye have faith as a grain of mustard seed, ye shall say unto this mountain, Remove hence to yonder place; and it shall remove; and nothing shall be impossible unto you. (21) Howbeit this kind goeth not out but by prayer and fasting." In verse 21:21 Jesus said "and doubt not" and in verse 17:20 "because of your unbelief" so it is easy to see that unbelief and doubt are two things that neutralize faith. If the volume of faith needed to move a mountain is equal to the volume of a mustard seed, we can see what a small amount of faith can do. It is easy to say Jesus could speak to mountains and they would obey because Jesus was God, but remember, Jesus was doing the speaking so it was God who said we could do it by speaking with faith, free of doubt and unbelief.

Jesus never performed a single miracle using the power of his office as the eternal Son of God. The power Jesus used to perform miracles is the same power available to every born-again Church member. That power is the Word of God and the Holy Spirit. Jesus was baptized by John in the Jordan River, at which time the Holy Spirit descended upon him in the form of a dove. It was after this point in the life of Jesus that he began doing miracles. If the Mark 16:17-18 signs are missing in your life or in your congregation, it is because of unbelief or doubt in the Word of God, or the absence of the Holy Spirit which is given in the rebirth. In either case, the situation is correctable, but it must be corrected by you. Our heavenly Father has given us his Word, Jesus, and the Holy Spirit. God isn't going to be giving us anything else, so that makes the next move ours. If your faith is based on a "firm belief in something for which there is no proof" your Christianity is founded on hear-say evidence. Your eternal salvation, or damnation, is too important to chance it to hear-say evidence. If your faith is based on the revealed will of God as recorded in the Holy Scriptures, then your faith and the faith of Jesus is based on the same foundation.

In Hebrews 11:6 we are told that without faith it is impossible to please God. In Romans 10:17 we are told where faith comes from, "So then faith cometh by hearing, and hearing by the word of God." Since God-pleasing faith comes from his Word, is it obvious the absence of his Word is the absence of faith. The faith that pleases God has always been based on what He said, on God's Word, never on a "firm belief in something for which there is no proof." If God said it, he is bound by it, and if God didn't say it, you can forget it. In fact, you *better* forget it. If you say the same thing God says, then both you and God are bound by the same word. You are in agreement with God. If God's Word says one thing, and your words contradict what God says, you are in disagreement with God, which puts you in agreement with Satan. A person who walks, talks, thinks, or believes contrary to the teachings of Jesus is called an antichrist not a Christian. In Amos 3:3 God asks the nation of Israel to consider a question, "Can two walk together, except they be agreed?" The difference between the nation of Israel walking with God or contrary to God can be seen in Leviticus chapter 26 and their history. They didn't get away with it and neither will the Church. During the Pergamos church era many false doctrines were introduced into Christendom. Some were condemned, but others were tolerated, and later became traditions. The only way to separate tradition from the factual Word of God is to get yourself a copy of the Bible and read it for yourself.

Although many errors were introduced into Christendom during the Pergamos church era, there was a portion of the congregation that remained faithful to Jesus and his teachings, "thou holdest fast my name, and hast not denied my faith." Since Jesus was doing the speaking, the pronoun "my" represents Jesus, so we could read the statement, "thou holdest fast Jesus' name, and hast not denied Jesus' faith." As we have already seen, faith comes from the Word of God, so Jesus' faith was based on the revealed will of his Father, as recorded in the Old Testament Scriptures. In John 5:39 Jesus said they testified of him, "Search the scriptures; for in them ye think ye have eternal life: and they are they which testify of me." Jesus was the promised Redeemer, so the New Testament portion of the Scriptures is the fulfillment of that promise. The New Testament is the record God gave us of his Son, 1 John 5:10, "He that believeth on the Son of God hath the witness in himself: he that believeth not God hath made him a liar; because he believeth not the record that God gave of his Son."

Those who reject Jesus are lost and in John 3:36 we are told the wrath of God abides on them, "He that believeth on the Son hath everlasting life: and he that believeth not the Son shall not see life; but the wrath of God abideth on him." How they reject Jesus is through unbelief in "the record that God gave of his Son" (1 John 5:10), or they refuse to believe the words of Jesus. In John 12:48 Jesus said those who refuse his words will be judged by those same words in the last day, "He that rejecteth me, and receiveth not my words, hath one that judgeth him: the word that I have spoken, the same shall judge him in the last day." If we sincerely believe Jesus, we are going to be obedient and do what he says, the way he says to do it. Jesus expects us to be doers of his Word and not hearers only. That's the difference between building a house on a rock foundation or dirt foundation. Luke 6:46-49, "(46) And why call ye me, Lord, Lord, and do not the things which I say? (47) Whosoever cometh to me, and heareth my sayings, and doeth them, I will shew you to whom he is like: (48) He is like a man which built an house, and digged deep, and laid the foundation on a rock: and when the flood arose, the stream beat vehemently upon that house, and could not shake it: for it was founded upon a rock. (49) But he that heareth, and doeth not, is like a man that without a foundation built an house upon the earth; against which the stream did beat vehemently, and immediately it fell; and the ruin of that house was great."

If you hear the words of Jesus and reject them through unbelief, your eternal salvation is in question. If you hear the words of Jesus and refuse to obey, your faith is in question, because you are neutralizing it through doubt. It is impossible to please God without faith (Hebrews 11:6) and the only kind of faith that pleases God is Bible faith, or literally, the faith that comes from his Word (Romans 10:17). Bible faith is the total and complete trust in the Word of God. There are many similarities between belief and faith but they are not the same thing. Faith is a spiritual force, but belief is a mental force.

One of the things of God is his Word, and the carnal mind has trouble with The Word because God is a spirit and so is his Word. In John 6:63 Jesus said, "It is the spirit that quickeneth; the flesh profiteth nothing: the words that I speak unto you, they are spirit, and they are life." The natural man is spiritually dead, which is why he cannot hear or understand the spiritual things of God. When a person is born-again the Holy Spirit enters his body and unites with his human spirit, to create a new creature. This spiritual birth is just as real as our physical birth, and the new creature resulting from the rebirth is as different as a child and its parents. This new creation has the ability to understand the spiritual things of God, hungers for his Word, and desires to do those things which please its heavenly Father. As the newborn feeds on the Word of God, he grows in the knowledge of Jesus Christ and his faith increases. He begins to see the Word of God as a weapon, not only the sword of the Holy Spirit, but the sword of his own spirit. As the newborn grows, the control center of his affairs changes from the old dead spirit received in his physical birth to the new living spirit he received in his rebirth. This new living spirit is capable of trusting God and his Word; recognizes Satan as the enemy, sin as sin, and the truth as the truth. The natural man would be as much out of place in heaven as the born-again believer is in this world.

The natural man is motivated by the desires of the flesh, the lusts of the soul, and is controlled by a human spirit who is dead toward God, his Word, and his ways, but very much alive toward Satan, his word, and his ways. This is why the natural man can see, understand, and believe in the things of this world, but the things of God are foolishness to him. Since faith comes from the Word of God, it is easy to see why the natural man has no God-pleasing faith. Since they view the Word of God as foolishness, they also view faith as foolishness. This is why the evolutionist rejects the Bible account of the creation as foolishness. When they say mother nature was the creator, the born-again believer says foolishness. When the born-again believer says Jesus was the creator, the evolutionist says foolishness. When the born-again believer explains Jesus accomplished the creation of the physical universe by speaking it into existence, the evolutionists are highly insulted. The problem is not that the evolutionists are born-again believers with a different point of view. The problem is they are neither born-again, nor are they believers, which is obvious when you listen to them calling God a liar by the words coming out of their mouth. They have rejected what God said, so they are without the faith and understanding of a born-again believing child of God, Hebrews 11:3, "Through faith we understand that the worlds were framed by the word of God, so that things which are seen were not made of things which do appear."

In Hebrews 11:1 we are told, "Now faith is the substance of things hoped for, the evidence of things not seen," and the chapter continues with examples of faith. When Jesus spoke the physical universe into existence, he called things which be not, as though they were, and they were. In Genesis 3:3, "And God said, Let there be light: and there was light." That's the way God operates, and that's the way faith operates. In Romans chapter 4 we are told Abraham's success was that he learned this principle of faith. God had made a promise to Abraham that he would have a son, and be the father of many nations through his son. When God made this promise Abraham was childless, and the only evidence he had was God's Word. When you understand faith, you will see that Abraham could have nullified the Word of God by speaking these words: "God promised me a son and I really believed him, but I am old now and my wife is past the age of childbearing, so I doubt if we ever have a son." How Abraham handled the situation is given in Romans 4:17-22, "(17) (As it is written, I have made thee a father of many nations,) before him whom he believed, even God, who quickeneth the dead, and calleth those things which be not as though they were. (18) Who against hope believed in hope, that he might become the father of many nations, according to that which was spoken, So shall thy seed be. (19) And being not weak in faith, he considered not his own body now dead, when he was about an hundred years old, neither yet the deadness of Sarah's womb: (20) He staggered not at the promise of God through unbelief; but was strong in faith, giving glory to God; (21) And being fully persuaded that, what he had promised, he was able also to perform. (22) And therefore it was imputed to him for righteousness."

In John 12:49 Jesus told us that he said only what the Father told him to say, "For I have not spoken of myself; but the Father which sent me, he gave me a commandment, what I should say, and what I should speak." The faith of Jesus was in his Father's Word. Since a Christian is a person who believes and follows the teachings of Jesus Christ their testimony is, "For I have not spoken of myself; but Jesus Christ which sent me, he gave me a commandment, what I should say, and what I should speak." Since we have a written record of what Jesus said and taught, we can compare what anyone says and teaches to that written record, and determine if they are in agreement with Jesus or contradicting Him. If they contradict what Jesus said and taught, they are antichrist, not Christians. When they contradict what Jesus said and taught, no matter how politely it is done, they are implying that Jesus is an untrustworthy liar. The contradiction should communicate to you that the person doing the speaking does not believe what Jesus said and taught, for if they believed Jesus they would be saying the same thing He said, not contradicting him. The contradictor is trying to turn you away from Jesus. If you follow the contradictor, you are denying Jesus. The synonym of contradict is deny. The contradictor has already denied Jesus, and if you believe and follow them you will also be denying Jesus. There is no neutral ground when it comes to Jesus. In Luke 11:23 Jesus said, "He that is not with me is against me: and he that gathereth not with me scattereth."

If we are living by the Word of God, we are living by faith. Christians demonstrate their faith both by what they do and what they don't do, what they say and what they don't say. Negative confessions or actions are contrary to the revealed will of God, while positive confessions or actions are in agreement with the revealed will of God. With negative reactions we limit the power of God and release Satan, which gives him the legal right to make our confessions a reality in our lives. With positive reactions we limit Satan and release the power of God, which gives him the legal right to make them a reality in our lives. Anything, any of us have from God, we have gotten through his word in the form of revelation knowledge or a promise. When we accepted that information as the truth, Satan was permitted to test us to determine our faithfulness to that truth in the baptism of fire. We can see the result of that judgment in the change in what a person says and does. When someone claims to have accepted Jesus as their Savior and Lord, they don't go around calling him a liar. Liars are on their way to hell, not heaven, Rev. 21:7-8, "(7) He that overcometh shall inherit all things; and I will be his God, and he shall be my son. (8) But the fearful, and unbelieving, and the abominable, and murders, and whoremongers, and sorcerers, and idolaters, and all liars, shall have their part in the lake which burneth with fire and brimstone: which is the second death." If you had to say what Jesus just said, could you have made it any plainer? Don't be led astray. You can trust what Jesus said. The overcomers are on their way to heaven, and the rest of that group are on their way to hell.

The Church is the Bride of Christ, but during this era she entered into a bigamy marriage with the state. Because Satan had political control of the government, he was able to use the power of the government to force the

Church into accepting the entire population of the Roman Empire as fellow Christians. The government did not force the population into becoming born-again believers, only church members. This single move changed the concept of Church and Christian. From God's viewpoint, the Church is the body of Christ, which is made up of born-again believers called Christians. From the government's viewpoint, the Church was the building, and the people inside the building were all Christians.

d. REBUKE: Some had the doctrine of Balaam and the Nicolaitanes.
Rev. 2:14-15, "(14) But I have a few things against thee, because thou hast there them that hold the doctrine of Balaam, who taught Balac to cast a stumbling block before the children of Israel, to eat things sacrificed unto idols, and to commit fornication. (15) So hast thou also them that hold the doctrine of the Nicolaitanes, which thing I hate."

The church in Pergamos was rebuked because some of its members held two false doctrines: the doctrine of Balaam, and the doctrine of the Nicolaitanes. The doctrine of Balaam taught: to cast stumbling blocks; to eat things sacrificed unto idols; and to commit fornication.

The historical record of Balaam and Balac is recorded in Numbers chapters 22 through 25. The doctrine of Balaam is Satanic in origin, so it reappears throughout Israel's history and the history of Christendom. Basically, "to cast stumbling blocks" is to teach errors and false doctrines, which causes God's people to stumble over the truth and fall short of God's promises, blessings, and provisions. They can be interjected into the intellect portion of the human soul by erroneous secular knowledge, or in the human spirit by perverting revelation knowledge. To understand the effects, consider what happens when something is placed in front of a physically blind person, which by the way is forbidden, Leviticus 19:14, "Thou shalt not curse the deaf, nor put a stumbling block before the blind, but shalt fear thy God: I am the Lord." The danger is the same regardless of whether it is spirit, soul, or body. Satan does not obey the commandments of God, so you can be sure the obstacles are there. The physically blind person has no way to see the danger of the obstacle placed in front of him, and may not know of it until he trips, falls, and perhaps gets hurt. It's too late then. We have a written record of the Word of God, so if we trip and fall spiritually or mentally we are without excuse. In Matthew 23:13-39 Jesus condemned the religious leaders for this very thing. He begins in verse 13 by saying, "But woe unto you, scribes and Pharisees, hypocrites! for ye shut up the kingdom of heaven against men: for ye neither go in yourselves, neither suffer ye them that are entering to go in." In verse 17 he called them blind fools, in verse 24 blind guides, and listen to verse 33, "Ye serpents, ye generation of vipers, how can ye escape the damnation of hell?"

"To eat things sacrificed unto idols" basically means to substitute the things of Satan for the things of God. It is deadly to feed your spirit perverted revelation knowledge. In Romans 8:6 we are told, "For to be carnally minded is death," so secular knowledge that contradicts revelation knowledge is just as harmful to your mind. To pursue and fulfill the lusts of the soul and desires of our physical bodies unrestrained by the commandments of God is to turn from the living God to eat things sacrificed to idols. Israel built and bowed the knee to literal idols, but the sin was that God told them "Thou shalt not" (Exodus 20:1-6), and they did it anyway. You don't have to worship a literal idol to be guilty of idolatry. Anything you exalt above God is your idol. Anything that comes between you and the revealed will of God is an idol. Satan wants us to eat the things he offers, not feed on the Word of God. If you won't eat the substitute, Satan is going to try to feed you compromise, and one is just as bad as the other.

The strategy used by Satan in the Garden of Eden to separate God from the human body was introduced into Christianity during the Pergamos era to prevent the Holy Spirit from reuniting with the human spirit. The members who ate Satan's junk remained spiritually dead, and in the process Christianity was changed from a victorious way of life to a unique paid-up fire insurance policy against going to hell at death. Without spiritual discernment Satan was also able to pervert revelation knowledge to something they could understand with the carnal mind, perceive as the truth, and put into their spirit to govern their religious worship. The absence of the Holy Spirit indwelling the human spirit restricts our worship to mental psychic, or soul worship, which is actually Satan worship. The only worship that is acceptable to God is the worship that comes from the spirit of a born-again person. "God is a Spirit: and they that worship him must worship him in spirit and in truth" (John 4:24).

Humans under the guidance of Satan and his demons brought humanism, intellectualism, and emotionalism into Christianity. Humanism says we humans can do it ourselves through self-improvement or self-sacrifice, and rejects all spiritual intervention, even to the point of denying the existence of spirits. Intellectualism says we are improving ourselves, and the human race, through education without realizing that reasoning rejects revelation knowledge. Emotionalism introduced personal feelings, which become the foundation on which appeals could be made to motivate and control the congregation. Appealing to human emotions, guilt feelings, fear tactics, and natural affections could be used to shame individuals into obedience. These are part of the doctrine of the Nicolaitanes or "people-controllers" which were hated by Jesus and the Churches in the Ephesus Era as we saw in Rev. 2:6. When the substitution is completed, worshipping God, in spirit and in truth, is replaced by unacceptable soul worship. Instead of the congregation being controlled spiritually by the Holy Spirit and the Word of God, they were controlled mentally by the Nicolaitanes and their doctrines. The Nicolaitanes then divided the congregation by making themselves the ruling clergy, and the people obedient layman.

The Pergamos congregation was rebuked because some held the doctrine of Balaam, which was to teach to cast stumbling blocks (errors which cause people to stumble over the truth); to eat things sacrificed unto idols (in essence to substitute the things of Satan for the things of God); and to commit fornication. As we have already seen, to commit spiritual fornication is to turn from worshipping God to worshipping something else. In both the spiritual and physical sense it means to turn from obedience to the revealed will of God. God revealed his will to Israel in the law and when they broke the Commandments God charged them with whoredom. One of the things forbidden by law was intermarriages between Israelites and Non-Israelites, or more specifically, covenant people with non-covenant people. This separation can be seen in Deuteronomy chapter 7.

Israelites are descendants of Abraham and were (and still are) covenant people because of the covenant God made to Abraham (Deuteronomy 7:6-9, 9:3-6). In review, God told Abram to leave his country and go to a land that God would show him (Genesis 12:1-7). Abram moved on the Word of God by faith and because he was obedient, God confirmed the promises by a covenant (Genesis 15:1-21, 17:1-27). Among other things, Abraham's descendants were to inherit the promised land, a piece of real estate that extended from the river of Egypt to the river Euphrates (Genesis 13:14-17, 15:18-21). God by the mouth of Moses gave specific instructions as to the treatment of the inhabitants of the promised land, Deuteronomy 7:1-3, "(1) When the Lord thy God shall bring thee into the land whither thou goest to possess it, and hath cast out many nations before thee, the Hittites, and the Girgashites, and the Amorites, and the Canaanites, and the Perizzites, and the Hivites, and the Jebusites, seven nations greater and mightier than thou; (2) And when the Lord thy God shall deliver them before thee; thou shalt smite them, thou shalt utterly destroy them; thou shalt make no covenant with them, nor shew mercy unto them: (3) Neither shalt thou make marriages with them; thy daughter thou shalt not give unto his son, nor his daughter shalt thou take unto thy son." The Israelites, led by Joshua, entered the promised land during the dispensation of law, but failed to do as God directed. Their failures are recorded in the first three chapters of the Book of Judges. Instead of destroying the inhabitants, the Israelites dwelt among them, Judges 3:5-7, "(5) And the children of Israel dwelt among the Canaanites, Hittites, and Amorites, and Perizzites, and Hivites, and Jebusites: (6) And they took their daughters to be their wives, and gave their daughters to their sons, and served their gods. (7) And the children of Israel did evil in the sight of the Lord, and forgat the Lord their God, and served Baalim and the groves."

Several passages refer to the real estate covenant as an everlasting covenant, which means that this property is given to Abraham's descendants as an everlasting possession. Genesis 17:7-8, "(7) And I will make thee exceeding fruitful, and I will make nations of thee, and kings shall come out of thee. (7) And I will establish my covenant between me and thee and thy seed after thee in their generations for an everlasting covenant, to be a God unto thee, and to thy seed after thee. (8) And I will give unto thee, and to thy seed after thee, the land wherein thou art a stranger, all the land of Canaan, for an everlasting possession; and I will be their God." Genesis 48:3-4, "(3) And Jacob said unto Joseph, God Almighty appeared unto me at Luz in the land of Canaan, and blessed me, (4) And said unto me, Behold, I will make thee fruitful, and multiply thee, and I will make of thee a multitude of people; and will give this land to thy seed after thee for an everlasting possession." 1 Chronicles 16:15-19, "(15) Be ye mindful always of his covenant; the word which he commanded to a thousand generations; (16) Even of the covenant which he made with Abraham, and of his oath unto Isaac; (17) And hath confirmed the same to Jacob for a law, and to Israel for an everlasting covenant, (18) Saying, Unto thee will I give the land of Canaan, the lot of your inheritance; (19) When ye were but few, even a few, and strangers in it."

When God promises something and says it is everlasting, we do not need to question when it will end. It will never end. People responding in obedience to the gospel during the Church Dispensation are promised everlasting life. I am amazed at the number of people who say their promise of everlasting life means everlasting, but the everlasting covenant God made with Abraham and his descendants does not mean everlasting. The disobedience of Abraham's descendants cannot nullify the promises made to Abraham any more than the disobedience of a church member can nullify God's promise of everlasting life to born-again believers. The believer's everlasting life is based on the righteousness of Jesus Christ, not his own righteousness. The promises made to Abraham's descendants were based on the righteousness God credited to Abraham, not the righteousness of his descendants. The real estate covenant will find its fulfillment in the Kingdom dispensation after the Church dispensation ends and it is on the horizon.

In this truth, the doctrine of Balaam does much damage. The real estate covenant, as well as the Jews being a covenant people is unconditional, but their presence in the promised land and their receiving of the blessings listed in Deuteronomy 7:12-26 is conditional, based on their obedience to the law. In Deuteronomy 11:26-28 the conditional part of the covenant is presented as a blessing or a curse, "(26) Behold, I set before you this day a blessing and a curse; (27) A blessing, if ye obey the commandments of the Lord your God, which I command you this day: (28) And a curse, if ye will not obey the commandments of the Lord your God, but turn aside out of the way which I command you this day, to go after other gods, which ye have not known." (Also see Deuteronomy 28:1-68). Israel believed (and they still do) the unconditional part of the covenant, but they stumbled over the conditional blessing or curse portion. They erroneously thought that because they were covenant people they could sin and not have to worry about God judging their sins. A look at their history shows how wrong they were.

Many Christians today are making the same error. The unconditional part of the New Covenant to the Church centers on the work of Jesus as the Redeemer–his suffering, death, burial, and resurrection. Because of the work of Jesus, this covenant is available to every individual on Earth, the "whosoever" of John 3:16, "whosoever will come" of Rev. 22:17, and "He that believeth and is baptized shall be saved" (Mark 16:16). The conditional part of the New Covenant can be seen in Matthew 7:21, "Not everyone that saith unto me, Lord, Lord, shall enter into the kingdom of heaven; but he that doeth the will of my Father which is in heaven." The "why" is recorded in Luke 6:46, "And why call ye me, Lord, Lord, and do not the thing which I say." The unconditional part of the New Covenant centers on "the work" of Jesus, while the conditional part centers on "the way" of Jesus, or more accurately, our obedience to the way He told us to go, what He told us to do, and the way He told us to do it. Whosoever will come can be born again and receive the Holy Spirit, but again, it is conditional based on our obedience to the Word, John 14:15-16, "(15) If ye love me, keep my commandments. (16) And I will pray the Father, and he shall give you another Comforter, that he may abide with you for ever;" That indwelling Holy Spirit is what makes the Christian a covenant person. It is our seal now and unto the day of redemption, Ephesians 4:30, "And grieve not the holy Spirit of God, whereby ye are sealed unto the day of redemption."

In Matthew 22:14 Jesus made this statement, "For many are called, but few are chosen" Many called but few chosen: The question is, What did the few chosen do or have that the many called missed? The answer is recorded in Rev. 17:14, "These (Antichrist and his ten-king kingdom) shall make war with the Lamb, and the Lamb shall overcome them: for he is Lord of lords, and King of kings: and they that are with him are called, and chosen, and faithful." The few were chosen because they were faithful. God has given us his will in his Word and Jesus communicates our faithfulness to his will in the results of the daily baptisms of fire. Ignoring the will of God or ignoring the test results will not change the facts. If you are going to be a Christian who dwells in the promised land (Heaven) and enjoys the blessings and provisions of God (on earth), it will cost you something, and that something is your sins. To think you can have them both is to be deceived by the doctrine of Balaam. When we ignore or turn from the revealed will of God to conform to the world, we actually make ourselves enemies of God, James 4:4, "Ye adulterers and adulteresses, know ye not that the friendship of the world is enmity with God? whosoever therefore will be a friend of the world is the enemy of God."

The "way of Balaam," cited in 2 Peter 2:15, concerns knowing the will of God and instead of letting the Word of God settle the issue once and forever, it is brought before God repeatedly in an attempt to get him to change or alter his Word. It is not only a waste of time, it makes God angry. In Psalms 119:89 we are told, "Forever, O Lord, thy word is settled in heaven." 2 Peter chapter 2 deals with false prophets and the damnable heresies they privately or secretly bring into Christendom. In verses 14-17 we are told they have gone astray to follow the way of Balaam, "(14) Having eyes full of adultery, and that cannot cease from sin; beguiling unstable souls: an heart they have exercised with covetous practices; cursed children: (15) Which have forsaken the right way, and are gone astray, following the way of Balaam the son of Bosor, who loved the wages of unrighteousness; (16) But was rebuked for his iniquity: the dumb ass speaking with man's voice forbad the madness of the prophet. (17) These are wells without water, clouds that are carried with a tempest; to whom the mist of darkness is reserved for ever." Balak, king of the Moabites (Numbers 22:1-4) feared the nation of Israel so he hired Balaam, a soothsayer, or diviner (Joshua 13:22), to put a curse on them (Joshua 24:9-10). In Numbers 22:5 Balak sends messengers to Balaam "with the rewards of divination in their hands" (verse 7) to persuade him to come and curse Israel. In verse 8 Balaam told the messengers to lodge with him that night while he sought God's will on the matter. In verses 9-11 God and Balaam discuss the matter and in verse 12, "God said unto Balaam, Thou shalt not go with them; thou shalt not curse the people: for they are blessed." The next morning Balaam (verses 13-14) sends the messengers home, "Get you into your land: for the Lord refuseth to give me leave to go with you." That should have ended the matter. Balaam had the Word of God and in that word, the will of God was unquestionable clear.

In Numbers 22:15, "And Balak sent yet again princes, more and more honourable than they" to Balaam in a second attempt to get him to come and curse the nation of Israel. Instead of Balaam sending them home with the words, "God's will is clear on the subject, I will not go with you and I will not curse Israel" he tells them, in verse 18, "I cannot go beyond the word of the Lord my God, to do less or more" and invites them to spend the night. In his actions it is clear that Balaam has already decided to ignore the revealed will of God, and in approaching God the second time on the same subject, all he was doing was trying to get God to change His mind. Notice Balaam had not decided to ignore all of God's will, only part of it. In Numbers 22:12 God told him, "Thou shalt not go with them" and "thou shalt not curse the people: for they are blessed." What Balaam said with his mouth is "I can't curse the people" and with his actions "It is my will to go with you." The additional honorable princes sent by Balac may have impressed Balaam, but the promise of honor and riches is what moved him, Numbers 22:17, "For I will promote thee unto very great honor, and I will do whatsoever thou sayest unto me: come therefore, I pray thee, curse me this people." This is the "error of Balaam" cited in Jude 1:11, "Woe unto them! for they have gone in the way of Cain, and ran greedily after the error of Balaam for reward, and perished in the gainsaying of Core." The subject in Jude is the apostate and one of their errors is that they use the Church and Christianity to acquire personal status or gain.

In Numbers 22:20 God told Balaam to go ahead, "but yet the word which I shall say unto thee, that shalt thou do." God didn't change his mind in the sense of saying don't go, then do go. The one who had a change of mind was Balaam. He didn't go with the first messengers Balak sent, but the second group changed his mind. This was the reason for God's anger in Numbers 22:22, "And God's anger was kindled because he went: and the angel of the Lord stood in the way for an adversary against him." After a discussion with his donkey (Numbers 22:23-41), Balaam meets Balak and tries three times to curse the nation of Israel. The first attempt to curse them is recorded in Numbers 23:1-13, the second in 23:14-26, and the third in 23:27-24:25. Each time God turned the curse into a blessing, Deuteronomy 23:1-6, Joshua 24:9-10, and Nehemiah 13:1-3. What Balaam and Balak learned was that Israel was a covenant people, and because of that covenant, God would not allow them to be cursed.

The same truth applies to members who have entered into the new Church Covenant through the rebirth. If a curse, black magic spell, or whatever, is spoken secretly against a born-again believer, God nullifies the curse. If the curse is spoken within hearing of the born-again believer, he is responsible to nullify it by refusing to accept it. Any negative response spoken by the born-again believer against the curse or curser will nullify it. If the curser is persistent tell them, "In the name of Jesus I bind you and your curse," then walk away and forget it. No one or no thing is above the Word of God or the authority of the name of Jesus. When you bind the curser or the curse in the name of Jesus, you are operating on the highest authority in the universe, and every authority is subject to the higher authority. When you rebuke a curser you nullify their power "because greater is he that is in you, then he that is in the world," or in the curser (1 John 4:4). Your words reveal your will and God honors the will of his children. Listen to Jesus in Matthew 18:18-19, "(18) Verily I say unto you, Whatsoever ye shall bind on earth shall be bound in heaven: and whatsoever ye shall loose on earth shall be loosed in heaven. (19) Again I say unto you, That if two of you shall agree on earth as touching any thing that they shall ask, it shall be done for them of my Father which is in heaven." On the other hand, if a born-again believer hears the curse and keeps his mouth shut, he confirms the curse. You can see this principle in Numbers Chapter 30 which deals with vows and oaths spoken by the lower authority and nullified or confirmed by the higher authority.

A vow or oath is a prophecy because it is something we speak in reference to a thing we are going to try to bring to pass. A curse or spell is a prophecy because it is something someone else predicts is going to happen to us in the future. When we think of spells and curses we usually think of sorcery, or one of the other Deuteronomy 18:9-14 forbidden practices, but damaging prophecies are not restricted to our enemies. In fact, the most damaging prophecies are the ones we speak against ourselves and our friends confirm, or our friends speak and we confirm. For example, we may wake up one morning feeling a little tired and comment to our spouse, "I don't feel too good today."

They respond with, "You look a little under the weather. The flu is going around, guess the bug got you."

We confirm the prophecy by adding, "Bill hasn't been to work all week because of the flu, guess I better call in sick today and go back to bed." Then we return to bed and catch the flu. When we realize we caught the flu from words, not people, we began to understand the power of words. In this example, Satan used the tongue of the spouse to suggest the flu as a remedy for your tired feeling, and you accepted the flu by responding favorably to that suggestion. Most of us will never meet a black magic witch doctor face to face, but we all face this situation every day. Innocent comments are not innocent if they instill fear or they are designed to steal, kill, or destroy.

Many times advice is nothing more than a prophecy. We seek advice today in order to change the future or to protect something we value in the future. A couple facing marital problems seeks the advice of a marriage counselor in hopes of making changes today to avoid a divorce in the future. A person about to invest money in the stock market seeks the advice of a broker in hopes of making a good investment today so they won't lose their money in the future. Regardless of whether we seek council, or receive unasked for advice, we need to consider the counselor before we consider their advice. The first question is whether the person is "of God" (a born-again believer) or of Satan (a non-believer). In doing this, you determine the source of the advice, and if it is "of Satan" disregard it as totally useless. If the counselor is "of God," compare his advice to the revealed will of God, and if the advice agrees with the Word, proceed with thanksgiving. Just because advice sounds good, appears intelligent, or seems logical, doesn't make it good advice.

Consider some advice given to Nehemiah. He returns to Jerusalem to rebuild the wall which was destroyed during the Babylonian invasion. Needless to say, Satan also had his crew on the scene to resist the efforts of Nehemiah. Their names were Sanballat and Tobiah. In Nehemiah 2:10 we find, "it grieved them exceedingly that there was come a man to seek the welfare of the children of Israel." In 2:17-20 Nehemiah reveals his intentions, and in verse 2:19 we are given the enemy reaction, "But when Sanballat the Horonite, and Tobiah the servant, the Ammonite, and Geshem the Arabian, heard it, they laughed us to scorn, and despised us, and said, What is this thing that ye do? will ye rebel against the king?" The restoration of the wall begins and in verse 4:1 we are given the enemy reaction, "But it came to pass, that when Sanballat heard that we builded the wall, he was wroth, and took great indignation, and mocked the Jews." In 4:8 they tried to raise an army to stop the restoration by force, "And conspired all of them together to come and to fight against Jerusalem, and to hinder it." When that failed they decided on sneak attacks, Neh. 4:11, "And our adversaries said, They shall not know, neither see, till we come in the midst among them, and slay them, and cause the work to cease." Work on the wall continued, with the laborers carrying a weapon in one hand and working with the other. In Nehemiah 6:1-4 they tried four times to lure Nehemiah into a conference away from the safety of Jerusalem to kill him. In Nehemiah 6:5-9 they threaten to report his efforts to restore the wall as a means of rebelling against the government, but Nehemiah refuses to meet with them to discuss the matter. In Nehemiah 6:10 he receives some advice, "Afterward I (Nehemiah) came unto the house of Shemaiah the son of Delaiah the son of Mehetabeel, who was shut up; and he said, Let us meet together in the house of God, within the temple, and let us shut the doors of the temple: for they will come to slay thee; yea, in the night will they come to slay thee." Nehemiah knew his enemies were trying to kill him, so at a glance the suggestion seemed to be good advice. If they would barricade themselves in the temple, a sneak attack would be impossible, and it would be most difficult for his enemies to catch him sleeping and kill him. The only problem was that if Nehemiah had acted on that advice, he would have been killed by Shemaiah. The source of the advice was Satan, the advisor was "of Satan," and the advice was a "prophecy" designed to destroy Nehemiah. He refused to react to fear and nullified the prophecy, Nehemiah 6:11-14, "(11) And I (Nehemiah) said, Should such a man as I flee? and who is there, that, being as I am, would go into the temple to save his life? I will not go in. (12) And, lo, I perceived that God had not sent him; but that he pronounced this prophecy against me: for Tobiah and Sanballat had hired him. (13) Therefore was he hired, that I should be afraid, and do so, and sin, and that they might have matter for an evil report, that they might reproach me. (14) My God, think thou upon Tobiah and Sanballat according to these their works, and on the prophetess Noadiah, and the rest of the prophets, that would have put me in fear."

When we left the historical account of Balaam and Balak in Numbers chapter 24 Balaam had tried three times to curse the children of Israel, and each time God turned the curse into a blessing. In verse 24:25 they part company and go home, "And Balaam rose up, and went and returned to his place: and Balak also went his way." If we would stop here it would appear that Balaam was unable to do damage to Israel. Both Balaam and Balak had learned that God would not allow his covenant people to be secretly cursed, but what is not visible at this point is that Balaam gave Balak some advice before they parted company. We do not have a record of the actual discussion, but from the events which followed we can see the council of Balaam. Balak feared the children of Israel and wanted to destroy them. He knew he could not defeat them in open warfare, so he hired Balaam to curse them. When God would not allow them to be secretly cursed, Balaam's advice to

Balak was to entice them into sinning against their God, and then their own God would curse them. Before we look at the results of the council of Balaam, let's look at some advice God gave to the children of Israel in Exodus 34:11-17, "(11) Observe thou that which I command thee this day: behold, I drive out before thee the Amorite, and the Canaanite, and the Hittite, and the Perizzite, and the Hivite, and the Jebusite. (12) Take heed to thyself, lest thou make a covenant with the inhabitants of the land whither thou goest, lest it be for a snare in the midst of thee: (13) But ye shall destroy their altars, break their images, and cut down their groves: (14) For thou shalt worship no other god: for the Lord, whose name is Jealous, is a jealous God: (15) Lest thou make a covenant with the inhabitants of the land, and they go a whoring after their gods, and do sacrifice unto their gods, and one call thee, and thou eat of his sacrifice; (16) And thou take of their daughters unto thy sons, and their daughters go a whoring after their gods, and make thy sons go a whoring after their gods. (17) Thou shalt make thee no molten gods."

God is the source of this advice, so Israel did not have to worry about whether it was good or bad advice. Nor did Israel need to wonder what would happen if they ignored the advice. This advice was given to protect Israel from danger, not to deprive them of something. The nations listed in Exodus 34:11 were enemies of God because they had chosen to reject revelation knowledge and align themselves with Satan. Israel needed to view the inhabitants of the promise land the same way God viewed them. The enemies were to be resisted, defeated, and driven out of the land. Their ideology as well as their idolatries were to be totally ignored, destroyed, and forgotten. If Israel made any covenants, the compromise would be a snare and result in future problems. If the covenant was a covenant of marriage, the inevitable result would be that the spouse would eventually turn the Israelite from obeying the true God to a life of disobedience and ruin. It was good advice then, and it is still good advice. If a born-again believer thinks he can join himself to a non-believer in marriage and live the more abundant life, he is deceiving himself. The same truth can be applied to the local Church congregation or to Christendom as a whole. Any Church organization or congregation that thinks it can operate effectively on a mixture of revelation knowledge and worldly ideology needs to compare what is happening in its midst to what Jesus said would happen in Mark 16:17-18.

The Moabites and the Midianites are not listed in the nations cited in Exodus 34:11 to be driven out of the promised land, because their dwelling place was on the west side of the Dead Sea. In reality, they were between Israel in the wilderness and Israel in the promised land. The Midianites were descendants of Midian, the son of Abraham and his concubine Keturah (Genesis 25:1-6). The Moabites were descendants of Lot and his oldest daughter (Genesis 19:30-38). Both had rejected the God of Abraham and Lot for the idol god Baal, worshipped as a deity by the Canaanites.

They renamed the idol god Baal-peor, but the demon and ideology are the same. The literal meaning of the Hebrew word *peor* is "a gap" or "opening," so the name of Baal-peor is actually "Lord of the gap." The word *peor* comes from the root word *paar* which means "to yawn," or literally, to "open wide." Our society has renamed Baal-peor, "New Morality," but the ideology is the same. Sexual gratification unrestrained by the commandments of God is immorality, and there is nothing new about it. The saddest parts of a nation worshipping Baal-peor are the unwanted conceptions, which end in mass murder. The early worshipers of Baal-peor didn't have our modern methods of abortion, so they waited until birth, put the baby in a jar or burnt it as a sacrifice to the idol. Today you are entitled to your private opinions, but when you stand in judgment before the One who said "Thou shalt not kill," your private opinion will mean absolutely nothing.

Twenty-four thousand men in Israel died because they refused to heed the good advice God provided in Exodus 34:11-17, and got snared in the counsel of Balaam. The word "And" in Numbers chapter 25 connects it with chapter 24 which ends with Balaam and Balak parting company. Numbers 25:1-9, "(1) And Israel abode in Shittim, and the people began to commit whoredom with the daughters of Moab. (2) And they called the people unto the sacrifices of their gods: and the people did eat, and bowed down to their gods. (3) And Israel joined himself unto Baal-peor: and the anger of the Lord was kindled against Israel. (4) And the Lord said unto Moses, Take all the heads of the people, and hang them up before the Lord against the sun, that the fierce anger of the Lord may be turned away from Israel. (5) And Moses said unto the judges of Israel, Slay ye every one his men that were joined unto Baal-peor. (6) And, behold, one of the children of Israel came and brought unto his brethren a Midianitish woman in the sight of Moses, and in the sight of all the congregation of the children of Israel, who were weeping before the door of the tabernacle of the congregation. (7) And when Phinehas, the son of Eleazar, the son of Aaron the priest, saw it, he rose up from among the congregation, and took a javelin in his hand; (8) And he went after the man of Israel into the tent, and thrust both of them through, the man of Israel, and the woman through her belly. So the plague was stayed from the children of Israel. (9) And those that died in the plague were twenty and four thousand."

The council of Balaam cost him his life, in Numbers chapter 31, when the Lord told Moses to avenge the children of Israel of the Midianites. If you are still uncertain as to God's feeling on sexual immorality consider His treatment of the Midianites. Numbers 31:1-18, "(1) And the Lord spake unto Moses, saying, (2) Avenge the children of Israel of the Midianites: afterward shalt thou be gathered unto thy people. (3) And Moses spake unto the people, saying, Arm some of yourselves unto the war, and let them go against the Midianites, and avenge the Lord of Midian. (4) Of every tribe a thousand, throughout all the tribes of Israel, shall ye send to the war. (5) So there were delivered out of the thousands of Israel, a thousand of every tribe, twelve thousand armed for war. (6) And Moses sent them to the war, a thousand of every tribe, them and Phinehas, the son of Eleazar the priest, to the war, with the holy instruments, and the trumpet to blow in his hand. (7) And they warred against the Midianites, as the Lord commanded Moses; and they slew all the males. (8) And they slew the kings of Midian, beside the rest of them that were slain; namely, Evi, and Rekem, and Zur, and Hur, and Reba, Five kings of Midian: Balaam also the son of Beor they slew with the sword. (9) And the children of Israel took all the women of Midian captives, and their little ones, and took the spoils of all their cattle, and all their flocks, and all their goods. (10) And they burnt all their cities wherein they dwelt, and all their goodly castles, with fire. (11) And they took all the spoil, and all the prey, both of men and of beasts. (12) And they brought the captives, and the prey, and the spoil, unto Moses, and Eleazar the priest, and unto the congregation of the children of Israel, unto the camp at the plains of Moab, which are by Jordan near Jericho. (13) And Moses, and Eleazar the priest, and all the princes of the congregation, went forth to meet them without the camp. (14) And Moses was wroth with the officers of the host, with the captains over thousands, and captains over hundreds, which came from the battle. (15) And Moses said unto them, Have ye saved all the women alive? (16) Behold, these caused the children of Israel, through the counsel of Balaam, to commit trespass against the Lord in the matter of Peor, and there was a plague among the congregation of the Lord. (17) Now therefore kill every male among the little ones, and kill every woman that hath known man by lying with him. (18) But all the women children that have not known a man by lying with him, keep alive for yourselves."

e. EXHORT: Repent by removing those practicing error.
Rev. 2:16, "Repent; or else I will come unto thee quickly, and will fight against them with the sword of my mouth."

Balaam died, but the doctrine of Balaam survived to enter Christendom during the Pergamos Church era. The remedy Jesus prescribed for those holding false doctrine was to repent; literally, to turn away from the false doctrines to the truth of the Word of God. To those who refuse to turn Jesus says, "or else I will come unto thee quickly, and will fight against them with the sword of my mouth." Anyone who thinks they can enter into a fight with Jesus and win is very close to the point of no return. The sword out of the mouth of Jesus is his Word, and speaks of that point in time when he will execute what he said he would do. When a person accepts a false doctrine, the lie actually hardens his spirit to the point where the truth of the Word of God cannot penetrate. The person will reach a point when the Word of God has no effect on his way of life and no influence in his thinking process. He puts himself in a position where Jesus has no choice but to take that sword of judgment and cut him off.

It was needful for Jesus to do the fighting because of the bigamy marriage relationship between the Church and State. When the Roman Government made church membership compulsory, it forced the Church to accept the entire population of the Roman Empire as fellow Christians. Because this situation was forced on Christendom by the government, the Church could no longer keep itself doctrinally clean by refusing admittance to those holding false doctrines. Like Balaam, these false teachers were eventually cut off, but their false doctrines survived and their influence is still visible in Christendom today. When the Church won the political power struggle with the State around A.D. 500, instead of correcting these false doctrines, they added some new ones and spent the next thousand years turning the whole package into tradition. Before we look at the Thyatira Church Era, let's read the promises Jesus made to the Christians of the Pergamos Era who were not overcome by the false doctrines.

f. PROMISES: The overcomer given hidden manna and a white stone.
Rev. 2:17, "He that hath an ear, let him hear what the Spirit saith unto the churches; To him that overcometh will I give to eat of the hidden manna, and will give him a white stone, and in the stone a new name written, which no man knoweth saving he that receiveth it."

The Letter to Thyatira

4. The Letter to Thyatira: The Papacy (500-1500).
Revelation 2:18-29, "(18) And unto the angel of the church in Thyatira write; These things saith the Son of God, who hath his eyes like unto a flame of fire, and his feet are like fine brass; (19) I know thy works, and charity, and service, and faith, and thy patience, and thy works; and the last to be more than the first. (20) Notwithstanding I have a few things against thee, because thou sufferest that woman Jezebel, which calleth herself a prophetess, to teach and to seduce my servants to commit fornication, and to eat things sacrificed unto idols. (21) And I gave her space to repent of her fornication; and she repented not. (22) Behold, I will cast her into a bed, and them that commit adultery with her into great tribulation, except they repent of their deeds. (23) And I will kill her children with death; and all the churches shall know that I am he which searcheth the reins and hearts: and I will give unto every one of you according to your works. (24) But unto you I say, and unto the rest in Thyatira, as many as have not this doctrine, and which have not known the depths of Satan, as they speak; I will put upon you none other burden. (25) But that which ye have already hold fast till I come. (26) And he that overcometh, and keepeth my works unto the end, to him will I give power over the nations: (27) And he shall rule them with a rod of iron; as the vessels of a potter shall they be broken to shivers: even

as I received of my Father. (28) And I will give him the morning star. (29) He that hath an ear, let him hear what the Spirit saith unto the churches."

a. TO: The church in Thyatira.
Rev. 2:18a, "And unto the angel of the church in Thyatira write."

The Thyatira Church Era is a period of history from approximately A.D. 500 to 1500. During this period of time, Christendom took on the form of the Roman Catholic Church headed by the papacy, or office of the pope. The organization became so politically strong that it was able to enthrone or dethrone the kings of Europe, wage its own wars, and kill those individuals who opposed its authority. I realize many denominations teach that their group was never part of the Roman Catholic Church. These groups trace their beginnings around the Catholic Church to the days of Jesus, Paul, John the Baptist, the day of Pentecost, or whatever. I also realize the Roman Catholic Church claims to have existed since the Apostle Peter, who it claims as its first Pope. God's analytical view of the Church Dispensation in Chapters 2 and 3 of the Book of the Revelation discredits both claims.

The Thyatira Church Era was followed by the Sardis Church Age, or the Reformation Era. It was at this time the Roman Catholic Church began to spawn the children mentioned in Rev. 2:23. These children gave birth to denominationalism. Actually, the first of her children came as a result of a Schism, or split, within the Church in the ninth century. The split in the Roman Catholic Church was a result of the split that occurred within the Roman Empire. The capital of the Roman Empire was the city of Rome until Constantine made Constantinople its capital in A.D. 330. Contention between the two cities increased, and by the year A.D. 395 the Roman Empire was divided into the Eastern Empire, with Constantinople as its capital under Emperor Arcadius, and the Western Empire with Rome as its capital under Emperor Honorius. The government of the Western Empire continued to weaken and in the year 410 the Ostrogoths, under Alaric, conquered the city of Rome. Conditions in the city deteriorated under the pirate raids of the Vandals, under Gaiseric, and the tribute demands of Attila the Hun. When Emperor Valenlinian stopped the tribute payments, Attila invaded Northern Italy. Pope Leo 1st pleaded for the city of Rome, and Attila abandoned his plan to take the city. In the year A.D. 476 the German conquerer Odoacer dethroned Romulus Augustulus and the Western Roman Empire fell. Romulus was the last Roman emperor of the Western Empire until the year 800 when the papacy enthroned Charlemagne as the emperor of the Holy Roman Empire.

The first human to exalt himself as the head of the Church was the Roman Emperor Constantine, who issued the edit of Milan, which ended the persecution of the Smyrna Era and introduced the Pergamos Era. He presided over the first Ecumenical Council (the first World Council of Churches) in the Council of Nicaea in A.D. 325. The bishops of the individual churches honored his claim by attending the council. By the end of the Pergamos Era the situation had reversed itself, and the Emperor of the Roman Empire honored the Bishop of Rome as the head of Christendom. In the year A.D. 445 Pope Leo I made the claim that his office was by divine appointment, and as such, he was the head of all bishops. He obtained formal government recognition from Emperor Valenlinian, and the stage was set for the transfer of political power to the papacy. This act prompted the bishops who attended the fourth Ecumenical Council at Chalcedon, in A.D. 451, to grant the Patriarch of Constantinople equal status with the Bishop of Rome. The popularity gained by Leo I for saving the city of Rome from Attila the Hun (A.D. 452), and Gaiseric the Vandal (A.D. 455), promoted the reputation of the office of the pope. The collapse of the Western Empire in A.D. 476 left Pope Simplicius free from all government authority and in a position to negotiate directly with the German invaders. They were converted to papal Christianity, and eventually the Pope became the most powerful figure in the West.

By the days of Pope Gregory I (A.D. 590-604) the papacy exercised complete control over the churches in Italy, Spain, England, France, Belgium, and parts of the Netherlands, Germany, and Switzerland. The Eastern churches, which included Greece, Western Asia, Turkey, Syria, Palestine, Egypt, and North Africa, still refused to honor the Pope of Rome as the head of the Church. In the days of Gregory I, the Patriarch of Constantinople was calling himself the Universal Bishop. The primary difference between the Western and Eastern churches was the political question, "Who is the head of the Church, the Pope at Rome, or the Universal Bishop of Constantinople. Doctrinally the churches were identical. Christendom had been paganized to the point of worshipping idols, images, relics, Apostles, Saints, Christian martyrs, and Mary, the mother of Jesus.

It was idolatry in Christendom that gave birth to Mohammedism. From Judaism and Christianity, Mohammed saw that idolatry was forbidden by God. In A.D. 610 he declared himself a prophet and spoke out against idolatry. He was rejected by the people in his home town of Mecca and fled to Medina where he raised an army. When Mohammed returned to Mecca in A.D. 630, with his army, the question was totally uncomplicated, "Become a Moslem, or die." Within three years, his army conquered Syria, and within 100 years, the cradle of Christianity, Palestine, Egypt, North Africa, and Persia. In the year A.D. 711, Moslems from North Africa entered and conquered Spain. In A.D. 732, Charles Martel defeated the Moslem army in the Battle of Tours, France, which saved the continent of Europe from becoming totally Islamic. As a result of the spread of Islamic, Christianity in the Eastern Empire was nearly eliminated, which left the Western churches headed by the papacy in a much stronger and influential position. It also explains why the Christianity that spread across the continent of Europe, and eventually into the Western World of the Americas, was Roman Catholic Christianity.

The papacy continued to exert its power and influence over the Eastern churches, but avoided a direct controversy by not claiming jurisdiction over them. After the threat of Islamic, the next threat to papal authority came from the Lombards, a Germanic people who invaded Italy, and by A.D. 751 were threatening the city of Rome. The events leading to the defeat of the Lombards actually started with the Merovingian, a dynasty of Frankish Kings (A.D. 481-751). The idleness of these kings left the government to the mayors of the palace. The daughter of Pepin of Landen, a Frankish mayor of the palace, married the son of Arnulf, Bishop of Metz. Their grandson, Pepin of Heristal, was the father of Charles Martel, who defeated the Moslem Army, and grandfather of Pepin the Short, who became mayor in A.D. 741. In A.D. 751, with the consent of the papacy, under Pope Zacarias (A.D. 741-752), Pepin the Short forced the last Merovingian king, Childeric III, into a monastery, and had himself proclaimed King of the Franks. When the Lombards attacked the city of Rome, the papacy under Pope Stephen II (A.D. 752-757), appealed to Pepin the Short for help. Pepin led his army into Italy, conquered the Lombards, and gave their land (Central Italy) to the papacy. This territory was the beginning of the papal States, under the civil control of the papacy. When Charlemagne replaced his father as King of the Franks, Desiderius, the last Lombard king, tried to reclaim his land from the papacy (Pope Adrian I A.D. 772-795). Charlemagne dethroned Desiderius and confirmed his father's land gift to the papacy. Pope Leo III rewarded Charlemagne by crowning him emperor of the new Holy Roman Empire. The relationship between Charlemagne and Pope Leo III was a mutual exaltation program. The papacy sanctioned Charlemagne's military achievements to enlarge the Empire, and Charlemagne promoted the papacy to the position of a world power.

The Holy Roman Empire was more a name than a reality. The historical record clearly shows there was nothing holy about it. We will have to wait until the return of Jesus to see the actual record of how much human blood was shed by the papacy in the name of Christianity. The arrangement between Charlemagne and the papacy was, basically, that the Pope would have complete control in the government of the Papal States and would be the sole spokesman for religious matters in the Empire. The Emperor was to honor Papal Christianity and have complete jurisdiction in governing the remainder of the Empire. The arrangement worked for them because neither overstepped his authority, but down through the centuries it has proven to be a bloody battleground between the papacy and European kings. The Treaty of Verdun in A.D. 843 divided Charlemagne's Empire into thirds, under three different emperors, which resulted in four different political leaders competing for top position in the Empire. The next 1000 years of European history is written in the blood of people slain in the political struggle for supremacy between over-ambitious kings and popes. In 1801 Napoleon made peace with the papacy in the Concordat of 1801. In 1804 he had himself proclaimed Emperor of the French, and was crowned at Notre Dame Cathedral by Pope Pios VII on December 2, 1804. In 1805 he was given the title of King of Italy, and went on to wage a war that made him master of the continent of Europe by 1809. After Napoleon's defeat, the papacy retained its Papal States until Italian troops annexed Rome in 1870. The popes cried until the Lateran Treaty of 1929 granted them a sovereign and independent papal State called Vatican City, with the guarantee of the pope's inviolability by the Italian government.

The word *icon* or *eikon* means image, a pictorial representation. According to Webster the second meaning is "a conventional religious image typically printed on a small wooden panel and used in the devotions of Eastern Christians." The World Book Encyclopedia reads, "icon or eikon, is a religious picture, usually painted on a flat surface such as wood or ivory. Icons in the Greek Orthodox churches are the pictures of Christ, the Virgin Mary, or the saints." Although icons may have been present in both the Western and Eastern churches, the Eastern churches exalted them to a position of idolatry. After the Eastern churches split from the Western churches, they called themselves Eastern Catholic, Eastern Orthodox, Greek Catholic, Greek Orthodox, but at this point in time, they are a single organization under the Patriarch of Constantinople. An *iconoclast* is "one who destroys religious images or opposes their veneration." *Veneration* is "respect or awe inspired by the dignity, wisdom, dedication, or talent of a person." The most advocate iconoclast in history was Mohammed. It was image worship in the Eastern churches that provoked him to declare himself a prophet from God. The Eastern churches paid for their folly by the sword of the Moslem army. Within 100 years after the army began to march, Spain, all of North Africa, Egypt, Palestine, Syria, Sicily, and Persia were turned from Christianity to Islamic. The only Eastern churches to survive the march were those in the area surrounding modern day Greece and Turkey.

It was Leo III, emperor of the Eastern or Byzantine Empire, in A.D. 717-718, was stopped the northern movement of the Moslem army and turned it eastward toward Persia. In A.D. 726 Emperor Leo III issued an order forbidding images and incense burning in the remaining Eastern churches. When the Eastern churches tried to impose the order on the Western churches, Pope Gregory II (715-31) and Pope Gregory III (731-41) resisted them, increasing the tension between the Eastern and Western churches. When Empress Irene (797-802) became ruler of the Eastern Empire, she concentrated all her efforts on the suppression of iconoclasm. Empress Irene called the II Council of Nicaea (7th Ecumenical Council) for the purpose of having images restored to all the churches. The council decreed that images ought to be venerated, not worshipped. Pope Adrian I sanctioned the degree which reversed Emperor Leo's order forbidding images in the Eastern Churches.

The final blow that caused the split, came in the reign of Pope Nicolas, when he interfered in the affairs of the Eastern churches. Ignatius, a son of

Emperor Michael I, was castrated and imprisoned by Leo V (813) to prevent his accession to Patriarch of Constantinople. In 846, he was made patriarch by Empress Theodora, who approved his zeal against iconoclasm. After her banishment, Ignatius was asked to resign, and Michael III made Photius patriarch. Photius was rushed through ordination and made patriarch, supposedly in one day. The papacy under Pope Nicolas refused to recognize him as patriarch. Photius called a synod and questioned the right of the Pope of Rome to pass judgment on the assignment of a patriarch to an office. Nicolas excommunicated Photius and he, in turn, excommunicated Nicolas. At the 8th Ecumenical Council held at Constantinople, in 869, the Eastern churches separated themselves from the papacy by rejecting the pope's claim to authority over them. Up to this point the only difference between the Western and Eastern churches was that the Western churches exalted the Pope at Rome as the head of the Church, and the Eastern churches exalted the Patriarch of Constantinople. One of the decrees of the II Ecumenical Council made the Bishop of Constantinople second only to the Pope of Rome. In the 4th Council he was granted equal status with the Pope of Rome. The 8th Ecumenical Council made the Patriarch of Constantinople free from all papal authority. It was at this point the Eastern churches introduced the idea that the "General Council," rather than the Pope, was the supreme governing body in the Church. It remained an idea, rather than a reality. The Eastern churches voted to honor the decrees of the first seven Ecumenical Councils, but from this point on, the Eastern churches had their Councils, and the Western churches had their Councils.

In reality, the 7th Council was the last Ecumenical Council. Never again would the Church meet under one roof in doctrinal agreement. Photius introduced the first actual doctrinal disagreement (besides who is the Big Boss of the Church). Photius condemned the papacy and the Western churches for adding the word *filioque* to the Nicene Creed. The Eastern churches held that the Holy Spirit proceeded directly from the Father. By adding the word *filioque*, the Western churches took the position that the Holy Spirit proceeded from the Father and the Son. From A.D. 869, the year of the 8th Ecumenical Council, all the way back to the first Council held by Emperor Constantine in A.D. 325, the Church had held to one doctrine. During this period of time several "-ism" Sects arose, and were labeled heretic by the Ecumenical Christian Church (both Western and Eastern churches). One of the first was Gnosticism, which taught that salvation was to be obtained through knowledge, rather than through faith, or good works. It goes all the way back to the revival of learning in the Hellenistic Era. Early Gnostics rejected the Jewish foundations of Christianity, and the Old Testament portion of the Bible. In the second century, Valentinus modified Gnosticism by dividing all people into three classes: the Gnostics, or elect, who were sure of salvation; Gnostics Christians, who might be saved through faith in Christ; and, all others, who were incapable of being saved. Gnosticism eventually merged with Manichaeism.

Manichaeism was started in the third century by a Persian named Mani. It was a mixture of Buddhism and Gnosticism, based on salvation by self-denial. The elect practiced strict celibacy and austerity, which assured them of everlasting happiness after death. The lower class laymen were called auditors or hearers. They could marry once, but had to restrict sensual pleasures to be reborn among the elect. Manichaeism was initially limited to the Byzantine Empire (area of the Eastern Churches), and was opposed so strongly by Christianity that by the year 500 it was nearly a dead religion. In Thrace (area north of Turkey) a sect called Paulicians revived Manichaeism by adding the rejection of sacraments, images, and most of the New Testament. In Bulgaria they united with the Bogomils, who preached political nationalism and resentment of Byzantine culture. As resentment of the papal priestly hierarchy increased several subgroups appeared, including the Cathari and Patarenes. Manichaeism rejects the Christian revelation of God, so when the Moslem army appeared, most of them were converted to Islamic. Manichaeism was revived in Southern France in the 12th and 13th centuries by a sect called Albigenses, who added the doctrine that Jesus lived only in semblance. The movement was suppressed by the papacy, but never completely eliminated. Manichaeism reappeared during the Reformation in John Calvin's doctrine of predestination.

Monarchianism is a Greek word meaning "belief in the rule of one." In essence, it is the denial of the Trinity (one God in three persons). The idea can be seen in the philosophy of Sabellius who taught the doctrine of the "economic Trinity," with God as one indivisible substance appearing successively as Father, Son, and Holy Spirit. Arianism (condemned at the first Ecumenical Council) taught that Jesus was a created creature, neither eternal or equal with the Father. Adoptionism teaches that Jesus was a mere human being adopted as the Son of God by baptism. Monarchianism, and many other "isms" were combated by the development of Christian creeds. The word *creed* is the Latin word *credo* meaning, "I believe." The creeds were a summary of the basic doctrines of the Christian faith. Among the most famous is the Apostles' Creed, "I believe in God, the Father almighty, maker of heaven and earth: And in Jesus Christ, his only Son, our Lord: who was conceived by the Holy Spirit, born of the virgin Mary, suffered under Pontius Pilate, was crucified, dead, and buried: he descended into hell, the third day he rose from the dead, he ascended into heaven, and is seated on the right hand of God, the Father almighty, whence he shall come to judge the living and the dead. I believe in the Holy Spirit, the holy Christian church, the communion of saint, the forgiveness of sins, the resurrection of the body, and the life everlasting. Amen." The phrase "the holy Christian church" originally read "the holy Catholic church" before the Reformation. Also, I believe the word *hell* should read "hades," place of the dead, instead of the word *hell*, the lake of fire.

The Thyatira Church era was a period of controversy in Christianity. The Ecumenical Councils were called to assemble the Church leaders

together in an attempt to settle these controversies. The place, date, and major controversy of the first eight Ecumenical Councils are as follows:
I Nicaea (325), condemned Arianism.
II Constantinople (381), Called to settle Apollinarianism. It taught that Jesus possesses Logos in place of a human mind. It was condemned.
III Ephesus (431), called to settle the Nestorian controversy. Nestorius, Patriarch of Constantinople, objected to calling the Virgin Mary, the Mother of God, saying that she bore him as a man. Followers of Nestorius, who retained the doctrine that Jesus was nothing more than a human being, formed the Nestorian Church.
IV Chalcedon (451), called to settle the Eutychian controversy. Eutyches had introduced the doctrine that Christ's humanity was absorbed in his one divine nature. Eutychianism was denounced.
V Constantinople (553), called to settle the Monophysitiam controversy. Monophysitism challenged the orthodox creed of Chalcedon by saying that Jesus Christ had only one nature. It produced the Coptic, Jacobite, and Armenian churches.
(The 3rd, 4th, and 5th councils clarified the orthodox position that the two natures of Jesus Christ [divine and human] are inseparable joined in one person, and partake of one divine substance.)
VI Constantinople (680), called to settle Monothelitism. Heraclius I introduced Monothelitism as a compromise between Monophysitism and orthodoxy. It declared that Jesus Christ had two natures, but operated with one will. It was condemned by the Council and died out after 680, except among the Syrian Maronite churches.
VII Nicaea (787), called to settle iconoclasm. It was opposition to the religious use of icons and images. Iconoclasm was rejected.
VIII Constantinople (869), called to define the authority of the papacy, and settle the controversy caused by the Western churches changing the Nicene Creed. No agreement was reached, which resulted in the Schism between the Eastern and Western churches.

Up to this point in time, the word Catholic Church meant the Universal Christian Church. It was the orthodox faith as opposed to the movements pronounced heretical. After the Schism, or split, in the Universal Christian Church, the Eastern and Western churches view each other as Schismatic (brothers in disagreement), but both consider the Nestorian, Coptic, Jacobite, Armenian, Syrian Maronite, and the various *ism* churches as heretical. The Western churches retained the name Roman Catholic Church, or Roman Universal Church, while the Eastern churches became known as the Orthodox Eastern Church. In the year 1123, at the council of Rome, it was decided that Bishops would be appointed by the Popes. In essence, this move by the Roman Catholic Church excommunicated all the Bishops, Patriarchs, and Pastors of the Eastern churches. In 1139, at the council of Rome, a second attempt was made to heal the Schism of the Eastern and

Western churches, which also failed. After the Reformation the term *Catholic Church* usually refers to the Roman Catholic Church. The reformation leaders were labeled protestors, which gave birth to the third division of Christendom, Protestantism. Today Protestants prevail in Western Europe and North America. Roman Catholic prevails in Southern Europe and South America. Greek Catholic prevails in Eastern and Southeastern Europe.

The Thyatira Church Era actually began in the year 445, when the government of the Roman Empire honored Pope Leo's claim that his office was by divine appointment, and as such, he was the head of the Church. The collapse of the government in the Western Roman Empire in 476 left the Pope as the strongest political figure in the West. From the year 445, until the 8th Ecumenical Council in the year 869, spans a period of 424 years. During this period the Bishop or Pope of Rome was the prime influence in Christendom. It was primarily his effort that kept the churches united against many heretical movements and external threats. The word *ecumenical* denotes the Christian Church as a whole, in the same manner as Christendom speaks of Christianity as a whole. In the 132 years preceding this 424 year period (edict of Milan, 313), we saw the Roman government force pagans and paganism into Christendom. In 445 when political control was restored to the church leaders, there were no major church reform movements within Christendom. The heretics did cause the leaders in Christendom to define the Christian faith and develop the Nicene, Athanasian, and the Apostles' Creed. The truths declared by these creeds still remain the fundamentals of the Christian faith. During this 424 year period a "heretic" was a person or group that held a religious belief or opinion opposed to the orthodox doctrines of the Church. "The Church" was the united, ecumenical, Eastern and Western churches of the Roman Empire. The word *orthodox* comes from the Greek words *orthos*, meaning "correct," and *dokeo*, meaning "thinking." There is no argument to the fact that there were errors in the Ecumenical churches. The thing to remember is that there were many more errors outside the Ecumenical churches, than there were inside.

The Thyatira Church Era ended on October 31, 1517, when Martin Luther posted his "95 Thesis" on the church door at Wittenberg, in open rebellion against the Roman Catholic Church. From the year 869, the 8th Ecumenical Council, to the year 1517, represents a period of 648 years. During this period of time the papacy turned the Roman Catholic Church into a powerful Italian political organization, and the Eastern churches decreased to near annihilation. The era opens at the 8th Ecumenical Council, when the Eastern churches rejected the universal jurisdiction of the pope and separated doctrinally by denouncing the changing of the Nicene Creed to include the word "filioque." The Eastern churches took the name "orthodox," claiming to have the "correct opinion" in Christianity. The papacy turned its back on the Eastern churches for 342 years (4th Crusade 1201-1204), and dedicated its efforts to ruling the European Continent. Beginning in 869 the history of the papacy is story of degeneration and bloodshed. It forced papal Christianity on Europe, and changed the definition of heretic to mean "any person or group that held a religious belief or opinion opposed to the teachings of the Roman Catholic Church."

Knowledge of the individual popes is common, available in most Church libraries and all civil libraries, so I will not go into much detail on their individual reigns. By the year 1012 the office of the pope was being bought and sold for money, an act called Simony. In 1033 some of the rich families in Rome united and bought the papacy for a twelve-year-old boy named Benedict IX. His murders and adulteries in broad daylight resulted in the people driving him out of the city of Rome. When Gregory VI bought the papacy, in 1045, it set off "gang wars" and three rival popes (Benedict IX, Gregory VI, and Sylvester III) did battle for the office of pope. The immorality of the Roman clergymen moved Emperor Henry III of Germany to appoint Clement II (1046-1047) as pope. This move set the stage for the Hildebrand reforms, aimed at correcting chief Church abuses of simony, lay investiture, and violations of clerical celibacy. It also resulted in transferring papal election from the Romans and Kings to the College of Cardinals in the year 1059.

To understand "lay investiture" we need a general idea of feudalism. In an ideal feudal society, ownership of all land was vested in the king. Under him was a hierarchy of nobles: highest holding from the king directly, lesser ones from the highest ones, and so on, down the ladder, to the seignior, holder of a single manor, to the manor peasants. The "investiture" was the formal ceremony of granting land to the seignior, who then swore to protect the interest and welfare of the nobility and the king. Gradation of nobility was based on both land-holding and military service. The knight was the typical military warrior. In this system it is easy to see the interest of kings and nobles in the assignments of bishops and abbots (a man who is head of a monastery). They wanted the men in authority within their realm to be mindful of their interests and loyal to their cause, right or wrong. This irritated the papacy in two ways. First, it undermined the authority of the papacy. Second, the offices were usually sold to the highest bidder or given to a person loyal to the king or nobility, without regard for their fitness or character.

When Hildebrand became Pope Gregory VII (1073-85), he challenged Henry IV, Emperor of Germany, on the lay investitures. Henry deposed Gregory, who in turn, excommunicated and deposed Henry. The war that followed ended in 1122 with the Concordat of Worms, an agreement between Pope Calixtus II and Emperor Henry V. The emperor conceded to the pope the right to invest bishops and abbots, but reserved the right to veto elections of prelates to whom he objected. William the Conqueror ran into the same problem when he conquered England. He began substituting foreign prelates for English bishops and established separate ecclesiastical courts. When his son, William II (Rufus), became king, he increased his wealth by selling churches and church land. When he died, Henry I, youngest son of William I, took the throne and continued the quarrel over investiture. The papacy won in 1107 when Henry I and Anselm, Archbishop of Canterbury, signed an agreement giving investiture power to the papacy. The papacy made it official at the council at Rome in 1123, when the attending bishops gave the pope the sole authority for investing or appointing bishops. This move made the papacy the strongest political force on the European continent. The papal hierarchy had the pope at the top. Under him were the archbishops, who were heads of an ecclesiastical territory. Under them were the bishops over towns or provinces. Under them were the abbots over monasteries, and priests over individual churches. Under the priests were the deacons.

Giving the pope the sole authority for appointing bishops excommunicated the bishops of the Eastern churches and put the abbots, priests, bishops and archbishops who had received their investiture from the state (kings or nobility) out of a job, unless they could obtain papal approval. Those deemed unworthy for office by the papal hierarchy began to preach rebellion against the papacy and the Roman Catholic Church. The pope's answer to the rebellion was the Inquisition. *Inquisition* is the seeking out of heresy and the punishment of heretics. At this point a heretic was any person or group that held a religious belief or opinion opposed to the teachings of the papacy or defiance of papal authority. The inquisition began in 1233, and was designed to crush opposition to papal authority by extermination. The only difference between the Inquisition and the Gestapo (or SS) is that one operated under the papacy and the other operated under Adolf Hitler.

The Spanish Inquisition was established in 1478 by Ferdinand and Isabella, not the papacy. The problem in Spain actually started in 630 with Mohammed. Islam conquered Syria and spread southward, conquering Palestine and Egypt. It continued westward conquering North Africa. It crossed the Mediterranean Sea, conquered Spain in 711, and was stopped in France in 732, when Charles Martel defeated the Moslem Army. The Moslems in Spain were called the *Moors*. There was almost continuous warfare between the Moors and the Spanish papal Christians. The victory at Navas de Tolosa, in 1212, put the papal Christians on the road to recovering Spain. The Spanish Inquisition was supposed to spy out converted Jews and Moors who were insincere. Like the papal inquisition, it turned into a blood bath. The year 1492 saw the last Moorish stronghold fall, the expulsion of the Jews from Spain, and the discovery of the New World by Christopher Columbus.

Islam also spread northward from Syria, until it was turned eastward by the army of Leo III. It conquered Persia in 640. Greece, Turkey, and Thrace (area north of Turkey) remained the Christian area, and the rest of the Eastern Roman Empire was Islamic. The Eastern churches that split from the Western churches in 869, were limited to the Christian area. The papacy irritated the situation in the East by the Crusades. The Crusades were a series of so-called Holy Wars, to recover Jerusalem and the Holy Land from the Moslems. The first Crusade (1095-99) was started by Pope Urban II, who promised that the journey would count as full penance. In 1095, several unorganized groups of French and German peasants began the march to Jerusalem. After massacring the Jews in the Rhineland, they were dispersed by the Bulgarians and Hungarians. Some reached Constantinople, crossed over to Asia Minor, and were defeated by the Turks. In 1097, a second group managed to reach, and conquer Jerusalem. They established the Latin Kingdom of Jerusalem. The second Crusade (1147-49) ended in failure. In 1187, Saladin, a Moslem warrior, recaptured Jerusalem. The third Crusade (1189-91) failed to capture Jerusalem, but resulted in Richard I of England negotiating a truce by which Christians were granted free access to the Holy Sepulcher. The fourth Crusade (1201-04) began in France and was led by Enrico Dandolo. To pay for their passage, the crusaders assisted the Venetians to recover the city of Zara from Hungary. After the papacy condemned their actions, the Crusaders went to Constantinople, sacked the city, divided the spoils with Venice, and set up the Latin Empire of Constantinople. The papacy (Pope Innocent III, 1198-1216) recognized the Empire, but his efforts to spread the Latin rite into the Greek churches only deepened the resentment between the Eastern and Western churches.

The Children's Crusade of 1212 was a disaster. Thousands of children led by Stephen of Cloyes, a French peasant boy, set out for the Holy Land, and were sold into slavery. Another group of German children perished of hunger and disease. The fifth Crusade (1217-21) was intended to recover Egypt from Islam, but failed. The sixth Crusade (1228-29) was undertaken by Emperor Frederick II. When they reached Jerusalem, Frederick made a truce with the Moslems, securing the surrender of the Holy Places. Sporadic fighting soon broke out and the Christians retreated to Gaza and Acre. The city of Jerusalem remained almost constantly under Moslem control until it was taken by the British in World War I. The Egyptian Mamelukes drove the Christians out of Gaza in 1244, which led to the seventh Crusade. The seventh (1248-54), eighth (1270), and ninth (1271-72) Crusades were total failures.

In 1291 Acre, the last Christian stronghold, fell to the Moslems. From 630 to 1058 the Moslem world was dominated by Arabians. From 1058 to modern times the Moslem world has been ruled by the Turks. The conversion of the Turks to Islam resulted in the Ottoman Empire. The growth of the Ottoman Empire was at the expense of the Christian portion of the Byzantine Empire. In 1361 Murad, an Ottoman sultan, took Adrianople and forced the Byzantine Empire to pay tribute (1373). In 1444, Murad II defeated the

Christian army at Varna. In 1453 Mohammed II conquered Constantinople, which ended the Byzantine Empire. Constantinople is the modern day city of Istanbul, Turkey. In 1456 Greece fell to the Moslem Turks and remained under Moslem rule until 1821. By the year 1456, the entire eastern portion of the Old Roman Empire, which was once under the Eastern Orthodox churches, had fallen to the Moslems and Islamic. This fall to the Moslem world took place sixty-one years before the Reformation leaders rebelled (October 31, 1517). From this, it should be obvious the reformation leaders were rebelling against the papacy and the Roman Catholic Church. When speaking of Christianity, Greece went out of the picture in 1456, and stayed out, until 1821. Asia Minor, Turkey, and the rest of the Arab states are still out of the picture.

b. FROM: The Son of God.
Rev. 2:18b, "These things saith the Son of God, who hath his eyes like unto a flame of fire, and his feet are like fine brass."

We have seen a brief outline of Christendom during the Thyatira Church Era. Now let's look at it through the eyes of Jesus, the Son of God. With those eyes like unto a flame of fire, he saw the Roman Government turn political control of the Church over to the Church leaders in A.D. 445. He saw the Church in a position to rid herself of the pagans forced on her by the Roman government. He saw her in a position to clean herself doctrinally by removing the false doctrines the pagans brought to Church with them during the Pergamos Era. Instead, he saw her turn them into traditions. He saw the anger in her face when the Reformation leaders said, "You are not saying the same things the Son of God said." He saw her pull away the shoulder and say, "I will not be reformed." Looking at her 479 years after October 31, 1517, she still hasn't changed. The government took the sword out of her hand, but she is still full of anger. Jesus hit the nail on the head when he rebuked her by saying, "I gave her space to repent of her fornication; and she repented not" (Rev. 2:21).

Jesus saw the churches united from A.D. 445 to 869 in an attempt to stop the various *isms* from entering Christendom. During this period he saw her struggle against many bearers of false doctrines. He saw the heavy burden she was already carrying, and said "enough is enough" in the exhort section of the letter, Rev. 2:24 25, "(24) But unto you I say, an unto the rest in Thyatira, as many as have not this doctrine, and which have not known the depths of Satan, as they speak; I will put upon you none other burden. (25) But that which ye have already hold fast till I come." If she had gotten rid of the burden forced on her by the Roman government in the space Jesus gave her to repent, he would not have had to watch his birthplace, the cradle of Christianity, and the Eastern and Southern portion of the Roman Empire fall to Islamic. She wasn't saying, "These things saith the Son of God," so the Moslem world heard, "These things saith the Prophet

Mohammed," and they buried Jesus under the Koran. She saw Mohammed promulgate his faith by the sword, and instead of condemning him, she copied him.

Four hundred twenty-four years after political control was returned to the Church, Jesus saw the 8th Ecumenical Council. He saw the Western churches open the Bible and read John 16:7, "Nevertheless I tell you the truth; It is expedient for you that I go away: for if I go not away, the Comforter will not come unto you; but if I depart, I will send him unto you." He saw them present the phrase "I will send him unto you" as clear evidence that the Holy Spirit proceeded directly from the Father, "and the Son" (filioque). He saw the stern look on the faces of the Eastern churches become more severe. He saw the discussion change to "Who is the head of the Church?" and watched as the discussion turned into a heated argument. It was out of this heat that Jesus saw the Universal or Catholic Church give birth to her first child, as the Eastern churches stomped out the door. Jesus looked toward the Reformation which was 648 years down the road, and knew the Eastern Greek Church was only the first of many children. The day is coming when the Roman Catholic Church and all her children will know who is the head of the Church. Rev. 2:22-23, "(22) Behold, I will cast her into a bed, and them that commit adultery with her into great tribulation, except they repent of their deeds. (23) And I will kill her children with death; and all the churches shall know that I am he which searcheth the reins and hearts: and I will give unto every one of you according to your works."

Jesus saw the blood that would be shed by the papacy during the next 648 years in its efforts to gain power over the nations. He saw the papacy at its prime, when most of the kings and rulers of the nations of Europe were in submission. The dominion of the papacy has been reduced from the European Continent to the 108.7 acres of Vatican City because of Rev. 2:21, "And I gave her space to repent of her fornication: and she repented not." When the Church leaves in the rapture and Antichrist sets fire to Vatican City, its epitaph will still read, "And I gave her space to repent of her fornication: and she repented not." Hear the warning Jesus gave in Rev. 2:22-23a, "(22) Behold, I will cast her into a bed, and them that commit adultery with her into great tribulation, except they repent of their deeds. (23a) And I will kill her children with death." She is still feeding her appetite for political power over the nations, without hearing the promises Jesus made to her in Rev. 2:26-29, "(26) And he that overcometh, and keepeth my works unto the end, to him will I give power over the nations: (27) And he shall rule them with a rod of iron; as the vessels of a potter shall they be broken to shivers: even as I received of my Father. (28) And I will give him the morning star. (29) He that hath an ear, let him hear what the Spirit saith unto the churches." Power over the nations is going to be given to "he that overcometh . . . and as many as have not this doctrine, and which have not known the depths of Satan, as they speak." (Rev. 2:24).

Jesus saw the Nicolaitanes (people controllers) trying to enter Christendom during the Ephesus Era, and commended the congregation for hating their deeds as much as he did (Rev. 2:6). In the Pergamos Era, Jesus still hated the doctrine of the Nicolaitanes, but the churches were beginning to take hold of the doctrine (Rev. 2:15). Jesus could see the change Christendom would undergo after the 8th Ecumenical Council. He saw the Nicolaitanes form the papal hierarchy, and change Christianity from "these things saith the Son of God" to "these things saith the Pope." There is only one Holy Father in the entire universe and his throne is in heaven, not in Vatican City. Antipas saw the papacy coming when the Nicolaitanes showed themselves in the Pergamos Era, and it cost him his life (Rev 2:13). They may have called him a heretic, but Jesus called him his "faithful martyr." The death of this individual was only a shadow of the thousands, maybe millions, who were killed under the Inquisition for opposing the Holy Father of the Roman Catholic Church. The cause of Antipas can be seen in what Jesus called him. Antipas is composed of the prefix *anti* meaning, opposite, instead of, opposed to, or against. *Pas* comes from the Greek word *pater* meaning "father." Antipas believed the words spoken by the Son of God in Matthew 23:8-10, "(8) But be not ye called Rabbi: for one is your Master, even Christ; and all ye are brethren. (9) And call no man your father upon the earth: for one is your Father, which is in heaven. (10) Neither be ye called masters: for one is your Master, even Christ." When Jesus says "Beware," you better stop and open your eyes. Luke 20:45-47, "(45) Then in the audience of all the people he said unto his disciples, (46) Beware of the scribes, which desire to walk in long robes, and love greetings in the markets, and the highest seats in the synagogues, and the chief rooms at feasts; (47) Which devour widows' houses, and for a shew make long prayers: the same shall receive greater damnation."

It is no accident that Jesus introduces himself as the Son of God to the Thyatira Church Era, especially when considering the virgin Mary and the position to which she had been exalted by the papacy. In the doctrine of the Immaculate Conception they made her born without original sin, which is a direct contradiction of 1 Corinthians 15:22, "For as in Adam all die, even so in Christ shall all be made alive." and Romans 3:23, "For all have sinned, and come short of the glory of God." In the doctrine of the Assumption, they got her "assumed" directly into heaven in her body, and anyone who has read the Bible knows that is tradition, not Scripture. They kept her a virgin all her life by denying the Biblical fact that she had other children, Matthew 12:46-50 and 13:53-58. She is prayed to as, Our Lady, Our Lady Queen of Heaven, Our Lady Star of the Sea or Stella Maris, Our Lady of the Immaculate Conception, and Our Lady of Sorrows. To pray to the Virgin Mary is to burn incense (Rev. 5:8) to the queen of heaven. It is a pagan idolatry that had its origin in the land of Babylon. It is identified in Jeremiah chapter 44 as a thing God hates, verse 4, "Oh, do not this abominable thing that I hate." Read the entire chapter from your Bible and notice the resistance to repentance this unique idolatry carries. One of the dominant characteristics of the Thyatira Church is Rev. 2:21, "And I gave her space to repent of her fornication; and she repented not." When Jeremiah warned the idolaters of the coming punishment, "by the sword, by the famine, and by the pestilence" (Jeremiah 44:13), they replied by saying, "(44:16) As for the word that thou hast spoken unto us in the name of the Lord, we will not hearken unto thee. (17) But we will certainly do whatsoever thing goeth forth out of our own mouth, to burn incense unto the queen of heaven, and to pour out drink offerings unto her, as we have done, we, and our fathers, our kings, and our princes, in the cities of Judah, and in the streets of Jerusalem: for then had we plenty of victuals, and were well, and saw no evil." When you pray or make appeals to the Virgin Mary, you are exalting her to the office of mediator between God and man. That office belongs to Jesus Christ, not his mother, 1 Timothy 2:5, "For there is one God, and one mediator between God and men, the man Christ Jesus." Those who heeded Jeremiah's warning escaped the judgment (44:14), and those who refused to repent perished by the sword, famine, and pestilence. Unlike the churches before her, the Thyatira churches are going to survive until Jesus comes and the great tribulation (Rev. 2:20-23). If you are a member of one of these churches and are guilty of this idolatry, you can repent and escape the coming judgment in the rapture. Refuse to repent and you can look forward to meeting four horsemen. The rider on the first horse is Antichrist (Rev. 6:1-2), the second has the sword (Rev. 6:3-4), the third is followed by famine (Rev. 6:5-6), and the fourth horseman, named Death, has your ticket to Hades, to await the white throne judgment and your second death in Hell.

c. COMMENDATION: Charity, service, faith, patience, but mostly works. Rev. 2:19, "I know thy works, and charity, and service, and faith, and thy patience, and thy works; and the last to be more than the first."

The church in Thyatira was commended on five points: works, charity, service, faith, and patience. Of these, the dominant characteristic is "works." Not every member of the Thyatira congregation was guilty of idolatry, nor did the total membership condone the deeds or doctrines of the Nicolaitanes. In fact, it was the deeds and doctrines of the papacy that caused the reformation, which gave birth to the rest of her children. Many Protestants today have trouble seeing the five points for which Jesus commended the Thyatira congregation in the Roman Catholic Church of the 1990s. The first thing for which Jesus commended the congregation was their works. Needless to say, not all works are good works. The works of the papacy are clear in its history. Weigh those works against the works Jesus told the papacy to do in Mark 16:15-18. If you find her wanting, don't make the same mistake Belshazzar made in Daniel chapter 5.

Another reason why Protestants have trouble seeing the five commendable points in the Roman Catholic Church is our vantage point in history. We are standing at the end of the space Jesus gave her to repent. We are looking at her just before Jesus throws her into the great tribulation and kills her children with death. She would look altogether different if she was dedicated to the Mark 16:15-18 Church Commission, and her works, charity, service, faith, and patience were all motivated by the Word of God, and directed by the Holy Spirit. We are looking at her as an old woman full of sins, adultery, fornication, idolatry, deceit, and murders, for which she has not repented. We are looking at her at the point in time when the Judge of all the earth has condemned her, and she is being led down the hall to the death chamber. Even now you can see the anger in her face because the reformation leaders were able to convince the government to take the sword out of her hand, and stopped her from killing people for reading and translating the Holy Bible. She still isn't telling the people to read the Bible and do as Jesus says, but because of the reformation blood, any member of the Roman Catholic Church can own and read the Bible. Any member can compare Bible Christianity to papal Christianity, by comparing what Jesus said to what the papacy said.

Another problem the Protestants have in looking for the five commendable points in the Thyatira congregation concern the length of its history. The total length of its history is from the year 445, when Emperor Valentinian surrendered political control of the churches to Pope Leo I (or the fall of the Western Roman Empire in 476, if you prefer), to the rapture, which will end the Church Dispensation. It was in the letter to the Thyatira churches that Jesus warns of his coming and the great tribulation. There were two major events in this time period which changed the course of history for Christendom. The first event was the Schism that occurred in the 8th Ecumenical Council in the year 869. The second event was the Schism that occurred in 1517, or the reformation. These two events divides the history of the Thyatira Era into three distinct time periods. The first period covers 424 years, from 445 to 869. The second period covers 648 years, from 869 to 1517. The third period covers from 1517 to the rapture.

During the first 424 years period there was no Roman Catholic Church or denominationalism. During this period Christendom was in unity, and the churches were universally one, united in doctrine, united against the infiltration of new false doctrines, and united in their cause. The churches had internal problems, but they also had millions of people dedicated to serving Jesus and the cause of Christianity. It was during this period of time that monasteries (monasticism) were introduced into Christendom. The idea was copied from Buddhism, where monks voluntarily seek the seclusion of a hermit's life in order to escape the pollution of this world. In essence, Monasticism is organized life in a community, as a retreat from worldly life, for religious purposes. Men who belong to these communities were called monks, and their establishments were called monasteries. Women who belong to these communities were called nuns, and their establishments were called convents. The idea was modified by the Christian community to be the establishment where people went to dedicate their lives to Christian work, charity, service, faith, and patience. Most of the Roman Empire was small farming communities, and Europe was in the Dark Ages, so the prime concern of the day was work and survival, not theological debates. What the common people knew about Jesus and how to serve Him, they learned by word of mouth from the abbots, bishops, and nuns. The local Bible book store simply did not exist.

During the next 648 years period (869-1517) the Papacy came into existence, and the Roman Catholic Church grew into a world power. The era began with the Schism between the Western churches, and what was left of the Eastern churches after Islam had claimed the southern and most of the eastern portion of the Old Roman Empire. Before this era ends, the remainder of the Eastern churches area falls to Islam (1456). During this period the papacy interposed itself between God and God's people, and exalted itself to the position of political ruler over the kings of Europe. By the reign of Pope Innocent III (1198-1216), the pope was claiming to be "infallible" (incapable of error in defining doctrines touching faith or morals), "Vicar of Christ and God," "Supreme Sovereign over the Church and the World," boasting that "All things on earth and in heaven and in hell are subject to the Vicar of Christ." The papal army was strong enough to enforce the Pope's claims, and the "Holy Office" kept the organization in unity by the "Inquisition." When Pope Boniface VIII (1294-1303) issued the "Unam Sanctam" saying, "We declare, affirm, define, and pronounce that it is altogether necessary for Salvation that every creature be subject to the Roman Pontiff," Jesus said, "And I gave her space to repent of her fornication; and she repented not." It was at this point in time Papal authority began to decline. The era ends in a second Schism, called the Reformation, which gave birth to Protestantism. Protestantism began as a movement within the Roman Catholic Church to reform the Church, by removing the numerous false doctrines being taught and practiced as Bible truth. When the papacy refused to let go of the false doctrines, the reformers left the Roman Catholic Church. The Papacy labeled them "protestors," hence, Protestants. This Schism was the beginning of the Sardis Church Era (1500-1700), Rev. 3:1-6.

Although the beginning of the Sardis Church Era ends the Thyatira Church Era, Jesus makes it clear in the letter to the Thyatira churches that they will continue to exist until he comes (Rev. 2:25), and unless there is repentance, both her and her offspring will be thrown into the great tribulation (Rev. 2:21-23). During the first period of Thyatira Church history (424 years, 445-869), the churches were universally one. During the second period (648 years, 869-1517), the Universal Church gave birth to the first of her children. The papacy took control of the Western churches and formed the

Roman Catholic Church. The bishops of the Eastern churches took control of their individual churches and formed the Greek Catholic churches. On October 31, 1517, the Catholic or Universal Church gave birth to her second child. The child called herself the Lutheran Church, her mother called her Protestor, and they agreed on the name Protestant. This event ended the Thyatira Church Era, but did not end the history of the Roman or Greek Catholic Church. From the year 1517, the Roman Catholic, Greek Catholic (or Orthodox), and the Protestant churches will continue to co-exist until Jesus comes, and ends the Church Dispensation with the rapture. In the rapture Jesus will snatch away from Earth all the born-again believers from all three organizations, and what remains on earth can rightfully be labeled "The One World Church." Antichrist will write the final chapter in Christendom in the next three and one-half years, as he eats her flesh, and burns her with fire (Rev. 17:16). The rapture will end the space Jesus gave the Thyatira churches, and all her children, to repent. The unrepentant will be faced with literal death in the great tribulation.

Listen to the rebuke, exhort, and promises, made by the rightful Head of the Church. His name is Christ Jesus, and "These things saith the Son of God."

d. REBUKE: Jezebel tolerated (Fornicators to go into great tribulation).
Rev. 2:20-23, "(20) Notwithstanding I have a few things against thee, because thou sufferest that women Jezebel, which calleth herself a prophetess, to teach and to seduce my servants to commit fornication, and to eat things sacrificed unto idols. (21) And I gave her space to repent of her fornication; and she repented not. (22) Behold, I will cast her into a bed, and them that commit adultery with her into great tribulation, except they repent of their deeds, (23) And I will kill her children with death; and all the churches shall know that I am he which searcheth the reins and hearts: and I will give unto every one of you according to your works."

e. EXHORT: Hold fast what you have, no other burdens added.
Rev. 2:24-25, "(24) But unto you I say, and unto the rest in Thyatira, as many as have not this doctrine, and which have not known the depths of Satan, as they speak; I will put upon you none other burden. (25) But that which ye have already hold fast till I come."

f. PROMISES: Overcomers to rule over the nations and given the morning star.
Rev. 2:26-29, "(26) And he that overcometh, and keepeth my works unto the end, to him will I give power over the nations: (27) And he shall rule them with a rod of iron; as the vessels of a potter shall they be broken to shivers: even as I received of my Father. (28) And I will give him the morning star. He that hath an ear, let him hear what the Spirit saith unto the churches."

Jezebel was the wife of King Ahab, one of the wickedest kings of the nation of Israel (1 Kings 16:29-33). The historical account of Jezebel and Ahab is recorded in 1 Kings chapters 17-22, and 2 Kings chapter 9. In brief, Jezebel worshipped the Canaanite god Baal, and when she became queen of Israel, she forced Baal worship on God's people. By Inquisition she killed all the prophets of God in the land, except 100 which Obadiah hid in caves (1 Kings 18:4, 18:13), and the Prophet Elijah. Jezebel's search for Elijah shows how an Inquisition operates, 1 Kings 18:10, "As the Lord thy God liveth, there is no nation or kingdom, whither my lord hath not sent to seek thee: and when they said, He is not there; he took an oath of the kingdom and nation, that they found thee not." Elijah could not be found because, after announcing to King Ahab it would not rain except by his word, Elijah fled into the wilderness. He was sustained by ravens till the brook of Cherith dried up, and then by a woman with a never empty meal barrel and cruse of oil. After a three and one-half year "sore famine in Samaria," Elijah was told to show himself to King Ahab. When Elijah met Ahab, he challenged him to gather 450 prophets of Baal on mount Carmel to demonstrate who was the true God in Israel. The question Elijah presented to the people and the prophets of Baal at mount Carmel is the same question the people living under the papacy were faced with, 1 Kings 18:21, "And Elijah came unto all the people, and said, How long halt ye between two opinions? if the Lord be God, follow him: but if Baal, then follow him, and the people answered him not a word." The demonstration is recorded in 1 Kings Chapter 18, and the peoples' response is recorded in 18:39, "And when all the people saw it, they fell on their faces: and they said, The Lord, he is the God; the Lord, he is the God." When the people repented, the rain came and ended the three-and-one-half-year famine.

Without argument, the sore famine in the land of Samaria was a literal physical famine. There is a famine that is much more dangerous than a physical famine. When God stops broadcasting the land with water a physical famine occurs, and the vegetation dries up and dies. When God's people stop broadcasting the Word of God in the land, a spiritual famine occurs, and the inhabitants of the land walk in spiritual darkness and perish. This is the famine Amos spoke of in Amos 8:11-14, "(11) Behold, the days come, saith the Lord God, that I will send a famine in the land, not a famine of bread, nor a thirst for water, but of hearing the words of the Lord: (12) And they shall wander from sea to sea, and from the north even to the east, they shall run to and fro to seek the word of the Lord, and shall not find it. (13) In that day shall the fair virgins and young men faint for thirst. (14) They that swear by the sin of Samaria, and say, Thy god, O Dan, liveth; and, The manner of Beersheba liveth; even they shall fall, and never rise up again."

When Jezebel killed the prophets of God, she stopped the Word of God from being proclaimed in the land. When the churches in the Thyatira Era stopped preaching the Word of God, Europe went through the Dark Ages.

It is because of this famine Jesus urges the members of the Laodicean churches to "anoint thine eyes with eyesalve, that thou mayest see" (Rev. 3:18). We are the generation living in the apostate Laodicean Church era, and the only way you are going to know if the person behind the pulpit is an apostate, or a man of God, is to compare what he says to the written Word of God. The Word of God is the only eyesalve that will heal spiritual blindness. Homosexuality is thriving and the famine is intensifying, but just wait. Consider the famine Jesus will cause on this planet when he calls away all born-again believers in the rapture, and the apostate's voice is the only voice you can hear. The rapture will introduce the most severe seven years of famine this planet has ever experienced.

In 1 Kings chapter 19, Ahab tells Jezebel of the demonstration, and that Elijah had killed her prophets. In 19:2 she swears to kill Elijah, which caused him to flee into the wilderness, where he asked God to let him die, 19:4, "But he himself went a day's journey into the wilderness, and came and sat down under a juniper tree: and he requested for himself that he might die; and said, It is enough; now, O Lord, take away my life; for I am not better than my fathers." The discouragement Elijah felt was the same discouragement God's people felt because of the papal Inquisition, 19:10, "And he said, I have been very jealous for the Lord God of hosts: for the children of Israel have forsaken thy covenant, thrown down thine altars, and slain thy prophets with the sword; and I, even I only, am left; and they seek my life, to take it away." There was a faithful remnant during the papacy reign, just as there was during Jezebel's reign, 19:18, "Yet I have left me seven thousand in Israel, all the knees which have not bowed unto Baal, and every mouth which hath not kissed him." They walked away from the papacy in the reformation when Martin Luther believed Romans 1:16-17, "(16) For I am not ashamed of the gospel of Christ: for it is the power of God unto salvation to every one that believeth; to the Jew first, and also to the Greek. (17) For therein is the righteousness of God revealed from faith to faith: as it is written, The just shall live by faith." Not the unquestionable, blind, obedient faith preached by the papacy, but faith in what God said, in his written Word. This is why the reformation leaders had to take the Bible out of the hands of the papacy and put it back in the hands of the people.

The papacy's use of deceit and murder to gain and exercise political power over the nations can also be seen in "that woman Jezebel, which calleth herself a prophetess." In 1 Kings Chapter 21, Ahab wanted Naboth's vineyard. In verse 21:2, Ahab offers to buy the land, "And Ahab spake unto Naboth, saying, Give me thy vineyard, that I may have it for a garden of herbs, because it is near unto my house: and I will give thee for it a better vineyard than it; or, if it seem good to thee, I will give thee the worth of it in money." In verse 21:3, Naboth tells him no, "And Naboth said to Ahab, The Lord forbid it me, that I should give the inheritance of my fathers unto thee." In verses 21:4-6, Ahab goes home depressed and tells Jezebel. Her reply is recorded in 21:7, "And Jezebel his wife said unto him, Dost thou now govern the kingdom of Israel? arise, and eat bread, and let thine heart be merry: I will give thee the vineyard of Naboth the Jezreelite." The means she used to put Ahab in control of the land is recorded in verses 21:8-16, "(8) So she wrote letters in Ahab's name, and sealed them with his seal, and sent the letters unto the elders and to the nobles that were in his city, dwelling with Naboth. (9) And she wrote in the letters, saying, Proclaim a fast, and set Naboth on high among the people: (10) And set two men, sons of Belial, before him, to bear witness against him, saying, Thou didst blaspheme God and the king. And then carry him out, and stone him, that he may die. (11) And the men of his city, even the elders and the nobles who were the inhabitants in his city, did as Jezebel had sent unto them, and as it was written in the letters which she had sent unto them. (12) They proclaimed a fast, and set Naboth on high among the people. (13) And there came in two men, children of Belial, and sat before him: and the men of Belial witnessed against him, even against Naboth, in the presence of the people, saying, Naboth did blaspheme God and the king. Then they carried him forth out of the city, and stones him with stones, that he died. (14) Then they sent to Jezebel, saying, Naboth is stoned, and is dead. (15) And it came to pass, when Jezebel heard that Naboth was stoned, and was dead, that Jezebel said to Ahab, Arise, take possession of the vineyard of Naboth the Jezreelite, which he refused to give thee for money: for Naboth is not alive, but dead. (16) And it came to pass, when Ahab heard that Naboth was dead, that Ahab rose up to go down to the vineyard of Naboth the Jezreelite, to take possession of it."

The papacy's use of military might and power to conquer and control the nations was also wrong. The papacy's ambition for territorial gain was motivated by the misconception that the end justifies the means and that the Church would conquer the world and usher in the Kingdom Dispensation. The papacy couldn't hear what God told Zerubbabel in Zechariah 4:6, "Then he answered and spake unto me, saying, This is the word of the Lord unto Zerubbabel, saying, Not by might, nor by power, but by my spirit, saith the Lord of host."

The Letter to Sardis

5. The Letter to Sardis: The Reformation (1500-1700).

Revelation 3:1-6, "(1) And unto the angel of the church in Sardis write; These things saith he that hath the seven Spirits of God, and the seven stars; I know thy works, that thou hast a name that thou livest, and art dead. (2) Be watchful, and strengthen the things which remain, that are ready to die: for I have not found thy works perfect before God. (3) Remember therefore how thou hast received and heard, and hold fast, and repent. If therefore thou shalt not watch, I will come on thee as a thief, and thou shalt not know what hour I will come upon thee. (4) Thou hast a few names even in Sardis which have not defiled their garments; and they shall walk with me in white: for they are worthy. (5) He that overcometh, the same shall be clothed in white raiment; and I will not blot out his name out of the book of life, but I will confess his name before my Father, and before his angels. (6) He that hath an ear, let him hear what the Spirit saith unto the churches."

a. TO: The church in Sardis.
Rev. 3:1a, "And unto the angel of the church in Sardis write."

The Sardis Church Era covers the period of history from the year 1517 to approximately 1700. It began on October 31, 1517, when Martin Luther stood in open rebellion against the Roman Catholic Church. It is followed by the Philadelphia Church Era, which began in the early 1700s as a great period of revival and evangelism called the Great Awakening. The Sardis churches are the Reformation churches, so the emphasis during this era was reform. The Sardis churches are the children (Rev. 2:23) or offspring of the mother Roman Catholic Church, called Protestantism. The Reformation began a movement within the Roman Catholic Church to reform the Church by removing numerous false doctrines being taught and practiced as Bible truth.

The Renaissance (rebirth or revival of learning) actually set the stage for the Reformation. Men began comparing what the Bible taught to what the Roman Catholic Church was teaching, and found that the church wasn't telling the truth. This happened in the secular world as well as the religious world. Many, if not all, the educated men in Europe during the Thyatira Era received their education through the papacy. For example: During the era the papacy taught that the earth was the center of the universe. The teaching went unchallenged until 1543 when Nicholas Copernicus described the sun as the center of a great system with the earth revolving around it. In 1632 when Galileo's astronomical discoveries confirmed the Copernican theory of our solar system, the papal Inquisition forced him to renounce his teaching.

To understand how the papacy was able to maintain the false doctrines they introduced into Christianity, we need to go all the way back to the last revival of learning during the Greek Empire. After the invasion of Alexander the Great (334-327 B.C.), the Greek language became the international language of the Mediterranean area. At this point the original Hebrew Bible was translated into the Greek language and modified by adding the fourteen Apocrypha books. This translation became known as the Septuagint. When the Roman Empire replaced the Greek Empire, the international language of the Mediterranean area changed from Greek to Latin. In A.D. 382, Jerome produced the Latin version of the Bible, called the Vulgate. When the Roman Empire split in A.D. 395, the Western churches retained the Latin Vulgate, and the Eastern churches retained the Greek Septuagint. Eventually, Islam conquered the Eastern Empire and silenced the Eastern Churches. The Western Empire was overrun and eventually conquered by the barbaric tribes dwelling north of the Roman Empire. The barbarians could not read, speak, or understand Greek or Latin, which left the papacy free to teach them whatever they wanted them to believe. Instead of translating the Bible from Latin to the languages of Europe, the papacy made translating or reading the Bible a crime punishable by death.

Taking the Bible away from the papal clergymen and putting it in the hands of the laymen was a bloody battle. John Wycliffe first made the whole Bible available in English. He produced the New Testament in 1380, and the Old Testament two years later. Wycliffe's translation was done from the Latin Vulgate, with the help of Nicholas of Hereford. For his part in the translation, Nicholas was put out of the Roman Catholic Church and imprisoned. On May 4, 1415, thirty-one years after John Wycliffe's death, the Council of Constance excommunicated him, ordered his bones dug up, burned, and the ashes thrown into a river.

The Gutenberg Bible was published by Johann Gutenberg, a German Printer, in 1456. This was probably the first Bible printed from movable types. Its folio pages of two columns, with forty-two lines each, were in Gothic type, and the language of the Gutenberg Bible was Latin. A copy was discovered in cardinal Mazarin's library. It is also called the Mazarin Bible, or 42-line Bible.

William Tyndale was the next great figure in the history of taking the Bible from the papacy. Tyndale translated the New Testament from Greek to the English language, which became the first printed English Bible. Tyndale began his work in England, but opposition forced him to flee to Germany. After he published his New Testament in 1525, it was banned by Cardinal Wolsey and the English bishops. On October 6, 1536, in the town of Vilvorde, near Brussels, Tyndale was seized and condemned for heresy. After a brief imprisonment, he was strangled and burned. His Bibles were gathered by the papal clergy and burned by the hundreds at St. Paul's Cross in London. Tyndale did his job so well that the King James Version reproduces about 90 percent of his New Testament.

The Reformation had the Christian world in a turmoil when Tyndale was translating his version of the Bible. The Reformation, and the Sardis Church Era, actually started on October 31, 1517, when Martin Luther, a Catholic monk, posted his 95 thesis on the Wittenberg Church door. In 1521, Luther was formally excommunicated and summoned before the Diet of Worms. When an edict demanded his seizure, he took refuge in Wartberg. There, he translated the New Testament into German, and began the translation of the entire Bible which was to be a great force in molding the German language. Luther had many other controversies, especially with Zwingli and later with John Calvin, which divided Protestants into the Luthern Church and the Reformed Churches. The mother Roman Catholic Church had spawned the second of her children, and now the children were reproducing, and denominationalism was introduced into the Sardis Church Era.

The Coverdale Bible was the first complete English Bible printed on the printing press. It was published in 1535. The title page stated that it had been translated out of the German and the Latin into English. In the dedication (to Henry VIII), Coverdale says that he used the work of five different translators. However, most of the New Testament and some of the Old Testament were actually the work of Tyndale. Coverdale's version of the Psalms still appears in the Book of Common Prayer, used daily in the ritual of the Church of England. In 1539, Coverdale collaborated in the Great Bible.

Matthew's Bible was the first "Authorized Version" of the Bible in English. It is a fusion of the Tyndale and Coverdale versions. It was printed in London by the Kings license in 1537, by the publishers Grafton and Whitchurch. The work on this version was done by John Rogers, who used the pen name Thomas Matthew for protection. In 1543, an act of Parliament forbade women "except Noble or Gentlewomen" from reading it, even privately, under penalty of death. Opposition to the Matthew's Bible began immediately and continued until Rogers was imprisoned in 1554 by Queen Mary. He was tried and burned as a heretic at Smithfield in 1555. Out of a study of this version came the first English Concordance by Marbeck, a church organist.

The next Bible to appear was a revision of the Matthew Bible, by Coverdale, called the Great Bible. The printing of this Bible began in Paris, but the Inquisition stepped in and the work had to be completed in England. It appeared in 1539 and was called the Great Bible because of its large size, approximately 15 inches by 9 inches. By 1547, great encouragement was given to the reading of the Bible, and to the printing of existing versions. An effort was made to place a copy of the Great Bible in every Church. It was chained to the reading desk in the churches, where it came to be known as the Chained Bible.

The religious freedoms granted by Edward VI ended when Mary Tudor (Mary I) became Queen of England. She was a Catholic and was determined to restore the Roman Catholic Church in England. The persecutions which she undertook made her known as "Bloody Mary." In her effort to make England a Roman Catholic land, anyone caught reading, translating, printing, or distributing the Bible lost their lives. Some of the English Reformers escaped to Geneva, where the leading figure was John Calvin. William Whittingham, who had married Calvin's sister, produced a revision in 1557 of the English New Testament, printed in Roman type, rather than Old English, with the text divided into chapters and verses. He and his associates then undertook the revision of the whole Bible. Their version appeared in 1560 and was known as the Genevan Bible.

Queen Elizabeth, who succeeded Mary Tudor, restored the arrangements of Edward VI. The Great Bible was again placed in the churches and people were encouraged to read the Scriptures. The excellence of the

Genevan Bible made obvious the deficiencies of the Great Bible, but some of its renderings and the marginal notes made it unacceptable to many of the clergy. Archbishop Parker, aided by eight bishops and several other scholars, made a revision of the Great Bible which was completed and published in 1568. It came to be known as the Bishop's Bible.

Queen Elizabeth was a Protestant, and when she became Queen, many Catholics fled from England. Some of the English exiles settled in France and in 1568 founded a college. Gregory Martin began the task of translating the Latin Vulgate into English for use in the Roman Catholic Church. The New Testament was published in 1582 and was done while the college was at Reims; hence this version is known as the Reims New Testament. The Old Testament was not published until 1609-1610, after the college had moved to Douai, and it is called the Dauai Old Testament. This translation was the first Roman Catholic Bible in English. The Rheims-Douay (Reims-Douai) Bible in use today is not the same as the one made by Gregory Martin, but a thorough revision of it made by Bishop Richard Challoner between 1749 and 1763. It was first authorized for use by American Roman Catholics in 1810 and has come to be known as the Authorized Roman Catholic Bible.

When Elizabeth I died in 1603, the crown passed to James I, who had been king of Scotland for thirty-seven years as James VI. Several months after he ascended the throne of England, he authorized a new translation of the Bible to replace the Bishop's Bible. Forty-seven of the best Hebrew and Greek scholars of the day were called together, and worked five years to produce the King James Version of the Bible. This Bible was not so much a new translation, as a careful revision of existing translations. In 1611 the new version was published. It does not contain the fourteen Apocrypha books of the Roman Catholic Bible, which were discredited by the Reformation as uninspired. Its excellence is shown by the fact that after 385 years it is still used in preference to any other version in the English-speaking Protestant world. It is most valuable because it was translated in a time period when there was little or no denominationalism bias. It was the Holy Bible during the Sardis (1517-1700) and the Philadelphia (1700-1900) Church Eras. During this 300 year period (1611-1900) it was the household Bible. When the Laodicean Church era began in 1900, men began revising, amplifying, paraphrasing, and condensing the Holy Bible to a point where its Holiness is questionable. If you keep in mind the Laodicean Church Era is the Apostate Church Age, you will exercise great care in selecting your Bible.

b. FROM: The one who has the seven Spirits of God.
Rev. 3:1b, "These things saith he that hath the seven Spirits of God, and the seven stars."

Jesus introduces himself to the Sardis Church as the one who has the seven Spirits of God and the seven stars. The seven stars are the same seven stars we saw in Rev. 1:20, identified as the seven angels of the seven churches. The seven Spirits of God is the Holy Spirit we saw in Rev. 5:5, the third person in the Trinity. By the fact that Jesus introduces himself as the one who has the Holy Spirit, we can see the problem facing the churches in the Sardis Era. They are the ones who should have the Holy Spirit, not Jesus. We saw the change Christendom underwent because of the big substitution in the Pergamos Church Era. Satan introduced enough errors and false doctrines into Christendom to nullify "the faith" and remove the Mark 16:17-18 signs, so the rebirth and indwelling Holy Spirit were no longer necessary to be called a Christian. Worshipping God was changed from worshipping Him in spirit and in truth, to worshipping Him in vain through soul worship and mental veneration. During the first part of the Thyatira Era the churches united to stop the infiltration of additional false doctrines, but refused to repent of their idolatry. When the papacy took control of Christendom during the last part of the Thyatira Era, they separated the Church members from the Bible. Since the only source of faith is the Word of God (Romans 10:17), and the sword of the Holy Spirit is the Word (Ephesians 6:17), it is easy to see why the Bible had to be returned to the Church membership. Now the members could hear the Word of God and "the faith" could be restored to the Church. With "the faith" restored, Jesus could transfer the Holy Spirit from his holding to their holding.

The Mark 16:17-18 church commission signs would become visible as well as the different spiritual gifts listed in 1 Corinthians 12:4-13, "(4) Now there are diversities of gifts, but the same Spirit. (5) And there are differences of administrations, but the same Lord. (6) And there are diversities of operation, but it is the same God which worketh all in all. (7) But the manifestation of the Spirit is given to every man to profit withal. (8) For to one is given by the Spirit the word of wisdom; to another the word of knowledge by the same Spirit; (9) To another faith by the same Spirit; to another the gifts of healing by the same Spirit; (10) To another the working of miracles; to another prophecy; to another discerning of spirits; to another divers kinds of tongues; to another the interpretation of tongues; (11) But all these worketh that one and the selfsame Spirit, dividing to every man severally as he will. (12) For as the body is one, and hath many members, and all the members of that one body, being many, are one body: so also is Christ. (13) For by one Spirit are we all baptized into one body, whether we be Jews or Gentiles, Whether we be bond or free; and have been all made to drink into one Spirit."

c. COMMENDATION: A few have not defiled their garments, they will walk in white.

Rev. 3:4, "Thou hast a few names even in Sardis which have not defiled their garments; and they shall walk with me in white: for they are worthy."

Only "a few" worthy ones leaves many unworthy ones who will not walk with Jesus in undefiled white garments. You don't accomplish much by taking the Bible from one unbeliever and giving it to another unbeliever. Nothing is accomplished when you stop one clergyman from teaching a group errors and false doctrine, and the group turns to another clergyman teaching different errors and false doctrines. Nothing is accomplished when you replace one error with another error, or leave one false doctrine to follow another false doctrine. The primary goal of the reformers was to remove errors and false doctrines from the Roman Catholic Church. That is the meaning of the word *reform*, "to make better by removing or correcting faults." However, regardless of whether we are looking at an organization or an individual, God's method doesn't change. When an individual turns to Jesus and accepts God's plan of salvation, his old spirit is not reformed. He is given a new Spirit and becomes a new creation in Christ. The reformation leaders had no chance whatsoever of reforming the mother church because she did not want to be reformed. Jesus gave "her space to repent of her fornication; and she repented not" (Rev. 2:21), so the only alternative was for the reformation leaders to come out of her and leave her. In order to turn to Jesus, they had to turn their backs on the Roman Catholic Church.

On October 31, 1517, when Martin Luther posted his 95 thesis on the Wittenberg church door, he stood in open rebellion against the Roman Catholic Church, and the Lutheran Church was born. Ulrich Zwingli (Swiss reformer 1484-1531) disagreed with Luther on the Church Sacraments of the Lord's Supper and infant baptism, which gave birth to the Reformed Church. Zwingli's view on communion was that it was purely symbolic. Then came John Calvin (1509-64), who imputed a spiritual meaning only to the words. Later, George Fox (1624-91) rejected the sacrament altogether. Fox's followers became known as Quakers. Zwingli organized a congregation in Zurich, Switzerland, in 1525. They rejected infant baptism and were labeled Anabaptists or Rebaptizers. Their doctrine was carried to Holland by Obbe Philips, who baptized Menno Simons in 1536. His followers became known as Mennonites, who baptized by pouring, only after a confession of faith. John Smythe accepted their teaching and organized the first English Baptist Church in 1609. Their belief in general atonement for all men was challenged by the predestination and limited atonement of John Calvin, which resulted in the General Baptist and Particular Church (British 1638). Internal strife resulted in another group known as Immersion Baptist who claimed baptism by total immersion only. In 1644 they wrote a confession of faith which is the basic foundation for most modern day Baptists.

John Calvin's doctrine of predestination questions the free will choice of humans to come to Jesus and be saved. In essence, it denies the "whosoever will" can come of Rev. 22:17, "And the Spirit and the bride say, Come. And let him that heareth say, Come. And let him that is athirst come. And whosoever will, let him take of the water of life freely." Predestination teaches that God's plans are absolute, that God elects or condemns people to salvation or damnation, and that it was all predetermined before the foundation of the world. It sanctifies immoral conduct by casting doubt on whether people are free to take responsibility for their actions, or whether their choice is controlled. John Calvin's preaching on predestination laid the foundation for the modern day Presbyterian Church.

Robert Brown (1550-1633), an English clergyman, preached nonconformity which gave birth to Congregationalism. In Congregationalism the authority of bishops and presbyters is rejected, and each congregation or local church has free control of its own affairs.

These splits and divisions within the Protestant Churches gave birth to denominationalism. The reformation leaders took the Bible from the Roman Catholic clergy and put it in the hands of the people. The invention of the printing press permitted wide distribution of the Bible, and with its reading came many different interpretations. The denominations began developing written "Confessions of Faith," or Catechisms, which later generations exalted to the position of the "Rule Book." These statements of faith became so rigid that they stopped the congregations from accepting and practicing spiritual truths which the reformation leaders could not see or did not understand. New spiritual insight causes an individual to grow in Christ, and it should do the same to a church or denomination. The danger here is not in their doctrinal stand on fundamental Bible truths, it is their inability to edify themselves because the "Rule Book" has been finalized and they will go that far, but no further. The end result of the finalized "Rule Book" can be seen in the rebuke section of the letter where Jesus says, "You are dead, living in name only."

d. REBUKE: Dead, living in name only.
Rev. 3:1c, "I know thy works, that thou hast a name that thou livest, and are dead."

Jesus says he knows three things about the Reformation denominations. First, Jesus says, "I know thy works." Second, Jesus says, "I know...that thou hast a name." Third, Jesus says, "I know . . . that thou livest, and are dead." Jesus can see they are dead; people looking for Jesus can look at Denominationalism and see the deadness; but, the pew-warmers inside the church building can't see themselves as dead. They are not going to be able to see themselves as Jesus sees them until they take their eyes off the rule book long enough to look at the Word of God. Since the Lutheran Church was the first actual Protestant denomination, let's take a closer look at it. In 1529 Martin Luther wrote his longer and shorter catechisms. Looking at his followers today, it becomes obvious that Luther either did not emphasize, did not understand, or did not believe the ending statement in the commission Jesus gave to the Church. "They (believers) shall lay hands on the sick, and they shall recover." Divine healing by the laying on of believers' hands is scriptural. I didn't just dream it up, Jesus spoke of it in Mark 16:15-18. If God is not confirming his word by this sign, it is because that Scripture is not being taught as the truthful Word of God. If this spiritual gift is not functioning in the Church, it is because of the pastor or congregation, not the Word of God. God's Word will accomplish for the believer exactly what God said it would accomplish. If Martin Luther was alive today and accepted "Divine healing by the laying on of believers hands" as scriptural truth, his own church, called by his name, would reject and excommunicate him. Martin Luther would have the same success trying to reform the Lutheran Church of today as he had trying to reform the Roman Catholic Church of his day.

It is obvious none of the reformation leaders understood the prophecies concerning the end of the Church Age. There was no visible evidence in their day that the Jews would be returned to their land to set the stage for the Gog invasion in Ezekiel chapters 38 and 39. There was no evidence that the Roman Empire would evolve into a ten nation economic world power. There was absolutely no way for the entire world to watch the killing of the two faithful witnesses in the streets of Jerusalem. The "order of the day" for the reformation leaders was reform, not prophecy. The cry in Christendom during Luther's day was Church reform, not the Church rapture. Martin Luther served his generation well. There was a job to be done and Luther was faithful to the task. Luther looked at what the Word of God said, compared it to what the Roman Catholic Church was saying, and was able to see she was telling lies. Had Luther compared what she was saying to the Roman Catholic rule book, he would have preached that she was telling the truth. Luther valued what the Scriptures said above what the papacy said. Luther not only stood against the papacy, he stood against the errors and false doctrine introduced in Christendom by Ulrich Zwingli, John Calvin, and the Anabaptists. Martin Luther believed the Word of God, and that is the reason his name lives today. That is why the name Martin Luther comes into the conversation when discussing the Lutheran Church or the Reformation. The Lutheran Church is still living on the name Martin Luther.

When the reformation took the Bible from the papal clergymen and put it in the hands of the laymen, it was both a blessing and a curse. It was a blessing because the people could now read the Word of God for themselves, choose obedience to that word, and allow Jesus to transfer the Holy Spirit from his holding to their holding. The curse lies in the fact that Satan never passes up an opportunity to pervert the Word of God. Some of the laymen were educated, others were illiterate, some were wise, others were fools, some believed the Word of God, others didn't, some preached the Word, others preached their own ideas. The "few" commended for not defiling their garments compared what was being taught to what the Bible taught. When the Sacrament of the Lord's Supper came under attack, they turned to Matthew 26:26-30, and saw where Jesus took the bread and said, "This is my body," and took the wine and said, "This is my blood." When

Zwingli, Calvin, and Fox, couldn't see it that way, a few knew either they, or Jesus had eye trouble. When Zwingli, Philips, Simons, Smythe, and the Anabaptist put an age limit on water baptism and excluded children from the kingdom of God, a few saw through the damnable heresy. A few believed the New Covenant promise of the indwelling Holy Spirit, saw the children's need for the Holy Spirit, and heard Jesus when he said, "Suffer little children, and forbid them not, to come unto me." The few who believed the Word of God read the Old Testament and saw what happens to children when God moves in judgment. They could see men like Zwingli and the Anabaptist standing outside Noah's Ark, when God shut the door, preaching, "The children are safe, no harm will come to the children." They could see the same type people standing in the streets of Sodom and Gomorrah, singing the same song, just before the Lord rained fire and brimstone on the cities. They could see them walking the streets of Egypt on the night of the first Passover telling the people that no harm will come to the first-born if they are children.

A few compared what the Word of God said to what John Calvin said, and saw that predestination calls God a liar in John 3:16, "(15) For God so loved the world, that he gave his only begotten Son, that whosoever believeth in him should not perish, but have everlasting life." It calls Jesus a liar in Mark 16:15-16, "(15) And he said unto them, Go ye into all the world, and preach the gospel to every creature, (16) He that believeth and is baptized shall be saved; but he that believeth not shall be damned." It calls Jesus, the Holy Spirit, the Church, and all Christians, liars in Rev. 22:17, "And the Spirit and the bride say, Come. And let him that heareth say, Come. And let him that is athirst come. And whosoever will, let him take the water of life freely." A few knew God's plan of salvation was finalized before the foundation of the world. It was predetermined that he would freely give eternal life to those who believed his Word and accepted his plan of salvation, and that he would judge and condemn to damnation those who rejected his word and plan of salvation. Jesus tells us how the few knew in John 7:16-17, "(16) Jesus answered them, and said, My doctrine is not mine, but his that sent me. (17) If any man will do his will, he shall know of the doctrine, whether it be of God, or whether I speak of myself."

During the Sardis Church Era the Protestants aligned themselves with whomever they chose to believe, developed the rule book to distinguish their group from all the other groups, and continued to read the Bible. As the knowledge of the Word of God increased in the Protestant population, the preaching turned to repentance, holy living, and obedience. The Sardis Church era ends with a whole new generation of Christians. Their heart's cry was, "Let's live like the word of God says, and let's go do what Jesus told us to do." By the year 1700, Christendom enters the Philadelphia Church Era, when Jesus opens the door that no man can shut (Rev 3:8), and the missionaries start going out. Every denomination heard Jesus say, "Go ye into all the world, and preach the gospel to every creature. He that believeth and is baptized shall be saved; but he that believeth not shall be damned." (Mark 16:15-16). The next 200 years of Church history is the Philadelphia Era, characterized by revival and evangelism. It was doing this period of history that Christians began reading and teaching the rest of the Church Commission, Mark 16:17-18, "(17) And these signs shall follow them that believe; In my name shall they cast out devils; they shall speak with new tongues; (18) They shall take up serpents; and if they drink any deadly thing, it shall not hurt them; they shall lay hands on the sick, and they shall recover." Manifestations of the indwelling Holy Spirit such as speaking in tongues, divine healings, and miracles were eventually rejected by established denominations, which gave birth to Pentecostalism. It just wasn't in the "Rule Book." That is why Jesus introduces himself to Reformation Denominationalism as the one holding the Holy Spirit, that they should be holding. That rejection of the last two verses of the Church Commission is what introduced the last period of Church history, the Laodicean Era, and killed denominationalism. This is the period in their history when Jesus will rebuke them with the words, "I know thy works, that thou hast a name that thou livest, and art dead."

e. EXHORT: Watch, strengthen, remember, and repent (coming as a thief). Rev. 3:2-3, "(2) Be watchful, and strengthen the things which remain, that are ready to die: for I have not found thy works perfect before God. (3) Remember therefore how thou hast received and heard, and hold fast, and repent. If therefore thou shalt not watch, I will come on thee as a thief, and thou shalt not know what hour I will come upon thee."

The "be watchful" exhort is "Be watchful, and strengthen the things which remain, that are ready to die, for I have not found thy works perfect before God." This exhort could not be heard by the reformation denominations during the Sardis or Philadelphia Church eras, which brought them the rebuke, "I know . . . that thou livest, and are dead" in the Laodicean Era. They are dead because of the absence of the Holy Spirit, which Jesus is holding instead of them. Jesus is the one who baptizes with the Holy Spirit. He is the one who holds the Holy Spirit until a person meets the requirements established for being born-again. When a person meets the requirements, Jesus baptizes them with the Holy Spirit. The determining factor in your salvation is who has the Holy Spirit, is he indwelling you, or is Jesus still holding him? If you are, in fact, a born-again believer, evident by the indwelling Holy Spirit, and Jesus says to you, "I have not found thy works perfect before God," you will lose rewards, but not your salvation. If you have been deceived into thinking you have been born-again, evident by the absence of the indwelling Holy Spirit, and Jesus says to you, "I have not found thy works perfect before God," you will be rejected at the rapture, because you were never saved in the first place. The indwelling Holy Spirit is what makes a person an overcomer, and the absence of the Holy Spirit is a clear indication that a person has been overcome by the deceiver. The promise Jesus made to the Sardis congregation in Rev. 3:5, is also a warning to those overcome by deceit. It reads, "He that overcometh, the same shall be clothed in white raiment; and I will not blot out his name out of the book of life, but I will confess his name before my Father, and before his angels."

The presence or absence of the Holy Spirit in a church congregation is a clear indication as to whether its members are born-again believers or dead unbelievers. If the Holy Spirit isn't manifesting his presence by the Mark 16:17-18 signs it is because he isn't there. Jesus said, "These signs shall follow them that believe," so if the signs are not there it is because they don't believe. You are not going to find the eternal life Jesus is offering you among the unbelieving. They can deceive you only after they convince you that they are telling you the truth and Jesus is not. Who you choose to believe will determine your eternal abode in heaven, or hell. Many modern day Christians don't care enough about what Jesus said to even look at what their denomination teaches. If you are already a member of a dead denominational church, listen as Jesus continues the letter, "Remember therefore how thou hast received and heard, and hold fast, and repent." Remember how your denomination got what you are receiving and hearing today, hold fast to the truth, and repent by removing the false doctrines and errors that are hampering your spiritual growth. The Lutheran, and many other churches, have the completed rule book that will not let them accept and do the Mark 16:17-18 works. The Presbyterians are still preaching predestination, and the Anabaptist doctrine is still being preached by the Baptist churches. What the Anabaptist doctrine teaches can be seen in the cliche, "Water baptism is an outward sign of an inward work." It sounds very religious, but the truth is that the Mark 16:17-18 signs are the outward signs of an inward work.

Like their mother Roman Catholic Church, the Protestant denominational children will continue to exist until the rapture, when Jesus takes the born-again believers off the planet and leaves the rest to be destroyed by Antichrist. This is why Jesus says, "If therefore thou shalt not watch, I will come on thee as a thief, and thou shalt not know what hour I will come upon thee." Jesus' coming as a thief in the night, and the activity of his servants is amplified in Matthew 24:36-51. You are either going to be taken or left, a faithful and wise servant or an evil servant, an overcomer or one that is overcome. Matthew 24:36-51, "(36) But of that day and hour knoweth no man, no, not the angels of heaven, but my Father only. (37) But as the days of Noe were, so shall also the coming of the Son of man be. (38) For as in the days that were before the flood they were eating and drinking, marrying and giving in marriage, until the day that Noe entered into the ark, (39) And knew not until the flood came, and took them all away; so shall also the coming of the Son of man be. (40) Then shall two be in the field; the one shall be taken, and the other left. (41) Two women shall be grinding at the mill; the one shall be taken, and the other left. (42) Watch therefore: for ye know not what hour your Lord doth come. (43) But know this, that if the goodman of the house had known in what watch the thief would come, he would have watched, and would not have suffered his house to be broken up. (44) Therefore be ye also ready: for in such as hour as ye think not the Son of man cometh. (45) Who then is a faithful and wise servant, whom his lord hath made ruler over his household, to give them meat in due season? (46) Blessed is that servant, whom his lord when he cometh shall find so doing. (47) Verily I say unto you, That he shall make him ruler over all his goods. (48) But and if that evil servant shall say in his heart, My lord delayeth his coming; (49) And shall begin to smite his fellowservants, and to eat and drink with the drunken; (50) The lord of that servant shall come in a day when he looketh not for him, and in an hour that he is not aware of, (51) And shall cut him asunder, and appoint him his portion with the hypocrites: there shall be weeping and gnashing of teeth."

f. PROMISES: Overcomers clothed in white raiment, will not blot out their names.

Rev. 3:5-6, "(5) He that overcometh, the same shall be clothed in white raiment; and I will not blot out his name out of the book of life, but I will confess his name before my Father, and before his angels. (6) He that hath an ear, let him hear what the Spirit saith unto the churches."

When Jesus comes as a thief in the night to get, rapture, or snatch away his Church from Earth, the event is limited to the Christian population of the planet. The participants in the rapture are limited to those born-again believing overcomers who have met the requirements of the New Testament, or Covenant. The remaining Christian population will be left on the planet to face Antichrist. The Christian population that will not participate in the rapture includes all those who did not meet the requirements of the New Covenant, the deceived Christians, the insincere who were playing Christian, the fake Christians who formulated their own Christianity, and all apostates. The rapture will end the Church Dispensation and all chances to be saved as a Church member. It does not end all chances to be saved, but they enter the tribulation without the guarantee, "I will not blot out his name out of the book of life." They got their names in the book of life by making a commitment to Jesus, but in the baptism of fire, had communicated their insincerity or unfaithfulness by failing the tests and yielding to Satan's temptations. Had they been faithful to that commitment by doing what Jesus said, the way He said to do it, they would have left Earth in the rapture with the Church congregation. Their unfaithfulness to Jesus has resulted in his rejection of them as Church members, but they can keep their names in the book of life and be saved as members of the fifth seal group (Rev. 6:9-11) by repenting and remaining faithful to Jesus in the baptism of fire unto death, when the Antichrist organization says "deny or die." A denial of Jesus, at this point, to keep your name in the book of the living will result in Jesus blotting your name out of the book of life, which condemns you to hell. If you refuse to deny Jesus, the Antichrist organization will blot your name out of the book of the living, but Jesus will not blot your name out of the book of life.

Don't confuse the Book of the Living with the Book of Life. They are two different books and neither was written in eternity past or before the foundation of the world, as predestination teaches. The difference between the two books can be seen in Psalm 69, which deals with the rejection of Jesus as the promised Redeemer. Verse 69:28 reads, "Let them be blotted out of the book of the living, and not be written with the righteous." Your name was recorded in the Book of the Living the instant you were conceived, Psalm 139:13-16, "(13) For thou hast possessed my reins: thou hast covered me in my mother's womb. (14) I will praise thee; for I am fearfully and wonderfully made: marvelous are thy works; and that my soul knoweth right well. (15) My substance was not hid from thee, when I was made in secret, and curiously wrought in the lowest parts of the earth. (16) Thine eyes did see my substance, yet being unperfect; and in thy book all my members were written, which in continuance were fashioned, when as yet there was none of them." Your name was written in the Book of Life, or "written with the righteous," when you acted on the Word of God, in accepting God's plan of redemption in Jesus Christ.

Also, don't confuse what was said about losing your salvation. If you have been born again, according to the gospel of Jesus Christ, He has baptized you with the Holy Spirit. That indwelling Holy Spirit is the token or seal of the New Covenant, and is your guarantee of eternal salvation. Listen to the promise Jesus made in John 14:15-21, "(15) If ye love me, keep my commandments. (16) And I will pray the Father, and he shall give you another comforter, that he may abide with you for ever; (17) Even the Spirit of truth; whom the world cannot receive, because it seeth him not, neither knoweth him: but ye know him; for he dwelleth with you, and shall be in you. (18) I will not leave you comfortless: I will come to you. (19) Yet a little while, and the world seeth me no more; but ye see me: because I live, ye shall live also. (20) At that day ye shall know that I am in my Father, and ye in me, and I in you. (21) He that hath my commandments, and keepeth them, he it is that loveth me: and he that loveth me shall be loved of my Father, and I will love him, and will manifest myself to him." If you have not loved Jesus and kept his commandments (Verse 15) tremble, because none of this applies to you. "That day" for the Church member is the rapture, the day of redemption. That indwelling Holy Spirit sealed you, and is your inheritance until the day of redemption, Ephesians 1:13-14, "(13) In whom ye also trusted, after that ye heard the word of truth, the gospel of your salvation: in whom also after that ye believed, ye were sealed with that holy Spirit of promise, (14) Which is the earnest of our inheritance until the redemption of the purchased possession, unto the praise of his glory." Ephesians 4:30, "And grieve not the holy Spirit of God, whereby ye are sealed unto the day of redemption."

In John 14:16 Jesus said "that he may abide with you for ever," so you don't have to worry about the Holy Spirit, your guarantee seal of eternal salvation, leaving you. The Church membership left behind at the rapture were never sealed by the Holy Spirit or they chose to sell their birthright in the daily baptisms of fire. Some were never born-again according to the gospel of Jesus Christ, so instead of being a child of God, they are bastards. Others are deceived by errors, false doctrines, or tradition into thinking they are born-again, but they never completed the rebirth and can only be described as miscarriages. They may not be able to see themselves as miscarriages today, but they will when they are rejected (prematurely developed) out of the Body of Christ at the rapture. Since the rapture will not occur until the end of the Laodicean Era, when the Bridegroom comes for his Bride, the condition of the reformation denominational churches can be seen in the five foolish virgins of Matthew 25:1-13. That oil missing from their lamps is the Holy Spirit, but before we look at how they went into the Laodicean Church Era without oil, let's look at them in the Philadelphia Church Era when their lamps were burning.

The Letter to Philadelphia

6. The Letter to Philadelphia: Revival and Evangelism (1700-1900).

Revelation 3:7-13, "(7) And to the angel of the church in Philadelphia write; These things saith he that is holy, he that is true, he that hath the key of David, he that openeth, and no man shutteth; and shutteth, and no man openeth; (8) I know thy works: behold, I have set before thee an open door, and no man can shut it: for thou hast a little strength, and hast kept my word, and hast not denied my name. (9) Behold, I will make them of the synagogue of Satan, which say they are Jews, and are not, but do lie; behold, I will make them to come and worship before thy feet, and to know that I have loved thee. (10) Because thou hast kept the word of my patience, I also will keep thee from the hour of temptation, which shall come upon all the world, to try them that dwell upon the earth. (11) Behold, I come quickly: hold that fast which thou hast, that no man take thy crown. (12) Him that overcometh will I make a pillar in the temple of my God, and he shall go no more out: and I will write upon him the name of my God, and the name of the city of my God, which is new Jerusalem, which cometh down out of heaven from my God: and I will write upon him my new name. (13) He that hath an ear, let him hear what the Spirit saith unto the churches."

a. TO: The church in Philadelphia.
Rev. 3:7a, "And to the angel of the church in Philadelphia write."

The Philadelphia Church Era began in the early 1700s as a great period of revival and evangelism called the Great Awakening. The era introduced the "Evangelist," who introduced "Revivals" which produced "Missionaries" who go out the "open door" to preach the gospel of Jesus Christ to the whole world. The Philadelphia Church Era ended around the year 1900 when the "open doors" started closing, but the Philadelphia churches will not end until the rapture, when Jesus closes the Church Door. The Philadelphia churches will continue to exist together with the Laodicean churches during the Laodicean Church Era, in the same manner as the Catholic and Protestant churches coexisted during the Sardis Church Era. At the end of the Laodicean Church Era the Philadelphia congregation is raptured and kept "from the hour of temptation, which shall come upon all the world, to try them that dwell upon the earth," and the Laodicean congregation is rejected, (I will spue thee out of my mouth) to enter the great tribulation.

The word *evangel* comes from the Greek word *euangelos* which means "bringing good news." It is constructed of *eu* meaning "well" and *angelos* meaning "messenger." In English the word *evangel* means "the gospel" or the good news of Jesus Christ. An evangelist is the messenger who preaches the gospel of Jesus. They evangelize by preaching the gospel of Jesus to the people, and converting them to Christianity. Those who hear and respond to the gospel or good news of Jesus are *revived.* The word *revive* is a Latin word constructed of the prefix *re* meaning "again," and *vivere* meaning "to live," hence the meaning "to live again." In English the word *revive* means "to come back to life or consciousness."

The life-giver in an individual, congregation, or denomination is the Holy Spirit, which was made available through the substitutionary death of the Redeemer, Jesus Christ, to whosoever will come to Him. The first four books of the New Testament–Matthew, Mark, Luke, and John–are called "The Gospels" because they record the life and ministry of Jesus Christ. They not only tell us what the Redeemer did, they are a written record of what He said. Jesus said there was life in his words in John 6:63, "It is the spirit that quickeneth; the flesh profiteth nothing: the words that I speak unto you, they are spirit, and they are life." Everlasting life or everlasting condemnation is dependent on what a person does in response to what Jesus said. The difference between hearing and doing is the difference between building a house on a rock or on sand (Matthew 7:24-27).

Christendom began "to live again" when men began to hear and say what Jesus said, instead of what tradition said. The churches going into the Philadelphia Church Era were the Catholic churches of the Thyatira Era and the Protestant denominations of the Sardis Era. The revival began within the churches when the evangelists began preaching the gospel of Jesus.

All the churches heard Jesus say, "Go ye into all the world, and preach the gospel to every creature. he that believeth and is baptized shall be saved; but he that believeth not shall be damned" (Mark 16:15-16). In response, the missionaries carried the gospel of Jesus through the open door to the entire world. In the Smyrna Church Era we saw missionaries scattered throughout the Roman Empire by the Church persecution, but not this time. These missionaries went of their own free will because they loved Jesus and because of Philadelphia, "brotherly love." Some of the church members began reading the remainder of the Church Commission and said, "We are still not doing all Jesus told us to do." What they read was Mark 16:17-18, "(17) And these signs shall follow them that believe; In my name shall they cast out devils; they shall speak with new tongues; (18) They shall take up serpents; and if they drink any deadly thing, it shall not hurt them; they shall lay hands on the sick, and they shall recover." The indwelling Holy Spirit began to manifest his presence in them when they began speaking in tongues and performing healing miracles. When they told the congregation of their experience, they were ridiculed, and driven from the Thyatira and Sardis churches, which gave birth to the Pentecostal and Evangelical Churches.

The Philadelphia Church Era ends with the Thyatira churches and the Protestant denominations of the Sardis Era returning to their traditional heritage. Their refusal to hear and do what Jesus told them to do in the last two verses of the Church Commission (Mark 16:17-18) is actually a rejection of the indwelling Holy Spirit. We saw Jesus introduce himself to the churches of the Sardis era as the One holding the Holy Spirit. Their rejection of the Holy Spirit during the Philadelphia era caused them to enter the final church era in a dead condition, as unbelieving members of the Laodicean Church. When Jesus raptures the Philadelphia churches, the Laodicean churches will enter the great tribulation to be destroyed by Antichrist. This will be the fulfillment of the promise Jesus made to the Catholic churches of the Thyatira era, Rev. 2:21-23a, "(21) And I gave her space to repent of her fornication; and she repented not. (22) Behold, I will cast her into a bed, and them that commit adultery with her into great tribulation, except they repent of their deeds; (23a) And I will kill her children with death." It is important to understand that not all of the churches formed during the Philadelphia era will be raptured. Many of the Pentecostal and Evangelical churches that came into existence during this era did so by placing the Mark 16:17-18 manifestations of the Holy Spirit on top of the foundation of error and false doctrines of their parent church and calling themselves by another name. Although they are closer to the truth than their parent, those errors and false doctrines are blemishes that will hamper their ministry until they are removed. What the Church and its members needs to do is start washing, and keep washing, until the glory starts showing, Ephesians 5:26-27, "(26) That he might sanctify and cleanse it with the washing of water by the word, (27) That he might present it to himself a glorious church, not having spot, or wrinkle, or any such thing; but that it should be holy and without blemish."

The Great Awakening that introduced the Philadelphia Church Era began in New Jersey with a Presbyterian clergyman named Gilbert Tennent preaching evangelism. His father, William, founded the Log College in 1726 to train evangelists for revival meetings. Jonathan Edwards, a Congregationalist, is credited with carrying the revival to New England, Samuel Davies to Virginia, and Samuel Kirkland westward to the Indians. The Great Awakening was not limited to the United States. The evangelistic preaching of John and Charles Wesley in England gave birth to the Methodist Church in 1729. The Great Awakening was spread by tours, where the evangelist would move from Church to Church holding revival meetings. As the movement gained momentum missionaries were sent to every country on earth. Great Britain took the lead and Jesus blessed that small island nation to the point where the sun never set on British soil. Eventually the United States took the missionary lead and Jesus has blessed this nation above all other nations, past or present. Protestant missionaries made Great Britain, the United States, and Canada what they are today. Roman Catholic missionaries made Central and South America what they are today. Asia and North Africa are what they are today because they rejected Christianity for Islam. India rejected Christianity for Hinduism which made India what it is today. Jesus closed the open door to China when it communicated its preference for Buddhism and Confucianism over Christianity in the Boxer Rebellion (1900). China put up the Bamboo Curtain to prepare its people for the invasion of the kings of the East in the Battle of Armageddon. Jesus closed the open door to Russia in 1918 when the Bolsheviks Revolution put the atheistic Communist Party into power. The Party put up the Iron Curtain to prepare its people for the Gog and Magog invasion of the Middle East. We have already discussed the Church doors closing as they reject what Jesus told them to do in the Mark 16:15-18 Church Commission. This is why Jesus is standing outside the Laodicean churches, knocking for admittance in Rev. 3:20, "Behold, I stand at the door, and knock: if any man hear my voice, and open the door, I will come in to him, and will sup with him, and he with me."

b. FROM: The Holy One who opens doors that no man can shut.
Rev. 3:7b, "These things saith he that is holy, he that is true, he that hath the key of David, he that openeth, and no man shutteth, and shutteth, and no man openeth."

Jesus presents himself as holy and true because that is how the Philadelphia churches recognize him. He presents himself as "he that openeth, and no man shutteth" to present the era as an opportunity for worldwide revival and evangelism. Although many doors close at the end of the era, and many more will continue to close during the Laodicean era, the revival and evangelism which marks this era will continue, to some degree, by the Philadelphia churches until the rapture. Jesus presents himself as he that "shutteth, and no man openeth" to communicate to the Philadelphia churches that the church age is coming to a close. One of the doors he shuts that no man can open is the Church door, which will be shut on the Laodicean churches at the rapture. He presents himself as "he that hath the key of David" to alert the Philadelphia churches that during their existence, they would see God continue his program with the Jews. This is the transition James spoke of in Acts 15:13-17, "(13) And after they had held their peace, James answered, saying, Men and brethren, hearken unto me: (14) Simeon hath declared how God at the first did visit the Gentiles, to take out of them a people for his name. (15) And to this agree the words of the prophets; as it is written, (16) After this I will return, and will build again the tabernacle of David, which is fallen down; and I will build again the ruins thereof, and I will set it up: (17) That the residue of men might seek after the Lord, and all the Gentiles, upon whom my name is called, saith the Lord, who doeth all these things."

In 1918 the Philadelphia congregation saw the Jews return to the Promised Land and the Communist Party take control of Russia. They could see the Gog and Magog invasion on the horizon. They heard the Jews announce to the world on May 14, 1948, that Israel was once again a nation. In 1967 they saw the Arab nations that pledged to annihilate Israel defeated in seven days, and the city of Jerusalem returned to the Jews. From the Book of Daniel they knew of the antichrist protection treaty to be confirmed with the Jews at Jerusalem, and saw that the only piece missing from the prophecy was the ten king kingdom. They stood in awe as the European Common Market grew from six nations in 1967, to nine nations in 1973, to completion in 1981. They could see the ministry of Jesus as High Priest to his Church coming to a close and his ministry as King Jesus on the horizon.

We are the privileged generation that has been permitted to watch God working with a generation of Christians and a generation of Jews at the same time, to bring his eternal purpose to pass. We are the generation that saw the world stage set for the fulfillment of a large portion of Bible prophecy, perhaps a third of the entire Bible. We are the generation watching the transition from the Church Dispensation to the Kingdom Dispensation. We are watching Christendom decrease, and the Jews increase, as the time of the Gentiles comes to its end. We are the generation seeing Jesus being thrown out of the churches, government, society, business, and out of the personal lives of millions of human beings. We are the generation who buys a Bible to take home, so we can bury it under a layer of dust. We are the apathetic generation that sits back with its mouth shut, and allows the apostate to pervert the Word of God, change truth to a lie, and light to darkness. Through apathy we allow the judges of our land to erase the laws of God from our judicial system, eliminate God's truth from our education system, and legalize murder through abortion. There has never been a generation of Christians on this planet with more light than our generation. It doesn't matter if you look at the prophecies in the Bible concerning the Church, the Jews, or the God rejecting world, they all say the same thing, "The time for judgment has arrived." The Philadelphia congregation is crying, "Behold, the Bridegroom cometh," and the Laodicean congregation is crying, "Don't bother us with the facts."

c. COMMENDATION: They kept the word and name, no hour of temptation for them.

Rev. 3:8, "I know thy works: behold, I have set before thee an open door, and no man can shut it: for thou hast a little strength, and hast kept my word, and hast not denied my name."

Rev. 3:10, "Because thou hast kept the word of my patience, I also will keep thee from the hour of temptation, which shall come upon all the world, to try them that dwell upon the earth."

Again, the statement, "I know thy works: behold, I have set before thee an open door, and no man can shut it." speaks of the Philadelphia Era as an opportunity for worldwide revival and evangelism. The opportunity arose in the early 1700s when men began preaching the gospel instead of the church tradition of the Sardis Era. When the era began, the emphasis was on the gospel of Jesus, so denominational tradition became secondary. Their strength was the gospel, their weakness was Sardis tradition, and mixing the two hampered their ministry to the point where Jesus had to say, "for thou hast a little strength." On that "little strength" the missionaries took the good news of Jesus to the entire world. As the people responded in repentance to the gospel message and became obedient to the Word of God, the Mark 16:17-18 manifestations of the indwelling Holy Spirit became a threat to the traditional doctrines of the Sardis denominational churches. By the year 1900, the Sardis churches had returned to their traditional heritage, which rejects miracles following believers. Speaking in tongues was declared unscriptural and attributed to Satan. The churches that rejected the manifestations of the indwelling Holy Spirit became the foundation of the Laodicean congregation in the next, and final, Church Era.

The members of the Sardis congregation who chose to believe Jesus were expelled from the established denominations, and became the Philadelphia churches entering the Laodicean Church Era. It was to these individuals, and these churches, that Jesus said, "for thou hast a little strength, and hast kept my word, and hast not denied my name." In the Laodicean Era they continue to compare the Word of God to traditional Christianity, and where tradition contradicts what Jesus said, they choose to believe Jesus. They realize they have to get Jesus' Word, before they could keep it, so they took Paul's advice to study the Bible, 2 Timothy 2:15, "Study to shew thyself approved unto God, a workman that needeth not to be ashamed, rightly dividing the word of truth." Their goal is to do what the

Holy Spirit said in Colossians 3:16, "Let the word of Christ dwell in you richly in all wisdom; teaching and admonishing one another in psalms and hymns and spiritual songs, singing with grace in your hearts to the Lord." They are obedient to Romans 12:2, "And be not conformed to this world: but be ye transformed by the renewing of your mind, that ye may prove what is that good, and acceptable, and perfect, will of God." They renew their minds by replacing their private opinions with Jesus' opinions, what they were taught with what the Bible taught, and what Church tradition said with what Jesus said. They live 2 Corinthians 10:5, "Casting down imaginations, and every high thing that exalteth itself against the knowledge of God, and bringing into captivity every thought to the obedience of Christ."

In the process they not only learn to think like Jesus, some start acting like him. When they run into a mountain, instead of reaching for a shovel, they speak to it as Jesus told them to do in Mark 11:23, "For verily I say unto you, That whosoever shall say unto this mountain, Be thou removed, and be thou cast into the sea; and shall not doubt in his heart, but shall believe that those things which he saith shall come to pass; he shall have whatsoever he saith." When they become sick or diseased, instead of building a hospital, they claim healing according to Mark 16:17-18. If they can't find a fellow believer to lay hands on them, they lay their own hands on themselves, and they recover. When they think like Jesus, they see things as Jesus saw them. They put the same faith in the words of Jesus, that Jesus put in his Father's words during his ministry as the Son of man, our Redeemer. They understand that Jesus operated on the authority of the Word and the power of the Holy Spirit to perform the miracles recorded in the Gospels. When they realize that the same Holy Spirit indwelt them, and that Jesus had given them the authority to use his name to perform miracles, the faith which was once commonplace in Christianity, revived. This was the faith nullified by the errors and false doctrines introduced into Christianity during the Pergamos Era and suppressed by traditions until the Philadelphia congregation revived the doctrine by removing the errors and false doctrines. Because of their faithfulness to Jesus and their obedience to the Word of God, they will be raptured before the great tribulation begins, Rev. 3:10, "Because thou hast kept the word of my patience, I also will keep thee from the hour of temptation, which shall come upon all the world, to try them that dwell upon the earth."

d. REBUKE: No rebuke whatsoever, enemies will know this Church was loved.

Rev. 3:9, "Behold, I will make them of the synagogue of Satan, which say they are Jews, and are not, but do lie; behold, I will make them to come and worship before thy feet, and to know that I have loved thee."

Of the seven letters to the seven churches, the letter to the Philadelphia congregation is the only letter containing no rebuke section, and the letter to the Laodicean congregation is the only letter containing no commendation section. The rebuke in the Philadelphia letter is not directed to the congregation, but to its enemies. The enemies of the Philadelphia congregation are not the world of unbelievers outside Christendom, but the world of unbelievers inside Christendom. The enemy is the Laodicean congregation, which says it is Christian but is not. They claim to be God's people, but in reality, they are of the synagogue of Satan. They are fakes, some by choice, others through deceit, but it doesn't make any difference, they are still fakes. Instead of repeating the words of Jesus, and telling the people that is the truth, they contradict what Jesus said, and preach those contradictions as the truth. Instead of preaching faith, they preach unbelief, and instead of making the congregation overcomers, they overcome them. Those outside Christendom look at the Laodicean congregation and compare what they do, say, and think to themselves, and can't see any benefits in Christianity. What those outside Christendom don't realize is that they are comparing themselves to another group of unbelievers. The sad part of the situation is that when a non-Christian opens the Bible and compares what it says, to the message and example of the Laodicean congregation, they close the Book and walk away from Christianity. When the same non-Christian hears a sermon from the Philadelphia pastor, they reject it with the attitude, "Same old song, just a different tune." You can see the same problem when the Philadelphia congregation sends a missionary to a foreign country to tell them of Jesus and the benefits of Christianity. The people look at the United States through the news media and all they see is violence, corruption, and moral decay in our country. They tell the missionary to take his Bible and go home, "If this is what Christianity will do for our country, you keep it."

Preaching unbelief not only closes doors, it produces a perverse and faithless generation that moves God to judgment. It is the duty of the Christian population to present the Jesus of the Church Covenant to the world, just as it was the duty of the Jews to present the God of the Abrahamic Covenant to the world. Hear what Moses told the Jews before they entered the Promise Land in Deuteronomy 32:15-38, "(15) But Jeshurun waxed fat, and kicked: thou art waxen fat, thou art grown thick, thou art covered with fatness; then he forsook God which made him, and lightly esteemed the Rock of his salvation. (16) They provoked him to jealousy with strange gods, with abominations provoked they him to anger. (17) They sacrificed unto devils, not to God; to gods whom they knew not, to new gods that came newly up, whom your fathers feared not. (18) Of the Rock that begat thee thou art unmindful, and hast forgotten God that formed thee. (19) And when the Lord saw it, he abhorred them, because of the provoking of his sons, and of his daughters. (20) And he said, I will hide my face from them, I will see what their end shall be: for they are a very froward generation, children in whom is no faith. (21) They have moved me to jealousy with that which is not God; they have provoked me to anger with their vanities: and I will move them to jealousy with those which are not a people; I will provoke them to anger with a foolish nation. (22) For a fire is kindled in mine anger, and shall burn unto the lowest hell, and shall consume the earth with her increase, and set on fire the foundations of the mountains (23) I will heap mischiefs upon them; I will spend mine arrows upon them. (24) They shall be burnt with hunger, and devoured with burning heat, and with bitter destruction: I will also send the teeth of beasts upon them, with the poison of serpents of the dust. (25) The sword without, and terror within, shall destroy both the young man and the virgin, the suckling also with the man of gray hairs. (26) I said, I would scatter them into corners, I would make the remembrance of them to cease from among men: (27) Were it not that I feared the wrath of the enemy, lest their adversaries should behave themselves strangely, and lest they should say, Our hand is high, and the Lord hath not done all this. (28) For they are a nation void of counsel, neither is there any understanding in them. (29) O that they were wise, that they understood this, that they would consider their latter end! (30) How should one chase a thousand, and two put ten thousand to flight, except their Rock had sold them, and the Lord had shut them up? (31) For their rock is not as our Rock, even our enemies themselves being judges. (32) For their vine is of the vine of Sodom, and of the fields of Gomorrah: their grapes are grapes of gall, their clusters are bitter: (33) Their wine is the poison of dragons, and the cruel venom of asps. (34) Is not this laid up in store with me, and sealed up among my treasures? (35) To me belongeth vengeance, and recompense; their foot shall slide in due time: for the day of their calamity is at hand, and the things that shall come upon them make haste. (36) For the Lord shall judge his people, and repent himself for his servants, when he seeth that their power is gone, and there is none shut up, or left. (37) And he shall say, Where are their gods, their rock in whom they trusted, (38) Which did eat the fat of their sacrifices, and drank the wine of their drink offerings? let them rise up and help you, and be your protection."

The very froward (perverse) generation of children without faith (Deuteronomy 32:20) was the generation of Jews who nailed Jesus to the cross. They couldn't recognize Jesus as the promised Redeemer because the religious leaders in Israel had distorted what God had said about the Redeemer. It was distorted so badly, that everything Jesus did, contradicted what they said He would do. The religious leaders had stopped telling the people what God said about the Redeemer and were presenting their own ideas of what the Redeemer would do. The Jewish religious leadership had perverted the Old Testament promises to the same point of perversion as the Laodicean clergymen have perverted the promises of the New Covenant. Their criticism of the Philadelphia congregation is the same criticism Jesus heard from the religious leaders when He walked through the streets of Jerusalem. Needless to say, the Jewish religious leaders were wrong, dead wrong.

When the Jewish religious leadership set aside the revelation God gave of his Redeemer and began promoting their own ideas of redemption, it was not a matter of "if" they would be judged, only "when." The same situation is true of the Laodicean congregation. We know from 1 Peter 4:17, "that judgment must begin at the house of God," but let's back up to 1 Peter 4:12-19, "(12) Beloved, think it not strange concerning the fiery trial which is to try you, as though some strange thing happened unto you: (13) But rejoice, inasmuch as ye are partakers of Christ's sufferings; that, when his glory shall be revealed, ye may be glad also with exceeding joy. (14) If ye be reproached for the name of Christ, happy are ye; for the spirit of glory and of God resteth upon you: on their part he is evil spoken of, but on your part he is glorified. (15) But let none of you suffer as a murderer, or as a thief, or as an evildoer, or as a busybody in other men's matters. (16) Yet if any man suffer as a Christian, let him not be ashamed; but let him glorify God on this behalf. (17) For the time is come that judgment must begin at the house of God: and if it first begin at us, what shall the end be of them that obey not the gospel of God? (18) And if the righteous scarcely be saved, where shall the ungodly and the sinner appear? (19) Wherefore let them that suffer according to the will of God commit the keeping of their souls to him in well doing, as unto a faithful Creator."

The Philadelphia congregation will see the glory of Jesus when they leave Earth in the rapture. This is when they will be glad with exceeding joy, 1 Peter 4:13b, "that, when his glory shall be revealed, ye may be glad also with exceeding joy." When the chief Shepherd appears, they will receive a crown of glory, 1 Peter 5:4, "And when the chief Shepherd shall appear, ye shall receive a crown of glory that fadeth not away." This is the crown mentioned in the exhort section of the Philadelphia letter in Rev. 3:11, "Behold, I come quickly: hold that fast which thou hast, that no man take thy crown." The rapture will be the fulfillment of Rev. 3:9, "Behold, I will make them . . . to know that I have loved thee." The rapture will be a time of glory and rejoicing for the Philadelphia congregation, and a time of shame and sorrow for the Laodicean congregation. It is also a judgment, in sequence, with 1 Peter 4:17, "judgment must begin at the house of God." The house of God during the Church Dispensation is the body of a born-again believer. Collectively, these born-again believers are the Church. They co-exist in Christendom with a group of fakes, who are not born-again believers. The rapture will be the beginning of a judgment limited to the house of God (the Church) where the born-again believers are separated from the congregation of unbelievers. The judgment will be completed by Antichrist destroying the remains of Christendom.

Those who died in Christ during the Church Dispensation, and the generation of born-again believers living at the time of the rapture, make up the bride of Christ in the Book of the Revelation. Her final dwelling place is the holy Jerusalem of Revelation Chapter 21, which is the same city as the new

Jerusalem in the promise section of the letter to the Philadelphia congregation, Rev. 3:12-13, "(12) Him that overcometh will I make a pillar in the temple of my God, and he shall go no more out: and I will write upon him the name of my God, and the name of the city of my God, which is new Jerusalem, which cometh down out of heaven from my God: and I will write upon him my new name. (13) He that hath an ear, let him hear what the Spirit saith unto the churches." Those killed by the Antichrist organization for their refusal to deny Jesus and the Word of God during the final phase of judgment on Christendom are the fifth seal group of Rev. 6:9-11. Although they are saved and resurrected to eternal life at the end of the tribulation period, they are not, nor will they ever be, Church members. The rapture will have ended the Church Dispensation and completed the bride of Christ. Those participating in the rapture were given their glorified eternal bodies at the instant the rapture occurred. They washed their robes in the blood of the Lamb, before the One who said, "Behold, I come quickly," came. Of them, Jesus could say they "kept my word, and hast not denied my name." Their testimony is that they communicated that fact to Jesus by their faithfulness in the daily baptism of fire prior to the rapture. The judgment that must begin at the house of God starts with you as an individual, judging yourself faithful or unfaithful to the Word of God in your daily baptism of fire. A record of faithfulness will result in your meeting Jesus in the rapture. A record of unfaithfulness will result in you meeting Antichrist in a 'get serious or get lost' situation. Today is the day of salvation, and the rapture will be payday. We have been told in advance the Philadelphia congregation will leave in the rapture, and the Laodicean congregation will be left behind. After you examine yourself, you need to examine the organization you support. If the Mark 16:17-18 signs aren't there, you shouldn't be there, either.

e. EXHORT: Coming quickly, hold fast that no man take thy crown.
Rev. 3:11, "Behold, I come quickly: hold that fast which thou hast, that no man take thy crown."

This coming of Jesus is as a thief in the night to rapture His Church. The event is recorded in 1 Thessalonians 4:13-5:3, "(13) But I would not have you to be ignorant, brethren, concerning them which are asleep, that ye sorrow not, even as others which have no hope. (14) For if we believe that Jesus died and rose again, even so them also which sleep in Jesus will God bring with him. (15) For this we say unto you by the word of the Lord, that we which are alive and remain unto the coming of the Lord shall not prevent them which are asleep. (16) For the Lord himself shall descend from heaven with a shout, with the voice of the archangel, and with the trump of God: and the dead in Christ shall rise first: (17) Then we which are alive and remain shall be caught up together with them in the clouds, to meet the Lord in the air: and so shall we ever be with the Lord. (18) Wherefore comfort one another with these words. (5:1) But of the times and the seasons, brethren, ye have no need that I write unto you. (2) For yourselves know perfectly that the day of the Lord so cometh as a thief in the night. (3) For when they shall say, Peace and safety; then sudden destruction cometh upon then, as travail upon a woman with child; and they shall not escape." The only people who will see Jesus are those participating in the rapture. The next time Jesus comes is at the end of the seven–year tribulation period, when every eye shall see him, Rev. 1:7, "Behold, he cometh with clouds; and every eye shall see him, and they also which pierced him: and all kindreds of the earth shall wail because of him. Even so, Amen."

f. PROMISE: A pillar in the temple and a place in new Jerusalem.
Rev. 3:12-13, "(12) Him that overcometh will I make a pillar in the temple of my God, and he shall go no more out: and I will write upon him the name of my God, and the name of the city of my God, which is new Jerusalem, which cometh down out of heaven from my God: and I will write upon him my new name. (13) He that hath an ear, let him hear what the Spirit saith unto the churches."

New Jerusalem will be the home address of the Church throughout eternity. It will be the centerpiece in the new heaven and new Earth after the millennial reign of King Jesus. We are given a glimpse of the city in Rev. 21:1-22:5. This is the "place" Jesus spoke of in John 14:1-4, "(1) Let not your heart be troubled: ye believe in God, believe also in me. (2) In my Father's house are many mansions: if it were not so, I would have told you. I go to prepare a place for you. (3) And if I go and prepare a place for you, I will come again, and receive you unto myself; that where I am, there ye may be also. (4) And whither I go ye know, and the way ye know." I am looking forward to living in this city. I have looked into the heavens on a clear night at the beautiful and vast physical universe Jesus made in only six days. He has been working on new Jerusalem for two thousand years. If He can create this in six days, can you imagine what He can create in two thousand years?

Before we leave the letter to the Philadelphia congregation, let's take a second look at Rev. 3:9, "Behold, I will make them of the synagogue of Satan, which say they are Jews, and are not, but do lie; behold, I will make them to come and worship before thy feet, and to know that I have loved thee." The letter is to the Philadelphia congregation, so the message is to the Church, but, there is also a message to the Jews. The Jews are significant to the Philadelphia congregation because it was during their days that God began to fulfill the covenant He made with Abraham in Genesis 15:18, "In the same day the Lord made a covenant with Abram, saying, Unto thy seed have I given this land, from the river of Egypt unto the great river, the river Euphrates." They returned to their homeland in the year 1918. Since that time the Philadelphia congregation has watched God set the stage for the fulfillment of the prophecies concerning the transition from the Church to

Kingdom Dispensation. The Jews are brought to mind in the Philadelphia letter instead of the Laodicean letter, because the Laodicean congregation, as well as the Jews, lacks the ability to see and understand what God is doing. The Jews rejected Jesus and alienated themselves from the New Covenant promise of the indwelling Holy Spirit. The Laodicean congregation did the same thing, and without the Holy Spirit they are as spiritually blind as the Jews. The Jews are also mentioned in the Philadelphia letter to alert the congregation of the blasphemy and tribulation they would suffer from the Laodicean congregation for preaching faith. They may not call it blasphemy, but that's what Jesus called it when the Roman Empire rejected the gospel and persecuted the Smyrna congregation in Rev. 2:8-11, verse 9, "I know thy works, and tribulation, and poverty, (but thou art rich) and I know the blasphemy of them which say they are Jews, and are not, but are the synagogue of Satan."

The blind Laodicean congregation can't see it, but the Jews had to be regathered and in control of the city of Jerusalem in order to confirm the protection treaty with Antichrist. This is the event that introduces the seven–year tribulation period. Because of their spiritual blindness the Jews will not be able to recognize the spokesman of that protection covenant as Antichrist. That same spiritual blindness is the reason the Laodicean congregation cannot recognize Antichrist as the spokesman of their protection covenant. Neither can they see their confidence as a covenant with death or that they are in agreement with hell (Isaiah 28:14-22). This is because they have made lies their refuge and hid themselves under falsehood. God nullifies the protection treaty of the Laodicean congregation during the first half of the tribulation period by Antichrist. He nullifies the Jews' protection treaty by the False Prophet during the last half of the tribulation period. During the first half, God will deal with the false Christians, and during the last half, he will deal with those "which say they are Jews, and are not, but do lie."

In the rebuke 'to them which say they are, and are not, but do lie,' Jesus also said, "Behold, I will make them to come and worship before thy feet, and to know that I have loved thee." The highest honor in the universe is to be called a son or daughter of the living God. There is absolutely nothing above being personally related to God. The new creation that resulted from the union of the Holy Spirit with your spirit, in the rebirth, is different than anything else in the Word of God. Under the Old Covenant, the Holy Spirit would come and rest upon people to equip them with gifts for a specific task, and then leave. This can be seen in the men that made the garment of the priest in Exodus 28:3, "And thou shalt speak unto all that are wise hearted, whom I have filled with the spirit of wisdom, that they may make Aaron's garments to consecrate him, that he may minister unto me in the priest's office." Bezaleel was given the gifts of wisdom, understanding, and knowledge to construct the tabernacle in Exodus 31:2-5, "(2) See, I have called by name Bezaleel the son of Uri, the son or Hur, of the tribe of Judah: (3) And I have filled him with the spirit of God, in wisdom, and in understanding, and in knowledge, and in all manner of workmanship, (4) To devise cunning works, to work in gold, and in silver, and in brass, (5) And in cutting of stones, to set them, and in carving of timber, to work in all manner of workmanship." (Also see Exodus 35:30-35). The ministry of Moses was under the same arrangement, Numbers 11:25-29, "(25) And the Lord came down in a cloud, and spake unto him, and took of the spirit that was upon him, and gave it unto the seventy elders: and it came to pass, that, when the spirit rested upon them, they prophesied, and did not cease. (26) But there remained two of the men in the camp, the name of the one was Eldad, the the name of the other Medad: and the spirit rested upon them; and they were of them that were written, but went not out unto the tabernacle: and they prophesied in the camp. (27) And there ran a young man, and told Moses, and said, Eldad and Medad do prophesy in the camp. (28) And Joshua the son of Nun, the servant of Moses, one of his young men, answered and said, My lord Moses, forbid them. (29) And Moses said unto him, Enviest thou for my sake? would God that all the Lord's people were prophets, and that the Lord would put his spirit upon them!"

Under the Old Covenant, God called the Jews his son because it was in that nation that his Word and the Holy Spirit could be found. God called the Jew, as an individual, his servant. Under the New Covenant, God calls his people, as a group, the Church, and individuals members his sons, if in fact, his Word and the Holy Spirit can be found in them. Otherwise, God calls them bastards (Hebrews 12:1-12). Under the New Covenant, God is actually taking people from the kingdom of Babylon and placing them in the kingdom of God. In the rebirth, God is legally adopting children from the family of Adam, and placing them in the family of God. This is why the Church member is called the child of God, and why the Church member can legally call God their Father. Under the New Covenant, as a born-again believer, every Church member is just as much a son (or daughter) of God as Jesus is. This is the promise of 2 Corinthians 6:14-18, "(14) Be ye not unequally yoked together with unbelievers: for what fellowship hath righteousness with unrighteousness? and what communion hath light with darkness? (15) And what concord hath Christ with Belial? or what part hath he that believeth with an infidel? (16) And what agreement hath the temple of God with idols? for ye are the temple of the living God; as God hath said, I will dwell in them, and walk in them; and I will be their God, and they shall be my people. (17) Wherefore come out from among them, and be ye separate, saith the Lord, and touch not the unclean thing; and I will receive you, (18) And will be a Father unto you, and ye shall be my sons and daughters, saith the Lord Almighty."

This is also why Jesus calls us brothers in Hebrews 2:9-18, "(9) But we see Jesus, who was made a little lower than the angels for the suffering of death, crowned with glory and honour; that he by the grace of God should taste death for every man. (10) For it became him, for whom are all things, and by whom are all things, in bringing many sons unto glory, to make the captain of their salvation perfect through sufferings. (11) For both he that sanctifieth and they who are sanctified are all of one: for which cause he is not ashamed to call them brethren, (12) Saying, I will declare thy name unto my brethren, in the midst of the church will I sing praise unto thee. (13) And again, I will put my trust in him. And again, Behold I and the children which God hath given me. (14) Forasmuch then as the children are partakers of flesh and blood, he also himself likewise took part of the same; that through death he might destroy him that had the power of death, that is, the devil; (15) And delivered them who through fear of death were all their lifetime subject to bondage. (16) For verily he took not on him the nature of angels; but he took on him the seed of Abraham. (17) Wherefore in all things it behoved him to be made like unto his brethren, that he might be a merciful and faithful high priest in things pertaining to God, to make reconciliation for the sins of the people. (18) For in that he himself hath suffered being tempted, he is able to succour them that are tempted."

The word *adoption* is used five times in the New Testament. The first time it is used is in Romans 8:15. Romans 8:13-19, "(13) For if ye live after the flesh, ye shall die: but if ye through the Spirit do mortify the deeds of the body, ye shall live. (14) For as many as are led by the Spirit of God, they are the sons of God. (15) For ye have not received the spirit of bondage again to fear; but ye have received the Spirit of adoption, whereby we cry, Abba, Father. (16) The Spirit itself beareth witness with our spirit, that we are the children of God: (17) And if children, then heirs; heirs of God, and joint-heirs with Christ; if so be that we suffer with him, that we may be also glorified together. (18) For I reckon that the suffering of this present time are not worthy to be compared with the glory which shall be revealed in us. (19) For the earnest expectation of the creature waiteth for the manifestation of the sons of God." Notice the word *Spirit* in the phrase "Spirit of adoption" (verse 15) is capitalized, which means the Spirit being discussed is the Holy Spirit. Since the Holy Spirit is the Spirit of adoption, it should be obvious you were repudiated until you received the Holy Spirit. Also notice, "the glory which shall be revealed in us" will be revealed at "the manifestation of the sons of God."

The second time the word *adoption* is used is in Romans 8:23, where we are told the adoption will be completed with the redemption of our physical body which is the rapture of the Church. Romans 8:22-23, "(22) For we know that the whole creation groaneth and travaileth in pain together until now. (23) And not only they, but ourselves also, which have the first fruits of the Spirit, even we ourselves groan within ourselves, waiting for the adoption, to wit, the redemption of our body."

The third time the word *adoption* is used in in Romans 9:4, where Paul tells of his sorrow because his nation, to whom the promises were made, rejected them. Romans 9:1-5, "(1) I say the truth in Christ, I lie not, my conscience also bearing me witness in the Holy Ghost, (2) That I have great heaviness and continual sorrow in my heart. (3) For I could wish that myself were accursed from Christ for my brethren, my kinsmen according to the flesh: (4) Who are Israelites; to whom pertaineth the adoption, and the glory, and the covenants, and the giving of the law, and the service of God, and the promises; (5) Whose are the fathers, and of whom as concerning the flesh Christ came, who is over all, God blessed for ever. Amen." The Jews, as a nation, had rejected Jesus as the promised Redeemer. After Jesus was resurrected to life, they also rejected the Gospel and alienated themselves from the New Covenant promise of the indwelling Holy Spirit. This can be seen in Acts 13:44-47, "(44) And the next sabbath day came almost the whole city together to hear the word of God. (45) But when the Jews saw the multitudes, they were filled with envy, and spake against those things which were spoken by Paul, contradicting and blaspheming. (46) Then Paul and Barnabas waxed bold, and said, It was necessary that the word of God should first have been spoken to you: but seeing ye put it from you, and judge yourselves unworthy of everlasting life, lo, we turn to the Gentiles. (47) For so hath the Lord commanded us, saying, I have set thee to be a light of the Gentiles, that thou shouldest be for salvation unto the ends of the earth." The final rejection is recorded in Acts 18:4-6, "(4) And he reasoned in the synagogue every sabbath, and persuaded the Jews and the Greeks. (5) And when Silas and Timotheus were come from Macedonia, Paul was pressed in the spirit, and testified to the Jews that Jesus was Christ. (6) And when they opposed themselves, and blasphemed, he shook his raiment, and said unto them, Your blood be upon your own heads; I am clean: from hence forth I will go unto the Gentiles."

The fourth time the word *adoption* is used is in Galatians 4:5, where we are told that the adoption could not take place until after the Redeemer redeemed. Galatians 4:1-9, "(1) Now I say, That the heir, as long as he is a child, differeth nothing from a servant, though he be lord of all; (2) But is under tutors and governors until the time appointed of the father. (3) Even so we, when we were children, were in bondage under the elements of the world: (4) But when the fulness of the time was come, God sent forth his Son, made of a woman, made under the law, (5) To redeem them that were under the law, that we might receive the adoption of sons. (6) And because ye are sons, God hath sent forth the Spirit of his Son into your hearts, crying, Abba, Father. (7) Wherefore thou art no more a servant, but a son; and if a son, then an heir of God through Christ. (8) Howbeit then, when ye knew not God, ye did service unto them which by nature are no gods. (9) But now, after that ye have known God, or rather are known of God, how turn ye again to the weak and beggarly elements, whereunto ye desire again to be in bondage?" As we have already seen, the Old Covenant was based on the atonement of sins, until the Redeemer paid the ransom. Under the New Covenant sins are forgiven–literally separated from the sinner–which allows the Holy Spirit to enter and reside in a sinless body. We also saw where the law was presented as a curse or a blessing. On the cross, Jesus not only paid the penalty for our sins and purchased forgiveness for us, He also redeemed us from the curse portion of the law. This is what guarantees the born-again believer good health and prosperity.

The last time the word *adoption* is used is in Ephesians 1:4, which deals with the fact that the Church Covenant was a dispensational mystery, meaning it was unrevealed in the Old Testament Scriptures. Ephesians 1:3-14, "(3) Blessed be the God and Father of our Lord Jesus Christ, who hath blessed us with all spiritual blessings in heavenly places in Christ: (4) According as he hath chosen us in him before the foundation of the world, that we should be holy and without blame before him in love: (5) Having predestinated us unto the adoption of children by Jesus Christ to himself, according to the good pleasure of his will, (6) To the praise of the glory of his grace, wherein he hath made us accepted in the beloved. (7) In whom we have redemption through his blood, the forgiveness of sins, according to the riches of his grace; (8) Wherein he hath abounded toward us in all wisdom and prudence; (9) Having made known unto us the mystery of his will, according to his good pleasure which he hath purposed in himself: (10) That in the dispensation of the fulness of times he might gather together in one all things in Christ, both which are in heaven, and which are on earth; even in him: (11) In whom also we have obtained an inheritance, being predestinated according to the purpose of him who worketh all things after the counsel of his own will: (12) That we should be to the praise of his glory, who first trusted in Christ. (13) In whom ye also trusted, after that ye heard the word of truth, the gospel of your salvation: in whom also after that ye believed, ye were sealed with that holy Spirit of promise, (14) Which is the earnest of our inheritance until the redemption of the purchased possession, unto the praise of his glory." It is the born-again Church member, sealed with the Holy Spirit who will be conformed to the image of Jesus at the rapture. They were foreknown of God because He adopted them as sons and daughters prior to the rapture. This is what it means to be predestinated in Romans 8:29-30, "(29) For whom he did foreknow, he also did predestinate to be conformed to the image of his Son, that he might be the firstborn among many brethren. (30) Moreover whom he did predestinate, them he also called: and whom he called, them he also justified: and whom he justified, them he also glorified." This Church Covenant is the same dispensational mystery discussed in Ephesians 3:1-11 and Colossians 1:25-27, "(25) Whereof I am made a minister, according to the dispensation of God which is given to me for you, to fulfil the word of God; (26) [Even] the mystery which hath been hid from ages and from generations, but now is made manifest to his saints: (27) To whom God would make known what [is] the riches of the glory of this mystery among the Gentiles; which is Christ in you, the hope of glory:"

In speaking of authority, this places the born-again, Spirit-filled, Church members directly under the Elohim (Trinity or Godhead), where they will function as kings and priests throughout eternity. Everything in the spirit and physical realm is subject to God, and everything that is subject to God will be subject to the Church member. This will be their position on the other side of the rapture, but what the Church has failed to realize is that this is their position on this side of the rapture. In reference to the authority of a Church member, the rapture will not change anything except your home address. God has given us his Word, the authority to use the name of Jesus, and the Holy Spirit to get a job done on earth, not in heaven.

The five signs Jesus said would follow them that believe in Mark 16:17-18 are to follow you in the earth, not in heaven. There will be no need for them to follow you to heaven. The first sign is "In my name shall they cast out devils" or demons. We have already seen in Rev. 12:7-12 that it is Michael and his angels who cast Satan and his angels out of heaven, not the Church. It is here, on Earth, that you need to defeat and overcome Satan and his angels. It is here you need to cast them out of yourself, the Church, and whosoever will come. If you are waiting till you get to heaven to take care of Satan, you will be one disappointed Laodicean Church member.

The second sign is "they shall speak with new tongues." This was the first sign to be manifest by the indwelling Holy Spirit after his arrival on the day of Pentecost, Acts 2:4, "And they were all filled with the Holy Ghost, and began to speak with other tongues, as the Spirit gave them utterance." The unbelievers in the crowd criticized them then (Acts 2:13), and they are still criticizing today. On the day of Pentecost, those filled with the Holy Spirit spoke in a language they had never learned, and the people from the various nations heard them in their native tongue. The Apostles came to recognize speaking in tongues as the initial receiving of the Holy Spirit. This can be seen with Cornelius and Peter in Acts 10:44-48 and in the ministry of Paul in Acts 19:1-7.

As the Church membership increased, the congregation became a mixture of people in different stages of spiritual growth. Those who spoke in tongues criticized those who didn't, while others hampered the effectiveness of the Church by not controlling themselves. This prompted 1 Corinthians chapters 12, 13, and 14, where the gift of tongues and the interpretation of tongues are explained, and guidelines are established for their use in a public church service. Chapter 12 begins with the statement, "Now concerning spiritual gifts, brethren, I would not have you ignorant." Chapter 14 ends with the statement, "(37) If any man think himself to be a prophet, or spiritual, let him acknowledge that the things that I write unto you are the commandments of the Lord. (38) But if any man be ignorant, let him be ignorant. (39) Wherefore, brethren, covet to prophesy, and forbid not to speak with tongues. (40) Let all things be done decently and in order." Be ignorant, if you choose, but also be very, very careful. To take something that is of

God and attribute it to Satan is blasphemy. When a person speaks or prays in tongues, it is the Holy Spirit speaking or interceding for the individual. To take a gift or something of the Holy Spirit and attribute it to Satan is blasphemy against the Holy Ghost. That is the only unforgivable sin in the Church Dispensation, Mark 3:28-30, "(28) Verily I say unto you, All sins shall be forgiven unto the sons of men, and blasphemies wherewith soever they shall blaspheme: (29) But he that shall blaspheme against the Holy Ghost hath never forgiveness, but is in danger of eternal damnation (30) Because they said, He hath an unclean spirit." (Also see Matthew 12:22-33, Luke 12:8-10, 1 John 5:16-17). The Church member will not need the Holy Spirit to do their talking after they meet God, face to face, in the rapture. Prophesying will also end with the Church Dispensation. (See Zechariah 13:6).

The next two Mark 16:17-18 signs concern your external and internal spiritual protection, "They shall take up serpents (external); and if they drink any deadly thing (internal), it shall not hurt them." The external protection is provided by the elect angels and the internal protection is provided by the indwelling Holy Spirit. The angelic protection can be seen in Hebrews 1:13-14, "(13) But to which of the angels said he at any time, Sit on my right hand, until I make thine enemies thy footstool? (14) Are they not all ministering spirits, sent forth to minister for them who shall be heirs of salvation?" These guardian angels protect your home, family, and possessions in your absence. They go before you and clear out any demonic threats or physical dangers you are not aware of. It is by these guardian angels that a thousand fall at your side, and ten thousand at your right hand, without your awareness. This is the protection guaranteed by Psalm 91, "(1) He that dwelleth in the secret place of the most High shall abide under the shadow of the Almighty. (2) I will say of the Lord, he is my refuge and my fortress: my God; in him will I trust. (3) Surely he shall deliver thee from the snare of the fowler, and from the noisome pestilence. (4) He shall cover thee with his feathers, and under his wings shalt thou trust: his truth shall be thy shield and buckler. (5) Thou shalt not be afraid for the terror by night; nor for the arrow that flieth by day; (6) Nor for the pestilence that walketh in darkness; nor for the destruction that wasteth at noonday. (7) A thousand shall fall at thy side and ten thousand at thy right hand; but it shall not come nigh thee. (8) Only with thine eyes shalt thou behold and see the reward of the wicked. (9) Because thou hast made the Lord, which is my refuge, even the most High, thy habitation: (10) There shall no evil befall thee, neither shall any plague come nigh thy dwelling. (11) For he shall give his angels charge over thee, to keep thee in all thy ways. (12) They shall bear thee up in their hands, lest thou dash thy foot against a stone. (13) Thou shalt tread upon the lion and adder: the young lion and the dragon shalt thou trample under feet. (14) Because he hath set his love upon me, therefore will I deliver him: I will set him on high, because he hath known my name. (15) He shall call upon me, and I will answer him: I will be with him in trouble; I will deliver him, and honour him. (16) With long life will I satisfy him, and shew him my salvation."

Three of the most obvious internal protections provided by the indwelling Holy Spirit are comfort against worry, anxiety, fear, etc., health insurance against plagues, diseases, sickness, etc., and His presence insures against demonic possession. The Holy Spirit operates on the Word of God, so the more Word you have in you, the more you will be able to enjoy that protection. This is especially true in the area of false teachers. Entering into a conversation with a false teacher without knowing God's opinion on the subject is like going to war without your weapon, and you limit the Holy Spirit by taking away his sword. The Word of God and the Holy Spirit are your only protection against the deadly poison of false doctrine and errors. Most Church members are familiar with the verse, "greater is he that is in you, than he that is in the world," but many do not realize that the statement was made in reference to overcoming false prophets, antichrists, and errors. 1 John 4:1-6, "(1) Beloved, believe not every spirit, but try the spirits whether they are of God: because many false prophets are gone out into the world. (2) Hereby know ye the Spirit of God: Every spirit that confesseth that Jesus Christ is come in the flesh is of God: (3) And every spirit that confesseth not that Jesus Christ is come in the flesh is not of God: and this is that spirit of antichrist, whereof ye have heard that it should come; and even now already is it in the world. (4) Ye are of God, little children, and have overcome them: because greater is he that is in you, than he that is in the world. (5) They are of the world: therefore speak they of the world, and the world heareth them. (6) We are of God: he that knoweth God heareth us: he that is not of God heareth not us. Hereby know we the spirit of truth, and the spirit of error." Needless to say, when you get to heaven it will be impossible for you to find the spirit of error, antichrist, false prophets, evil, or the plague we saw in Psalm 91.

The fifth sign in Mark 16:17-18 is "they shall lay hands on the sick, and they shall recover." Again, if you are going to wait until you get to heaven to look for a sick, diseased, crippled, or mutilated body to lay hands on, you are going to be very disappointed. Where is your faith, Christian, in Jesus, the Great Physician, or the medical profession? That medical procedure is so simple that most five-year-old children can understand it. How could Jesus have made the procedure more simple? The problem is not a complicated procedure, but one of unbelief. The truth is, you don't handle medical problems the way which Jesus told you because you don't believe him. What faith says is that you are exactly what the Word of God says you are, and you can do exactly what the Word of God says you can do. Unbelief says the Word of God is untrustworthy, or literally, God is a liar. God's best for you is to walk through this world in a strong, healthy body. If you live in a body that is sick, diseased, crippled, or mutilated, it is a good indication that you have rejected the more abundant life Jesus offers. If the condition is persistent, there is a strong possibility that you are living in unbelief. Your testimony to an unbelieving world is you are serving a very small, inadequate god. No wonder they reject your testimony and god. That is the god of the Laodicean congregation, and his name is Antichrist. Think! What kind of father would confine his child to a sick, diseased, crippled, or mutilated body if it is within his power to put the child in a strong healthy body? If your child knew beyond any doubt you could change his situation and you don't do it, do you honestly believe your child would cherish you with pure, undiluted love? Your Heavenly Father has done everything necessary for you to enjoy the abundant life in a strong healthy body maintained by the great physician named Jesus. Can you imagine the hurt He feels after providing the way and we refuse to walk in it?

What do you do, shepherd of the flock, when a member of your congregation who is immature in the faith alerts you of a medical problem? Are you obedient to James 5:14-15, "(14) Is any sick among you? let him call for the elders of the church; and let them pray over him, anointing him with oil in the name of the Lord: (15) And the prayer of faith shall save the sick, and the Lord shall raise him up; and if he have committed sins, they shall be forgiven him." In these two verses alone, you can see how far traditional Christianity is from the truth. You should be ashamed to call yourself a Christian if you don't believe and practice what Jesus Christ said. You should be just as ashamed to belong to, or support, an organization that teaches, by word or example, that Jesus is an untrustworthy liar. How are you going to answer Jesus when he says, "Give account of yourself, Why didn't you believe and do what I said?" The embarrassment you suffer that day will be far greater than anything your friends or denomination can give. You better realize quickly that Jesus is not going to judge you on your faithfulness to your denomination. You will be judged on your faithfulness to what Jesus said, John 12:48, "He that rejecteth me, and receiveth not my words, hath one that judgeth him: the word that I have spoken, the same shall judge him in the last day." It becomes more apparent, the closer we get to the rapture, that Mark 16:17-18 is the dividing line between the Philadelphia congregation and the Laodicean congregations. Mark 16:17-18, "(17) And these signs shall follow them that believe; In my name shall they cast out devils; they shall speak with new tongues; (18) They shall take up serpents; and if they drink any deadly thing, it shall not hurt them; they shall lay hands on the sick, and they shall recover."

The Letter to Laodicea

7. The Letter to Laodicea: The Apostate Church (1900-?).
Revelation 3:14-22, "(14) And unto the angel of the church of the Laodiceans write; These things saith the Amen, the faithful and true witness,

the beginning of the creation of God; (15) I know thy works, that thou are neither cold nor hot: I would thou wert cold or hot. (16) So then because thou art lukewarm, and neither cold nor hot, I will spue thee out of my mouth. (17) Because thou sayest, I am rich, and increased with goods, and have need of nothing; and knowest not that thou art wretched, and miserable, and poor, and blind, and naked: (18) I counsel thee to buy of me gold tried in the fire, that thou mayest be rich; and white raiment, that thou mayest be clothed, and that the shame of thy nakedness do not appear; and anoint thine eyes with eyesalve, that thou mayest see. (19) As many as I love, I rebuke and chasten: be zealous therefore, and repent. (20) Behold, I stand at the door, and knock: if any man hear my voice, and open the door, I will come in to him, and will sup with him, and he with me. (21) To him that overcometh will I grant to set with me in my throne, even as I also overcame, and am set down with my Father in his throne. (22) He that hath an ear, let him hear what the says Spirit saith unto the churches."

a. TO: The church of the Laodiceans.
Rev. 3:14a, "And unto the angel of the church of the Laodiceans write."

As we have already seen, the Laodicean congregation has co-existed with the Philadelphia congregation since the era began near the year 1900. The Laodicean Church Age is the seventh and final era of Church history. The era ends with the rapture of the Philadelphia congregation and the destruction of the Laodicean congregation by Antichrist during the first half of the seven–year tribulation. The era opens with a controversy in Christendom concerning the indwelling Holy Spirit manifesting itself through miracles and the Mark 16:17-18 Church Commission signs. The traditional view held by the Thyatira (or Catholic) churches and the children spawned in the Sardis Era (Protestant churches) is that miracles can only be performed by God, and only if, and when, He chooses. These "Traditional Christianity" churches enter the Laodicean Church Age as part of the Laodicean congregation. The Philadelphia congregation was the members who came out of traditional Christianity with the view that Jesus gave the Church and its members the authority and responsibility to perform miracles as part of the gospel message. In looking at the Mark 16:15-18 Church Commission, the dividing line, between traditional Christianity and the Philadelphia congregation, is between verse 16 and verse 17. Both groups believe and actively participate in Mark 16:15-16, "(15) And he said unto them, Go ye into all the world, and preach the gospel to every creature. (16) He that believeth and is baptized shall be saved; but he that believeth not shall be damned." The Philadelphia congregation believes and actively participates in Mark 16:17-18, while traditional Christianity rejects them, "(17) And these signs shall follow them that believe; In my name shall they cast out devils; they shall speak with new tongues; (18) They shall take up serpents; and if they drink any deadly thing, it shall not hurt them; they shall lay hands on the sick, and they shall recover."

As the reasons for the controversy came into focus the underlying problem centered on faith. The Philadelphia congregation claims people are exactly what the Word of God says they are, and they can do exactly what the Word of God says they can do. If Jesus says the believer can use his name to cast out devils (or demons), he can. If Jesus says you can lay your hands on the sick, in his name, and they will recover, they will. What the Word of God says supersedes what our bodies say, what our mind says, what circumstances say, and what the world says. That's the difference between walking by faith and walking by sight (2 Corinthians 5:7). It is also the difference between being spiritually minded or carnally minded, Romans 8:6-9, "(6) For to be carnally minded is death; but to be spiritually minded is life and peace. (7) Because the carnal mind is enmity against God: for it is not subject to the law of God, neither indeed can be. (8) So then they that are in the flesh cannot please God. (9) But ye are not in the flesh, but in the Spirit, if so be that the Spirit of God dwell in you. Now if any man have not the Spirit of Christ, he is none of his." There is nothing new about walking by faith; it has been in the Book for nearly two thousand years. Traditional Christian teaching has suppressed the faith walk since the Pergamos Era (Rev. 2:13), but it's not suppressed today.

God never gave a Christian the prerogative of accepting part of what he said and rejecting the rest. God never intended a Christian to become a babe in Christ and stay a baby the rest of their lives. A baby either eats and grows up, or he stops eating and dies. This is obvious if you continue reading in Romans Chapter 8 to verse 13, "(13) For if ye live after the flesh, ye shall die: but if ye through the Spirit do mortify the deeds of the body, ye shall live. (14) For as many as are led by the Spirit of God, they are the sons of God." In discussing the Ephesus Era we saw that the Holy Spirit reprehended the church at Corinth for being a bunch of babies playing church. The reprimand is recorded in 1 Corinthians 3:1-3, "(1) And I, brethren, could not speak unto you as unto spiritual, but as unto carnal, even as unto babes in Christ. (2) I have fed you with milk, and not with meat: for hitherto ye were not able to bear it, neither yet now are ye able. (3) For ye are yet carnal: for whereas there is among you envying, and strife, and divisions, are ye not carnal, and walk as men?"

Traditional Christianity presents the Corinth congregation as Carnal Christians and teaches that is the normal Christian lifestyle. This teaching presents salvation as a quick trip to the altar, sometime during your lifetime, to receive a paid up fire insurance policy against going to hell at death. After the trip to the altar the Christian is to patiently wait for the rapture or death (whichever comes first), when Jesus is going to straighten out everything. The errors and false doctrine introduced into Christendom during the Pergamos Era dimmed the light of the gospel to the point where the more abundant life wasn't even taught. Yet even during the Dark Ages the average person on the street had more reverence toward God than most modern day Christians.

Nearly all the Christians who lived during the Dark Ages were baptized as infants and taught to fear God and trust in the redemptive work of Christ. They received the Holy Spirit in their water baptism as infants, which gave them the ability to hear, see, and understand that portion of the Word of God being published by the papacy. The indwelling Holy Spirit produced their reverence toward God and allowed them to trust Jesus. They never enjoyed the more abundant life, but they were born again, and that is why God could honor their fire insurance policy when the believers closed their eyes in death.

During the Reformation Era, Martin Luther led a rebellion against the Roman Catholic Church on the foundation of "The just shall live by faith." The reformation leaders took the Bible out of the hands of the papal clergymen and put it in the hands of the Church members. This is the point in time when Satan sent the Anabaptist to Church to pervert the rebirth process. They refused water baptism to infants, which denied them the indwelling Holy Spirit, and made them incapable of hearing, seeing, or understanding the spiritual truths in the Word of God. Their entire education on the Word of God was restricted to learning about Bible stories and historical accounts without any understanding of the spiritual significance behind the event. Without the spiritual insight provided by the indwelling Holy Spirit, a Bible story, or in fact, the entire Bible, is perceived as foolishness and stays carnal knowledge. By the time the Anabaptist children were deemed old enough for water baptism, most of them were already spiritually deaf. The Bible carnal mindfulness they were taught in their youth actually hampered the Bible spiritual mindfulness the Holy Spirit was attempting to instill. The Bible training they received in their youth made it most difficult for them to be led by the Holy Spirit, because carnal mindfulness is diametrically opposed to spiritual mindfulness.

As the Protestant churches gained spiritual insights into the Word of God, the Anabaptist congregations were forced to reject more revelation knowledge. Later generations reached the point of spiritual deafness and blindness where they began rejecting water baptism as necessary for salvation. They kept the traditional fire insurance policy for salvation, but when they close their eyes in death, they will be very disappointed to find that the policy is invalid because it was never signed or sealed by the Holy Spirit in water baptism. They will also be surprised to find that they are primarily responsible for producing the generation of unbaptized parents and children in the Laodicean Church Era, who are almost totally insensitive to the Word of God, Old Testament law or New Testament faith. Their spiritual blindness also contributed to many divisions in the Church. When Christendom entered the Laodicean Era in 1900 there were less than fifty major denominations. By 1994 there were 1200 plus, with a large portion built on the foundation of Anabaptist doctrine. Some replaced the traditional fire insurance salvation package with a less complicated "Only

Believe" package. Others changed the gospel to a message totally foreign to Christianity. By the end of the Laodicean Era their deafness will be incurable, and because of the damnable heresies they introduced into Christendom the gospel of Jesus will fall on the ears of a generation unable to hear.

In 1 Corinthians 3:1-3, the Corinth congregation were actually newborn Christians being warned to grow up. The danger of not growing up can be seen in the deafness described in Hebrews 5:11-14, "(11) Of whom we have many things to say, and hard to be uttered, seeing ye are dull of hearing. (12) For when for the time ye ought to be teachers, ye have need that one teach you again which be the first principles of the oracles of God; and are become such as have need of milk, and not of strong meat. (13) For every one that useth milk is unskillful in the word of righteousness: for he is a babe. (14) But strong meat belongeth to them that are of full age, even those who by reason of use have their senses exercised to discern both good and evil." As we have already seen, this deafness was the method Jesus used in John 8:41-47 to distinguish between those of Satan and those of God. If we continue reading in the Book of Hebrews we can see that the ultimate danger in refusing to grow up is apostasy. *Apostasy* is the renunciation (a disclaiming) of a religious faith, and that is a prime characteristic of the Laodicean Church era. It is the deafness and blindness of the apostate to the truth of the Word of God that makes it impossible to renew them again unto repentance. The Holy Spirit lists six of the principles (primary or fundamentals) of the doctrine of Christ, and the danger of falling away, turning from the truth of the Word of God, or disclaiming them in Hebrews 6:1-6, "(1) Therefore leaving the principles of the doctrine of Christ, let us go on unto perfection; not laying again the foundation of repentance from dead works, and of faith toward God, (2) Of the doctrine of baptisms, and of laying on of hands, and of resurrection of the dead, and of eternal judgment. (3) And this will we do, if God permit. (4) For it is impossible for those who were once enlightened, and have tasted of the heavenly gift, and were made partakers of the Holy Ghost, (5) And have tasted the good word of God, and the powers of the world to come, (6) If they should fall away, to renew them again unto repentance; seeing they crucify to themselves the Son of God afresh, and put him to an open shame."

If we continue reading in the third chapter of 1 Corinthians, where the congregation was warned to grow up, we can see where they would lose rewards that could have been theirs. 1 Corinthians 3:10-15, "(10) According to the grace of God which is given unto me, as a wise master builder, I have laid the foundation, and another buildeth thereon. But let every man take heed how he buildeth thereupon. (11) For other foundation can no man lay than that is laid, which is Jesus Christ. (12) Now if any man build upon this foundation gold, silver, precious stones, wood, hay, stubble; (13) Every man's work shall be made manifest: for the day shall declare it, because it shall be revealed by fire; and the fire shall try every man's work of what sort it is. (14) If any man's work abide which he hath built thereupon, he shall receive a reward. (15) If any man's work shall be burned, he shall suffer loss: but he himself shall be saved; yet so as by fire."

The Corinth congregation was in no danger of losing their salvation, but if they refused to grow up, they would never enjoy the abundant life Jesus purchased for them at Calvary. Because of where they stood in history their sojourn on Earth would terminate in physical death. If their sojourn was to be terminated by the rapture, the reward they would lose is their Church membership. There would be no guarantees (Rev. 3:5-6), but some might be saved as part of the fifth seal group, through their own death, instead of being saved as a Church member through the death of Jesus. The spiritual gifts were visible in the Corinth congregation (1 Corinthians 12:1-14:40), so it is obvious the false prophets and teachers had not changed the born-again requirements. Had they not been born again, they would have no rewards or salvation to lose. The Corinth congregation had completed the rebirth, except the baptism of fire, in which they were failing. That failing was causing them to be overcome. Had the rapture occurred in the days of the Corinth churches, the overcomers would have left in the rapture, the overcome would face Antichrist in a get serious situation, and any unbelieving in the congregation would face Antichrist in a 'get serious or get lost' situation. The unbelieving will, more than likely, get lost or more accurately stay lost. The overcome will get serious, get killed, and get salvation, and while they are on earth making up their minds, the Church members will be in heaven receiving their rewards.

b. FROM: The Amen, the faithful and true witness.
Rev. 3:14b, "These things saith the Amen, the faithful and true witness, the beginning of the creation of God."

We end our prayers with the word "amen," meaning truly, let it be so. Jesus introduces himself to the Laodicean congregation as the "Amen" because it is time to end the Church Age. The time has arrived to let it be so. He introduces himself as "the faithful and true witness" because the Laodicean congregation has a problem figuring out who "the faithful and true witness" really is. He introduces himself as "the beginning of the creation of God," because he was the beginning of the new creation called the Church. Jesus was the first begotten from the dead, the first member of the human family to be resurrected to eternal life in a glorified human body. The time has arrived for his brothers and sisters to join him.

c. COMMENDATION: Nothing whatsoever commendable.

There was nothing commendable or worthy of praise in the Laodicean congregation. They may have called themselves a church, but it is only a name, not a reality. They may have called themselves Christians, but

Gentile is a more accurate description, Ephesians 4:17-19, "(17) This I say therefore, and testify in the Lord, that ye hence-forth walk not as other Gentiles walk, in the vanity of their mind, (18) Having the understanding darkened, being alienated from the life of God through the ignorance that is in them, because of the blindness of their heart: (19) Who being past feeling have given themselves over unto lasciviousness, to work all uncleanness with greediness."

God is going to deal with the Laodicean congregation severely because no people has ever had as much light on the revelation of God as our generation has had. Our nation was founded on Judeo-Christian concepts which we have almost totally abandoned. If our nation hasn't already past the point where God has to give up on us, we are approaching it with accelerated speed. Listen to how the Holy Spirit describes this condition in Romans 1:16-32, "(16) For I am not ashamed of the gospel of Christ: for it is the power of God unto salvation to every one that believeth; to the Jew first, and also to the Greek. (17) For therein is the righteousness of God revealed from faith to faith: as it is written, The just shall live by faith. (18) For the wrath of God is revealed from heaven against all ungodliness and unrighteousness of men, who hold the truth in unrighteousness; (19) Because that which may be known of God is manifest in them; for God hath shewed it unto them. (20) For the invisible things of him from the creation of the world are clearly seen, being understood by the things that are made, even his eternal power and Godhead; so that they are without excuse: (21) Because that, when they knew God, they glorified him not as God, neither were thankful; but became vain in their imaginations, and their foolish heart was darkened. (22) Professing themselves to be wise, they became fools, (23) And changed the glory of the uncorruptible God into an image made like to corruptible man, and to birds, and fourfooted beasts, and creeping things. (24) Wherefore God also gave them up to uncleanness through the lusts of their own hearts, to dishonour their own bodies between themselves: (25) Who changed the truth of God into a lie, and worshipped and served the creature more than the Creator, who is blessed for ever. Amen. (26) For this cause God gave them up unto vile affections: for even their women did change the natural use into that which is against nature: (27) And likewise also the men, leaving the natural use of the woman, burned in their lust one toward another; men with men working that which is unseemly, and receiving in themselves that recompense of their error which was meet. (28) And even as they did not like to retain God in their knowledge, God gave them over to a reprobate mind, to do those things which are not convenient: (29) Being filled with all unrighteousness, fornication, wickedness, covetousness, maliciousness; full of envy, murder, debate, deceit, malignity; whisperers, (30) Backbiters, haters of God, despiteful, proud, boaster, inventors of evil things, disobedient to parents, (31) Without understanding, covenant breakers, without natural affection, implacable, unmerciful: (32) Who knowing the judgment of God, that they which commit such things are worthy of death, not only do the same, but have pleasure in them that do them."

Homosexuality is a clear indication that God has given up a person and turned them over to a reprobate mind. When homosexuality is practiced openly and uncondemned by a society, it is a clear indication that God has given up on the society, and turned it over to reprobates. When the Church welcomes homosexuals with open arms, it's time for God to burn down the building. That is the degenerate state our nation and the Laodicean church congregation have reached. How much intelligence does it take to know, if God gave them up, they are hopeless? Anyone who has ever read past Chapter 19 in the Bible, knows how much God hates homosexuality. You can call it gay, an alternate lifestyle, lesbianism, homosexuality, or sodomy, but God calls it sin. He demonstrated his hatred of it when he rained fire on Sodom and Gomorrah. They are your example so you can expect the same treatment, and the same final abode, Jude 1:7, "Even as Sodom and Gomorrah, and the cities about them in like manner, giving themselves over to fornication, and going after strange flesh, are set forth for an example, suffering the vengeance of eternal fire." The sad thing about the whole situation is that while the Laodicean churches were busy molding this generation we just sat back and watched.

We have educated ourselves to the point where we are a nation of fools. Just a hundred years ago we hung people for stealing a twenty-dollar horse. When our government set the Bible aside, they decided it was wrong to punish criminals and our most intelligent supreme court made a royal commandment to rehabilitate them. They put rotating doors on luxurious prisons and honestly believed the problem would go away. How intelligent they were can be seen a little further down the road when repeat offenders are responsible for eighty percent of the crime in our country. We are too intelligent now to get a rope and reduce the crime rate by 80 percent within the week. Our government in all its wisdom will solve the problem with a another royal commandment: raise the taxes, employ more police, build more prisons. When that doesn't work, they will raise taxes and try it again, and again, and again. Have you every wondered why our government does not tell us monthly what the national budget is for security guards and systems, law enforcement, prisons and repeat offender judicial cost? If rehabilitation is the answer to the sin problem, somebody needs to tell God so he can rewrite the Bible. If God would write a book that would solve all the problems in our country, do you think our government would have the intelligence to make it top priority in our educational system?

d. REBUKE: Works replaced with apathy, motivated by gain, spiritual blindness.

Rev. 3:15-17, "(15) I know thy works, that thou are neither cold nor hot: I would thou wert cold or hot. (16) So then because thou are lukewarm, and neither cold nor hot, I will spue thee out of my mouth. (17) Because thou sayest, I am rich, and increased with goods, and have need of nothing; and knowest not that thou are wretched, and miserable, and poor, and blind, and naked."

The lukewarm Laodicean church prides herself of, being rich, being increased with goods, and having need of nothing. Jesus looks on this church as being wretched, miserable, poor, blind, and naked. They are wretched and miserable because they failed in the baptism of fire by submitting to temptations. Instead of being overcomers, they have been overcome, and because of their ignorance of the Word of God, they don't know the difference. The word *happy* is used only six times in the New Testament. The first is in John 13:17, where Jesus explains that he is our example, John 13:15- 17, "(15) For I have given you an example, that ye should do as I have done to you. (16) Verily, verily, I say unto you, The servant is not greater than his lord; neither he that is sent greater than he that sent him. (17) If ye know these things, happy are ye if ye do them." The second time is in Acts 26:2, when Paul defended the gospel before king Agrippa, "(2) I think myself happy, king Agrippa, because I shall answer for myself this day before thee touching all the things whereof I am accused of the Jews: (3) Especially because I know thee to be expert in all customs and questions which are among the Jews: wherefore I beseech thee to hear me patiently." The third time is in Romans 14:22-23, where we are told the difference between operating in faith or doubt, "(22) Hast thou faith? have it to thyself before God. Happy is he that condemneth not himself in that thing which he alloweth. (23) And he that doubteth is damned if he eat, because he eateth not of faith: for whatsoever is not of faith is sin." The fourth time is in James Chapter 5:10-11, in connection with the rich oppressing the poor, and the poor enduring the affliction with patience, "(10) Take, my brethren, the prophets, who have spoken in the name of the Lord, for an example of suffering affliction, and of patience. (11) Behold, we count them happy which endure. Ye have heard of the patience of Job, and have seen the end of the Lord; that the Lord is very pitiful, and of tender mercy." The fifth time is in 1 Peter 3:14-16, where we are told that happiness comes by suffering for righteousness' sake, "(14) But and if ye suffer for righteousness' sake, happy are ye: and be not afraid of their terror, neither be troubled; (15) But sanctify the Lord God in your hearts: and be ready always to give an answer to every man that asketh you a reason of the hope that is in you with meekness and fear: (16) Having a good conscience: that, whereas they speak evil of you, as of evildoers, they may be ashamed that falsely accuse your good conversation in Christ." The last time is in 1 Peter 4:14-16, where we are told that happiness comes when suffering as a Christian, (for the name of Christ), "(14) If ye be reproached for the name of Christ, happy are ye; for the spirit of glory and of God resteth upon you: on their part he is evil spoken of, but on your part he is glorified. (15) But let none of you suffer as a murderer, or as a thief, or as an evildoer, or as a busybody in other men's matters. (16) Yet if any man suffer as a Christian, let him not be ashamed; but let him glorify God on this behalf."

They are wretched and miserable because they are living a lie. They are staggering through life, saying, "Peace, Peace, when there is no peace." Listen to how the Holy Spirit describes this crowd in Jeremiah 6:13-17, "(13) For from the least of them even unto the greatest of them every one is given to covetousness; and from the prophet even unto the priest every one dealeth falsely. (14) They have healed also the hurt of the daughter of my people slightly, saying, Peace, peace; when there is no peace. (15) Were they ashamed when they had committed abomination? nay, they were not at all ashamed, neither could they blush: therefore they shall fall among them that fall: at the time that I visit them they shall be cast down, saith the Lord. (16) Thus saith the Lord, Stand ye in the ways, and see, and ask for the old paths, where is the good way, and walk therein, and ye shall find rest for your souls. But they said, We will not walk therein. (17) Also I set watchmen over you, saying, Hearken to the sound of the trumpet. But they said, We will not hearken." They are spiritually poor because of their ignorance of the Word and ways, of God. They are spiritually blind because they have never completed the rebirth, are not indwelt by the Holy Spirit, and refuse to be led by the Holy Spirit. They are spiritually naked because they are without excuse. They have the Romans 10:3 righteousness problem, "For they being ignorant of God's righteousness, and going about to establish their own righteousness, have not submitted themselves unto the righteousness of God."

Apathy means indifference. They are lukewarm, neither cold nor hot. Satan and his crew are guilty of many things, but apathy is not one of them, so let's set aside the Antichrist element in the Church and discuss the pew-warmer. If you have been warming that pew long enough that "ye ought to be teachers" (Hebrews 5:12), and are not, you will be in trouble at the time of the rapture. If you blow on something that is smoldering, one of two things happens: it bursts into flame, or you blow it out. If the person behind your pulpit is blowing the Word of God, either you will conform and burst into flame, or you will become "dull of hearing" (Hebrews 5:11), and sit there till Jesus spews you out of his mouth at the rapture. The pew-warmer is the smoking flax (dimly burning) of Matthew 12:20, "A bruised reed shall he not break, and smoking flax shall he not quench, till he send forth judgment unto victory." Matthew 12:20 is a quote from Isaiah 42:3, and speaks of the coming of Jesus as Redeemer. When Jesus returns, he is coming as the Judge to execute judgment. By sitting there doing nothing when there is so much to be done, you are judging yourself lukewarm. To you, Jesus says, "So then because thou are lukewarm, and neither cold nor hot, I will spue thee out of my mouth." The word translated as *spue*, is the Greek word *emeo*, meaning to vomit. You are nauseating Jesus, not pleasing him.

The letter to the Laodicean congregation, like all the other letters, is addressed to those in the Church, not those outside. If you call yourself a Christian and are contradicting the Word of God by your words or actions, you are a liar. That may make you hot, but not near as hot as you are going to be when Rev. 21:7-8 is history, "(7) He that overcometh shall inherit all things; and I will be his God, and he shall be my son. (8) But the fearful, and unbelieving, and the abominable, and murderers, and whoremongers, and sorcerers, and idolaters, and all liars, shall have their part in the lake which burneth with fire and brimstone: which is the second death." If you call yourself a member of the Church, and are lukewarm, Jesus calls you vomit, and promises to rid his body of you in the statement, "I will spue thee out of my mouth." If you used to be a Christian and have turned from Christianity, you are the cold apostate. Your second state is worse than your first, Matthew 12:43-45, "(43) When the unclean spirit is gone out of a man, he walketh through dry places, seeking rest, and findeth none. (44) Then he saith, I will return into my house from whence I came out; and when he is come, he findeth it empty, swept, and garnished. (45) Then goeth he, and taketh with himself seven other spirits more wicked than himself, and they enter in and dwell there: and the last state of that man is worse than the first. Even so shall it be also unto this wicked generation."

e. EXHORT: Buy his gold, put on his clothes, use his eyesalve.
Rev. 3:18-20, "(18) I counsel thee to buy of me gold tried in the fire, that thou mayest be rich; and white raiment, that thou mayest be clothed, and that the shame of thy nakedness do not appear; and anoint thine eyes with eyesalve, that thou mayest see. (19) As many as I love, I rebuke and chasten: be zealous therefore, and repent. (20) Behold, I stand at the door, and knock: if any man hear my voice, and open the door, I will come in to him, and will sup with him, and he with me."

Gold, in prophecy symbolizes deity, while fire denotes judgment. The Deity tried by judgment was Jesus Christ. The Laodicean congregation rejected Jesus by refusing to buy what he was selling. In other words, they rejected what Jesus said to do, and thereby rejected Jesus. They want to go to heaven and have eternal life, but they don't want to acquire it from Jesus. They want to do it their way, instead of the way Jesus told them to do it. The problem is that if they accept what Jesus said as the truth, they would have to be obedient to that truth. It is all right to be called a Christian, as long as they don't have to live like one. They want the more abundant life Jesus promised, but they want to buy it with gold or money, not through Jesus, the rebirth, and obedience to the Word of God. In John 14:6, Jesus said he was "the way, the truth, and the life." He provided the way for us to purchase eternal life when he died at Calvary, so buy that truth, and like it says in Proverbs 23:23, sell it not, "Buy the truth, and sell it not; also wisdom, and instruction, and understanding." It is that truth that will make you free,

John 8:31-32, "(31) Then said Jesus to those Jews which believed on him, If ye continue in my word, then are ye my disciples indeed; (32) And ye shall know the truth, and the truth shall make you free." To "continue" means 24 hours a day, 7 days a week, 52 weeks a year, not just two hours on Sunday, and one hour on Wednesday night. When Satan, or one of his crew, tries to turn you from that truth in the baptism of fire through temptations, don't sell out. The Laodicean congregation valued their temporary gold above the eternal gold Jesus was selling. They bought the lie, and sold the truth. Like Esau, they sold a very precious birthright to satisfy fleshly appetites.

The Laodicean congregation failed in the baptism of fire unto life, will lose their Church membership at the rapture, and then will face the baptism of fire unto death. In the trial of their faith they tested unfaithful. Had they tested faithful, they would have found what they received was much more precious than gold, 1 Peter 1:7, "That the trial of your faith, being much more precious than of gold that perisheth, though it be tried with fire, might be found unto praise and honour and glory at the appearing of Jesus Christ." The white raiment that Jesus is offering the Laodicean congregation will correct their nakedness problem. As we have already seen, their nakedness problem is the Romans 10:3-4 righteousness problem, "(3) For they being ignorant of God's righteousness, and going about to establish their own righteousness, have not submitted themselves unto the righteousness of God. (4) For Christ is the end of the law for righteousness to every one that believeth." That "white garment" is Jesus, but like the Jews, traditional Christianity has erred in claiming salvation by keeping the law, instead of faith in God's Redeemer. The law condemns us and is designed to show us our need for a Redeemer, which leads us to Jesus. The law makes you a sin fighter and puts you in a war you cannot win. The Laodicean congregation is wearing the "white garment" of their own righteousness. From God's point of view, they are wearing filthy rags, not a white garment, Isaiah 64:6, "But we are all as an unclean thing, and all our righteousnesses are as filthy rags; and we all do fade as a leaf; and our iniquities, like the wind, have taken us away." Fig leave garments didn't hide Adam and Eve's nakedness from God, and they won't hide your nakedness either. Your righteousness will not get you to heaven and neither will the rightcousness of the law.

In John, Chapter 3, Jesus tells Nicodemus that unless a person is born again of water and the Spirit, he cannot see or enter into the kingdom of God. Until you have been baptized into Christ, you have not put on Christ, so you cannot see, understand, or enter into the good fight of faith. Listen to how the Holy Spirit describes the difference between law and faith in Galatians 3:22-29, "(22) But the scripture hath concluded all under sin, that the promise by faith of Jesus Christ might be given to them that believe. (23) But before faith came, we were kept under the law, shut up unto the faith which should afterwards be revealed. (24) Wherefore the law was our schoolmaster to bring us unto Christ, that we might be justified by faith. (25) But after that faith is come, we are no longer under a schoolmaster. (26) For ye are all the children of God by faith in Christ Jesus. (27) For as many of you as have been baptized into Christ have put on Christ. (28) There is neither Jew nor Greek, there is neither bond nor free, there is neither male nor female: for ye are all one in Christ Jesus. (29) And if ye be Christ's, then are ye Abraham's seed, and heirs according to the promise." This is why Galatians 2:16 says no one will be justified by the works of the law, "Knowing that a man is not justified by the works of the law, but by the faith of Jesus Christ, even we have believed in Jesus Christ, that we might be justified by the faith of Christ, and not by the works of the law: for by the works of the law shall no flesh be justified."

The "works of the law" means walking in obedience to all the "Thou shalt not's" given to the Nation of Israel in the Old Covenant. Break any one of them and you are guilty of breaking the whole law, James 2:10-11, "(10) For whosoever shall keep the whole law, and yet offend in one point, he is guilty of all. (11) For he that said, Do not commit adultery, said also, Do not kill. Now if thou commit no adultery, yet if thou kill, thou are become a transgressor of the law." In 1 John 3:4 we are told "sin is the transgression of the law," but the only way God can forgive sin is through Jesus Christ. The redemptive work of Jesus on Calvary was God's plan of salvation, and it is the only way he has to forgive our sins. Jesus is the mediator of the New Covenant that Church members enter into by being born again. It is in that rebirth that our sins are forgiven, God credits us with the righteousness of Jesus, and we are given the Holy Spirit, which enables us to walk by faith and mortify the deeds of the flesh condemned by the Old Testament law. That is the difference between walking after the flesh and walking after the Spirit we saw in Romans 8:1-14. The Laodicean congregation has taken water baptism, which is part of the New Covenant rebirth, and reclassified it as "works." That goes a long way in explaining the absence of the Holy Spirit in the members of its congregation.

The remedy for this spiritual blindness is "anoint thine eyes with eyesalve, that thou mayest see." The only thing that will cure spiritual blindness is the Word of God (Rev. 19:13), and his name is Jesus Christ. Jesus was the truth and he spoke the truth. The major problem in the Laodicean congregation is that they refuse to believe what Jesus said. The sin that is condemning people to hell during the Church Dispensation is unbelief. They demonstrate their unbelief by contradicting what Jesus said and refusing to do what He told them to do. When Jesus says, "He that believeth and is baptized shall be saved," they say, "Only believe." When Jesus says, "Except a man be born of water and of the Spirit," they say, "Water baptism is not required." When Jesus says, "These signs shall follow them that believe," they say, "No, they won't." When Jesus says, "The thief cometh not, but for to steal, kill, and destroy," they say, "It is the will of God, give God the credit," thereby making God the thief. Jesus said exactly what he meant, and meant exactly what he said. They present an untrustworthy Jesus by perverting what he said. They discredit Jesus, call his Father a liar, and alienate themselves from the Holy Spirit, all in the same breath, 1 John 5:10, "He that believeth on the Son of God hath the witness in himself: he that believeth not God hath made him a liar; because he believeth not the record that God gave of his Son."

Laodicean church members are quick to tell you what their denomination says Jesus said. The sad part is that most pew-warmers don't care enough about what Jesus said to even look at the record. Their ignorance of the Word of God is by self-choice because God's will may interfere with their plans. Someone once described the modern Church member by saying, "If they were arrested for being a Christian, there wouldn't be enough evidence to convict them." That is an accurate description. Most of them don't know enough about the Word of God to carry on an intelligent conversation about Jesus. No wonder the organization is repulsive to Jesus. He called it right when he named them Laodicean. The Greek word *laos* means "a people," while *dikiea* is a complicated word which basically implies judgment. In essence, Jesus called them a people who have prepared themselves for judgment. Teaching in Christendom in the past was that Jesus was calling a people out of the world and putting them in the Church. Then, when Jesus comes back these good Church people will be taken to heaven and non-church people would go to hell. That is the truth as long as you understand the Laodicean Church is not his Church. Jesus will not rapture the Laodicean congregation. He will vomit them out of his body.

Instead of being in the Laodicean Church, Jesus is presented as being outside, at the door, knocking for admission. Rev. 3:19-20, "(19) As many as I love, I rebuke and chasten: be zealous therefore, and repent. (20) Behold, I stand at the door, and knock: if any man hear my voice, and open the door, I will come in to him, and will sup with him, and he with me." It is truly a sad situation when an individual turning to Jesus must turn his back on the so-called church, and go outside the organization to find Jesus. Some present this passage as Jesus calling individuals out of the Church and working with them as individuals, outside the organized Church. That could be true in areas where there are no Philadelphia churches. The Philadelphia congregation and the Laodicean congregation will continue to co-exist until the rapture. Until that point in time, Jesus will continue knocking for admittance, and the congregation that will open the door to Him will be changed from a Laodicean to a Philadelphia Church, as they throw the false teachers, deceivers, and antichrists out of the congregation. If the congregation ignores the knocking, and individuals hear Him knocking, if they want to be with Jesus, they have no other choice but to get on the other side of the door. Don't be deceived into thinking you can change them. If they won't listen to what Jesus said, there is nothing you can say that they can hear. Get out, and get out quickly, because when Jesus stops knocking it will be too late. We are so close to the rapture, last Sunday may have been the last time Jesus knocked.

If you are a new born Christian, or a ninety-nine-year-old pew-warmer who just saw the Light, and you are looking for a Philadelphia Church, just compare what they believe and do, to the Mark 16:15-18, Church Commission. Satan can't duplicate the signs, the faithless can't work them, and they will not follow them that don't believe Jesus. In fact, most Laodicean congregations will readily admit they are unbelievers if you ask them for their opinion on the signs. Of course, these are not all the signs, but they are five unmistakable signs, by which Jesus said we could identify believers. The word translated as *signs* is the Greek word *semeion* which means to indicate, or an indication. It contains the Greek word *sema* meaning, a mark. We use instrument gauges to show us the internal condition of machinery and to measure all sorts of things. By these signs you know your condition and the condition of your church. More importantly, everyone can see the condition, so there is no excuse for anyone joining a false church or following a false teacher. These signs are outward evidences of the indwelling Holy Spirit. It doesn't matter if we apply them to an individual or a group. Jesus gave us these signs so we could distinguish between believers and non-believers, the truth and the lie, His Church and the apostate church. If we claim to be a believer and deny these signs we make Jesus a liar. After all, Jesus is the one who said, "These signs shall follow them that believe." You are either one of "them that believe" or one of them that doesn't. By that decision you make yourself a member of the Laodicean Church or a member of the Philadelphia Church. There is no third choice. A person in a vehicle who ignores the instrument panel is headed for trouble. A person in a church who ignores the Mark 16:17-18 instrument panel is already in trouble. The person who designed the vehicle and the person who designed the church put the instrument panel there to tell you something. You are headed for a disaster if you don't understand what the instrument panel is saying.

Among the Laodicean congregation is a group of churches labeled "New Testament Only." They are assisting the Anabaptist in conditioning a generation of people outside the Church who will not respond to the Word of God. The people outside the Church cannot understand the law of faith. The only thing they can understand is Old Testament law. They need to be taught the law and the punishment for breaking the law, until they are convinced that the commandments of God are good and that they need to keep them. That is the point when the Holy Spirit can convict them of sin, and the law schoolmaster can bring them to the Redeemer Jesus. Stop preaching law and punishment for disobedience, and you take the schoolmaster out of society, which results in the lawless generation we see in the United States today. A person who walks with no fear of God before his eyes cannot see the need for redemption. Society cannot see any need to be reconciled to God if there is no law, no punishment for breaking the commandments of God, and no judgment day. There is no need for our country to go up in smoke, but there is no choice if the Church refuses to put the lawless under law, put the judges who are perverting judgment behind bars, and replace the godless people in authority with born-again believers. The ungodly can't even recognize sin until they know the commandments of God. Listen to how the Holy Spirit describes the situation in Romans 7:7-12, "(7) What shall we say then? Is the law sin? God forbid, Nay, I had not known sin, but by the law: for I had not known lust, except the law had said, Thou shalt not covet. (8) But sin, taking occasion by the commandment, wrought in me all manner of concupiscence. For without the law sin was dead. (9) For I was alive without the law once: but when the commandment came, sin revived, and I died. (10) And the commandment, which was ordained to life, I found to be unto death. (11) For sin, taking occasion by the commandment, deceived me, and by it slew me. (12) Wherefore the law is holy, and the commandment holy, and just, and good."

From God's point of view there is no such thing as a "New Testament Only Church." The Church Commission begins with the statement, "Go ye into all the world, and preach the gospel to every creature." The word *Gospel* means, "good news," and the good news is that we have been redeemed. The whole story of redemption is the whole Bible, not just the New Testament. If we are going to reject the Old Testament, we should also reject all New Testament passages which make reference to the Old Testament. It is *all* the Word of God and it should all be preached. The same thing applies to the Church Commission–we should be doing all of it, not just part of it. All the Old Testament passages referring to the Messiah are referring to Christ Jesus. All Old Testament passages referring to the Redeemer are referring to Jesus Christ. All Old Testament promises to the redeemed are promises to you, if you are in fact, redeemed. It is the Old Testament that elaborates on the curses from which the redeemed are freed, such as death, poverty, sickness, diseases, and all other forms of demonic oppression. All these satanic things came upon the human family as sin in the garden of Eden through the fall of Adam and Eve. Without an understanding of the Old Testament you are like a person trying to solve a complicated mathematical equation with no knowledge of arithmetic.

The New Testament teaches in the death and resurrection of Jesus Christ, Satan was defeated. Jesus died to pay the penalty for our sins, and to deliver us from the effects of sin. In 1 John 3:8-10, we read, "(8) He that committeth sin is of the devil; for the devil sinneth from the beginning. For this purpose the Son of God was manifested, that he might destroy the works of the devil. (9) Whosoever is born of God doth not commit sin; for his seed remaineth in him: and he cannot sin, because he is born of God. (10) In this the children of God are manifest, and the children of the devil: whosoever doeth not righteousness is not of God, neither he that loveth not his brother." The "works of the devil" that Jesus destroyed were sin, death, poverty, sickness, diseases, and all other forms of demonic oppression such as worry, fear, doubt, blindness, dumbness, lameness, etc. These works are the manifestations of the devil. If these signs are visible in you or your Church, it is time to reevaluate your Christianity. There are only two sets of signs: One set reveals the works of the Holy Spirit, and the other set reveals the works of the devil. What the person behind the pulpit is preaching will make you either an overcomer or one that is overcome. What Jesus commanded the person behind your pulpit to do, in the Church Commission, is to continue doing what He started, Acts 10:38, "How God anointed Jesus of Nazareth with the Holy Ghost and with power: who went about doing good, and healing all that were oppressed of the devil; for God was with him." If the person behind the pulpit isn't doing it, or the congregation refuses to acknowledge their responsibility to do the whole Mark 16:15-18 Church Commission, you have no choice but to leave and find yourself an obedient congregation. There is no way you can sit there and listen to them preach unbelief and be an overcomer. The last generation of Christians is facing a situation that none of the previous generations faced, and that is the rapture. If you are not an overcomer before the rapture occurs, Jesus will cancel your Church membership and leave you behind to face death by the Antichrist in the tribulation period.

f. PROMISE: Co-rulers with Christ by overcoming as he overcame.
Rev. 3:21-22, "(21) To him that overcometh will I grant to sit with me in my throne, even as I also overcame, and am set down with my Father in his throne. (22) He that hath an ear, let him hear what the Spirit saith unto the churches."

The rapture of the Church is history. It occurred between Revelation Chapter 3 verse 20 and verse 21. All born-again believers and all water baptized children under the age of responsibility have been removed from Earth to meet Jesus in the air. The prophecy in 1 Thessalonians 4:13-18 has now been fulfilled. Church members who died in Christ since the arrival of the Holy Spirit on the day of Pentecost, have been resurrected to eternal life in their glorified bodies. All the prophecies concerning the coming of Jesus as a thief in the night have now been fulfilled. The living who participated in the rapture, fulfilled the prophecy in 1 Corinthians 15:51-55. Mortals put on immortality and instantly disappear from view. They heard someone call their name, looked up, and saw Jesus standing in outer space, with his arms open, and a smile on his face. What a time of rejoicing, and it is only the beginning of an eternity of rejoicing.

Meanwhile, back on Earth, it will be an altogether different story. Parents will scream in horror as they see their children disappear from the middle of a group of children playing in the yard. Wives will scream in horror as their husbands disappear from before their eyes, and vice versa. Cold chills will run up the backs of people who see the person speaking to them disappear in the middle of a sentence. The worst horror will come with the realization that the rapture of the Church is history. Pastors and priests will frantically try to explain to their congregations why they were not taken in the rapture. Members of the congregations will try to figure out why some were taken, and they were left behind (Matthew 25:1-13). Wives will sink into despair as they realize the bread winner is gone and his life insurance policy is void because she cannot produce his body or his death certificate. Pew-warmers who have attended Church all their lives will be on their knees, in tears, praying to a heaven of brass. Deceived Christians will fall into despair as they realize they have been deceived and Jesus has closed the Church door. Jesus stopped knocking on the Laodicean church door and the foolish procrastinators join in the cry of the five foolish virgins (Matthew 25:1-13). To their cry, "Lord, Lord, open to us," Jesus answers, "Verily I say unto you, I know you not." The midnight cry "Behold, the bridegroom cometh" meant about as much to them as Jesus saying, "Strive to enter in at the strait gate." They will fulfill the prophecy Jesus gave in Luke 13:24-27, "(24) Strive to enter in at the strait gate: for many, I say unto you, will seek to enter in, and shall not be able. (25) When once the master of the house is risen up, and hath shut to the door, and ye begin to stand without, and to knock at the door, saying, Lord, Lord, open unto us; and he shall answer and say unto you, I know you not whence ye are: (26) Then shall ye begin to say, We have eaten and drunk in thy presence, and thou hast taught in our streets. (27) But he shall say, I tell you, I know you not whence ye are; depart from me, all ye workers of iniquity."

The promise section of the Laodicean letter is for those individuals who had their Church membership canceled by Jesus at the rapture. Every denominational church that existed just prior to the rapture will continue to exist after the rapture, with one major change. They will all be non-believing members of the one world church that Jesus formed when he removed the Christians in the rapture. The name of the one world church is Laodicean, a people who have prepared themselves for judgment. The judgment will not come at the hands of Jesus. He has already judged the unfaithful and unworthy of Church membership by leaving them behind at the rapture. Their judgment will come at the hands of Antichrist, the god they chose to believe instead of Jesus. When his organization begins setting fire to the church building and killing the members who refuse to deny Jesus, the flight of the Christian population for a safe hiding place will be very real. There will be no safe place to hide because Jesus will help them find you. He wants to offer you salvation as a member of the Rev. 6:9-11 fifth seal group. During the first half of the seven–year tribulation, every person who has ever named the name of Jesus, messed around with his Church, or played around with Christianity, will be tested in the baptism of fire unto death, in the 'deny or die' situation presented by the Antichrist organization. When the last person has denied, or died, the Church will be a dead issue on Earth. At this point the False Prophet will be reincarnated from Hades, and Jesus will turn his attention to the city of Jerusalem and the Jews who must now face the 'deny or die' situation presented by the False Prophet.

For the Laodicean congregation (who missed the rapture) to overcome, they must overcome, "even as I (Jesus) overcame." It is no secret, anywhere in Christendom, that Jesus overcame and defeated Satan by his death on the cross at Calvary. If you refused to accept that offer of salvation, you will have to pay for your unbelief by sacrificing your own life. You lost your Church membership by denying Jesus. Don't make the same mistake twice, because this time it will cost your salvation. When Jesus puts you in the baptism of fire unto death there is no second chance. You either deny and get your name blotted out of the Book of Life, or you refuse to deny, die, and receive salvation as one of the fifth seal group, Rev. 6:9-11. At the end of the first half of the tribulation you will be told to wait until you are joined by your brethren who must face the False Prophet during the last half of the era. When the last one arrives you will all be included in the great multitude of Rev. 7:9-17. When Jesus returns to Earth at the end of the tribulation era, you will accompany him, be resurrected to eternal life, and reign as a king with Jesus during the Kingdom Dispensation (Rev. 20:4-6).

We are living in the latter days of the Church Dispensation. The Bible has much to say about this period of time. The events quoted from the Bible will take place. The names may change or they may occur in a slightly different sequence, but they will happen. Your destination is either heaven or hell and the decision is yours to make. You can either follow the Holy Scriptures and Jesus to heaven or you can put yourself in the unrighteous crowd listed below and follow the apostate to hell. This crowd has already turned from the faith to follow the latter times seducing spirits and the doctrine of demons, 1 Timothy 4:1-5, "(1) Now the Spirit speaketh expressly, that in the latter times some shall depart from the faith, giving heed to seducing spirits, and doctrines of devils; (2) Speaking lies in hypocrisy; having their conscience seared with a hot iron; (3) Forbidding to marry, and commanding to abstain from meats, which God hath created to be received with thanksgiving of them which believe and know the truth. (4) For every creature of God is good, and nothing to be refused, if it be received with thanksgiving: (5) For it is sanctified by the word of God and prayer." They are going to get worse instead of better, 2 Timothy 3:13, "But evil men and seducers shall wax worse and worse, deceiving, and being deceived."

The Mark 16:17-18 signs will not follow them because of their unbelief. Instead of being born-again members of the kingdom of God, they are miscarriages, deceived into thinking they have inherited something they have not. They refused to be obedient and inherit the kingdom of God on this side of the rapture and now they are on the other side with the same righteous problem, 1 Corinthians 6:9-10, "(9) Know ye not that the unrighteous shall not inherit the kingdom of God? Be not deceived: neither fornicators, nor idolators, nor adulterers, nor effeminate, nor abusers of themselves with mankind, (10) Nor thieves, nor covetous, nor drunkards, nor revilers, nor extortioners, shall inherit the kingdom of God." Galatians 5:19-21, "(19) Now the works of the flesh are manifest, which are these; Adultery, fornication, uncleanness, lasciviousness, (20) Idolatry, witchcraft, hatred, variance, emulations, wrath, strife, seditions, heresies, (21) Envyings, murders, drunkenness, revellings, and such like: of the which I tell you before, as I have also told you in time past, that they which do such things shall not inherit the kingdom of God." Rev. 21:8, "But the fearful, and unbelieving, and the abominable, and murderers, and whoremongers, and sorcerers, and idolaters, and all liars, shall have their part in the lake which burneth with fire and brimstone: which is the second death."

As it is written, so let it be. Even so, come, Lord Jesus.